Art of Siberia

Text: Maria Czaplicka,
Valentina Gorbatcheva,
Marina Federova

Layout:
Baseline Co Ltd,
33 Ter - 33 Bis Mac Dinh Chi St.
Star Building, 6th Floor
District 1, Ho Chi Minh City
Vietnam

ISBN: 978-1-84484-562-0

Printed in Korea

Art of Siberia

PARKSTONE
INTERNATIONAL

CONTENTS

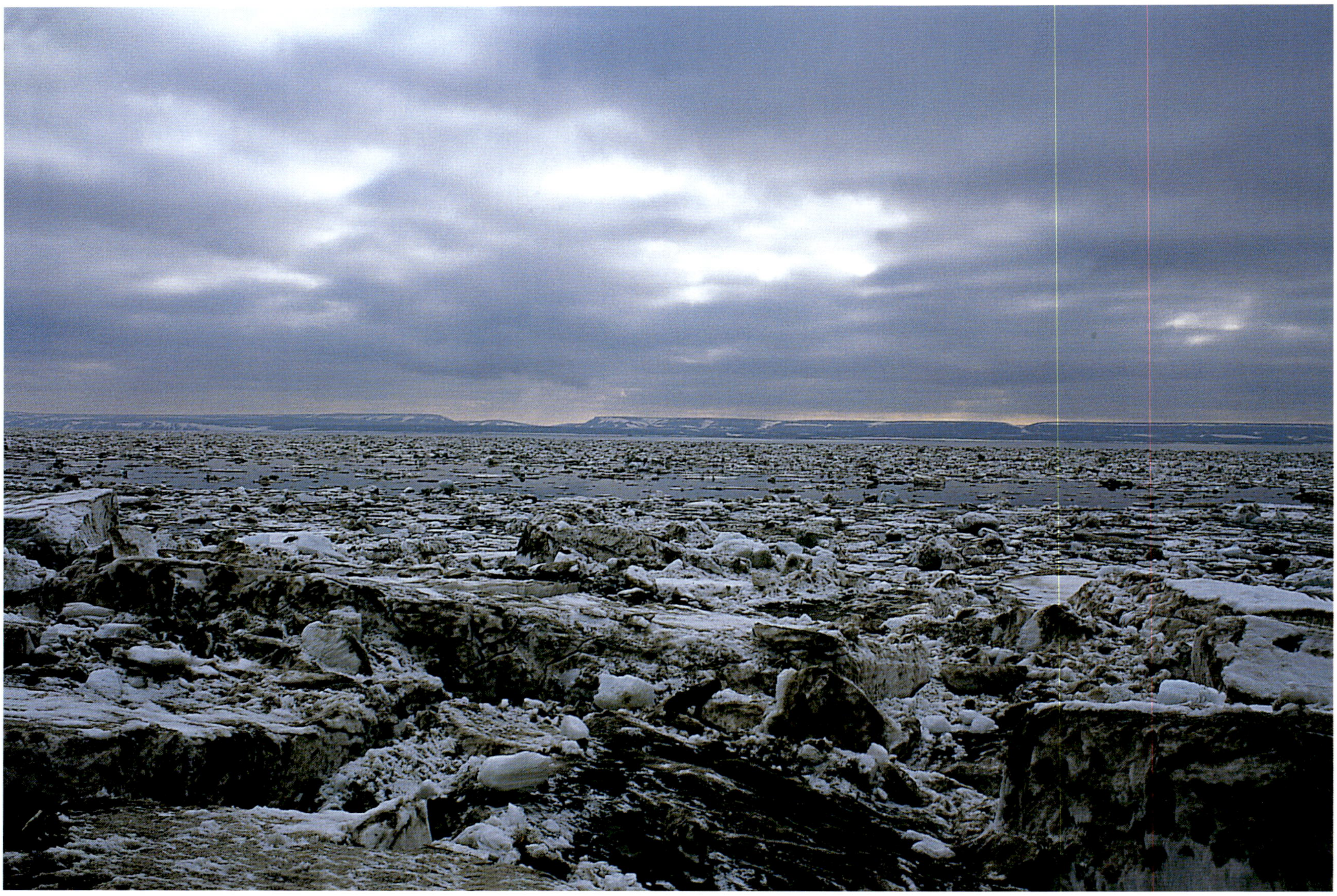

INTRODUCTION

The Evenki, the Yukaghirs, the Chukchi, the Koryaks, the Nenets, the Nanai people, the Yakuts, the Tuva people . . . Cradle of many cultures, Siberia constitutes an area that is rich in human traditions, as diverse and changeable over time as the region itself. The native inhabitants of Siberia, dwellers in the lands of far-northern and far-eastern Russia – by tradition reindeer-herders, horse-breeders, hunters of marine mammals and fishermen-hunters – have, over the millennia, evolved the means by which human communities may survive in this vast desert of extreme climatic conditions in northern Asia. Through their prolonged proximity to nature, the native inhabitants of the icy, Arctic expanses have learned to make a home in the wasteland, using every natural element at their disposal to create more than rude tents and campfires: they have become artists. The tribal cultures of Siberia express themselves in everything from the intricate designs on a walrus tusk, to the many-coloured glass beads on a woman's dress, to the delicately carved child's toy, to the ambiguously haunting shaman's mask. In an environment in which utility and survival are everything, these rapidly disappearing communities release their artistic cry into the wilderness.

Unfortunately, colonization by incoming cultures has in many cases caused a significant decline in the fortunes of such groups. Confronted with the more destructive aspects of Russian expansion and the Industrial Revolution, both the indigenous cultures and their all-important environment are threatened. As reindeer and fish disappear and the native populations dwindle, we are losing the opportunity to observe these profoundly simple and diverse communities. Those with the fewest numbers today may yet witness for themselves the extinction of their ancestral cultures.

What follows is an overview of the relationship between Siberia's extraordinary climate, the varied terrain and the peoples, along with a summary of the background from which those peoples stemmed, and accounts of historical events that dramatically altered their way of life. In the descriptions of shamanic principles, practices, and the essential role that the shaman plays in the daily lives of Siberian groups, we may glimpse the spiritual and artistic yearnings of these cultures. This book's constant endeavour is to enable the reader to enter fully into the traditional world and shamanist mindset of the original inhabitants of 'Russian' Asia.

The Lena on the break-up of the ice.

Ivan Shishkin,
Hiver, 1890.
Oil on canvas, 125.5 x 204 cm.
Russian Museum, St. Petersburg.

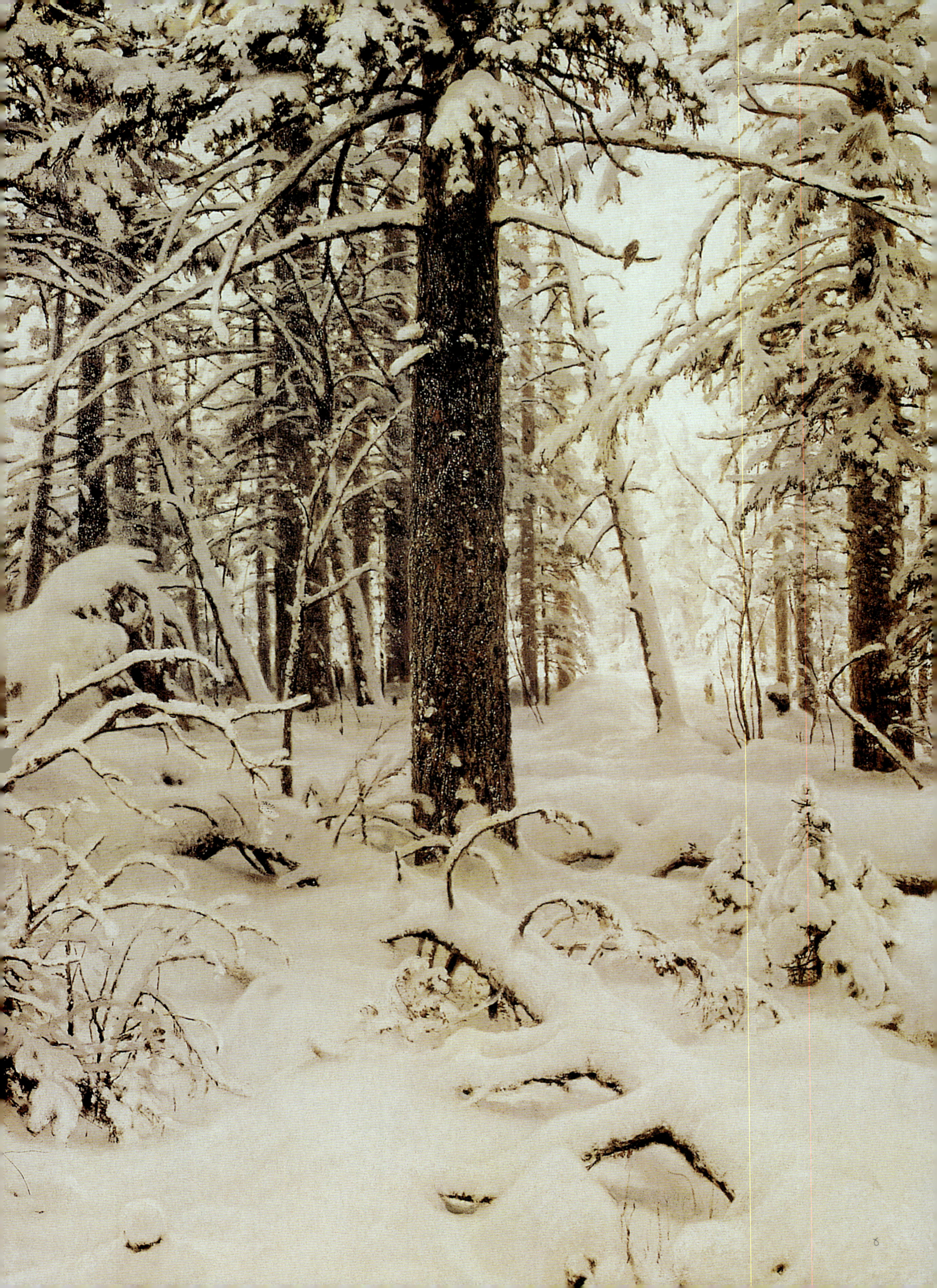

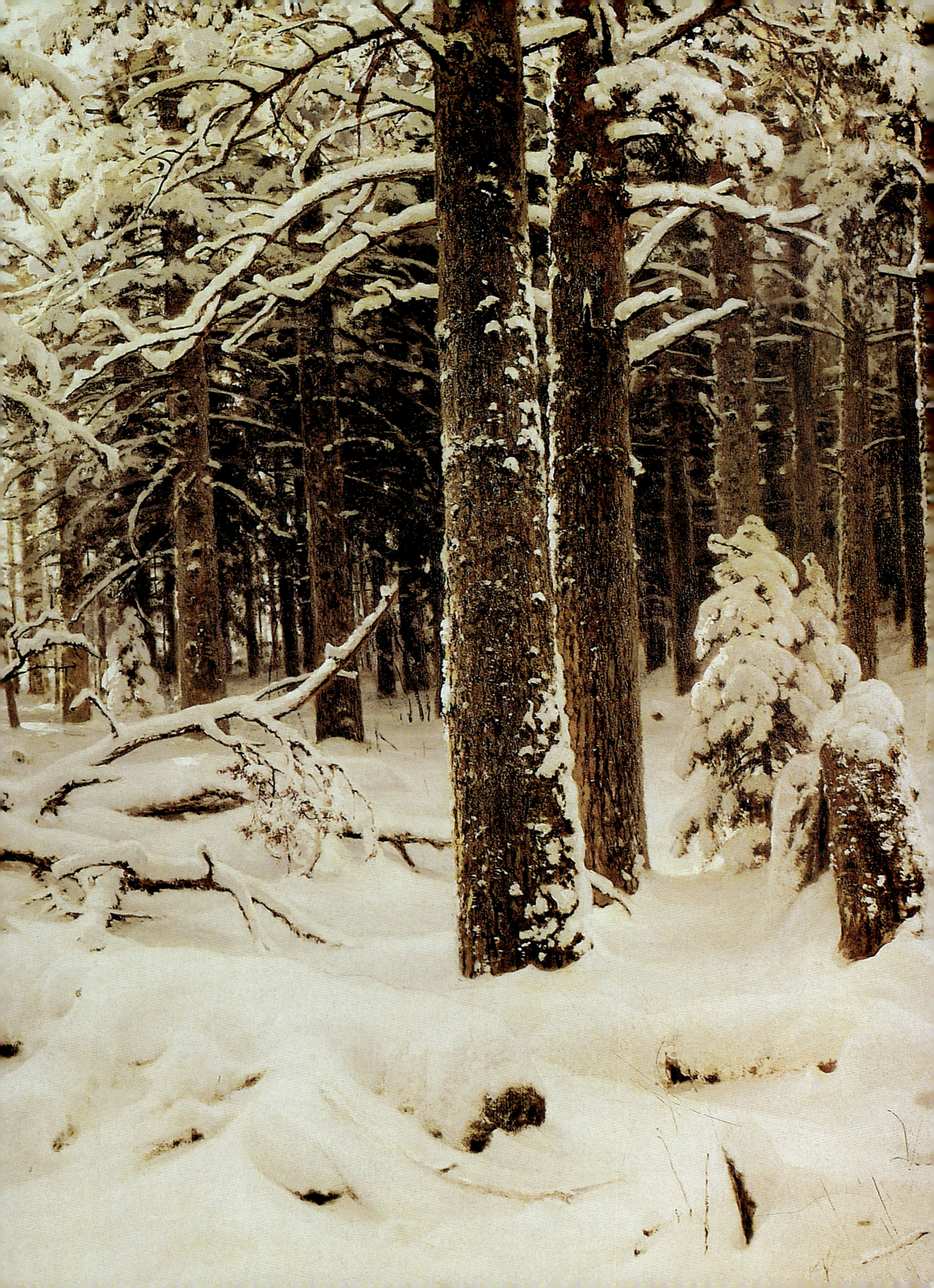

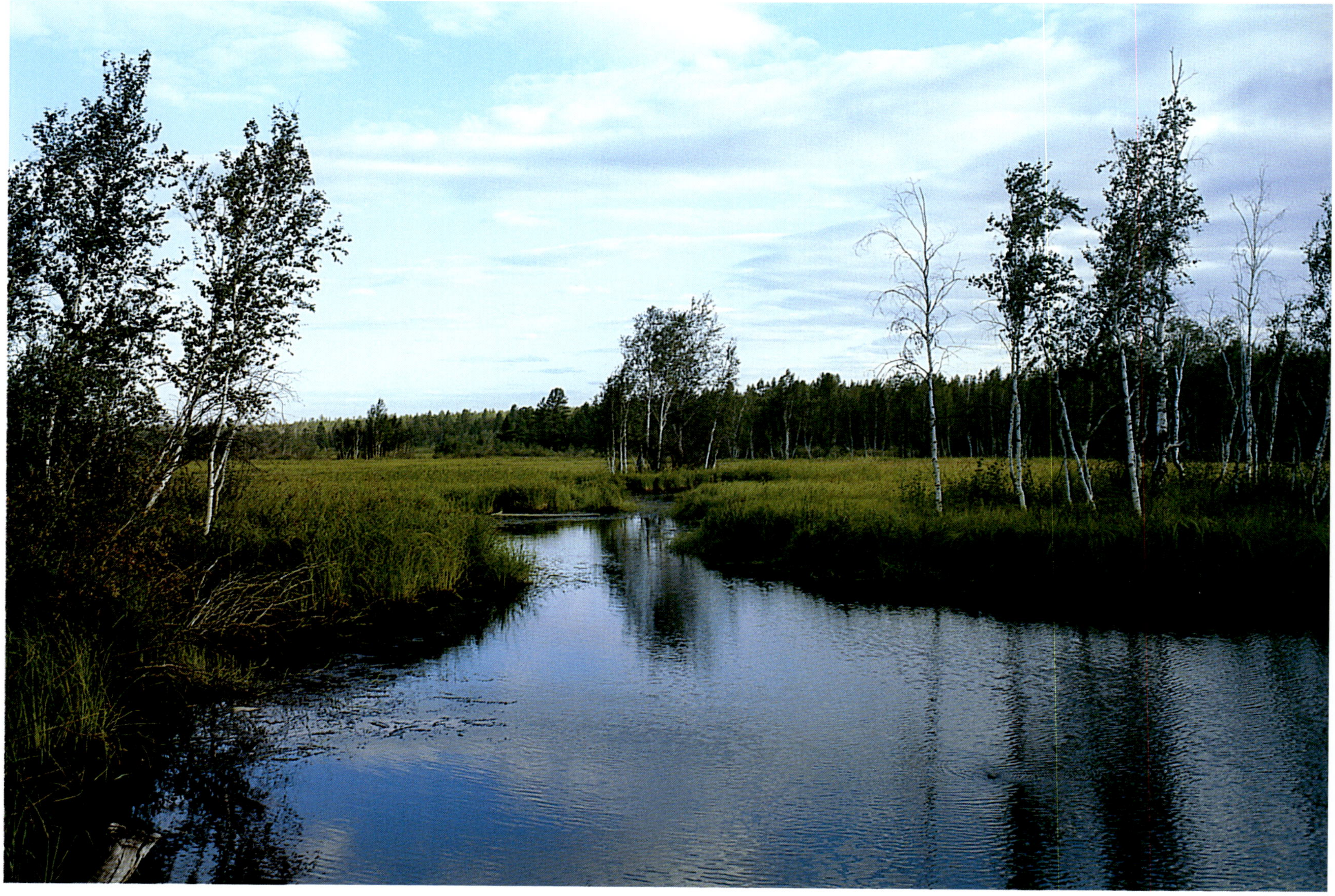

I. SIBERIA: GEOGRAPHY AND HISTORY

A. AN INHOSPITABLE CLIMATE

"A country of intense cold and great heat. A country outwardly wretched, but hiding in its bosom incalculable treasure."

Understood for almost three centuries to be no more than a geographical extension of the Russian state, Siberia stretches from the icy Arctic Ocean in the north to borders with Kazakhstan, Mongolia and China in the south, from the great chain of the Ural Mountains in the west to the Pacific Ocean in the east. Siberia lies (roughly) between the 45th and 77th parallels of north latitude, and extends from the 60 to the 190 of east longitude. Its most northern point is Cape Severo, or North-East Cape, a tongue of land between the estuaries of the great rivers Yenisey and Lena; Cape Vostotchni, its eastern extremity, is only forty-eight miles from Cape Prince of Wales in North America, from which it is separated by Bering Strait. Its greatest length from East to West is about 3,600 miles, and its greatest breadth from North to South a little less than 2,000 miles, forming an area which is 30% larger than Europe.

Many Europeans think of Siberia as a huge wilderness, remote and hostile to human habitation, mostly iced over, darkened by the polar night for a good part of the year. And yet Siberia is nothing if not diverse. From north to south there are a number of large areas that are completely different from each other in climate, terrain, flora and fauna. As you move southward, the Arctic wastes gradually transform into the tundra with its permafrost; further south, the tundra in turn transforms into the slightly warmer zones where scrubby trees will grow; further south still is the evergreen coniferous forest of the taiga; continuing south, there are the fertile steppes and then the arid steppes – and all these various ecological areas come with their own topographical relief, from low-level flatlands to massively towering peaks.

Occupying the greater part of this vast landmass, the central Siberian plateau is bound to the north, east and south by an enormous amphitheatre of mountain chains. To the north and east are the mountains of Verkhoyansk, which at their highest reach 9,097 feet (2,389 metres). Forming Siberia's southern boundary are the Sayan mountains (9,612 feet/2,930 metres) and the ranges of the Altai (which at Mt Belukha top out at 14,783 feet/4,506 metres). Within these various chains lie the sources of the three great Siberian rivers, the Ob, the Yenisey (a name derived from Evenki *ioanessi* 'great river'), and the Lena. These rivers are frozen over for much of the year – between October/November and May/June – but at other times flow powerfully across Siberia for about 2,500 miles (4,000 kilometres) until they reach the cold Arctic Ocean.

The peninsula of Kamchatka, an important center of Siberian aboriginal life, is a long, irregular tongue of land lying east of the Okhotsk Sea, between the fifty-first and sixty-second degrees of north latitude, and measuring in extreme length about seven hundred miles. It is almost entirely of volcanic formation, and the

Swampy area in the region of Yakutsk.

great range of rugged mountains by which it is longitudinally divided includes five or six volcanoes that are still active today. This immense chain of mountains stretches from the fifty-first to the sixtieth degree of latitude in one almost continuous ridge, and at last breaks off abruptly into the Okhotsk Sea, leaving to the north a high level steppe called the *dole* or desert, which is the wandering ground of the reindeer-herding Koryaks. The central and southern parts of the peninsula are broken up by the spurs and foot-hills of the great mountain range into deep sequestered valleys of the wildest and most picturesque character, and afford scenery whose majestic and varied beauty is difficult to match in all northern Asia. The climate everywhere, except in the extreme north, is comparatively mild and equable, and the vegetation has an almost tropical freshness and luxuriance to it.

The Arctic Ocean to the north of Siberia is divided into several regional seas –from west to east, the Kara Sea, the Laptev Sea and the East Siberian Sea – which are likewise choked with a thick blanket of ice for at least ten months of the year. The summer period of remission is brief: just the remaining two months, July and August.

Orographically, Siberia may be naturally divided into two parts: the lowland west of the Lena, through which only a few less important mountain ridges run, and the immense region to the east of that river, traversed by the great chain of the Jablonoff mountains, which in some places to the south-east reach a height of nearly 7000 feet, giving to this part of the province the character of a mountainous region. Shut off by mountain-chains from the warmer currents of air coming from the south and the south-east, and exposed to the Arctic winds from the north, this immense country has possibly the severest climate in the world. The winter commences early.

The smaller rivers and the numberless lakes begin to freeze in September. In the first or second week of October the whole country is covered with snow. The cold increases day by day. In the middle of the winter the temperature may remain for weeks together below the freezing-point of mercury, and at times will sink to 80 degrees below zero Fahrenheit. Such a low temperature gives a keen and penetrating sharpness to the air, and all life seems to have congealed. The Siberian winter does not rage and roar, as does that of northern Europe, but suppresses all motion. Neither the sun, which only for a few hours appears above the horizon, nor the earth, which is frozen to an unknown depth and in the summer melts only two or three feet, can withstand its power. The constantly growing cold compresses the air more and more, until it finally threatens, as it were, to suffocate all life beneath its weight. The strongest currents of air from the Arctic sea, from the Pacific, or from the immense continental regions lying to the south are unable to move this inert and compressed mass of air.

In these northerly latitudes, the ground surface – permanently frozen – is mostly shingle, perhaps covered in algae, lichens and mosses. This is the true Arctic wilderness and characterizes most of the islands, especially those off the coast of the Taimyr Peninsula. Seals, walruses, belugas and polar bears populate the coastline.

As distance increases from the north pole southwards, the Arctic wilderness turns into the tundra – a bare region in which only lichens, mosses, and short, scrubby trees (dwarf species of birch or willow, mainly) shroud the ground, with some spiky plants and Arctic grasses. Winter in the tundra is lengthy – between eight and ten months – and cold. At the end of November the sun dips below the horizon and does not return. This is the polar night, which in the tundra lasts for

The tundra under the spring snows (May).

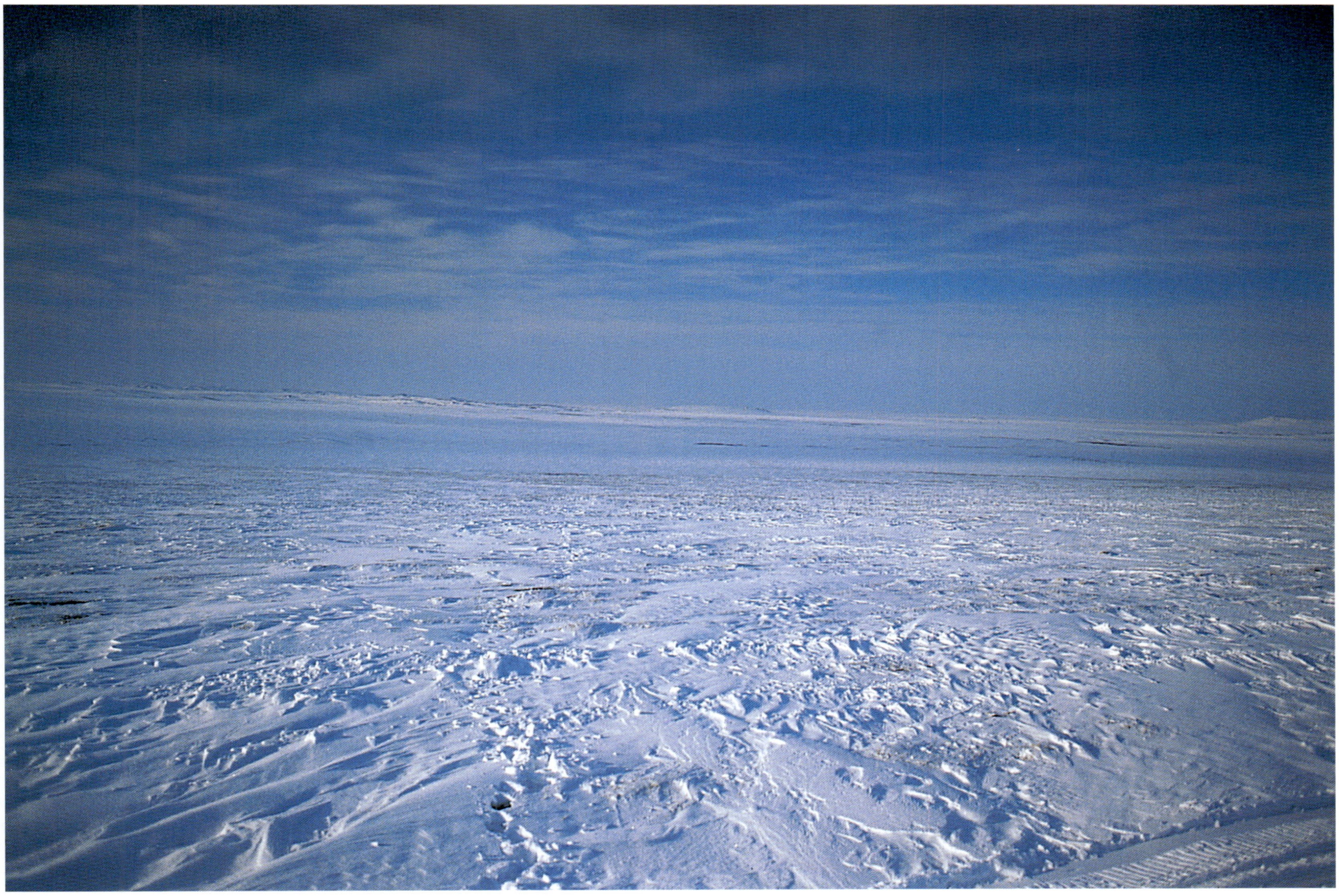

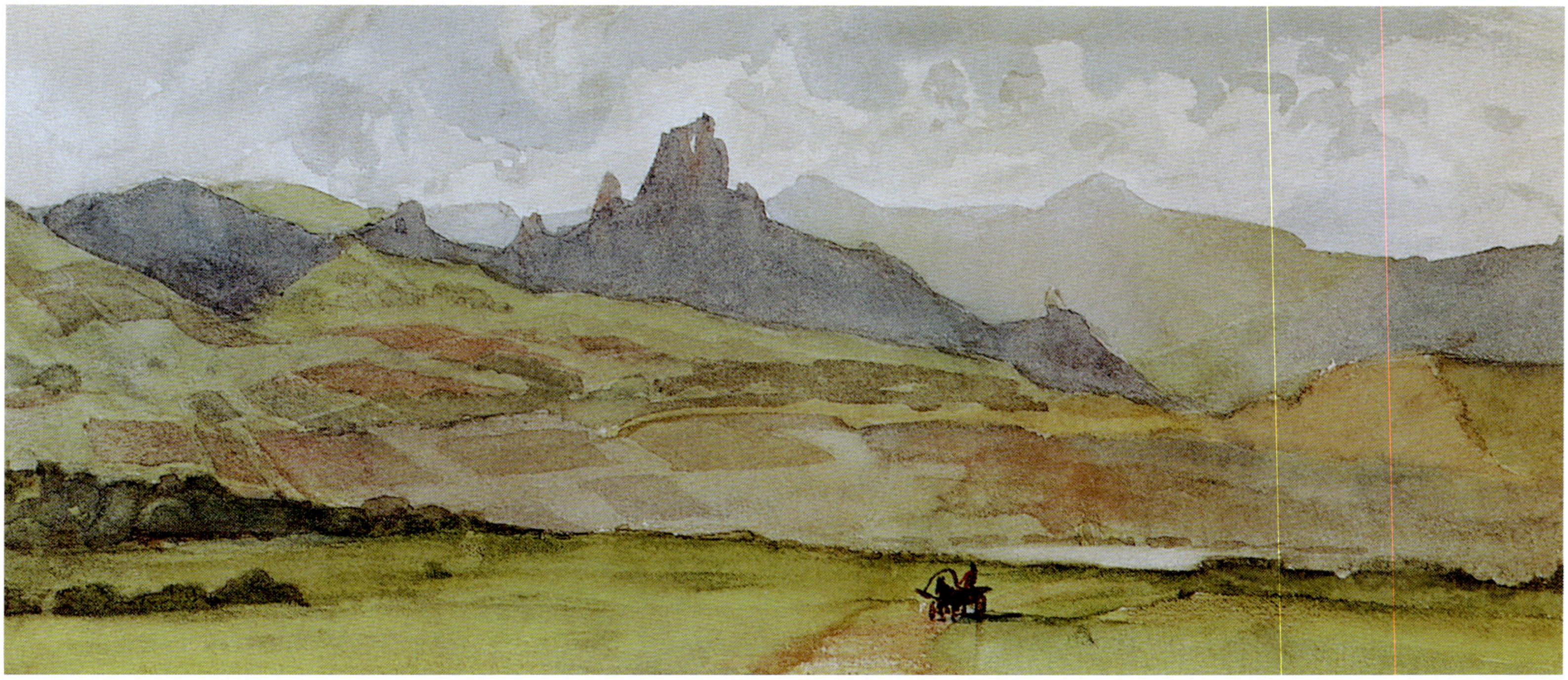

Vasily Surikov,
Steppes near Minussinsk, 1873.
Watercolour on paper, 136 x 31.8 cm.
Tretyakov Gallery, Moscow.

two or three months (compared with up to six months in the Arctic wilderness). Then finally, in January, the sun reappears once more, and the days little by little lengthen even as the nights little by little become shorter. This goes on until, from sometime in May to sometime in July, the sun doesn't leave the sky at all.

Summer in the Arctic is not so much warm as brisk – temperatures average from 5-12°C (40-68°F) – and short. Towards mid-August, heralding the end of summertime, the tundra takes on its autumnal coloration. Leaves on the woody plants turn golden, the lichens and mosses turn grey, while the wild mushrooms sprout in abundance and the berries ripen in a vast moving red and orange carpet.

The tundra is the home of the reindeer (caribou), of the Arctic wolf, the wolverine (glutton), the Arctic fox, the lemming, the great white owl, and the ptarmigan (the gallinaceous bird that, unlike any other, winters by hiding itself under the snow). In spring, the tundra welcomes the arrival of the many migratory birds – geese, swans, ducks, terns, gulls and others – that come to breed.

The terrain tends to be marshy, with a scattering of thousands of little lakes of no real depth. Baron Eddel, a traveller who a hundred years or so ago explored the lower reaches of the Indigirka and the Kolyma Rivers, recalled in his memoirs that 'to draw a map of all these lakes, all you need to do is dip a paintbrush in blue watercolour and bespeckle the paper all over with it'. The tundra is swampy because of the presence beneath the topsoil of permafrost – a stratum of soil frozen solid over thousands of years sometimes to a depth of 1,000 feet (300 metres) or more, whereas the topsoil itself may be no more than a foot (30 centimetres) deep. The permafrost is impervious, which means that although annual rainfall may be comparatively low, the water cannot drain away or be absorbed. Nor does it evaporate, because the air is already extremely humid and the heat is not sufficient.

The southern boundary of the permafrost – a line that actually runs through a little less than two-thirds of the area covered by the Russian state – lies north of the valleys of the lower Tunguska (a tributary of the Yenisey) and the Vilyuy (a tributary of the Lena). It is in the north-east of Siberia that the permafrost is most extensive. To the north of Yakutia the subsoil keeps turning up the fossilized remains of animals – whole cemeteries of mammoths trapped in thick layers of frozen sediments, their bones and their ivory tusks forming colossal repositories. It is also in Yakutia that the coldest place in the Northern hemisphere is located – at Oymyakon, in the Verkhoyansk mountains. Here, the average temperature in January is somewhere between -48°C and -50°C (-54°F and -58°F), occasionally getting down to as low as -70°C (-94°F). However, the air is so dry, and there is no wind at all, so these temperatures do not feel as extreme as they might.

Further south, a change in vegetation indicates a difference in the prevailing climate and conditions. The number of dwarf trees and bushes increases greatly. This is an intermediate zone between tundra and taiga (which many people think of as an individual zone in its own right). Continuing south, the vegetation diversifies. The trees become more numerous and grow much taller. Finally, the environment is that of the taiga – the huge northern forest that cloaks the greater part of Russia.

Comprised mostly of conifers (larch, pine and Siberian cedar) but also the north birch, willow and aspen, in the south and west deciduous species, the taiga forests are home to an important group of larger predatory animals (bears, wolverines, wolves and lynxes), foraging omnivores (foxes, sables, polecats, weasels, ermines, mink and martens), ungulates (deer and elk) and birds (capercaillies, partridges, woodpeckers and nutcrackers). Winters in this region are very long and very cold. Summers, however, can be warm in the central part of the region, where the annual range of temperatures can be as wide as 100 degrees on the Celsius scale (180 degrees on the Fahrenheit scale). The warm months are propitious times for the insects, especially mosquitoes, midges and flies for which the tundra, with its multitudinous marshes and lakes, has been the ideal breeding-ground.

Further south still, the taiga gives way first to the fertile steppes and then to the arid steppes – areas typical of northern Central Asia and Mongolia. Here, the climate is by no means unpleasant: summers are fairly long and warm, and the rainfall is light although the prevailing winds tend to be strong. Much of the steppes is covered by vast prairies of tall grasses growing on humus-rich fertile soil. It is an area well suited to farming, both of crops and of livestock. But there is plenty of wildlife too: marmots, voles and fieldmice, hamsters, jerboas, hares, foxes, saiga antelopes and badgers. Birds of the steppes include bustards, kestrels, Asiatic white cranes and many more.

Amid the arid steppes north of Mongolia, over a length of an extraordinary 400 miles (635 kilometres), stretches the largest inland source of fresh water in the world: Lake Baikal. In places it is 5,300 feet (1,620 metres) deep. A miracle of nature, Lake Baikal provides essential water for all kinds of local populations – including of course the creatures that live in it, which are now regrettably under severe threat from the pollution exuded into the lake as effluent from the timber workings up the rivers that flow into it.

The most easterly part of Russia is an area drained largely by rivers that flow out into the Pacific Ocean – rivers such as the Anadyr in the north and the Amur in the south. In the area around the Amur (which for a time forms the boundary with China), the climate and the overall humidity are favourable to the growth of mixed forest, particularly of broadleaved trees like limes, aspens or oaks. The wildlife here is much the same as in the taiga, with the addition of the Asiatic tiger, the leopard, the civet, the genet, the goral (a goat-like antelope related to the chamois), the sika deer and a great number of bird species.

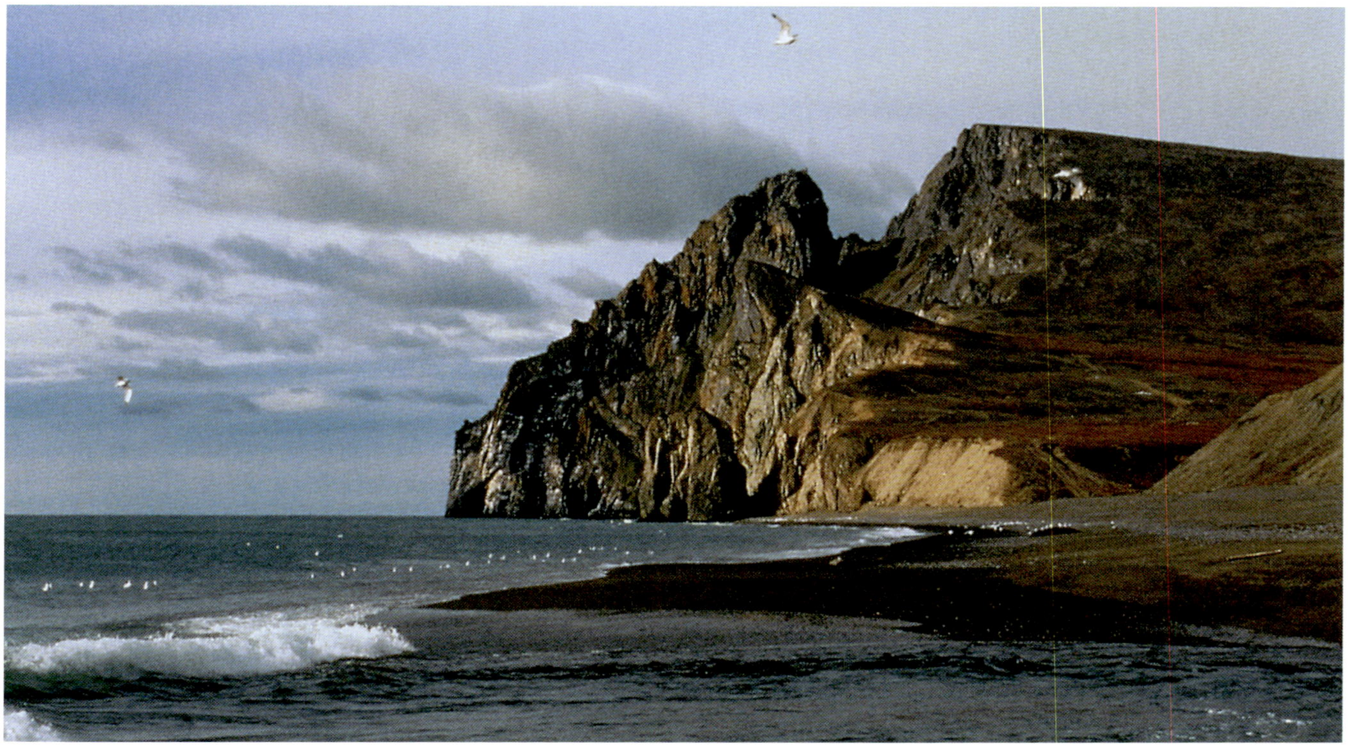

Siberia is rich in natural resources. It has minerals that can be extracted – gold, silver, tin, diamonds, nickel and phosphates; it has abundant means for supplying energy – huge reserves of oil and petroleum and of natural gas, extensive coal seams, and a great number of fast-flowing waterways; and it has a wealth of other useful and commercial materials – the timber in its forests and the pelts of its animals. In many ways, then, it is Russia's warehouse of goodies, contributing around one-fifth of the state's overall gross national product. One western traveller in Siberia commented,

> *"[Abundant animal life was there] to complete the picture. Wild ducks, with long outstretched necks, shot past us, continually in their swift level flight, uttering hoarse quacks of curiosity and apprehension; the honking of geese came to us, softened by distance, from the higher slopes of the mountains; and now and then a magnificent eagle, startled from his solitary watch on some jutting rock, expanded his broad-barred wings, launched himself into air, and soared upward in ever-widening circles until he became a mere moving speck against the white snowy crater of the Avachinski volcano. Never had I seen a picture of such wild primitive loneliness as that presented by this beautiful fertile valley, encircled by smoking volcanoes and snow-covered mountains, yet green as the Vale of Tempe, teeming with animal and vegetable life, yet solitary, uninhabited by man, and apparently unknown."*
>
> —George Kennan (1845-1924)

And yet this is the territory used by the Tsars as a penal colony, a vast concentration camp for 'internal exiles'. This too is where, simply because it contained all those goodies, massive migrations of people were organized and resettled during the whole of the period of Soviet domination, despite the generally inhospitable nature of much of the territory to human occupation. Almost 32 million people were sent to take part in exploiting Siberia's resources, and many of them (and their descendants) are still there, in the thousands of towns, industrial centres and mining camps set up specifically for this purpose – places like Vorkuta, Noril'sk, Novosibirsk, Krasnoyarsk, Bratsk, Irkutsk, Kemerovo, Prokop'yevsk, Angarsk, Komsomolsk-on-Amur, Yakutsk, Petropavlovsk-Kamchatskiy, Magadan, Khabarovsk, Vladivostok and Ussuriysk.

Northeastern edge of the Chukotka Peninsula, 1998.

Lake Lama, on the Taimyr Peninsula.

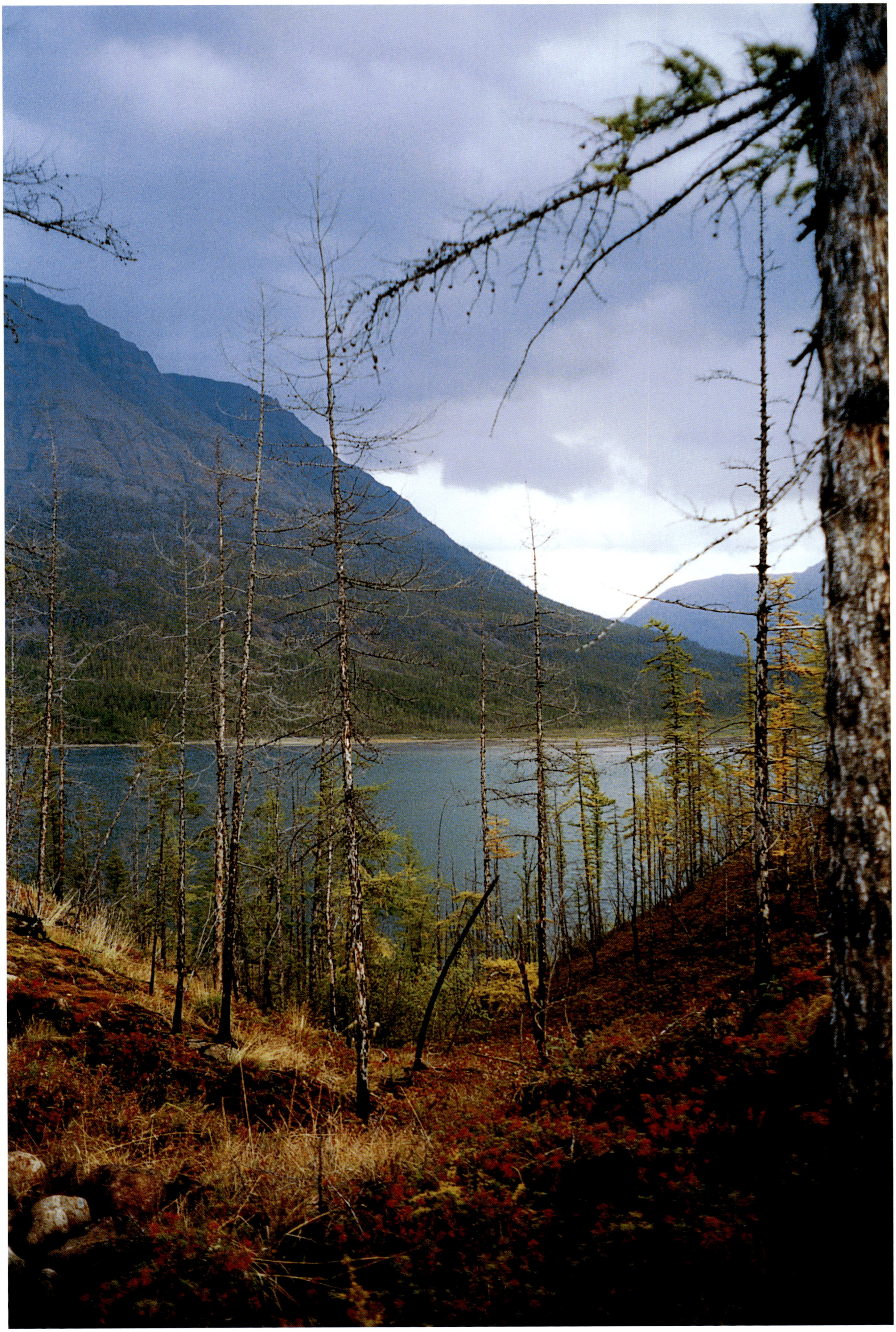

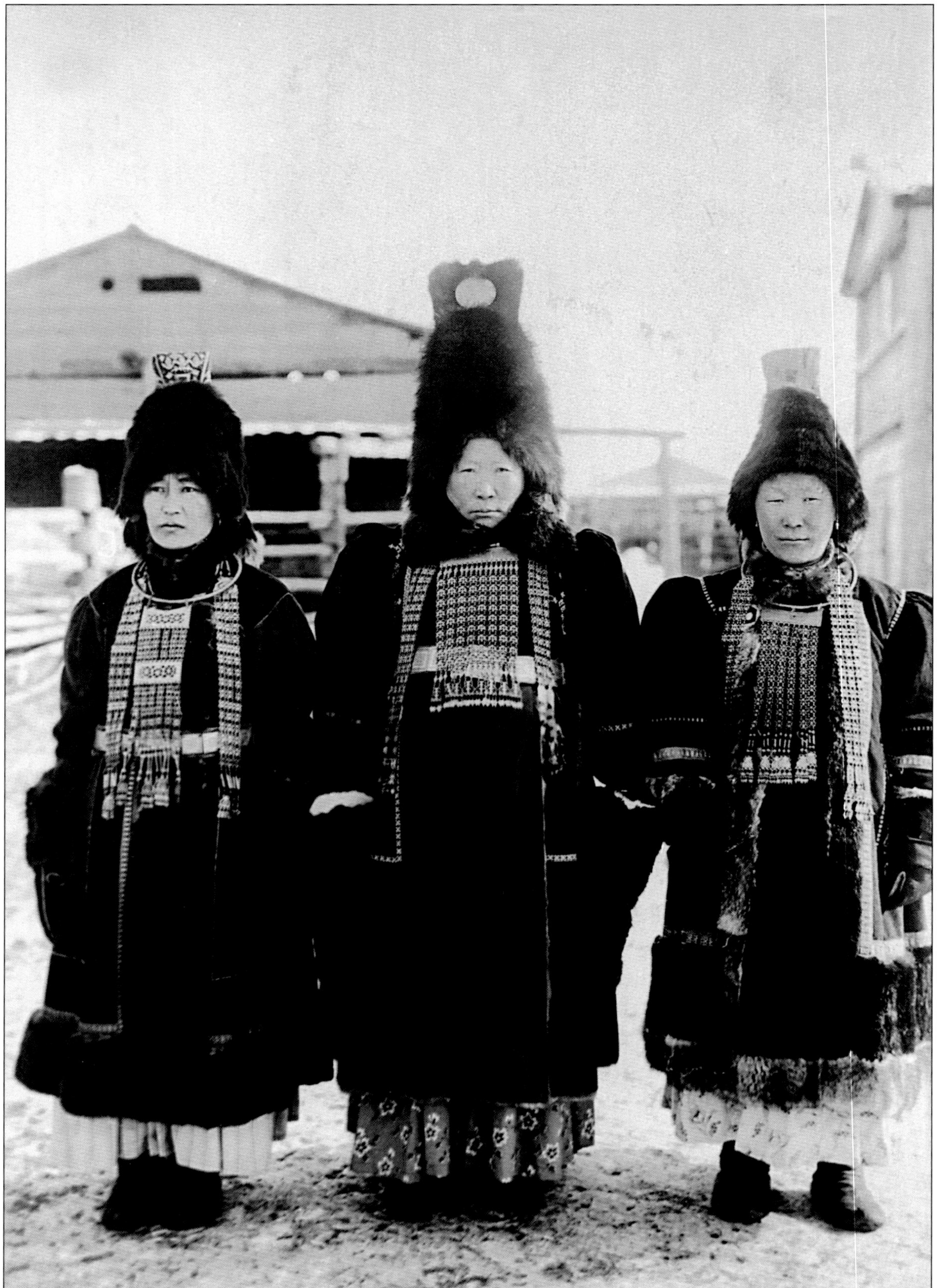

B. PEOPLE IN THE WASTELAND

"These people manage to live in a country which holds out to the ordinary traveller no inducement commensurate with the risk and hardship which its exploration involves."

Penal colony, place of banishment, 'northern Eldorado' for millions of Soviet migrants – Siberia today is populated by members of considerably more than a hundred different ethnic groups from all over what used to be the Soviet Union. It is not altogether surprising, then, that this vast northerly and easterly area is far less well known for being the cradle of cultures some of which are many thousands of years old. Representatives of around thirty of these aboriginal groups still live in the region, although some of the groups now comprise very few individuals (and are accordingly lumped together by some anthropologists under misleadingly generalizing descriptive names, like 'the northerly folk').

The fact is that from the far north down to the southern steppes and across to the most easterly region, Siberia displays a rich panorama of local cultures, traditions, languages and different ways of life. The history of these aboriginal groups, however, has in general been as misunderstood, or as unconscionably misinterpreted, as has the heritage of other aboriginal peoples, such as the Native American Indians or the Australian Aborigines, in times more recent than most care to remember. Now, at the dawning of the 21st century, this legacy of human endeavour through the millennia is rapidly eroding and may soon be lost for ever.

1) The First Siberians

Archaeologists have turned up evidence of the presence of human residents in this part of the world as early as in the Upper Palaeolithic age between 20,000 and 25,000 years ago. Scattered remains throughout Siberia and along the northerly coastline indicate that by Neolithic times much of northern Asia was inhabited by people with some pretensions to culture, for they certainly seem, all those thousands of years ago, to have differentiated between the material and the spiritual sides of life, and to have appreciated their own forms of art.

The steppes of southern Siberia and the area around Lake Baikal were first settled by tribes who were livestock-herders and crop-growers. In the neighbouring regions of the taiga, people lived instead by hunting and fishing. It is probable that the communities in what is now Yakutia and the residents of the Baikal area maintained fairly close connections, which would account for the well-established cultural group that occupied the area between the Angara and Lena rivers. Archaeological evidence relating to this group is fairly plentiful, and includes rock carvings that appear to reveal particular aspects of their spiritual beliefs (involving rites of passage, Neolithic hunting rituals, and so forth).

The regions of the tundra to the north-east of Siberia were occupied by nomadic tribes who lived by hunting reindeer (rather than herding them) and by fishing. Sites discovered between the rivers Olenëk and Kolyma have proved that the ancestors of today's Yukaghirs lived by hunting and fishing, in total isolation,

Yakuts in traditional festive costume,
1906.
Yakutia.

from the Neolithic period for at least another thousand years. Elsewhere in the north-east were regions occupied by ancestors of the present-day Chukchis and Eskimos, who were able to live a settled, residential life because they depended on the resources of the sea. In time, the way of life of these marine predators became widespread, from the shores of the Bering Sea over the length of the Arctic coastline.

Inland, many communities at first lived a nomadic form of existence based upon hunting wild reindeer. The 'domestication' of the reindeer – or at least the discovery of the way of life that involved herding the semi-domesticated creature – was a highly progressive stage in the overall history of humans' successfully taking up residence in the tundra and the taiga.

The great age of human migration in Central Asia fell between the 10th and 13th centuries AD. This was the time when an influx of new people into Siberia from the south pushed the original inhabitants there northwards and eastwards. Palaeo-Asiatic groups such as the Chukchis and Koryaks, and Tungusic tribespeople such as the Evenki and the Eveni, formerly resident in what today is Yakutia, thus found themselves hounded from their homelands and forced towards the northern and eastern margins by the ancestors of modern Yakuts – who had themselves been pushed northwards by Mongol-speaking invaders.

Until the 16th and 17th centuries, the peoples of Siberia had no contact at all with any European civilization. All were isolated, each community generally maintaining some form of relations only with neighbouring communities, and then often only if those communities were from the same cultural background. The names these people of the north give themselves in their own languages frequently bear witness to this aspect of primal isolation: most of the tribal names mean simply 'the people'. In this way, the Chukchis call themselves the *Lyg'oravetlat*, and the Eskimos think of themselves as the *Uit*, *Yuit* or *Yupik*, all of which mean 'the (real) people'.

Likewise, the Nenets know themselves as *Khasava* 'people', whereas the Olchi people, the Oroki and the Orochon people reckon that they are all *Nani* which, like *Nanai* – for several decades now the official name of their neighbouring tribal group, otherwise known as the Gold people – would seem to mean 'the people of the soil' (just as in English *human* may be related to *humus*).

When the Russians took over Siberia and its inhabitants, they tended to rechristen the groups they came across, often borrowing the neighbouring people's name for each community rather than the indigenous name. This is, for example, how the peoples now known as Yakuts and Yukaghirs got their current names. As far as they are concerned, they are the *Sakha* and the *Odul* respectively – but in Evenki they were the *Yakut* 'the yak (or cow) people' and the *Yukaghirs* 'the ice dwellers' – and that is the way they are now known all over the world. Similarly, the peoples known by much of the world (but not in countries where there are Lapps) as Khanty and Mansis recognize themselves only as *Ostyaks* or *Vogul* people. The Eveni think of themselves as the *Lamut*.

From west to east inside the zone of the tundra that borders the coast of the Arctic Ocean, nomadic groups who live by herding reindeer, by hunting and by fishing, successively neighbour and occasionally overlap with each other. In that part which is in Russian Europe, on the Kola Peninsula, live the *Saami* (or Sami), better known as the Lapps, who also live in the north of Finland, Norway and Sweden. From the banks of the Dvina to the Yenisey, and particularly on the Yamal Peninsula, live the *Nenets*, whose territory thus just reaches into the Taimyr

Eskimo (Uit) children.

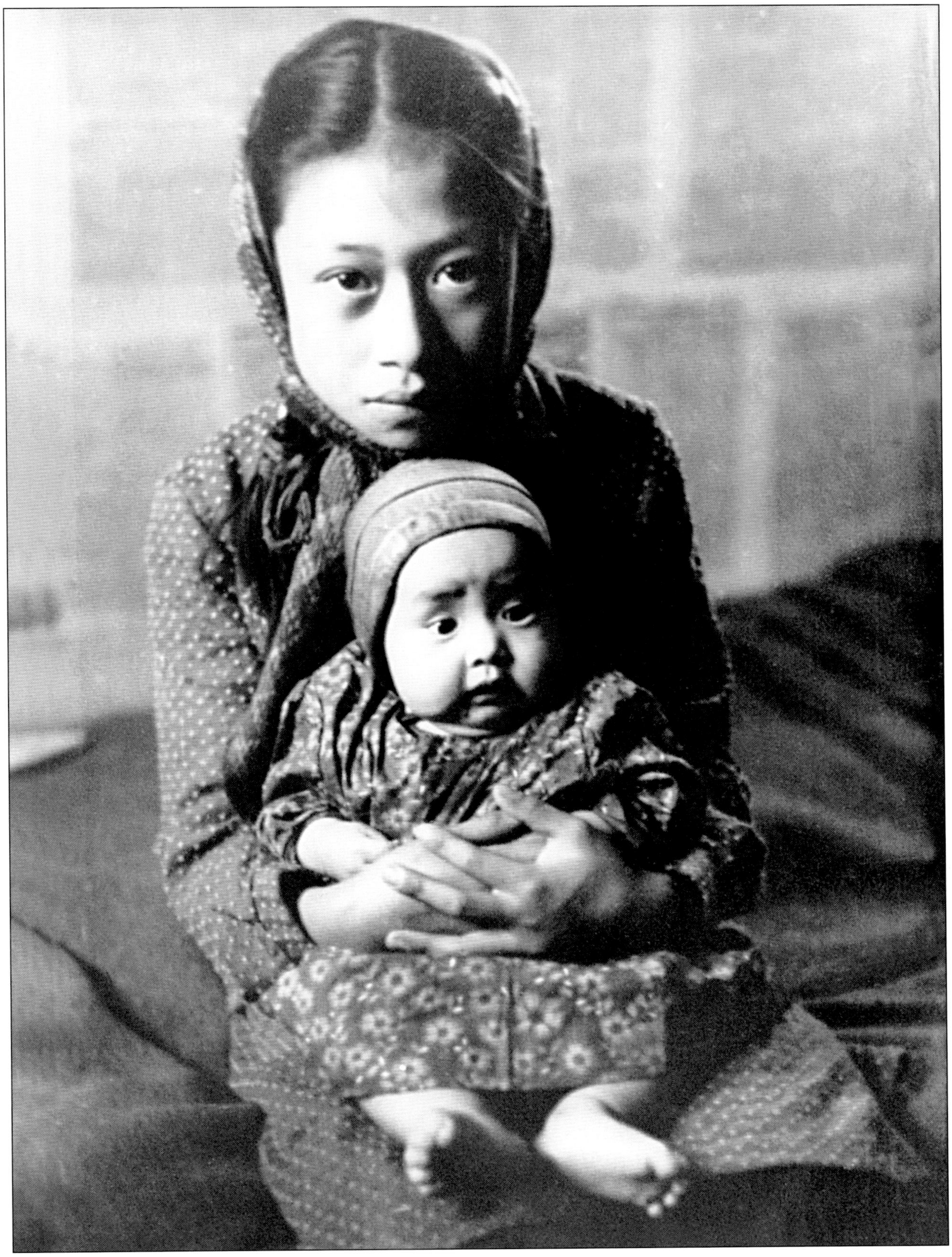

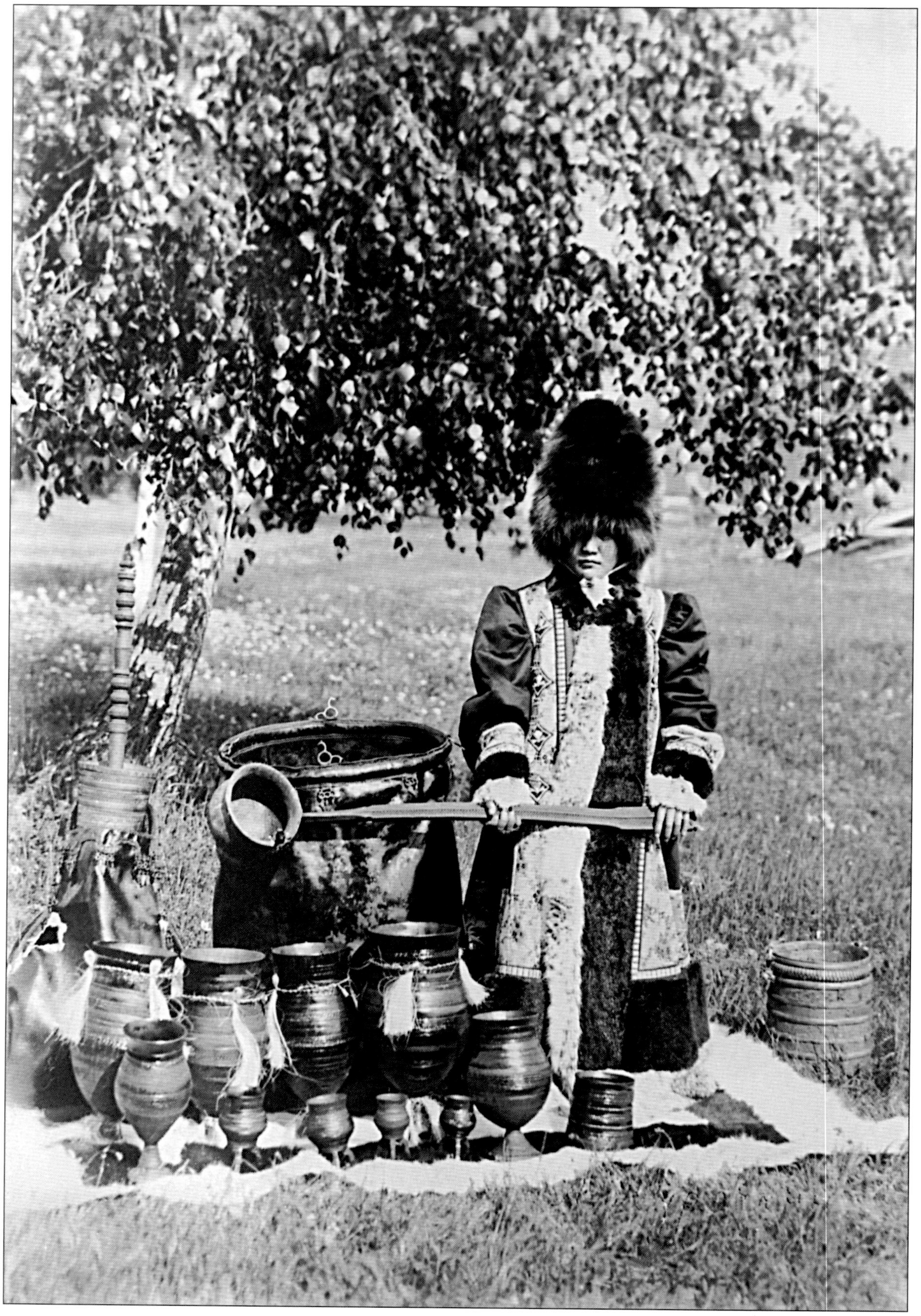

Peninsula – the area which, since prehistoric times, has been the home of the *Nganassani*, the most northerly-based people in the whole of Russian Asia. The area from the River Taz to the River Turukhan (a tributary of the Yenisey) is the home of the *Selkup*. Now almost disappeared, the *Enets* – culturally closely related to both the Nenets and the Nganassani – live along the banks of the Yenisey, where they come into contact with the *Dolgans*, a relatively new ethnic group which have not been around for much more than a couple of centuries, and which derive from combined Yakut, Evenki and Russian antecedents. The Dolgans are also prevalent in the north-east of Yakutia. Displaced ever northwards by the Yakuts infiltrating from the south, groups of *Evenki* established themselves on the lower courses of the Lena, which forms the western boundary of an enormous territory dominated for at least one millennium, as far as the River Kolyma, by the *Yukaghirs*. Of the Yukaghirs there are now only a few hundred left, generally in the Kolyma Basin not far from the mouth of the Alazeya, although some live further south in the taiga on the banks of the River Yasachnaya (Upper Kolyma). The *Eveni* people, also displaced by incoming Yakuts, once lived in what are now the lands of the Yukaghirs in northern Yakutia, and as late as the 19th century found themselves pushed all the way to the extreme north-east to live among the *Chukchis* and their neighbours to the south, in Kamchatka, the reindeer-herding *Koryaks*.

Some of these ethnic groups of the tundra are also represented in the more southerly zones of the taiga, including, for instance, the Nenets, the Eveni and the Evenki. The Evenki, in fact, are scattered across a vast area bounded in the west by a line between the Rivers Ob and Irtysh, in the east by the coastline of the Sea of Okhotsk, and in the south by the Upper Tunguska (a tributary of the Yenisey), the Angara, Lake Baikal, and by the Amur River.

The taiga affords a fairly good living for the nomadic peoples who hunt and fish, or who hunt when they are not herding reindeer. In the west, on the plain of the Ob, is the land of the *Khanty* and the *Mansis* – closely related culturally and linguistically – who have a variety of lifestyles, based on hunting, fishing, herding reindeer and breeding other livestock. The non-nomadic (residential) *Kets* hunt and fish on the edges of the Yenisey. Pouring up from the south during the 14th century, the *Yakuts* established themselves firmly on the middle courses of the Lena. This horse- and cattle-breeding people finally occupied an area as large as the Indian subcontinent, bordered to the north by the Arctic Ocean, pushing before them to the north and east those groups that had been there first – the Evenki, the Eveni, the Yukaghirs and the Chukchis.

In the south of Siberia, towards the frontier with Mongolia between the Ob and the Yenisey, the *Altai* people (or *Oirot*), the *Tuva* people (or Tuvinians or *Soyot*), a little further northwards the *Khakass* people and, to the east of Lake Baikal, the *Buryats* are all specialists in raising horned animals Mongolian-style. Yet the *Karagas* people (or *Tofalars*) – a very small ethnic group to the west of Lake Baikal – herd reindeer and live by hunting and fishing in the taiga. The peoples of the Pacific coastline, from the Bering Strait in the north down to the Chinese border, mostly hold to a traditionally non-nomadic (residential) lifestyle that involves hunting marine mammals. These include the *Aleuts* of the Commander (Komandorski) Islands, separated from their ethnic brethren on the other islands to the east, the Aleutian Islands, not only by the Russian-American border but also by the international date-line. In this way they are very like the *Uit* (*Yuit* or Eskimos) who live on the shores of the Bering Strait, cut off from their ethnic cousins in Alaska and Canada. Inhabitants here additionally include communities of

Yakuts in national costume making koumiss for the festival of Isyakh, 1910.
Russian Museum of Ethnography, St. Petersburg.

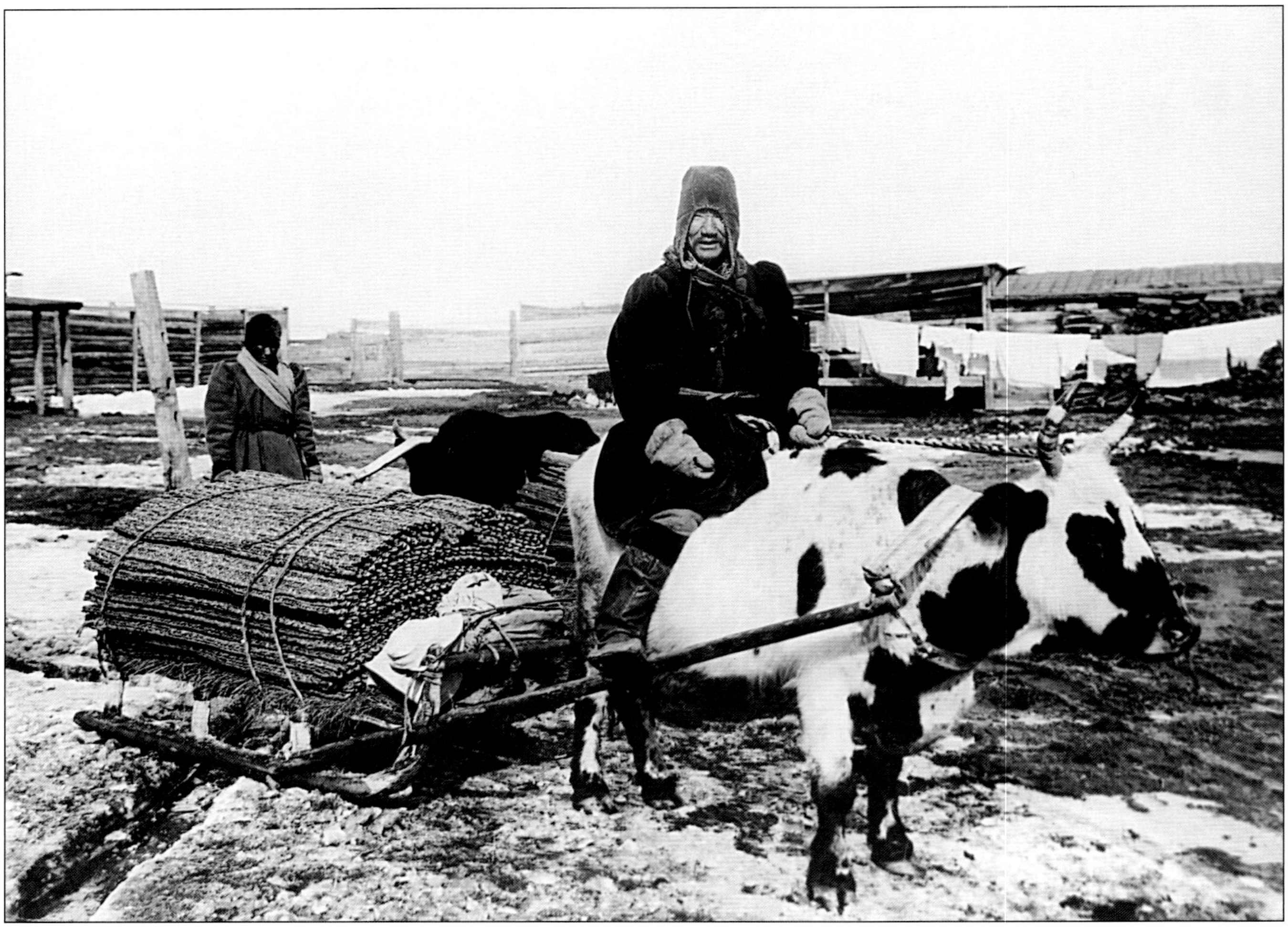

Yakut carrying straw for sale.

Chukchis and Koryaks, smaller groups of semi-nomadic Eveni people living on the shores of the Sea of Okhotsk (in the Magadan region), and, on the island of Sakhalin, the *Nivkhi* (or *Gilyaks*). Finally, still in the extreme east of Siberia, but further south around the border with China, is where the Eveni and the Evenki live, in close touch with the *Olchi,* the *Orochon* people, the *Oroki*, the *Negidal* people and the *Udekhe*, all originally inhabitants of the Amur Basin. Before the Russians took over, these semi-nomadic groups who depend on hunting and fishing were for centuries, if not millennia, under the thumb of their equally dominant neighbours, the Chinese.

2) Cultures on the Edge of Extinction

Although the peoples of Siberia may no longer live in what used to be their ancestral territories and are scattered in groups here and there in no particular pattern, they may nonetheless be regarded as stemming ultimately from only eight independent 'nations,' based not on racial characteristics but on language families. Most, in fact, belong to one or other of just two – the Uralic and the Altaic language super-families.

In the west of Siberia, the Uralic super-family is represented by the Khanty and the Mansis who are related to the Finno-Ugric branch (which includes Lapps and Finns), and by their northern neighbours the Nenets, the Enets, the Nganassani and the Selkup who make up the Samoyedic branch. The Evenki, the Eveni and

Chukchi,
Hunter with the skin of a fox he has killed, 1979.
Magadan, village of Vankarem.

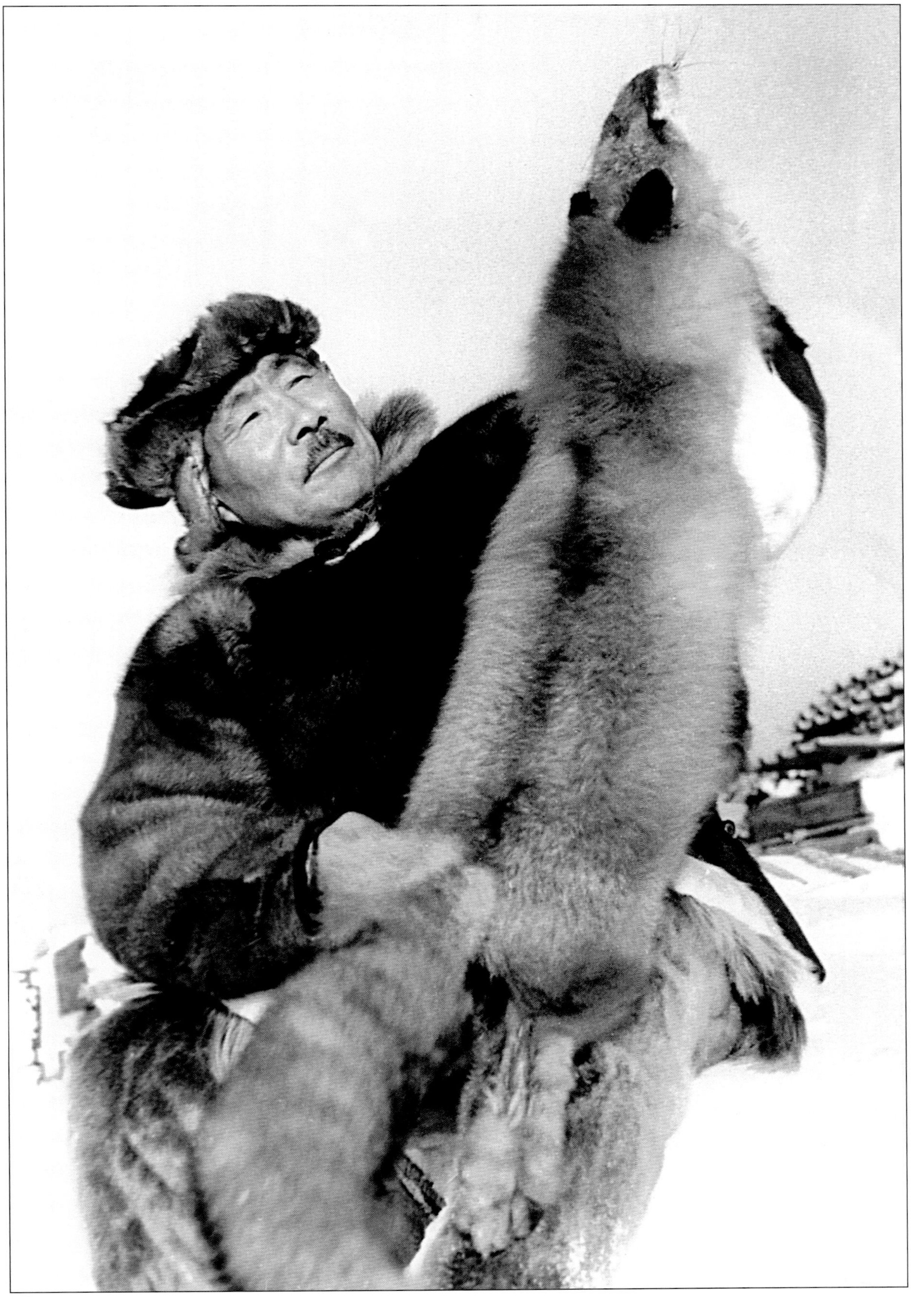

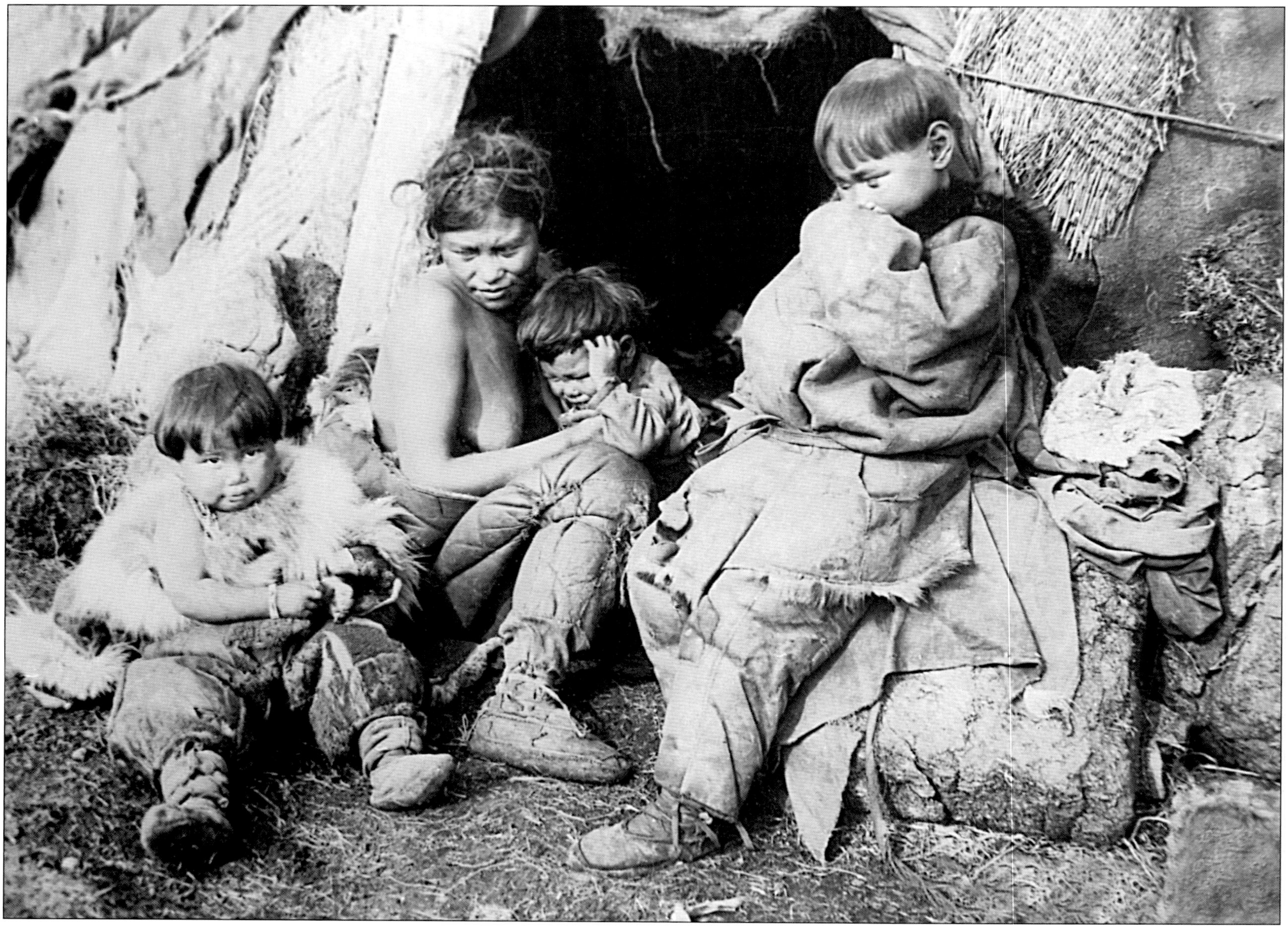

Chukchi woman with children at the entrance to the yarang, 1925-1926. Yakutia.

the peoples of the Amur region all belong to the Tungusic family, a branch of the Altaic super-family, which also includes in its Turkic branch the Yakuts, the Khakass people, the Tuva people, the Altai people, the Dolgans, the Shorians and the Karagas people, and in its Mongolian branch the Buryats. The Kets around the Yenisey and the Nivkhi on Sakhalin each speak a language that appears not to be related to any other.

Independent of the Uralic and Altaic super-family communities listed above, the peoples of north-eastern Siberia form three different linguistic groups: Chukchi-Koryak-Kamchatka (occasionally referred to as 'palaeo-Asiatic') which includes the tongues of the Chukchis, the Koryaks, the Kereks and the Itelmen (the latter of whom speak Kamtchatka); the Eskimo-Aleut group which combines the Uit and the Aleuts; and finally the Yukaghir-Chuvantsi group which self-evidently comprises the languages of the Yukaghirs and the Chuvantsi, although these two may be said to be grouped together only by convention.

The majority of the ethnic groups in Siberia have a couple of major factors in common: an area of dispersal so wide as to be significant for the continuing

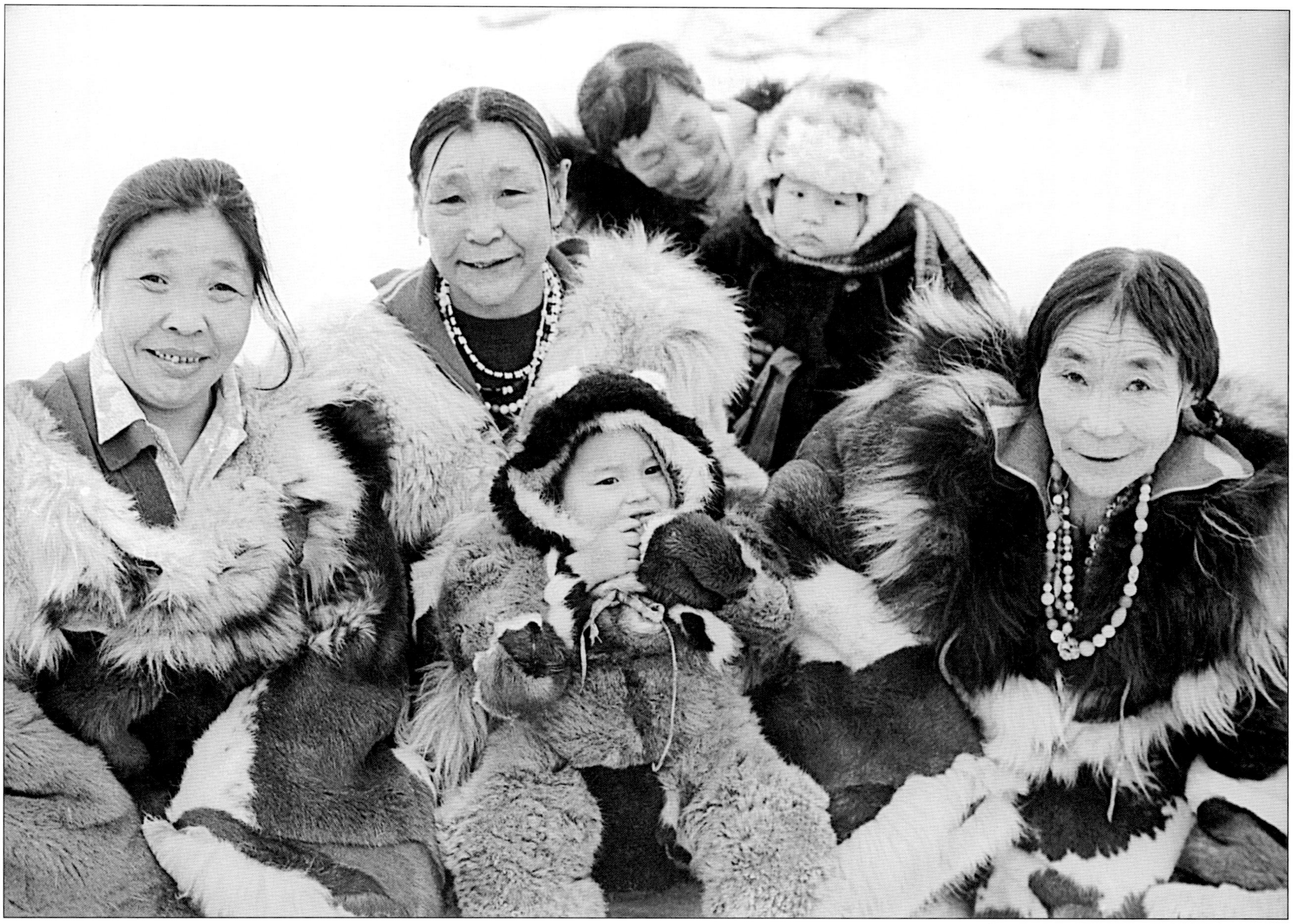

survival of each group, and the varying influences of unrelated neighbouring groups on the larger groups that do live as ethnic communities. So, for example, the Koryaks – like the Chukchis or the Eveni people – may themselves be divided into two groups: one that lives on the coast by hunting marine mammals and by fishing, the other that lives as nomads who herd reindeer and follow them inland in due season. Such groups, although originally speaking precisely the same language tend after all this time to speak different dialects of the parent language. And in the case of the Yukaghirs, the dialects have become so different and so mutually unintelligible that some linguistic anthropologists prefer to regard the Yukaghirs of the taiga who live by hunting and fishing as a completely different ethnic group from the Yukaghirs of the tundra who live by herding reindeer.

Regardless of how different the languages and the corresponding dialects have become, regardless of the many linguistic barriers existing between the residents of Siberia, it remains a salient fact that today it is (and has been for some time) the Russian language that has in many areas displaced the ancestral languages for

Chukchi,
The people of the tundra, 1986.
Anadyr area.

ordinary daily purposes. The result of compulsory assimilation programmes and the deliberate blurring of ethnic differences, it may well be that even now the numbers of speakers of some of these tongues are so few as not to be able to prevent them from dying out altogether.

With a total of some 32 million inhabitants, Siberia can nonetheless boast no more than a million and a half of the aboriginal populations. Indeed, apart from the Buryats, the Yakuts, the Tuva people, the Khakass people, the Shorians and the Altai people, no fewer than 26 other ethnic groups are officially (according to figures taken from the Soviet census in 1989) recorded as 'ultra-minorities', comprising between them no more than around 180,000 individuals, and thus as groups 'doomed to certain extinction'.

The most numerous ethnic group of these is that of the Nenets who, in the same census, were counted at 34,190 persons. Now the Nenets are one of the peoples of Siberia who have best preserved their traditional way of life and culture. The Evenki, almost as numerous (29,901 persons), have on the other hand been subject to considerable assimilation, especially into Yakut groups. Next in order of numerical importance are the Khanty (22,283 persons), then the Eveni (17,055), the Shorians (16,652), the Chukchis (15,107), the Nanai people (11,833), the Koryaks (8,942), the Mansis (8,279), the Dolgans (6,584) and the Nivkhi (4,631). The remaining ethnic groups are undoubtedly 'ultra-minorities':

· The Selkup, the Olchi, the Itelmen and the Udekhe make up between 2,000 and 4,000 people

· The Chuvantsi, the Nganassi, the Yukaghirs, the Kets, the Saami of western Siberia and the Uit of eastern Siberia number between 1,000 and 2,000 people

· Some ethnic groups comprise no more than a few hundred men and women: these are the Orochon people (883 persons), the Karagas people (722), the Aleuts of eastern Siberia (644), the Negidal people (587), the Enets (198) and the Oroki (179)

· One really tiny ethnic group – so small that it was not even counted separately in the census – was that of the Kereks of southern Chukotka, who in total numbered fewer than 50 representatives.

Assimilation of language and of culture has affected all of these small ethnic groups to one extent or another, but so has such assimilation also affected – if less seriously – the more numerously significant groups, such as the Buryats (listed in the census as numbering 417,425 persons), the Yakuts (380,242), the Tuva people (206,160), the Khakass people (78,500) and the Altai people (69,409). Today, just one small proportion of Siberia's original inhabitants preserves an ancient and traditional way of life, continues on a daily basis to practise and to teach its ancestral rituals and language. But such efforts are puny in the face of what is massed against them, notably the effects of 'modern life' and 'technological development' (which include an increased mortality rate, severely depressed morale, stress disorders and diseases, alcoholism, high unemployment, soaring suicides and other measures of progress). It was the frenetic pace at which assimilation was overtaking all these various ethnic groups that caused them to be featured in *The Red Book of Ethnic Groups on the Verge of Disappearing*, published during the last years of the Soviet Union.

To understand how this demographic and cultural erosion came about, it is necessary to turn back and look once more at history.

Vasily Surikov,
Siberian Beauty, 1891.
Oil on canvas, 50 x 39 cm.
Tretyakov Gallery, Moscow.

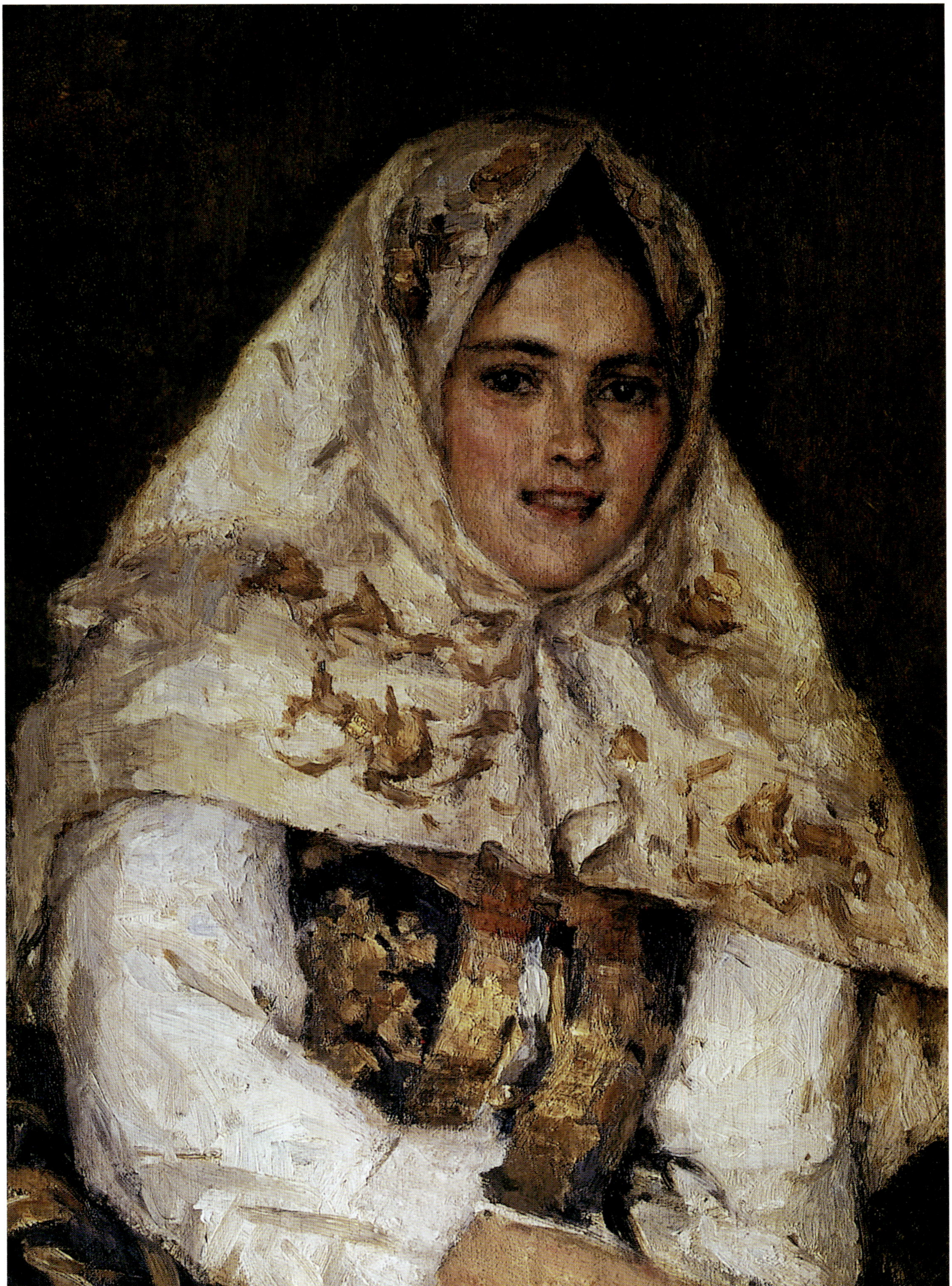

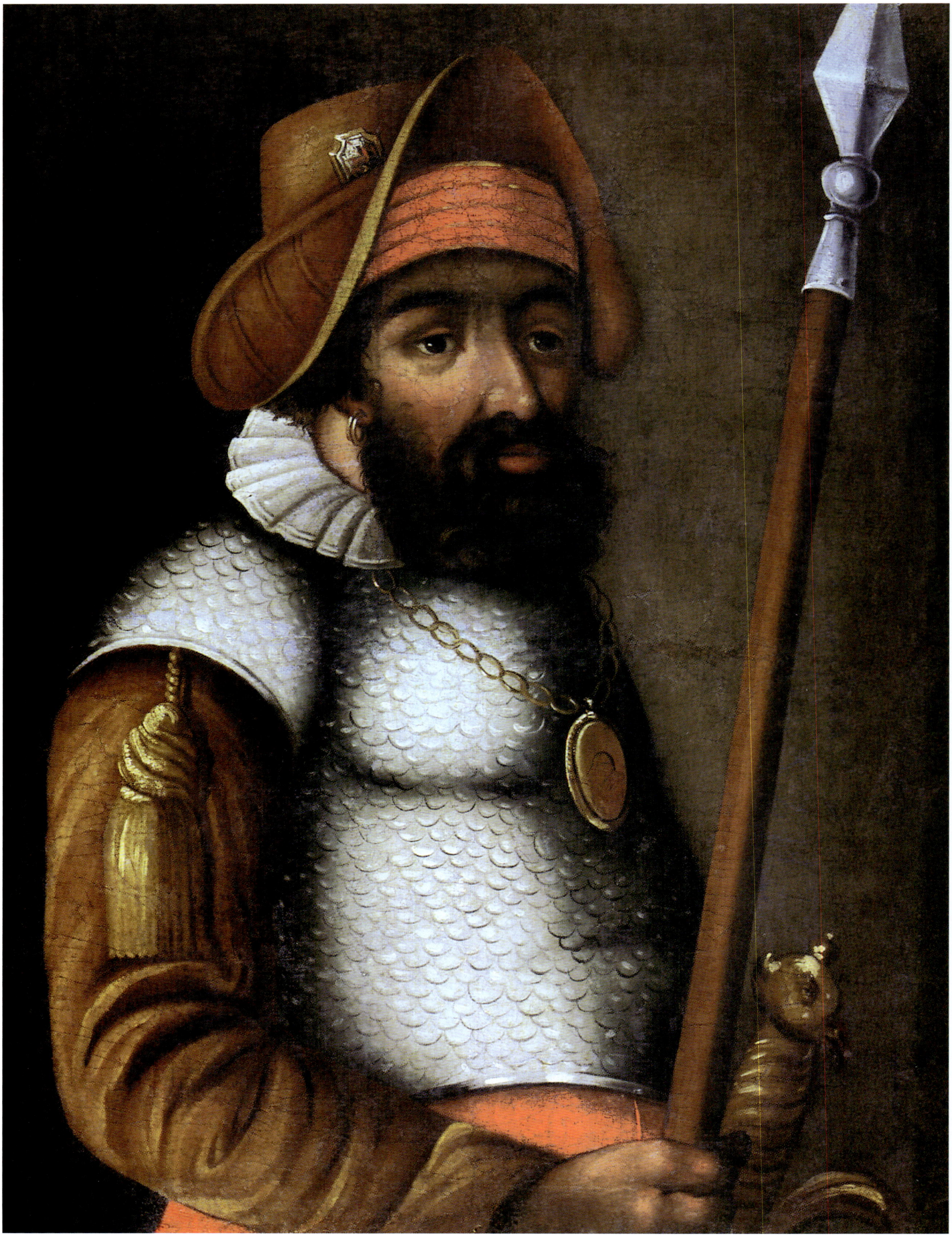

C. THE TRANS-SIBERIAN RAILWAY

"The Trans-Siberian Railway featured Europe and Western civilisation at the one extremity, China and Eastern civilisation at the other. In between, the greatest of the continents, and across that continent the unbroken band of iron."

1) The Conquest of Siberia

For a long time blocked by the unwelcome presence of the Tatars, the extension of the Russian Empire on the far side of the Ural Mountains was made possible only by the eventual defeat of the Tatar khan, Kuchum, at the hands of Yermak and his Cossack forces in 1582. The great Asiatic empire established by Jenghiz Khan began to go to pieces in the fifteenth century, and various more or less independent governments were established on the site of the ancient realm. Dissensions among these people caused some of them to spread northward, and in the beginning of the sixteenth century, before Yermak's expedition, the Tartars had occupied much of the territory east of the Ural Mountains. They had found it easy to overcome the scattered inhabitants who had lived there previously, but they found more difficulty with the Russians with whom they came in contact in the Urals, so that in 1555 the Tartar Prince Ediger agreed to pay a yearly tribute of 1,000 sable skins to the Tsar, though otherwise still preserving a nominal independence. His successor, however, the Khan Kutchum, rebelled against this tribute shortly before Yermak's arrival, and the Stroganoffs, a powerful family in the Ural Mountains, encouraged Yermak to make his invasion.

When Yermak crossed the Urals he found several well-established Tartar communities, and he first carried on operations successfully on the east slope of the mountains. He moved then eastward and easily captured Isker, the stronghold of Khan Kutchum, in the valley of the River Tobol, near where the town of Tobolsk now stands. He sent messengers to the Tsar describing his victories, and announcing that he held the conquered regions subject to his commands. The Tsar, Ivan IV, surnamed "the Terrible," greatly pleased with the services of Yermak, raised him in royal favor, and sent him a hundred rubles, a silver cup and two cuirasses, as well as a fur robe which he had worn himself, a sign of special favor. The Tartar legend relates that a small black animal like a hound emerged from the Tobol River, while a large white shaggy wolf emerged from the Irtish. They met on a sandy island near the confluences of the two streams and fought, the smaller animal finally killing the larger one; then both disappeared in the Irtish. The native soothsayers interpreted this as meaning the overthrow of the Tartars by the Russians.

Yermak continued his work of invasion, but in 1584 was defeated by the Tartars, and was drowned in the River Irtish. After his death, however, the Russians promptly followed up the conquests that he had begun, and rapidly occupied the vast regions to the east. In 1587 the now flourishing city of Tobolsk was founded near the site of the old Tartar stronghold of Khan Kutchum. In 1604 the Russian advance had progressed so far to the east that

Unknown artist,
Portrait of Yermak, early 18th century.
Oil on canvas, 70 x 57 cm.
V. P. Sukachev Art Museum, Irkutsk.

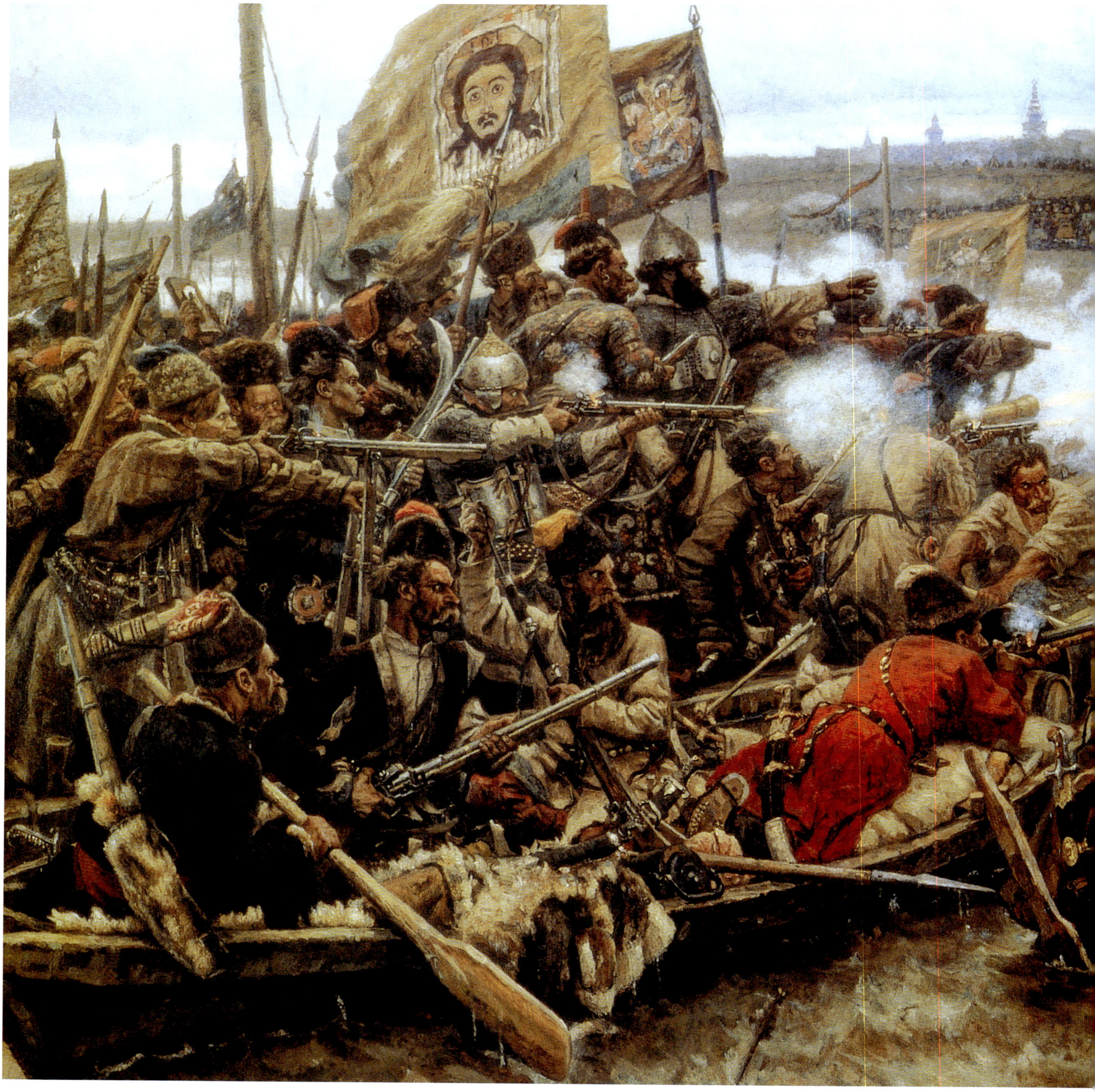

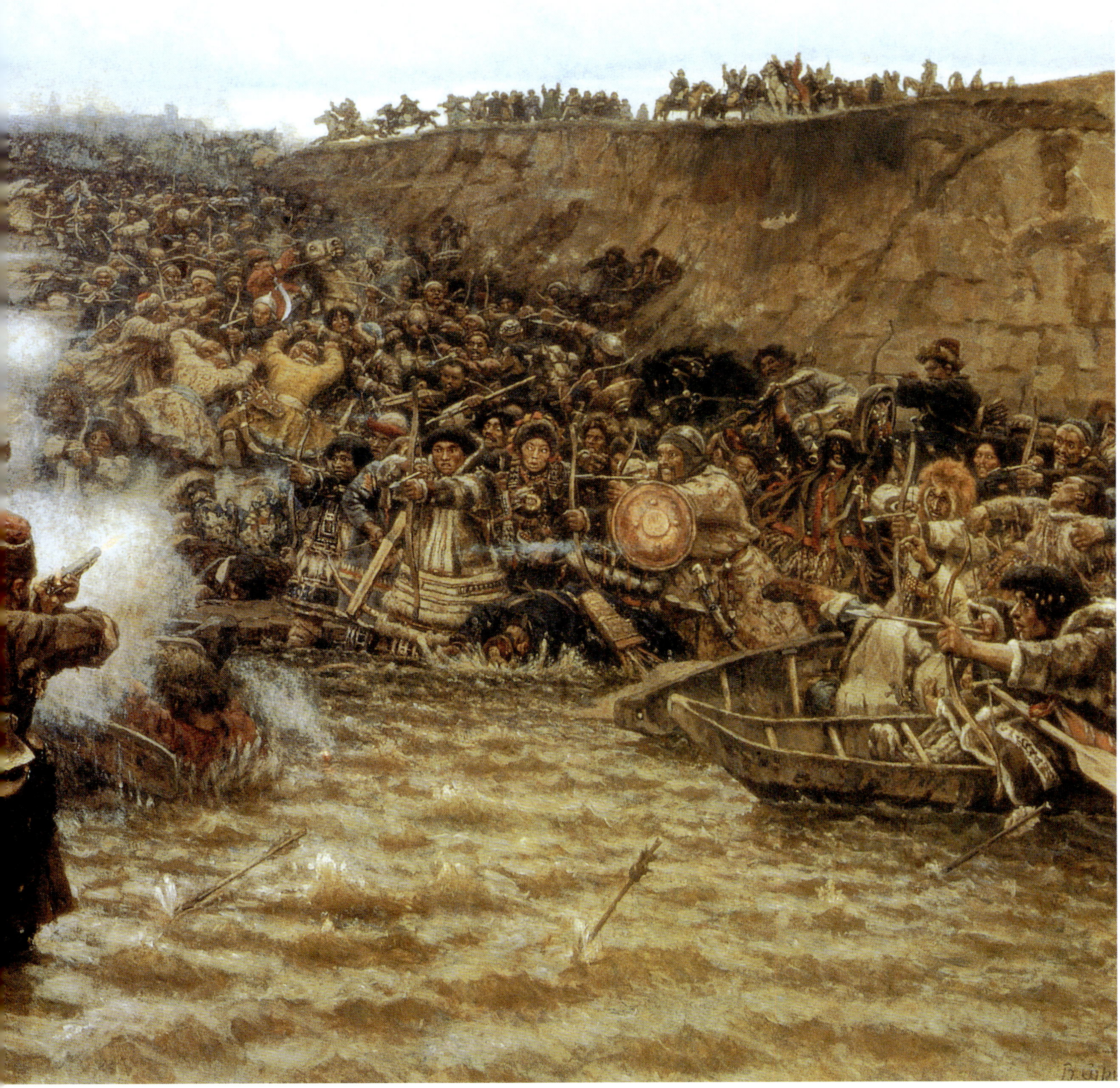

the town of Tomsk, almost 1,000 miles from the Urals, now one of the most flourishing commercial centers of northern Asia, was founded; and in 1622 the town of Yakutsk, over twice that distance, was founded; while in 1647 the Cossack Dezhneff crossed Bering Straits, over 4,000 miles east of the Urals. In 1643 the explorer Poyarkoff discovered the Amur region in southeastern Siberia; and in 1649-52 the celebrated Khabaroff entered this same vast region and defeated the natives and the Chinese armies that defended it. It was, however, subsequently returned to the Chinese by the treaty of Nerchinsk in 1689, and was not again recovered by the Russians until 1858, when, by the skill and diplomacy of Count Muravioff, it was ceded to them by the treaty of Aigun without any fighting. Shortly after the middle of the seventeenth century the town of Irkutsk, west of Lake Baikal, and the town of Nerchinsk, east of Lake Baikal, were founded.

Thus within less than a hundred years after the campaigns of Yermak the Russians had carried their explorations and conquests across Asia to the farthest points on the Pacific Coast ; and all the northern part of the continent, from the Urals to the Pacific, and from the Turko-Mongolian possessions and the Chinese frontier on the south, to the Arctic Ocean on the north, was under Russian control.

The conquest of Siberia had been accomplished at remarkable speed, but at the expense of a great deal of blood.

As they continued in their warlike progress ever eastwards, the Cossacks demanded tribute from the populations they overran – tribute not in the form of money but of furs: the yassak. They also constructed forts to control these new subjects of the Russian Tsar and in which to stockpile the precious tribute. Some of the tribespeople, such as the Yakuts, surrendered without much resistance (the Russians were excellent at knowing whom to treat gently and offer gifts to), only to rise in revolt soon afterwards. It was more common, however, for the tribal groups – like the Khanty and the Mansis, the Khakass people, the Evenki and the Eveni people – to act with the utmost ferocity in staving off for as long as possible this hated colonization. The pacification of the north-east of Siberia, from the end of the 17th century, thus took place amid horrifically bloody scenes of combat. The Yukaghirs, and then the Itelmen, sustained heavy losses; whole communities of them were wiped out. The Koryaks kept up their defiant opposition for nearly 25 years. And only after a full 60 years were the pertinacious Chukchis – a warrior nation – finally subdued, and even then only at the wrong end of the cannons brought in especially by the Russians, forced to adopt unusual methods.

The incorporation of Siberia into the Russian Empire was accompanied by an influx of colonists and the inauguration of a social system designed to exploit the indigenous populations. The consequences were manifold and immediate: the aboriginal peoples were forcibly suppressed, and made thoroughly aware of their insignificant numeric strength. As happened in the Americas, the colonists who came to Siberia brought with them all kinds of viral and bacterial diseases against which the aboriginal peoples had no immunity – smallpox, measles, and syphilis among them. Recurrent epidemics racked the defenceless communities. Smallpox alone accounted for the deaths of several thousand Yukaghirs.

The *yassak* system likewise, over time, was to have repercussions that were all but catastrophic for the peoples of Siberia. Together with the diseases it represented a principal reason for the declining numbers in the population of the

Vasily Surikov,
The Conquest of Siberia by Yermak, 1895.
Oil on canvas, 285 x 599 cm.
Russian Museum, St. Petersburg.

Vasily Surikov,
The Conquest of Siberia by Yermak, detail *(indigenous archers)*, 1895.
Oil on canvas, 285 x 599 cm.
Russian Museum, St. Petersburg.

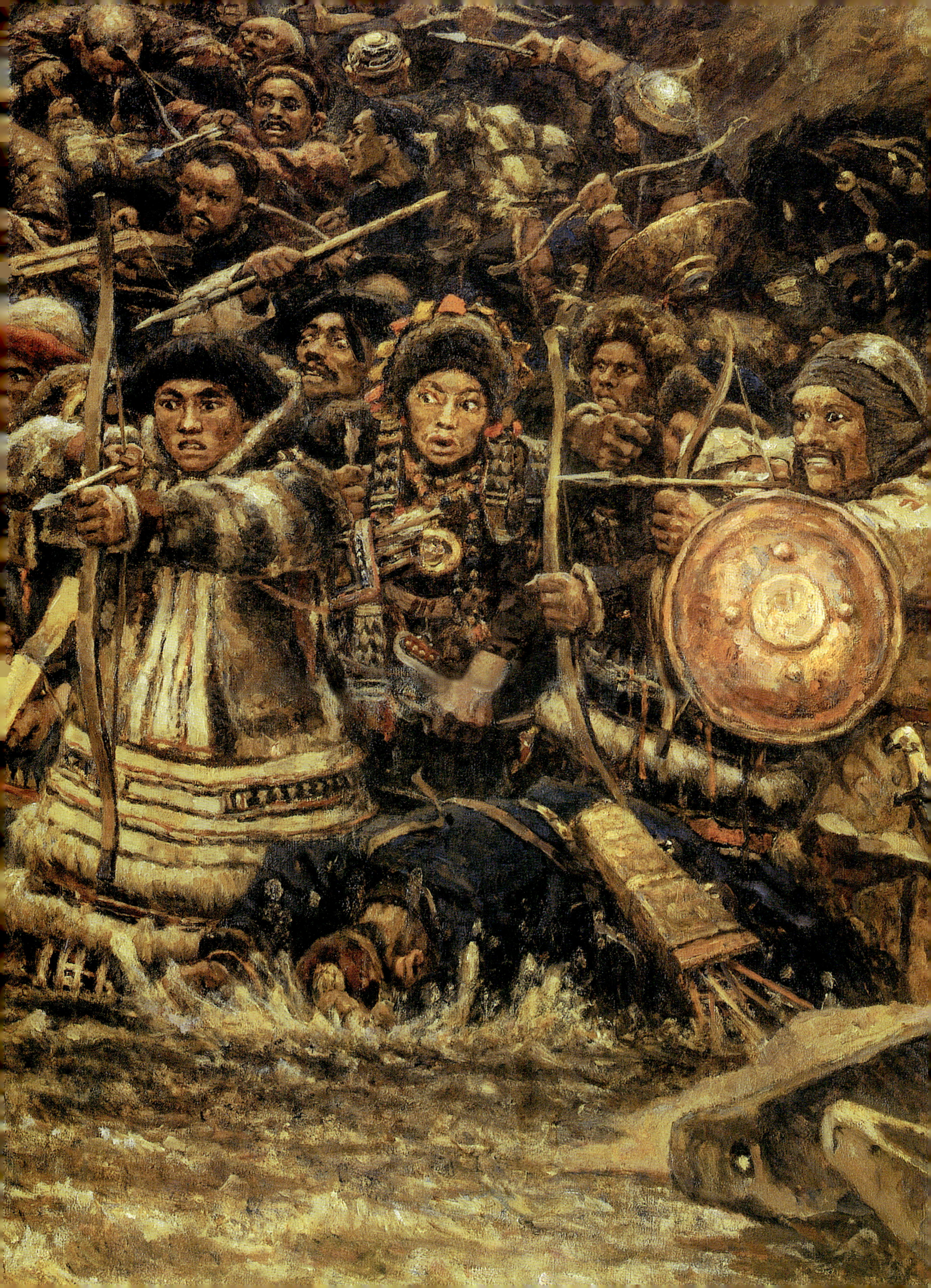

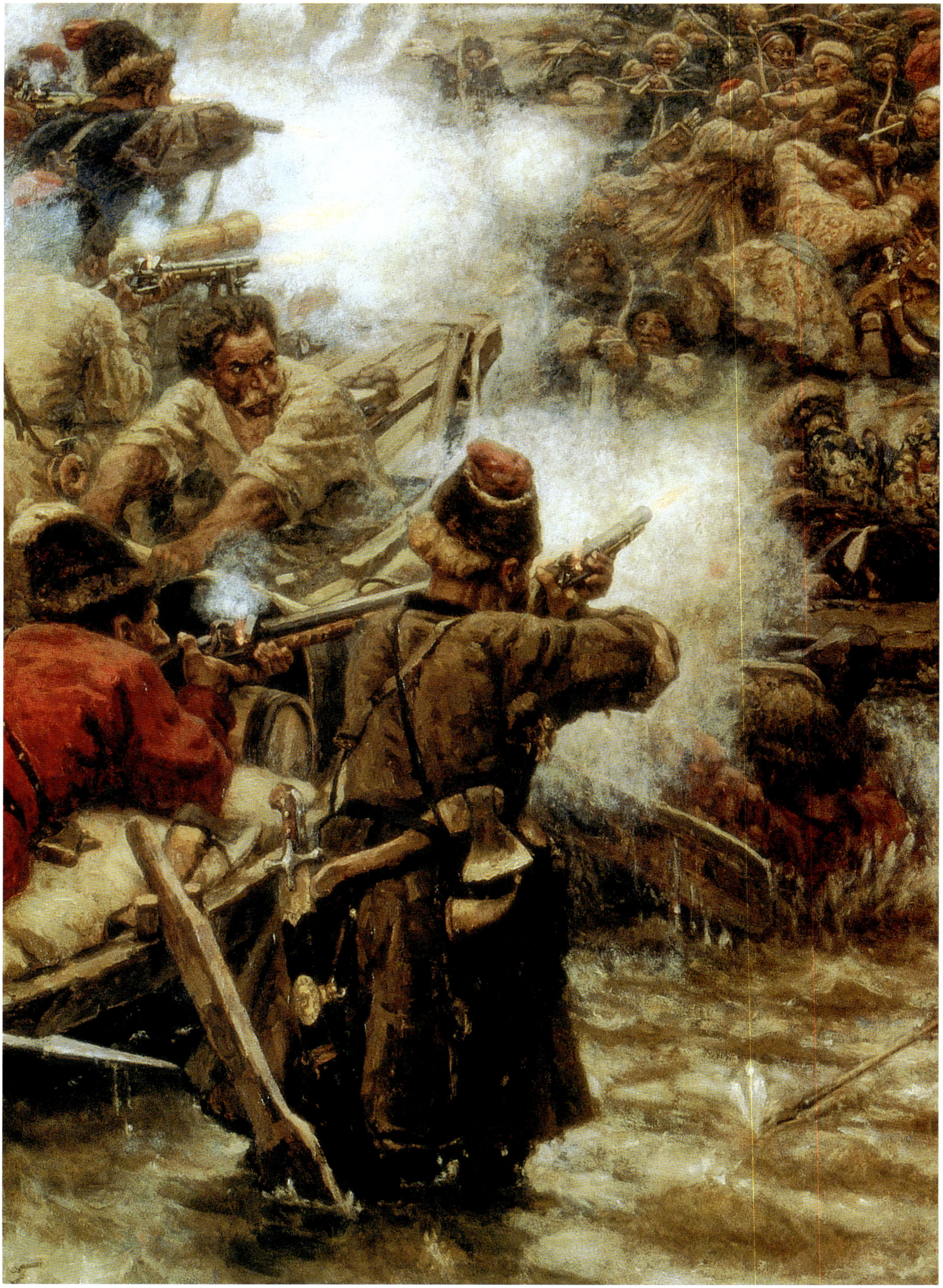

ethnic groups during the Tsarist period. So oppressive was the levy of furs that local inhabitants were often forced to go to extreme lengths to get hold of 'the golden pelt'. If the levy had not been fully supplied by the due date, the officers responsible for collecting it had various additional methods of extracting it. One of the more common was to kidnap someone and hold him or her to ransom until it was forthcoming, usually someone important in the community of whoever was defaulting on the tax – perhaps one of the best hunters, a headman, possibly one of the tribal elders. In this way quite often having insufficient time to see to keeping themselves properly fed, exhausted, obliged to do without their leaders or the people most required for the survival of their group, the local people all too frequently underwent periods of famine which, in the environmental conditions natural to the cold north and to Siberia in general, were particularly, insidiously, destructive.

At the beginning of the 18th century, brutality and massacres accompanied the forcible conversion to Christianity of the indigenous peoples. The Russians had realized that 'gentle' methods did not seem to be working. Simultaneously, the colonists continued to exploit the people shamelessly. It was nonetheless only a little later, in 1824, that an official Code of Practice was promulgated by the authorities that was meant to protect the peoples of Siberia from abuses of these kinds. Nothing much came of it.

In the space of two centuries, the conquest and the colonization of Siberia caused a general – in some cases, even permanent – decline in the fortunes of the aboriginal populations. By the end of the 19th century some of the ethnic groups were in such a sorry state (by way of depletion in numbers, wretched health, poverty and low morale) that even then their disappearance altogether was regarded as being only a matter of time – and a short time at that.

On the 9th of November 1901, the following telegram flashed along the wires from Sergei Witte, the Director of Railway Affairs, to his Imperial master, the Tsar :

> *"On May 19, 1891, your Majesty at Vladivostok turned with your own hand the first sod of the Great Siberian Railway. Today, on the anniversary of your accession to the throne, the East Asiatic Railway is completed. I venture to express to your Majesty, from the bottom of my heart, my loyal congratulations on this historic event. With the laying of the rails for a distance of 2,500 kilometres, from the Transbaikal territory to Vladivostok and Port Arthur, our enterprise in Manchuria is practically, though not entirely, concluded.*
> *Notwithstanding exceptionally difficult conditions, and the destruction of a large portion of the line last year, temporary traffic can, from day to day, be carried on along the whole system. I hope that within two years hence all the remaining work to be done will be completed, and that the railway will be opened for permanent regular traffic."*

In ten years, four thousand miles of railway had been laid down, averaging more than a mile a day: a record.

A huge country covering five million square miles of swamp and forest and rich corn land, and mountains, and deserts. A country of mighty rivers flowing from the central mountains of Asia to the Arctic Ocean, frozen solid half the year, but at certain seasons among the most magnificent waterways of the world. A country that was once inhabited by a great population, and then for ages the

Vasily Surikov,
The Conquest of Siberia by Yermak,
detail *(front line)*, 1895.
Oil on canvas, 285 x 599 cm.
Russian Museum, St. Petersburg.

abode of a few wandering tribes; now receiving fresh life from tens of thousands of emigrants, who poured into it from Russia over the iron way. Suddenly, Siberia had leapt into notice as a new Land of Promise, to which were turned the eager and inquiring eyes of half the world.

2) An Enormous Undertaking

In the second half of the 19th century, the Russians had acquired an important province in the Far East, washed by the waters of a great ocean, and traversed by a noble river. They determined that it should be joined to their European possessions by something more commodious and more safe than the ill-made, bandit-infested post-road that had previously wound its muddy or frozen length across the steppes and mountains. The government was also becoming more concerned about the fact that the populations of Russia, European and Asiatic, were very disproportionate. The nomadic tribes of Siberia, such as the *Bashkires, Khirghiz, Evenks, Buryats, Votiaks, Kamchakdales,* and *Samoyedes* were of small numbers in comparison to the millions of acres comprising Asiatic Russia, the official computation of the population being (including both Russians and aboriginals) one man to every five square miles. The first cause of the extremely slow progress in populating Siberia may be set down to its distance and inaccessibility from the congested districts of Russia. The only means of reaching its heart, up till the commencement of the Trans-Siberian Railway work, was by the lonely tarantass or the occasional steamers playing the tortuous waterways of the Irtish and Obi systems. The Siberian railway, however, promised to considerably alter this state of things.

Another stumbling-block to the rapid development of Siberia until this time been the great prejudice existing against it throughout European Russia, a prejudice which may be said to be far greater than that among foreigners. For many years Siberia had been the dumping-ground for criminals of the worst class. Although the want of communication may be set down as the first, the chief cause undoubtedly existed in Siberia having been made a penal colony.

It is said that the great famine of 1890-1891 which spread throughout Southern Russia, turned the eyes of the Russian government towards Siberia as a possible outlet for surplus population. Tsar Alexander II had always taken a kindly interest in his Asiatic possessions, and it was the dream of his life to see Siberia developed to its fullest extent. The wish was commendable, but the means were lacking.

It was in order to see with imperial eyes what Siberia was that Tsar Nicholas II (then Tsarevitch) took his memorable journey across the steppes and mountains from the Pacific coast. The first sod was cut and the first barrow-load wheeled at Vladivostok by Nicholas at the end of this grand tour of the East in 1891. His royal contribution was laid in that town as the foundation-piece of what would, in the course of a few years, rank as the monumental railway enterprise of the nineteenth century. Alexander, right up to his death, cherished his colonization scheme, and the heritage he left his son was energetically pushed forward. A start was made at the Cheliabinsk end in the following year. Following its commencement, construction steadily progressed in the face of physical and other difficulties at a pace which eclipsed the laying of the great trunk lines of the United States and Canada.

Vasily Surikov,
Stenka Razin, detail, 1906.
Oil on canvas, 318 x 600 cm.
Russian Museum, Moscow.

O. Kurliukov,
Tabernacle, 1901-1906.
Silver, gilding, cloisonné enamel, porcelain, 33 x 9 x 14 cm.
St. Michael Cathedral, Sitka, Alaska.
Moscow.

Unknown artist,
Icon: Kazan Mother of God,
mid-19th century.
Wood, oil paint, 45 x 57 cm.
Irkutsk Regional Museum, Irkutsk.

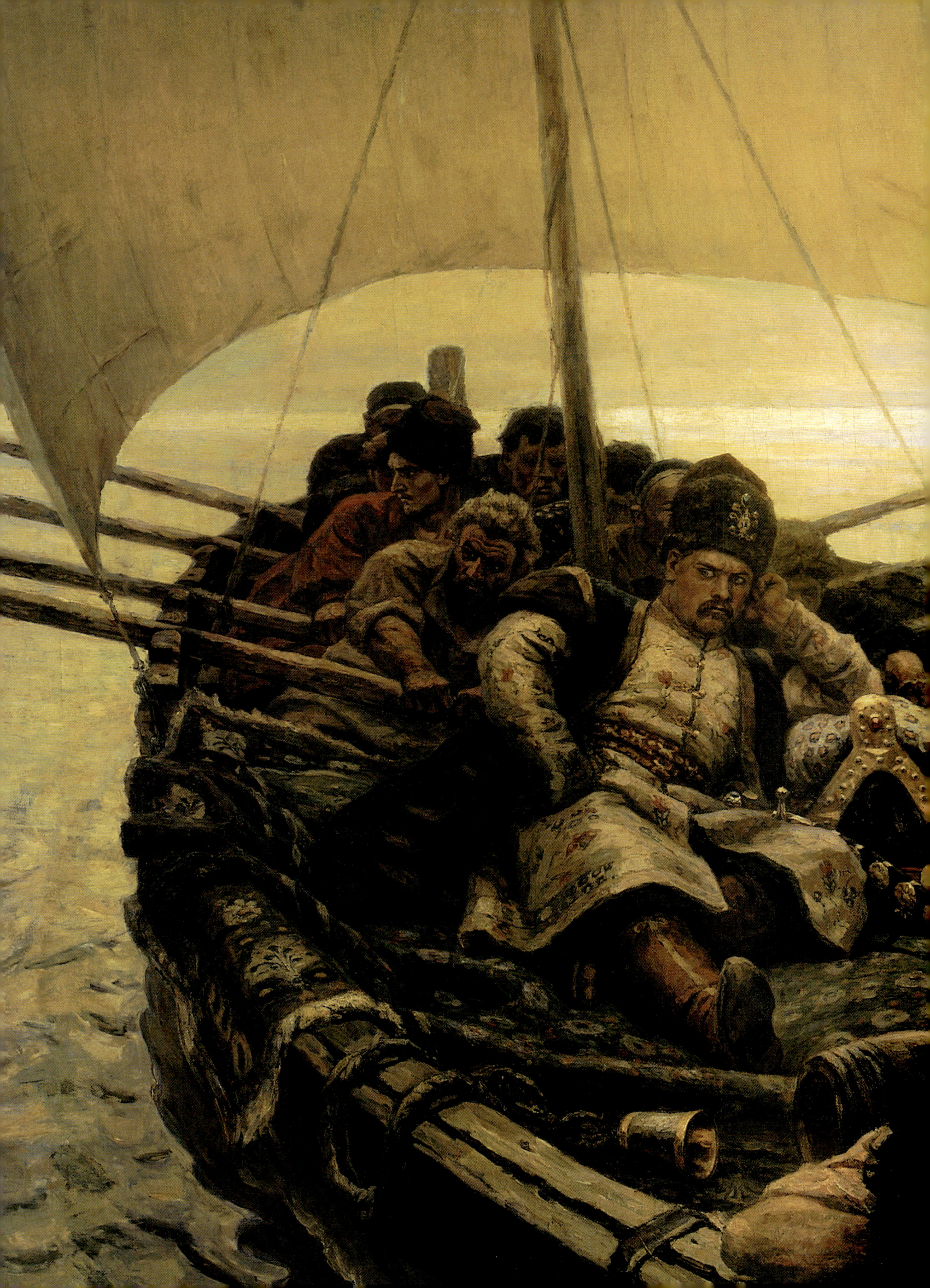

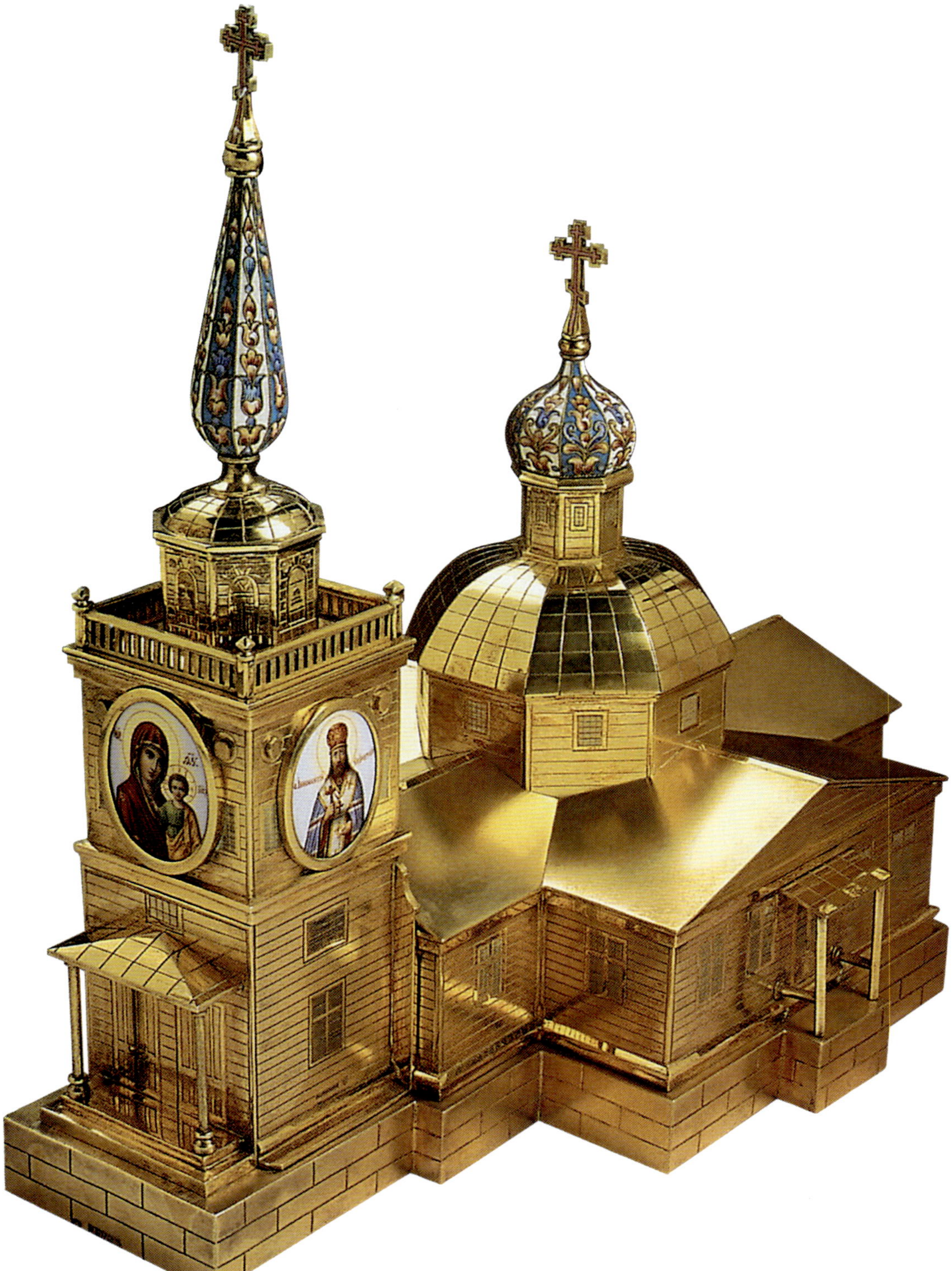

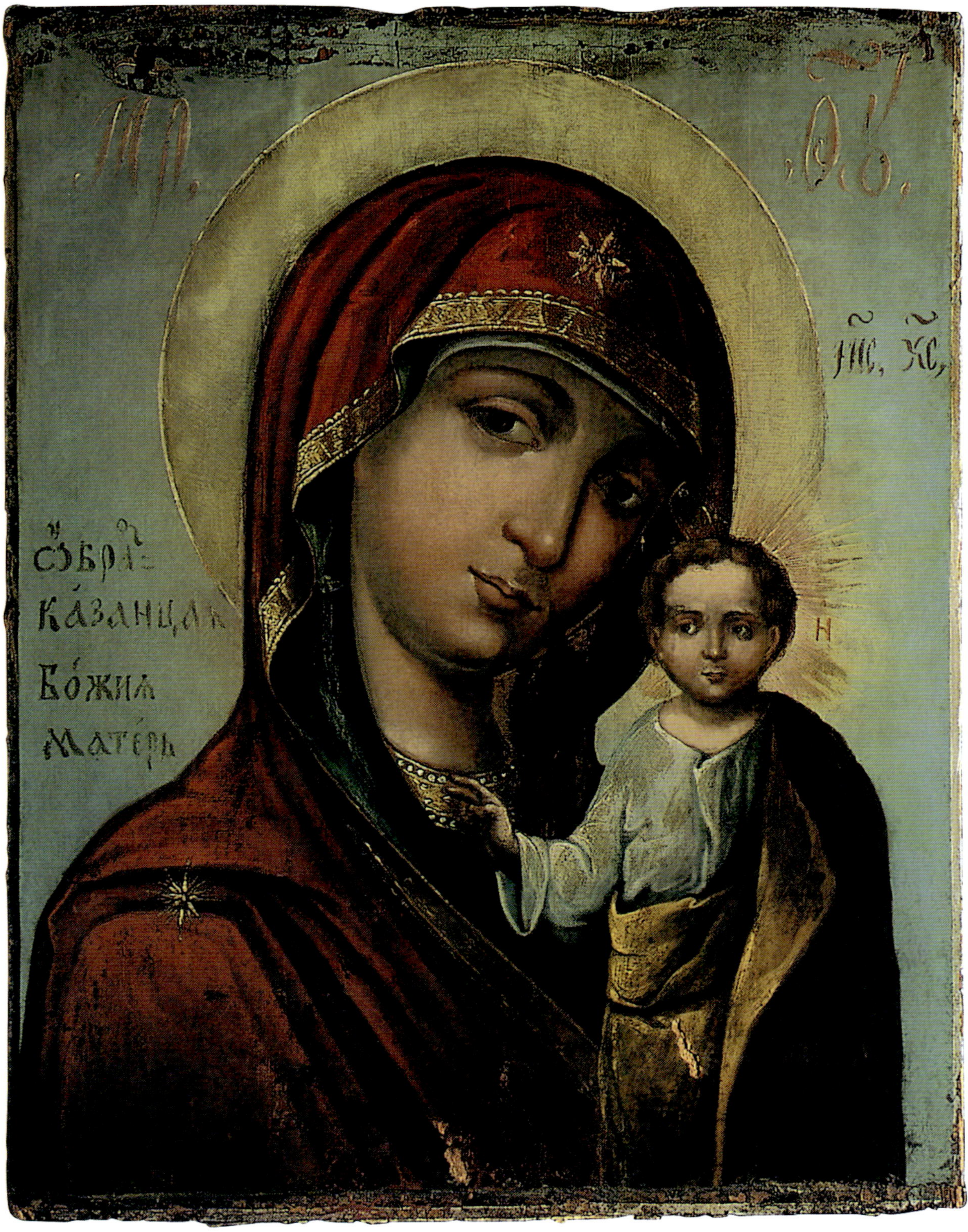

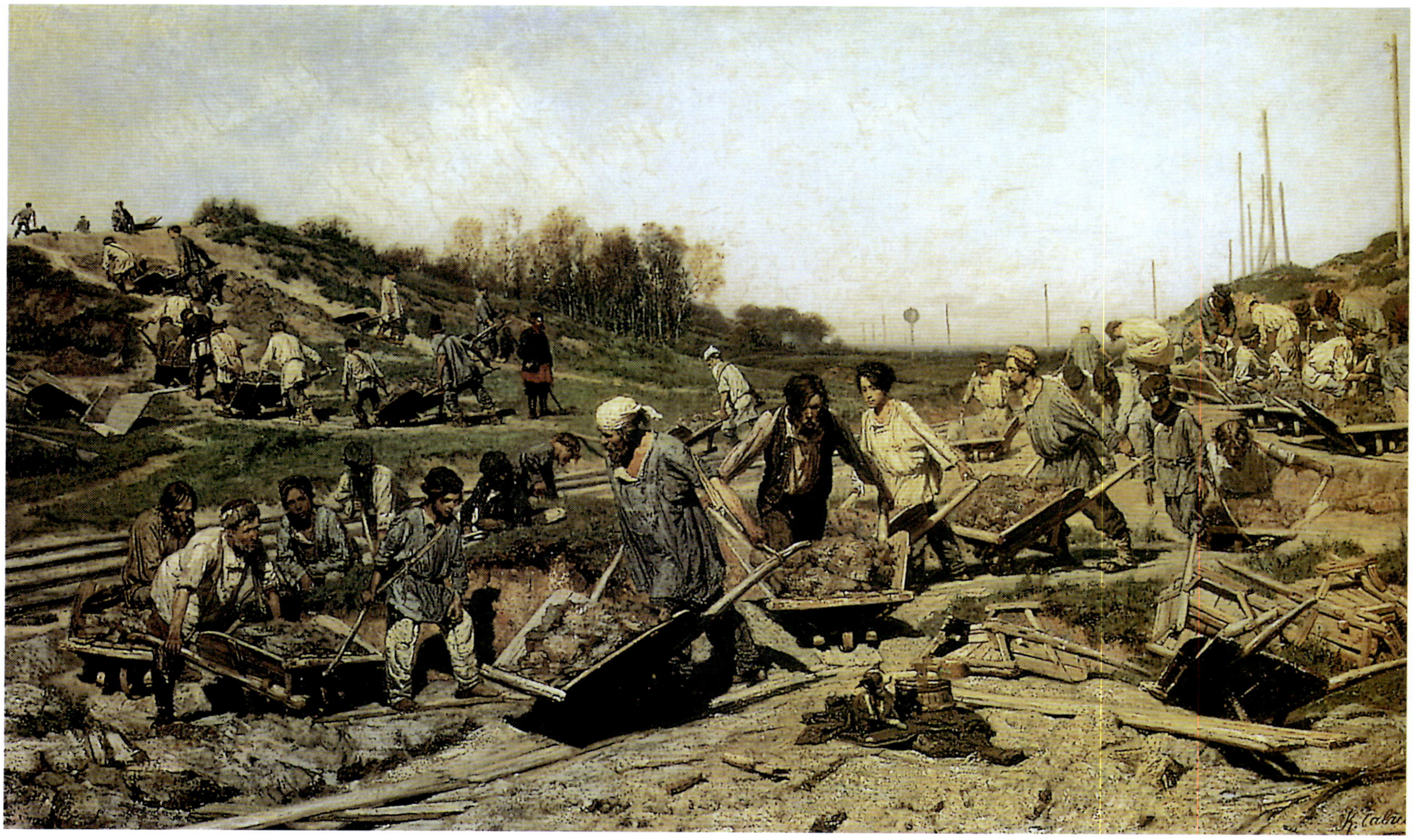

Konstantin Savitsky,
Repairing the Railroad, 1874.
Oil on canvas, 100 x 175 cm.
Tretyakov Gallery, Moscow.

In December 1895, the Trans-Siberian railway was completed to Omsk; in 1896 to Obi; in 1896 to Irkutsk, 3371 miles east of Moscow. Stretensk was reached in July 1900, and there the original scheme terminated. To avoid carrying the line along the Amur, an arrangement was come to with the Chinese Government in 1896, by which the engineers were given rights to drive the track across North Manchuria in an almost straight line to Vladivostok; and in 1898 the Russo-Chinese Bank (alias Russian Government) obtained a concession to make a branch due south from the Manchurian section to Port Arthur on the Gulf of Pechili. These sections were pushed forward with the greatest possible speed, owing to political events in the Far East, which demanded the presence of large bodies of troops to protect or extend Russian interests.

Many Russians once supposed that the construction of the Great Siberian Railway would ruin the traffic of the river systems; but it was found, on the contrary, that with the coming of the railway the river traffic was actually very greatly increased. This was due partly to the great stimulus given to business generally throughout Siberia, and also to the fact that these rivers, excepting the

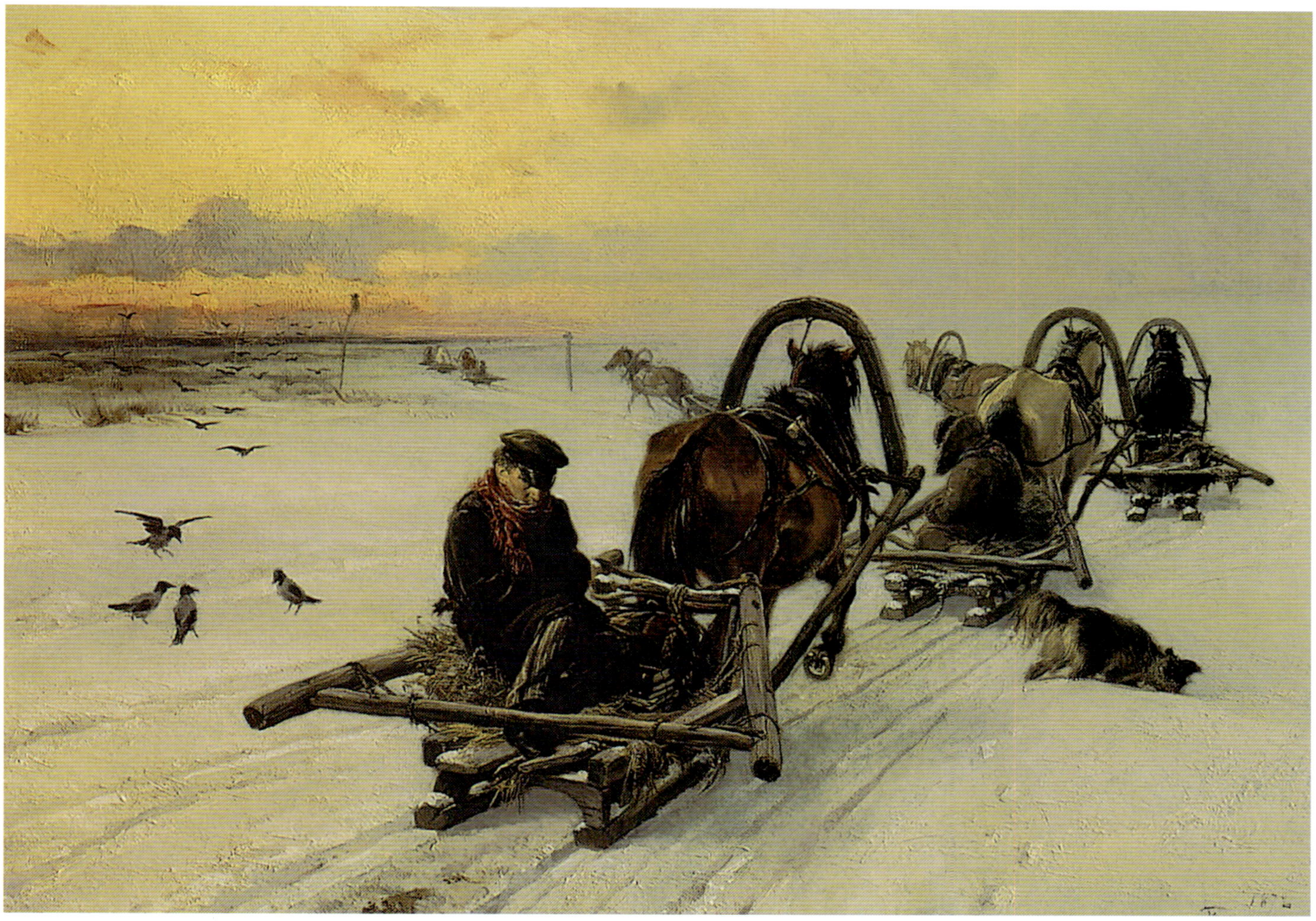

Amur, were dangerous to access by the cold sea route of the Arctic Ocean, and until the railway came, had no ready outlet for their traffic. Ocean steamers could readily enter the mouth of the Amur, but very few entered the great rivers which empty into the Arctic, on account of the difficulty and danger of navigating the Arctic Ocean north of the continent of Europe and Asia. Occasionally vessels from Russian ports and some from English and other ports in Europe made the trip; but the service was not regular and many of them were compelled to turn back, while not a few were lost. Hence the railway was of peculiar benefit to the traffic of these rivers by supplying a connection with the outside world which could not be gotten satisfactorily by sea.

Though the rivers and military postroads offered ready means of local travel before the railway was built, yet the distances in Siberia are so great that these methods, even under the most favorable circumstances, were slow and tedious; and, moreover, during a large part of the year the rivers are frozen and sleighs had to be used. The journey to different places took many months, and sometimes years, and was accompanied by great hardships and dangers, not only from the intense cold of the winter, but also from the intense heat of the

Illarion Pryanishnikov,
Empties, 1872.
Oil on canvas, 48 x 71 cm.
Tretyakov Gallery, Moscow.

short summer, and from wild beasts and famine. In early days the journey from Moscow to Irkutsk took about a year, while to Kamchatka it took six months more. Later on, however, the improvements on the military postroads and in the service on them made travel much more rapid, and a distance of 200 miles a day was not an unusual rate. Nevertheless, it became yearly more evident that more rapid communication was necessary for the proper development and protection of this vast region; and by about 1860 the project of railways in Siberia was much discussed. Many schemes to connect different river systems by short lines of railway, thus facilitating transcontinental traffic, were considered; but it was finally decided to build a continuous line from European Russia across Siberia to the Pacific. The discussion over the route of this line lasted for over twenty-five years, until finally, in 1891, the Tsar Alexander III chose the present one.

An elaborate monument at Vladivostok commemorates the arrival of the Tsarevitch at that place in 1891, and his inauguration of the Great Siberian Railway. The road was to be started from both ends and to be pushed as rapidly as possible. In the meantime the railway system of European Russia had already been continued east from Moscow to the Urals, and in 1892 the extension to Tchelyabinsk on the Asiatic side of the Urals was opened. This town was considered the starting point of the Great Siberian Railway, and from here the line was built eastward, passing through the region of Orenburg, along the southern border of the region of Tobolsk and the northern border of the Kirgiz Steppe; thence through the regions of Tomsk, Yenisey, and Irkutsk to Lake Baikal, reaching the town of Irkutsk in 1898. The passengers and freight were then transferred across the lake by boat, though the railway was later constructed around its south end. The road begins again on the other side of the lake, and has been completed eastward through Transbaikalia to Stretensk, on the Shilka River, to which point it was opened for travel in 1901. In the meantime, the East-Chinese Railway, built under Russian auspices through Manchuria, was completed. This line connected the line in Transbaikalia with the Ussuri Railway, thus establishing a through route from St. Petersburg and Moscow to the Pacific Coast port of Vladivostok. A branch line also connected the East-Chinese Railway with Port Arthur and the splendid Russian seaport of Dalny.

One of the principal objects of the railway was the transportation of emigrants to the fertile valleys of Central Siberia. The train-bound traveller passed train load after train load of outward-bound emigrants. At the principal stations of Chelabinsk, Kurgan, Omsk, Kainsk, and Atchinsk, emigrants by the hundreds disembarked, and could be seen encamped by the roadside awaiting their further transportation north, south, or east. The numbers were evidence that the attractions offered by the Government entirely outweighed prejudice and the discomfort of a long journey.

The agents of the Russian government were sent to the most thickly populated or distressed portion of European Russia, and there the desirability of emigrating to Siberia was impressed upon the more industrious of the peasantry, who could scarcely make ends meet in the overcrowded cities. The Russian Government offered inducements to the willing, and at the same time fixed a nominal fare to Siberia, in order to keep out the dangerous or dissolute. This fare was fixed at the rate of about one-twentieth of a penny per kilometer; and thus it was possible for a peasant to travel three thousand kilometers (two thousand miles) for the moderate sum of six roubles. From Southern Russia this would land the emigrant in the heart of Siberia.

Boris Yakovlev,
Transport Returns to Normal, 1923.
Oil on canvas, 100 x 140 cm.
Tretyakov Gallery, Moscow.

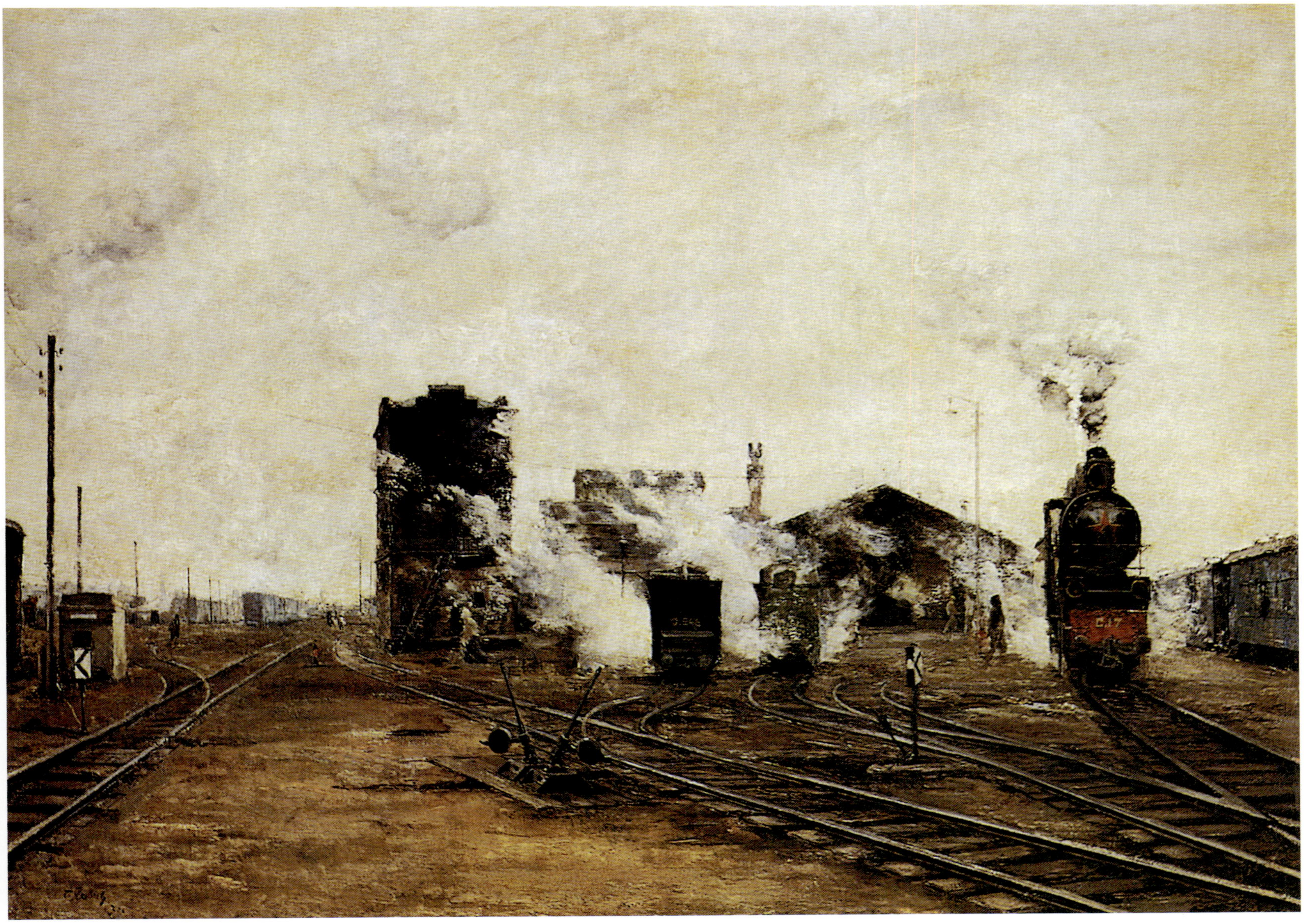

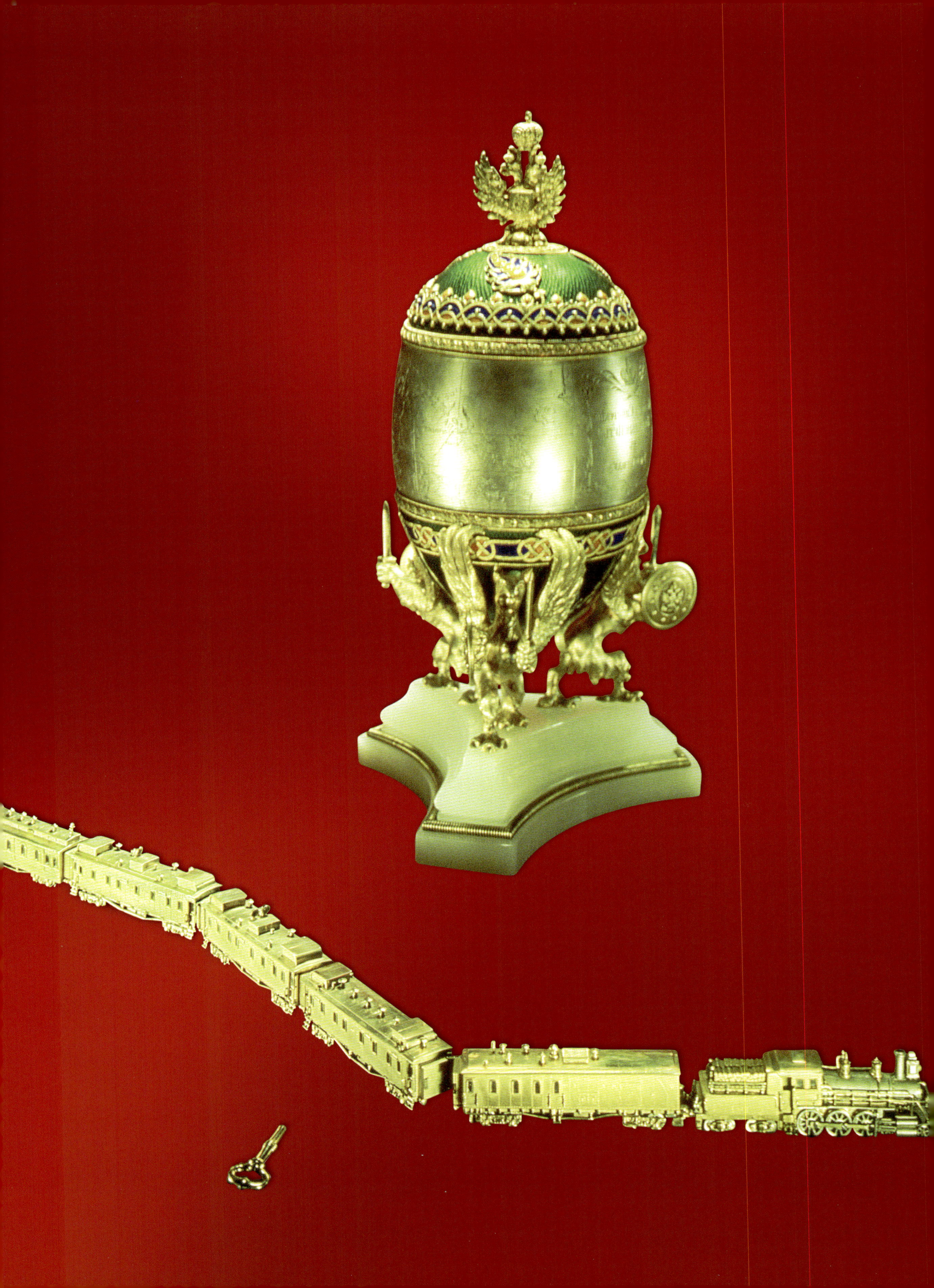

In 1896 alone nearly a quarter of a million peasants left Russia for Siberia. At that time, neither the railway nor the colonizing department could cope with the rush, and the Tsar was compelled to issue the edict commanding the officials of the various Siberian governments to drop all other State work and devote their efforts to the colonization movement. For a time things were in a completely chaotic state, and a large number of emigrants, finding no land ready for them, returned to Russia.

The Trans-Siberian Railway, as measured from Moscow, has a length to Vladivostok of 9,288 miles. The railway in its course crosses the upper waters of the Obi, Yenisey, Lena, and Amur at points where they begin to be easily navigable by vessels of considerable size. Up to the commencement of the Siberian railway, the only means of communication with interior Siberia were by horse. Such enormous distances had to be covered between towns that, in order to accommodate the large number of travellers, the Government erected, on the great high-road which pierced the heart of Siberia, stations at intervals of twenty-five to thirty miles. At these stations, horses could be hired at rates set down on a Government schedule, but beyond this and the shelter afforded, nothing was provided. It was thus necessary at the outset of the system for the traveller to provide everything requisite for the journey himself. In addition to his luggage, the wise Siberian traveller carried his bed, bed-clothing, food, and, in short, everything that he might require, rendering himself absolutely independent of hospitality on the way. On his arrival at a post-station, he wanted nothing but the *samovar*, or machine for boiling water, with which he made his tea. The charge for the samovar was minimal. No charge whatever was made for the use of the post-house, where the traveller in Siberia would break his journey for the night. If one, therefore, excluded the cost of horses, the traveller's expenses were wonderfully low.

However, with the opening of the country by means of the railway, it stood to reason that a new class of travellers would spring up, and thus better accommodation had to be provided. More comfortable hotels and inns appeared, and towns materialised from nothing where the Trans-Siberian Railway's stations were constructed, as the increased traffic brought money to the region. Already by the end of the nineteenth century, before the completion of the Trans-Siberian Railway's unbroken route from Moscow to Vladivostok, adventurous travellers from America and western Europe were entering Russia in droves, eager to embark on the uniquely long voyage across the Siberian steppes, which was still a notoriously uncertain and perilous one. One such early traveller reported:

> *"Gratuitous information concerning the Trans-Siberian Railway was freely offered by our fellow-passengers, and we began to fear the worst. Tales about three hours' stoppages at small stations; half a day here and a day there. No bridges over the Obi and Chulim rivers; so that the monotonous train journey should be relieved by a little sledging."*
>
> (Robert L. Jefferson, *Roughing it in Siberia*)

Unfortunately, the railway's influence was restricted to the southern part of Siberia and left thousands of square miles to both the north and the south completely untouched by its economic prosperity. The less positive contributions of disease and corruption, however, were brought from the crowded cities and spread amongst the native Siberian peoples with ease and

House of Carl Fabergé,
Model of the Imperial Trans-Siberian Railway and a Fabergé Egg, 1901.
Egg: onyx, silver, gold, quartz, enamel; Train: gold, platinum, 13 cm.
Armoury Museum, Moscow.

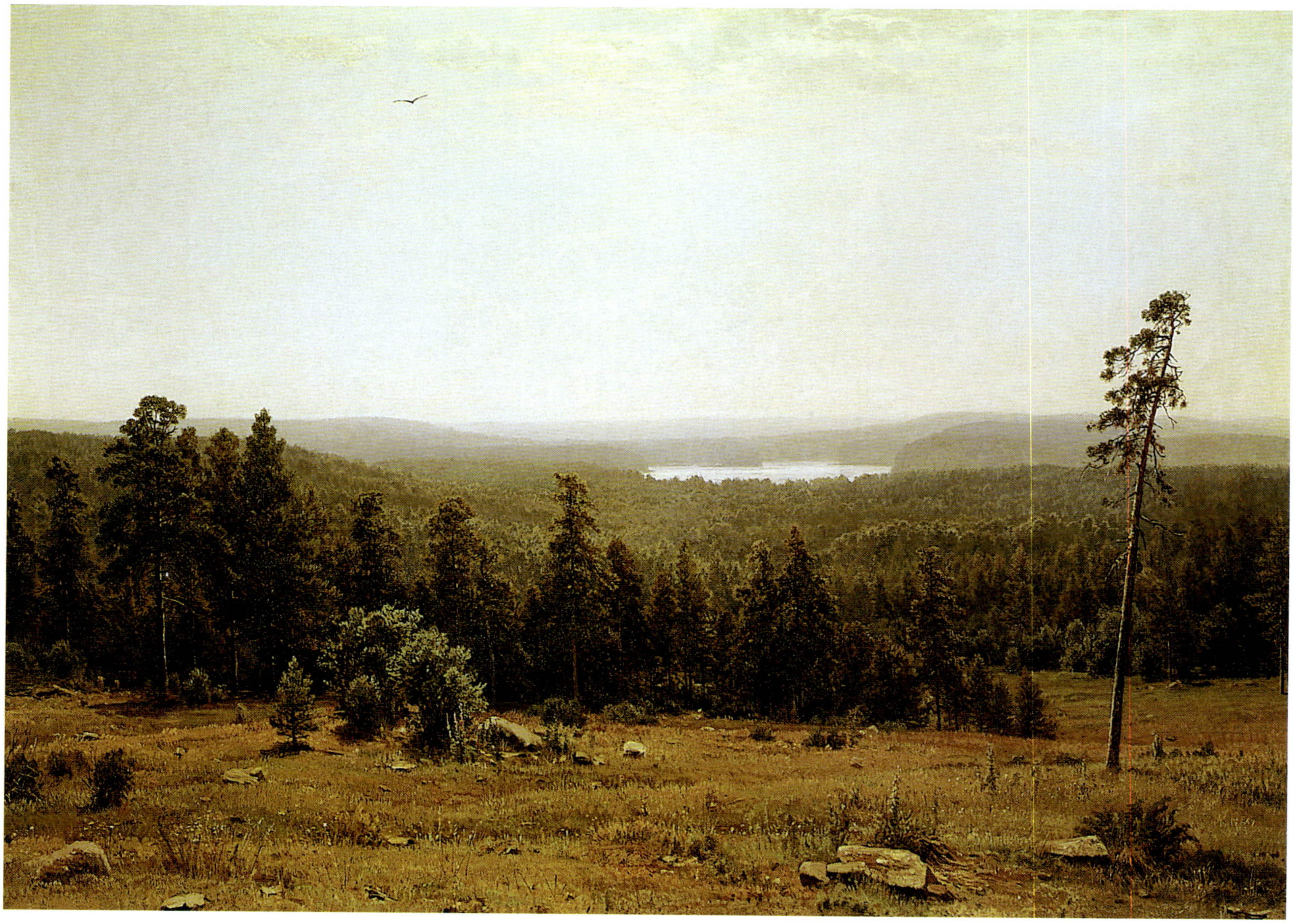

Ivan Shishkin,
Distant Forests, 1884.
Oil on canvas, 112.8 x 164 cm.
Tretyakov Gallery, Moscow.

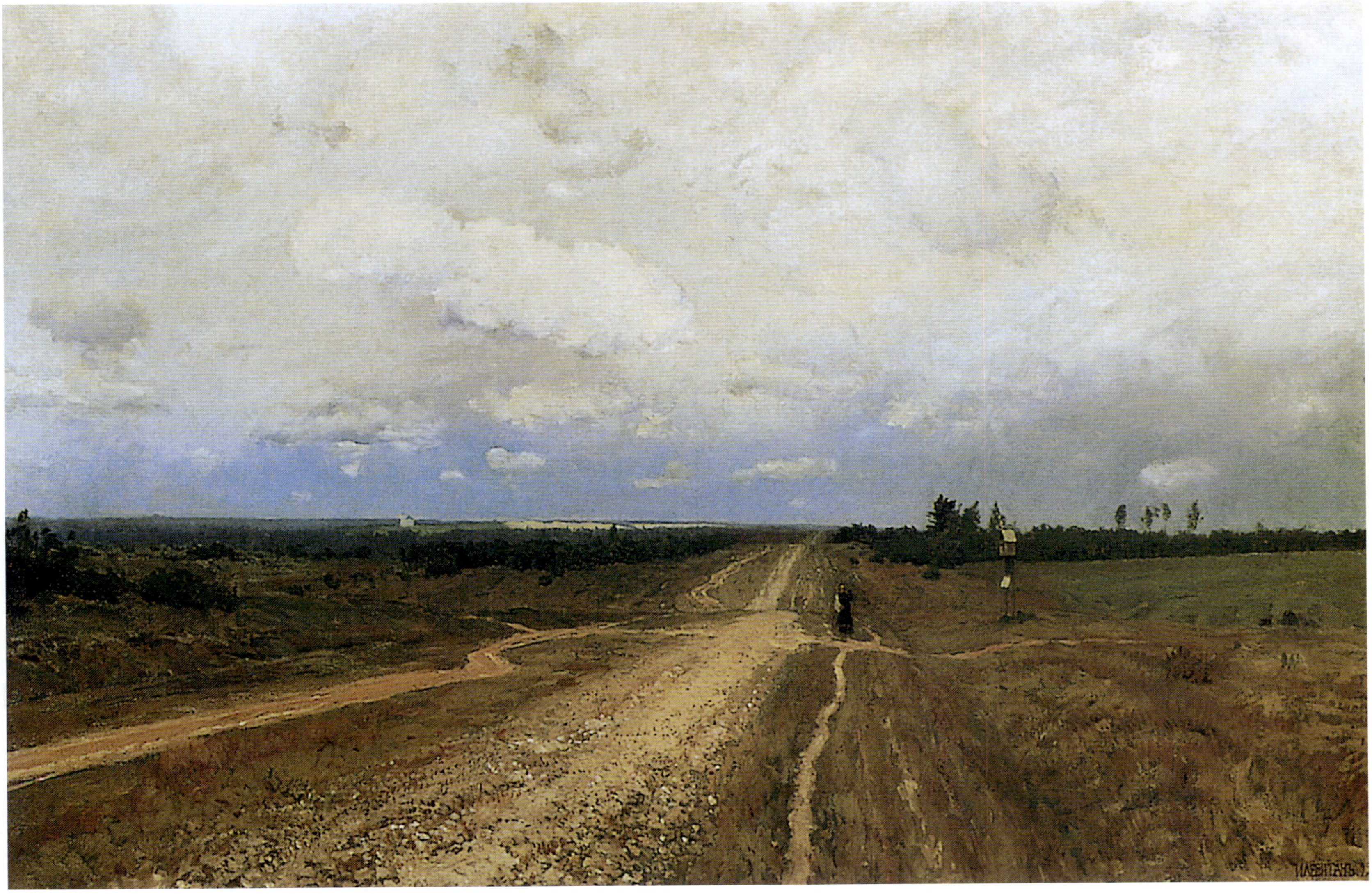

Isaac Levitan,
The Vladimirka, 1892.
Oil on canvas, 79 x 123 cm.
Tretyakov Gallery, Moscow.

rapidity, devastating entire races and permanently endangering the very existence of tribal culture in the Arctic.

3) The Price of Progress

With the increasing influence and pressure imposed by the waves of emigrating Russians, the culture of the tribal people of Siberia suffered greatly. Throughout the 20th century, confronted by industrialization and the insistence on assimilation, each generation of native Siberian youth found itself more at odds with parents and relatives, unable to find a place in what had once been home, knowing nothing about the ancestral way of life and incapable of living in the manner best suited to the taiga or the tundra. In the space of just a few years, the precious practical knowledge transmitted from generation to generation for centuries on end was deliberately obliterated.

But there was an even more vexatious consequence of the industrialization of Siberia and the influx into the northern and eastern regions of massive numbers of immigrants: environmental destruction. The list of ruinous effects is long – deforestation in the most easterly zone and on the Pacific coastline; pollution of rivers and lakes (the Ob, the Yenisey, the Vilyuy, Lake Baikal, and so on); acid rain (the High Altai, the area around Lake Baikal); air pollution (Norilsk, the Kuzbass Basin, Magadan, Vladivostok, Khabarovsk); and more. Such forms of pollution of course hit first and hardest the local populations who lived almost exclusively on natural produce in the affected areas. The spoiling of pasturage similarly led to an immediate reduction in the numbers of livestock and reindeer. Places where the hunting was known to be good suddenly became much smaller – and much emptier once the poachers arrived there. Fish became scarce, and those that were caught might often be dangerous to eat.

Since the 1970s, many of the different communities in Siberia have discovered among themselves writers, poets and artists, all intimately concerned with the catastrophic fate of their fellow aboriginals, and all refusing to admit even the possibility of their own ancestral culture's extinction. They include people whose names are today well known, such as Vladimir Sanghi (of the Nivkhi), Yuri Rytkhe (Chukchi), Anna Nerkagi (Nenet), and the Kurilov brothers (Yukaghir).

The realities of life for the peoples of the north today are far from simple. A good third of the aboriginal populations have become entirely urbanized and are no longer distinguishable from other members of the public. The remainder live as best they can in their rural surroundings, perhaps half-engaged in traditional activities, perhaps half doing other things or simply unemployed.

For all the pain of assimilation, and for all the traditional ancestral practices with which the younger generation has failed to become familiar, the essential contribution bequeathed to the world by the ethnic cultures of Siberia seems, nonetheless, to have been maintained. That contribution is made up of a way of life founded directly on closeness to and dependence on nature, and on a holistic vision of the world and of humankind's place in it, both recognizable even now in the persistence of animist rituals (or less often, shamanist rituals).

The next section of this book makes contact with such original ways of life, original ways of thinking – original, that is, in the sense both of being primeval and unlike anything else – so characteristic of the aboriginal peoples of Siberia.

Sergei Ivanov,
On the Road, the Death of a Resettler,
1889.
Oil on canvas, 71 x 122 cm.
Tretyakov Gallery, Moscow.

The taiga (central Yakutia).

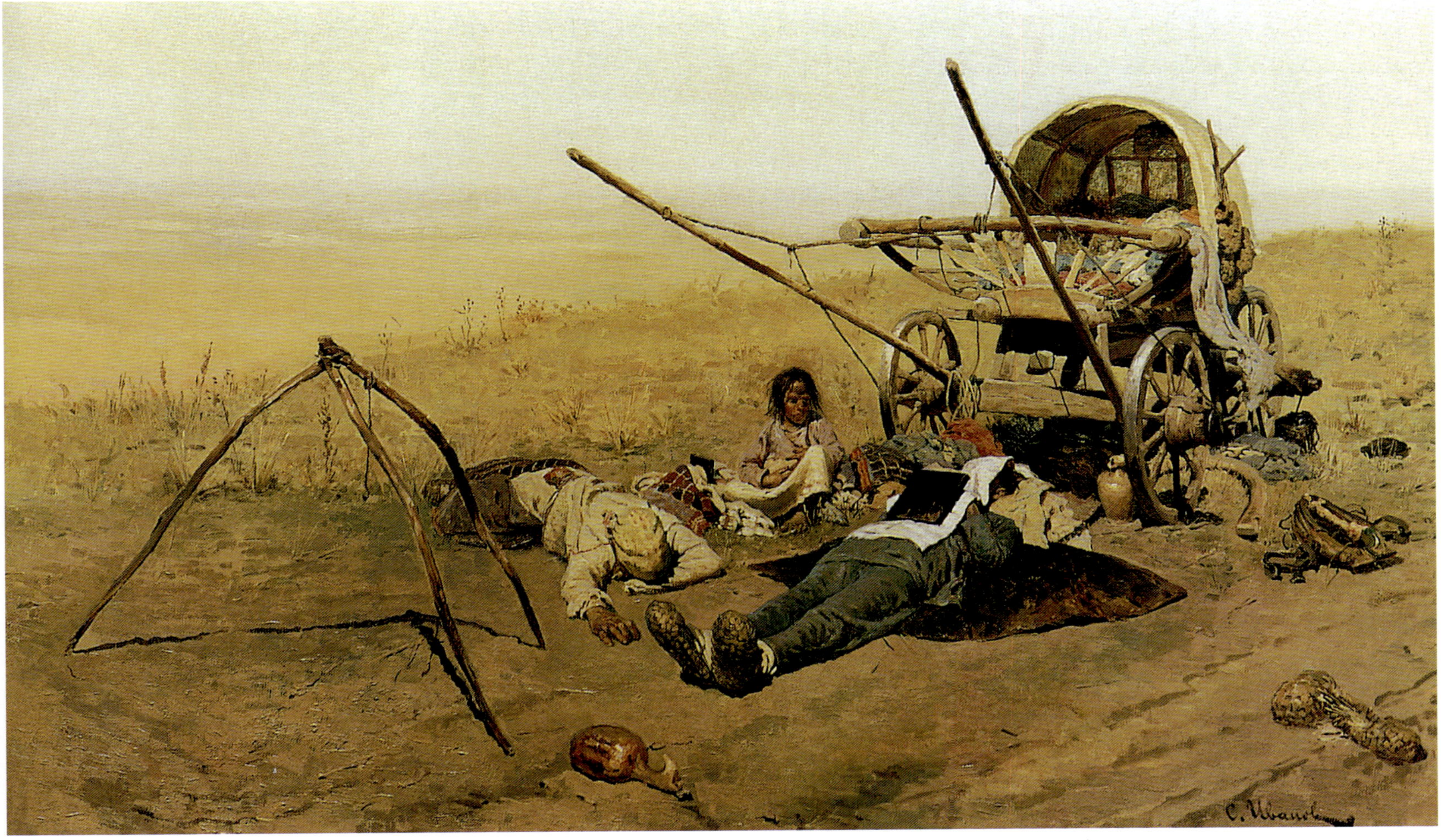

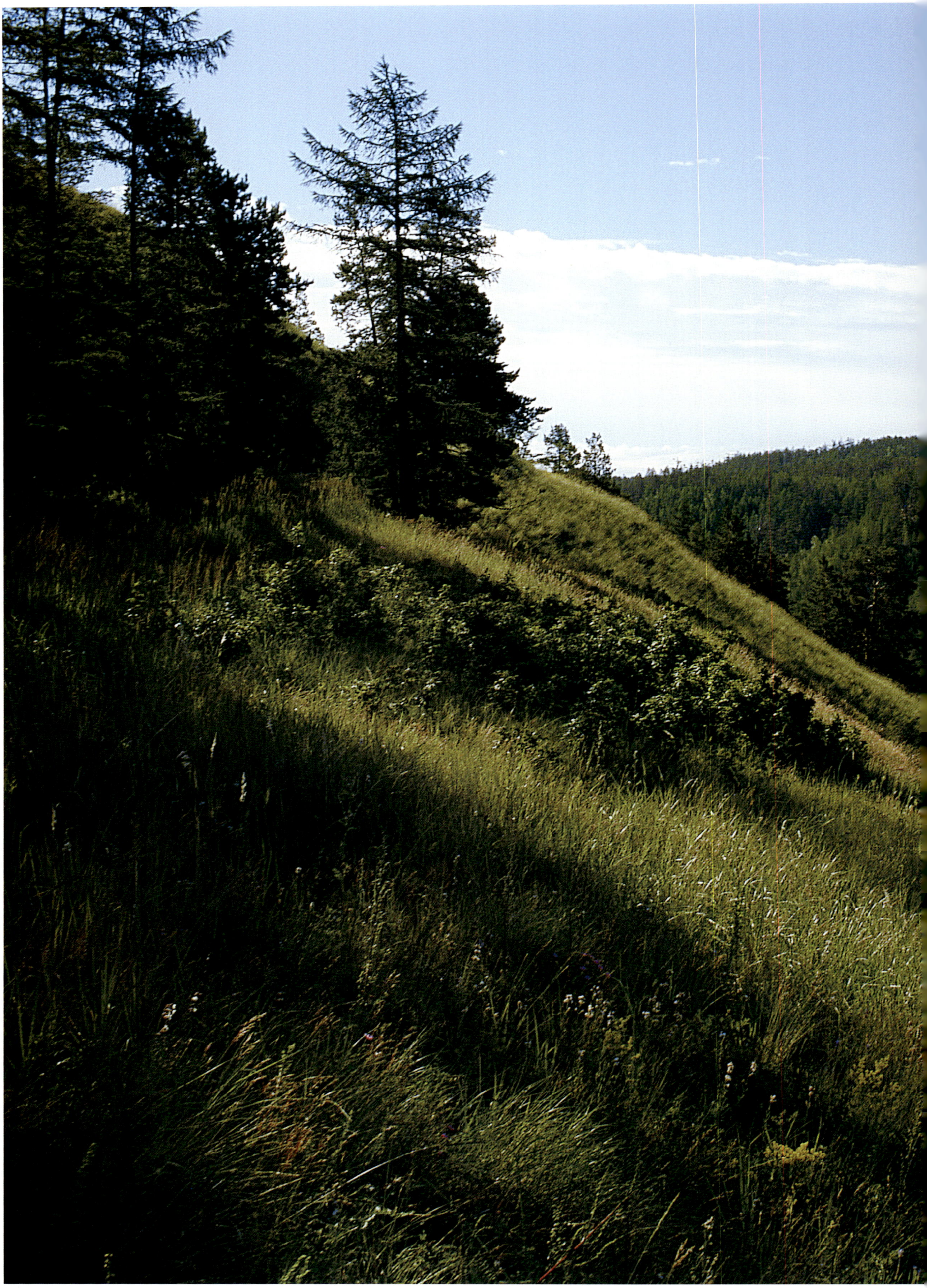

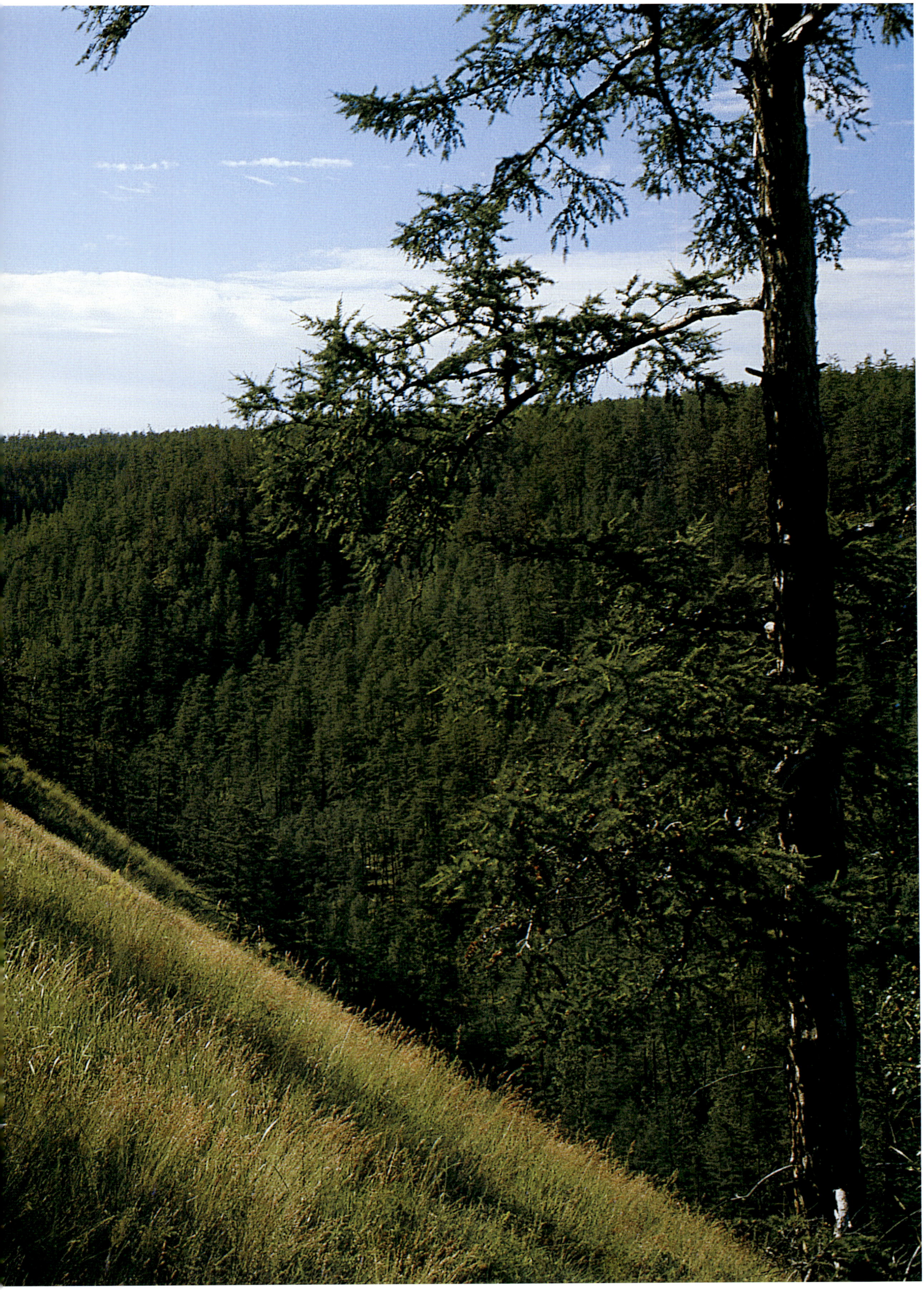

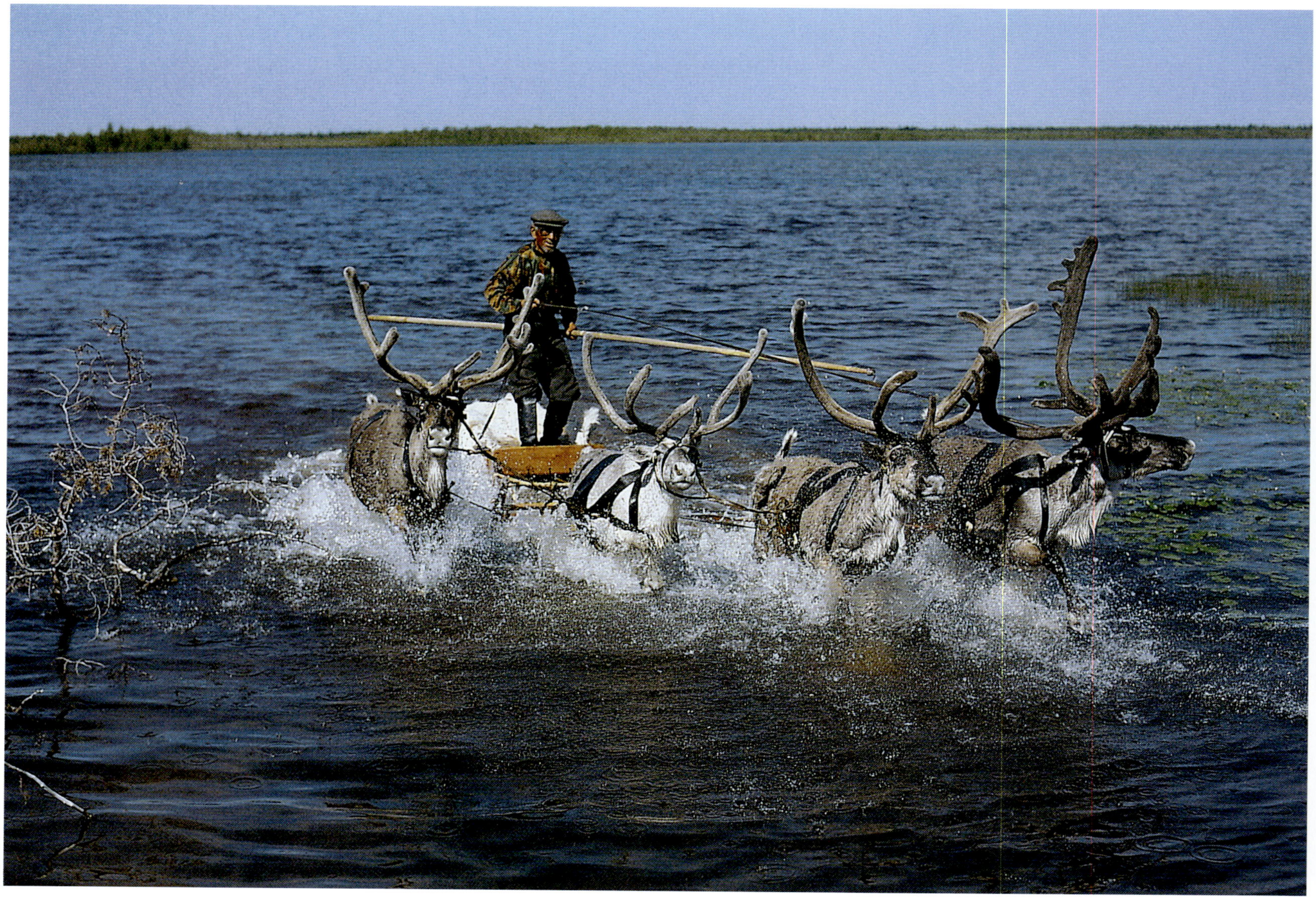

II. TRADITIONAL DAILY LIFE

A. THE ROUTINE OF SURVIVAL

"In every aspect of their daily life, in the midst of their interminable struggle against the unrelenting landscape and weather, we may glimpse the expression of an irrepressible aesthetic."

The traditional lifestyles of the various communities that live in Siberia depend on one or more activities – fishing, hunting, the herding of reindeer or the breeding of cattle – that are specific to their locality, but also subject to regional variations, some of them significant, even within a single ethnic group. For example, the Evenki may herd reindeer and hunt, may hunt and fish, or may instead farm cattle and breed horses depending on where they live. The Eveni people, on the other hand, herd reindeer and hunt in the tundra and the taiga, while on the shores of the Sea of Okhotsk they rely solely on catching marine creatures.

Communities in Siberia tend by tradition to live on the resources available to them, making the best of the geographical and climatic conditions. Factors that have a far-reaching influence on their everyday lives include fragile ecosystems; the long, cold, dark northern winter; the migration of herds; the hibernation of species upon which they rely for food; the brevity of the crop-growing period.

Reindeer herders thus take it for granted that when the reindeer make their annual move to seek out new pasturage, they must go with them, so becoming nomads. The arrival in the far north of migrant birds in May marks the beginning of the most bountiful hunting season of the year. In spring and autumn various species of fish swim up the rivers to spawn. Each has its own preferred riverine destination – salmon, for instance, find their way far upriver to the shallow headstreams. The fishermen naturally follow season after season to where their preferred fish are most plentiful, to make their best catches while the fish are at their meatiest and while the females are full of roe. In summer, the brief period of plant growth is punctuated by the ripening of different types of berry, one after the other, in their preferred surroundings.

At the coasts, however, there are always animals and birds to catch, which means that littoral communities, at least during peaceable times, have never needed to become nomadic.

The fauna and the flora, the regenerative cycle of nature in Siberia – all determine the rhythm of life of the aboriginal people, and embody an annual calendar of things to do and things to go and get for individual groups and, indeed, for individuals.

The peoples of Siberia are the inheritors of highly practical and specific traditions that distinguish one group from another but contain elements

Khanty,
Reindeer sled crossing a shallow lake,
1998.

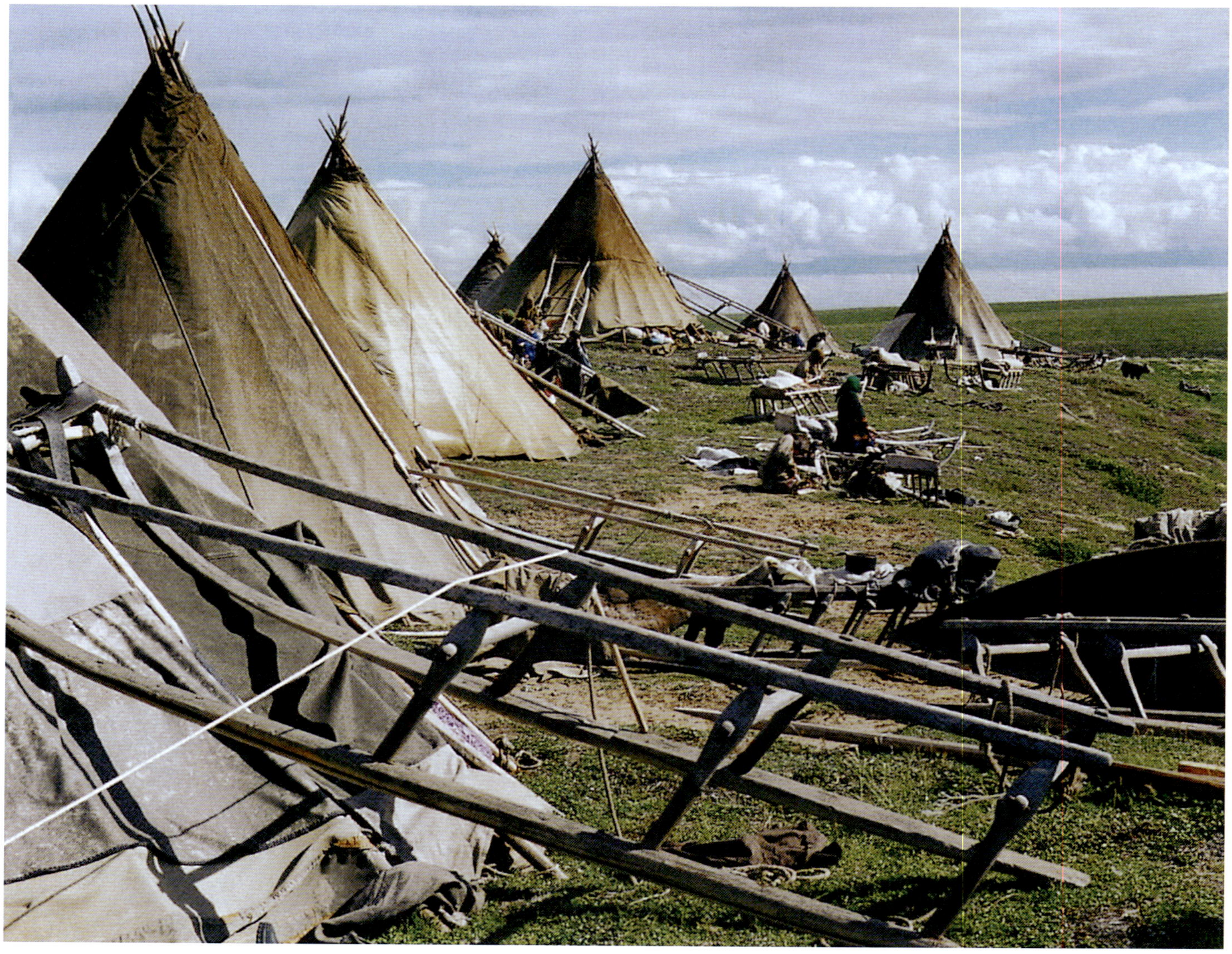

common to all. For example, almost all the inhabitants of Siberia eat fish, although it is prepared in various fashions. The most widespread recipe – known from north to south and from east to west – is undoubtedly *yukola*, in which the fish is dried on large wooden frames in the summer sun to preserve it for the winter. Highly nourishing, the *yukola* has for centuries taken on the same role for Siberian groups that bread plays elsewhere in the world. Similarly, *stroganina* is the dish of choice for inhabitants of some of the coldest regions: it is fish caught in winter and frozen the instant it leaves the water in air temperatures of under -40°C (-40°F), preserved, and eaten just as it is, cut into fine strips. A favourite of all dwellers in the north, Russians as well as indigenous peoples, *stroganina* is mostly kept for special occasions. In the smaller villages, the fish may be stored frozen on the outdoor porches and balconies of the houses over the winter (for the average temperature outside is usually lower than that of electric freezers anyway).

Another constant among the differing traditions is the use of natural materials – wood, bark, furs and skins – to make clothing, handicraft-work and/or a shelter. Throughout all the regions of Siberia, reindeer-skin is most used for winter clothing, in particular for knee-boots fashioned from strips of hide taken from the

Nenet,
Mobile chums, 1998.
Skin and fabric.

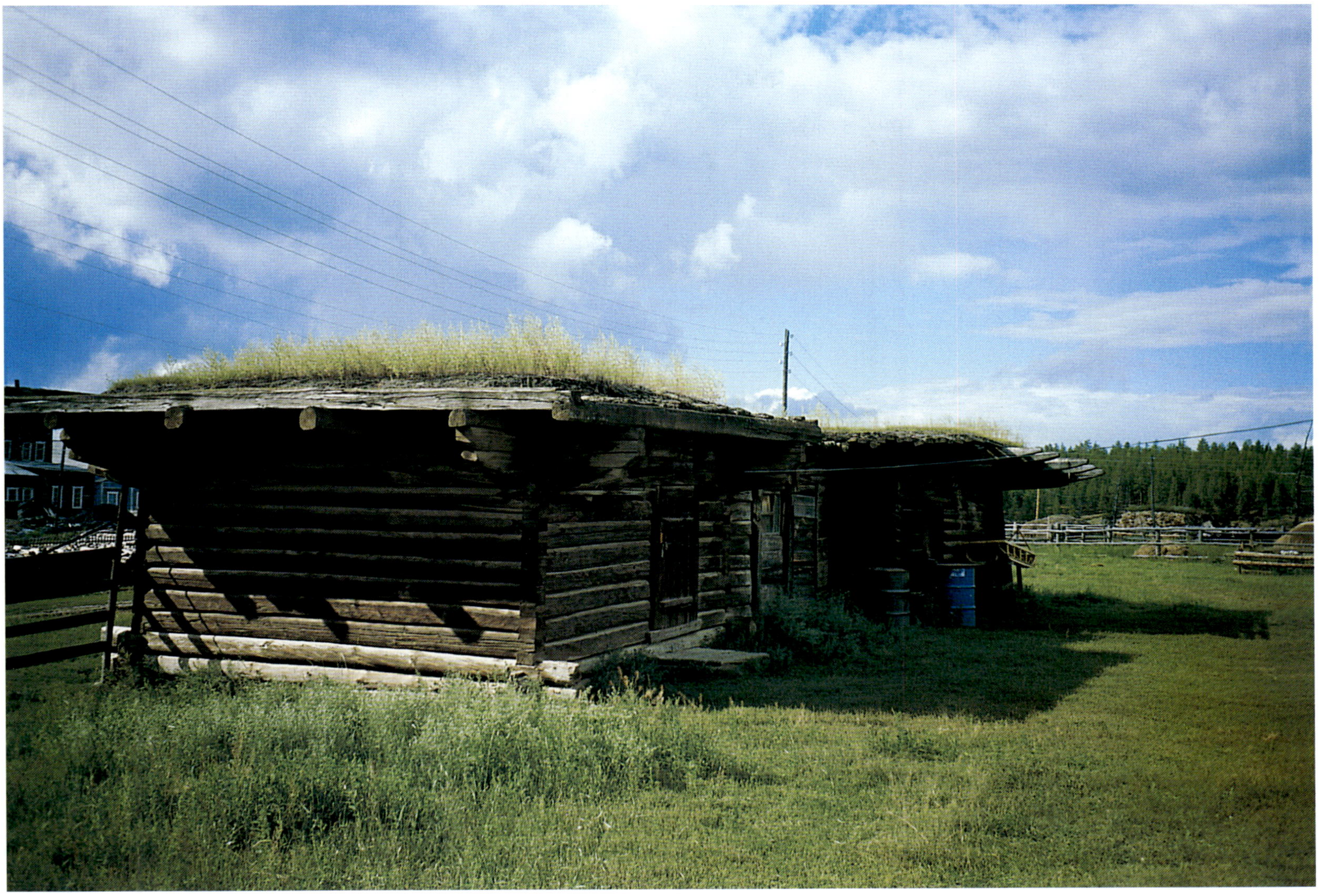

lower limbs of the reindeer. The more northerly peoples – the Nenets, Nganassani, Yukaghirs, Chukchis, and so forth – tend to make their shoes and boots from the little piece of roughened skin that lies between the large and the small parts of the hoof of the reindeer. Although an inordinate quantity of such pieces is required for even one pair, the resultant shoes are guaranteed to keep the feet warm and dry.

As means of transport, the people of many regions in Siberia use dogs instead of reindeer to pull their sleds. To each sledge with its ordinary load of up to 450 lbs., twelve or thirteen dogs are as a rule attached. Unlike the Samoyedes and the Greenlanders, who fasten each dog to the sledge by means of a separate leather rope, the natives in the region of the lower Lena use one common trace, made of leather, to which the dogs are attached on each side by means of short thongs, while at the end is harnessed the peredovoi, or leader. This plan has the advantage of preventing the dogs from becoming entangled in a multiplicity of ropes, but, on the other hand, a certain amount of traction-power is lost owing to the trace of each dog forming an angle to the common trace. The dogs are steered, not by reins, but by word of command from their lord and master, which they obey very well as long as they do not scent any game; but if they are hungry

Ambar (cereal granaries).

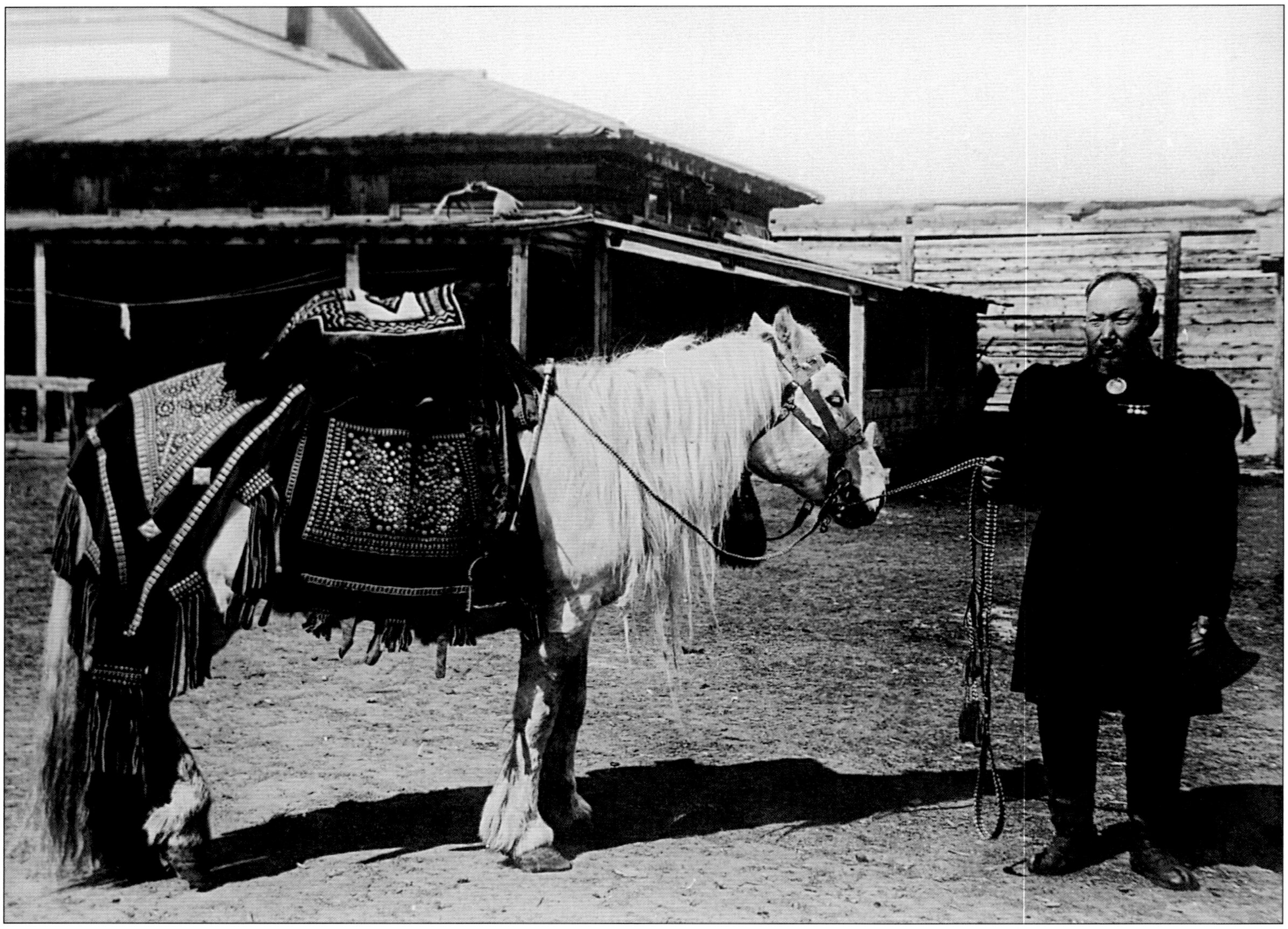

and get the scent, for instance, of a reindeer, they will rush away after it until little is left of the sledge behind them but splinters. To check the pace or stop the dogs the driver ordinarily uses an iron-shod pole as a brake.

The importance of a conscious, deliberate lifestyle on the icy tundra cannot be adequately stressed. The indigenous Siberians have mastered the art of balancing their diet and activity in accordance with the climate. A traveller relates his observations of the essential behavior of hunters in the wasteland:

> *"A man who will eat a hearty supper of dried fish and tallow, dress himself in a Siberian costume, and crawl into a heavy fur bag, may spend a night out-doors in a temperature of -70 degrees without any serious danger; but if he is tired out, with long travel, if his clothes are wet with perspiration, or if he has not enough to eat, he may freeze to death with the thermometer at zero. The most important rules for an arctic traveller are: to eat plenty of fat food; to avoid over-exertion and night journeys; and never to get into a profuse perspiration by violent exercise for the sake of temporary warmth. I have seen Chukchis in a region destitute of wood and in a dangerous temperature, travel all day with aching feet rather than exhaust their strength by trying to warm them in running."*

Urban Yakut on horseback, 1906.
Yakutia.

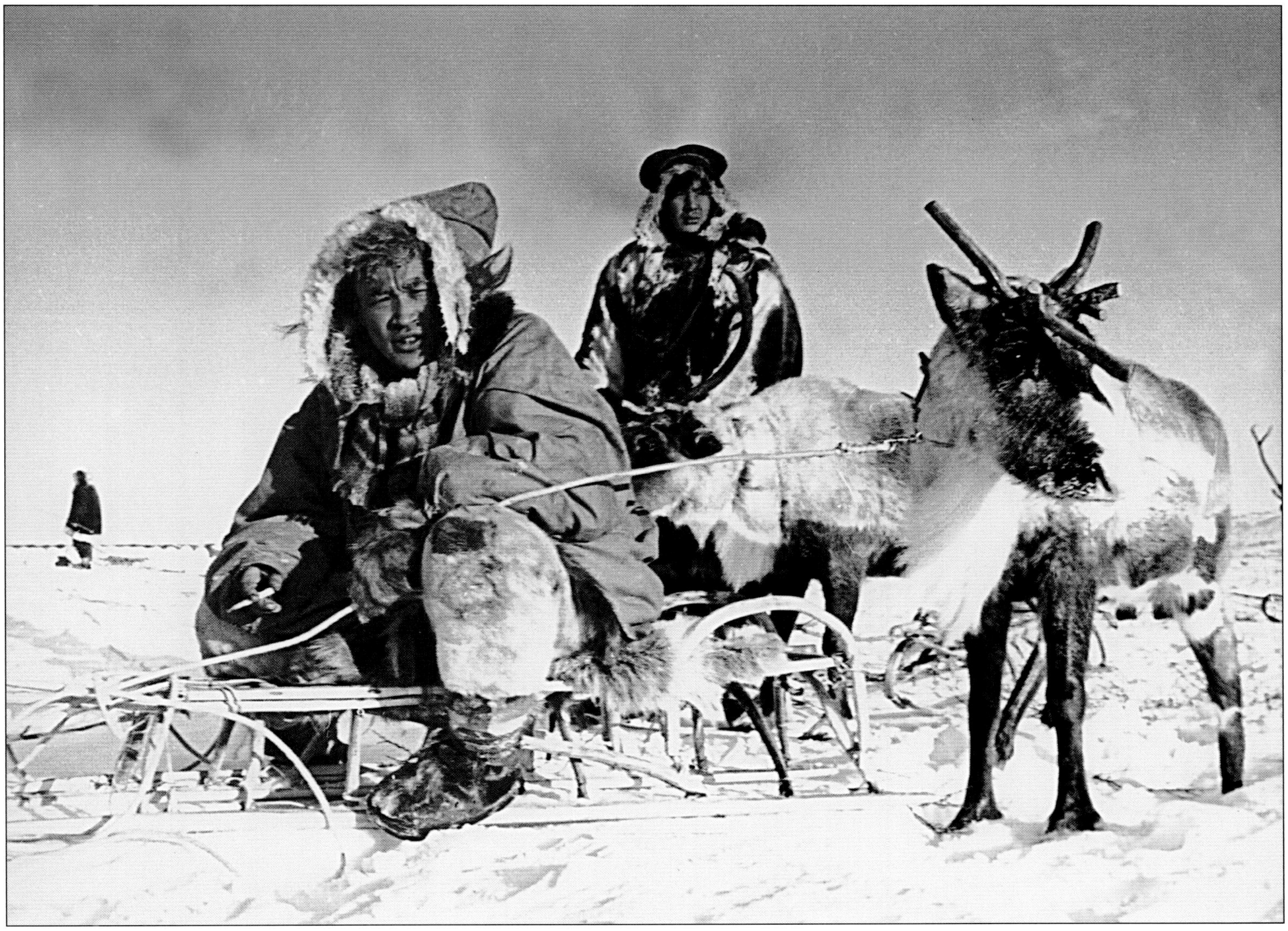

The traditional lifestyles of the peoples of Siberia, many aspects of which have in recent times changed or indeed been lost altogether, have one other thing in common: the ability to adapt to a hostile environment. Such practical knowledge, vital to these northern ethnic groups, represents a heritage that ought to be precious to all humankind – knowledge of northern environments, of the animals and plantlife, of the climate; knowledge, gained over thousand of years and handed down from generation to generation, that not only enables people to survive in such conditions but also represents an expression of their artistic creativity. The aboriginal people of Siberia are fairly clever handicraftsmen as carpenters and above all as smiths, a craft which has old and high traditions, and is inherited. At the time of their subjugation by the Russians, they knew how to produce iron from the ore, and their traditions show that the metal has been known to them from time immemorial. They are also clever carvers of wood and bone. The Chukchis and Koryaks are talented workers in ivory. They produce animal representations well cut in ivory, and spear-heads of masterful strength and design. Their hunting knives, made from hoop-iron, are well fashioned, and some of the handles are tastefully inlaid with copper, brass, and silver.

Chukchi,
Reindeer-herders in the tundra, 1979.
Anadyr area.

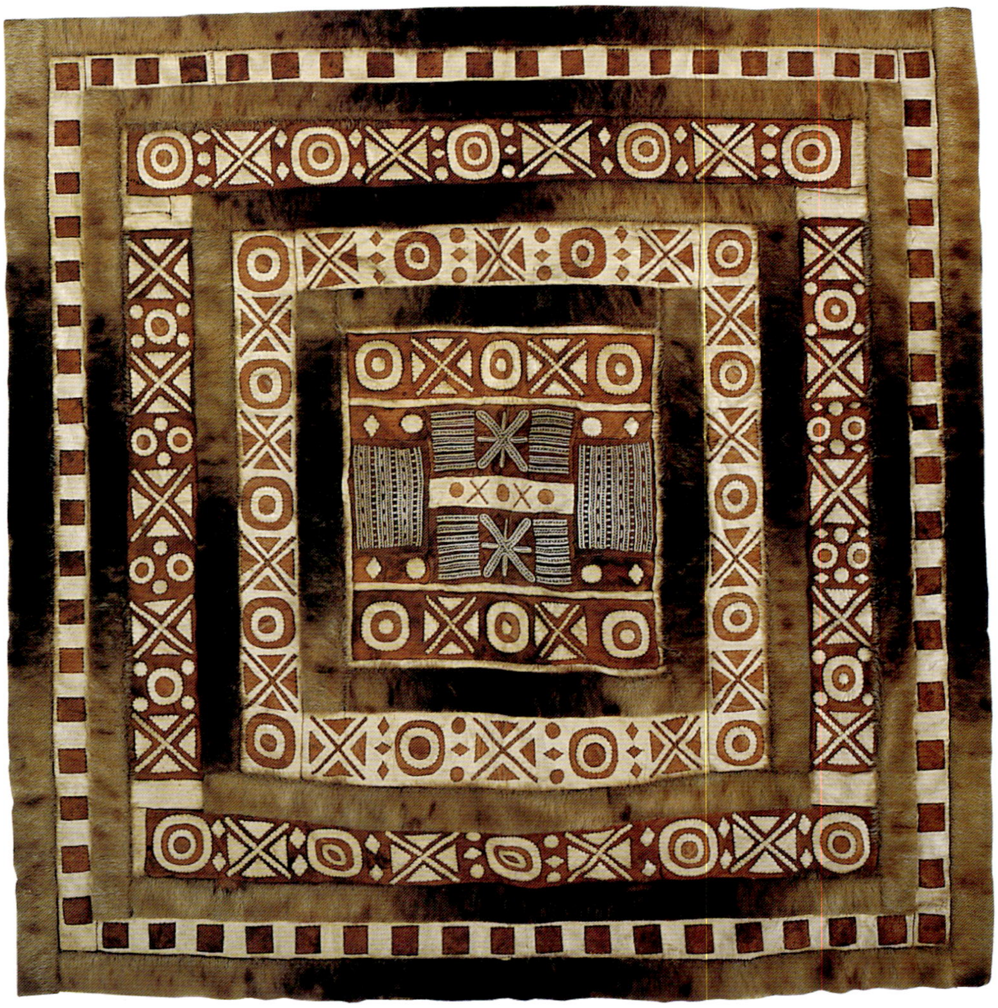

Eskimo,
Rug, 1909.
Seal hide and skin, reindeer underneck hair, 70 x 68.5 cm.
Russian Museum of Ethnography, St. Petersburg. Kamchatka Okrug, Chukchi District.

Chukchi,
Small plastic artwork 'Journey, riding the reindeer', 1906.
Walrus tusk ivory, 7.5 x 7 cm.
Russian Museum of Ethnography, St. Petersburg. Primorskaya Oblast, Anadyr Krai.

Yakut,
Sculpture 'Reindeer breeder on the sledge', 1955.
Mammoth bone, 17 x 4.5 x 5.5 cm.
Russian Museum of Ethnography, St. Petersburg. Yakut ASSR.

Many indigenous Siberian tribes are passionately fond of music of any kind, and will accompany themselves upon a three-cornered guitar with three strings, called a *ballalaika*. Some of them play quite well upon roughly-crafted home made violins. They indulge in amusements such as dancing, playing football on the snow in winter, and racing with dog-teams.

Often, their furniture and tools consist of a large kettle, knife, wooden bowls, platters, spoons or ladles, and an axe, with flint and steel. The Chukchis have a kettle or cooking utensil, in their language called *cookie*. To these vessels, which are of iron, they are much attached, and the stronger and stouter they are, the better; usually, no consideration will induce them to take or purchase a copper vessel, although lined with tin, as they consider it poisonous. Plain raw iron utensils are preferred, and these they will fearlessly, and with impunity, handle in a temperature of forty degrees below zero, Fahrenheit. Other bowls, dishes and much of the household utensils are made mostly of wood or of birch bark. A bucket made of this bark, for carrying water, a basin formed of the same rude material, a few wooden spoons, and some skins of the reindeer, are all that is required to supply the wants of an Ostyak family.

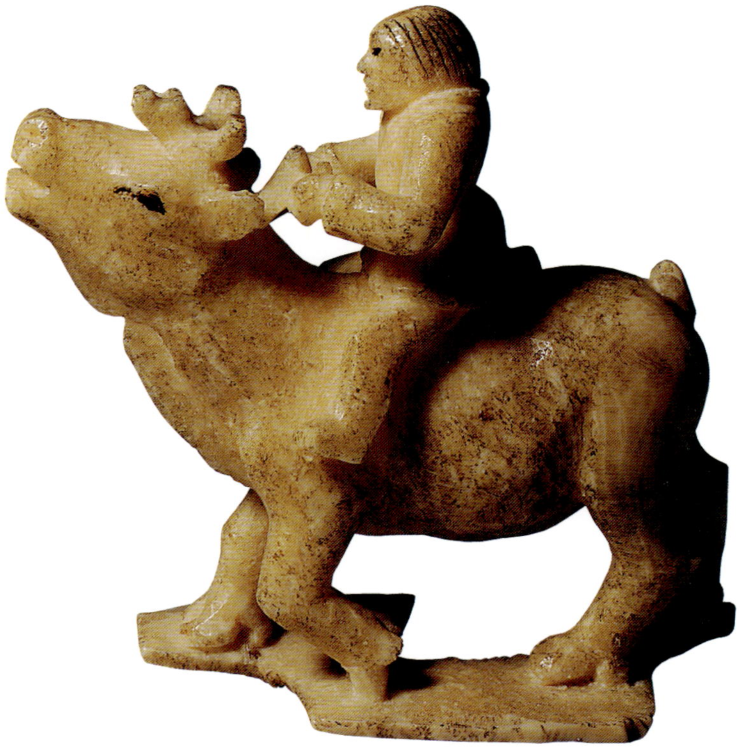

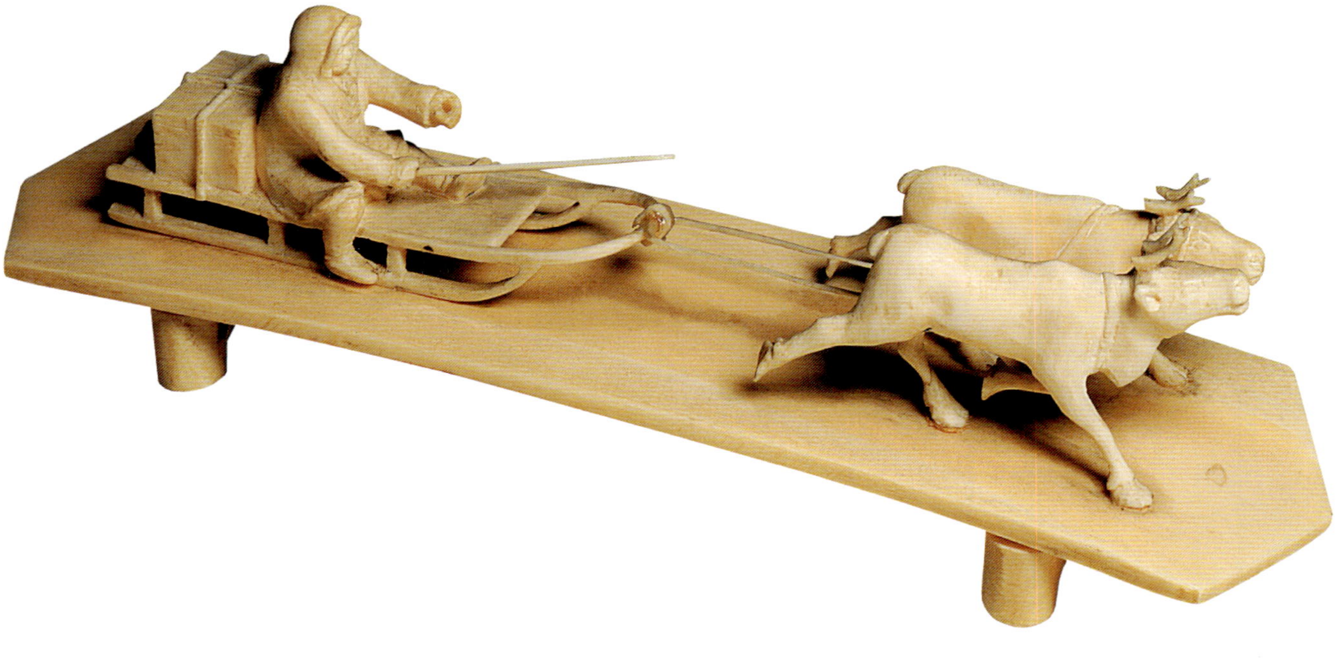

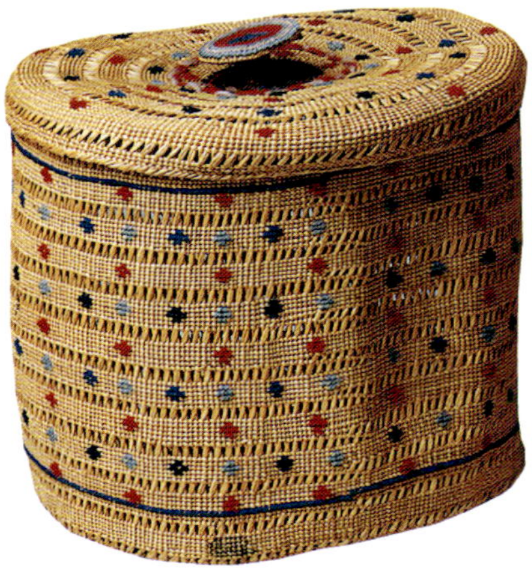

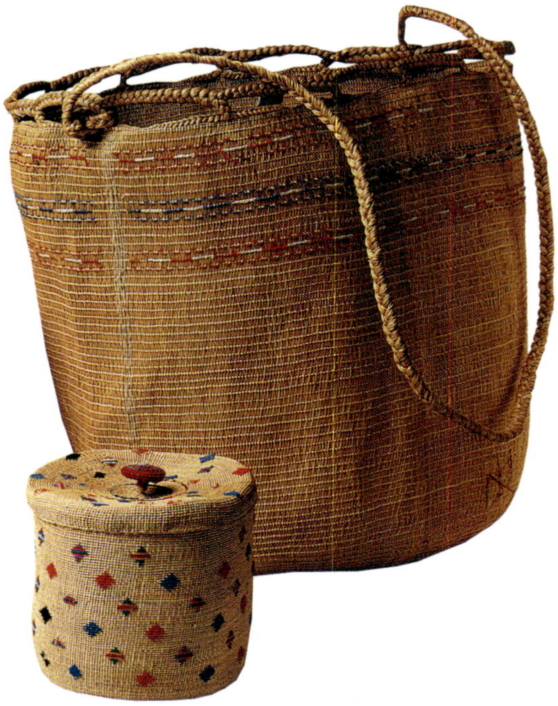

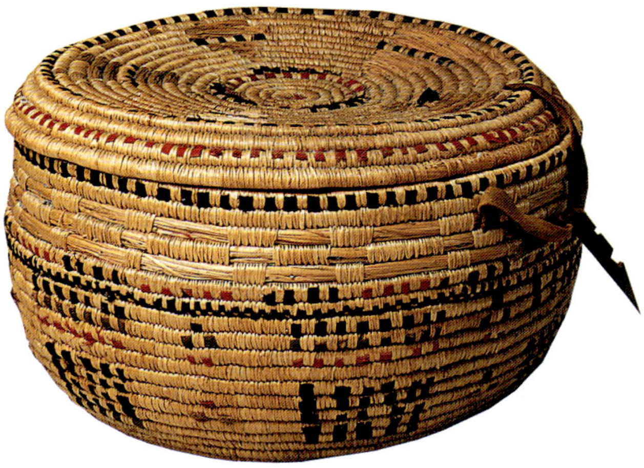

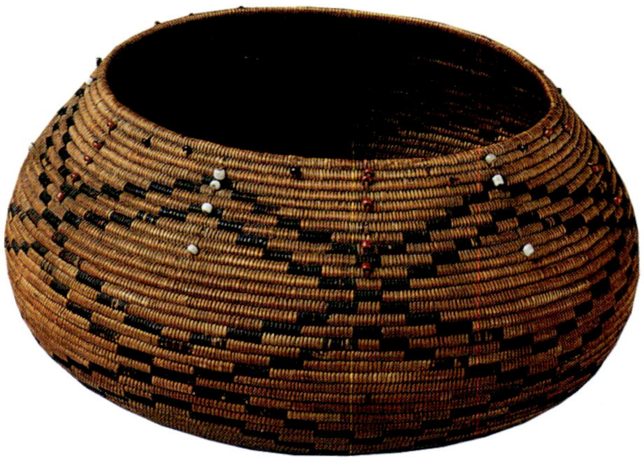

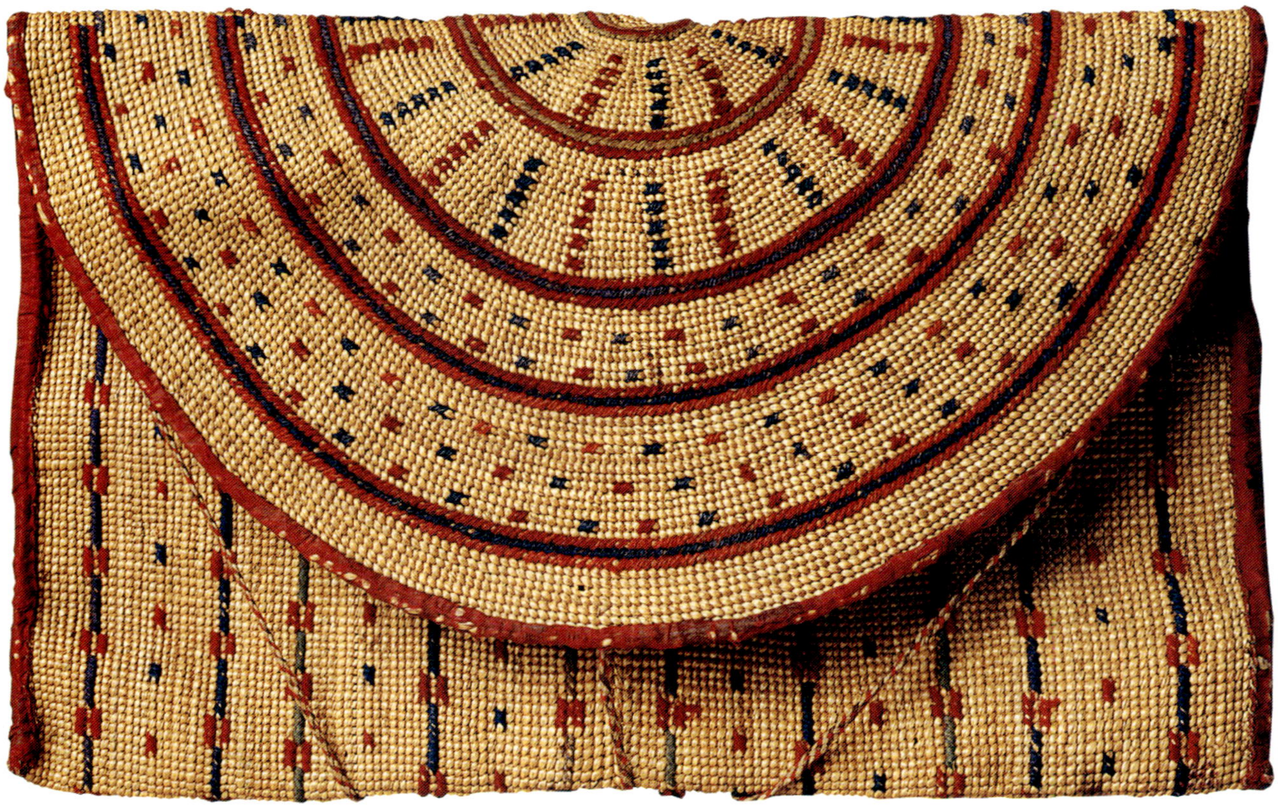

Among all the natives of Siberia the cattle breeding Buryats have best preserved the ancient custom of the community of goods. A poor Buryat, for example, has the right to receive food or shelter from his well-to-do brethren. When a Buryat kills game, his neighbours first receive their share of the meat, and the host gets only what is left. In like manner the Buryat girl simply goes to the village smith and selects metal ornaments for her hair and dress without paying; and the crops on the fields are gathered in by the community, each member of which has the right to take what he needs from the common store. This principle of communism also finds expression in the large communal hunting-parties which at certain periods take place and are accompanied by great festivities.

The town of Kiakhta, in the Selenga valley, near the frontier, was the great international market where the Russians and indigenous groups would meet and trade. A major industry in the area near Lake Baikal was the catching and domesticating the *maral*, or wild deer, for the sake of its horns, which were once considered a very valuable medicine by the Chinese.The maral sheds its horns once a year, and they were collected and sold at high prices to the Chinese merchants, who shipped them south to China. In a similar manner, the Siberian found ready purchasers among Chinese merchants for the bones, claws, and other parts of the northern tiger, which was once in abundance in Ussuri on the Pacific Coast. These parts, when ground up and administered to a patient, were supposed to have wonderful effects and the Chinese are said to have given this medicine to their soldiers to keep up their courage.

Aleut,
Baskets, 1909-1910.
Grass-wrack, woolen yarn, Diameters of the bottoms: 1) 12.2 cm 2) 21 cm 3) 33 cm.
Russian Museum of Ethnography, St. Petersburg. Aleutian Islands, Umnak Island.

Aleut, Koryak,
Baskets, early 20th century.
Grass-wrack, seed beads, woolen yarn, paint, dressed reindeer skin, 1) 25.5 and 17.2 x 12 cm; 2) 22 x 13 cm.
Russian Museum of Ethnography, St. Petersburg. Commander Islands, Kamchatka Peninsular.

Aleut,
Small woman's bag, 1909-1910.
Grass-wrack, woolen yarn, fabric, 27 x 24 cm.
Russian Museum of Ethnography, St. Petersburg. Aleutian Islands, Unalaska Island.

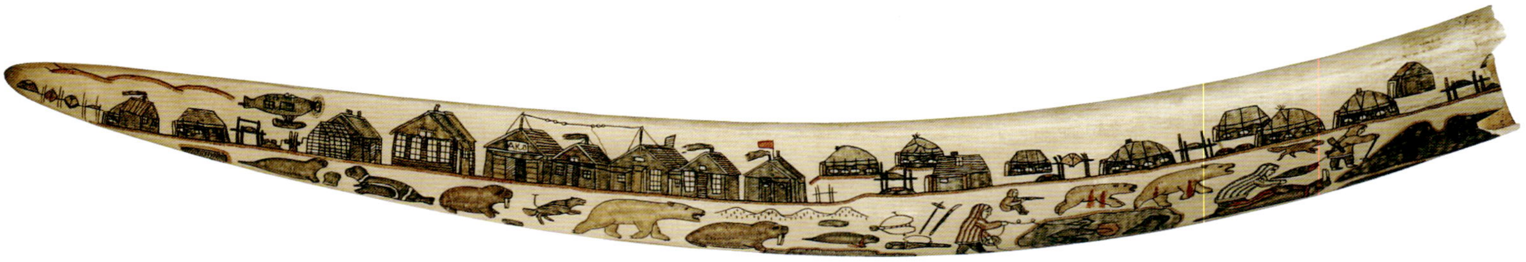

Chukchi,
Tusk with coloured engraving (1st side),
1930s.
Walrus tusk ivory, 62 x 6 cm.
Russian Museum of Ethnography,
St. Petersburg. Chukchi Peninsular.

Chukchi,
Tusk with coloured engraving (1st side),
1930s.
Walrus tusk ivory, 57 x 6 cm.
Russian Museum of Ethnography,
St. Petersburg.

Chukchi,
Tusk with coloured engraving (2nd side),
detail, 1930s.
Walrus tusk ivory, 57 x 6 cm.
Russian Museum of Ethnography,
St. Petersburg. Chukchi Peninsular.

Chukchi,
Tusk with coloured engraving (2nd side),
1930s.
Walrus tusk ivory, 57 x 6 cm.
Russian Museum of Ethnography,
St. Petersburg. Chukchi Peninsular.

The following description of a traditional Yakut wedding demonstrates customs of the northern Yakuts that differ from those of the people in the southern parts of the province. The process of marriage in indigenous Siberia usually goes as follows: When a father wants a wife for his son, he either goes himself or sends some one of his trusted friends to find a suitable girl. When one is found, the price to be paid for her must be settled with her father. When the parties have agreed as to the price, the first instalment is paid. The second instalment is paid at the wedding, and the full payment is concluded when the married couple live together. In spite of the mercantile character of marriage among the tribal cultures, there are, of course, many instances of real and warm affection between man and wife, and still more so between parents and children.

The wedding, which is attended by many guests, both invited and uninvited, takes place both in the home of the bride and that of the bridegroom; the relatives and friends of the bride congregating at her home, and those of the bridegroom at his. The bride and bridegroom do not sit at the table, but in a corner behind the door, with their faces turned towards the wall, the bride on the women's side, and the bridegroom on the men's side of the yurta. Both are dressed in their best clothes. Thus they sit for three days, which is as long as the festival continues, without looking at one another. The young people, both girls and boys, are all the time singing, dancing, and playing. Prominent guests and old men sit on the nares along the wall, smoking and drinking tea, koumiss, and vodka. Food is eaten every now and then all the time, but the principal festival meals are the dinner and supper. In front of each guest, on a horse-hide which serves as table-cloth, is placed a large piece of boiled meat with the bones attached. The relatives of the young couple exchange these pieces of meat, and this performance is the principal part of the Yakut marriage ceremony, symbolising the union between the families, which henceforth are to forget all enmity, and for the future be "flesh of one flesh and bone of one bone." Formerly, when the custom of "robbing the bride"

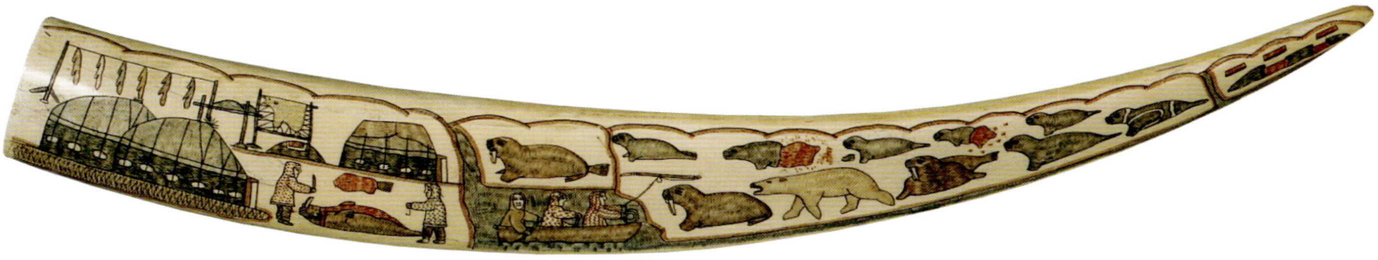

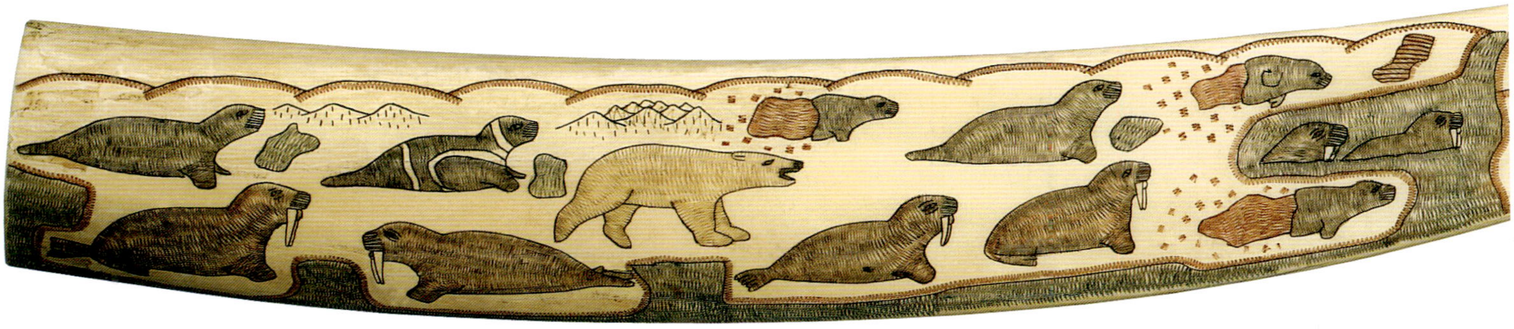

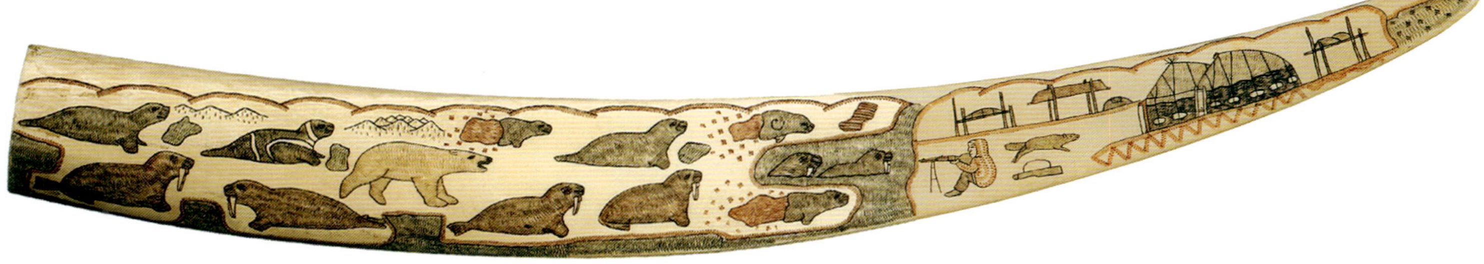

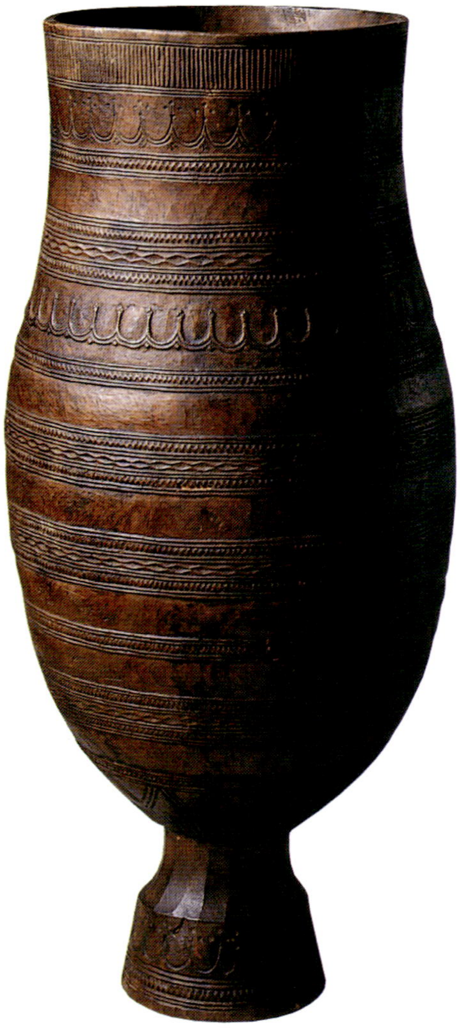

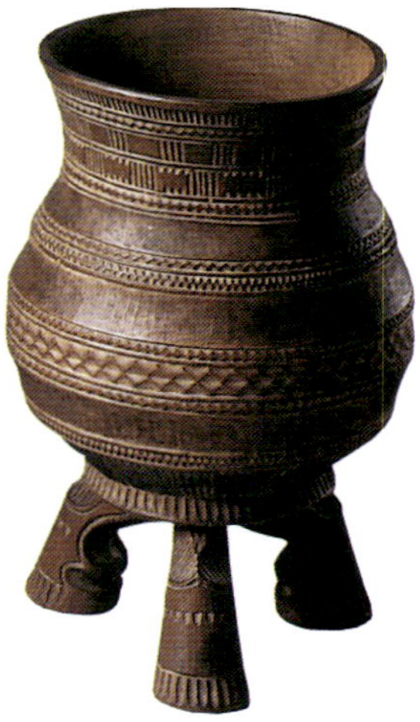

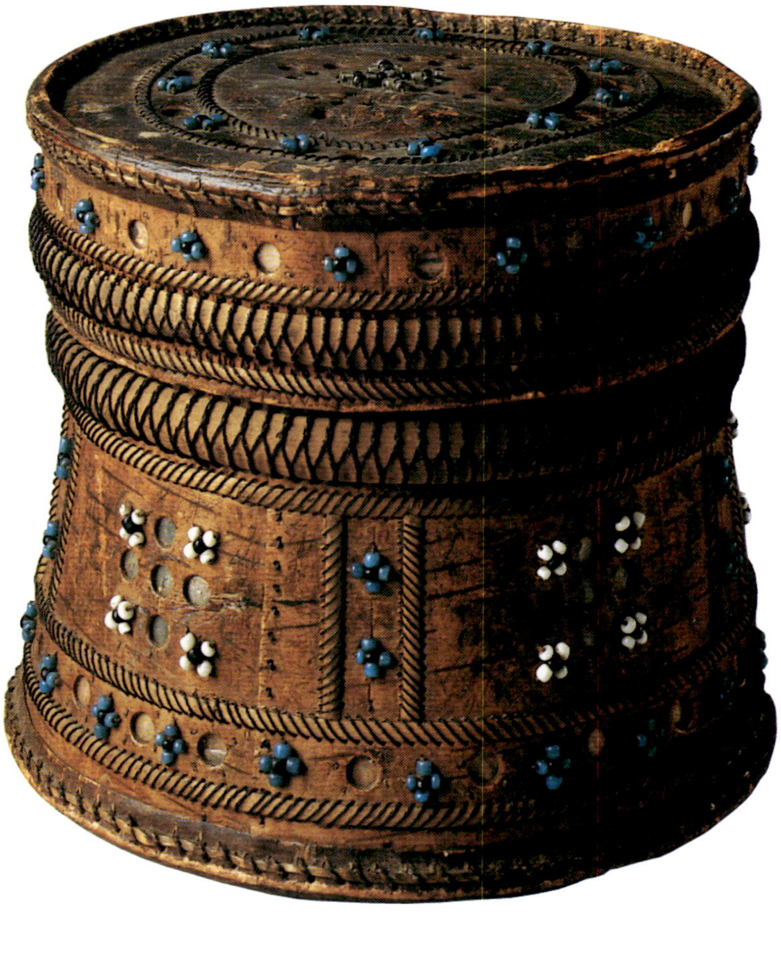

Yakut,
Chorons – cups for koumiss (fermented mare's milk), 1903, end of the 19th and beginning of the 20th century.
Wood, 1) 21 x 13 cm; 2) 56 x 21 cm.
Russian Museum of Ethnography, St. Petersburg. Yakut Oblast.

Yakut,
Box for sewing appliances, 1908.
Birch bark, beads, horsehair, wood, leather, 14 x 17 cm.
Russian Museum of Ethnography, St. Petersburg. Yakut Oblast, Vilyuy Okrug.

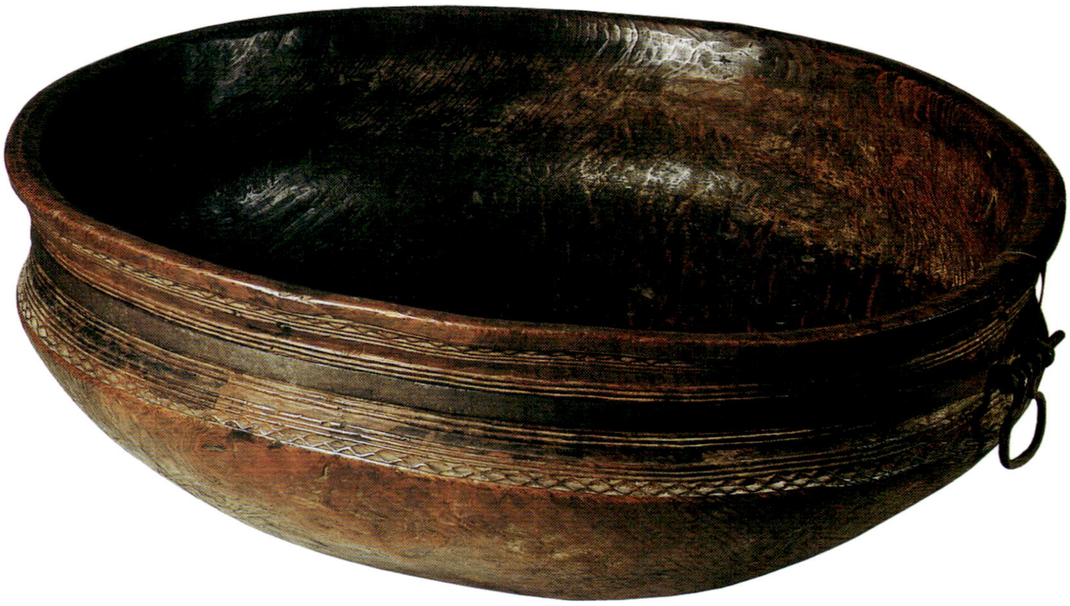

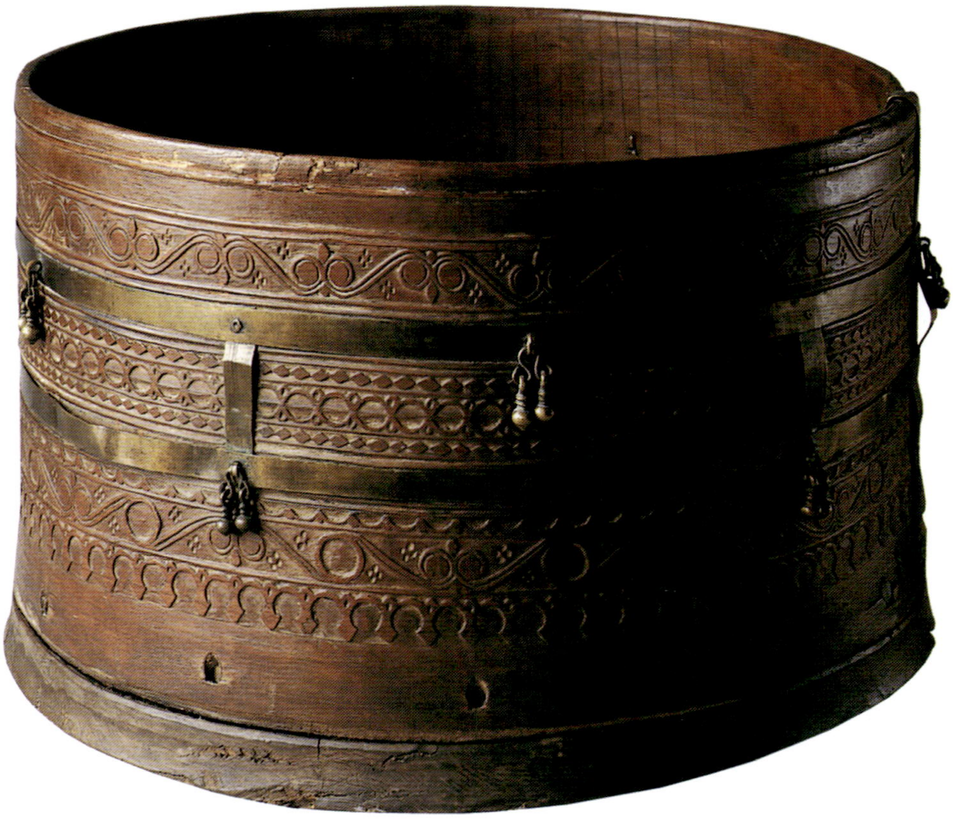

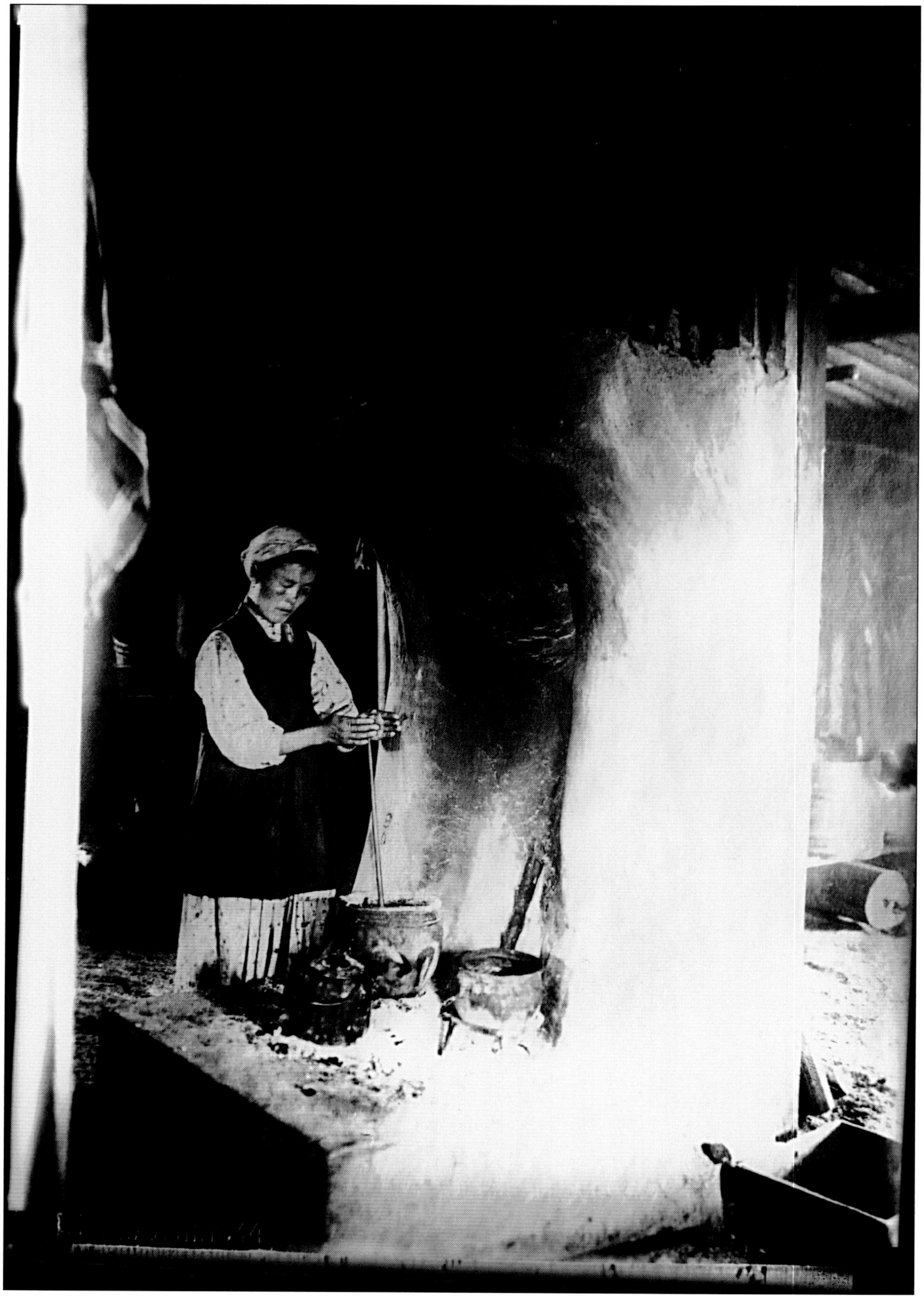

still continued, this ceremony consisted in the exchange of gifts as a token of reconciliation and as compensation for losses sustained during mutual feuds. When the wedding is over and the guests are ready to leave, the following ceremony takes place. Holding a goblet of koumiss in their hands, the guests are conducted by the host and hostess three times around the poles standing outside the yurt, to which horses are tied, and which are considered sacred. Then the guests mount their horses, drink part of the koumiss, and pour the rest on the manes of their steeds.

The role of the married woman is undoubtedly a challenging one among these people. Her duties are not only to bear and bring up children, but to make and mend the clothes for the whole family, make tents and pitch them, gather and chop wood, take up ice and melt it into water for family use, prepare food, and help the men in their hunting, fishing, and trapping occupations.

Until the beginning of the 18th century the Buryat people, like all the peoples of northern Asia belonging to the eastern branches of the Ural-Altaic group (i.e. all the Evenki, Mongol, and Turki tribes), were practitioners of a religion that we generally call Shamanism. At the time of the advent of the Dai-Tsin dynasty to the throne of the Chinese Empire, Shamanism was introduced in China under the name of Tjao-Shen, but the new religion did not meet with any success there. The fact, however, deserves to be mentioned, because a description of the ceremonies of Shamanism was published in China in 1747, in the Manchu language, and was for centuries the only printed account existing of the ancient religion of the Mongols.

In 1727 Buddhist missionaries came to Mongolia and converted the Transbaikalian Buryats and the inhabitants of the Tungkin valley to Buddhism, which, however, became very much mixed up with Shamanism. At one time the Buddhist monasteries in the area near Lake Baikal and the southern parts of Irkutsk were counted by hundreds. By the dawn of the twentieth century, their number was much smaller, almost insignificant. These Buddhist missionaries exerted a great civilising influence on the Buryats by introducing the art of writing among them, and by translating several Tibetan religious books into the Mongolian language. The Buddhist monastery at the Goose Lake was the most important, because it was the residence of the chief of the Siberian adherents of the Lama faith. At the same place was a library containing a very valuable collection of books and manuscripts in the Tibetan and Mongolian languages. Great annual religious festivals also took place at this monastery. The Buryat people were fond of making pilgrimages to Urga, where there is a "living Buddha." So great is this devotion that a Buryat will frequently surrender the whole of his property to some shrine on condition that he receives just enough to live upon.

More recently, on the tops of the hills near the river, native graves are often to be seen, with a simple wooden cross as their headstone, proclaiming the dominance of Russian-imported Christianity. The majority of the natives are nominally Christians, and pagan burials without crosses are now forbidden. Besides, there is the belief spreading among the "Christian" natives, that the Resurrection Angel will not recognise their graves if he does not see the cross over them. But even these "Christian" burial-places attest to the more ancient and traditional religious practices in the children's toys, the skulls of the reindeer, the sleighs which were used in transporting the dead to their last resting-place, and other belongings of the deceased with which the graves are decked.

Yakut,
Dish for treating of guests, 1909.
Wood, metal, 23.5 x 65 cm.
Russian Museum of Ethnography, St. Petersburg. Yakut Oblast, Boturuski ulus.

Yakut,
Ware for koumiss (fermented mare's milk), used during the Ysyakh holiday, 1906.
Wood, metal, 22 x 32.5 cm.
Russian Museum of Ethnography, St. Petersburg. Yakut Oblast, Yakut Okrug.

Woman preparing food near a stove inside a yurt, 1913.

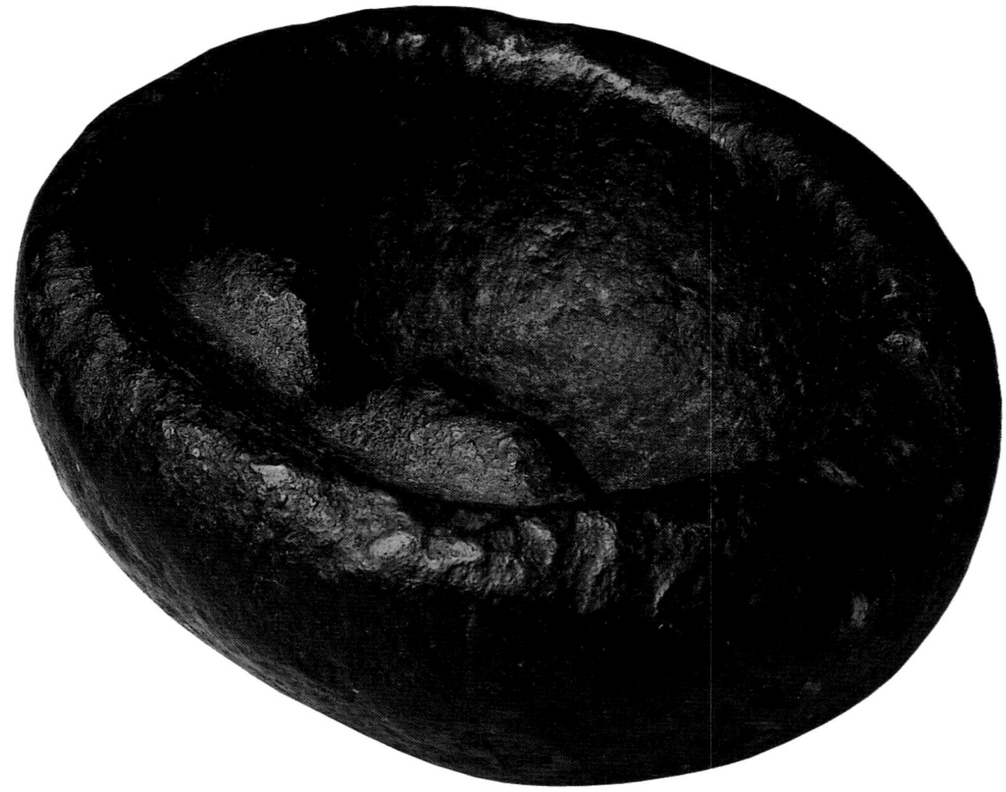

Chukchi,
Blubber lamp for heating and lighting of the lodge, early 20th century.
Stone, diameter: 16 cm; height: 7 cm.
Russian Museum of Ethnography, St. Petersburg. Primorskaya Oblast, Anadyr Krai.

Yakut,
Scoop for pouring koumiss (fermented mare's milk), early 20th century.
Wood, 103 x 18 cm.
Russian Museum of Ethnography, St. Petersburg. Yakut ASSR.

Aleut,
Spoon, early 20th century.
Wood, 28.5 cm.
Russian Museum of Ethnography, St. Petersburg. North-Western America.

Koryak,
Spoon, 1909-1911.
Argali horn, 15.9 cm.
Russian Museum of Ethnography, St. Petersburg. Kamchatka.

Many Siberian tribes are surprisingly hospitable to strangers, often enthusiastic about the opportunity to exhibit their wealth, whether it is in terms of cattle or furs. In Bulun, the "capital" of the district of Schigansk, an area where the Evenki live, there is a church with a priest, a civil officer and police-court, about 40 yurts with some 200 natives, and in the midst of these towers, the palace of the king, in the shape of a large Russian izba. A stranger to this part of Siberia is courteously invited into the palace, and shown much hospitality in the shape of vodka and dried reindeer-meat, vodka and *jukkala* (dried fish), vodka and boiled fish, vodka and *stroganina* (frozen fish), and vodka and *ikra* (caviar). The walls of the reception-hall in the palace are covered with costly and shining icons, and in the right corner, a lamp is constantly burning in front of the image of St. Nicolas. The treasure vaults of the king contain an immense heap of carved and decorated mammoth tusks, worth many thousand roubles, and a large pile of skins of white foxes, blue foxes, and even black foxes, also worth great amounts of money.

Wandering, nomadic peoples such as the Chukchi developed ways of communicating with one another across the vast, icy expanses. Throughout the tundra were once poles, placed in groups or singly in a certain order, at various distances from each other, some of which had mysterious marks cut on them, others incisions in which splinters were stuck, pointing in different directions.

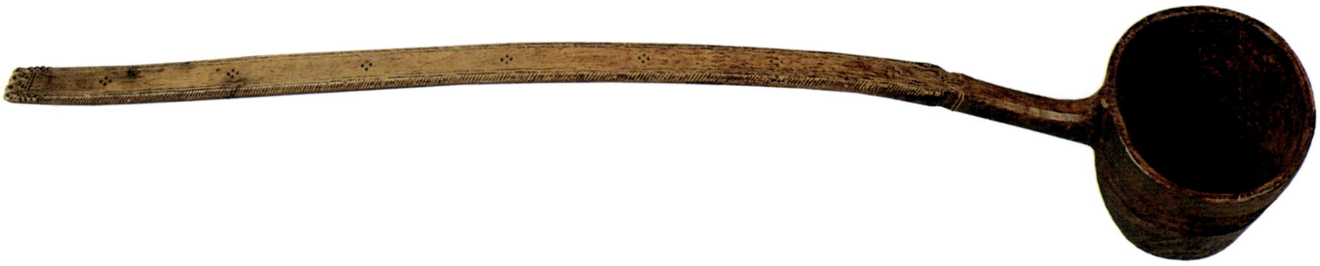

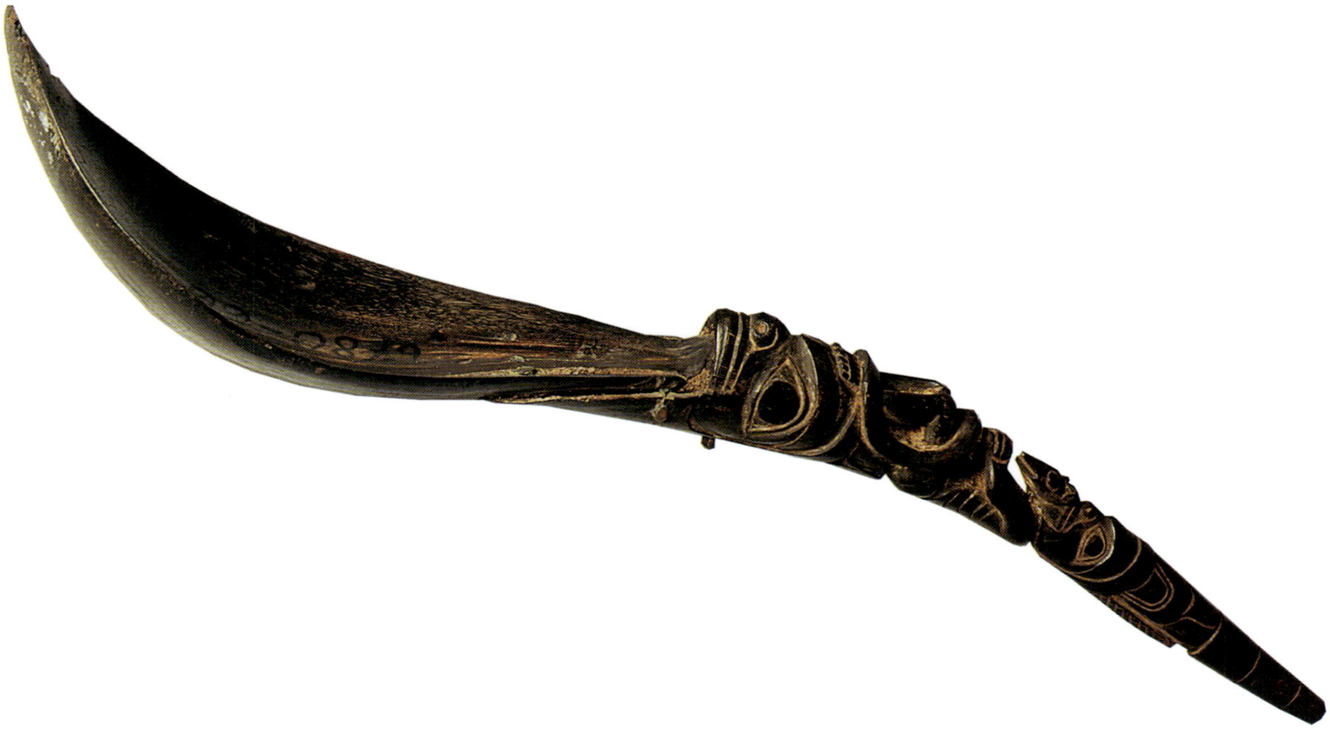

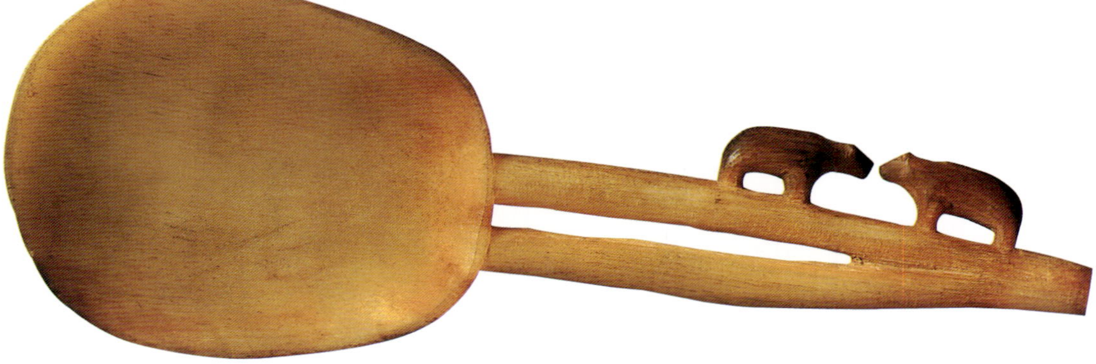

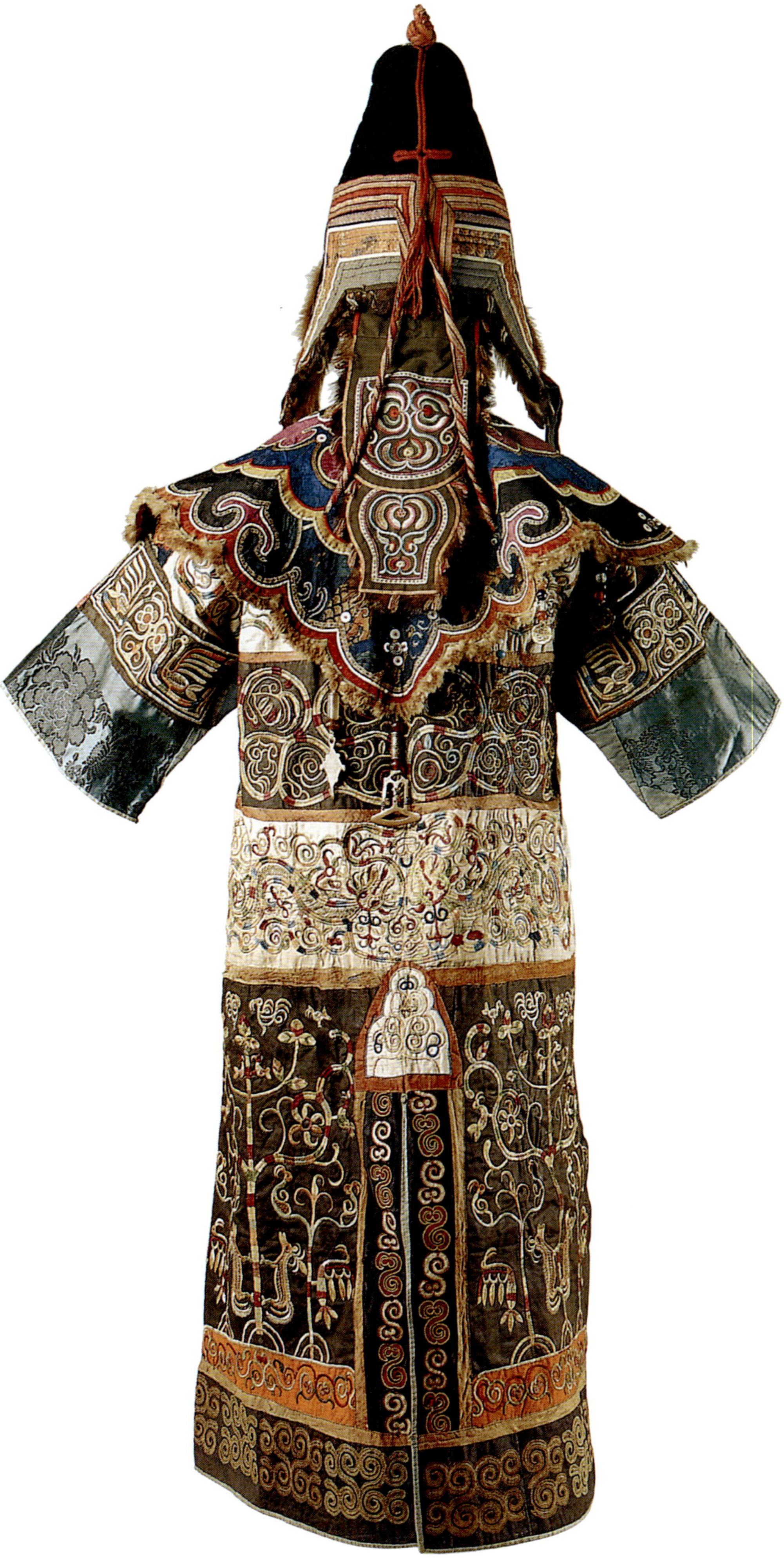

Nanai,
Wedding robe.

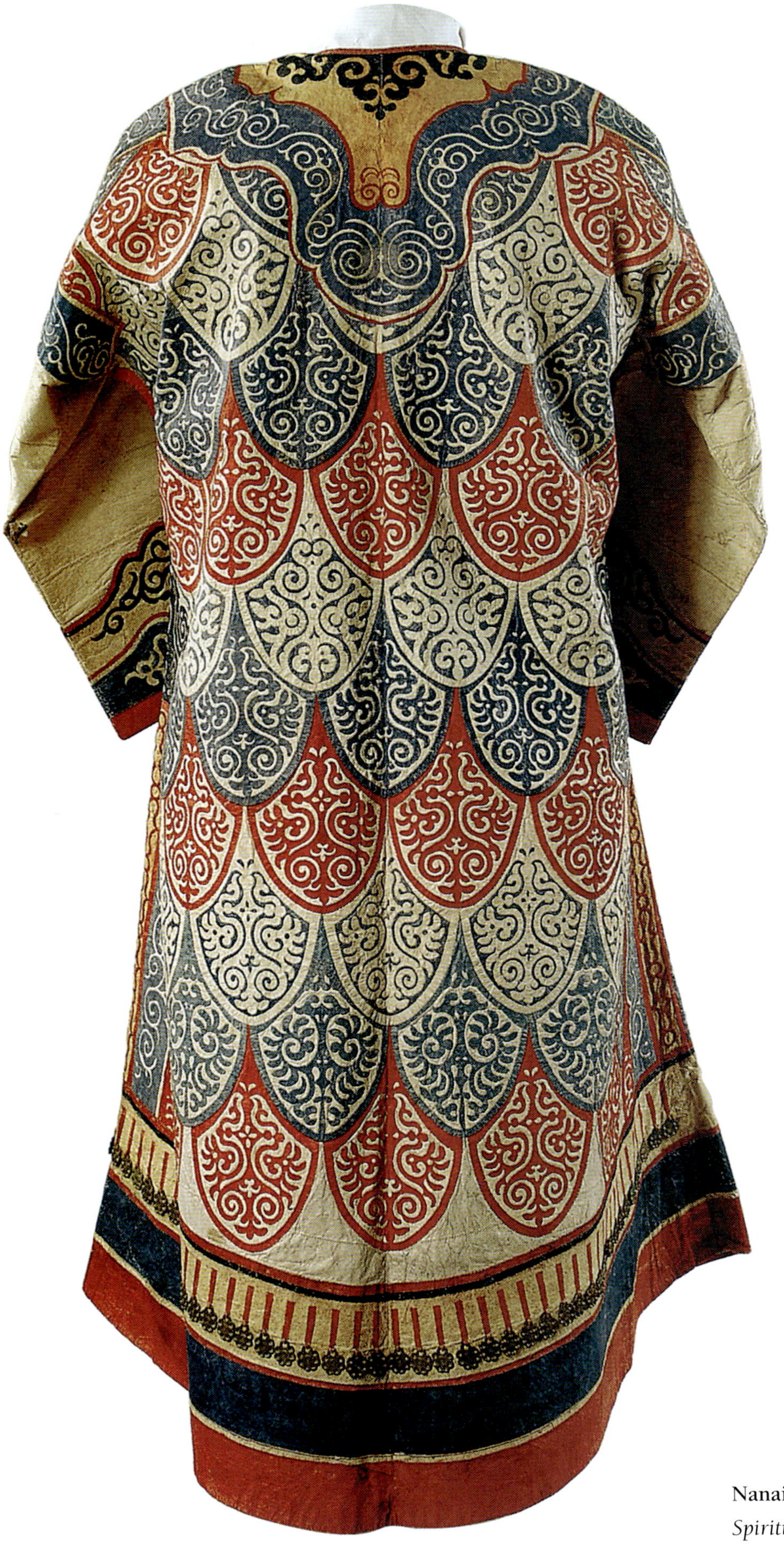

Nanai,
Spiritually protective robe.
Fish scales, fabric.
Russian Museum of Ethnography,
St. Petersburg.

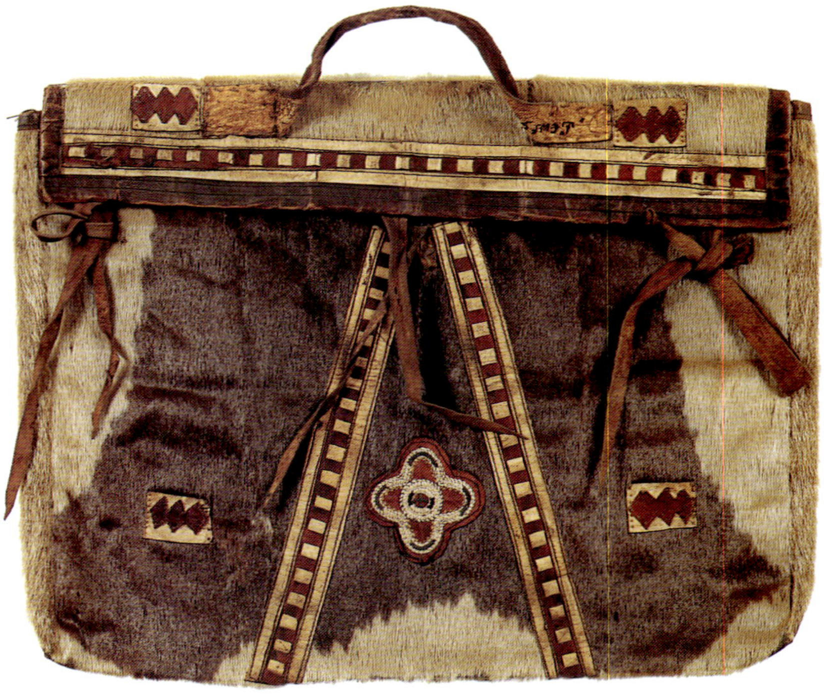

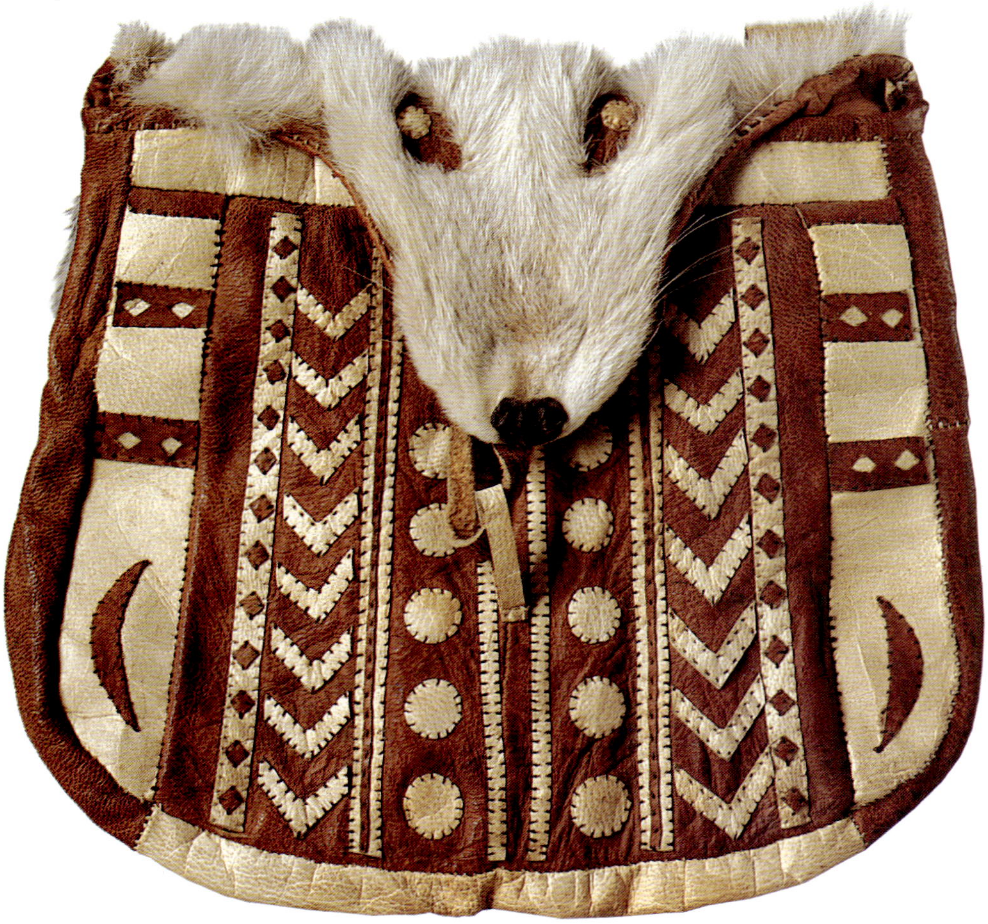

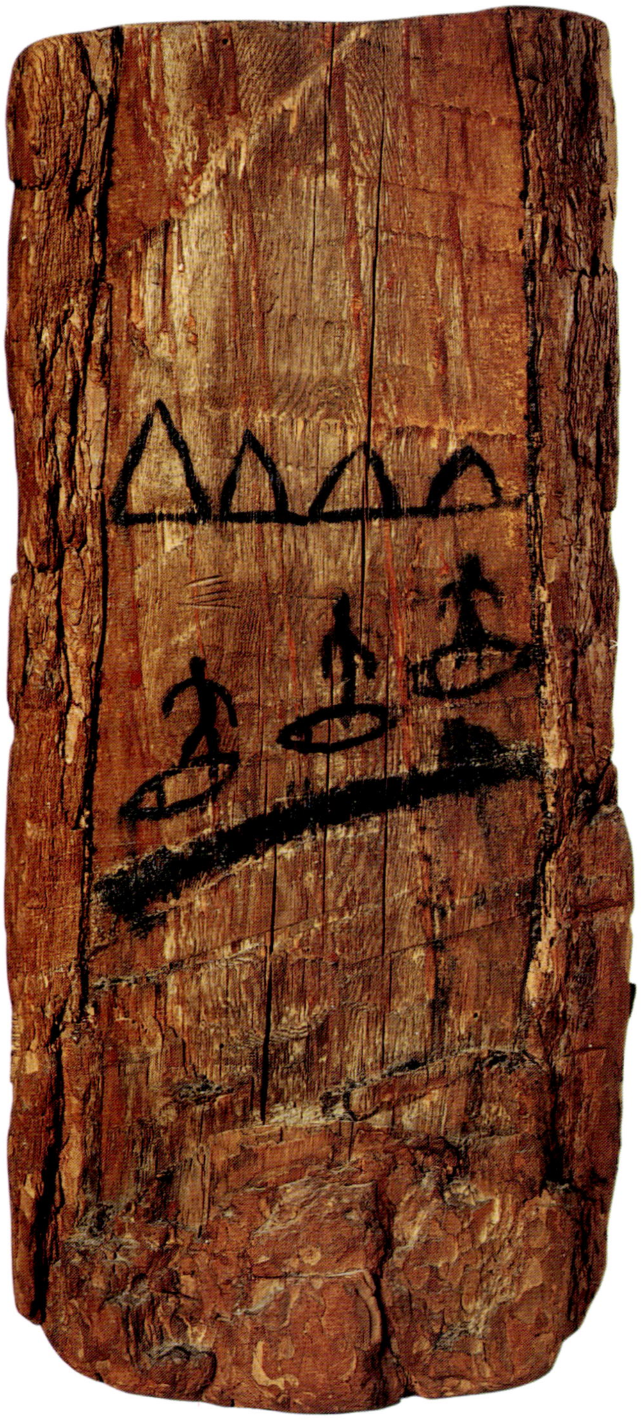

Eskimo,
Woman's bag, early 20th century.
Seal hide and skin, reindeer underneck hair, 37 x 49 cm.
Russian Museum of Ethnography, St. Petersburg. Chukchi Peninsular.

Aleut,
Woman's bag, 1909-1910.
Eared seal intestines, bird fluff, woolen yarn, bird skin, 34 x 36 cm.
Russian Museum of Ethnography, St. Petersburg. Aleutian Islands.

Evenki,
Pictographic letter, 1908.
Wood (pine), coal, 59 x 26 cm.
Russian Museum of Ethnography, St. Petersburg. Yenisey Gubernia (province), Yenisey Uyezd (district), the Podkamennaya Tunguska river basin.

These sticks and poles represented the letters and newspapers of the desolate land, and traveling parties studied them carefully. From them they learnt, for example, that this place had been visited during the summer by Evenki, hunting the wild reindeer; that a fox-trapper from Olenek had passed a few weeks before on his way westward; or that someone who had visited the place had seen polar-bears in the vicinity. The drivers in their turn contributed to these "open letters," putting up new sticks and poles in order to inform future travellers about their journey.

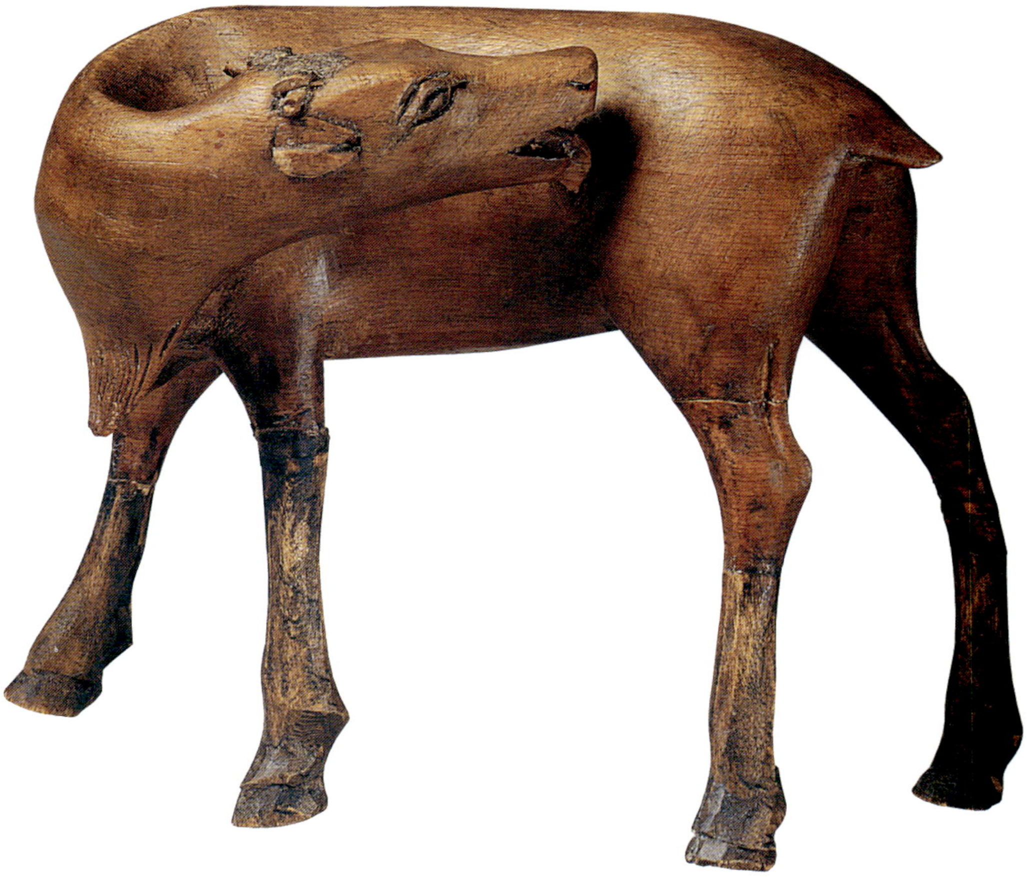

B. EARTH AND WATER

"The fauna and the flora, the regenerative cycle of nature in Siberia – all determine the rhythm of life of the aboriginal people, and embody an annual calendar of things to do and things to go and get for individual groups and, indeed, for individuals."

1) REINDEER HERDERS

It was the Evenki and the Eveni people who made the first attempt to domesticate the reindeer, which even now they use as a form of transport particularly well adapted to the region of the taiga, especially in hunting other ungulates. The reindeer is the focus around which the world revolves for these two communities, who often call themselves in their own languages 'the people of the reindeer'.

An activity typical of Siberia, reindeer-herding is practised – more or less intensively – by ten ethnic groups: the Nenets, the Nganassani people, the Chukchis, the Koryaks, the Evenki, the Eveni, the Dolgans, the Yukaghirs, the Khanty and the Karagas people. Methodologies differ in the tundra and the taiga.

In the taiga, herds are comparatively small, averaging between 20 and 25 head, with perhaps 50 head in the largest herds. Here, the reindeer is used primarily as a means of transport, the people for the most part living by hunting and fishing. The Khanty, for example, herd reindeer (which in fact was something they copied from the Nenets) only as a sideline. Reindeer are credited with more importance in the tundra, where herds are larger and of variable size – from a hundred or so to several thousand head. The semi-domesticated reindeer represents an essential source of livelihood for the peoples of the far north.

Lichens and mosses, the main diet of the reindeer, tend only to grow some 3 millimetres (an eighth of an inch) per year. When all have been consumed in an area, the reindeer have to leave and find new pasturage. This seasonal migration of the reindeer is naturally reflected in the life of their herders and those who go hunting with them. The journeys involved in the migrations are proportional to the overall size of the herds, for the more head of reindeer there are in a herd, the more important it is to find a large area of fresh lichens and mosses (from the taiga or the intermediate zone between taiga and tundra in the wintertime – where the reindeer can more easily find their food under the snow and the men can find firewood to keep themselves warm – to the vast bare expanses of the north in summertime). Small herds, in tundra or taiga, tend to cover short distances when travelling from summer to winter pastures – an average of perhaps 25 to 37 miles (40 to 60 kilometres), 60 miles (100 kilometres) at the most. In the taiga, the reindeer-herders who use reindeer for hunting select migratory paths that accord with migratory patterns of the animals they want to hunt or with places known to be the habitat of the fish they want to catch.

In western Siberia, the largest of the reindeer-herders are the Nenets; in the east the Chukchis and the Koryaks. Less well organized than the Nenets, the 'Chaochus' and the 'Chavchuven' (which is what the Chukchi and Koryak

Koryak,
Toy-reindeer, 1897.
Wood, 18 x 12 cm.
Russian Museum of Ethnography, St. Petersburg. Kamchatka.

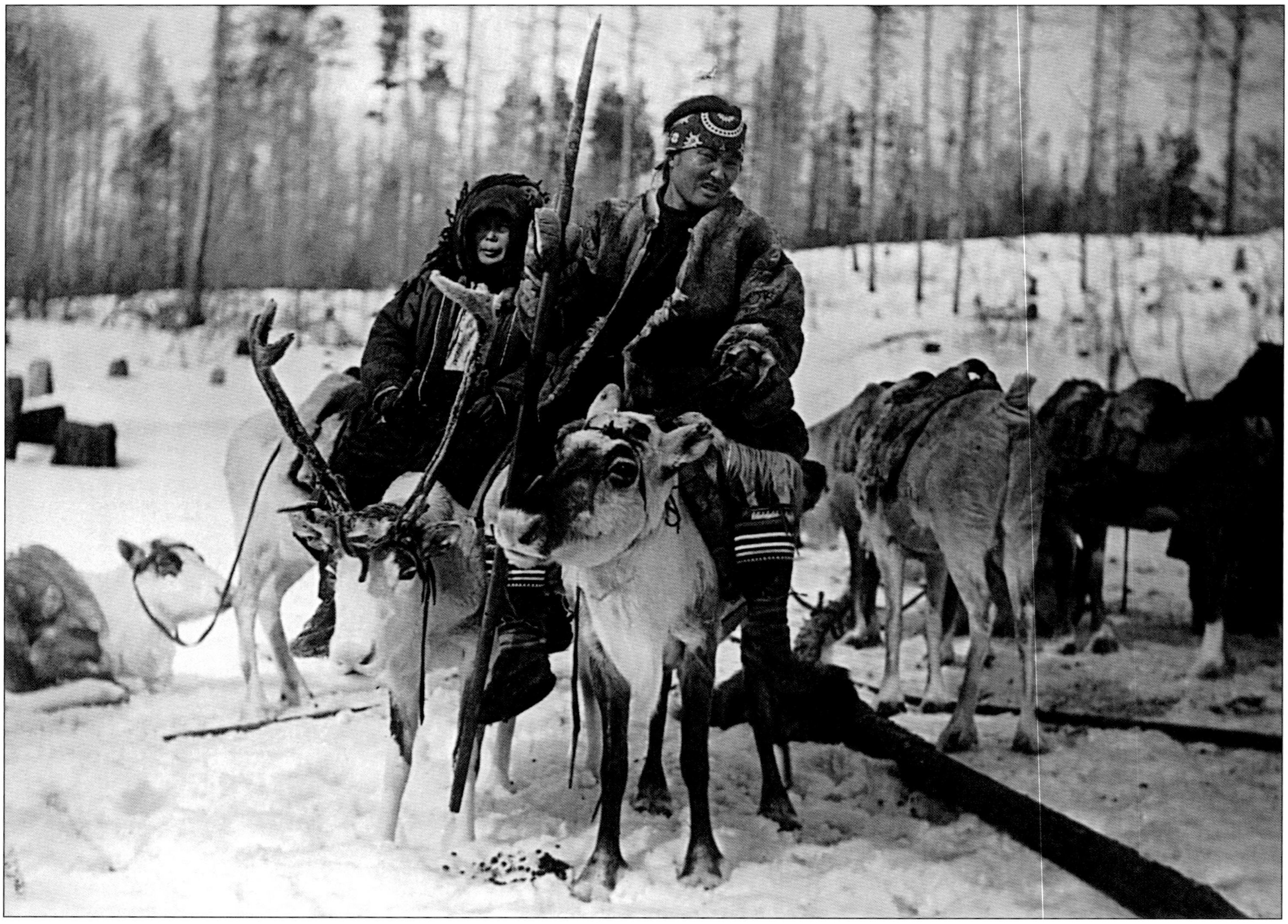

reindeer bosses call themselves) keep the numerically most prolific herds in the whole of Siberia. The Nenets tend to the grazing of the reindeer all the year round: the herds are kept under observation day after day by herdsmen with the help of dogs trained to round up any stray animals. With the Chukchis and the Koryaks, at least until the 1950s, the herd was left to its own devices once it reached pasturage, with the result that the herdsmen – who had no dogs – often had to spend a considerable time rounding up stray reindeer.

The reindeer of the Eveni people are regarded as particularly valuable by the Chukchis and the Koryaks, who were once willing to exchange two of their own animals for one of the Eveni's. It was the same in respect of all the reindeer of the taiga, highly appreciated for their larger overall size by the herders of the tundra.

The tundra herders do not ride their animals but harness them to sledges (sleighs) for the transportation of goods and passengers. In the taiga, riding reindeer is the primary means of transport for the Evenki and the Eveni. The reindeer makes an excellent mount in wooded and mountainous terrain, as the Tuva people – who breed cattle and horses down in the south of Siberia – can attest, for they too use them to get around in their mountains.

Evenki,
Evenki on reindeer-back,
early 20th century.
Yenisey Province.

Reindeer-herding is a testing business physically, and not just in winter, because of hunger and cold. After the fawning season (which takes place in May),

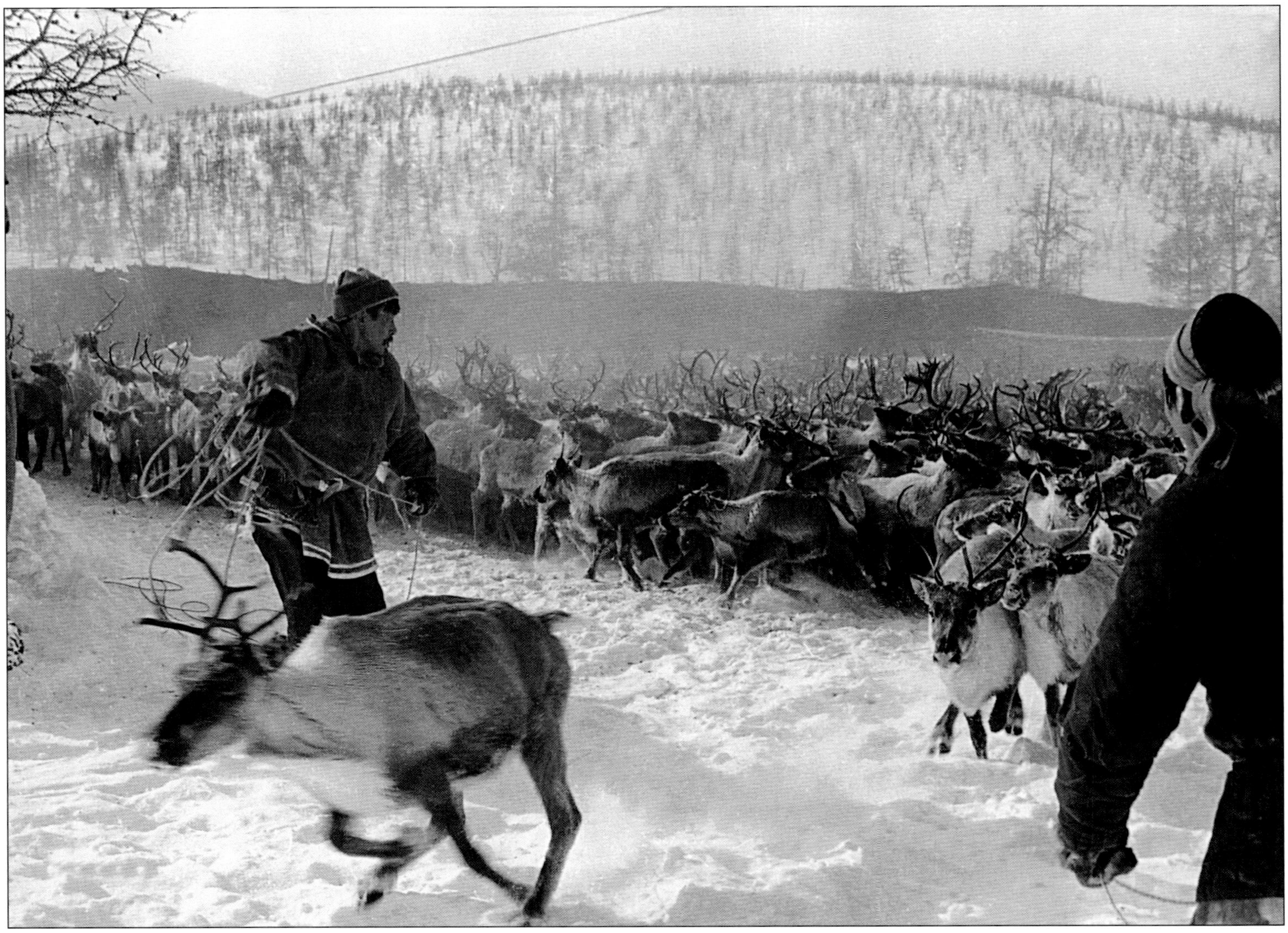

the herdsmen have to watch day and night over the young fawns to make sure they are not snatched by wolves. Towards the end of summer, when the wild mushrooms appear everywhere, they have to be even more vigilant, for reindeer adore such potentially harmful delicacies. And so, for their own health and security, the herd of animals has gradually to be more restricted, until they are penned every night (the Arctic day is already coming to its end) in an enclosure next to the encampment.

The diet of the herders of the taiga for the most part consists of items they have hunted, caught (in the form of fish) or gathered (in the form of berries and fungi). The proprietors of the largest reindeer herds, on the other hand, live almost entirely on the resources provided by their own animals, beginning with the slaughter of one of the herd at the beginning of the autumn. Every bit of the reindeer has its own use: nothing at all goes to waste. The meat is eaten boiled, raw or frozen. To preserve it, it may be smoked. The blood is drunk still lukewarm from the slaughter, and the raw marrow is regarded as the herdsmen's treat. The fat is usually eaten with the meat but may alternatively be used to provide lighting – the Nenets make candles out of it. From the tendons and sinews comes a thread useful in making clothes and as string or cord. The skin can be plied into thongs and then turned into a lasso, into straps or reins for the harnesses or into bridles.

Koryak,
Reindeer-herder,
late 19th-early 20th century.
Kamchatka Peninsula.

Ulchi,
Reindeer herder, 1992.

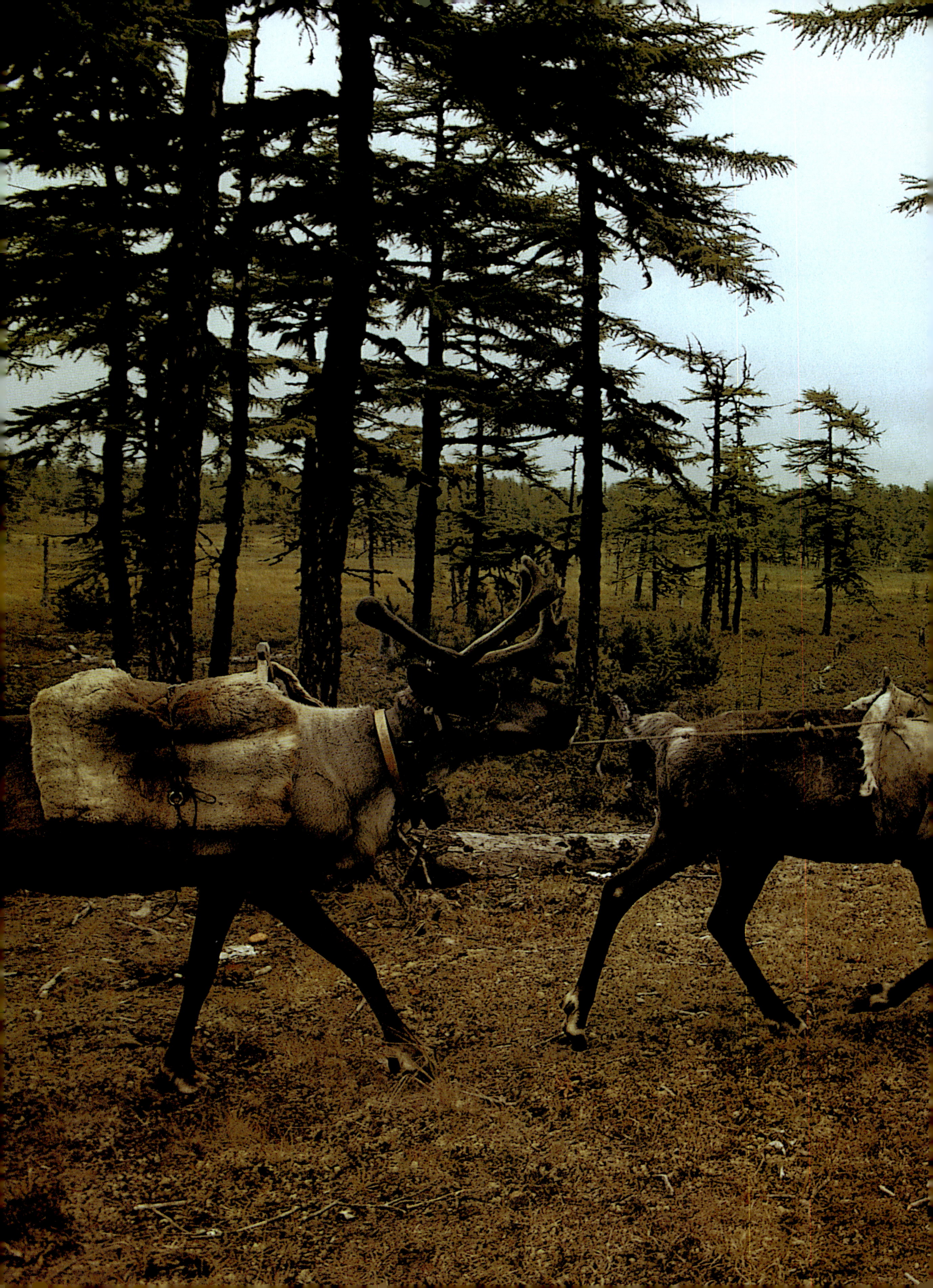

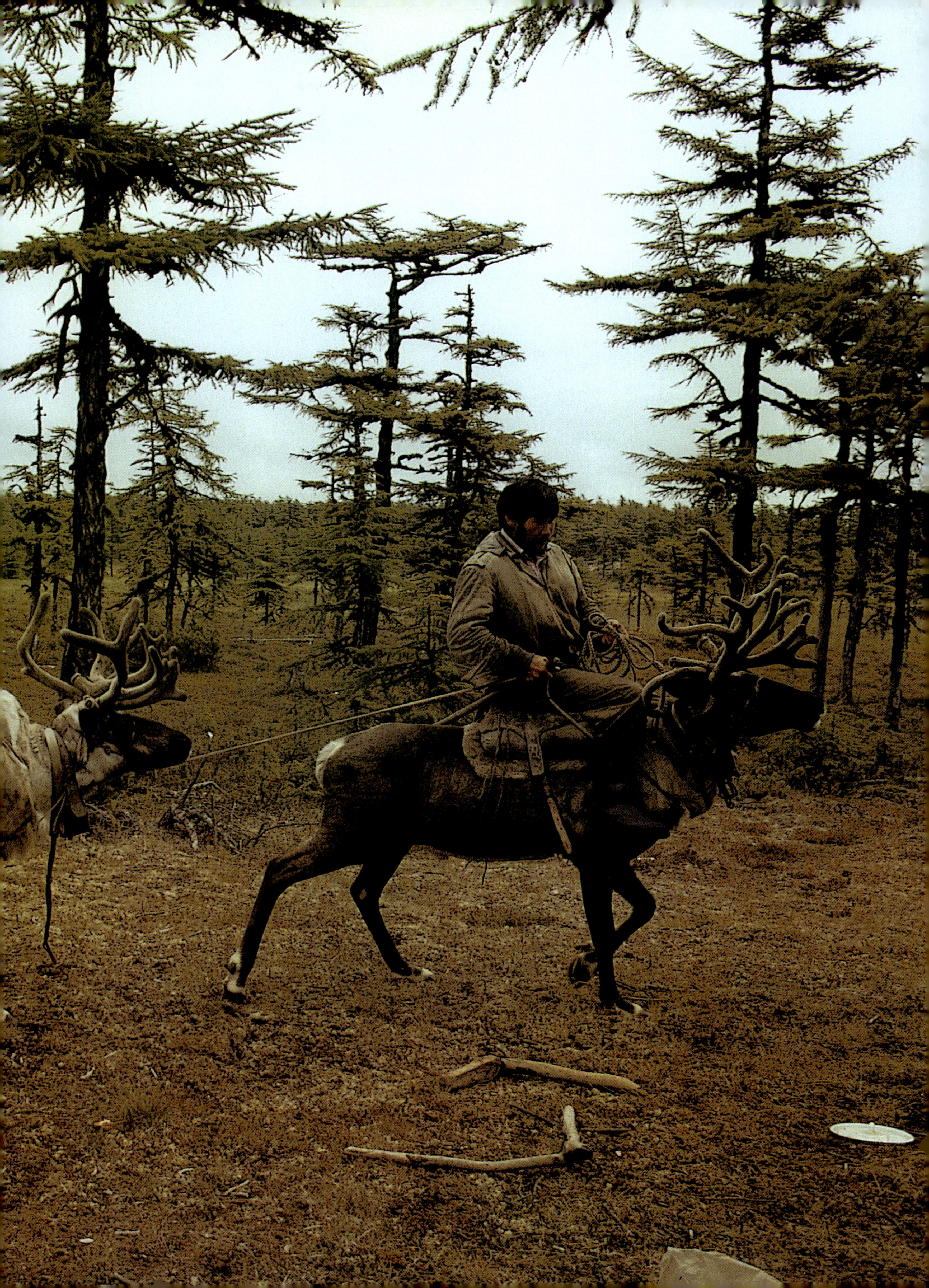

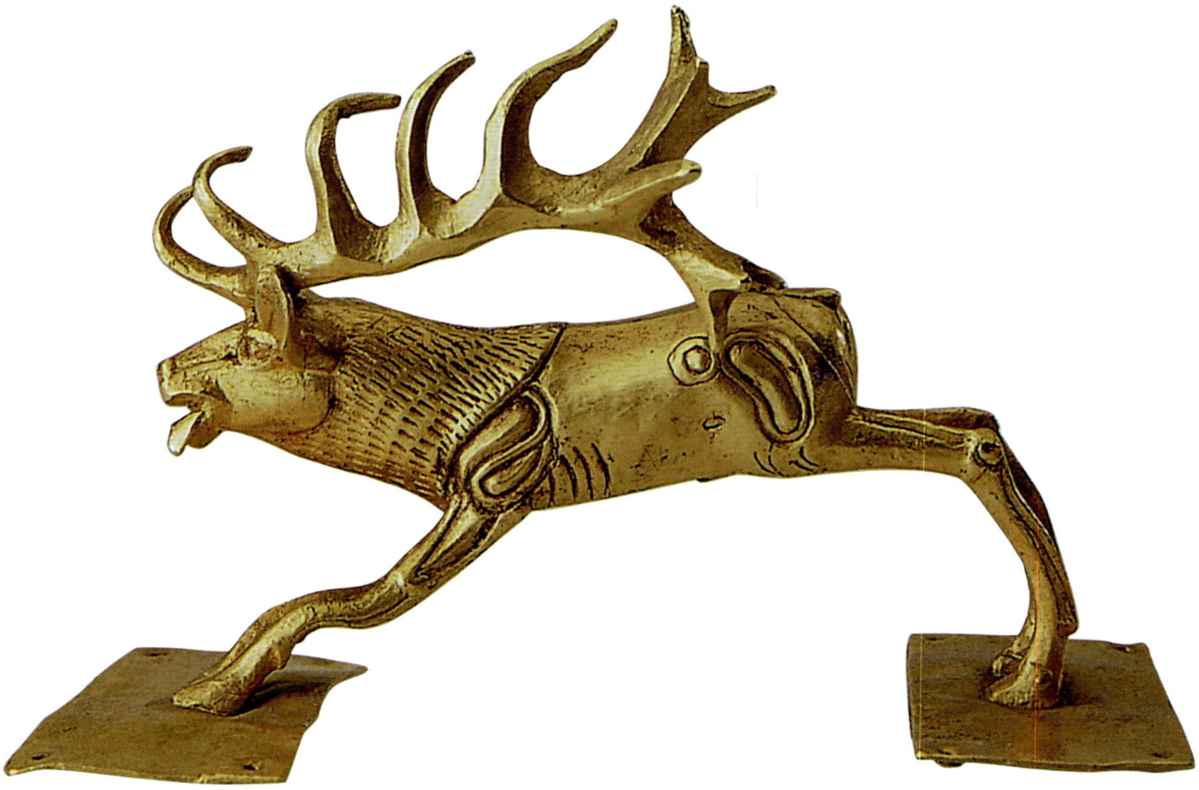

The furry parts of the skin of the reindeer are ordinarily used to fashion garments or to make up the huge, heavy carpet-coverings that insulate the tent or wigwam-like dwellings of the nomadic hunter-herders.

The dwellings of Siberian aboriginals differ greatly from community to community and reflect the close relationship that the people have with nature. The houses of the reindeer herding tribes of the tundra and taiga come in two varieties. The Nenets, the Nganassani people, the Dolgans, the Evenki and some others in central and western Siberia make use of what they call a *choom*, whereas the peoples to the north and east of them – the Chukchis, Koryaks, Eveni – make their temporary home in a *yarang*.

The *choom*, which is conical in shape, is a sort of movable wigwam set up around a framework of between 20 and 50 poles stuck in the ground in a circle and tied together at the top. In the winter this framework is covered with two layers of reindeer-hide, furry sides out, so that the interior of the *choom* is lined with fur and the outside also presents fur to the elements, and there is a minimal insulation space between the two. In summertime, instead of the skins, the *choom* is tightly encased in strips of birch-bark or densely-packed moss. The open area in the middle of the *choom* is occupied by two horizontal poles some 5 feet (1.5 metres) or so off the ground, from which all kinds of things can be suspended over the fire – urns, cauldrons, billycans, clothing, footwear and just about anything else. For the Nenets, the living space in the *choom* is to the left and right of the entrance, each side of the hearth. On the ground, the floor is

Buryat,
Reindeer figurine, 5th-4th century B. C.
Gold, 4.5 cm.
State Hermitage Museum,
St. Petersburg. Amur region.

Evenki,
Cradle, 1907.
Wood, fabric, glass beads, metal, deer skin, 68 x 27 x 20 cm and 16 cm.
Russian Museum of Ethnography,
St. Petersburg. Yenisey Province,
Khatanga River (camp).

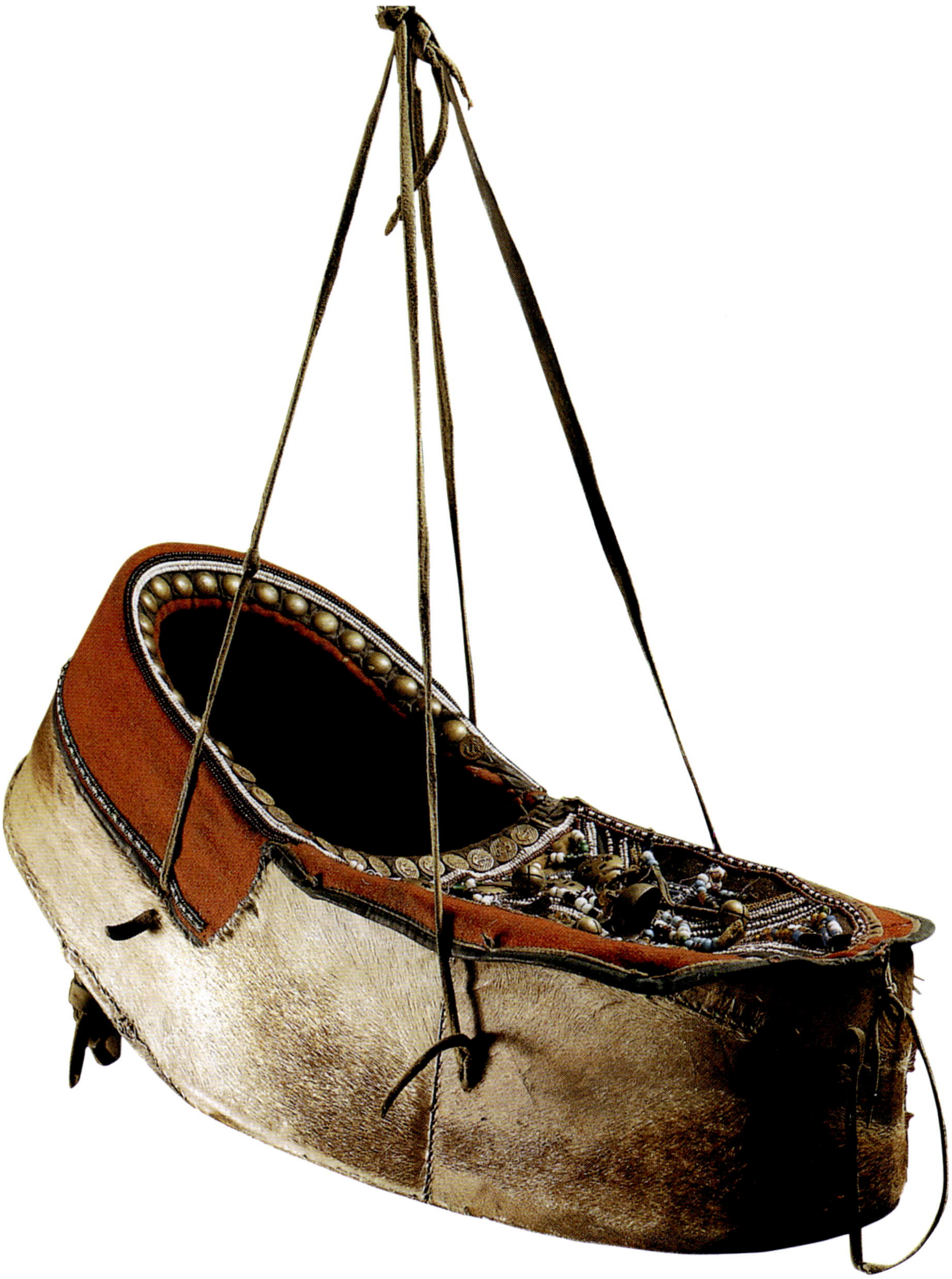

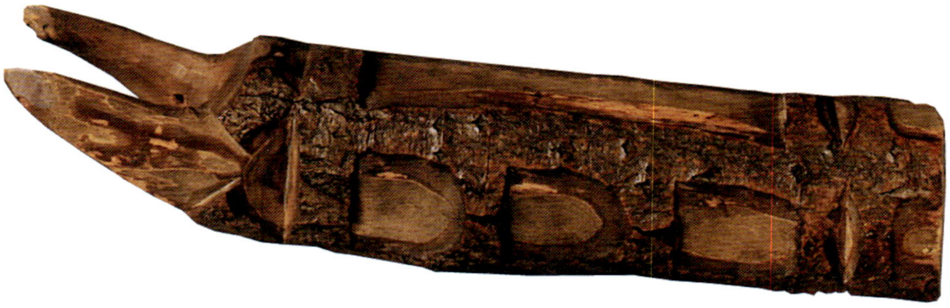

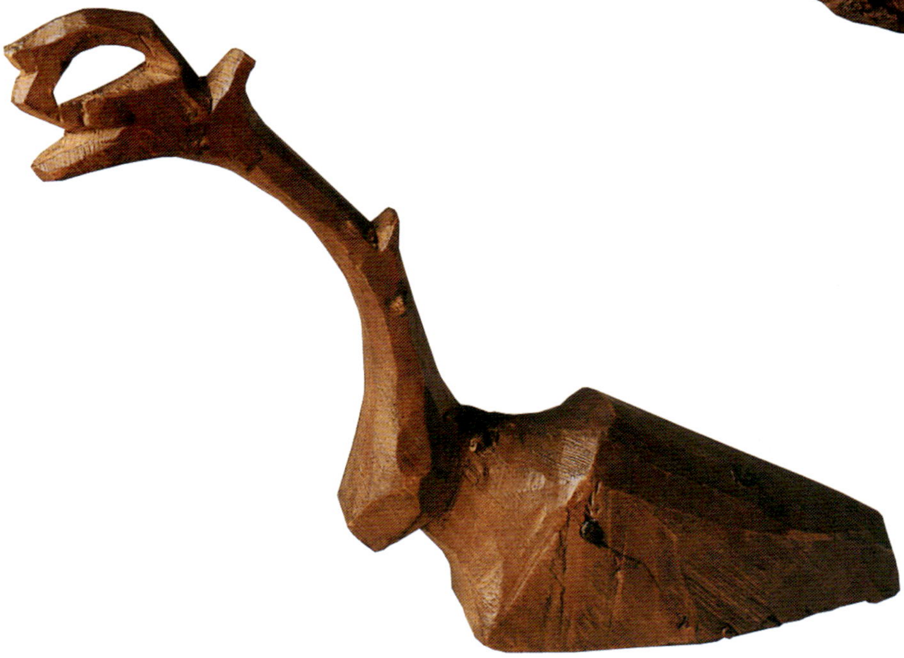

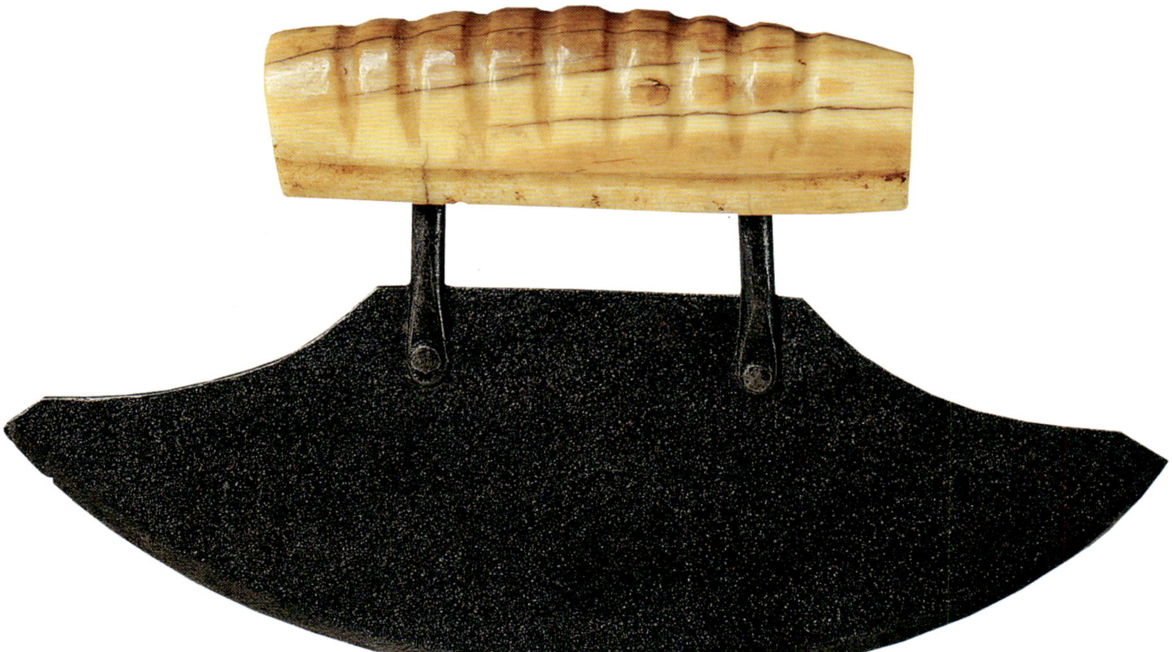

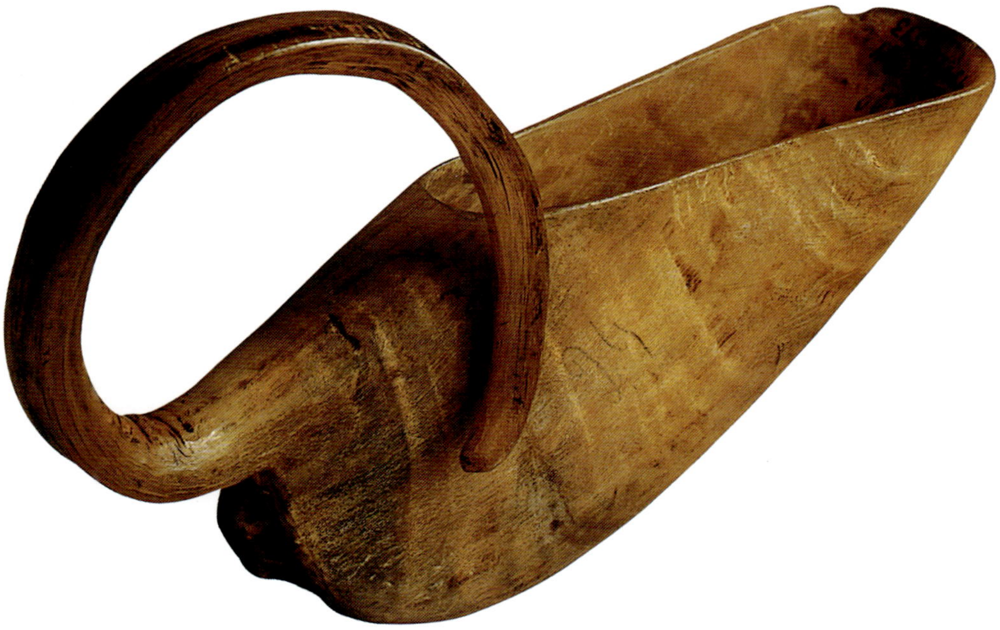

strewn with willow stems and dry grass and carpeted with reindeer skin. The side of the choom opposite the entrance is the area that has to be kept 'pure' and clean at all times, for this is where the family's sacred objects are located, together with the cooking and eating vessels and the food stocks. For the Evenki, the side either to the right or to the left of the entrance is reserved for women, the central area is reserved for other members of the family, and the back – opposite the entrance – is for male guests.

The *yarang* is rather different, though still wigwam-like. It is cylindrical from the ground up but tapers to a cone at the top – a shape that is particularly effective in withstanding squalls and Arctic storms. During winter the framework of poles is hung around with reindeer hides that are held down with heavy stones or with sledges pegged into the snow. The entrance to the *yarang* is traditionally to the east or north-east. Putting it up and taking it down, collecting and packing up all its bits and pieces (the coverings, hangings, carpets, poles and the rest) ready for moving is a job for the women. Among the Koryaks and the Chukchis, an encampment comprises between five and ten *yarangs*, each accommodating one or two families who are blood-relations or are related by marriage. It takes around twenty sledges to move one *yarang* and its complement of occupants. The largest of the reindeer-herders in former times, some of whom owned up to 5,000 reindeer, might need 150 sledges.

Yakut,
Toys: 1) reindeer 2) bull-calf, 1908, 1903.
Wood, 1) 22 x 4 cm; 2) 18 cm x 13 cm.
Russian Museum of Ethnography, St. Petersburg. 1) Yakut Oblast, Vilyuy Okrug; 2) Turukhan Krai, Litovie settlement.

Chukchi,
Woman's knife for cutting of animal carcasses, cutting out of hides, umbilical cord cutting of a new-born child (in the past), early 20th century.
Metal, walrus tusk ivory, Knife: 20 cm; Haft: 11 cm.
Russian Museum of Ethnography, St. Petersburg. Chukchi National Okrug (region), Magadan Oblast.

Koryak,
Dipper for water, 1909-1911.
Argali horn, 14.5 x 12 cm; diameter of reservoir: 10.4 cm.
Russian Museum of Ethnography, St. Petersburg. Kamchatka.

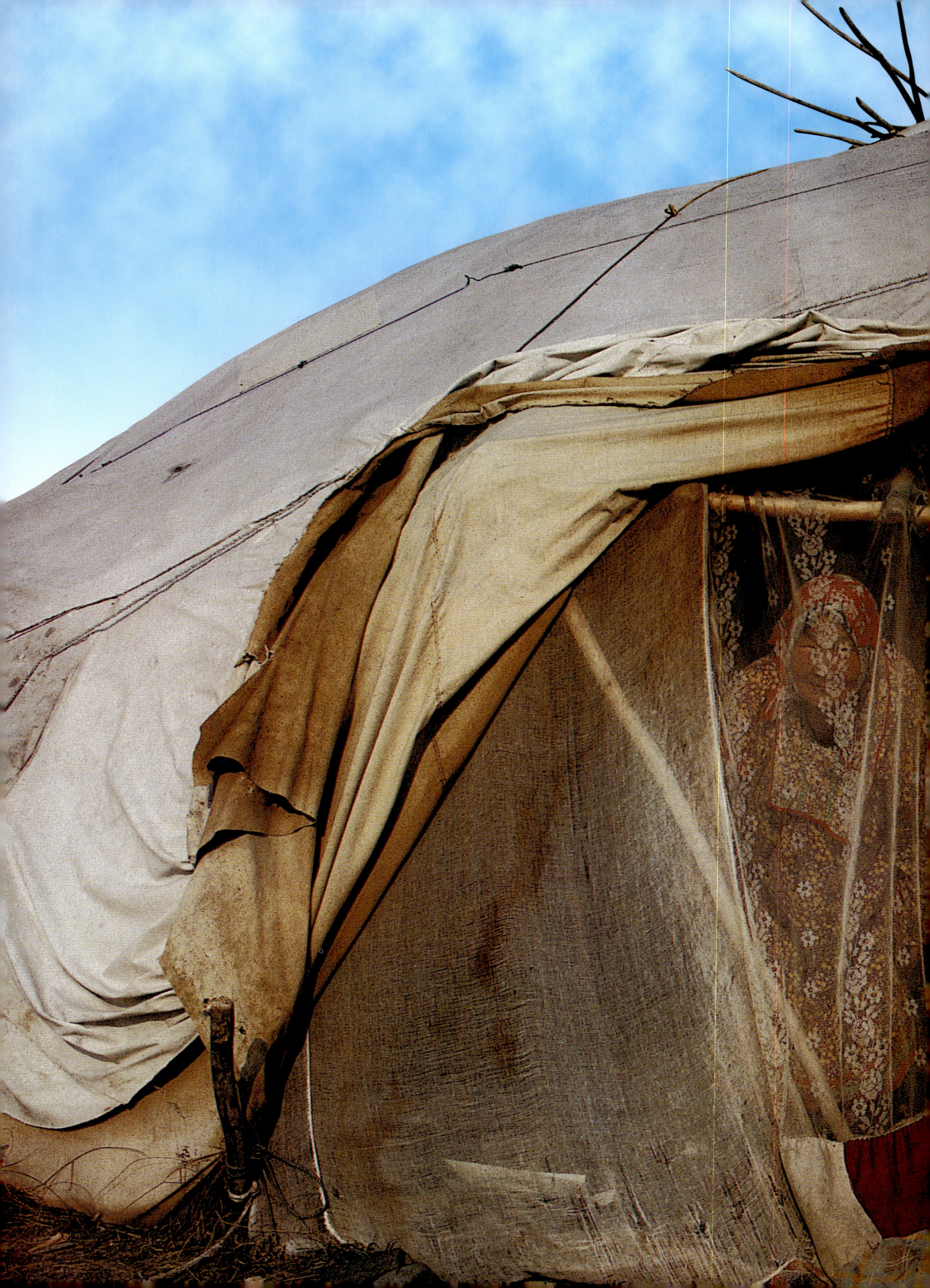

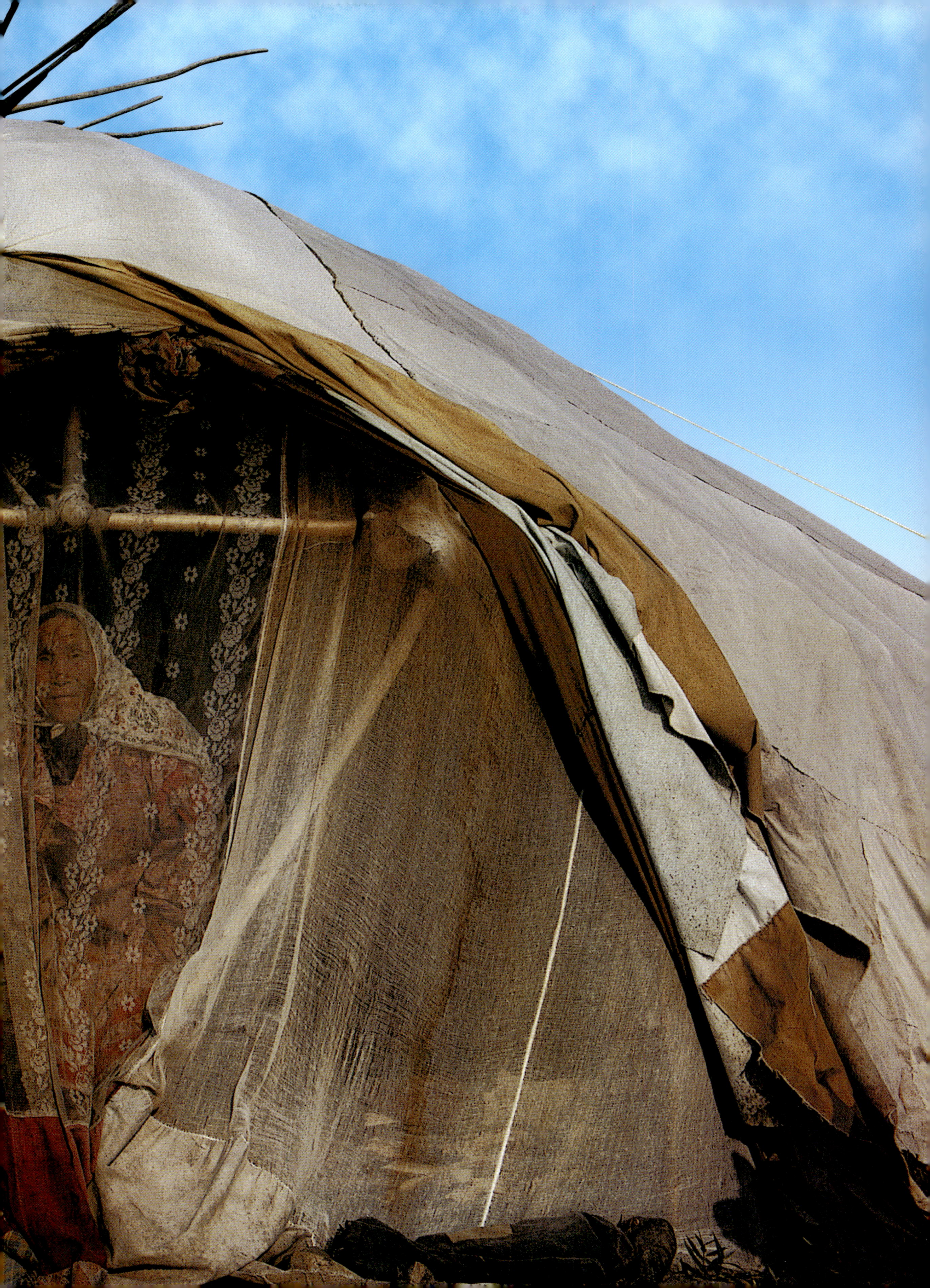

The population of the Kamchatka peninsula, home to both the Koryaks and much of the Chukchi population, is made up of three distinct classes—the Russians, the Kamchatkas or settled natives, and the nomadic tribes. The Kamchatkas are settled in log villages throughout the peninsula, near the mouths of small rivers which rise in the central range of mountains and fall into the Okhotsk Sea or the Pacific. Their principal occupations are fishing, fur-trapping, and the cultivation of rye, turnips, cabbages, and potatoes, which grow thriftily as far north as fifty-eight degrees north latitude. Their largest settlements are in the fertile valley of the Kamchatka River, between Petropavlovsk and Kluchei. The Russians, who are comparatively few in number, are scattered here and there among the Kamchatka villages, and are generally engaged in trading for furs with the Kamchatkas and the nomadic tribes to the northward.

The nomadic Koryaks, who were once the wildest, most powerful, and most independent natives in the peninsula, seldom come south of the 58th parallel of latitude, except for the purpose of trade. Their chosen haunts are the great desolate steppes lying east of Penzhinsk Gulf, where they wander constantly from place to place in solitary bands, living in large fur tents and depending for subsistence upon their vast herds of tamed and domesticated reindeer. The government under which all the inhabitants of Kamchatka nominally lived was administered by a Russian officer called an *ispravnik* or local governor who is supposed to settle all questions of law which may arise between individuals or tribes, and to collect the annual yassak, which was levied upon every male inhabitant in his province. He resided in Petropavlovsk, and owing to the extent of country over which he had jurisdiction, and the imperfect facilities which it afforded for getting about, he was seldom seen outside of the village where he had his headquarters. The only means of transportation between the widely separated settlements of the Kamchatkas were packhorses, canoes, and dog-sledges.

A Kamchatka village is often situated on a little elevation near the bank of some river or stream, surrounded by scattered clumps of poplar and yellow birch, and protected by high hills from the cold northern winds. Its houses, which are clustered irregularly together near the beach, are very low, and made of logs squared and notched at the ends, and chinked with masses of dry moss. The roofs are covered with a rough thatch of long coarse grass or with overlapping strips of tamarack bark, and project at the ends and sides into wide, overhanging eaves. The window-frames, although occasionally glazed, are more frequently covered with an irregular patchwork of translucent fish bladders, sewn together with thread made of the dried and pounded sinews of the reindeer. The doors are almost square, and the chimneys are nothing but long straight poles, arranged in a circle and plastered over thickly with clay. Here and there between the houses stand half a dozen curious architectural quadrupeds called "balagans" (bah-lah-gans'), or fish storehouses. They are simply conical log tents, elevated from the ground on four posts to secure their contents from the dogs, and resemble as much as anything small haystacks trying to walk away on four legs. High square frames of horizontal poles stand beside every house, filled with thousands of drying salmon; and "an ancient and fish-like smell," which pervades the whole atmosphere, betrays the nature of the Kamchatkas' occupation and of the food upon which they live.

The settled natives of northern Kamchatka have generally two different residences, in which they live at different seasons of the year. These are respectively called the "zimovie" or winter settlement, and the *letovie* or summer

Eveni,
Yurt, 1992.

Herds of reindeer in Siberia, 1998.

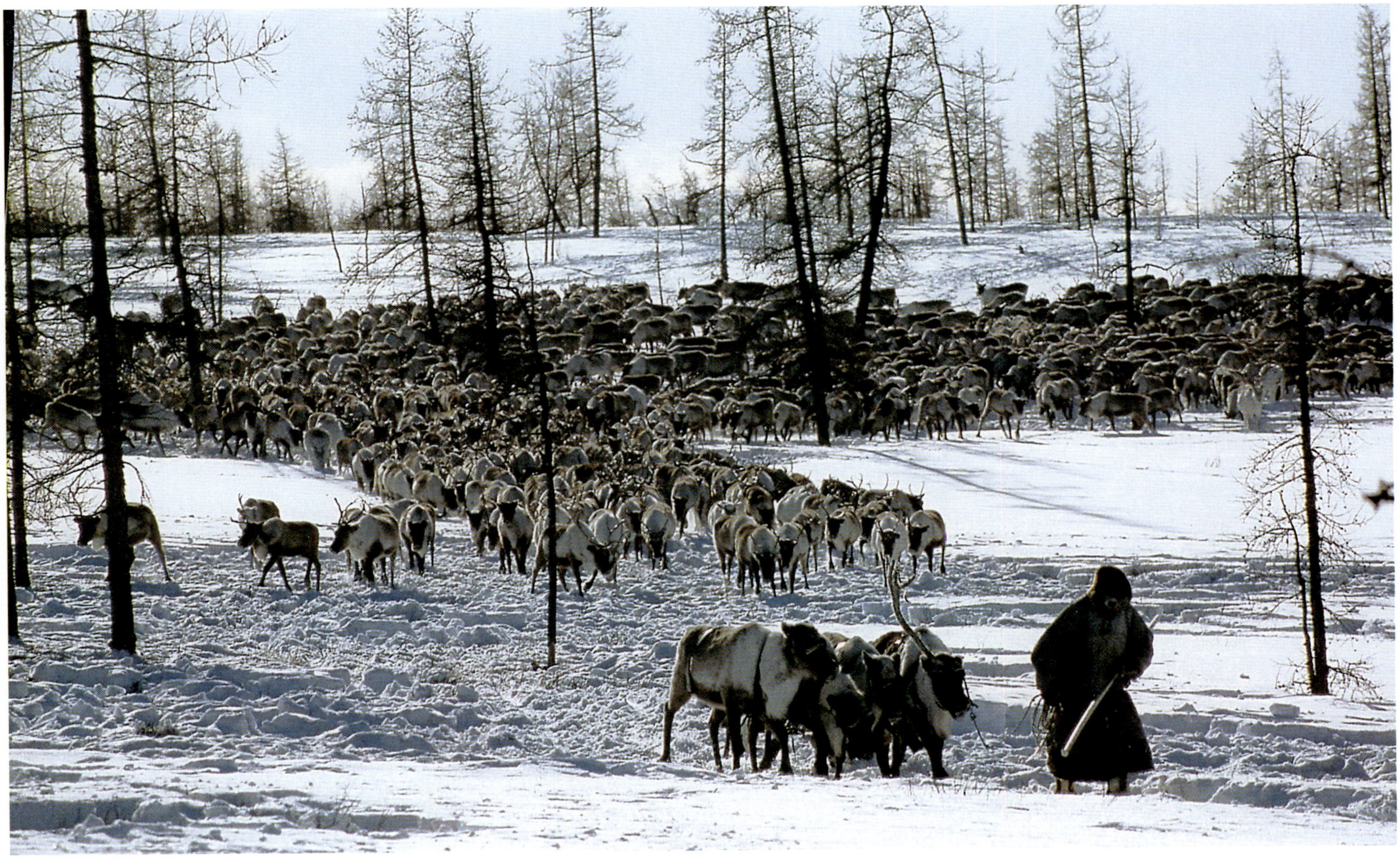

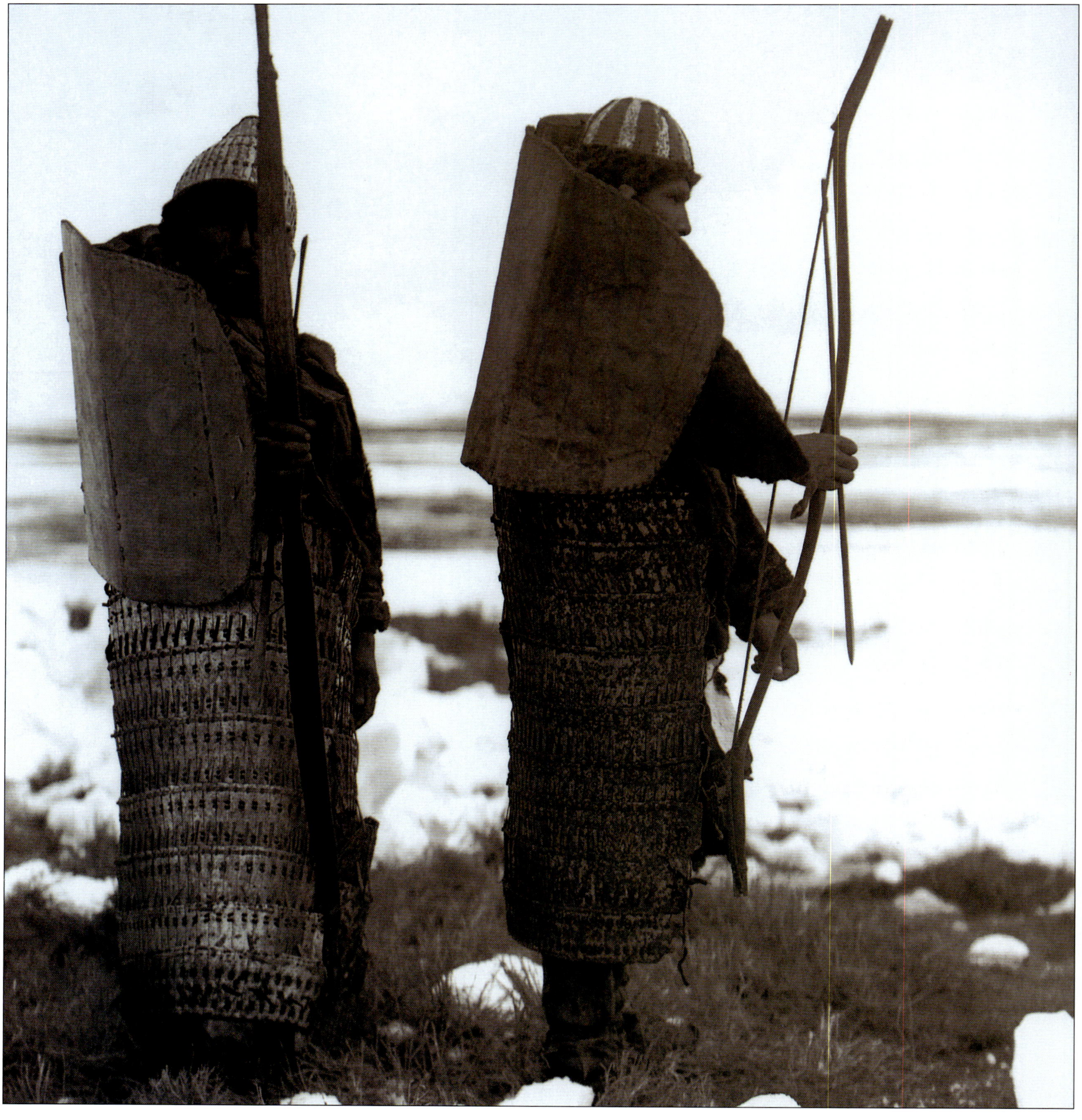

fishing-station, and are from one to five miles apart. In the former, which is generally situated under the shelter of timbered hills, several miles from the seacoast, they reside from September until June. The letovie is always built near the mouth of an adjacent river or stream, and consists of a few *yurts* or earth-covered huts, eight or ten conical *balagans* mounted on stilts, and a great number of wooden frames on which fish are hung to dry. To this fishing-station the inhabitants all remove early in June, leaving their winter settlement entirely deserted. Even the dogs and the crows abandon it for the more attractive surroundings and richer pickings of the summer balagans.

Besides their all-important reindeer, the Kamchatka peninsula natives depend mainly for subsistence upon the salmon, which every summer run into these northern rivers in immense numbers to spawn, and are speared, caught in seines, and trapped in weirs by thousands. These fish, dried without salt in the open air, are the food of the Kamchatkas and of their dogs throughout the long, cold northern winter. During the summer, however, their bill of fare is more varied. The climate and soil of the river bottoms in southern Kamchatka admit of the cultivation of rye, potatoes, and turnips, and the whole peninsula abounds in animal life. Reindeer and black and brown bears roam everywhere over the mossy plains and through the grassy valleys; wild sheep and a species of ibex are not unfrequently found in the mountains; and millions upon millions of ducks, geese, and swans, in almost endless variety, swarm about every river and little marshy lake throughout the country. These aquatic fowls are captured in great multitudes while moulting by organised "drives" of fifty or seventy-five men in canoes, who chase the birds in one great flock up some narrow stream, at the end of which a huge net is arranged for their reception. They are then killed with clubs, cleaned, and salted for winter use.

Bread is now made of rye, which the Kamchatkas raise and grind for themselves; but previous to the settlement of the country by the Russians, the only native substitute for bread was a sort of baked paste, consisting chiefly of the grated tubers of the purple Kamchatkan lily. The only fruits in the country are berries and a species of wild cherry. Of the berries, however, there are fifteen or twenty different kinds, of which the most important are blueberries, *maroshkas*, or yellow cloud-berries, and dwarf cranberries. These the people pick late in the fall, and freeze for winter consumption. Cows are kept in nearly all the Kamchatka settlements, and milk is always plenty. A curious native dish of sour milk, baked curds, and sweet cream, covered with powdered sugar and cinnamon, is a particular treat.

2) FISHERMAN-HUNTERS

On the shores of the Arctic and the Pacific Oceans, some nomadic or semi-nomadic groups tend to hunt marine mammals (occasionally even in the summer) for their skins, their fat or just for a change of meat in the daily diet. Such groups include the Nenets – should they happen to travel as far north as the Arctic coast during their seasonal summer migration – and the Nganassani people, and on the Pacific coast the Evenki, the Olchi, the Oroki and the Orochon people. For the Nivkhi people of Sakhalin island and especially in the extreme north-east for the Aleuts, the Uit (Eskimos) and for the coastal groups of Chukchis (the *Ankaliniy*), of Koryaks (the *Nymylany*) and of Eveni (the *Nemeh*), the hunting of marine mammals is the basis of their way of life, the foundation of their traditional culture in a temporal and spiritual sense.

Chukchi men in armour.
Walrus and seal skins.

The Bering Strait, the shores of the bay at Lavrentiya and the environs of Novoye Chaplino are locations where the hunting of marine mammals is a speciality. In this area (on the Chukotskiy Peninsula), the villages of the hunters follow the coastline, winding in with the bays and out with the promontories. From their own houses the hunters have a full view of the sea, and may even be able to mark down individual animals that would make suitable targets: walruses, seals, belugas and whales.

The traditional weapons for the hunt are the harpoon and the spear, long replaced now, of course, by the rifle. The techniques and traditional methods of hunting, which are numerous, differ according to the season, to the animal that is the quarry – and to the ancestral beliefs about that animal.

The beginning of winter, while the ice is still fairly thin, is the time to catch seals, using baited lines lowered through the top of the ice-floe where an animal has made a hole through which to breathe. The same technique is employed in catching fur-seals. What usually happens is that the hunter remains completely motionless next to the hole, facing the wind, waiting for the creature to emerge. As soon as it does, he gaffs it with his harpoon, and kills it with a rifle shot. Among the Chukchis, dogs are specially trained to sniff out the breathing-holes.

At the beginning of spring, when the seals take to basking in the sunshine on top of the ice-floes, the hunters get as close as they can to them by humping along on their stomachs, mimicking the awkward movements and even the sounds of the animals themselves, sometimes also assisted by being camouflaged with sealskin.

For the Aleuts and the Eskimos the hunting season begins when the ice melts and they take to sea in their kayaks. The Chukchis and the Koryaks do the same in their bidarkas. Both types of boat are of variable length but particularly light and strong, made as they are of flexible sealskin or walrus-skin stretched over a wooden frame. A traveller at the end of the nineteenth century describes a Siberian water-craft:

> *"We saw a raft, ready for our reception. It was composed of three large dugout canoes, placed parallel to one another at distances of about three feet, and lashed with sealskin thongs to stout transverse poles. Over these was laid a floor or platform about ten feet by twelve, leaving room at the bow and stern of each canoe for men with paddles who were to guide and propel the unwieldy craft in some unknown, but, doubtless, satisfactory manner. On the platform, which was covered to a depth of six inches with freshly cut grass, we pitched our little cotton tent, and transformed it with bearskins and blankets into a warm living space."*
>
> —George Kennan (1845-1924)

Catching seals may be something that can be done by one person, but catching walruses or whales has to be a group activity and with several bidarkas. Each bidarka is occupied by a crew of between six and ten men – one or two with harpoons at the prow, five or six oarsmen in the body of the boat, and on the rudder at the stern the owner of the bidarka. Once a walrus is spotted, the oarsmen hastily propel the boat towards the creature, and the men at the prow hurl their harpoons, which are attached to their belts by a long cord. If the point of one or both harpoons is firmly fixed in the body of the walrus, the cord attached drags on the creature, preventing its movement and tiring it, allowing the hunters to close in. It is finally despatched, either

Eskimo,
Small plastic artwork: 'Killer-whale holding a seal with its teeth',
early 20th century.
Walrus tusk ivory, 7.5 x 2.7 cm.
Russian Museum of Ethnography, St. Petersburg. Kamchatka Okrug, Chukchi District.

Chukchi,
Small plastic artwork: 'Hunting for walrus', 1906.
Walrus tusk ivory, 17.8 x 2.8 cm.
Russian Museum of Ethnography, St. Petersburg. Primorskaya Oblast, Anadyr Krai.

Koryak,
Small plastic artwork 'Before cutting of the walrus carcass'.
Walrus tusk ivory, 5.8 x 3.8 cm.
Russian Museum of Ethnography, St. Petersburg. Primorskaya Oblast, Anadyr Krai.

Chukchi, Eskimos,
Canoe, weapons and appliances for collective hunting of sea hunters. Scene of the exhibition 'My friends – sea hunters', dedicated to the memory of the Director of the Museum D.A. Sergeev, 1970-1974.
Russian Museum of Ethnography, St. Petersburg. Chukchi National Okrug, Magadan Oblast.

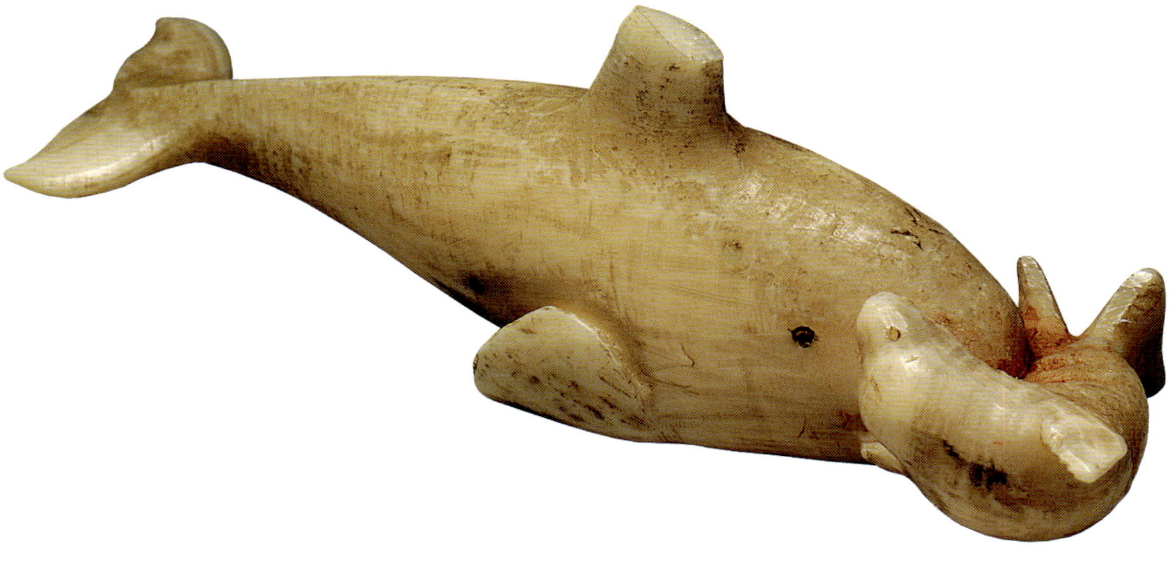

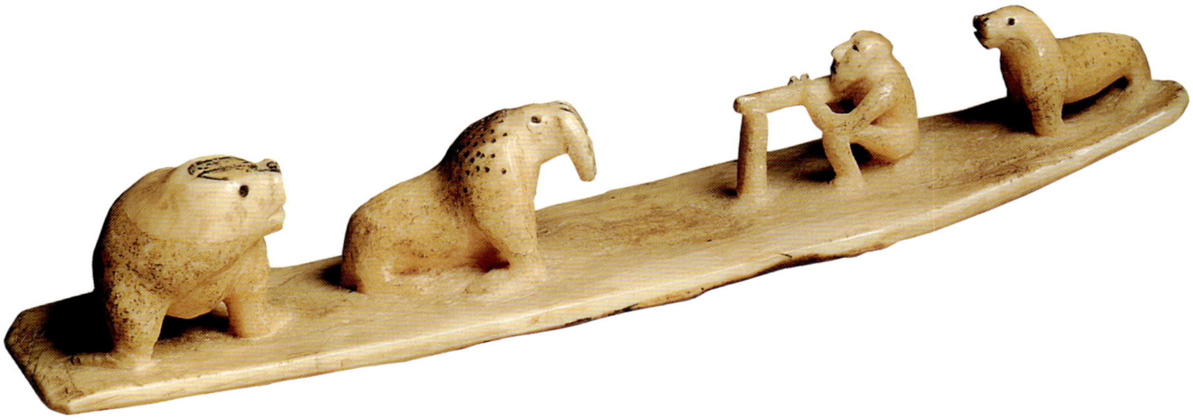

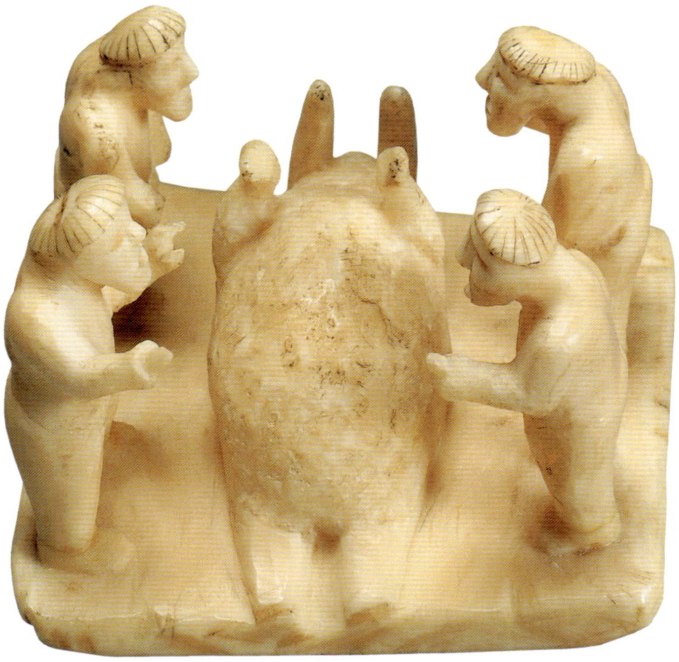

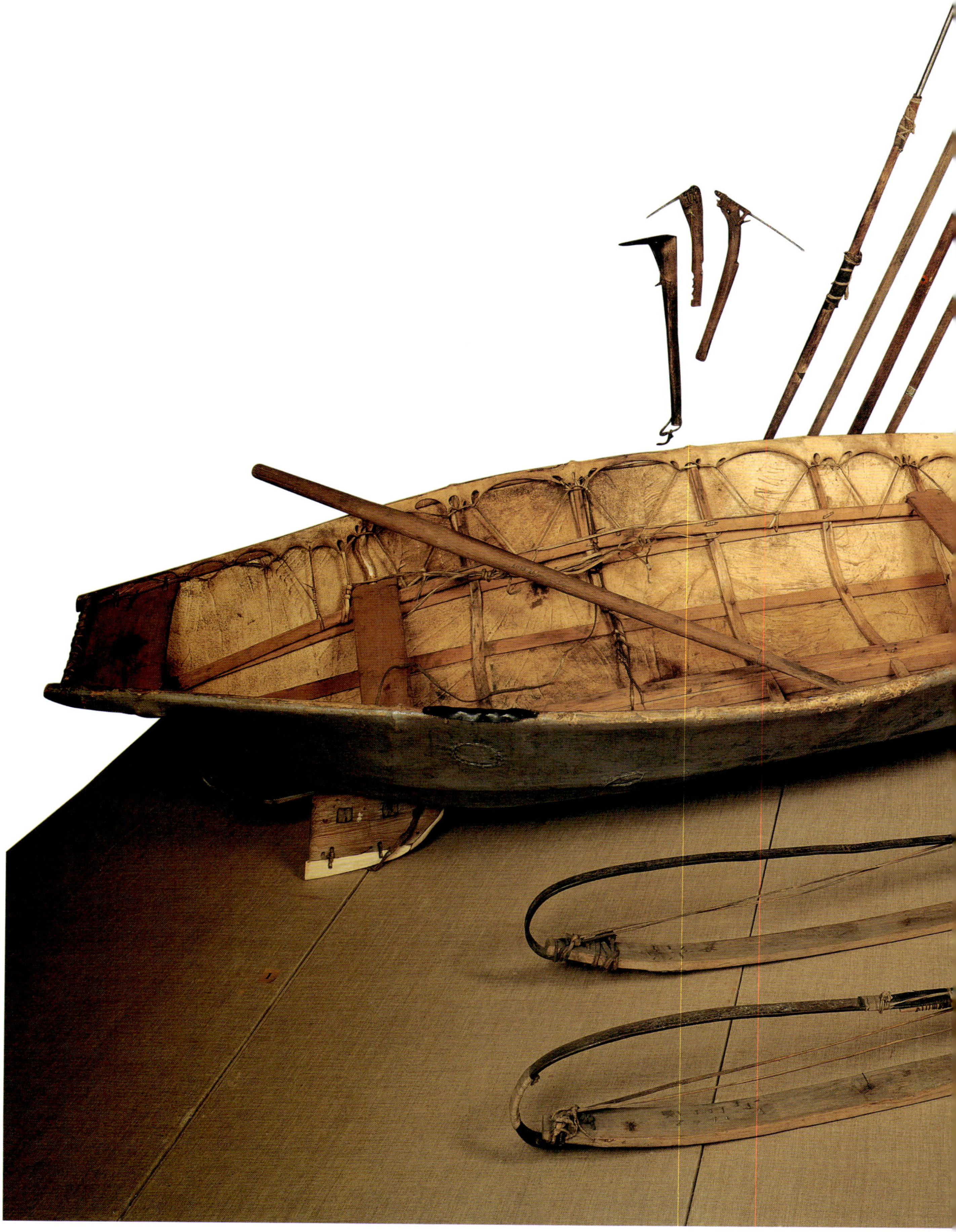

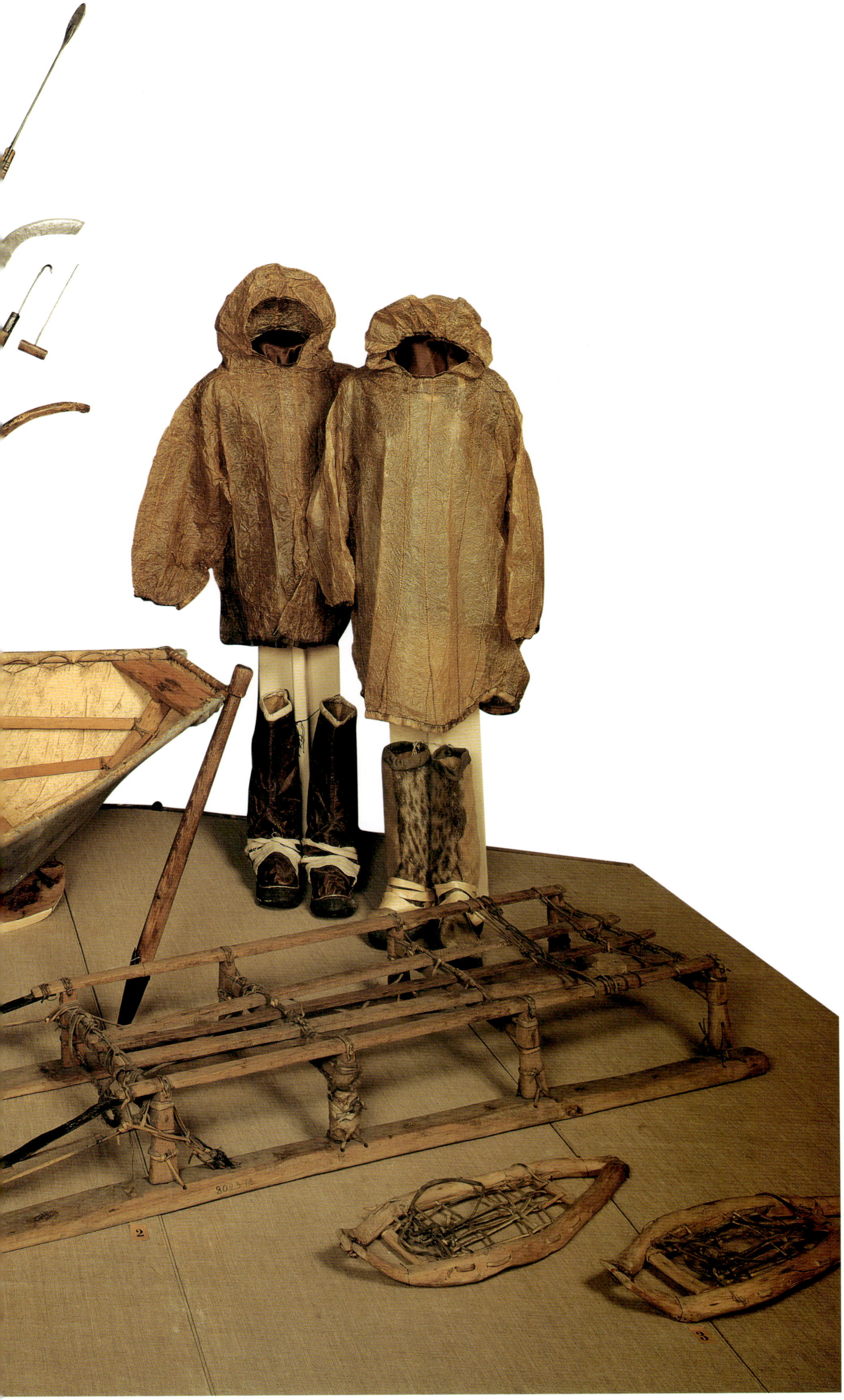
2
3

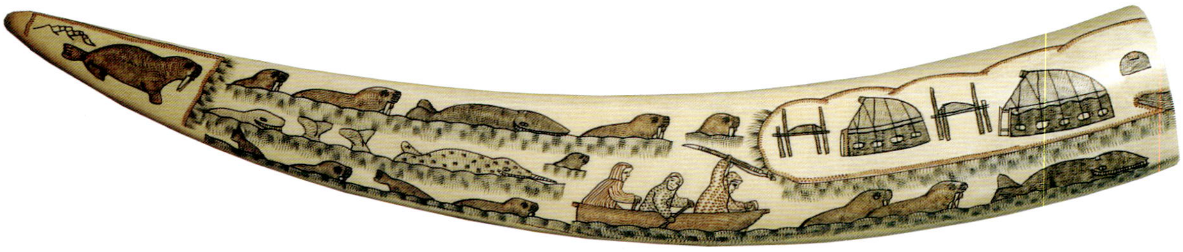

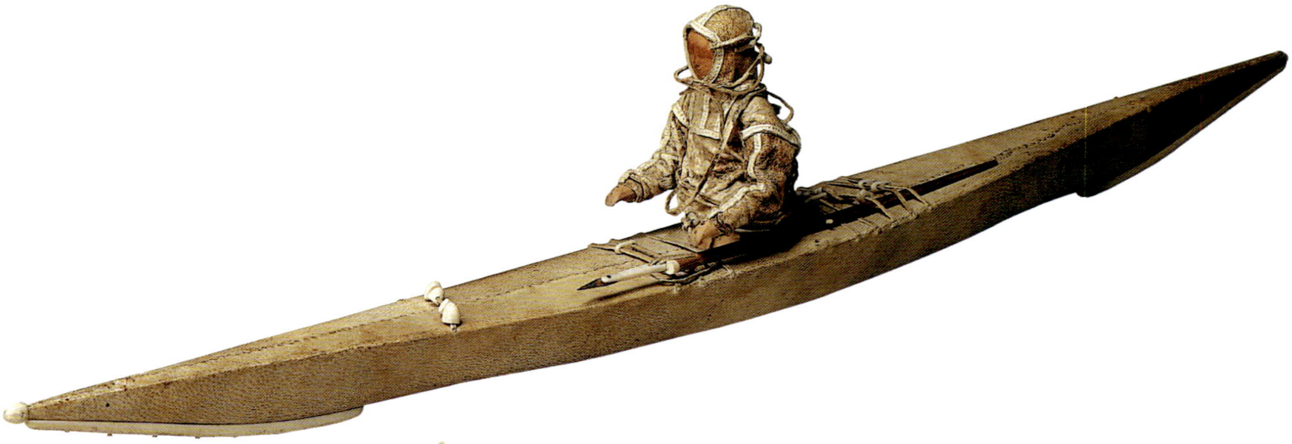

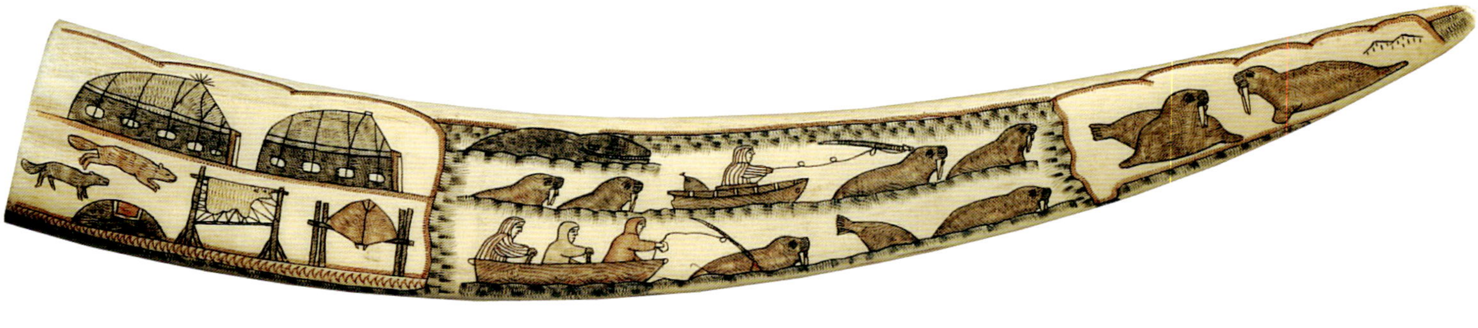

with a spear or, more often now, by rifle shot. Back on dry land, the corpse is cut up and its flesh shared out in an equitable manner between all the members of the community.

Much the same techniques are used when hunting the whale, but of course many more bidarkas are required (for the animal is that much bigger). The capture of a whale is cause for great celebration, for just one of these mammals provides enough food and other resources for an entire village for a year. The bounty of the sea thus bestows indispensable gifts on the coastal populations: things to eat, things to burn and things for the household (including materials for handicrafts and clothing).

In the diet of these coastal dwellers, the meat and fat of marine mammals not unnaturally occupies a dominant position. The meat is eaten raw, smoked, boiled, frozen or even in a state of fermentation. To preserve walrus or whale meat for the winter, the Chukchis get it to ferment by hermetically enclosing it inside a sealskin pouch and burying it in the summertime in a place that remains covered in snow all year. In this way they assure themselves of a supply of fermented meat in winter that has also been kept naturally frozen in the permafrost. The blackened and stringy skin of the whale, with its fine layers of pinkish fat, is a real treat for hunters of sea creatures.

The food of the coastal peoples also includes reindeer meat, fish (from which they make *yukola*), berries and the occasional vegetable. Fat is a particularly precious, if not indispensable, substance – the Eskimos used to keep it in containers made out of the bladders of whales or walruses, the Chukchis in sealskin pouches – for it could also be used as a bartering medium to obtain furs or reindeer meat from passing nomads.

Finally, the bones. The tusks of the walrus and the ribs and jawbones of the whale now principally serve to supply the medium for a form of art that has reached a surprisingly high standard. All the coastal peoples have long practised it, and are expert at it. It is the carving of statuettes – of people or of animals, of hunting scenes or of scenes of family and social life – in 'marine' ivory. These solid down-to-earth representations in tusk and bone are at the same time representations of the internal world of the dwellers of the far north.

The hunters of marine creatures lay up their bidarkas over the winter, and their sledges over the summer, on solid supports some 6.5 feet (2 metres) high. In the past, these supports were whale ribs driven into the ground. Whale ribs and jawbones also used once to form the rounded framework of the traditional dwellings of the coastal communities in the north-east of Siberia – the ancient half-buried lodges covered over with earth and moss. Among the Uit such lodges could shelter an entire community of some 40 people. Among the Chukchis and the Koryaks, the entrance to a half-buried lodge like this in summer was through an opening in the roof leading to a ladder carved from the trunk of a tree. In winter, in order to maintain the warmth inside the lodge, entry was via a long passage that started at ground-level. Seal skins were used as floor-carpeting and/or to cover the walls of the dwelling. For light and heat, moss was burned with whale fat or walrus fat on a hearth made of stone or fireclay. This setup also facilitated the cooking of food.

Today, only the dilapidated ruins of such lodges remain, abandoned now for almost 150 years in favour of the *yarang* or of wooden houses. Inside the *yarangs*, candles have replaced the whale-oil lamps.

If hunting and fishing are only sidelines for most Siberians, they nonetheless constitute the very foundation of certain cultures, reflecting their original

Chukchi,
Tusk with coloured engraving (1st side),
1930s.
Walrus tusk ivory, 51 x 7 cm.
Russian Museum of Ethnography,
St. Petersburg. Chukchi Peninsular.

Eskimo,
Model 'Hunter in the canoe',
early 20th century.
Wood, sealskin, walrus tusk ivory,
46 x 8.5 cm.
Russian Museum of Ethnography,
St. Petersburg.

Chukchi,
Tusk with coloured engraving (2nd side),
1930s.
Walrus tusk ivory, 51 x 7 cm.
Russian Museum of Ethnography,
St. Petersburg. Chukchi Peninsular.

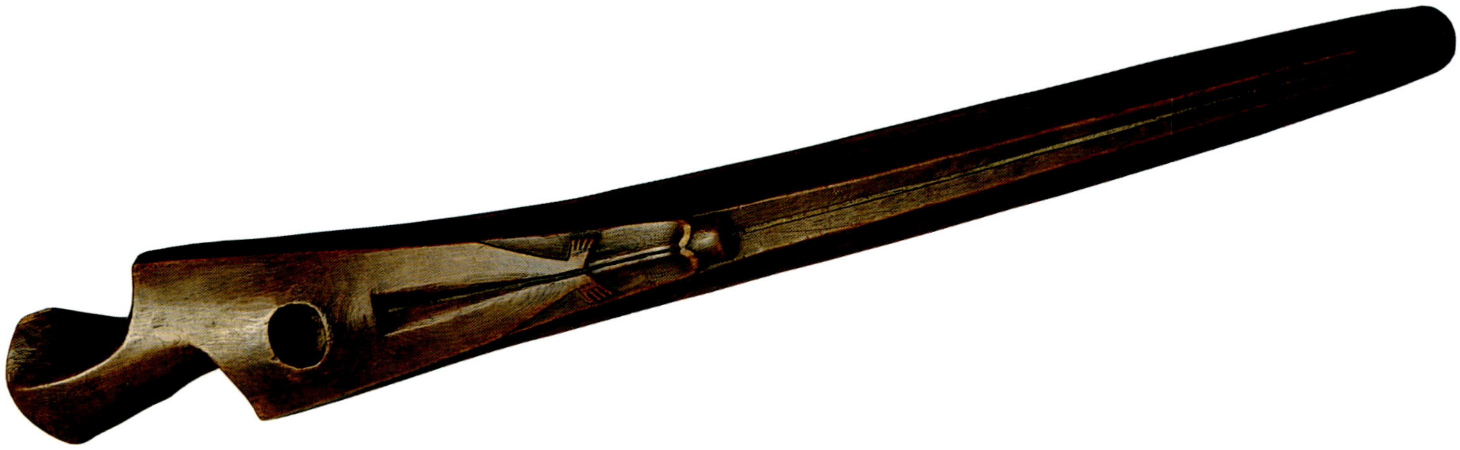

Aleut,
Small plank for throwing of harpoons and darts, late 19th-early 20th century.
Wood, bone, 49.8 cm.
Russian Museum of Ethnography, St. Petersburg. Commander Islands.

Eskimo,
Adz, comb for grass, scraper for processing of marine mammal intestines, 3rd-4th century AD (adz, scraper); 17th century AD (comb).
Walrus tusk ivory, nephrite, wood,
Adz: 10.3 cm; comb: 11.9 cm; scraper: 9 x 4.3 cm.
Russian Museum of Ethnography, St. Petersburg. Chukchi Peninsular.

lifestyles. Cultures of this kind include those of the Kets, the Selkup, the Mansis and the Yukaghirs in the taiga, the Shorians, many groups of Evenki and of the Khanty, and the peoples of the Amur River: the Nanai people, the Olchi, the Negidal people, the Oroki, the Orochon people and the Udekhe.

A natural frontier between Russia and China, the Amur River contains more than a hundred species of fish. Fishing has always therefore been of extreme importance to the local populations. Catching salmon in summer and autumn, and different types of sturgeon and carp in winter, effectively enables the aboriginal communities of the area to live in relative security. It is hunting that in winter is rather the sideline.

When the salmon begin to swim back from the open sea up the Amur River, climbing ever upstream in their urgency to spawn, the local people organize huge fishing parties in the course of which techniques tried and tested over the years bring in truly vast catches. By raising the level of the riverbed with large stones and constructing a large barrier of stones on the upstream side, the men prevent the incoming shoal of salmon from continuing on their course. All at once the stones on the riverbed are removed and the riverbed returns to its normal height, leaving the fish trapped in a much lower pool behind a much taller barrier. The natives originally caught the fish by means of small floating nets, usually made of horse-hair. Sitting in his *vetka* or dug-out canoe, the fisherman floats along with his net, watching it carefully. When he observes that a fish is fast in it, he quickly pulls up the net, gaffs the fish with an iron gaff, kills it with a small wooden mallet, throws out the net again, and floats on as before.

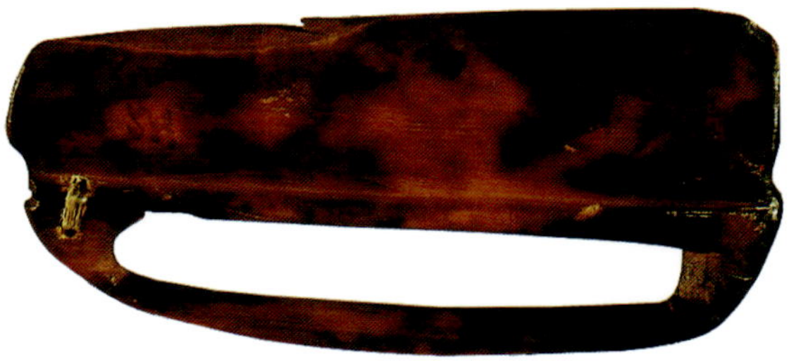

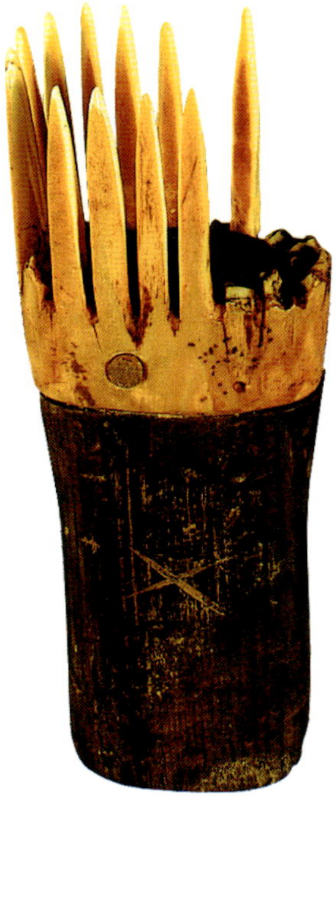

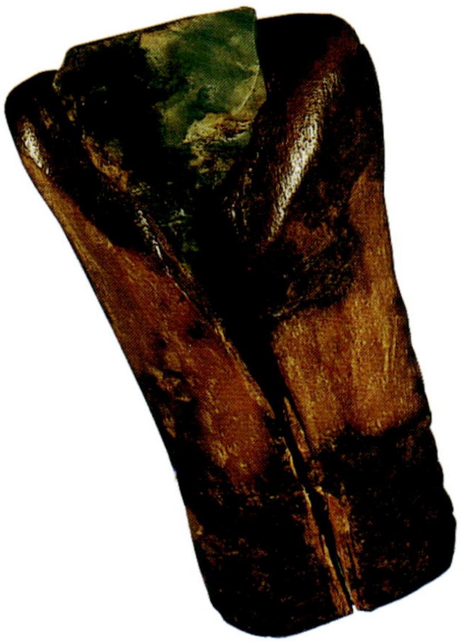

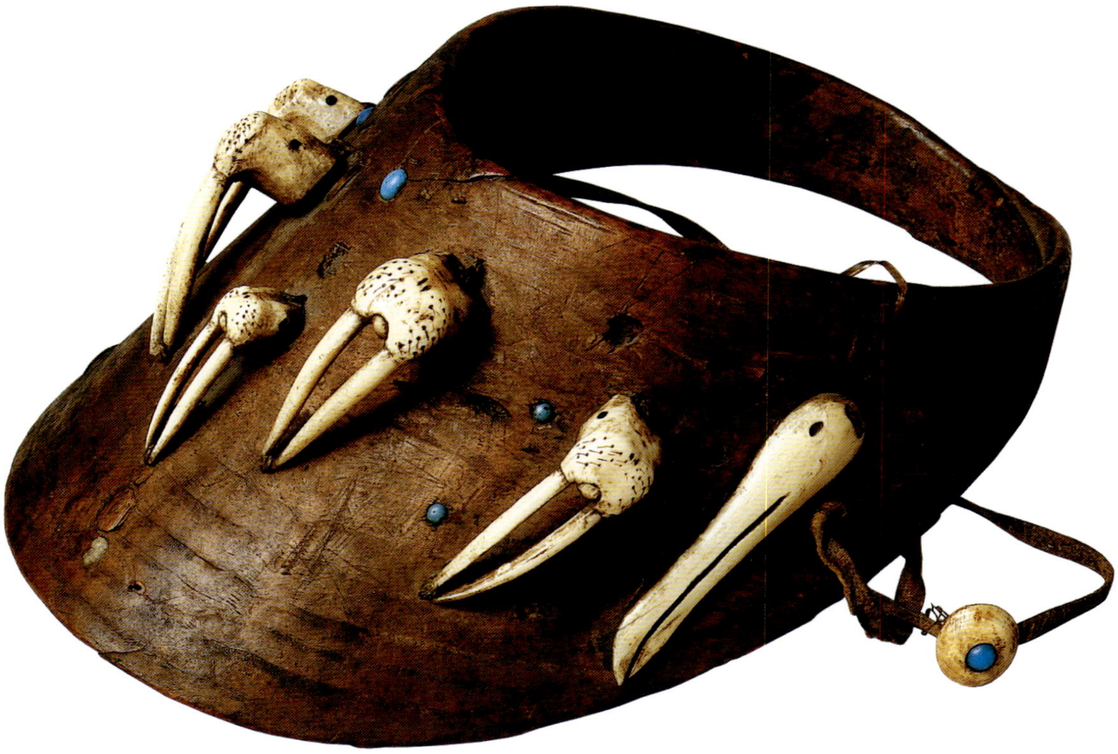

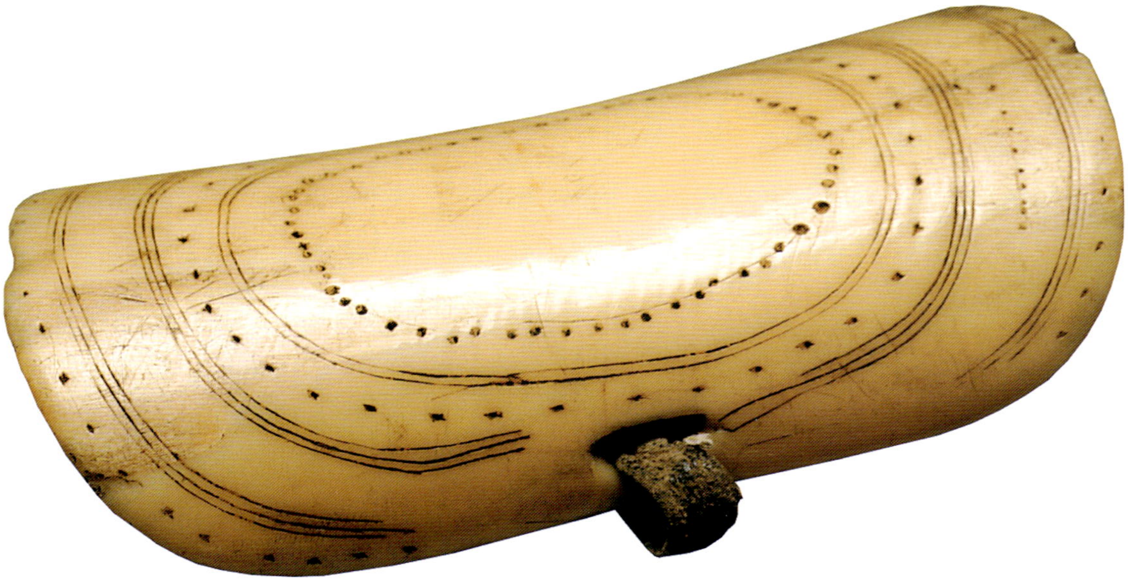

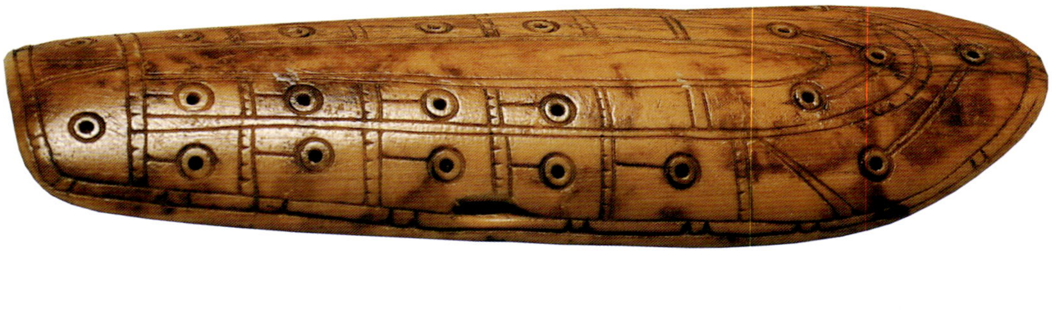

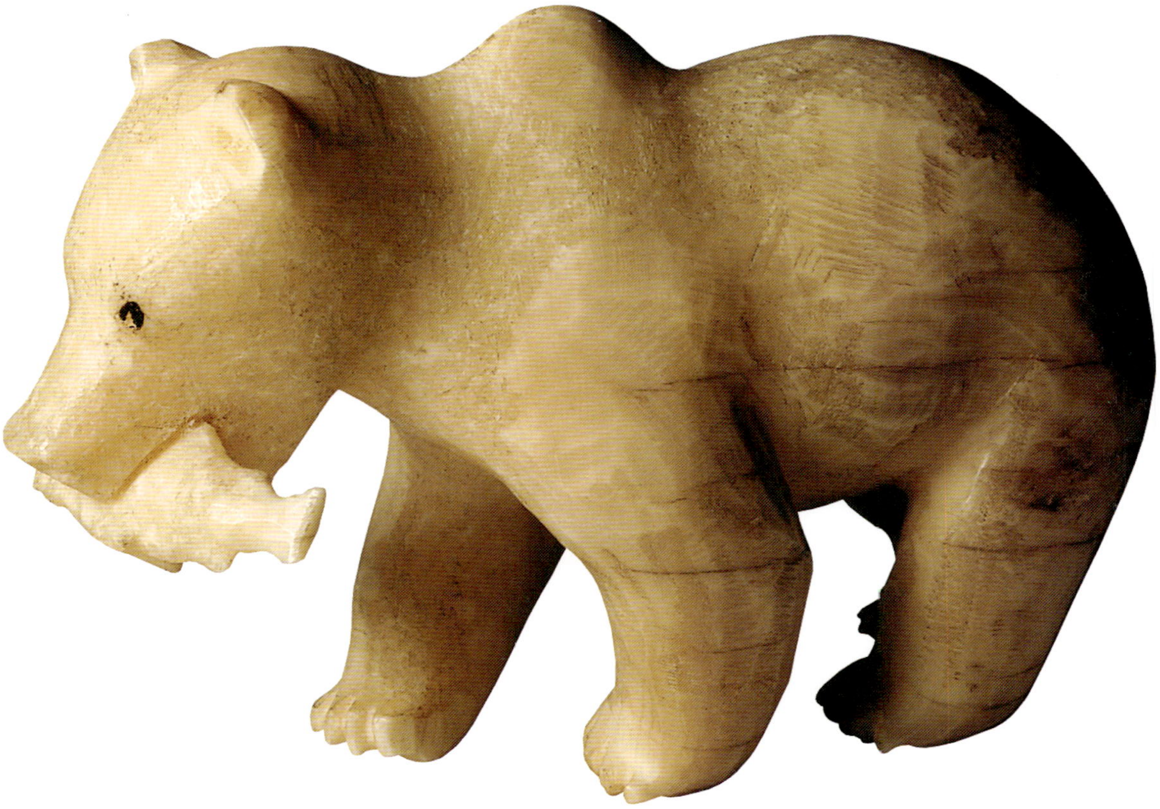

Aleut,
Hunter's visor, 1912.
Wood, leather, walrus tusk ivory.
Lower diameter: 21.8 cm; Height: 8.7 cm.
Russian Museum of Ethnography,
St. Petersburg. Aleutian Islands.

Chukchi, Eskimos,
Accessories for protection of archer's arm during shooting, 1) 3rd-4th century AD; 2) 1904-1907.
Walrus tusk ivory, leather, 1) 11.3 cm 2) 10 cm.
Russian Museum of Ethnography, St. Petersburg.
Primorskaya Oblast, Anadyr Krai, Chukchi Peninsular.

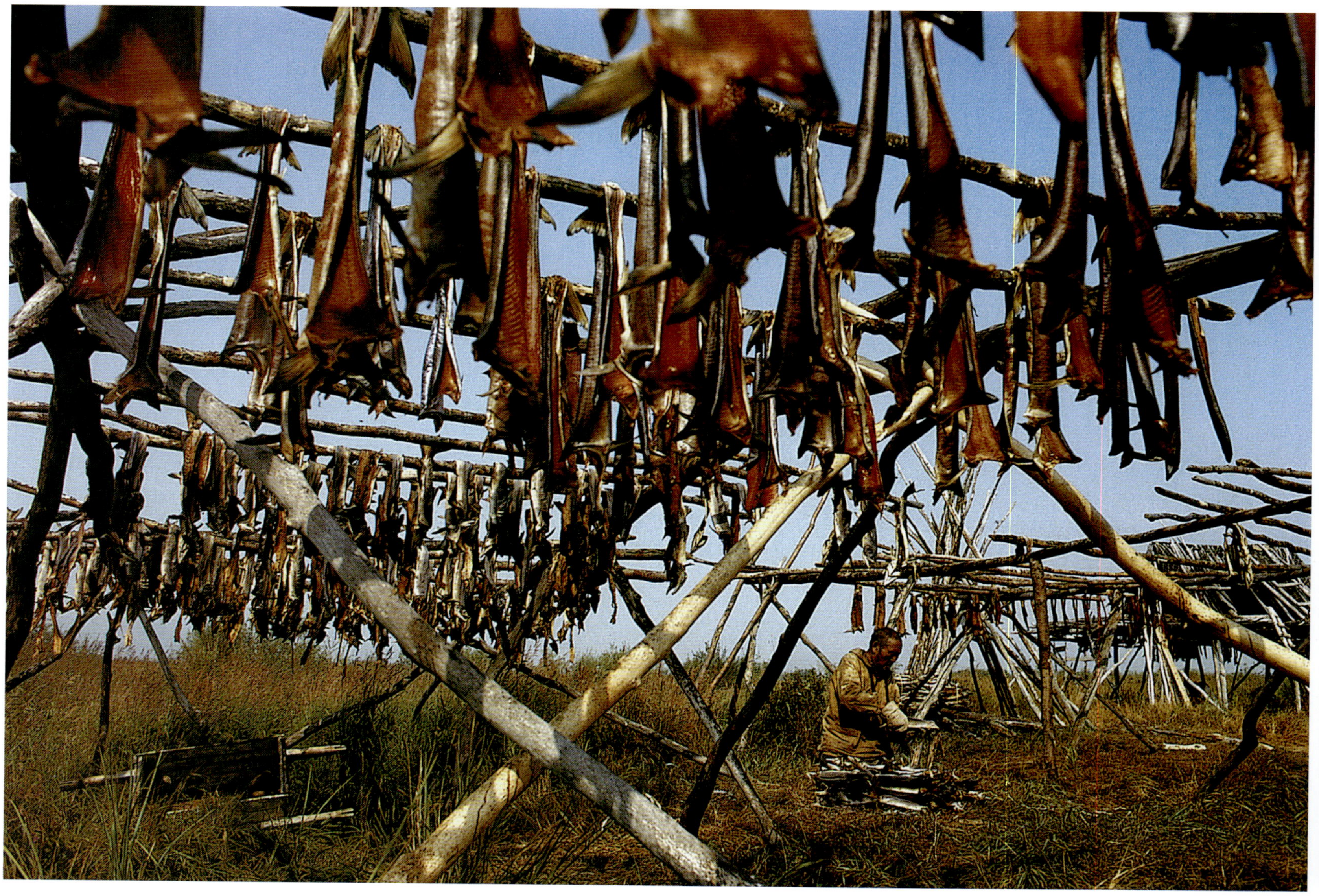

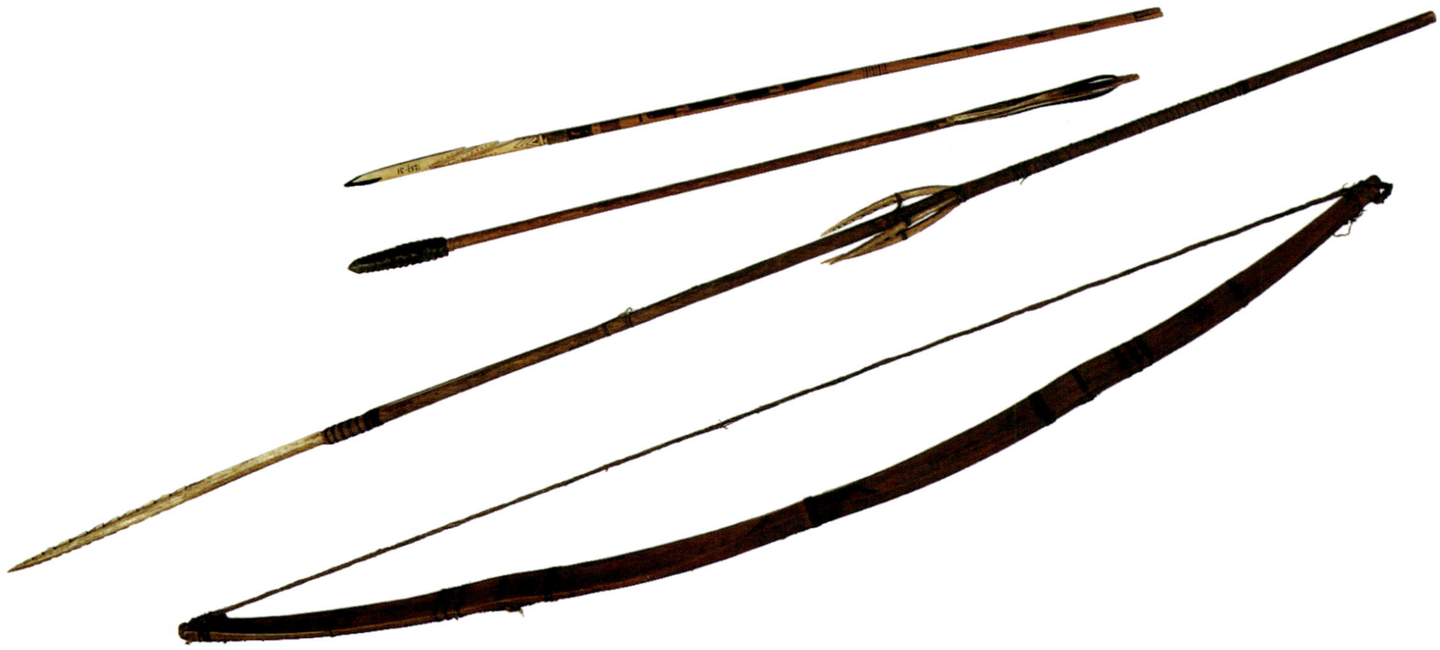

When the ice between the islands and the delta become sufficiently strong to walk on, coastal tribes set their small nets beneath the frozen surface of the water. Early every morning they are overhauled, and usually a fisherman has the good luck to catch three or four fish, weighing from one to three pounds or more, and in this way a man is daily provided with one form, at least, of excellent diet.

An element central to traditional cultures of the Amur, fish fulfil a multitude of uses in local daily life. Primarily, of course, they constitute the basic staple diet of the area. They are eaten raw, frozen, smoked, boiled, fried and, particularly, dried. Stocks of salmon and carp, from which *yukola* is prepared, visibly demonstrate the wellbeing of the residents of the Amur's banks, for in summertime, when *yukola* is prepared for the winter, the villages are transformed – from just about anywhere that projects over an empty space hang fish topped and tailed and sliced lengthways into two flat pieces. The Olchi people have no fewer than eight different words and expressions in their language for *yukola*. What is left over from preparing the fish is given to the sledge dogs to eat.

In addition to fish, the people of the Amur like to eat the meat of the elk (moose), bear, reindeer, and even dog. One of the Nanai people's favourite dishes is *magdan*, which is based on dried caviar crushed and mixed with water or birch sap. In the north, the Yukaghirs of the taiga delight in a rather similar speciality, the *kul'ibakha* – a combination of whortleberries (a type of bilberry), fresh caviar and fish-oil.

Koryak,
Small plastic artwork 'Bear holding fish in his mouth', 1903.
Walrus tusk ivory, 8 x 5 cm.
Russian Museum of Ethnography, St. Petersburg. Primorskaya Oblast, Gizhiginski Okrug.

Evenki,
Yukola drying, 1992.

Aleut,
Weapons of hunting on land (bow, arrows and spear),
late 19th-early 20th century.
Wood, bone, sinew, bird feather, flint
Lengths: 1) arrow: 82.5 cm 2) arrow: 71 cm 3) spear: 149 cm 4) bow: 135.5 cm.
Russian Museum of Ethnography, St. Petersburg.

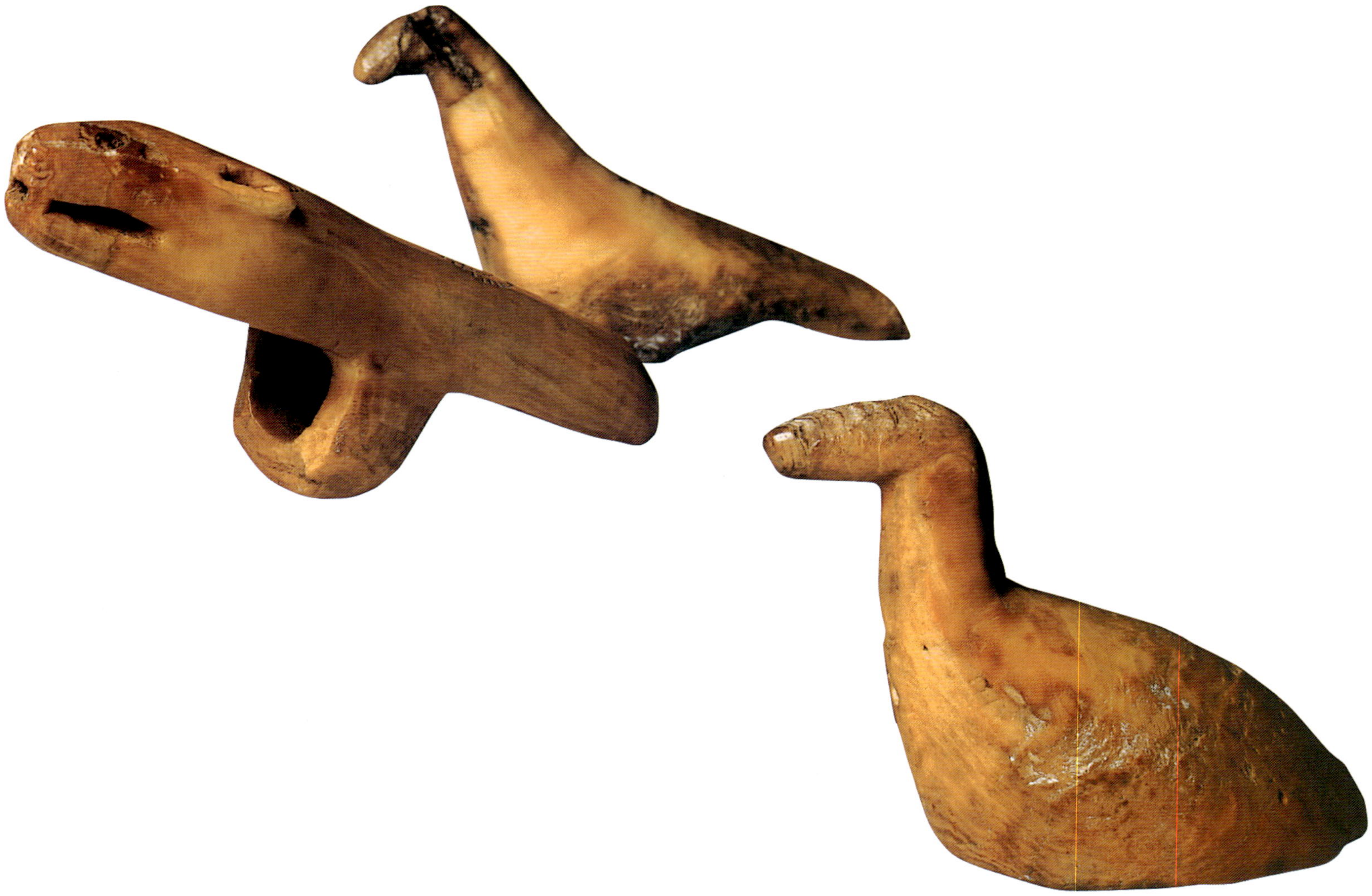

Eskimo,
Small plastic artwork – picture of water birds and fastener in the form of bear, 3rd-4th century AD.
Walrus tusk ivory, Birds:
1) 3.2 x 3.2 cm; 2) 3.5 x 2.8 cm;
Fastener: 5.7 cm.
Russian Museum of Ethnography, St. Petersburg. Chukchi Peninsular.

The women have a unique process for making something special of the skins of pike, salmon and carp. For several days the skins are left to dry in a particularly shady place. Then they are put on wooden trays and beaten out flat with a mallet. Next, they are rolled around a stick of absinthe, moistened a little, and left for several hours. They are then carefully unrolled, and stretched to their maximum length. Finally, the skins are hung above the hearth and smoked there for two weeks, being taken down before they begin to turn yellow.

Fish-skin also goes into making sails for the birch-bark fishing boats, and can be used in windproof drapes for the windows of wooden houses. In summertime the fishermen go off to live in such cabins in the wetlands. If instead they go hunting or fishing at a distance inland, they take their conical wigwams with them and put them up as and when needed.

Water pollution and other serious problems caused by Soviet domination have badly disrupted the ethnic cultures that depend on fishing. All too many of their traditional and ancestral ways of going about things have now been lost forever.

For thousands of years the elk and the (wild) reindeer have been the primary game animals in Siberia. The people who live by hunting ungulates lead a nomadic life based upon the seasonal migrations of these animals in spring and in autumn. In winter, the inhabitants of the taiga tend instead to hunt fur-bearing prey, such as squirrel or the marten-like sable. Most Evenki legends revolve around hunting, either alone or as a group, for reindeer, for elk, and for birds – and they make no mention whatever of tracking down fur-bearing animals, an activity that spread into the area only after the arrival of the Russians and the imposition of the yassak (the requirement of tribute paid in furs).

The summer heat and the mosquitoes in the taiga of the south drive thousands upon thousands of wild reindeer to the shores of the Arctic Ocean, and especially to the delta with its innumerable islands. In the fall these beautiful animals, now fattened, return southwards, swimming in large herds over the channels at certain fixed places, known to the natives from time immemorial.

At these places the natives lie in wait for the animals, and when the herd is swimming over, the hunters in their vetkas make a sudden attack upon them, killing the deer sometimes by scores at a time with their iron-pointed wooden spears. At the end of the nineteenth century, at least 1000 reindeer were killed in this way in the Lena delta every year. Then there is the white polar fox, which the natives catch in traps. Late in the fall, in September, when the reindeer-hunts are ended, the Evenki go in their *vetkas* to the islands and the shores of the Arctic Ocean, putting up their fox-traps for the winter. Later still, when the channels and the sea have frozen, they move to their large winter-villages, such as Bykoff-Myss, in the eastern part of the delta, Turak at its western border, and Balkalak near the mouth of the Olenek. All these villages are situated at places where there is winter fishing, with which the natives occupy themselves during this season, using ice-nets. Sometimes the winter fishing fails, and then their dogs are decimated by famine, which means great losses, and the native Siberians themselves also suffer famine from the same cause. A famine may be caused by the absence of strong northerly winds, which seem to drive the fish up to the mouths of the large rivers.

Elk and reindeer hunting provides the Evenki and the Eveni with all the essentials for eating, housing, clothing, and making objects for everyday use. The most intensive hunting takes place at the beginning of spring. Wearing skis, the hunters chase the quarry down, on and on until it is exhausted. Of course there are other techniques. Some use the lure – perhaps a male reindeer cunningly arranged with its antlers entwined within a leather thong. In a confrontation with another male, a male generally locks horns – and doing so now will entrap those antlers in the leather thong too. The hunters, who have been following their live lure by keeping it on a very long leash, take immediate advantage of the entanglement by killing the wild reindeer. In the region around the Amur and Lake Baikal, the Evenki have another method: they use a decoy made of birch-bark (*orevun*) to imitate the rutting-call of the male reindeer. Other (real) reindeer race to remonstrate with this upstart trespasser on their territory . . . and pay the price. Formerly armed with long spears and metal bows, the aboriginal hunters have, since the advent of the Russians, adopted the rifle.

Most of the peoples of the taiga hunt fur-bearing animals for the money in it. From autumn on, they take to areas where there are plenty of squirrels and sables,

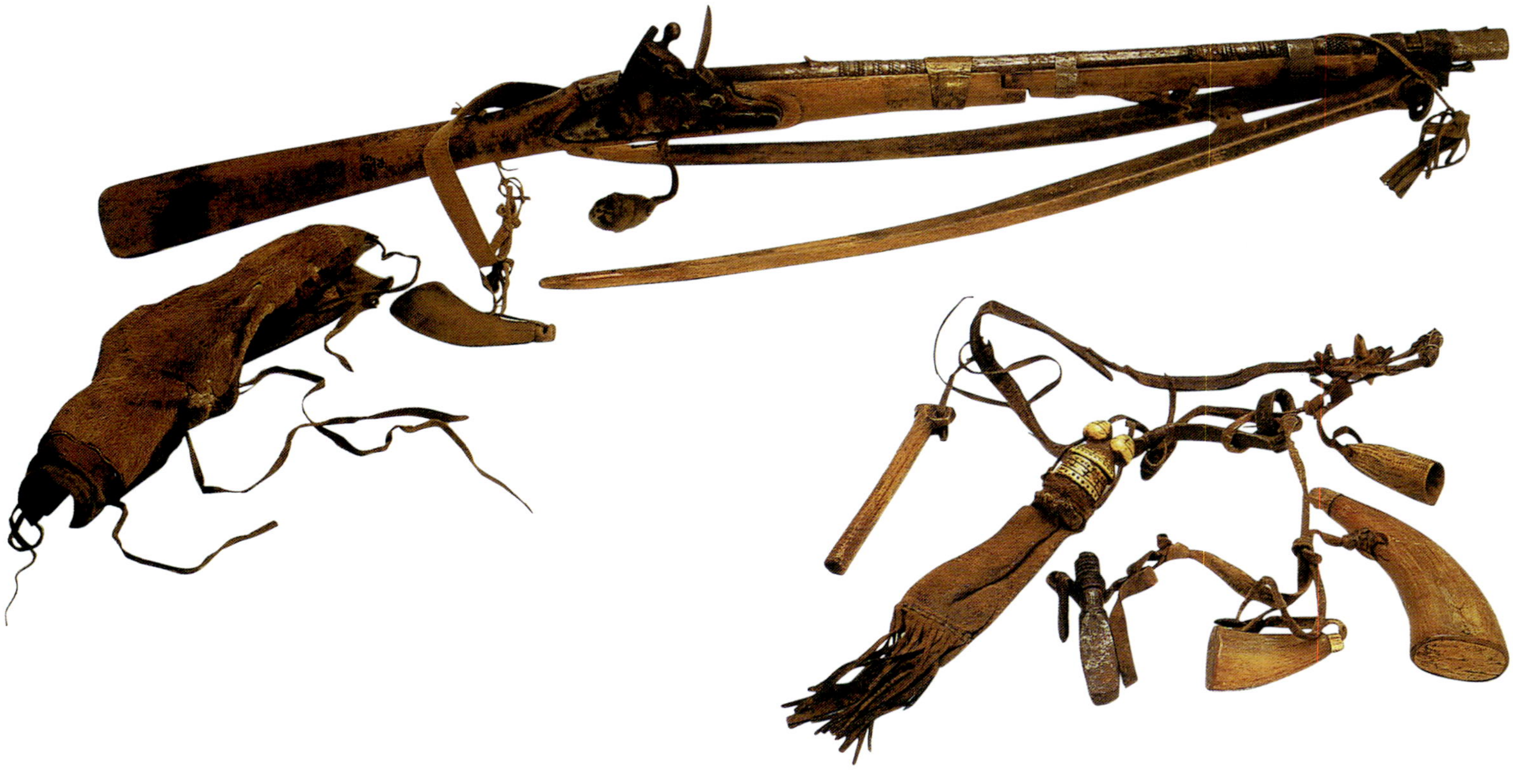

Chukchi,
Flintlock with stand and powder kit, gun kit, 1900-1901.
Wood, metal, skin; metal, leather, bone, ivory, wood, 99 cm; 33 cm.
American Museum of Natural History, New York. Markovo.

Chukchi,
Small plastic artwork 'Hunting for bear', 1906.
Walrus tusk ivory, 14 x 5.7 cm.
Russian Museum of Ethnography, St. Petersburg. Primorskaya Oblast, Anadyr Krai.

Koryak,
Small plastic artworks 'Tea-drinking' and 'Meal', 1911.
Walrus tusk ivory, 1) 6 x 4.5 cm; 2) 6.7 x 7 cm.
Russian Museum of Ethnography, St. Petersburg. Kamchatka Oblast.

and spread themselves out all over the taiga. Those hunters who possess reindeer travel as nomads with the whole of their families. Those hunters who don't instead group up in twos and threes for the duration of the winter, leaving their wives back at the encampment. They go on skis as long as a man's height and as broad as two thumbs – skis in Siberia are usually made of thin conifer wood, although when the snow is particularly deep a layer of reindeer-skin may be added underneath (as with boots, the reindeer skin is from the lower part of the legs of the animals). With the aid of a stick the hunters supervise matters from a sledge mounted on ski-runners.

Apart from ungulates (elk and reindeer) and fur-bearing animals, which are hunted all over Siberia, there are some creatures that are not hunted because – at least among certain ethnic groups – they have totemic associations with the people. Such creatures include the eagle, the swan, the owl, the stork, the bear, the wolf and the tiger.

Rarely undertaken, the hunting of the bear is in any case strictly regulated, for this animal – so sympathetic in appearance, and so human in intelligence – inspires both fear and respect among the ethnic communities of Siberia. So much so that for many it is taboo to use the ordinary word for 'bear' and kennings (pseudonymous phrases) are used instead: 'the old man of the forest', 'the grandfather', 'the master of the taiga' and so forth. Indeed, the bear is the focus of a highly developed cult among certain peoples, notably the Nivkhi, the Negidal people and the Khanty.

The wolf, because it hunts down the same quarry as men, is considered by them to be their equal, and in consequence is seldom hunted itself. The Evenki of the east call the animal 'son', 'greyhair' or 'naughty boy', and believe that it is a heinous crime to cause the death of wolfcubs. In winter, however, the Chukchis

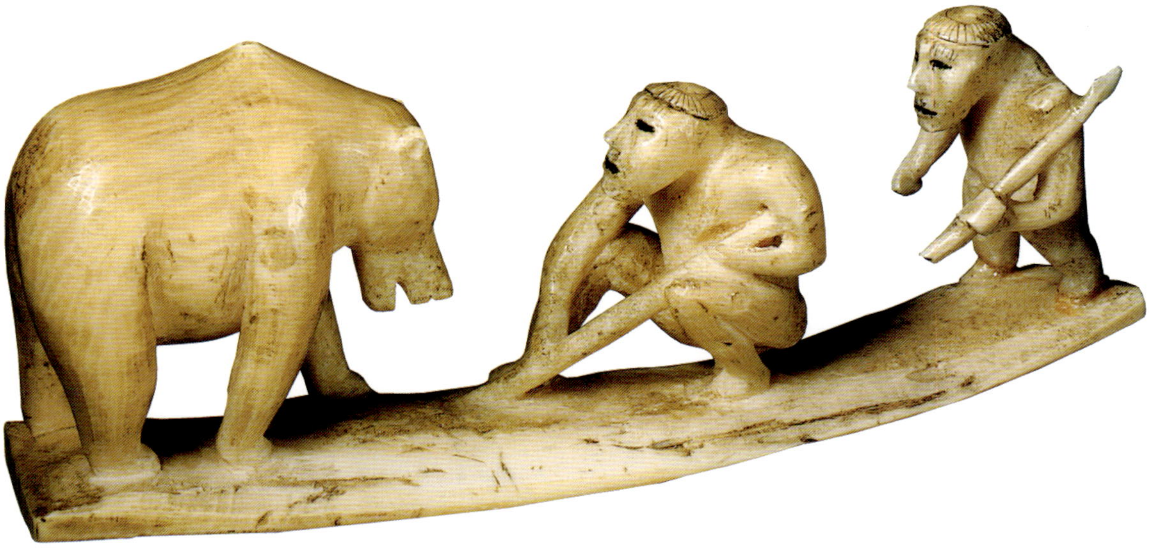

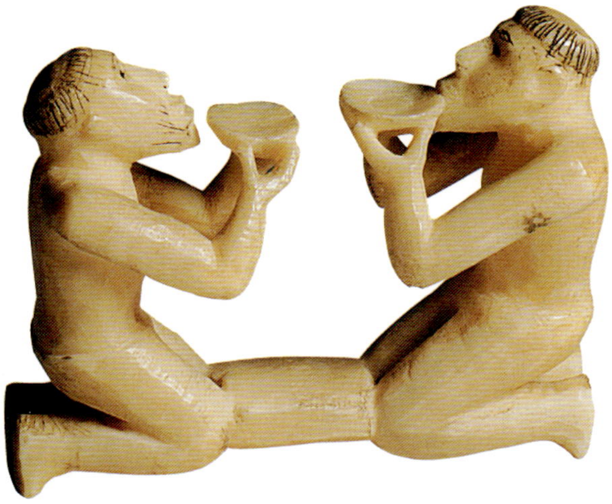

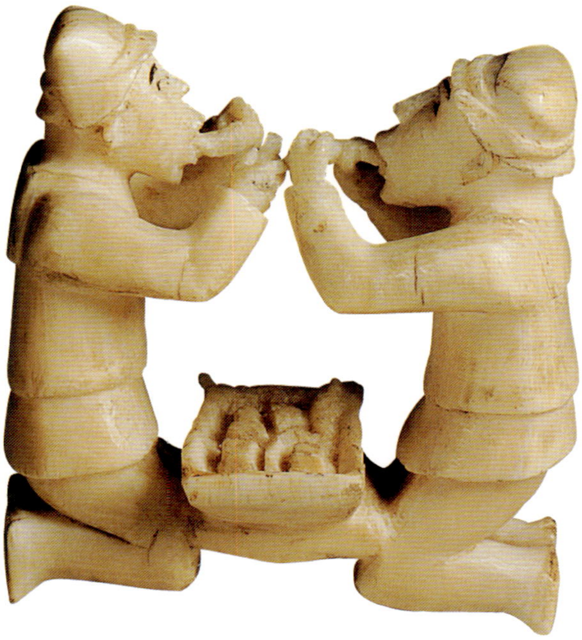

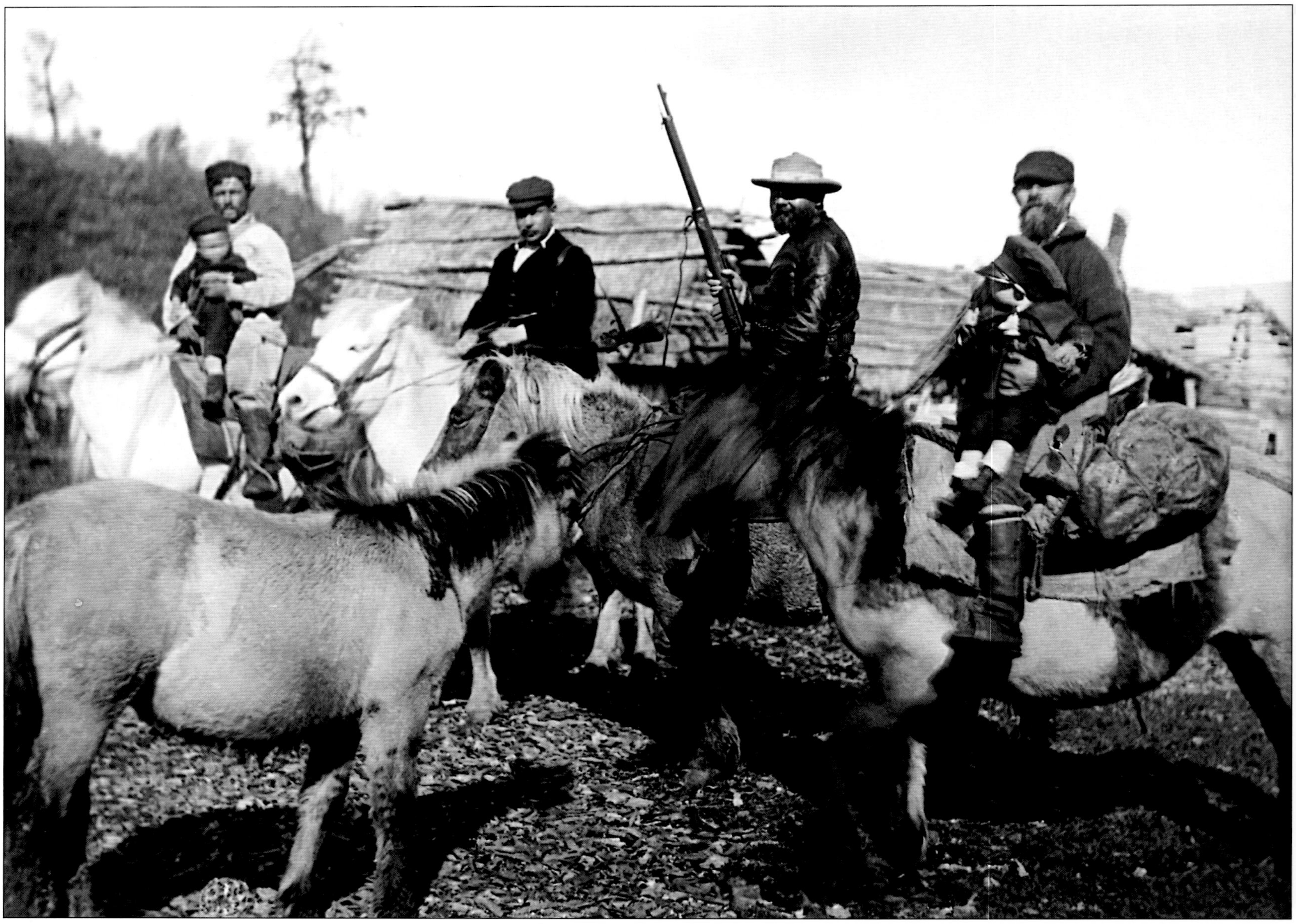

Kamtchatka,
1897.

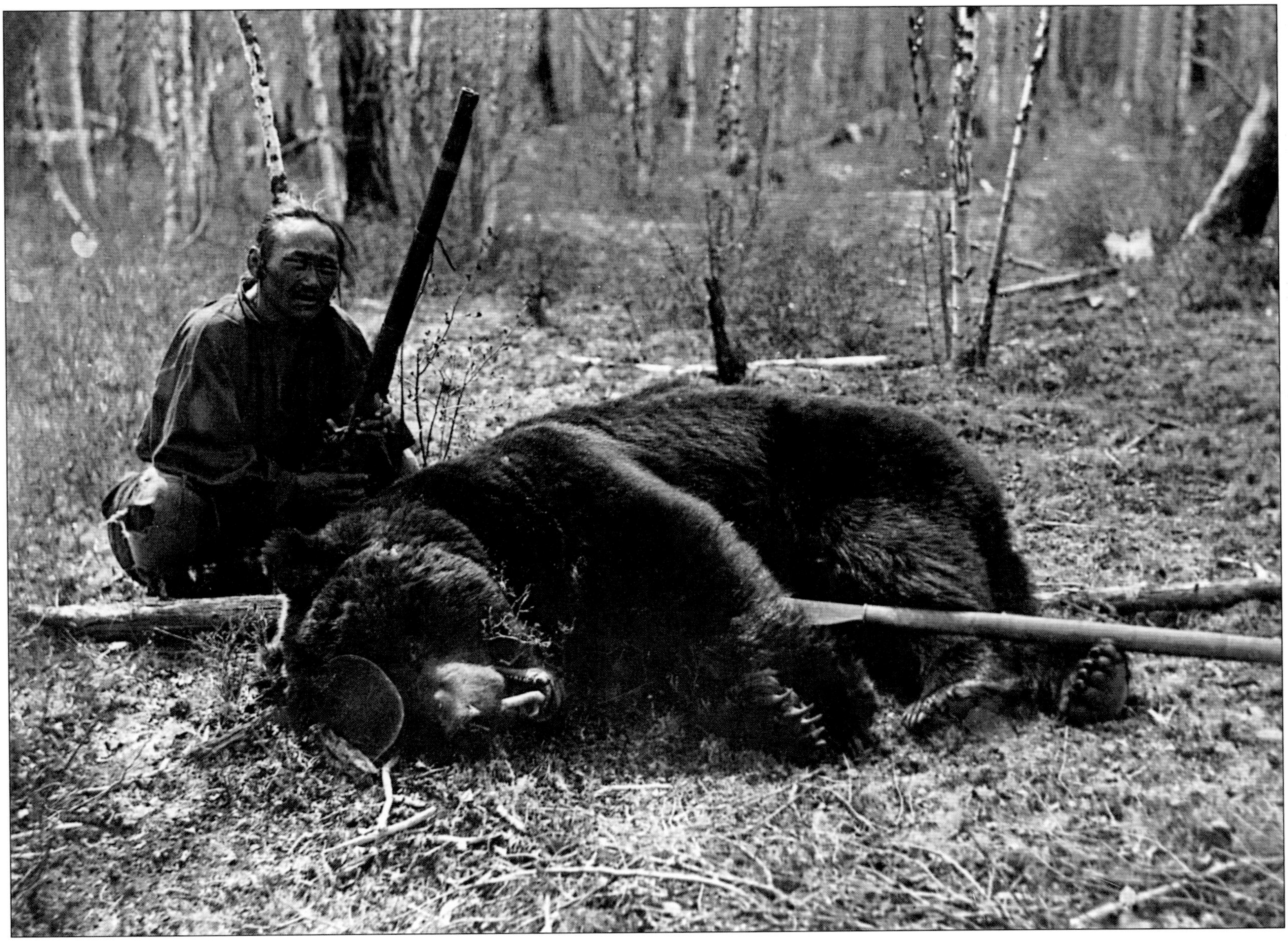

Evenki,
Hunter performing a ritual over a slain bear, early 20th century.
Yenisey Province.

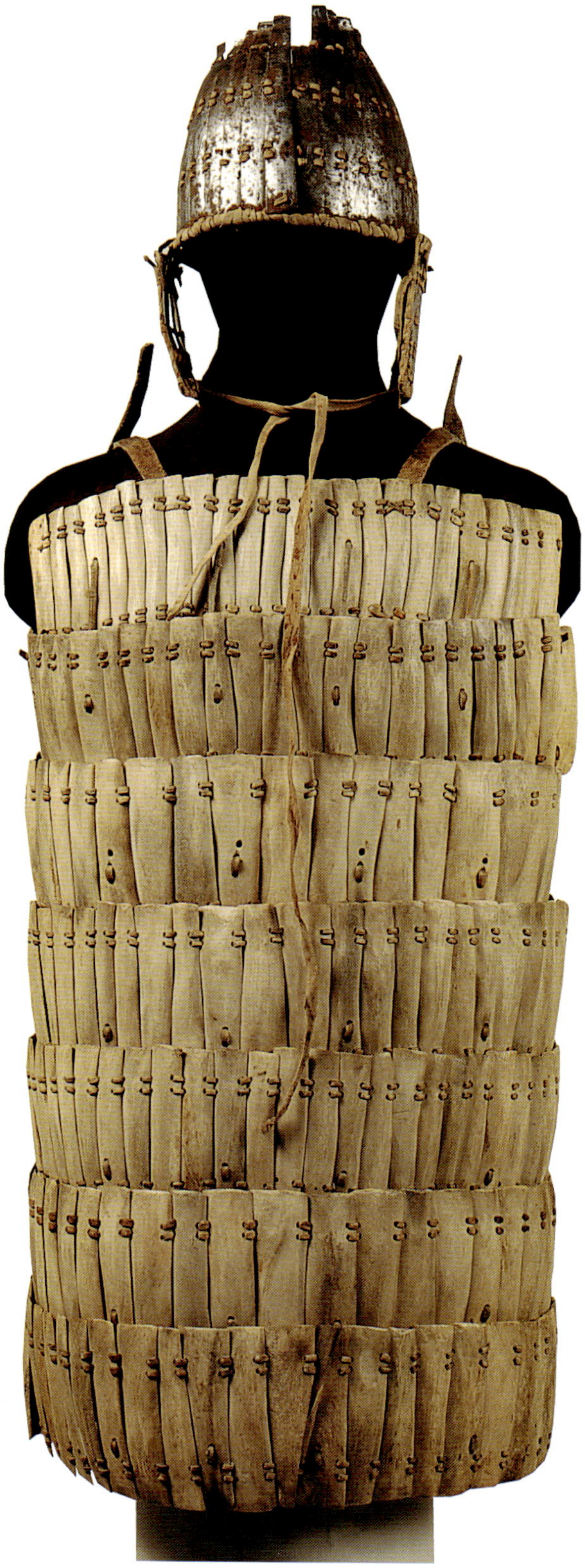

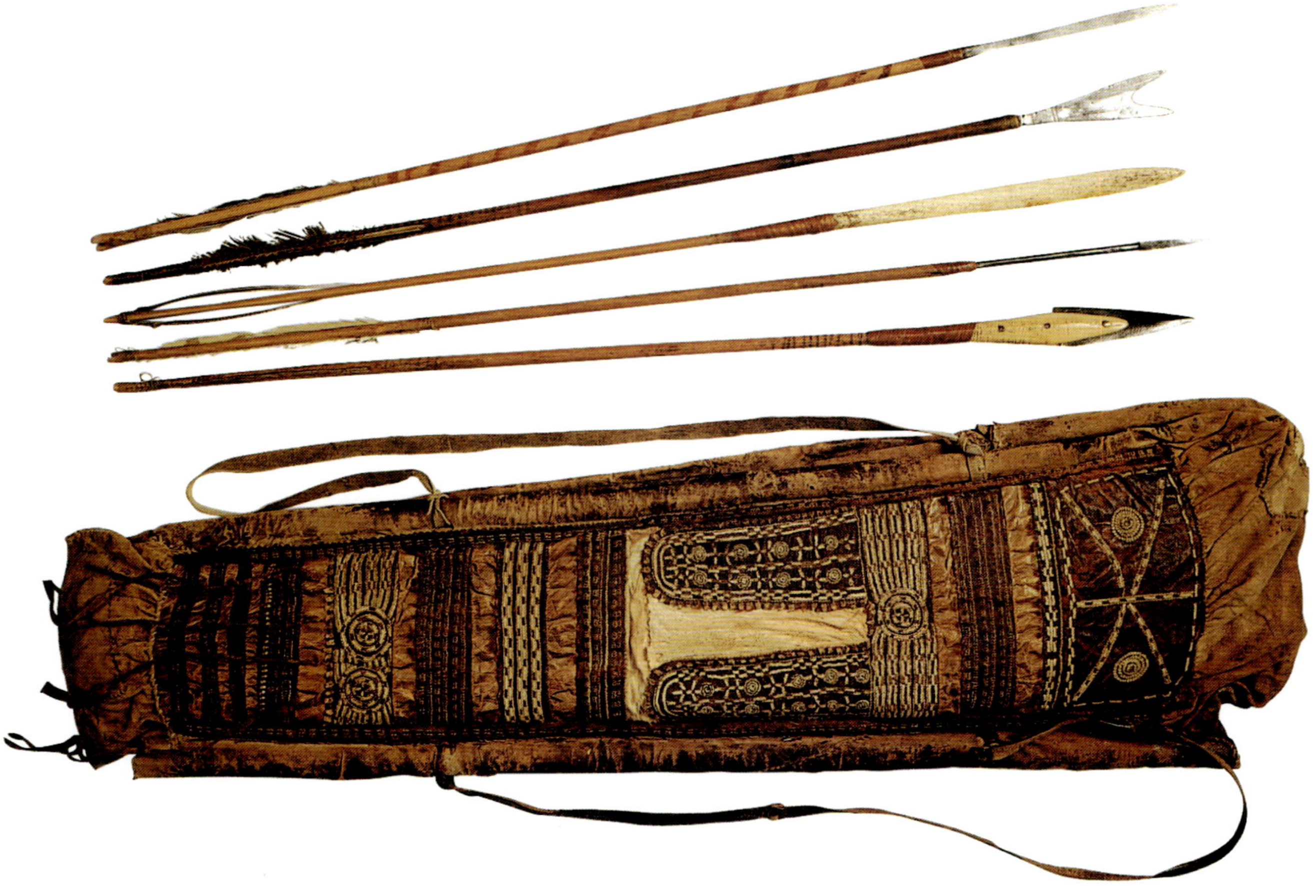

hunt the wolf with the aid of a redoubtable weapon. A piece of bony cartilage from a whale's head is carved into an extremely spiky shape, rolled up small and tied in that position with string. It is then steeped in water until it ices up. The string that kept it together is drawn off, and the resultant iced ball is smeared with animal fat. It is then placed in the path of the wolf which, when it finds it, swallows it. The ice melts quickly in the internal warmth of the stomach, the sharp spikes emerge and unbend to pierce the stomach wall of the wolf, and so cause its death.

By tradition it is the men, in Siberia, who devote themselves to hunting and fishing, while the women are charged with domestic duties – keeping the fire going, putting up and taking down the *choom*, tanning the hides, stitching together the clothes, looking after the children... Yet among many of the peoples it is by no means unusual for women to go hunting, alone or together with the men – and to be as successful at it. That is certainly the case among, for example, the Yukaghirs. Some of their old women are renowned for their hunting prowess, and include even bears among their hunting trophies.

3) ANIMAL BREEDERS

In the steppes of southern Siberia, the Khakass people, the Altai people, the Tuva people, the Buryats and, further north and just into the tundra, the Yakuts

Chukchi,
Armour and helmet of a warrior,
1904-1907.
Antler, metal, sealskin, Armour:
74.5 x 129 cm;
Helmet: 22 cm x 11.2 cm.
Russian Museum of Ethnography,
St. Petersburg. Primorskaya Oblast,
Anadyr Krai.

Chukchi,
Quiver and arrows, 1904-1907.
Dressed reindeer skin, sealskin,
metal, reindeer underneck hair,
wood, metal, bone, bird feather,
Quiver: 88 x 21.5 cm; Arrows: 76.5 cm;
78 cm; 77.3 cm; 76.5 cm; 79 cm.
Russian Museum of Ethnography,
St. Petersburg.
Primorskaya Oblast, Anadyr Krai.

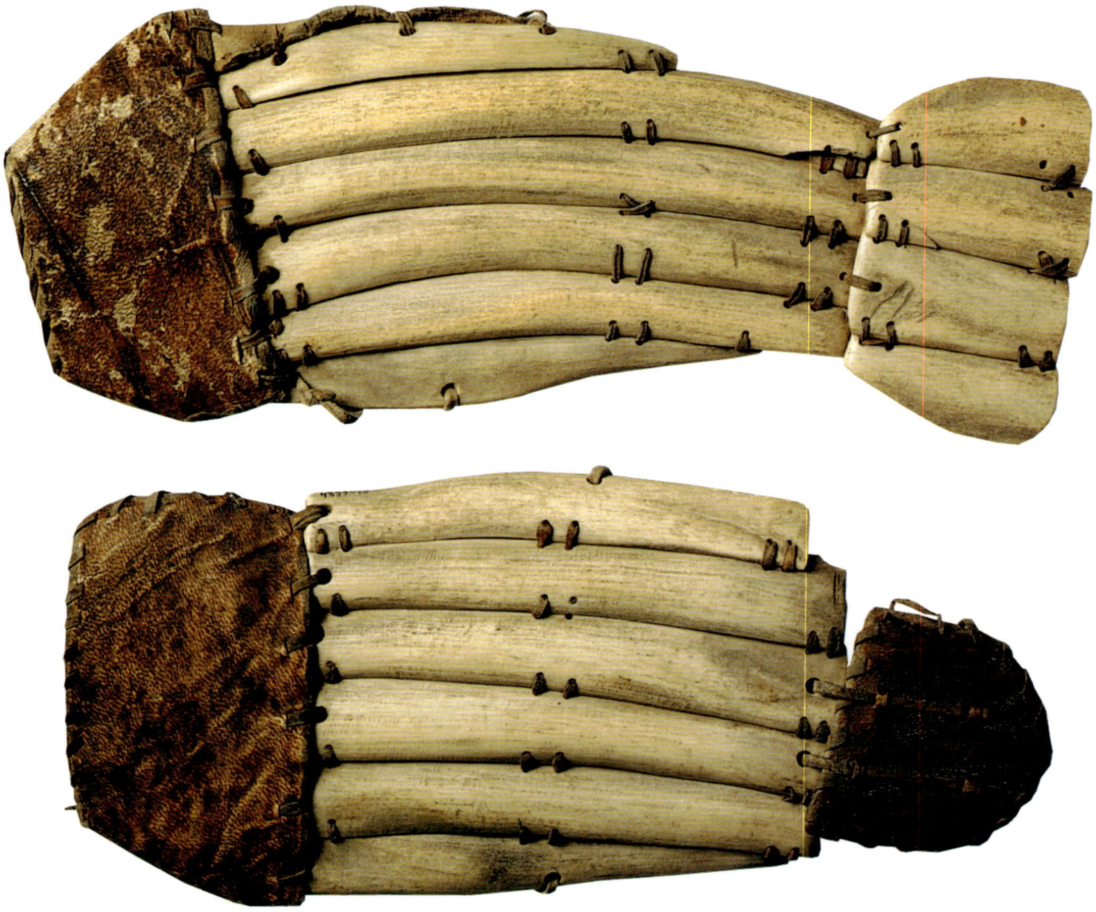

Chukchi,
Oversleeves of a warrior, 1904-1907.
Antler, sealskin, 1) 36.5 cm; 2) 37 cm.
Russian Museum of Ethnography,
St. Petersburg. Primorskaya Oblast,
Anadyr Krai.

Aleut,
Hunter's hat, early 20th century.
Wood, bone, eared seal whiskers,
38.5 x 22 cm.
Russian Museum of Ethnography,
St. Petersburg. Aleutian Islands.

Aleut,
Hunter's hat, early 20th century.
Wood, 54 x 17 cm.
Russian Museum of Ethnography,
St. Petersburg. Commander Islands.

have for centuries based their culture on raising horses and breeding horned animals. These Turkic and Mongolian peoples also farm sheep on the southern plains, while in the mountainous regions they additionally herd reindeer – strictly for transportation purposes. Further north still, in Arctic zones, the Yakuts have copied reindeer-herding methods from the Evenki.

Nomadic in former times, these communities have during the course of the 20th century become partly – well, totally – residential in habit. To be sure, a few groups lead a sort of semi-nomadic way of life with their animals, divided between winter pasturages and summer pasturages.

Summertime among these groups is dedicated to agricultural activities, and there is much to do, especially the hay-making which ensures reserve supplies of food for much of the livestock. In the winter the cattle and horses, left to their own devices in grasslands, have to find food for themselves under the snow.

Breeding cattle and horses for adaptation to the conditions of Siberia has been the work of the Yakuts. Indeed, the physical particulars of a Yakut horse bear witness to its adaptation to the rigours of the climate in the Siberian north – compact and small in stature, with a long shaggy coat, the animal can withstand extremely low temperatures (below –50°C/–58°F) and is quite capable of turning up its food independently by stamping on the frozen

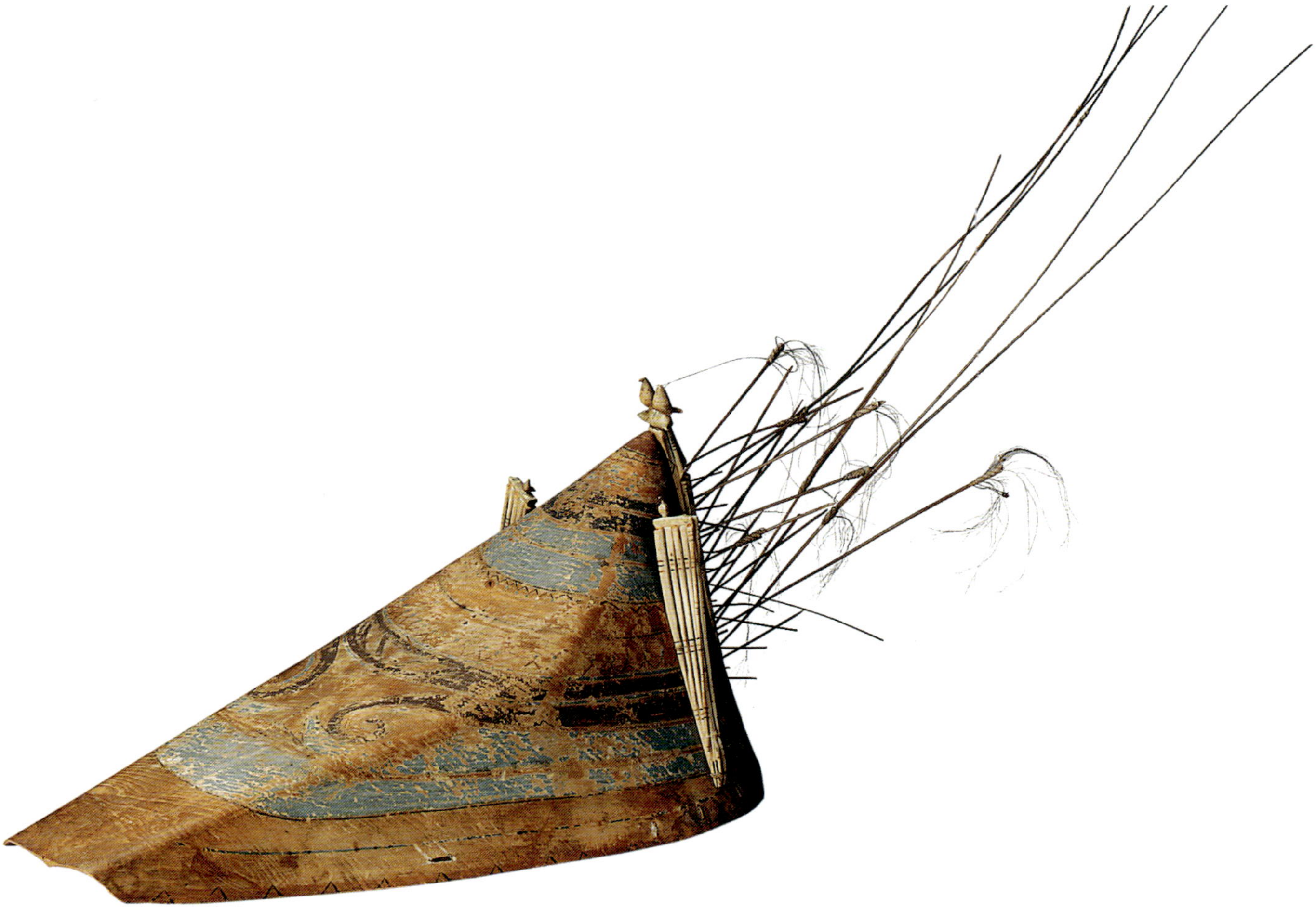

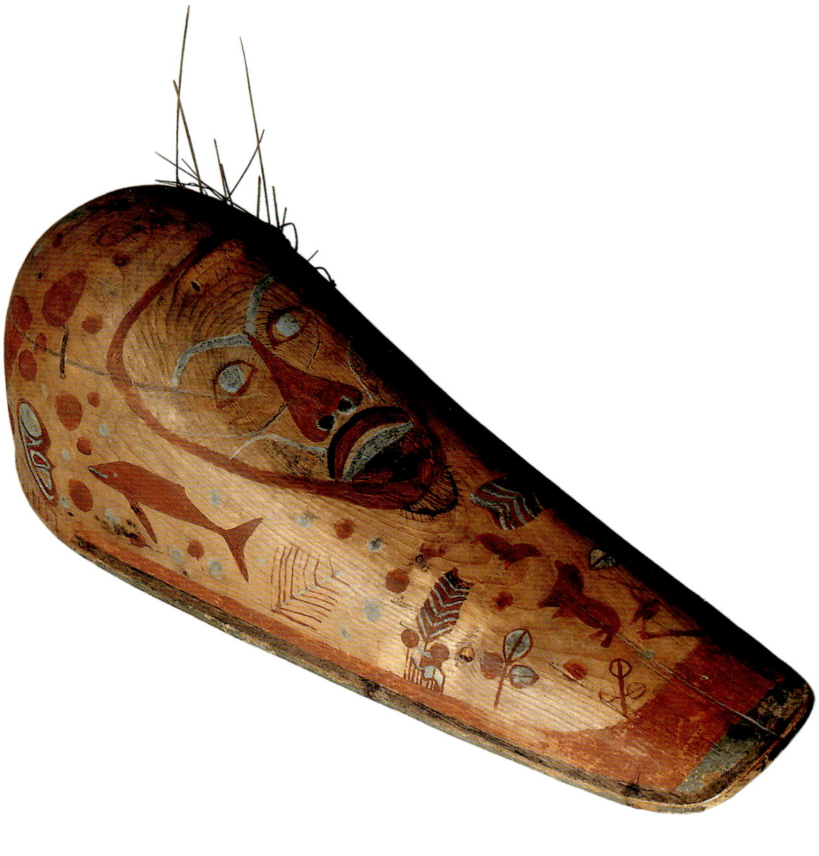

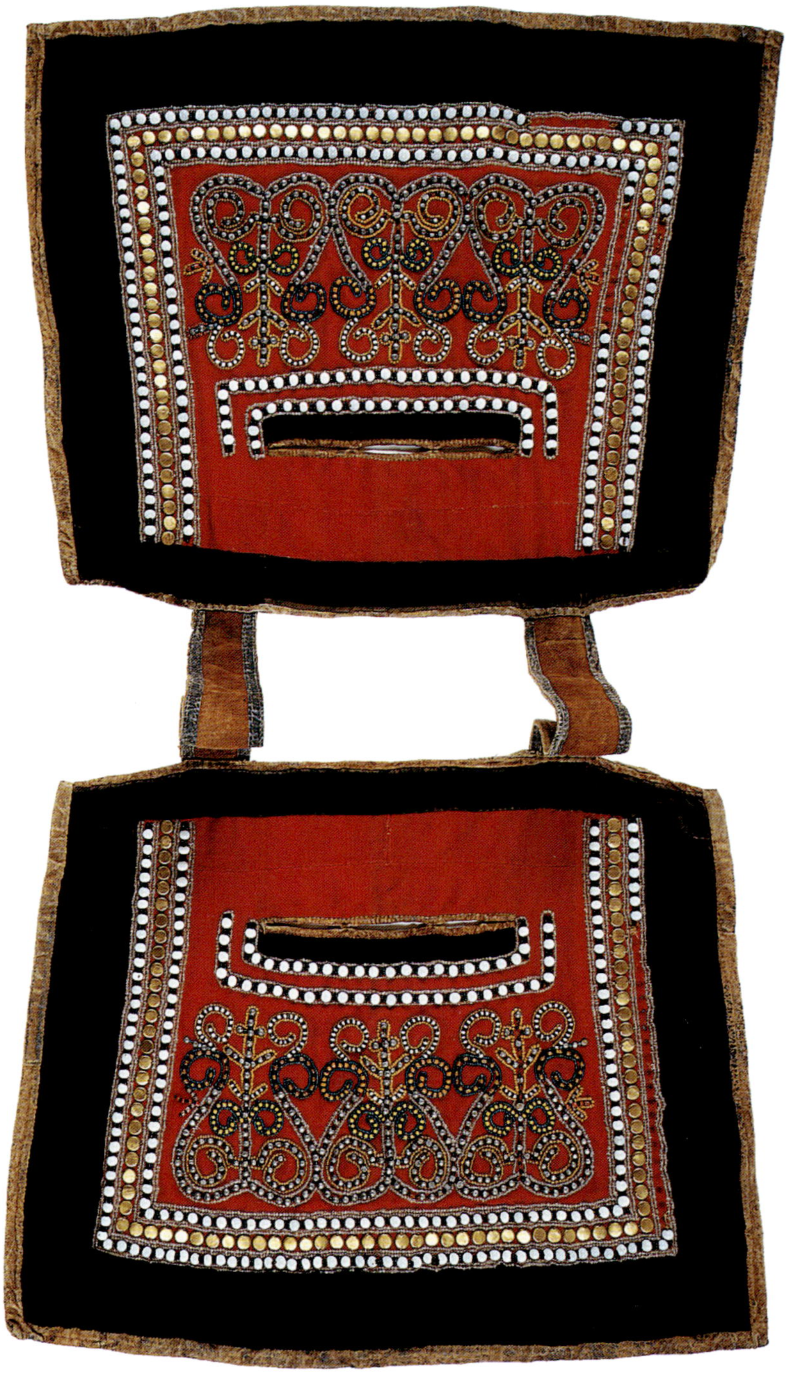

ground with its hoofs. It is the horse that is the focus of the Yakut cultural heritage. According to one legend it was the first creature on the earth, the ancestor of humankind. And certainly in former times the horse provided the Yakuts with all the resources needed for their lifestyle – meat, leather, hide, transportation, everything. Cattle, introduced by these same Yakuts into the northern regions of Siberia rather later, have since taken over as the central pillar of their way of life. Nonetheless, the breed of cattle developed by them over the centuries is today on the edge of extinction. They possess the very same qualities as the Yakut horse – small, hardy, with a shaggy hide and a reproduction rate that is relatively slow – although their milk is particularly rich, in terms of nutritive value, in comparison with that of ordinary cows. But it was because of the sluggishness in the overall rate of reproduction that the Soviet authorities decided that other types of cattle must be brought in, and following the resultant multiple cross-breeding that then ensued, the Yakut cattle have today all but vanished completely.

The semi-nomadic way of life of the Turkic and Mongolian peoples of Siberia is closely linked with the herds of horses they move with twice every year – in spring and in autumn – to new areas of pasturage.

In Yakutia, horses live in a semi-wild state. On festive occasions the Yakuts pay special attention to the tack – by tradition, the standard equestrian accoutrements comprise a saddle ornamented with plaques of embossed silver, a pair of stirrups, a bridle and a smallish saddle-blanket also decorated with bright bits and pieces. In the summertime, both horses and cattle wander freely over the great plains that characterize the traditional countryside of the Yakuts – the alas, a vast heathland bestrewn with scattered lakes surrounded by forests. In the evenings, the cattle return to the byre for milking, either following a leader or driven there by boys on horseback.

Left to roam the pastures in summer, the cattle in winter are fed on hay in *khoton* – sheds specifically adapted for extreme temperatures. In past centuries the *khoton* were pretty well no more than extensions of the yurt, and indeed still retain similarities. Like the Yakut style of yurt (*balaghan*), the *khoton* is made of wood, has sloping sides and a flat roof covered with earth. Its walls are shored up from the outside with clay and cow-dung. It is a system that ensures the cows are warm in winter – and in summer the blocks of dried cow-dung are removed and burned to keep the multitudinous mosquitoes at bay.

The Yakuts used to live in groups, scattered here and there in the forests or on the tundras, each family living in a yurt, or, if on the tundra, in tents. In central Yakutia, despite the Sovietization, the Yakut villages preserve their local colour thanks both to the *khoton* and to the *ambar* (cereal granaries), rectangular buildings of wood with flat roofs covered in earth and, in summertime, with vegetation. Winter yurts and the summertime tents (*urasa*) have, on the other hand, now completely disappeared in favour of Russian-style wooden houses. Yurts nonetheless remain in use in some southern regions of Siberia. The yurts are wooden huts with sloping walls covered with a thick layer of turf. In the place of window-glass ox-bladders are used in summer-time and ice in winter. The window-openings are usually not more than a foot square in size. The fireplace is in the middle of the yurta, and is made of poles, placed close together and covered with mud or clay. Along the walls inside the dwelling run low nares or benches, between the wooden pillars, serving as sitting-places during the daytime and as bedsteads at night. The yurt is divided into two parts: to the right from the entrance is the women's

Yakut,
Tebenki (horse-cover), 1904.
Woolen cloth, dressed reindeer skin, beads, seed beads, metal, 62 x 51 cm.
Russian Museum of Ethnography, St. Petersburg.
Yakut Oblast, Yakutsk.

and children's apartment, where, among the poorest classes, the cattle are also housed ; and to the left that of the men. To the women's apartment men not belonging to the family are not allowed to go. The Yakuts generally have special yurtas for winter and summer, the latter usually situated near their meadows and haystacks. In the far north they often live in tents or huts resembling those of the Lapps.

They prefer to settle in groups, where there is plenty of pasture, or in the neighbourhood of lakes and rivers abounding with fish, or in forests where game is to be had. Such groups or communities are called *aga-usa* ("paternal families," or made up of people who are related). The members of these communities of relatives do not marry within the community, but they keep together to help and protect each other. They elect an "elder" and form a council, which decides their common affairs, settles disputes, and performs other offices. These communities in their turn associate themselves into larger groups, forming the so-called *naslegi* (association of family communities), which again are organised into *ulus*, corresponding to the Russian village-districts (*volost*). At the head of the ulus stands the *golova* or chief, with an *uprava* or kind of police- court. The *naslegi* are administered by a district-council and a district-elder having the title of *kujas* (prince), which was conferred on these tribal chiefs by Catherine II. The taxes are collected by the local authorities of the ulus, which are by law connected with the officials and the police authorities. The taxes (yassak) were formerly paid in the shape of furs, but after the sable were to a great extent exterminated, they were paid in money, the amount of which, plus communal taxes, varied, depending on the decision of the local authorities and the economical condition of the tax-payer.

The Yakuts are generally poor. Their principal possessions consist of cattle and horses. The Yakut horses are small and shaggy, but very hardy, strong, and good-tempered animals. Throughout the long and terrible winter they subsist on the grass underneath the snow, which, like the reindeer, they remove with their feet, the strongest horses going in front, and the weaker ones following them, eating the uncovered grass. The Yakuts, like other Tatar peoples, are very fond of horse-meat, and from the horses ' milk they prepare the well-known *koumiss*. The number of horses they own, however, is diminishing, and only well-to-do Yakuts as a rule now keep them, the great majority having cattle instead. The Yakut cattle are very small and of inferior quality. The cows give very little milk; a family of ordinary size needs for its subsistence from 10 to 15 head of cattle, of which 7 to 9 are milk cows. The great majority of Yakut families, however, have not so many, and want and famine are very common among them. Their principal work consists in gathering hay on the meadows and marshes.

The food-products of cattle-raising – meat and milk – constitute the primary diet of the Turkic and Mongolian peoples. Specialities involving meat and milk dominate their eating habits, topped up with fish, which in turn form an appreciable proportion of the diet of those who live on the shores of Lake Baikal and on the banks of the Lena. Additional delicacies are those brought home after hunting and, in summer, after scavenging for berries and fungi. A drink consumed amid some ritual by the Yakuts is the famous *koumiss*, fermented mare's milk, quaffed in large quantities at the height of the festival of *Isyakh* in June from huge bowls carved in wood – the *ayakh* or *choron*. Quite different is the daily dish of the Yakuts out in the fields: *kuortchekh* – whipped cream embellished with whortleberries. The preferred meat dishes of these northerly people are frozen raw foal meat and *stroganina* (frozen raw fish).

Yakut,
Toys in the form of horses, 1908, 1910.
Wood, 1) 30 x 15 cm; 2) 23 x 22 cm.
Russian Museum of Ethnography, St. Petersburg. 1) Yakut Oblast, Vilyuy Okrug; 2) Yakut Oblast, Vilyuy Okrug, Boturuski ulus (settlement).

Yakut,
Boxes, 1959, early 20th century.
Wood, 1) 31 x 11 x 7.5 cm;
2) 17 x 5 cm.
Russian Museum of Ethnography, St. Petersburg. Yakut ASSR, Vilyuysk town.

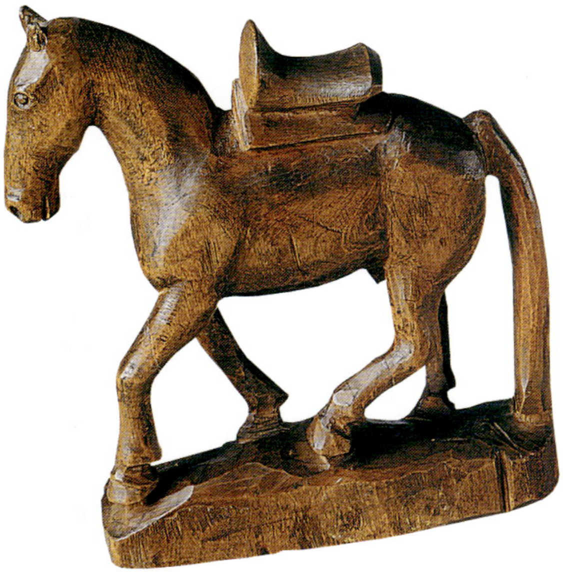

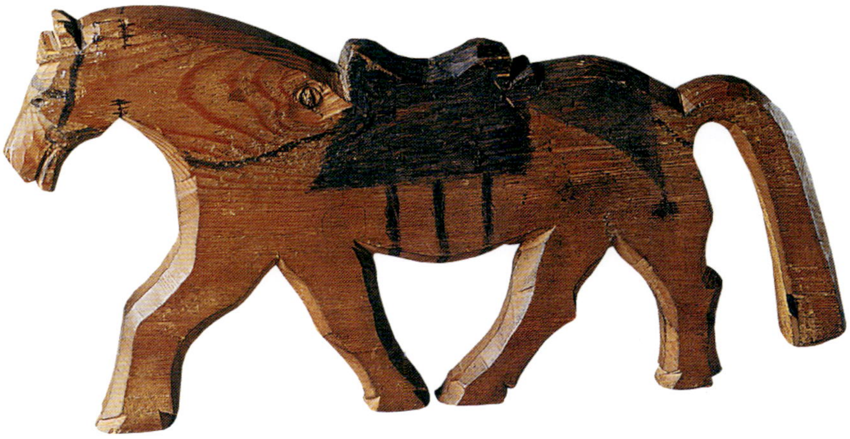

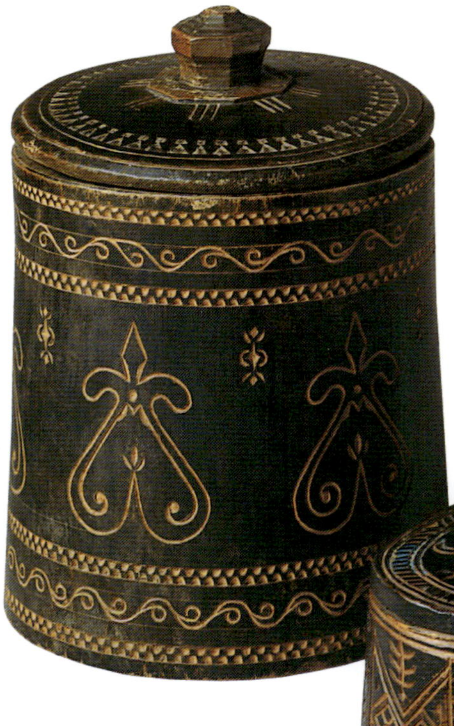

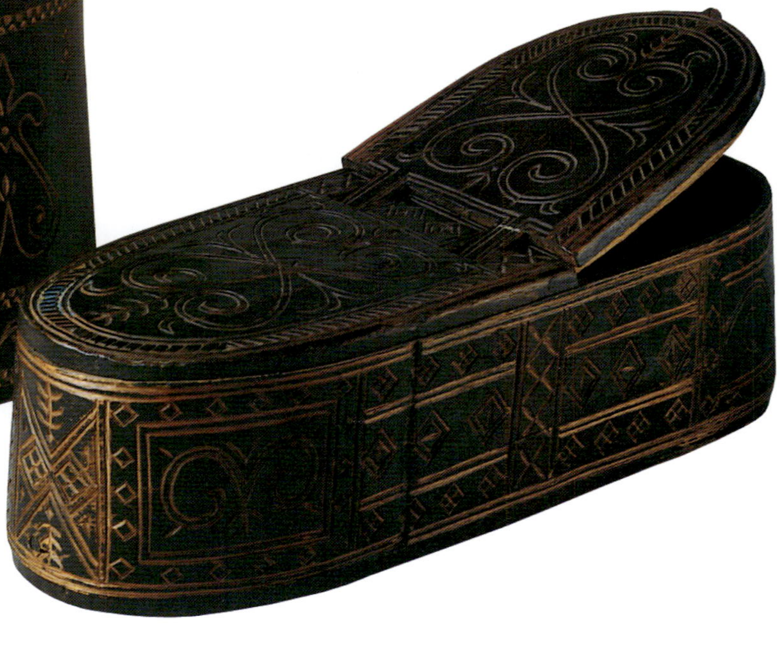

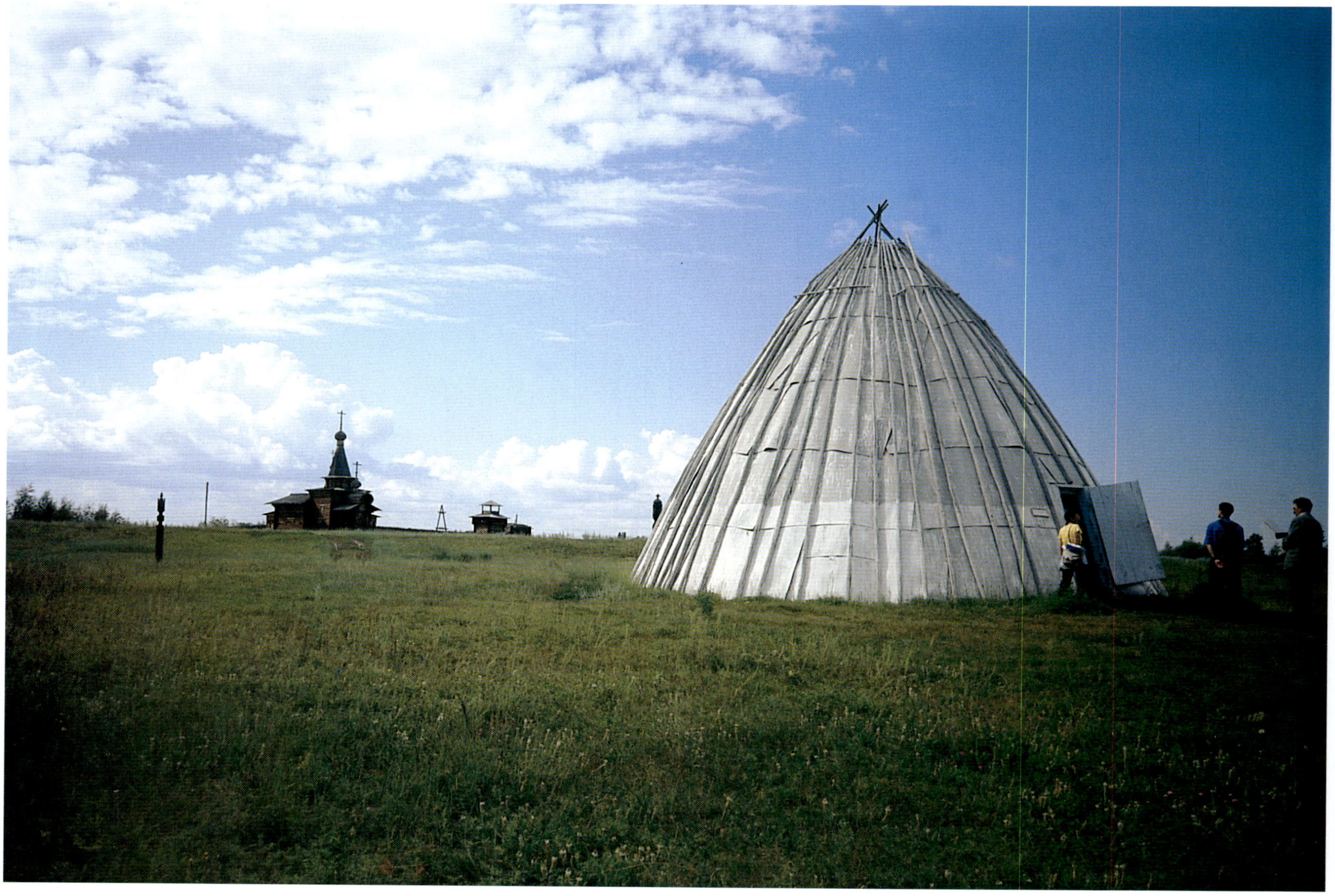

Summer tent.

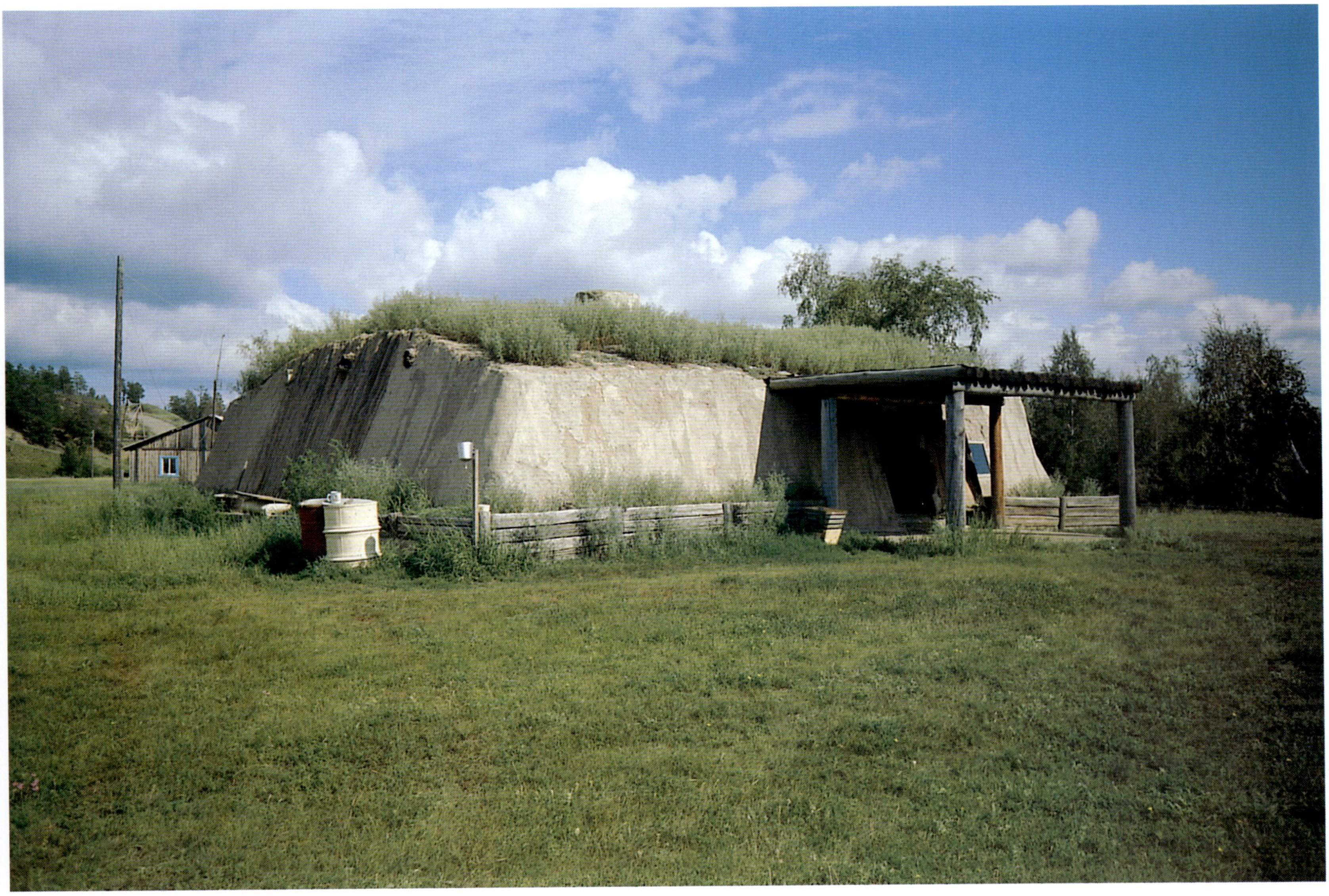

Yurt (traditional Yakut winter residence).

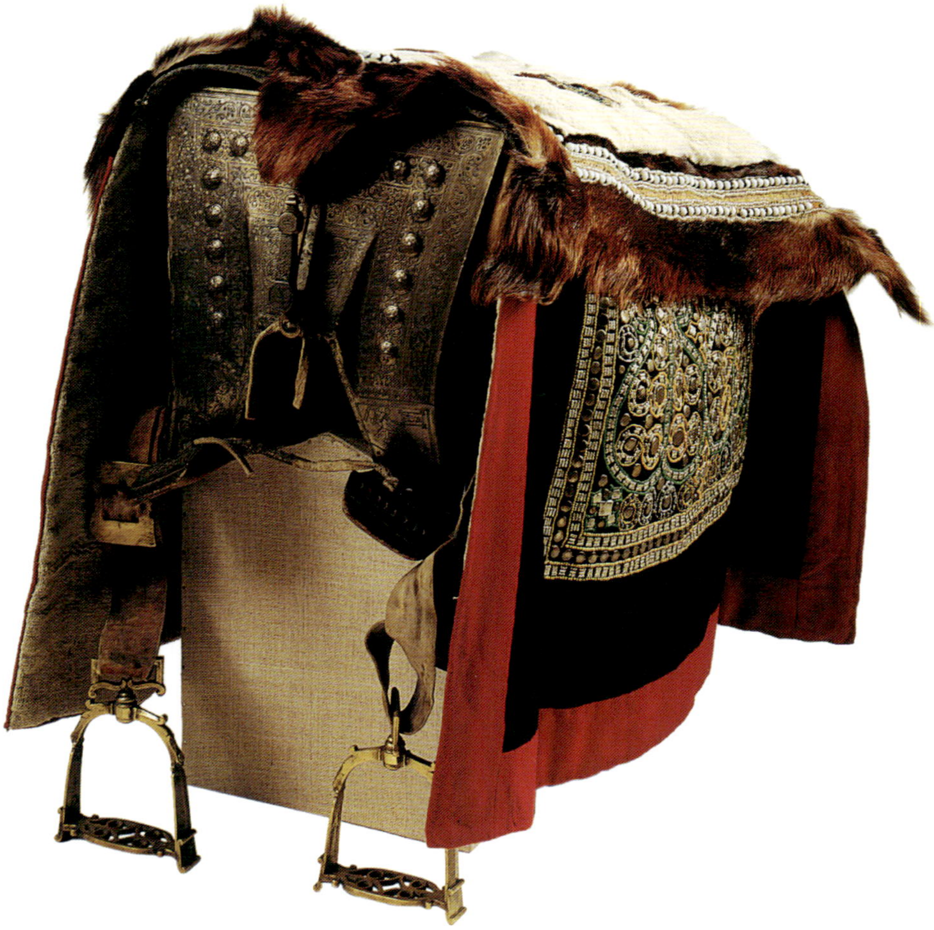

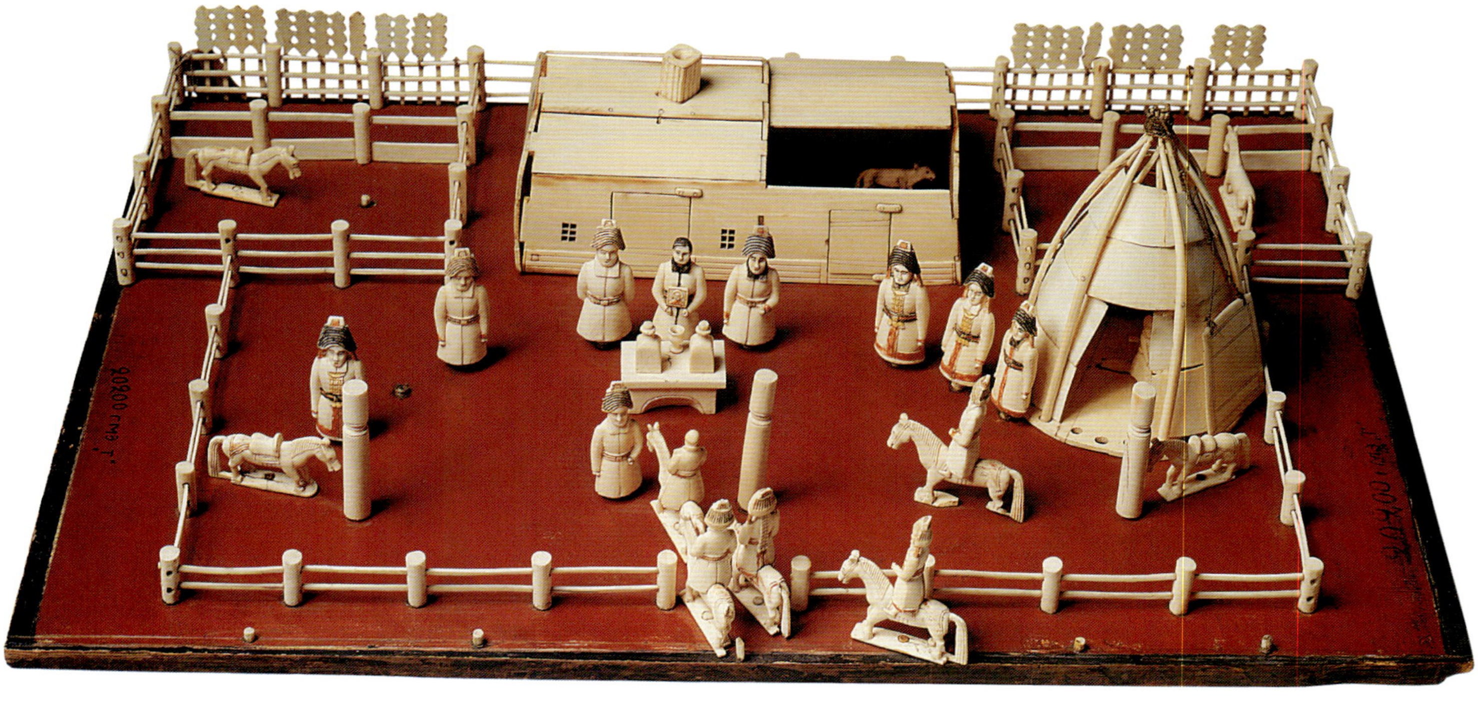

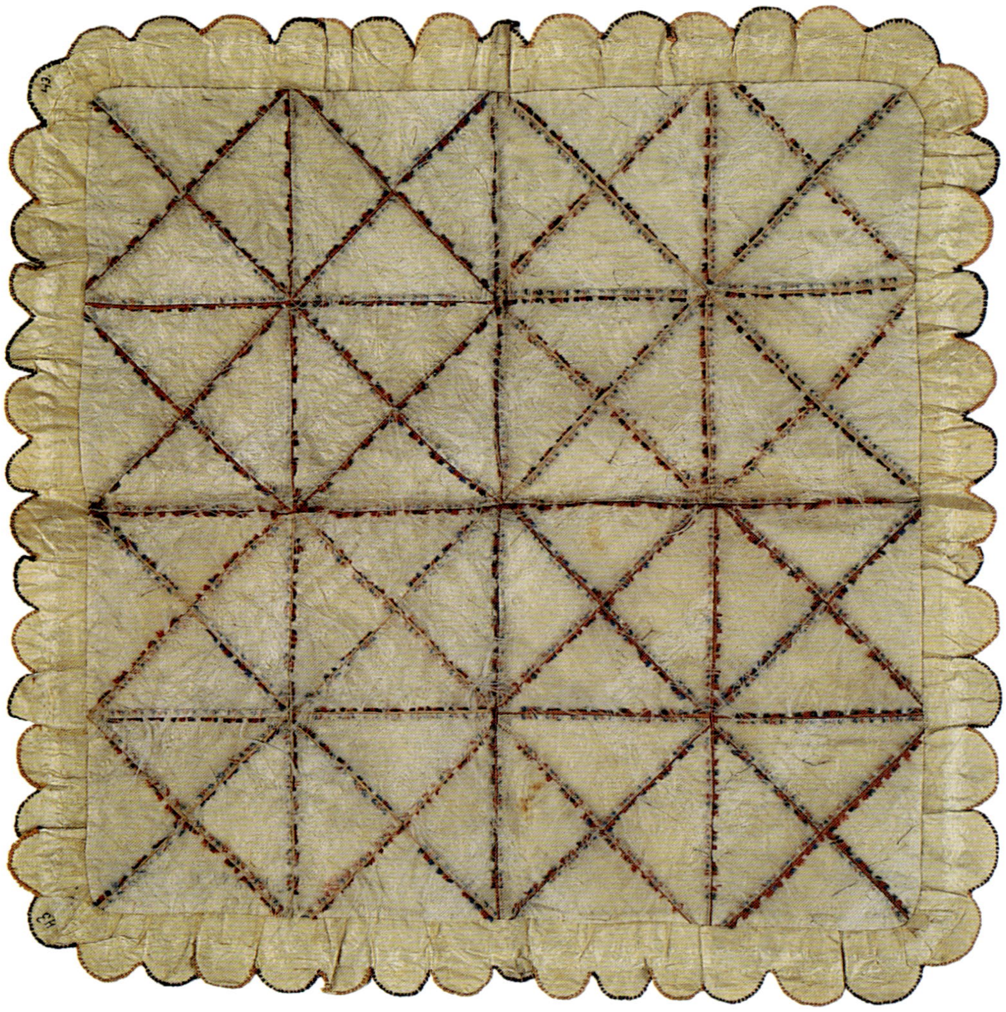

Yakut,
Woman's wedding saddle, 1959, 1909, 1925-1926.
Wood, metal, elk leather, horsehair, fabric, woolen cloth, horse fur, beads, seed beads. Saddle: 55 x 27 x 34 cm;
Stirrups: 19 x 14 cm;
Horse-cover: 156 x 89 cm;
Saddle cover: 93 x 69 cm.
Russian Museum of Ethnography, St. Petersburg. Yakut ASSR, Vilyuy District, Boturuski Ulus, Yakutsk.

Model of Yakut homestead, early 20th century.
Mammoth bone, wood, 54 x 36 cm.
Russian Museum of Ethnography, St. Petersburg. Yakutia.

Aleut,
Rug, 1909-1910.
Eared seal intestines, fabric, bird fluff, woolen yarn. 33 x 28 cm.
Russian Museum of Ethnography, St. Petersburg. Aleutian Islands.

The usual food of the great majority of Yakuts is the so-called "*tar*" which is a mixture of meat, fish, various roots, grass, and pine-bark. This is put into skimmed milk mixed with water, to which is added a little flour, if such is to be had, and the whole is boiled into a kind of porridge. The Yakuts drink a great deal of tea, and are very fond of strong spirits. The wealthy eat meat every day and a kind of thick pancake, made of water and barley-flour.

Only in the past two centuries has the culture of cereals been introduced among the Yakuts by the Russians, especially the "Skoptsi" and other sectarians. Instead of flour, they formerly used the juicy part of the bark of the pine and different kinds of roots. Before the middle of the nineteenth century, no one believed it would be possible to cultivate cereals in Yakutsk, due to the inhospitable climate. In the first experiments the crops were frost-bitten, but eventually the corn became acclimatised, and now in favorable years good crops are secured. In the short space of two months from sowing, thanks to the usually hot summers, the grain ripens and is harvested. In the neighbourhood of the city of Yakutsk are thus grown barley, oats, wheat, potatoes and even water-melons. The implements and methods of agriculture were originally very primitive, wooden ploughs and harrows being exclusively used, but the more efficient products of the Industrial Revolution have since been introduced.

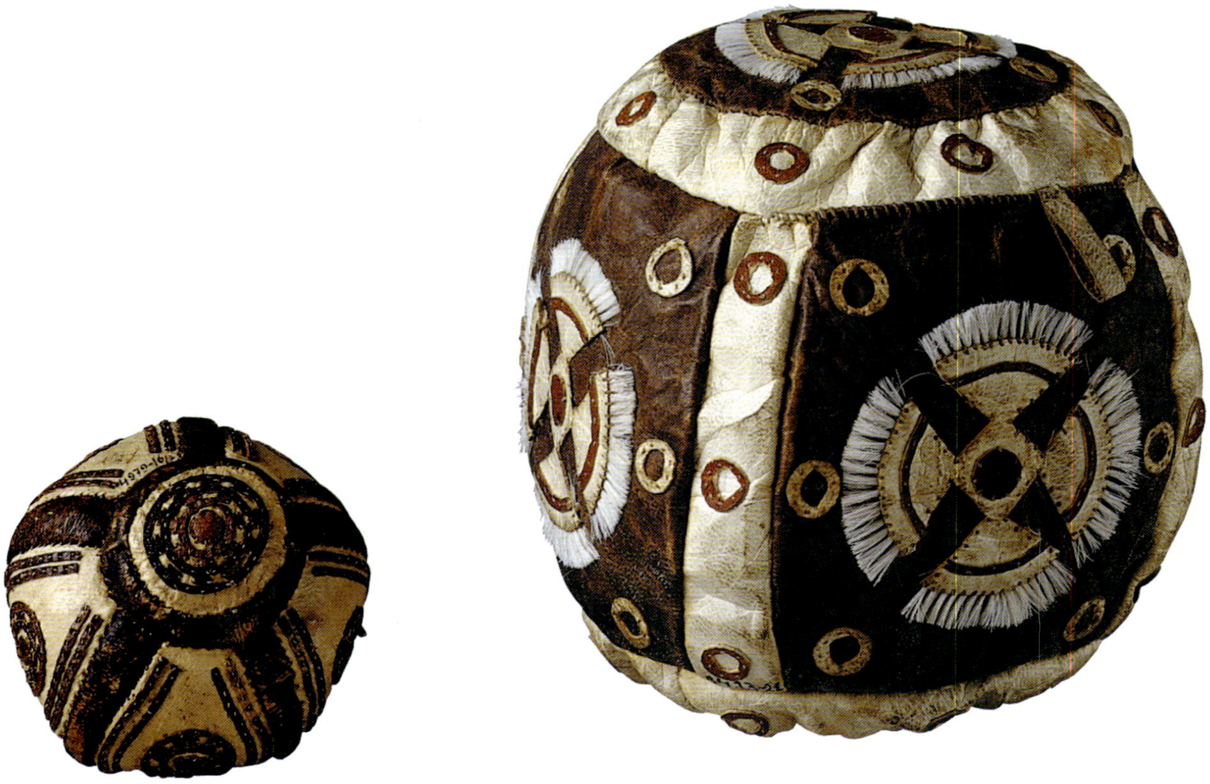

Chukchi, Eskimos,
Balls for games: 1) foot 2) hand,
1) 1974; 2) 1904-1907.
Seal skin and wool, reindeer underneck hair, Circumference: 1) 58 cm; 2) 25 cm.
Russian Museum of Ethnography, St. Petersburg. Chukchi Peninsular.

Evenki,
Doll-woman, 1907.
Fabric, reindeer ankle-bone, beads, 11 cm.
Russian Museum of Ethnography, St. Petersburg. Yenisey Gubernia (province), Yenisey Uezd (district), the Katonga river basin.

The Buryats, animal-breeders who share some characteristics with the Yakuts, live in *ulus*. An ulu is, literally, a group of families (*ail*) constituting a tribe or part of a tribe (*aimak*). The yurts or cabins of the families are not built in regular rows like the houses of the European Russian villages, but are scattered in picturesque confusion and surrounded by a large common enclosure. At a distance from the village are the so-called *ugugi*, immense enclosures where the cattle graze in winter and whence in summertime the Buryats gather splendid crops of hay. By the side of the houses are seen high poles resembling maypoles. On these are hung sacrificial gifts to the Buryatic divinities in the shape of goat-skins with head and horns attached, rags, and different kinds of clothing.

Besides the villages, in which they spend the winter, the Buryats also have their summer stations, between which they move with their herds of cattle. Up to the beginning of the twentieth century, they lived only in yurts or earth-cabins; but now well-to-do Buryats have comfortable houses, and only a few families live in yurts. The traditional mode of dwelling for the cattle-breeding communities in Siberia is this Mongolian-style *yurt*. Mobile when made mainly of cloth, pretty solidly static when built of wooden logs, the yurt varies

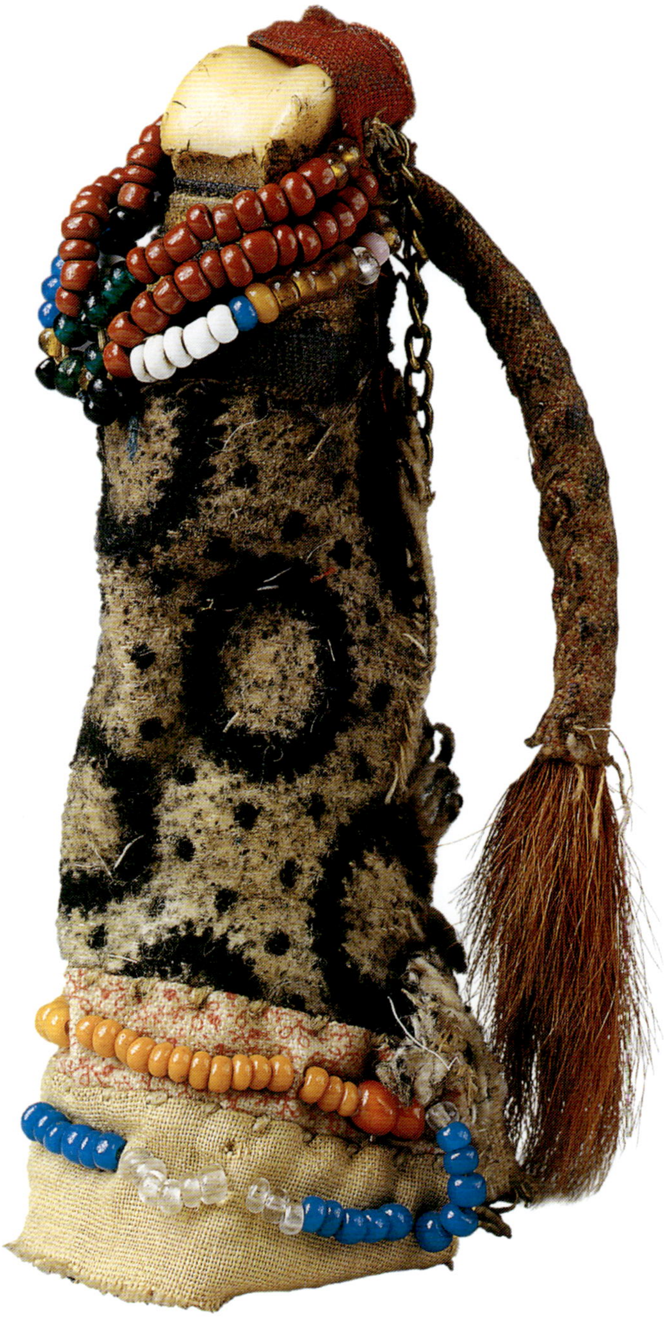

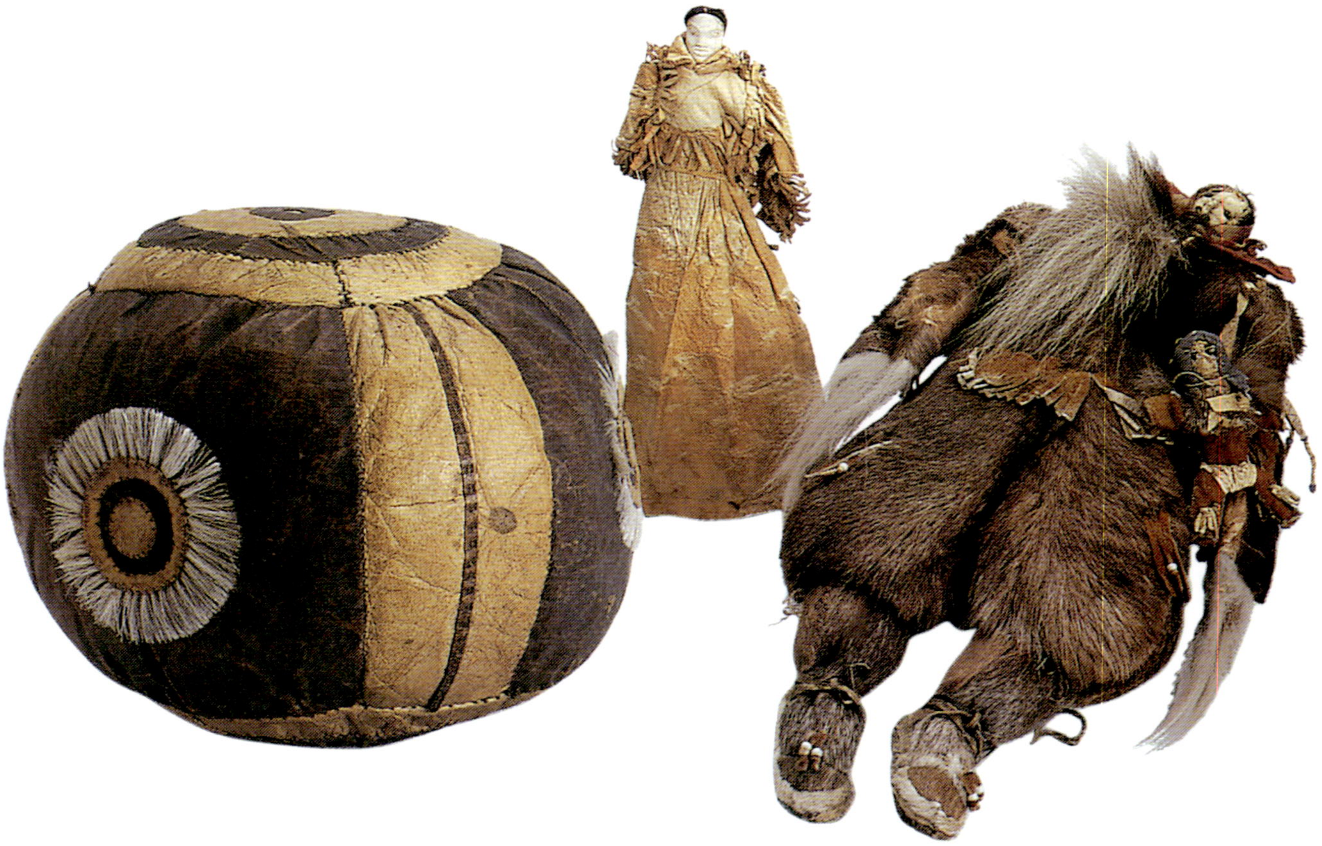

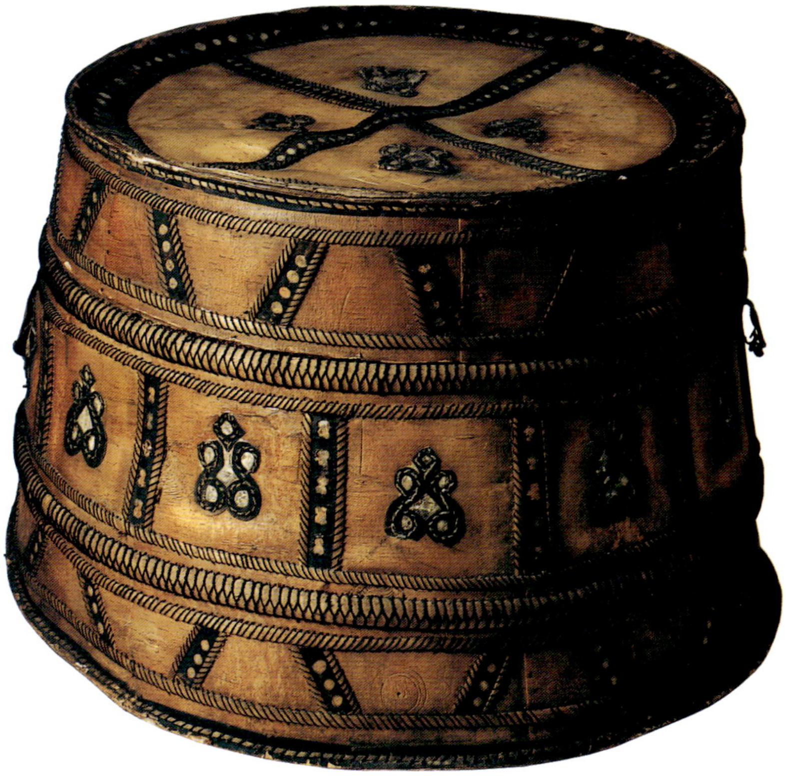

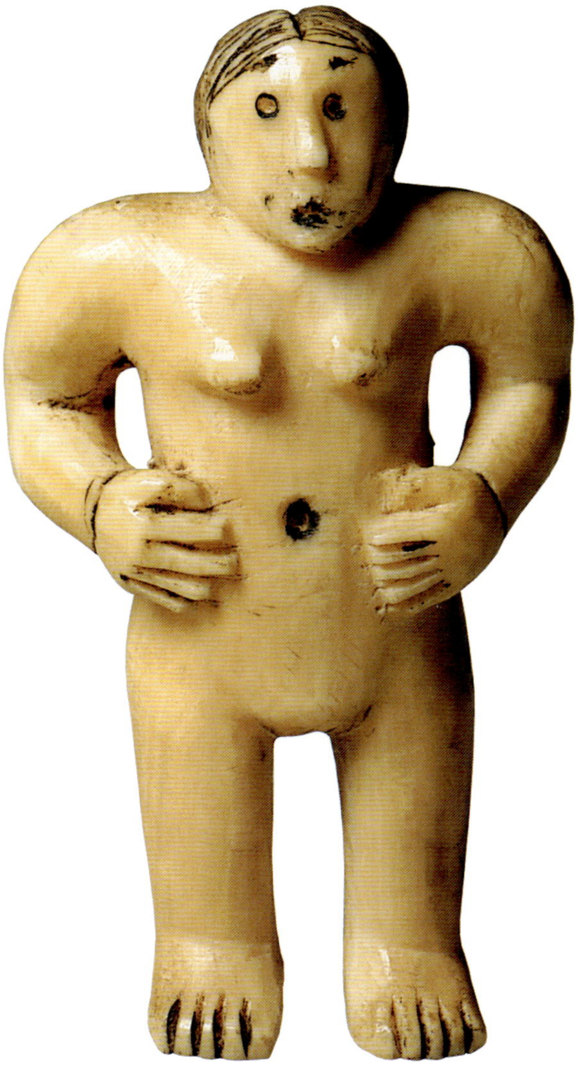

Chukchi, Tlingit,
Leather kickball and dolls, 1898, 1901.
Ball: sealskin, hair; Dolls: 1) marble, hair, cloth, buckskin; 2) reindeer skin, cotton cloth, beads, sinew, Ball: 17 cm; Dolls: 1) 25 cm; 2) 38 cm.
Museum of Anthropology and Ethnography, Moscow. Anadyr district.

Yakut,
Box for fur and silver things, 1906.
Birch bark, mica, paper, horsehair, leather, 37 cm x 57 cm; opening diameter: 48 cm.
Russian Museum of Ethnography, St. Petersburg. Yakut Oblast, Yakut Okrug.

Koryak,
Small plastic artwork 'Nude woman', 1911.
Walrus tusk ivory, 5.3 cm.
Russian Museum of Ethnography, St. Petersburg. Kamchatka Oblast.

from region to region not only in construction materials but also in shape – round, square, octagonal, and more besides. The roof of the yurt is held up in the centre by a wide post at an angle, which also acts as a chimney-flue. The entrance to the yurt, among the Buryats, is oriented towards the south; among the Yakuts it is towards the east. In some areas in summer, the yurt is replaced by a wigwam-like conical tent.

Buryats, even when they live in tents, are not really nomads, but keep to one particular district. Although the children of Mongols, once the terror of the world, there is nothing of the warrior about them, except their splendid horsemanship. Their saddles look high banked and uncomfortable, but they manage their horses, which are light brown with black manes and very swift, with wonderful agility. The Buryats live chiefly on milk, millet, and sheep killed on feast days. Their wealth consists in immense herds of cattle; some of them even possess four to five thousand head.

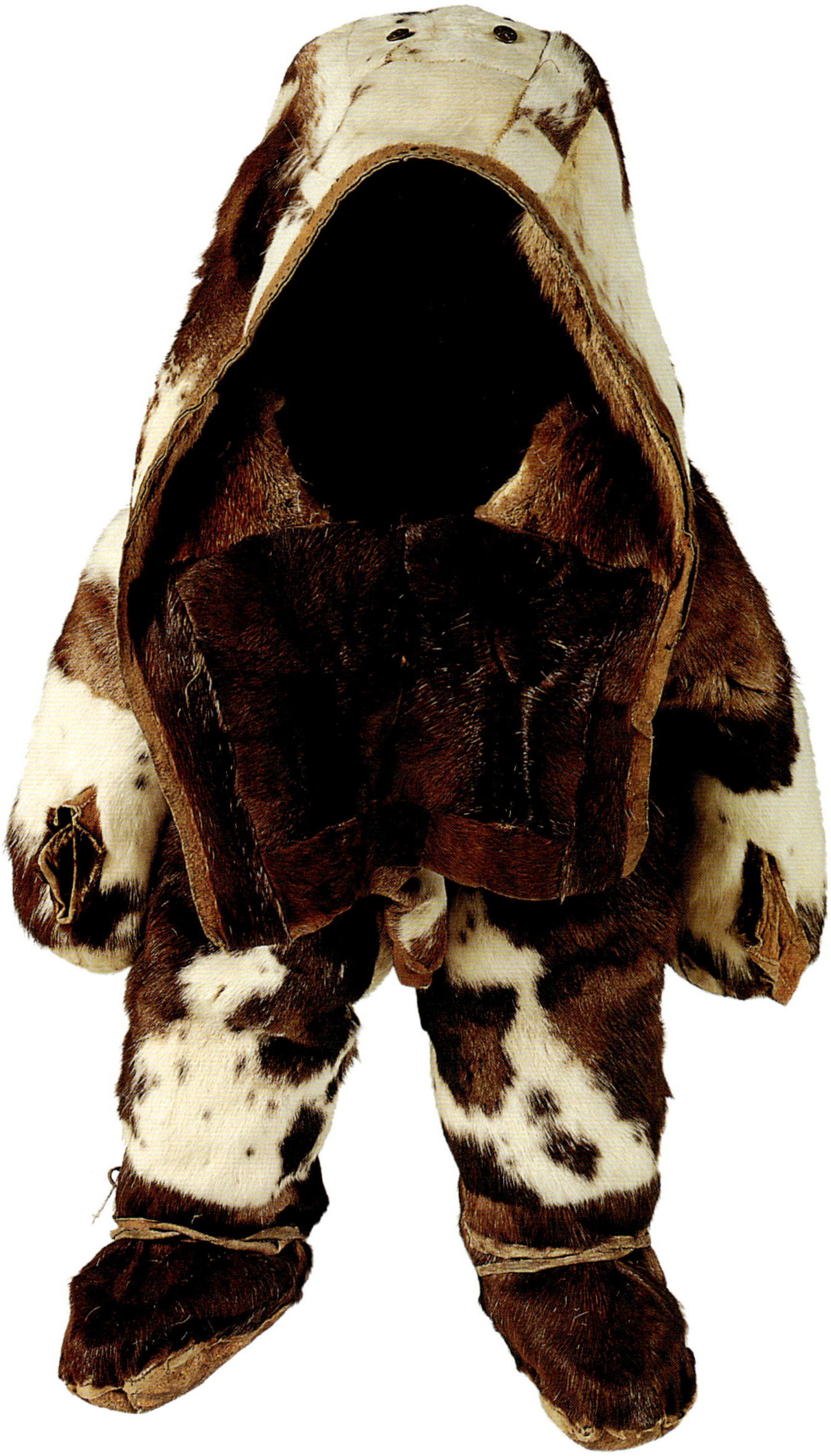

C. INDIGENOUS CLOTHING

"The tribal peoples have become masters of creating, with artistic skill and thoroughness, clothing that defies Nature's elements and expresses the human spirit."

As in many cultures, clothing is an essential aspect of the indigenous Siberian life. What a person wears is at once an indication of his or her status or rank, a means to artistic expression, and, of course, protection against the elements. Whether a garment is loose-fitting or tight, made from squirrel-skin, bear-skin or fish-skin, covered in elaborate decorations or plainly sewn, it serves a purpose in the physical and social life of the wearer. A wealthy Siberian native might wear a silver belt over his cloak; a reindeer hunter might prefer liberating, close-fitting leggings to the wide-legged skin trousers of the sledge driver; a woman awaiting her wedding might wear particular pieces or jewellry and part her hair a certain way, according to tradition.

The dress of the Kamchatkas in winter and summer is made for the most part of skins. Their winter costume consists of sealskin boots or *torbasses* worn over heavy reindeerskin stockings and coming to the knee; fur trousers with the hair inside; a foxskin hood with a face border of wolverine skin; and a heavy *kukhlianka*, or double fur overshirt, covering the body to the knees.

This is made of the thickest and softest reindeerskin, ornamented around the bottom with silk embroidery, trimmed at the sleeves and neck with glossy beaver, and furnished with a square flap under the chin, to be held up over the nose, and a hood behind the neck, to be drawn over the head in bad weather. In such a costume as this the Koryaks and the Chukchis defy for weeks at a time the severest cold, and sleep out on the snow safely and comfortably in temperatures of twenty, thirty, and even -40 degrees Fahrenheit.

When they leave the settlement to hunt, heavy *kukh-lankas*, or hunting-shirts of spotted deerskin, confined about the waist with a belt, and fringed round the bottom with the long black hair of the wolverine, cover the bodies of the Kamchatka people from the neck to the knee, ornamented here and there with strings of small coloured beads, tassels of scarlet leather, and bits of polished metal. Fur trousers, long boots of sealskin coming up to the thigh, and wolfskin hoods, with the ears of the animal standing erect on each side of the head, complete the costume, which enables free movement while keeping the body warm and covered.

The dress of the Buryats is partly Mongol and partly Russian, adapted for the specific conditions and activities of the people. Their caps are often conical in shape, made of quilted cloth and ornamented with a silken tassel attached to the apex. Their trousers have a Chinese appearance, but their coats were generally of sheepskin, after the Russian model. They decorate their belts with colorful bits of steel or brass.

Like many indigenous groups in Siberia, the Buryats favor a garment called the *dehar*. The Russian dehar is generally made of antelope or deer skin, and forms an admirable defence against cold. Often reaching to the heels, it touches the floor when the wearer stands erect. When the collar is turned up and brought

Koryak,
Children's overall, 1958.
Reindeer hide, dressed reindeer skin, 105 cm.
Russian Museum of Ethnography, St. Petersburg. Koryak National Okrug, Tigilski District, Sedanka village.

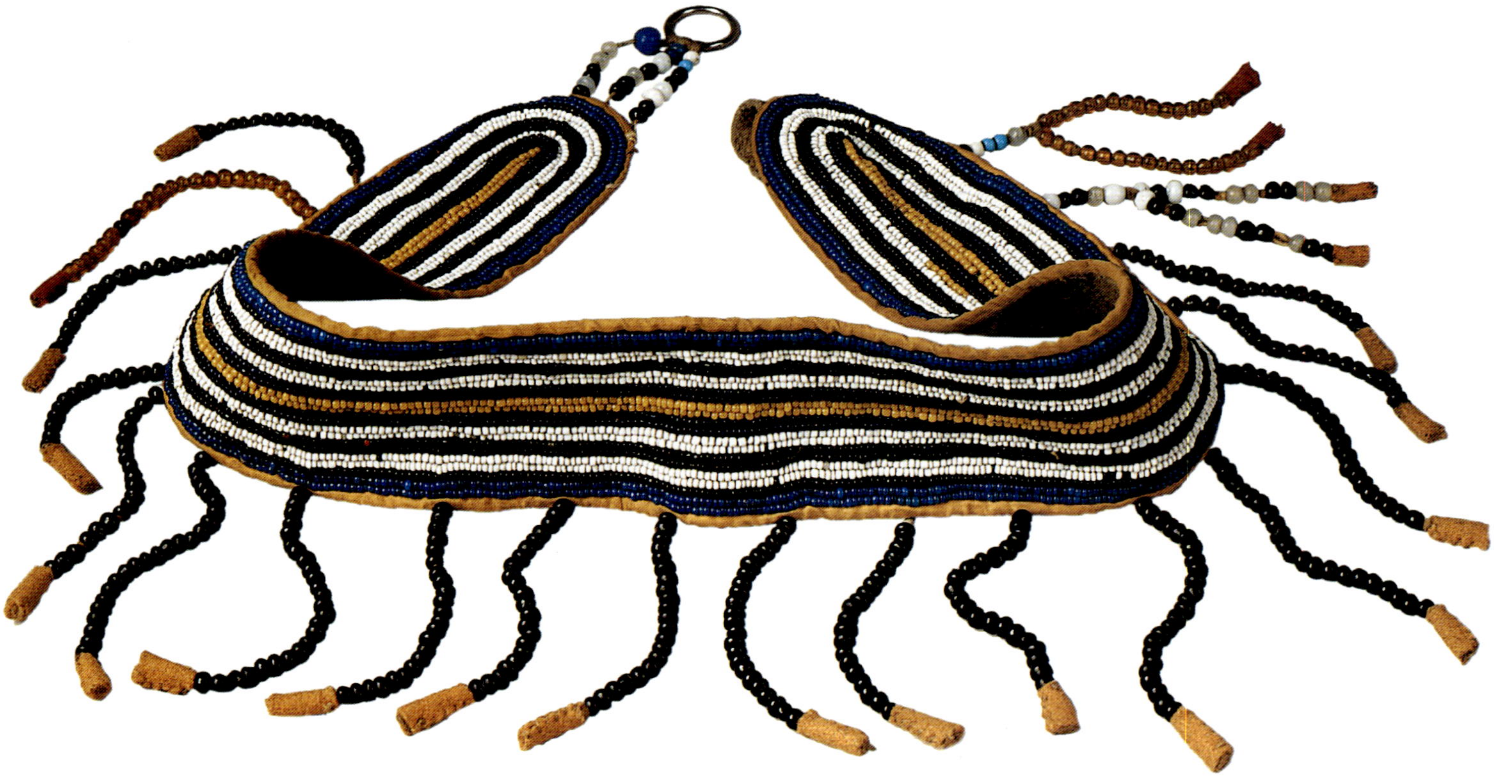

Evenki,
Woman's belt, early 20th century.
Dressed reindeer skin, beads and seed beads, metal, 91 x 9 cm.
Russian Museum of Ethnography, St. Petersburg. Siberian Krai, Turukhan district, the Nizhni (Lower) Tunguska river basin.

Chukchi,
Winter outfit of an elderly man, back view, 1904-1907.
Reindeer fur and leg fells, dog fur, seal undercoat, fabric, Parka: 93 cm; Cap: 27 cm.
Russian Museum of Ethnography, St. Petersburg. Primorskaya Oblast, Anadyr Krai.

together in front, the head is barely visible. The sleeves are four or five inches longer than the wearer's arms, and the width of the garment can be enough for two people. Walking is very difficult in a dehar, and its wearer often has a limited range of movement. However, the warmth of the garment atones for its cumbersome character, and its gigantic size is fully intentional. The length protects the feet and legs, the high collar warms the head, and the great width of the dehar allows it to be well wrapped about the body. The long sleeves cover the hands and preserve fingers from frostbite.

The costume of the Lamout is very effective, and has a theatrical character. It is made of the skin of very young deer, and is embroidered in fanciful designs with beads and dyed deer sinews. The fur cap and high moccasins reaching to the belt are also embroidered with beads. The waist is encircled by a belt, from which hangs the hunting knife, powder horn, and bag with bullets.

Reindeer fur is beautifully warm, which of course is why it is utilized so much by the aboriginal peoples of Siberia not only as an insulating covering for the ground and for the linings of the *chooms* and *yarangs*, but also in the making of clothing – especially clothing for the reindeer herdsmen and the hunters who are required to spend considerable periods of time out of doors during the winter.

The Nenets wear the *malitsa*, a large reindeer-fur tunic with an integral hood and mittens – the fur on the inside. When it becomes really cold, they put on, over the *malitsa*, another garment made of reindeer-hide called the *sokwi*, which

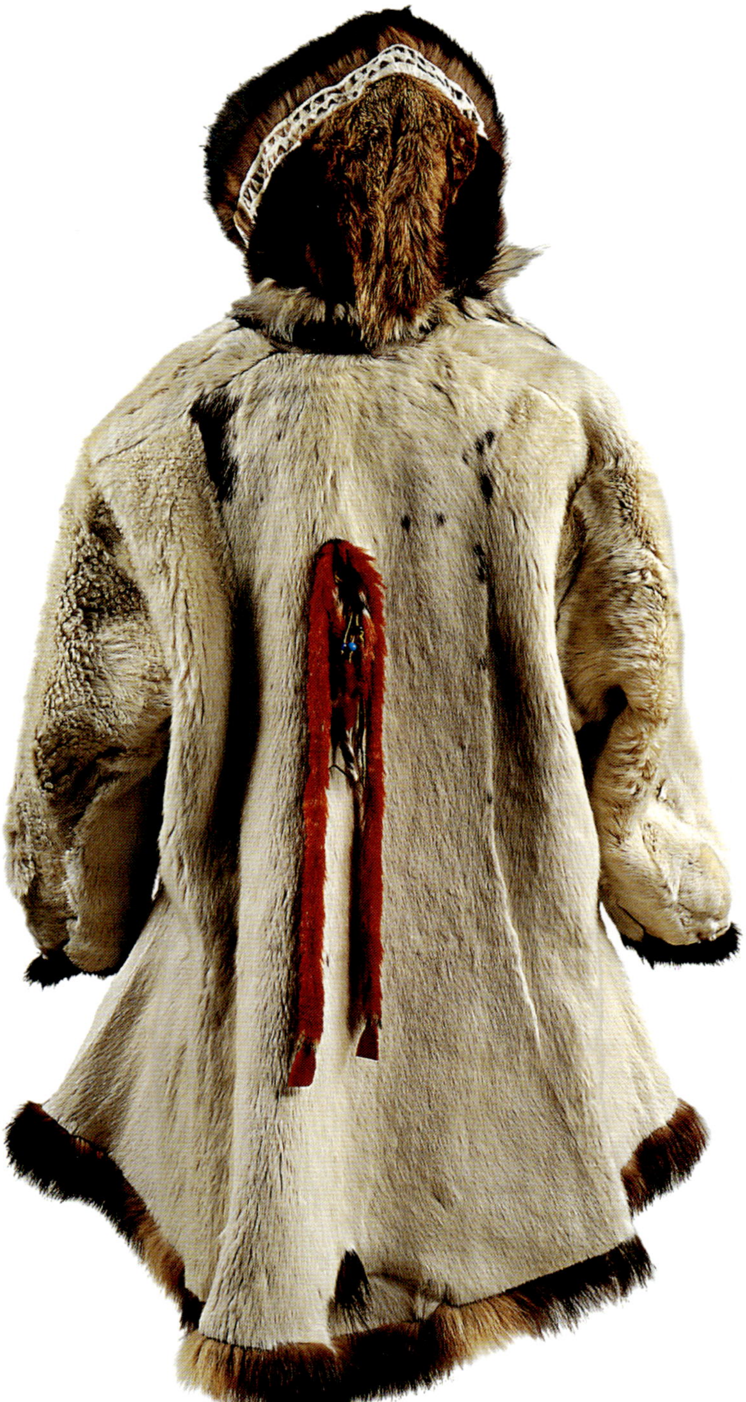

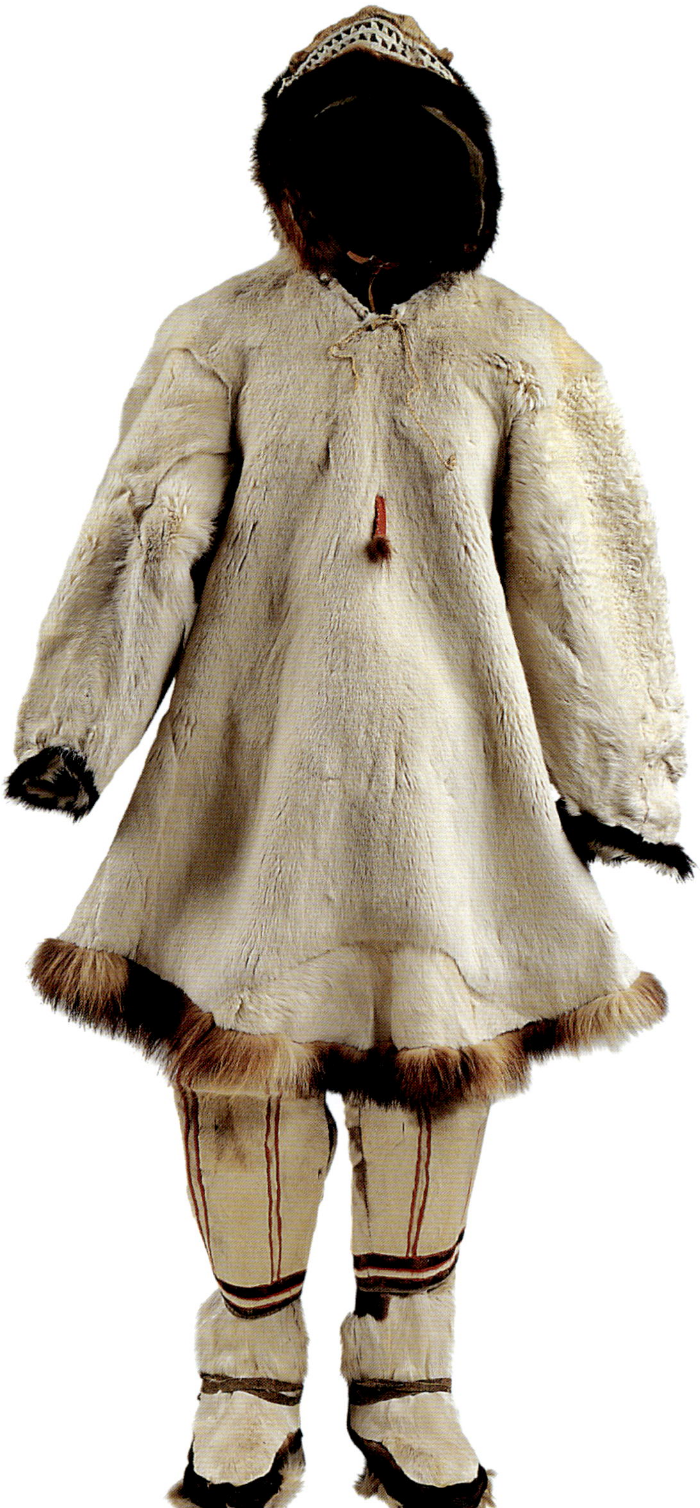

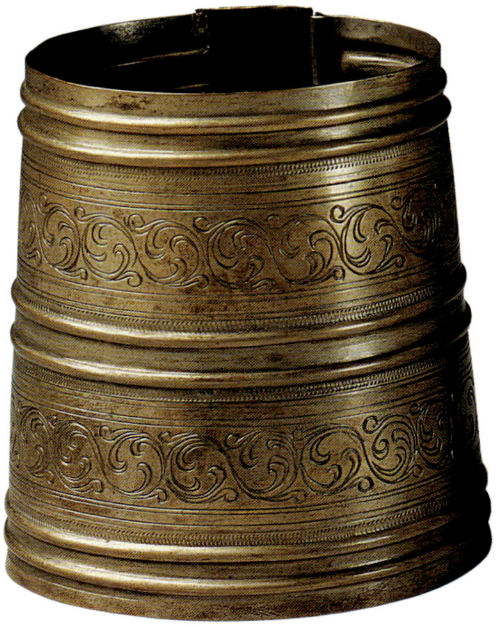

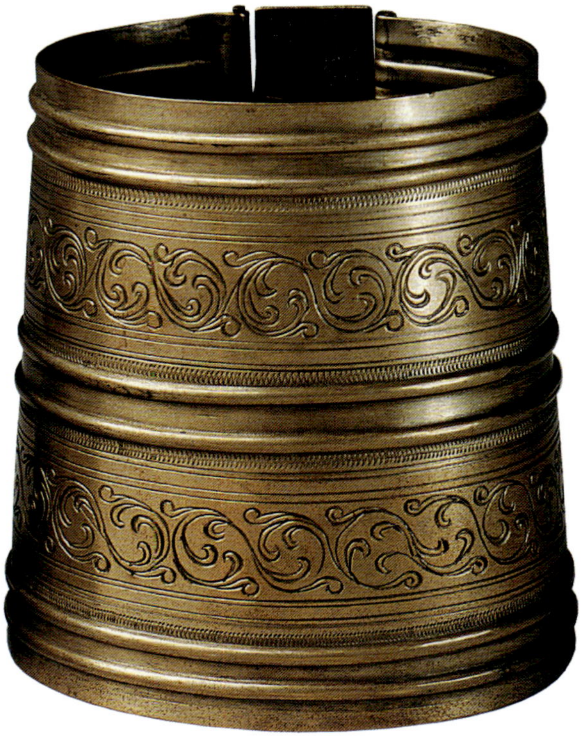

has its own hood. The *sokwi* of the Nenets and the Nganassani hunters is stitched together from different materials: from reindeer-skin at the back in order to keep the shoulders and lumbar region warm, and from dog-skin at the front in order to soundproof the movements of the hunters as they go. The costume of Nenet women is, with some trifling distinctions, nearly the same as that of the Ostyak women. They wear girdles around the waist, ornamented in front with large plates of brass, emblazoned with various figures. The plates are commonly of a circular form, and broad enough to cover nearly the whole of the chest. From these hang strings of beads and sounding pieces of metal, which dangle in front. Bells of metal are often fastened as ornaments to the elbows. The Nenets depend on furs for trade as well as clothing. Various specimens of foxes, which fetch high prices, come from this district, as do blue ermine, and ducks, the down of whose necks is very much prized for its exquisite beauty, and, after undergoing a certain process, is used to ornament pelisses.

The dress of the Koryaks is also of deer skin, and comprises a frock, pantaloons, and boots or leggings. Both sexes dress alike, and wear ornaments of beads in their ears. The Chukchis and the Koryaks wear the *kukhlianka*, a reindeer-fur double tunic – double because it is made in two pieces so that there is fur on the inside *and* on the outside, but summer clothing is of dressed skins alone. The neck and the sleeves of the *kukhlianka* are sometimes decorated with strips of dog or wolverine fur. The persons of the Chukchi are not peculiarly large, though their dress, which is of enormous size, gives them a gigantic appearance. Many men wear a long fur

Chukchi,
Winter outfit of an elderly man, front view, 1904-1907.
Reindeer fur, leg fells and bristle, dog and wolverine furs, dressed reindeer skin, fabric, Parka: 85 cm; Trousers: 101 cm; Sleeves: 53 cm; Shoe soles: 27 cm; Cap: 27 cm; Boot height: 17 cm.
Russian Museum of Ethnography, St. Petersburg. Primorskaya Oblast (region), Anadyr Krai (territory).

Yakut,
Woman's bracelets, 1904.
Metal, 8 cm.
Russian Museum of Ethnography, St. Petersburg. Yakut Oblast.

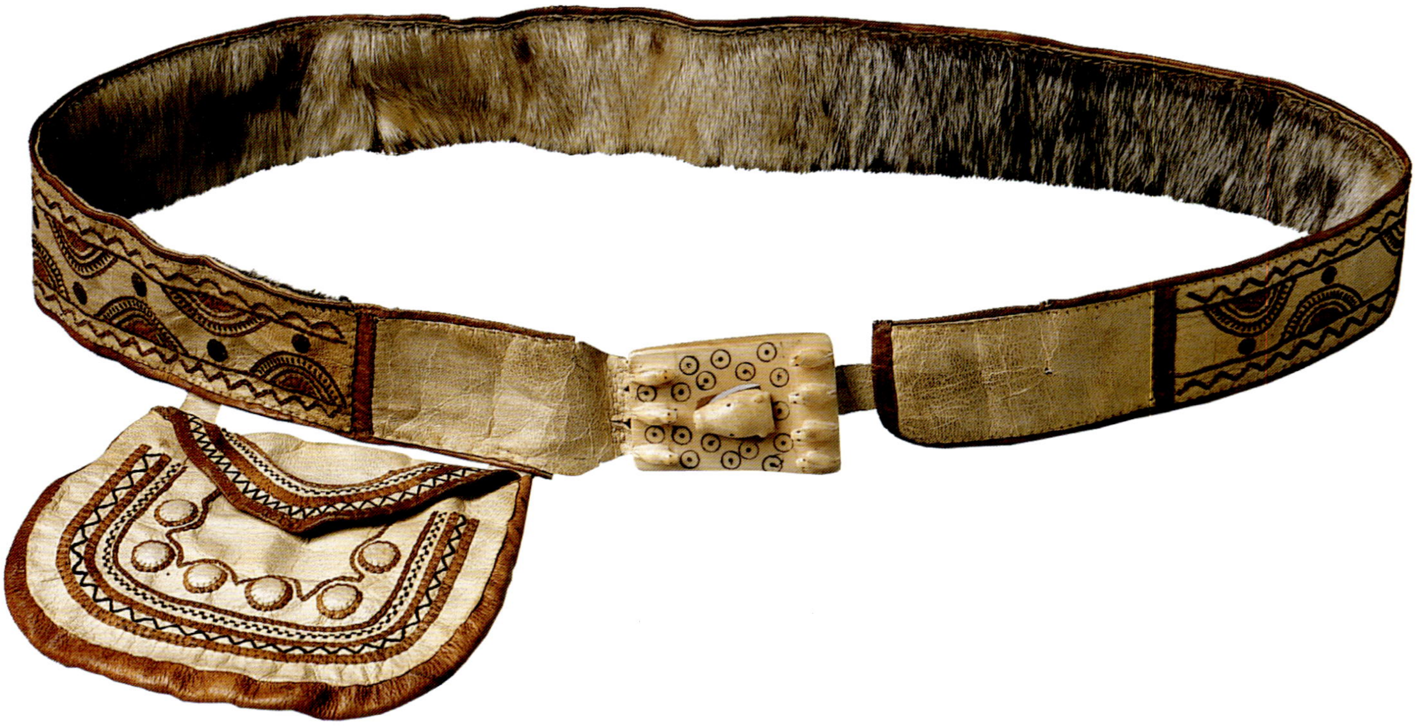

Eskimo,
Man's belt, 1909.
Seal hide and skin, walrus tusk ivory,
Belt: 100 cm; small bag: 5.8 x 3.9 cm.
Russian Museum of Ethnography,
St. Petersburg. Kamchatka Okrug,
Chukchi District.

Eveni,
Woman's outfit, back view, 1910, 1907.
Dressed reindeer skin, gopher and dog furs, seal and reindeer hair, beads,
Outfit: 91 cm; Cap: 30 x 28 cm.
Russian Museum of Ethnography,
St. Petersburg. Primorskaya Oblast,
Anadyr Krai.

coat of deerskin, fur trousers, moccasins, boots bordered with beaver, fur hood bordered with fox paws, and gloves of fox-fur. The clothing of the Chukchi is often embroidered with the skins of mice.

In these groups, the dress of either sex differs from that of other nations chiefly in their mode of ornamenting it. Often, it consists of trousers of the reindeer skin, with the hair inside, and stockings and boots of the same animal. A coat or jacket also of leather, sometimes lined with white foxes' or with hares' skins, supplies the place of a thick sort of short overcoat of double leather without the hair; and lastly, for the severity of winter, of a single or double frock with hair in and outside, the two leather sides being together. A warm cap and large gloves, with sometimes a guard for the breast, of white fox, called *nagroodnick*, or breast-cover, and a comforter round the neck, formed of the tails of the squirrel; such is their costume, which is almost wholly furnished from the skins of reindeer. Foxes' skins serve for caps and linings, and a wolf's is considered valuable, as the warmest of all outside garments. They have also a guard for the forehead, ears, nose, and chin. In summer, they wear nankeens, and at present most of the Koryaks and Chukchis wear a shirt. The women have also adopted the Russian head-dress. In trimming their garments, they are very skillful, and cut bits of deerskin into various fantastic shapes.

In general, winter costumes consist of the following garments: stockings made of the skins of reindeer, with the hair turned inward; high boots made of the skins

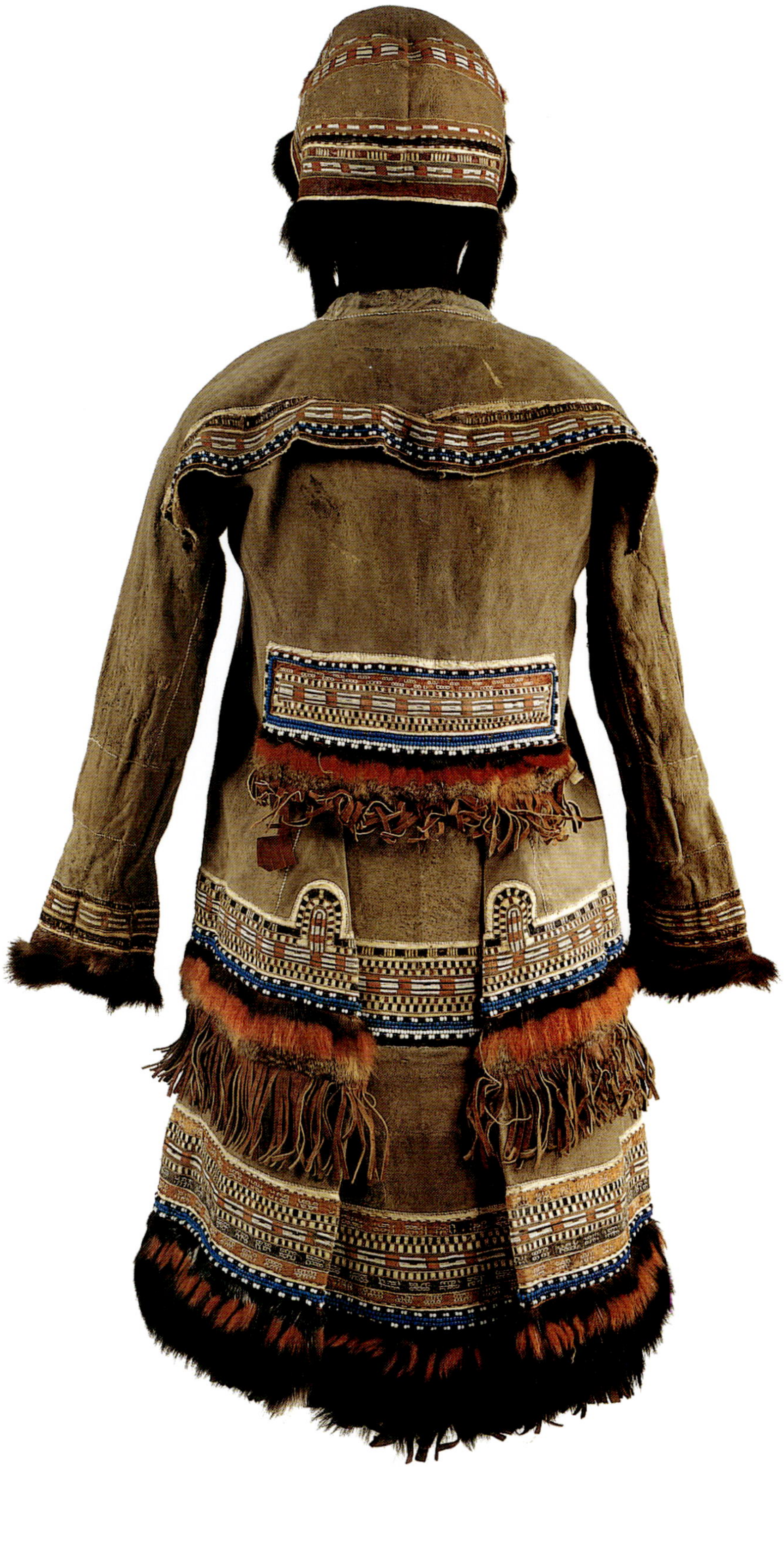

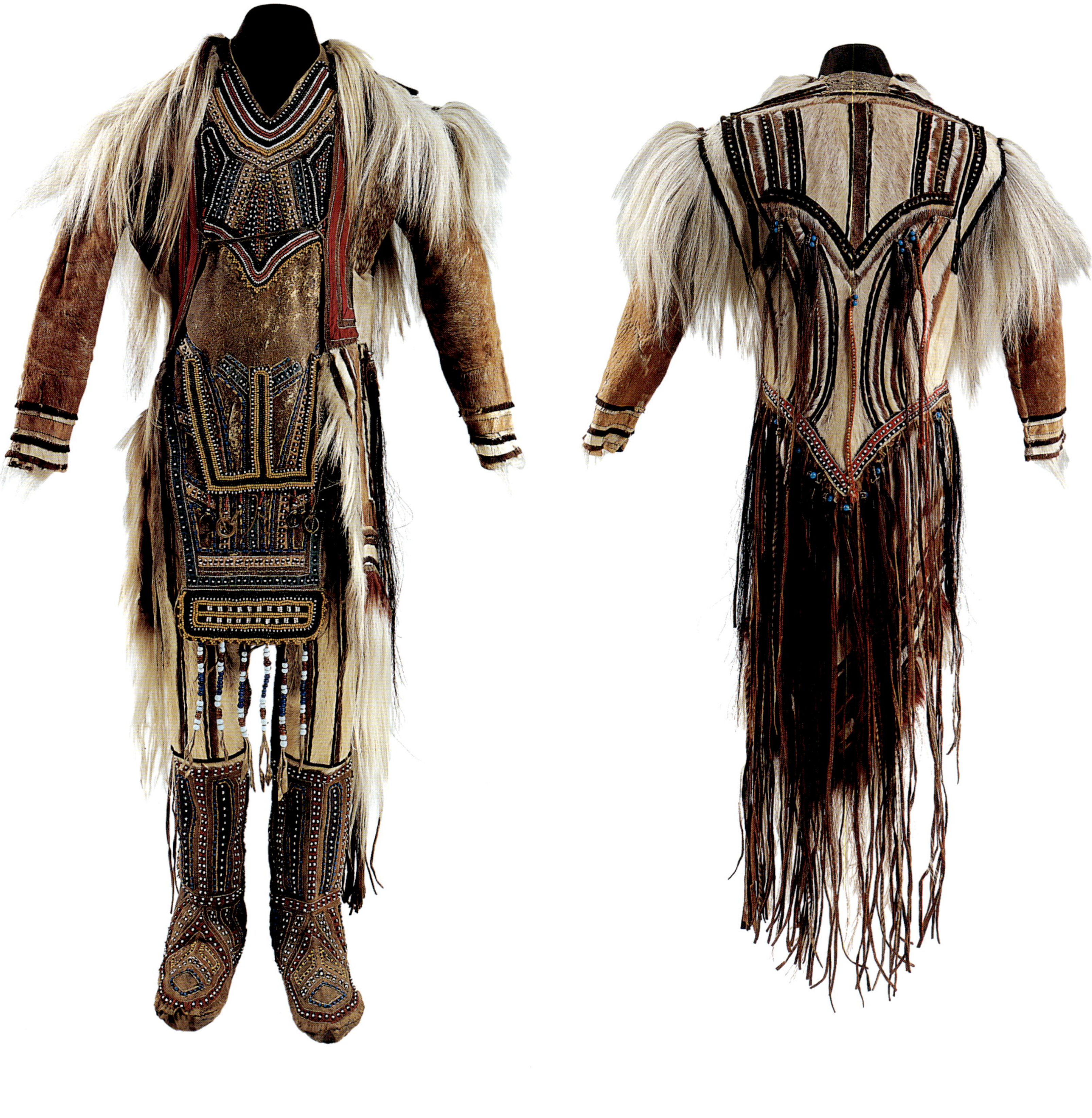

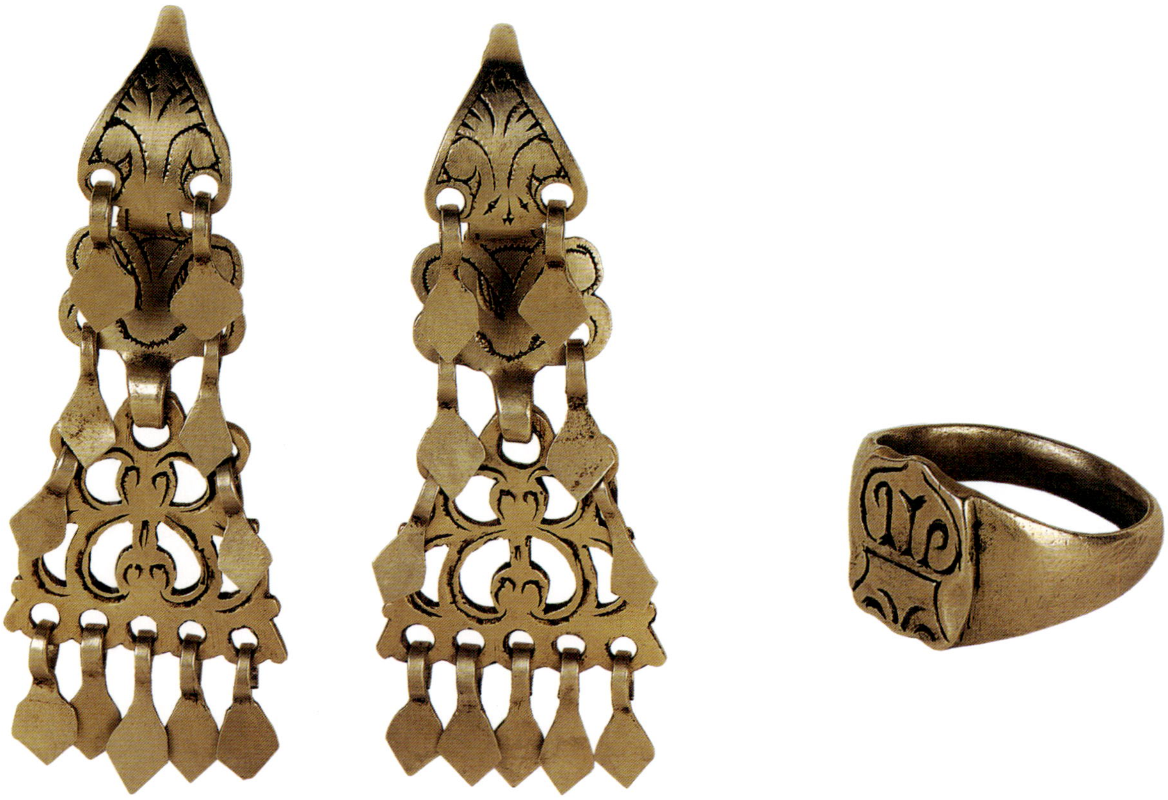

of the legs of the reindeer, and very roomy, so as to afford plenty of space for hay, with which they are well stuffed and which serves as insulation; under-clothes, trousers and vest of woollen cloth; an inner coat of the skins of reindeer, and a large overcoat of reindeer-skin. The coats are put on over the head like shirts; on the head, one frequently wears a large hood, covering the whole face, leaving an opening only for the eyes, a feature of the costume which enables one to travel long distances in the biting wind and blinding glare of the snowy expanses. The hands are protected by gloves of reindeer-skin. In particularly severe weather, a sledge-driver may wear two heavy kukhliankas, two thick reindeerskin hoods with long fringes of black bearskin pulled up over his head, and a squirrelskin mask to protect his nose and mouth from the driving snow.

Reindeer-skin snow-boots (*untiy*, *torbaza*, and other technical terms), ornamented with glass beads on the front and most often with a felt sole, are worn in all the regions of northern Siberia, even in the towns. Most articles of clothing made from reindeer skin are soaked and smeared with fish fat to further strengthen the material against the wind and wet weather.

The skin of the semi-domesticated reindeer varies from snow-white to dark grey or nut-brown. A brown skin with white spots is most sought-after for making festive clothes, which differ from ordinary everyday clothes in that they tend to be covered in metal ornaments or strands of multicoloured glass beads, or hung about with all kind of pendants (for instance, little furry animals dressed in the ethnic costume of the Eveni people).

From the month of April, the inhabitants of the tundra and the taiga have to shield their eyes against the reflection of the sun on the snow and against the wind. In the past they used to use special eyeshades split into two sections horizontally, made in metal, birch-bark or wood, or otherwise just lengths of coarse hair.

Evenki,
Girl's outfit, front view, 1905.
Dressed reindeer skin, horsehair, beads, seed beads, reindeer fur, cotton fabric, Caftan: 88 cm; Chest panel: 90 x 38 cm.
Russian Museum of Ethnography, St. Petersburg. Yenisey Gubernia.

Evenki,
Girl's caftan, back view, 1905.
Dressed reindeer skin, horsehair, beads, seed beads, 88 cm.
Russian Museum of Ethnography, St. Petersburg. Yenisey Gubernia.

Yakut,
Woman's earrings, man's ring, 1959.
Metal, Earrings: 8.7 cm; Ring: 2.2 cm.
Russian Museum of Ethnography, St. Petersburg. Yakut ASSR, Vilyuy District, Chochunsk village, Yakutsk.

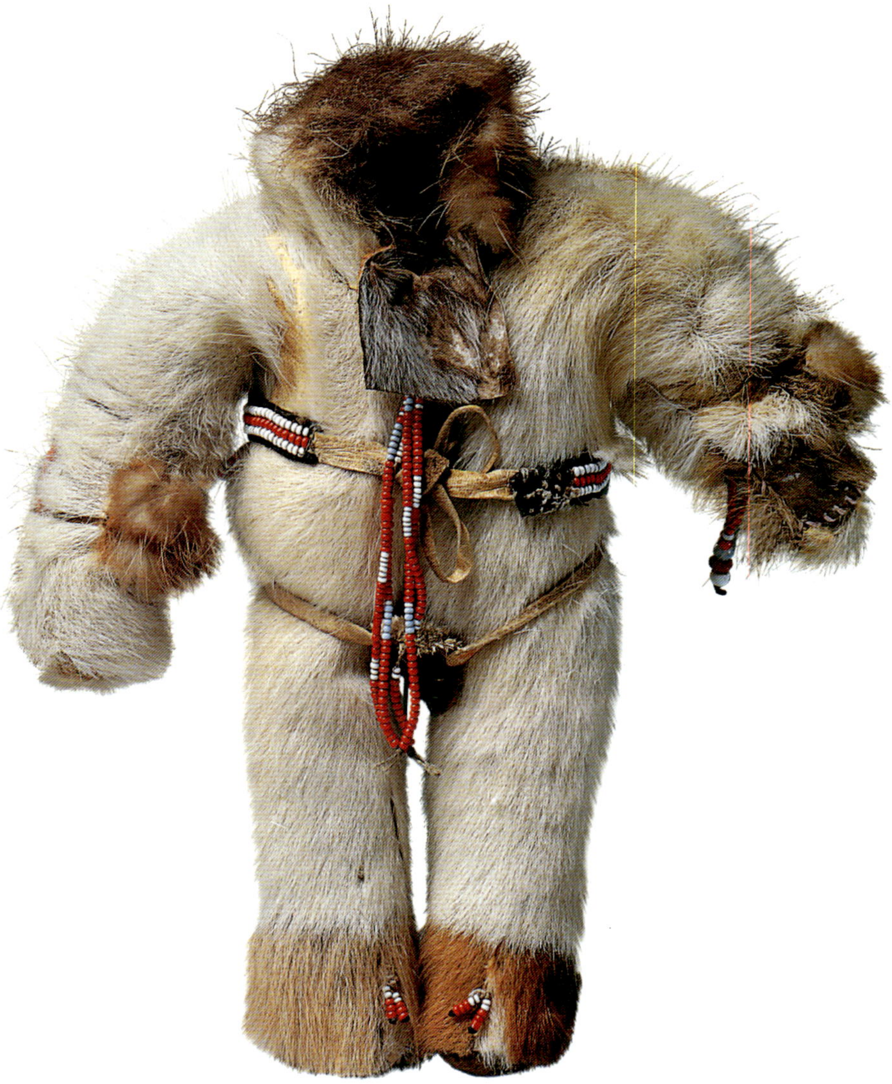

Koryak,
Doll-child, 1988.
Reindeer fur, beads, seed beads, dressed reindeer skin, 23.5 cm.
Russian Museum of Ethnography, St. Petersburg. Koryak Autonomous Okrug, Kamchatka Oblast, Achai-Vayam settlement.

Buryat,
Necklace with swans,
5th-4th century B. C.
Wood, leather, gold, 60 x 28 cm.
State Hermitage Museum, St. Petersburg.

By tradition, the summer clothing of the coastal people was always made of the skins (or various internal parts) of seals, walruses or bears, whereas winter clothing was made of reindeer-hide. Before they began to barter with the reindeer-herders, however, the Eskimos also used the skins and feathers of birds in their clothing. Today they wear fur socks and stockings, over which are knee-boots and trousers made of sealskin with the fur on the inside. In extremely cold conditions, like the Chukchis and Koryaks they wear the reindeer-skin *kukhlianka*. On top of all other clothing they can wear the *kamleyka*, a garment stitched together with the completely waterproof intestinal membrane of the walrus: it is particularly commonly used for hunting trips at sea where its remarkable waterproof and humidity-proof qualities are especially appreciated. The costume of the Amur river tribes consists of a fur hood, tight fur trousers, short deerskin boots, a Masonic apron, made of soft flexible buckskin and elaborately ornamented with beads and pieces of metal, and a garment similar to a frock-coat cut in very civilised style out of deerskin, and ornamented with long strings of coloured reindeer hair made into chenille.

Various parts of the fish are utilized in making summer clothes and footwear. The Nanai people and the Olchi wear vests and shirts made of fish-skin, decorated with embroidery and ordinarily having a round, Chinese-style collar

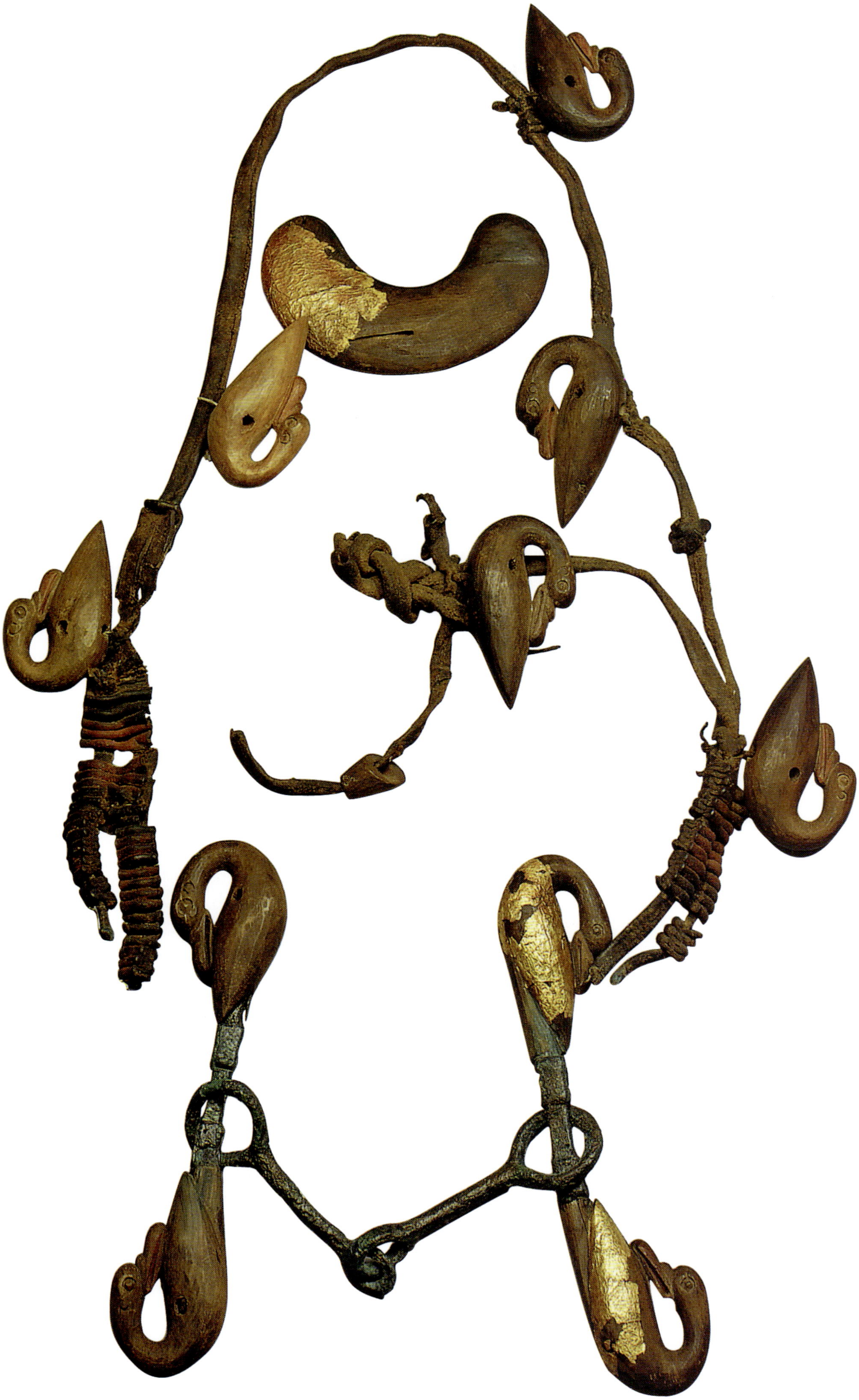

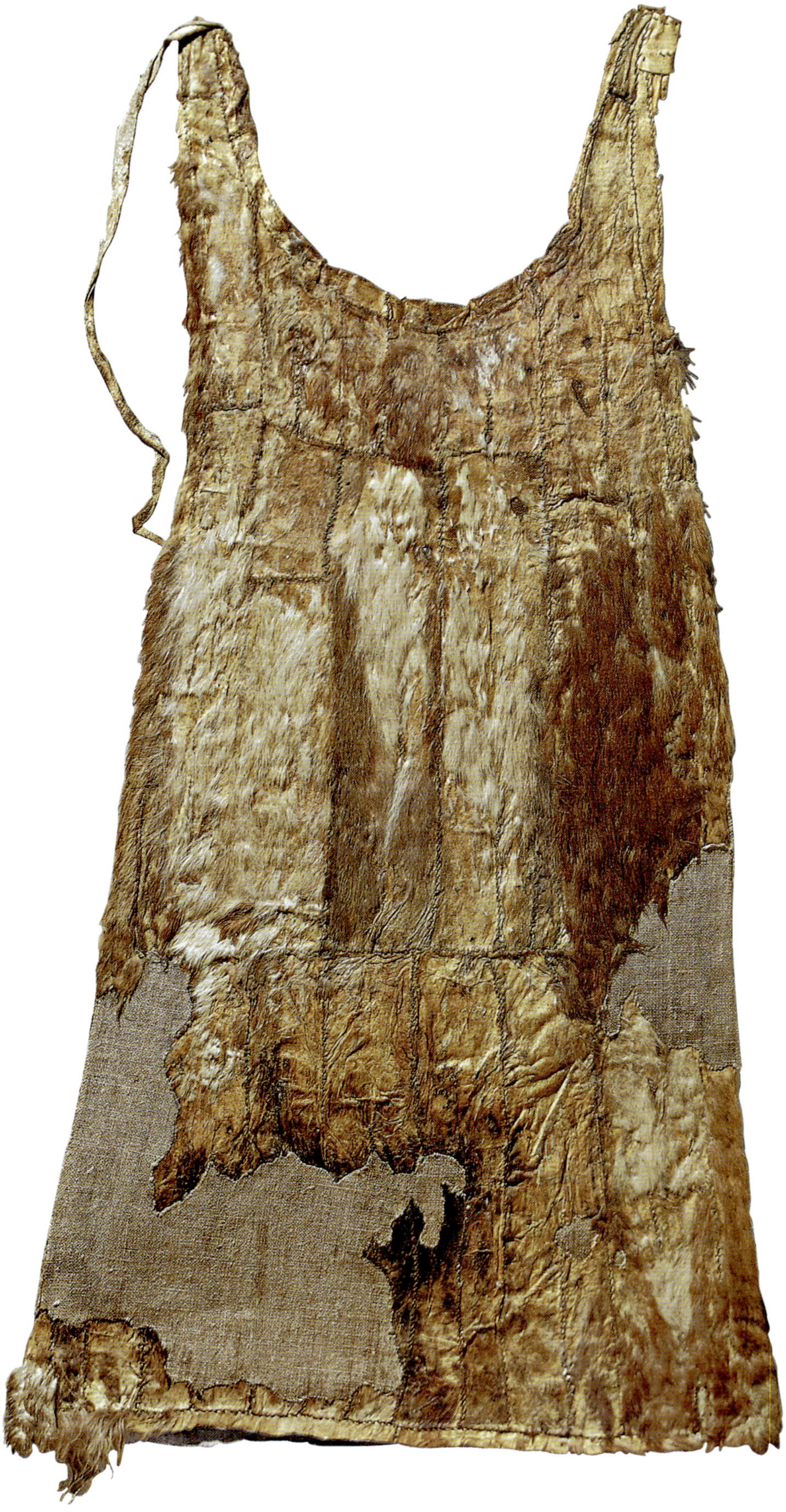

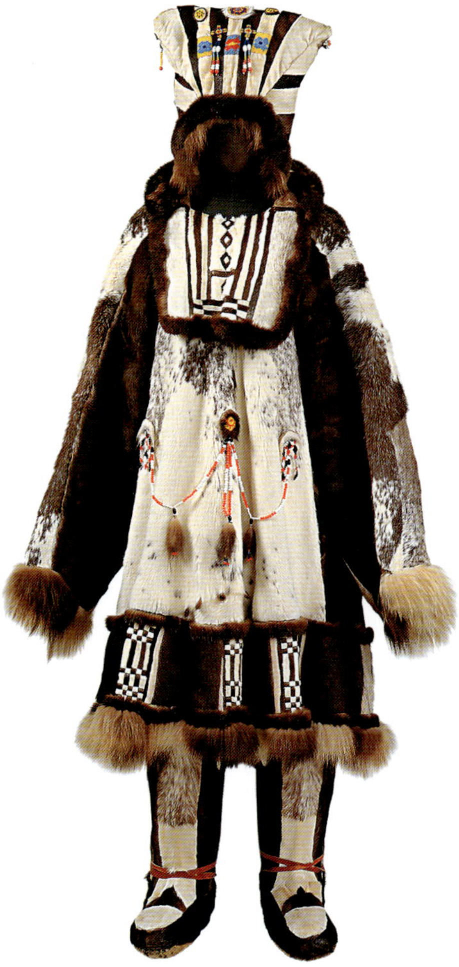

that does up on the right-hand side. The method of preparation of fish skins for clothing is fairly simple. The skins are dried and afterward pounded, the blows making them flexible and removing the scales. This done, they are ready to be sewn into garments. A coat of this material embroidered and otherwise decorated can be extremely beautiful, and sheds water remarkably well. Fish-skins are also used in making sails for boats. During festivals, young girls of the coastal areas adorn themselves in holiday dress, and wear large breastplates, made of rounded discs of metal linked together, over tunics embroidered with deer sinews dyed in various colours.

In winter, the traditional headgear of the Nanai people is conical in shape with a fur border; it is worn with round fish-skin ear-muffs that are furry on the inside and embroidered on the outside. In winter, the fish-skin clothes are lined with cotton. That is the time too for cloaks made of dog-fur or, more often, of reindeer-skin. Shoes, and even boots, made of fish-skin are light, waterproof and surprisingly heat-insulated: during the wintertime they can be padded with dry grasses that keep the feet beautifully warm. This is the customary practice of the peoples not only of the Amur but also of Manchuria and northern China.

The summer dress of the Yakuts consists of the *robasehka* (the Russian "over-shirt"), and the *balachbn*, a kind of blouse, both of cloth, long boots of soft leather, and wide breeches of the same material. The dress of the women differs from that of the men only by its greater length and its ornaments. In the winter

Buryat,
Apron, first century B. C.
Feathers, fabric, 60 x 33 cm.
State Hermitage Museum,
St. Petersburg.

Koryak,
Man's winter clothes, 1970s.
Reindeer hide and leg fells, dog fur, dressed reindeer skin, bearded seal skin, beads, Parka: 126 cm; Trousers: 106 and 110 cm; Footwear: 71 and 74 cm; Shoe soles: 32 and 31 cm; Cap: 32 cm x 33 cm.
Russian Museum of Ethnography, St. Petersburg. Koryak National Okrug, Kamchatka Oblast.

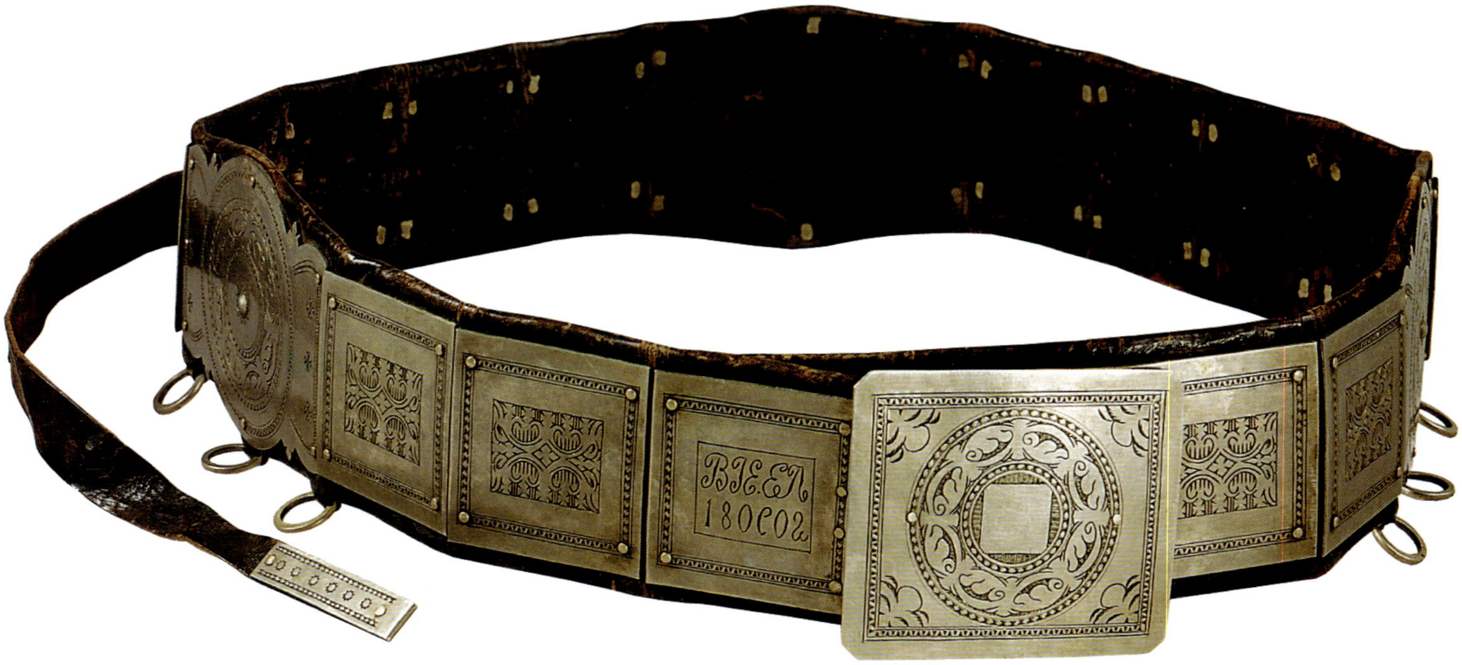

they dress in fur, more or less costly according to their circumstances. The warm skin of the polar hare is very much in use as lining. The fur-coat, which is made like a shirt and put on over the head, has usually a hood of the same material attached to it. Many Yakuts wear a tobacco-pouch with pipe and flint and steel, together with the indispensable long knife, attached to the belt about their waist. Frequenters of the taigas or Siberian forests are obliged to wear veils to protect their necks and faces against the massive swarms of mosquitos, gnats, and other vicious insects.

On their gala-days and festivals, the summer dress of the Khanty people consists of a shirt, commonly of red or yellow cloth, and sometimes of white linen. In the latter case, the collar as well as the borders below are of black cloth, trimmed with divers-coloured beads, and shining-tin or brass plates; shoes of cloth, of all colours, complete this costume. The every-day apparel of a Khanty woman resembles in all points that of the man, except that she wears a veil, which cannot be laid aside even when in her own yurt. Khanty men and women alike plait their hair in braids, one on either side of the head; but the woman's braids admit of much more adornment. Hanging down from her shoulders, their ends are united by a string, or flattened cord, about three inches broad, richly studded with beads. From this point the two braids fall together; and at certain distances, several other strings of beads are attached, and in that manner the hair descends almost to the heels. Each string of beads is, at its termination, fastened to a circular metal plate of the size of a coin, which, at the least movement of the head or body, striking against the glass beads, keeps up a constant, musical noise.

For such an occasion as a wedding, a man sometimes wears a richly-coloured yellow and crimson tunic, with a pair of black velvet trousers embroidered in various-coloured silks. He may sport a valuable green shawl round his waist. On

Yakut,
Man's belt, 1971.
Metal, leather, 126 x 7 cm.
Russian Museum of Ethnography, St. Petersburg. Yakut ASSR.

Nanai woman's fishskin coat, 1898-1899.
Dyed and undyed fishskin, thread, 104 cm.
American Museum of Natural History, New York. Amur River Region.

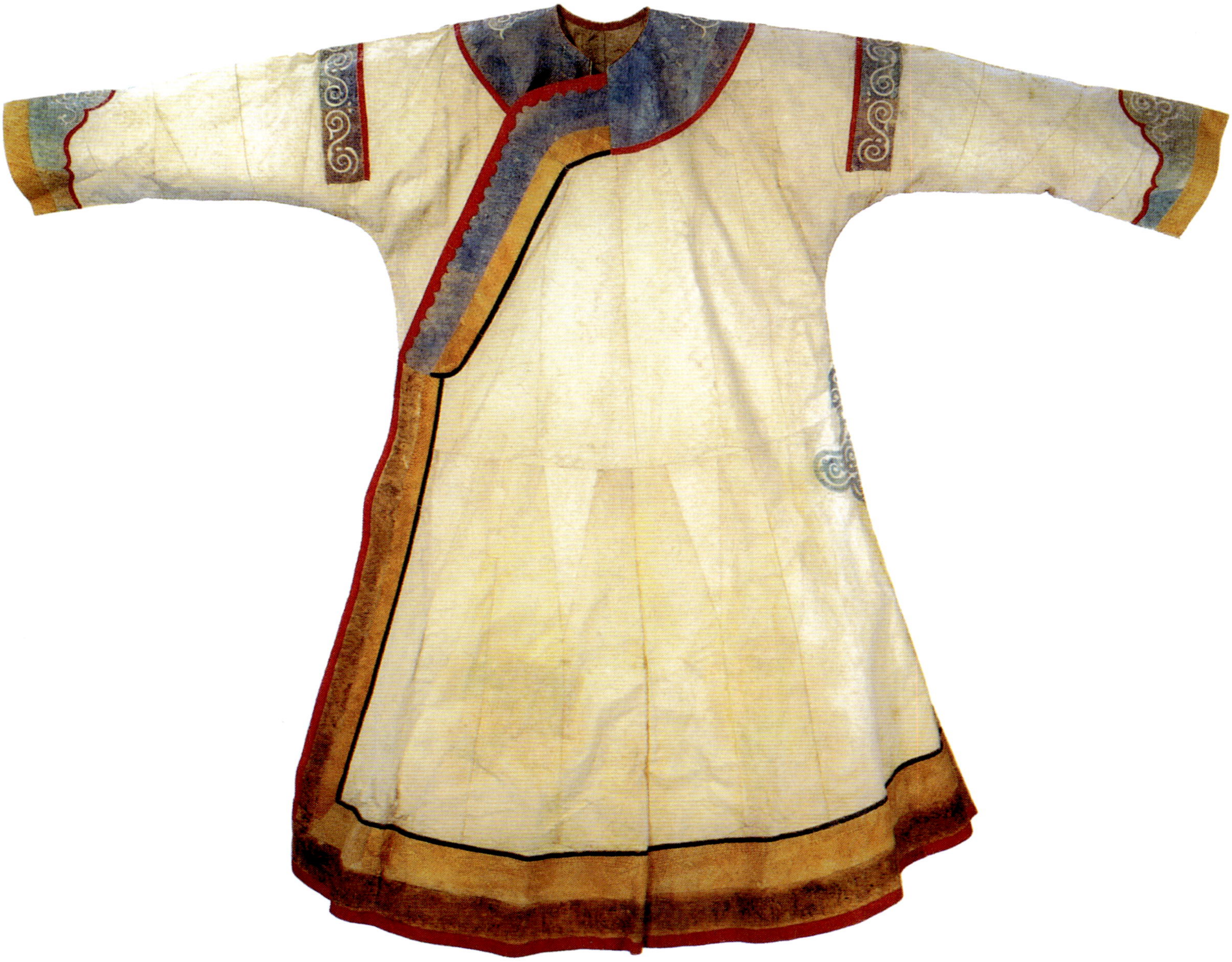

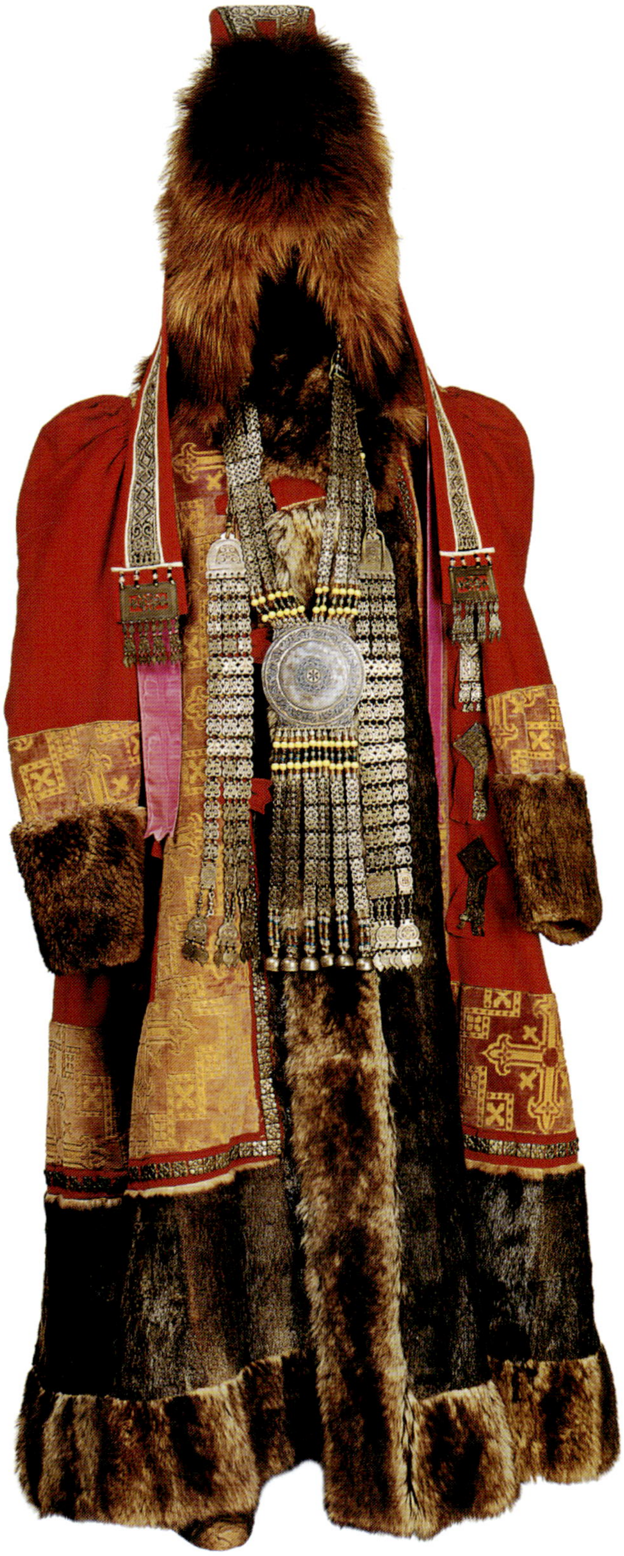

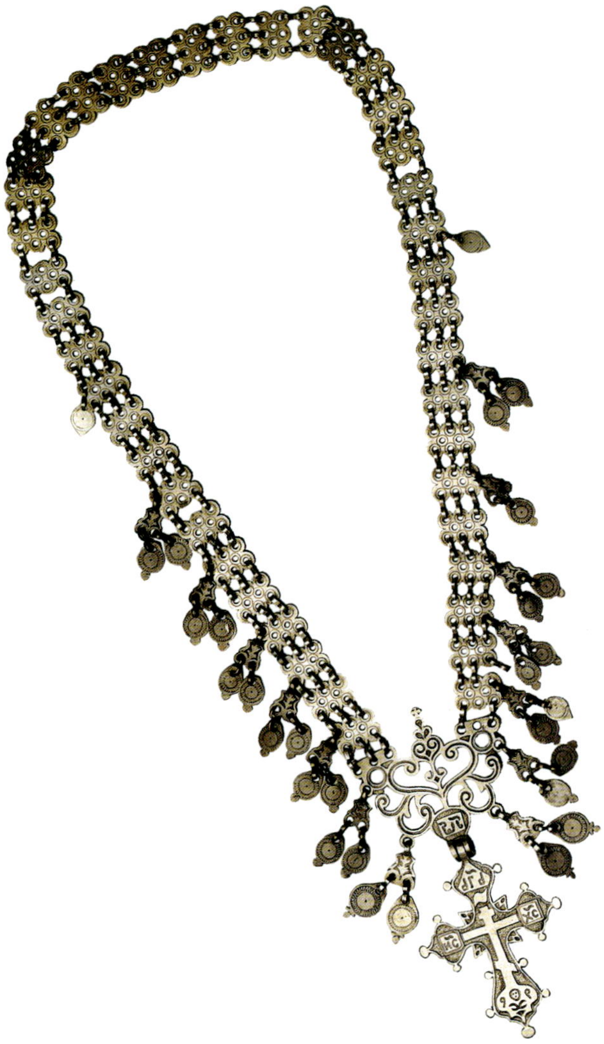

his head, the man wears a crimson cap, turned up with black fox-skin. His leather pouch is usually decorated with iron, inlaid with silver; in this he carries his flint, steel, tinder, and snuff bottle. A knife, pipe, and a whip, stuck in his sash, complete the outfit of the Siberian bridegroom.

As strange as the costume of the indigenous peoples of Siberia may seem to western observers, it was once even more elaborate. A traveller amongst the Kirghis community in 1860 was amazed by the savage beauty of the native dress. He recounts,

> *"Several [of the men] had horse-skin coats, with flowing manes down the centre of their backs; the skirts tucked into their trousers of yellow leather. On their heads they had horse-skin caps, with part of the mane on the top falling back like a helmet, which gave them a most ferocious aspect. Others had sheepskin coats, leather and fox-skin caps, with lappets hanging over their ears."*
>
> —Thomas W. Atkinson (1799-1861)

Much has changed, however, and among most of the peoples of Siberia, traditional costume is no longer worn at any time other than on ceremonial

Yakut,
Woman's holiday outfit, 1903, 1908.
Woolen cloth; brocade; furs of beaver, seal, gopher, wolverine, sable, lynx; metal; silver; silk; fabric; beads, Fur coat: 134 cm; Head gear: 70 cm; Head adornment: 97 cm.
Russian Museum of Ethnography, St. Petersburg. Yakut Oblast, Yakut Okrug, Boturuski Ulus (settlement).

Yakuts,
Cross, worn on the body, 1906.
Metal, 49 cm.
Russian Museum of Ethnography, St. Petersburg. Yakut Oblast, Yakut Okrug, Vostochno-Kangalaski Ulus.

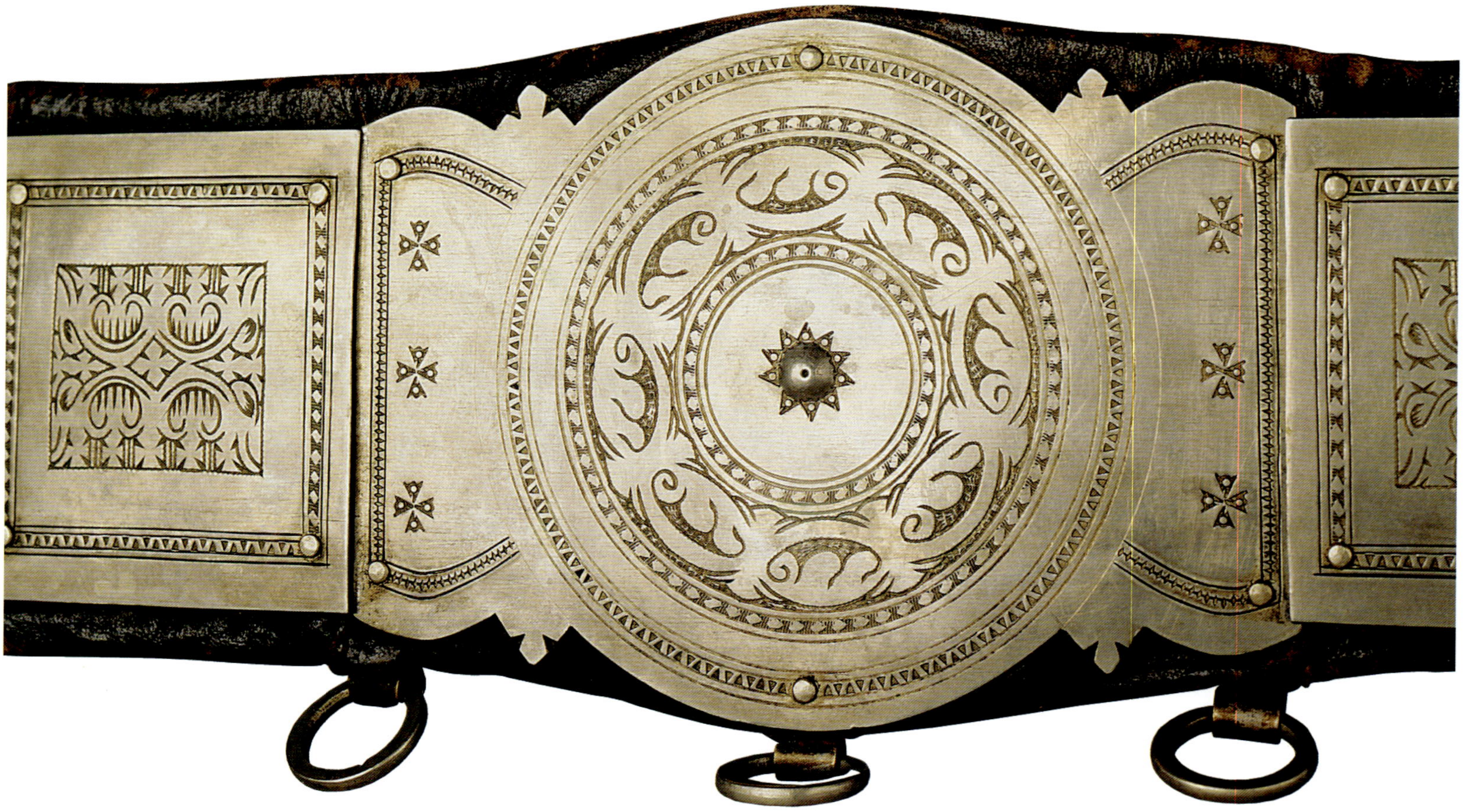

Yakut,
Man's belt, fragment, 1971.
Metal, leather,
Russian Museum of Ethnography,
St. Petersburg. Yakut ASSR.

Chukchi,
Woman's winter outfit, 1970s.
Reindeer fur and leg fells, dog fur, bearded seal skin, dressed reindeer skin, Length: 103 cm; Spread of sleeves: 170 cm.
Russian Museum of Ethnography,
St. Petersburg. Chukchi Peninsular.

occasions. Among the Yakuts it is the women who are then more colourfully dressed, for onto their costumes are sewn the furs of marmot, beaver and sable. The lining is of red and green cloth or even Chinese silk. The outside is decorated with embroidery, beads and silver ornaments. This form of costume, which in the old days was passed down from mother to daughter, is completed by a fur hat crowned with a little cloth top-piece with pointed edges. On the hat are many silver decorations, while similar carved silver ornaments of more complex design hang from the wearer's ears and as wider panels over the breast and back.

With the influence of European Russia, indigenous people have been exposed to western dress, and will chose it for daily wear. For dancing and festivities, many Siberians appear in full dress with fur-boots, wide fur trousers and fur-lined velveteen coats. In groups bearing significant Mongol influence, the women wind their hair in a peculiar knot, near the nape of the neck. They pierce this knot with two long pins like knitting needles, and trim it with bright ribbons and real or artificial flowers. They have earrings, bracelets, and finger rings in profusion, displaying considerable taste and care in the adornment of their bodies.

Metalworking, particularly silversmithing, is a craft that has been much practised over the centuries and that flourishes even now in Yakutia. Women there continue to wear their traditional jewellery – especially rings, necklaces and decorated earrings. The head-coverings of some are in the shape of tablets, falling

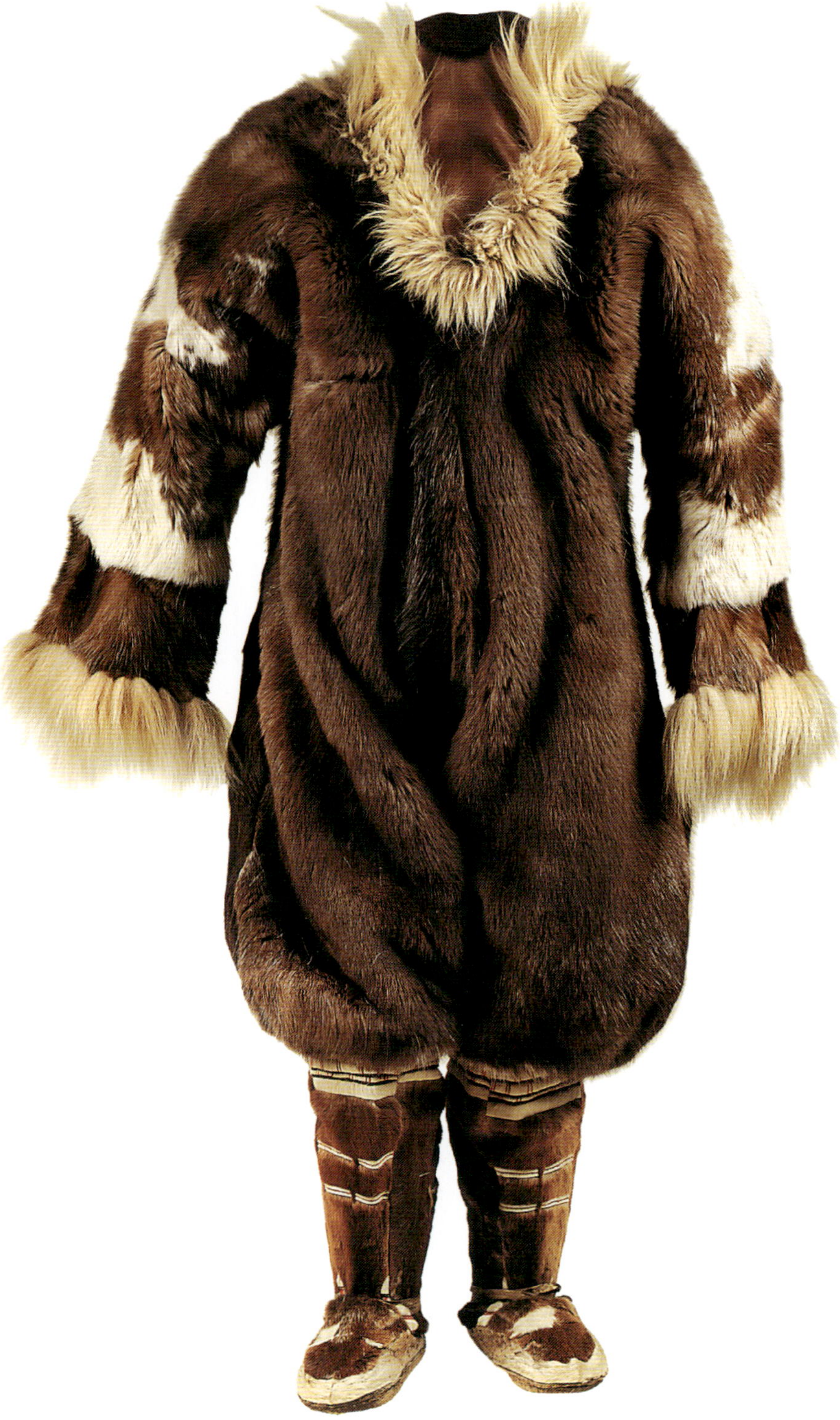

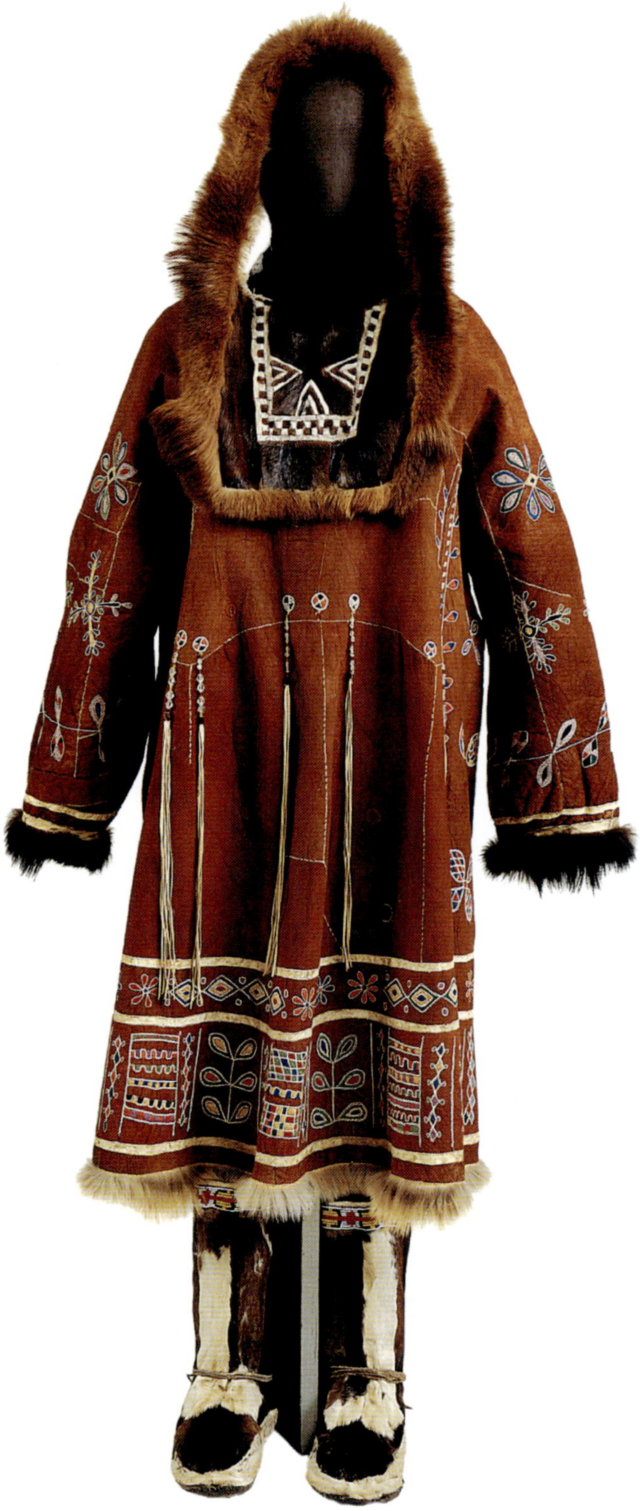

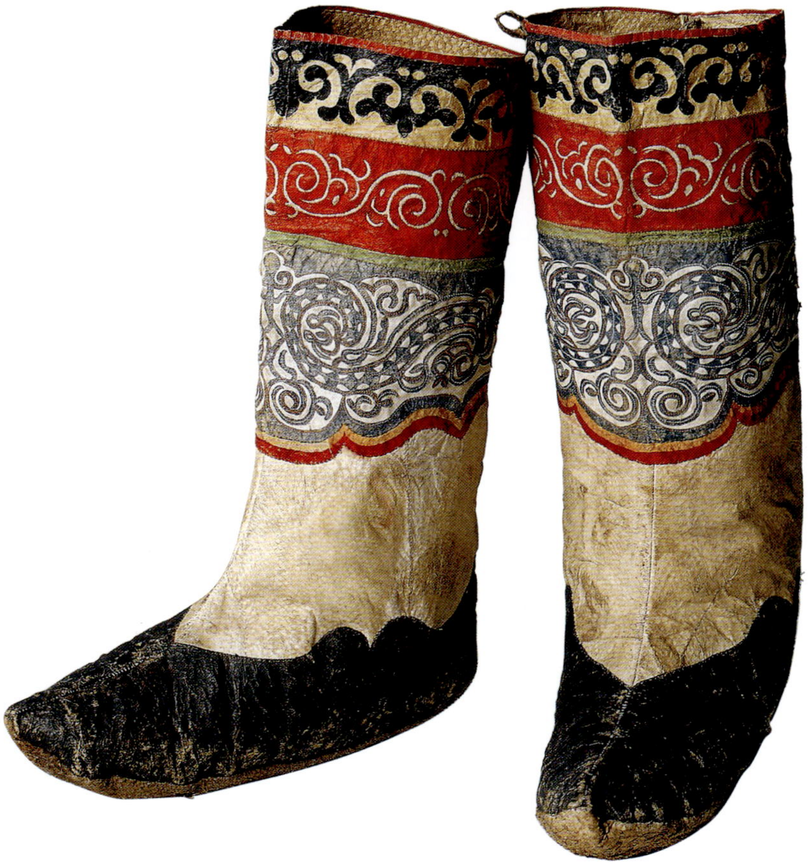

in a perpendicular line on the forehead. Some women's costumes are studded with a quantity of silver and gold coins, giving forth a sound at every movement of the head. Other head-dresses are fashioned in the shape of diadems, cut out at the top in the form of a crescent, the ends of which projected on both sides, like two horns. These diadems, like the tablets, are adorned with a number of plates and studs of brass and of other metals. Some women have their bosoms and necks covered with silver and gold medals of various sizes, and a portion being bored and strung together to form a sort of costly necklace.

In addition, the Yakuts carve and make sculptures out of wood and, from the 18th century, out of mammoth-tusk ivory – earrings, bracelets, ornamental combs and trinket-boxes, little statuettes, and so on. Such handicrafts merely add lustre to the skills they demonstrate in working with skins and furs.

The indigenous people of Siberia exhibit considerable talent and efficiency in their creation of clothing. Centuries of life in the challenging climate of the tundra or taiga have taught them how to use every resource available to them, every scrap of reindeer fur or fish skin, in order to protect their bodies from the cruel weather. But besides these strictly practical considerations, the garments and lifestyles that represent the cultural heritage of the peoples of the north revolve around many traditions, rituals, customs, rules and taboos that flow from a specific way of thinking, a highly particular conception of the world: the beliefs and practices associated with Shamanism.

Koryak,
Woman's holiday clothes, 1970s.
Reindeer hide and leg fells, dog fur, dressed reindeer skin, embroidery thread, beads, Parka: 127 cm; Shoe soles: 26 cm; Boot height: 28 cm; Span of sleeves: 130 cm.
Russian Museum of Ethnography, St. Petersburg. Koryak National Okrug, Kamchatka Oblast, Karaga village.

Amur region,
Boots.
Reindeer skin, fish scales, fabric, eggs, soot.
Russian Museum of Ethnography, St. Petersburg.

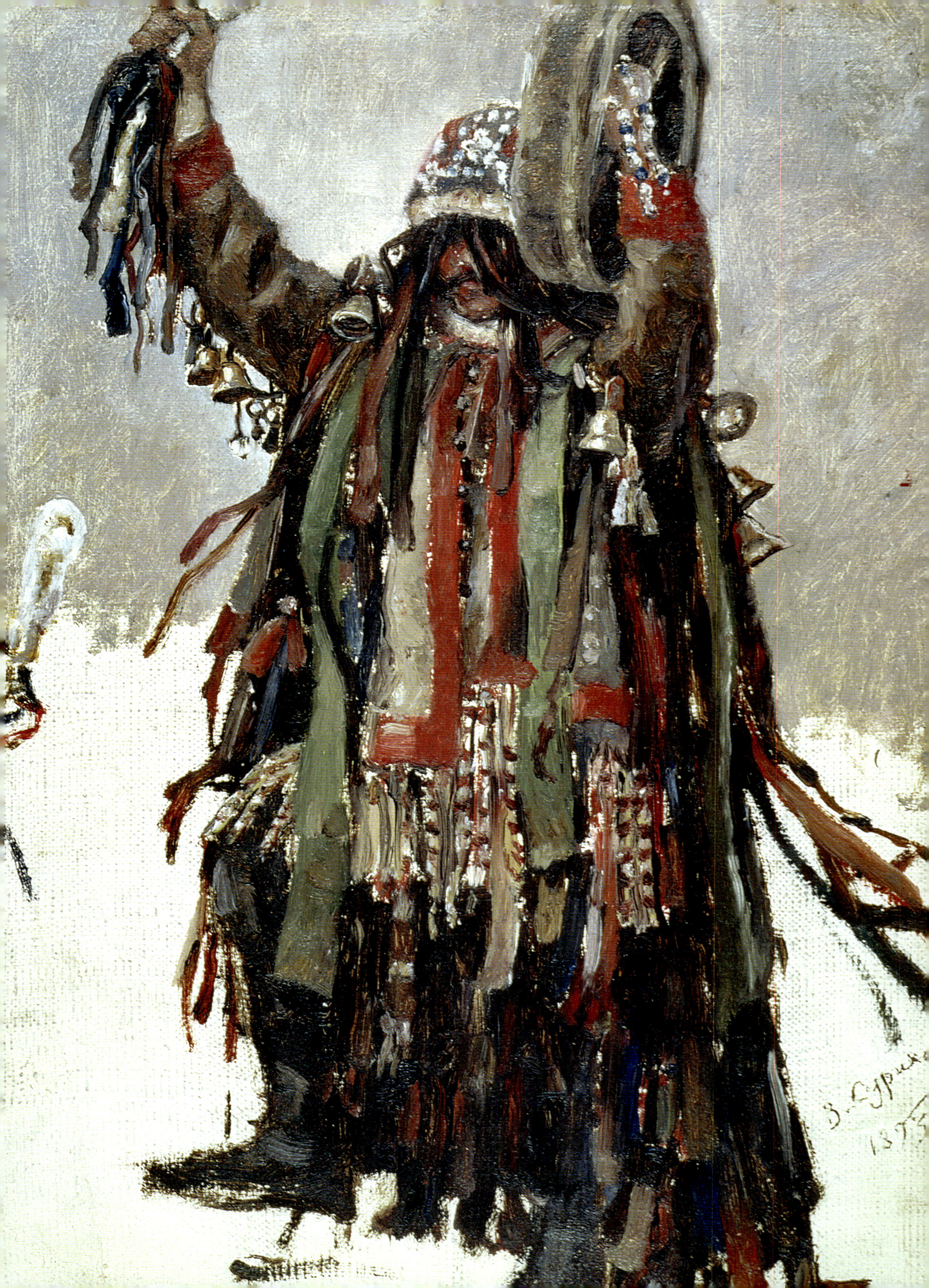

III: SHAMANISM

INTRODUCTION

Shamanism is understood by some people to be a primitive form of religion or religio-magic practised by the aborigines of northern Asia as well as by all other aborigines in other parts of the world. Shamanism was only one form of expression of the religious cult of northern Asia, practised in order to avert the evil spirits.

One must not lose sight of the fact that in the various beliefs of the Siberian tribes a very close connexion is noticeable, and, there can also be observed an uninterrupted identity in the foundations of their mythology, and in their rites, even extending as far as the nomenclature - all of which gives one the right to suppose that these beliefs are the result of the joint work of the intellectual activity of the whole north of Asia.

The old national religion of the Mongols and the neighbouring nations is known in Europe as "Shamanism," whereas among those who are not its followers it has no special name.

Shamanism was called "The Black Faith" (*Khara Shadjin*), in contradistinction to Buddhism, which they called "Yellow Faith" (*Shira Shadjin*). The Chinese call Shamanism *Tao-Shen* ("gambolling before the spirits").

Those names, however, do not give any idea of the true character of Shamanism. Some are of the opinion that it originated alongside with Brahminism and Buddhism, while others find in it some elements in common with the teachings of the Chinese philosopher Lao-Tze. Many hold that Shamanism is nothing but Nature-worship, likening it to the faith of the followers of Zoroaster. Careful study of the subject shows that the Shamanistic religion did not arise out of Buddhism or any other religion, but originated among the Mongolic nations, and consists not only in superstitious and shamanistic ceremonies, but in a certain primitive way of observing the outer world – Nature – and the inner world - the soul.

We find Shamanism all over northern and part of central Asia. As we see them now, the Palaeo-Siberians may be considered as possessing the simplest, and the Neo-Siberians the most complex, form of Shamanism. Thus among the former we see more 'family' than 'professional' Shamanism; that is, the ceremonials, beliefs, and shamans are practically limited to the family. Professional Shamanism, that is, ceremonies of a communal kind performed by a specialized or professional shaman, was here only in its infancy, and, being weaker, has been more affected by Christianity.

Among the Neo-Siberians, where professional Shamanism is strongly developed (for example, among the Yakut), family Shamanism has been more affected by European influences. We cannot, however, argue from this that the Palaeo-Siberian form is the more primitive. Professional Shamanism may be a development of family Shamanism, or it may be a degenerate form, where environment is such that communal life is no longer possible.

That the dissimilarity between the Shamanism of the Palaeo and Neo-Siberians is no doubt due to the differences in the geographical conditions of

Vasily Surikov,
A Shaman, sketch for 'The Conquest of Siberia by Yermak', 1893.
Oil on canvas, 25 x 23 cm.
Krasnoyarskiy Kraevoy Musey, Krasnoyarsk.

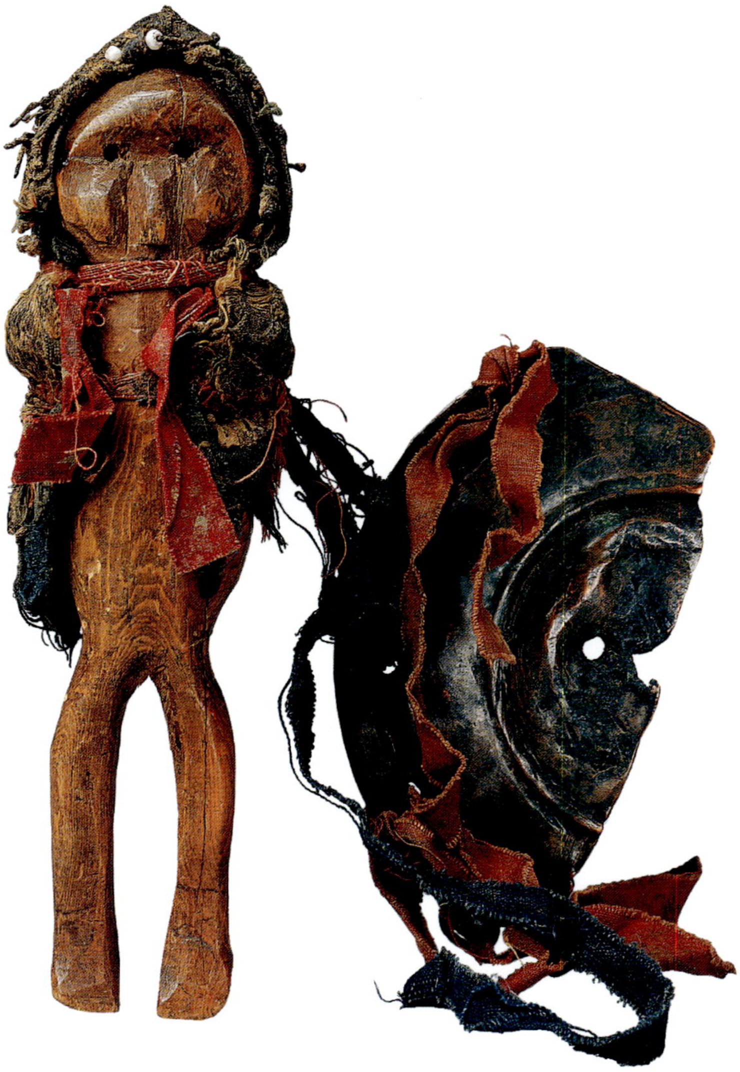

Evenki,
Amulet, 1910.
Wood, cotton fabric, beads, metal, 17 cm.
Russian Museum of Ethnography, St. Petersburg. Yenisey Gubernia (province), Yenisey Uezd (district), the Angara river basin.

northern and southern Siberia seems to be proved by the result of a careful study of certain Neo-Siberian tribes (Yakut) who migrated to the north, and of certain Palaeo-Siberians (Gilyak) who migrated to the south. The ease with which they absorbed the customs and beliefs appertaining to their new surroundings shows that there was no fundamental difference between their shamanistic practices. The differences, being due to environment, disappear in migration. It cannot be said that the change is due to contact, since this, in many cases, is very slight. Indeed, Shamanism seems to be such a natural product of the continental climate with its extremes of cold and heat, of the violent *burgas* and *burans*, of the hunger and fear which attend the long winters, that not only the Palaeo-Siberians and the more highly cultivated Neo-Siberians, but even Europeans, have sometimes fallen under the influence of certain shamanistic superstitions. Such is the case with the Russian peasants and officials who settle in Siberia, and with the Russian Creoles.

According to the official census, only a small part of the aborigines are 'true Shamanists,' but, as a matter of fact, we see that though they are registered as Orthodox Catholics and Buddhists, they are in reality nearly all faithful to the practice of their old religion.

A. THE SHAMAN

"When I was twenty years old, I became very ill and began 'to see with my eyes, to hear with my ears' that which others did not see or hear."

As among all primitive religions, the role of the priest, as the repository of religious beliefs and traditions, is of the greatest importance. The organization of the shamanhood varies slightly in different tribes. In some cases this office is hereditary, but everywhere the supernatural gift is a necessary qualification for becoming a shaman. As we should expect from the generally higher culture of the Neo-Siberians, their shamanhood is more highly organized than that of the Palaeo-Siberians. The family shamans predominate among the Palaeo-Siberians, and the professional shamans among the Neo-Siberians. In modern times the importance of family Shamanism is losing ground among all the tribes named, with the exception of the Chukchi, and there is a tendency to its being replaced on all occasions by individual Shamanism. These individual or professional shamans are called among the Chukchi 'those with spirit' (*enenilit*), from *enen*, 'shamanistic spirit.'

Although hysteria (called by some writers 'Arctic hysteria') lies at the bottom of the shaman's vocation, at the same time the shaman differs from an ordinary patient suffering from this illness in possessing an extremely great power of mastering himself in the periods between the actual fits, which occur during the ceremonies. A good shaman ought to possess many unusual qualities, but the chief is the power, acquired by tact and knowledge to influence the people round him. His reserved attitude has undoubtedly a great influence on the people among whom he lives. He must know how and when to have his fit of inspiration, which sometimes rises to frenzy, and also how to preserve his high 'tabooed' attitude in his daily life.

In speaking of the shaman's vocation, we do not include the family shaman of the Koryak, Asiatic Eskimo, Chukchi, and Yukaghir, whose position and capacity are rather vague, as we see from the following description of his duties: Each family has one or more drums of its own, on which its members are bound to perform at specific periods: that is, to accompany the beating of the drum with the singing of various melodies. Almost always on these occasions one member at least of the family tries to communicate with "spirits" after the manner of shamans. Sometimes he even tries to foretell the future, but he receives no attention from his audience. This is done in the outer room and in daylight, whereas the "shaman's," or professional shaman's, actions are performed in the inner room and at night.

Besides this, every adult Chukchi will occasionally take his drum, especially in the winter, and beat it for a while in the warm shelter of the sleeping-room, with the light or without it, singing his melodies to the rhythm of the beats.

We see from the above that one member of the family has the duty of beating the drum during certain ceremonials, and amuses himself sometimes by shamanizing just as he amuses himself by beating the drum at any time, apart from ceremonials. Of course, we cannot call this member of the family a shaman, but a master of the ceremonies, who imitates the shaman; we can call shamans only those individuals who possess special skill and vocation, whether or not they are shamans by heredity.

However, the same Koryak, Asiatic Eskimo, Chukchi, Yukaghir and practically all the Palaeo-Siberians possess the professional shaman, sometimes in decadence, but still there is no doubt of his existence. Among the Itelmen there is only one great annual ceremony, in November, and the chief roles at this ceremony belonged to old men.

From this meagre information we can scarcely decide whether among the Itelmen there is or not a family shaman, because as the old men play the role not at ceremonials in separate families, but at communal ceremonies, we must rather call them communal shamans. But there was some form of professional Shamanism, though not specialized, since every old woman could shamanize.

The female sex is nicer and probably cleverer, therefore there are more women and *koekchuch* among the shamans than there are men.

Among the Itelmen there are no special shamans, as among other nations, but every old woman and *koekchuch* (probably women in men's clothes) is a witch, and explains dreams.

The Itelmen had no professional shamans, but every one could exercise that art, especially women and Koekehuch; there was no special shaman garb; they used no drum, but simply pronounced incantations and practised divination, which description appears more like the family Shamanism of the present day. It is unlikely that the Itelmen should form an exception among the rest of the Asiatic and American tribes in having had no professional shamans.

It may be said that professional Shamanism does seem to have existed, at least in germ, among the Itelmen, alongside of the communal Shamanism which was in the hands of the old men. That those who could shamanize most effectually were women, 'nice and clever,' points to the fact that some sort of standard was already set up for those who aspired to be special practitioners of this extra-communal Shamanism, and that women most nearly approached this ideal.

1. THE SHAMAN'S VOCATION

Whether his calling be hereditary or not, a shaman must be a capable - nay, an inspired person. Of course, this is practically the same thing as saying that he is nervous and excitable, often to the verge of insanity. So long as he practises his vocation, however, the shaman never passes this verge. It often happens that before entering the calling persons have had serious nervous affections.Thus a Chukchi female shaman, Telpina, according to her own statement, had been violently insane for three years, during which time her household had taken precautions that she should do no harm to the people or to herself.

People about to become shamans have fits of wild paroxysms alternating with a condition of complete exhaustion. They will lie motionless for two or three days without partaking of food or drink. Finally they retire to the wilderness, where they spend their time enduring hunger and cold in order to prepare themselves for their calling.

To be called to become a shaman is generally equivalent to being afflicted with hysteria; then the accepting of the call means recovery. There are cases of young persons who, having suffered for years from lingering illness (usually of a nervous character), at last feel a call to take up shamanistic practice and by this means overcome the disease.

Yukaghir,
Shaman's outfit, 1900-1901.
Reindeer skin, fur, leather, hair embroidery, sinew, flannel, dyed seal pup fur, Coat: 96 cm; Apron: 94 cm; Hat: 91 cm.
American Museum of Natural History, New York. Markovo.

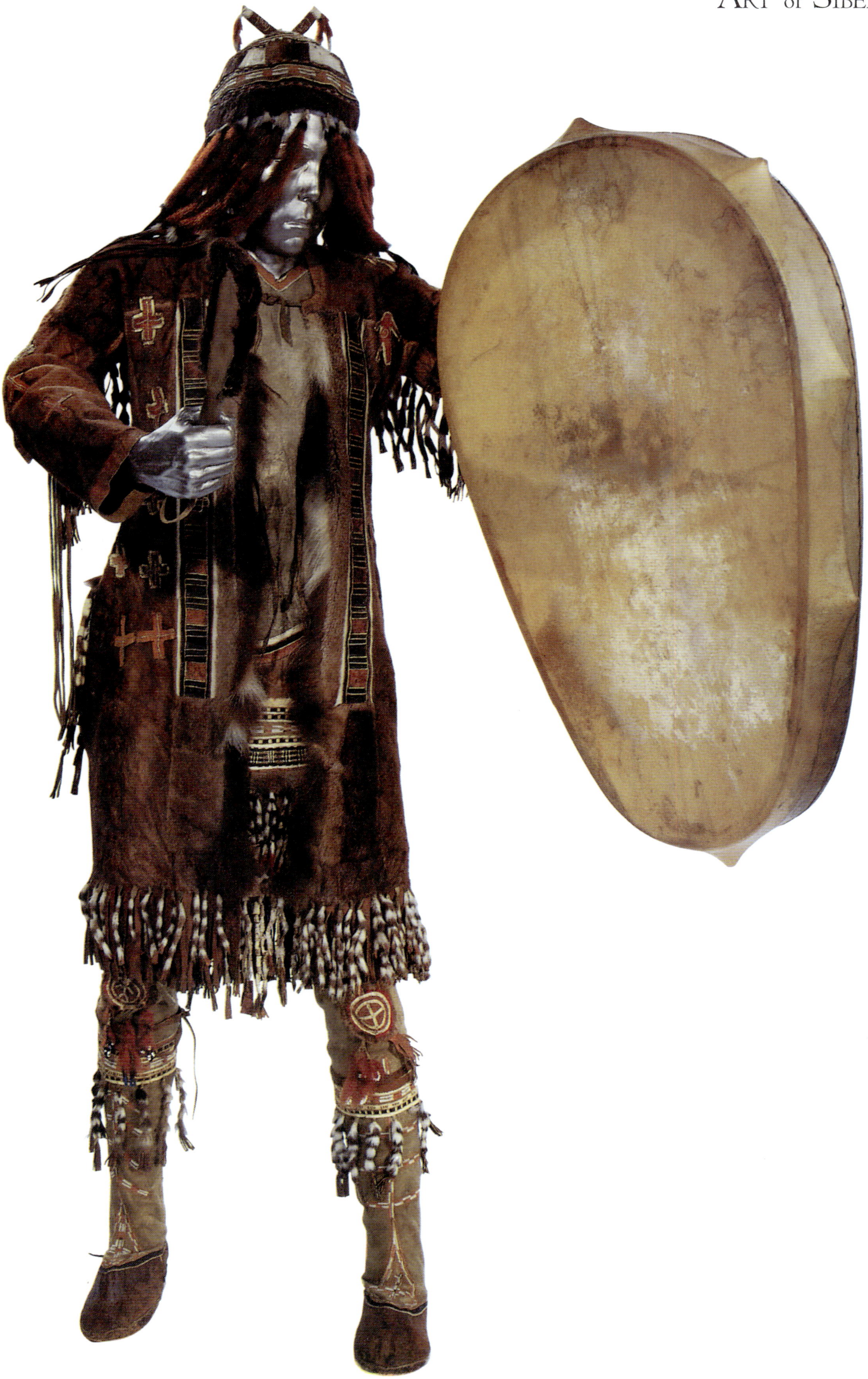

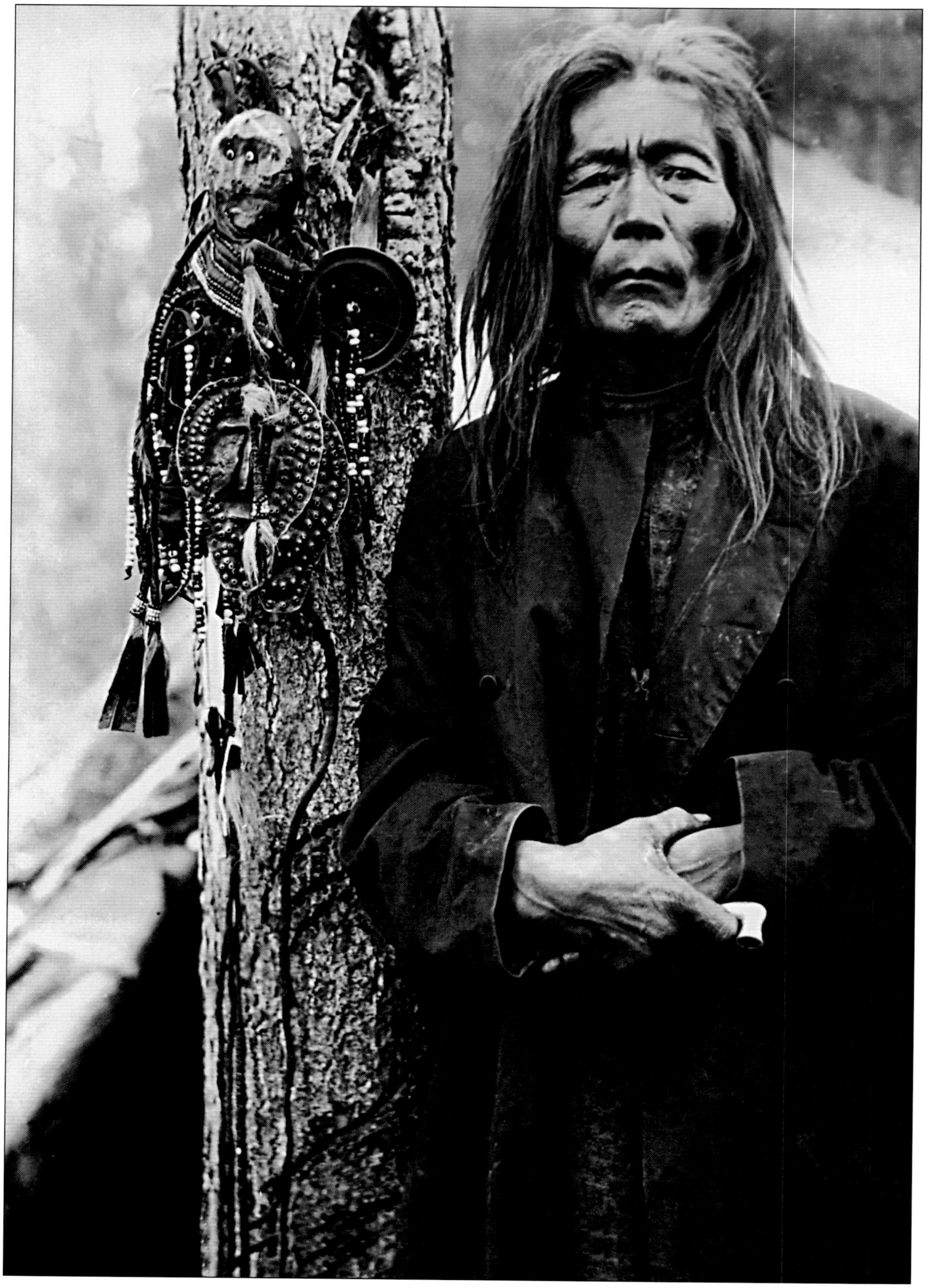

To the believer, the acceptance of the call means accepting several spirits, or at least one, as protectors or servants, by which means the shaman enters into communication with the whole spirit world. The shamanistic call sometimes manifests itself through some animal, plant, or other natural object, which the person comes upon at the 'right time,' i.e. when very young, often in the critical period between childhood and maturity (or else when a person more advanced in age is afflicted with mental or physical troubles). Sometimes it is an inner voice, which bids the person enter into intercourse with the 'spirits.' If the person is dilatory in obeying, the calling spirit soon appears in some outward visible shape, and communicates the call in a more explicit way. One story tells of a shaman named Ainanwat who, after an illness, saw several 'spirits,' but did not pay much attention to them; then one 'spirit' came, whom Ainanwat liked and invited to stay. But the 'spirit' said he would stay only on the condition that Ainanwat should become a shaman. Ainanwat refused, and the 'spirit' vanished.

A Yakut-Evenki shaman, Tiuspiut ('fallen-from-the-sky'), tells of how he became a shaman: "I was ill and for nine years I struggled with myself, and I did not tell any one what was happening to me, as I was afraid that people would not believe me and would make fun of me. At last I became so seriously ill that I was on the verge of death; but when I started to shamanize I grew better; and even now when I do not shamanize for a long time I am liable to be ill."

Tiuspiut was sixty years of age and had been shamanizing thirty-one years when he told his story. He was a man of medium size, thin, but muscular, with signs of former beauty. In spite of his age he could shamanize and dance the whole night. He was an experienced man, and travelled a great deal both in the south and in the north. During the shamanistic ceremonies his eyes had a strange expression of madness, and a pertinacious stare, which provoked to anger and excitement those on whom his look rested.

Generally in the features of a shaman there is something peculiar which enable an observer, after a short experience, to distinguish them from the other folk present.

A similar observation may be made about the Chukchi shamans. The eyes of a shaman have a look different from that of other people, and they explain it by the assertion that the eyes of the shaman are very bright (*nikeraqen*), which, by the way, gives them the ability to see "spirits" even in the dark. It is certainly a fact that the expression of a shaman is peculiar - a combination of cunning and shyness; and it is often possible to pick him out from among many others.

The Chukchi are well aware of the extreme nervousness of their shamans, and express it by the word *ninirkilqin*, "he is bashful." By this word they mean to convey the idea that the shaman is highly sensitive, even to the slightest change of the psychic atmosphere surrounding him during his exercises.

The Chukchi shaman is diffident in acting before strangers, especially shortly after his initiation. A shaman of great power will refuse to show his skill when among strangers, and will yield only after much solicitation: even then, as a rule, he will not show all of his power.

The shamanistic call comes sometimes to people more advanced in years. To people of more mature age the shamanistic call may come during some great misfortune, dangerous and protracted illness, sudden loss of family or property. It is generally considered that in such cases a favourable issue is possible only with the aid of the 'spirits,' therefore a man who has undergone some extraordinary trial in his life is considered as having within himself the possibilities of a shaman,

Evenki,
Shaman with representations of the spirits, early 20th century.
Russian Museum of Ethnography, St. Petersburg. Yenisey Province.

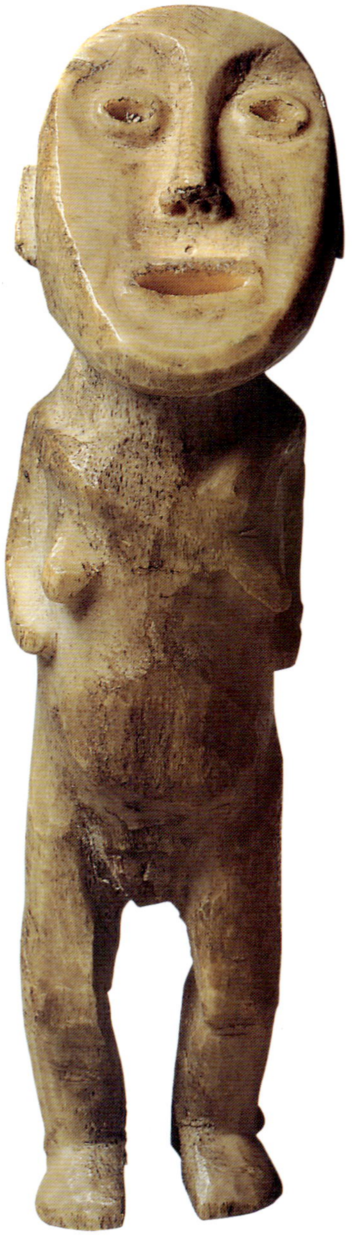

Koryak,
Image of a woman, 1906.
Antler, 10.7 cm.
Russian Museum of Ethnography, St. Petersburg. Primorskaya Oblast, Anadyr Krai.

Ivan Shishkin,
Backwoods, 1872.
Oil on canvas, 209 x 161 cm.
Russian Museum, St. Petersburg.

and he often feels bound to enter into closer relations with the 'spirits,' lest he incur their displeasure at his negligence and lack of gratitude.

Katek, a shaman from the village of Unisak at Indian Point, entered into relations with the 'spirits' when he was of mature age, during a terrible adventure he had while hunting seal.

He was carried away on the piece of ice on which he was standing, and only after a long time of drifting came upon an iceberg, on to which he climbed. But before he encountered the iceberg, he had tried to kill himself with his belt-knife, when a large walrus-head suddenly appeared out of the water quite close to him and sang: "O Katek, do not kill yourself! You shall again see the mountains of Unisak and the little Kuwakak, your elder son." When Katek came back home he made a sacrifice to the walrus-head, and from that time on he was a shaman, much respected and very famous among his neighbours.

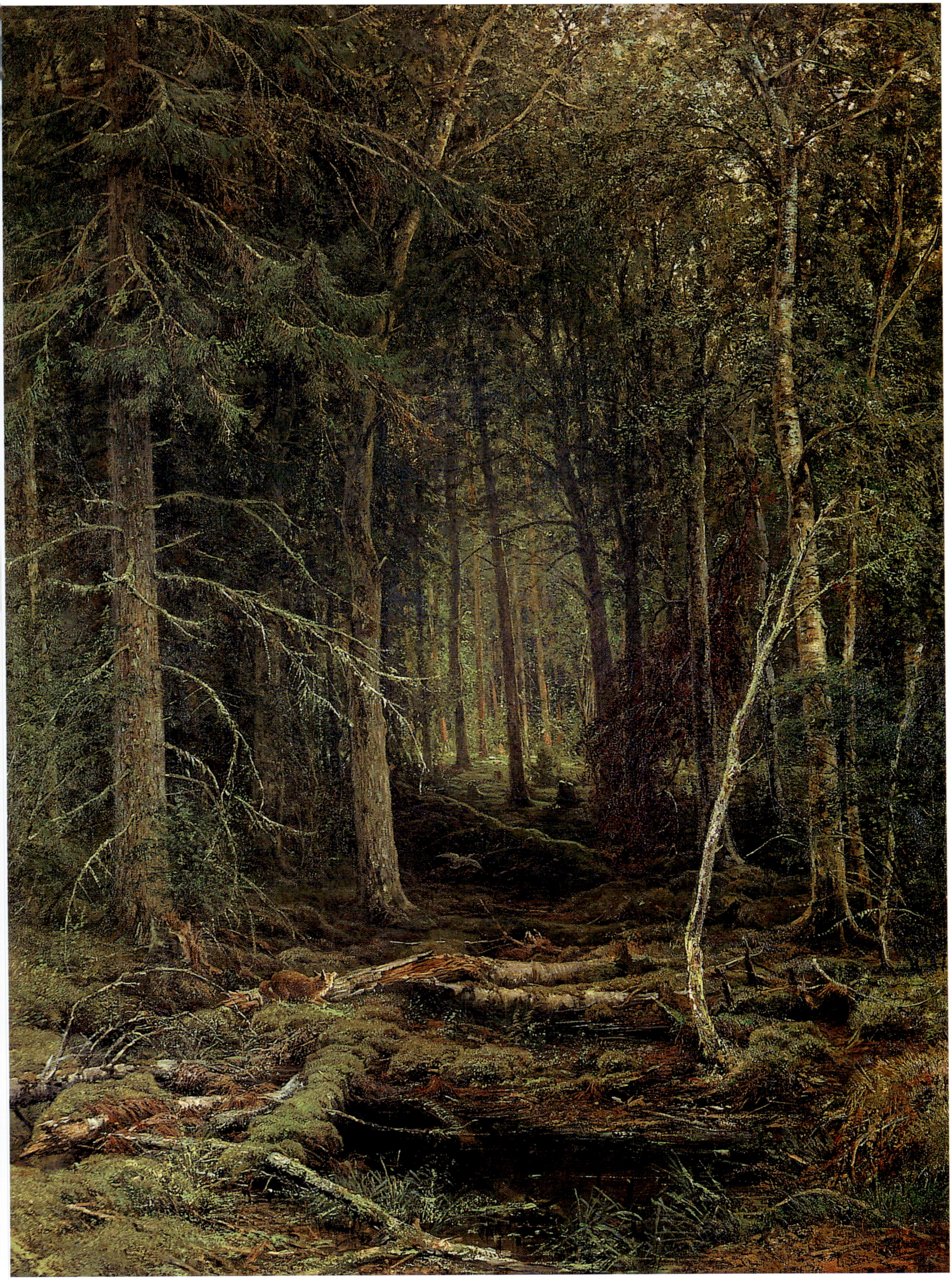

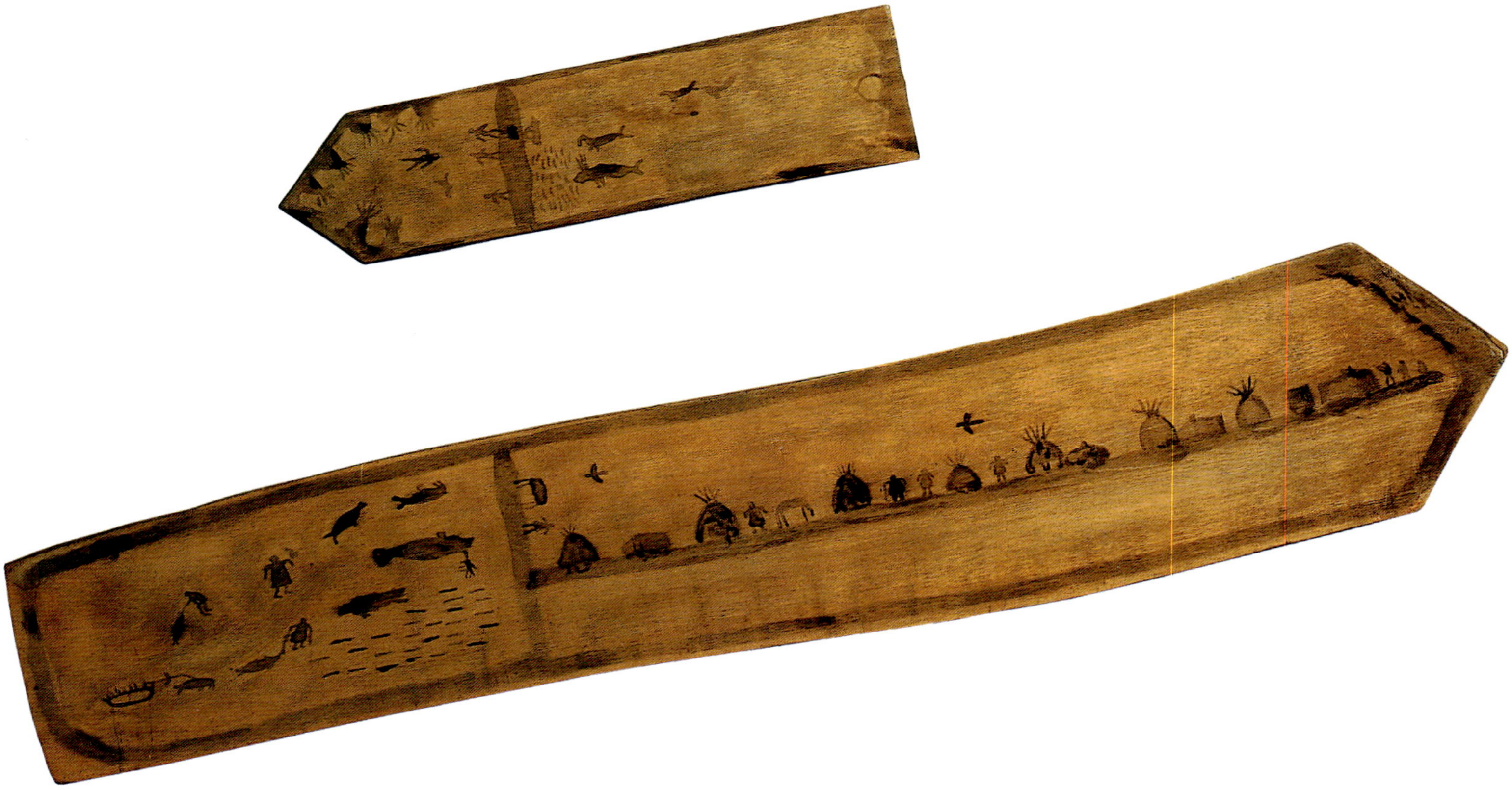

Chukchi,
'Boards of conjuration' for performing of rites at holidays, 1904 - 1907.
Wood, paint, 1) 62.2 x 10 cm;
2) 29.5 x 7.8 cm.
Russian Museum of Ethnography, St. Petersburg. Chukchi Peninsular.

However, very old people are not supposed to hear the shamanistic call. In a Koryak tale, when Quikinnaqu (who had already a grown-up daughter) unexpectedly makes for himself a drum, and becomes a shaman, his neighbours say sceptically: "Has the old Quikinnaqu really become a shaman? From his youth up he had no spirits within his call."

But young people when they get into trouble also call for the help of 'spirits;' when the latter come to them, such youths also frequently become shamans.

A man named Yetilin, who belonged by birth to an Arctic maritime village, but afterwards married into a reindeer-breeding family on the Dry Anui River, and joined its camp, describes how in his early childhood his family perished from a contagious disease (probably influenza), and he was left alone with his small sister. Then he called to the 'spirits.' They came and brought food and said to him: "Yetilin, take to beating the drum! We will assist you in that also."'

The Chukchi tales contain accounts of poor and despised orphans, who were protected by 'spirits,' and turned into shamans. The shamanistic call among the Evenki of Trans-Baikalia shows itself in the following manner: a dead shaman

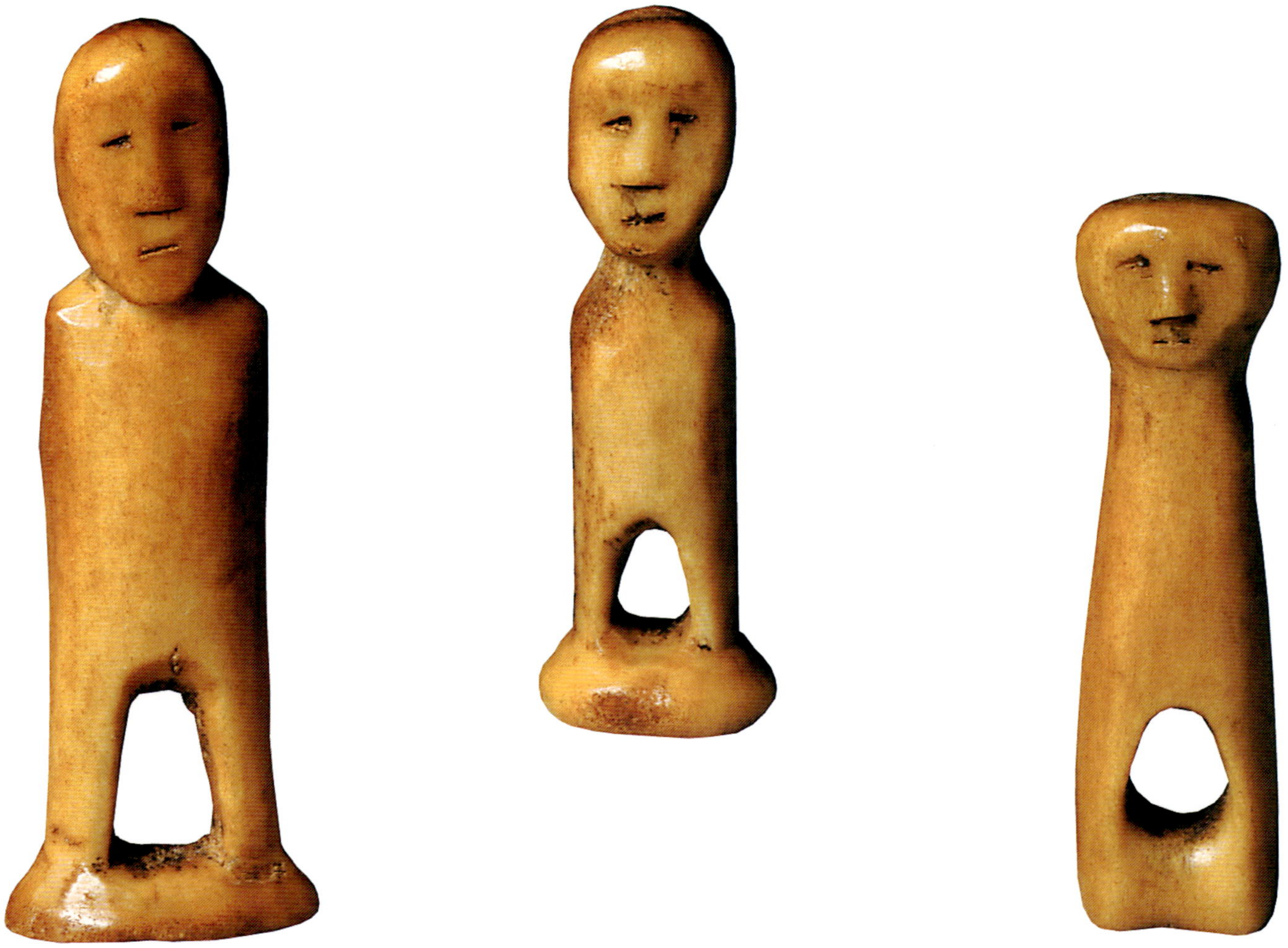

appears in a dream and summons the dreamer to become his successor. Similar instances are to be found in the records of all Siberian tribes.

As to the shamanistic office being hereditary, this is the case wherever a descendant of a shaman shows a disposition for the calling.

Among the Ostyak, the father himself chooses his successor, not necessarily according to age, but according to capacity; and to the chosen one he gives his own knowledge. If he has no children, he may pass on the office to a friend, or to an adopted child.

The Ostyak shaman occasionally sells his familiar spirit to another shaman. After receiving payment, he divides his hair into tresses, and fixes the time when the spirit is to pass to his new master. The spirit, having changed owners, makes his new possessor suffer; if the new shaman does not feel these effects, it is a sign that he is not becoming proficient in his office.

Among both the Yakut and the Buryat, although the office is not necessarily hereditary, it is usually so in part; for it will generally happen that the shamanistic spirit passes from one to another of the same family.

Eskimo,
Sketches of man, 3rd-4th century AD.
Walrus tusk ivory, 1) 4.7 cm;
2) 3.7 cm; 3) 3.8 cm.
Russian Museum of Ethnography,
St. Petersburg. Chukchi Peninsular.

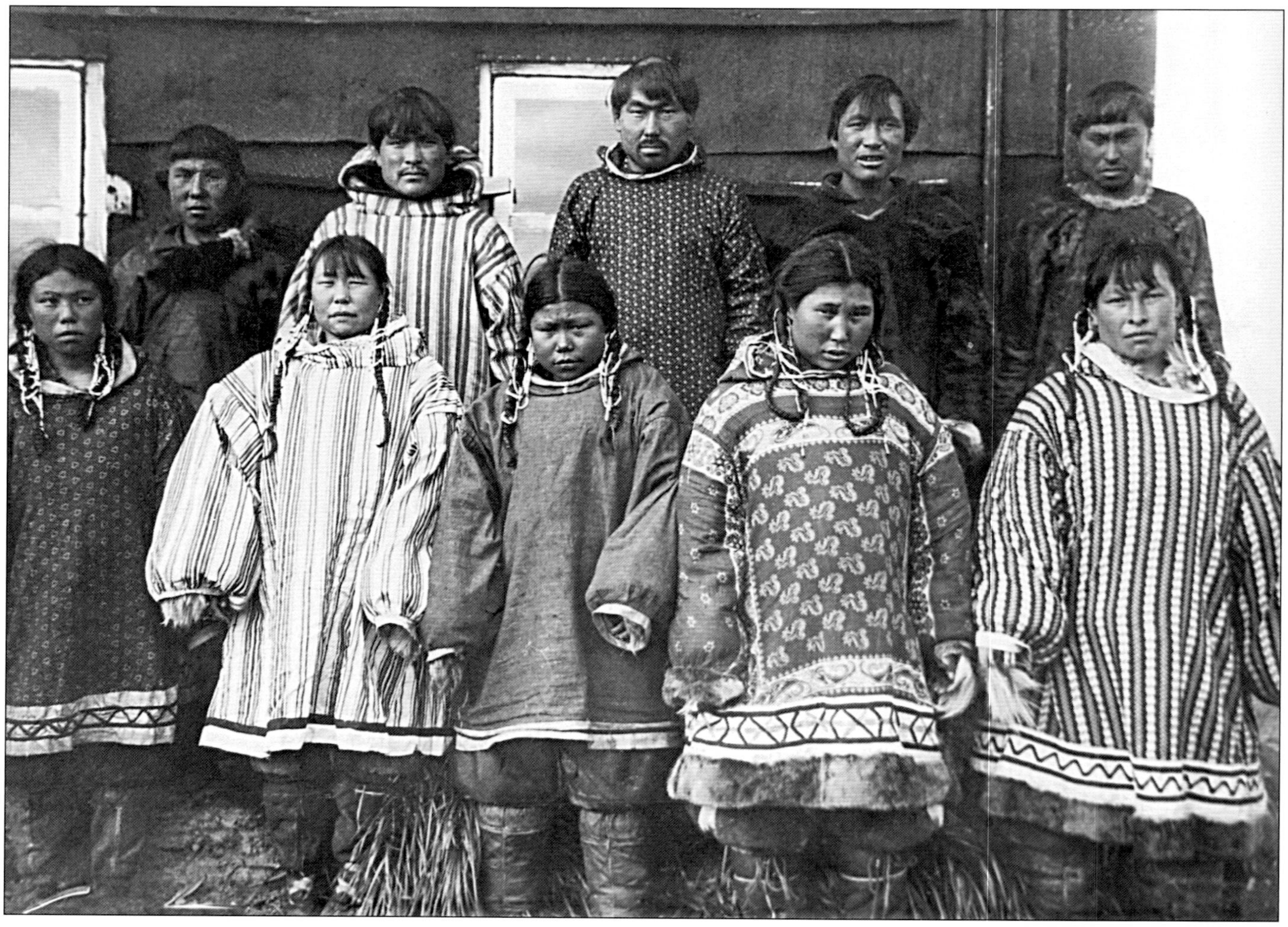

The Altaians believe that no one becomes a shaman of his own free will; rather it comes to him *volens volens*, like a hereditary disease. They say that sometimes when a young man feels premonitory symptoms of the call, he avoids shamans and shamanistic ceremonies, and by an effort of will occasionally cures himself. The period when the shamanistic call comes to the descendant of a shamanistic family is known as *tes bazin-yat*, 'the ancestor (spirit) leaps upon, strangles him.'

The vocation of the shaman is attended with considerable danger: the slightest lack of harmony between the acts of the shamans and the mysterious call of their 'spirits' brings their life to an end. This is expressed by the Chukchi, when they say that 'spirits' are very bad-tempered, and punish with immediate death the slightest disobedience of the shaman, and that this is particularly so when the shaman is slow to carry out those orders which are intended to single him out from other people.

Chukchis in traditional costume.

Eveni,
Reindeer herders in the taiga,
1896–1897.
Okhotsk region.

We have similar statements from the more advanced tribes. The duties undertaken by the shaman are not easy; the struggle which he has to carry on is dangerous. There exist traditions about shamans who were carried away still living from the earth to the sky, about others killed by "spirits," or struck down at their first meeting with the powers whom they dared to call upon. The wizard

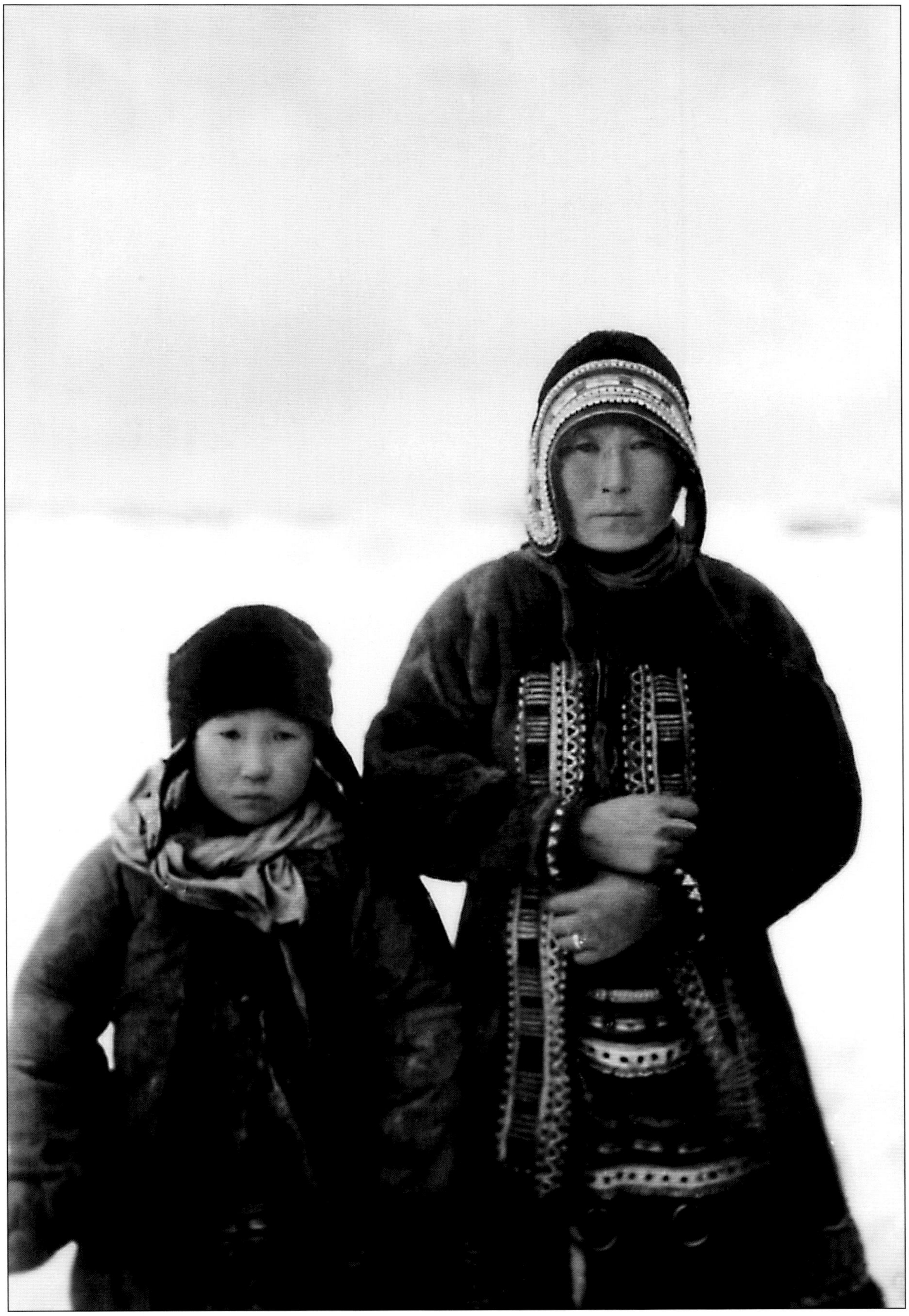

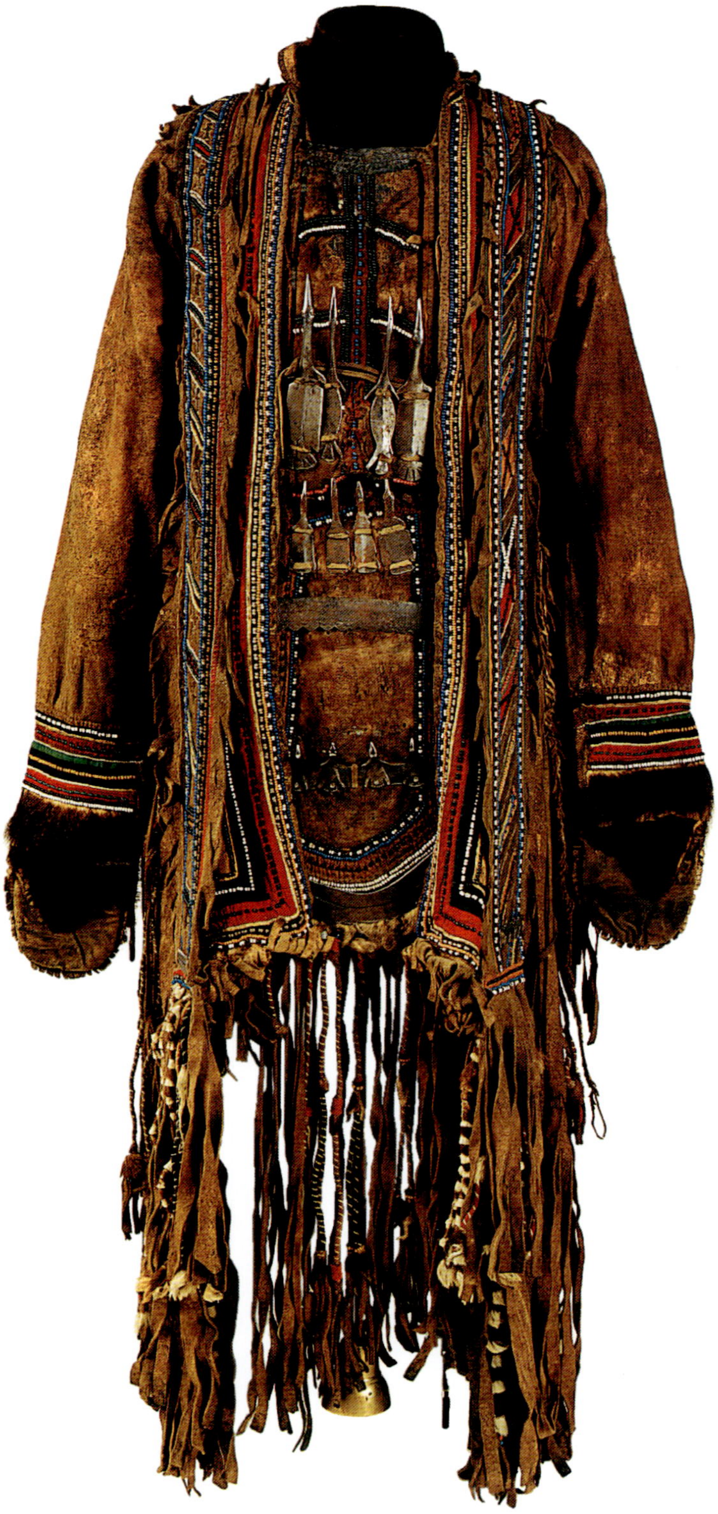

who decides to carry on this struggle has not only material gain in view, but also the alleviation of the griefs of his fellow men; the wizard who has the vocation, the faith, and the conviction, who undertakes his duty with ecstasy and negligence of personal danger, inspired by the high ideal of sacrifice, such a wizard always exerts an enormous influence upon his audience. The distinction that the natives draw between the 'Great,' 'Middling,' and 'Mocking' or deceitful shamans is apparent immediately upon meeting a shaman. Although exposed to danger from supernatural powers, the shaman is supposed to be safer from human anger than any other person.

One Chukchi tale says that a murderer came to her neighbour, a woman who was busy with her fireboard, trying to make a fire. She stabbed her from behind. But the girl continued to work on the fire, because she was a shaman-girl, a woman able to stab herself in a shamanistic performance. Therefore she could not kill her, but only severed the tendons of her arms and legs.

A man who can pierce himself through with a knife, so that its end shows at his back, or cut his head off, put it on a stick, and dance round the yurt, is surely strengthened sufficiently against an enemy's attacks. Yet the shaman, Scratching-Woman, when he refused to drink the alcohol offered to him by his host and which he had previously demanded, explained as follows: "I will be frank with you. Drink really makes my temper too bad for anything. Usually my wife watches over me, and puts all knives out of my reach. But when we are apart, I am afraid."

On the whole, the shamans are very much attached to their vocation, in spite of the persecutions which they have to suffer from the Russian Government. Tiuspiut was many times punished by the Russian officials and his shamanistic dress and drum were burned; but he returned to his duties after each of these incidents. "We have to do it, we cannot leave off shamanizing,' he said, 'and there is no harm in our doing it."

Another shaman, who was old and blind, affirmed that he had been a shaman some time before, but after he became convinced that it was a sin he stopped shamanizing, and although another very powerful shaman took from him the "sign," *ämägyat*, still the spirits made him blind.

In the village of Baigantai one encounters with another instance of a shaman who, however many times he vowed to abstain from Shamanism, still returned to it when the occasion arose. He was a rich man, who did not care for material gain, and he was so wonderful that his eyes were said to jump out on his forehead during shamanistic performances.

One rarely meets shamans among the Palaeo-Siberians who could be said to live solely on the profits of their art. It is only a source of additional income to them. Among the Evenki and Yakut the shaman is recompensed only when his arts are successful. Tiuspiut was poor and cared for money, but he was proudly regardful of his reputation, and when some of his neighbours called in another shaman, one who lived farther away than Tiuspiut, he became quite offended.

2. THE SHAMAN'S PREPARATORY PERIOD

The Chukchi.

The Chukchi call the preparatory period of a shaman by a term signifying 'he gathers shamanistic power.' For the weaker shamans and for female shamans the preparatory period is less painful, and the inspiration comes mainly through dreams.

Evenki,
Shaman's outfit, early 20th century.
Dressed reindeer skin, beads, metal, bear fur, cotton fabric, Caftan: 96 cm; Chest panel: 73 x 17 cm.
Russian Museum of Ethnography, St. Petersburg. Siberian Krai, Krasnoyar Okrug, Turukhan District, the Nizhni (Lower) Tunguska river basin.

But for a strong man this stage is very painful and long; in some cases it lasts for one, two, or more years. Some young people are afraid to take a drum and call on the 'spirits,' or to pick up stones or other objects which might prove to be amulets, lest the 'spirit' should call them to be shamans. Some youths prefer death to obedience to the call of spirits. Parents possessing only one child fear his entering this calling on account of the danger attached to it; but when the family is large, they like to have one of its members a shaman. During the time of preparation the shaman has to pass through both a mental and a physical training. He is, as a rule, segregated, and goes either to the forests and hills under the pretext of hunting or watching the herds, often without taking along any arms or the lasso of the herdsman; or else he remains in the inner room the whole time. The young novice, the "newly inspired" (*turene nitvillin*), loses all interest in the ordinary affairs of life. He ceases to work, eats but little and without relishing his food, ceases to talk to people, and does not even answer their questions. The greater part of his time he spends in sleep. This is why a wanderer must be closely watched, otherwise he might lie down on the open tundra and sleep for three or four days, incurring the danger in winter of being buried in drifting snow. When coming to himself after such a long sleep, he imagines that he has been out for only a few hours, and generally is not conscious of having slept in the wilderness at all.

However exaggerated this account of a long sleep may be, we learn that the Chukchi, when ill, sometimes fall into a heavy and protracted slumber, which may last many days, with only the necessary interruptions for physical needs.

The Koryak.

The mental part of the training consists in coming into contact with the right spirits, i.e. with the spirits who are to be the shaman's protectors in his shamanistic practice. Every Koryak shaman has his own guardian spirits, who help him in his struggle with disease-inflicting *kalau* in his rivalry with other shamans, and also in attacks upon his enemies. The shaman spirits usually appear in the form of animals or birds. The most common guardian spirits are the wolf, the bear, the raven, the sea-gull, and the eagle. One shaman among the Koryak related how the spirits of the wolf, raven, bear, sea-gull, and plover appeared to him (the shaman) in the desert - now in the form of men, now in that of animals - and commanded him to become a shaman, or to die. Thus we see that, while they are in solitude, the spirits appear to them in visible form, endow them with power, and instruct them. Often, however, the process of gathering inspiration is so painful to young shamans, because of their mental struggle against the call, that they are sometimes said to sweat blood on the forehead and the temples. Afterwards every preparation of a shaman for a performance is considered a sort of repetition of the initiative process: hence it is said that the Chukchi shamans during that time are easily susceptible to haemorrhage, and even to bloody sweat.

As to the physical training of a novice, he must learn singing, dancing, various tricks, including ventriloquism, and how to beat the drum.

The beating of the drum, notwithstanding its seeming simplicity, requires some skill, and the novice must spend considerable time before he can acquire the desired degree of perfection. This has reference especially to the performer's power of endurance. The same may be said of the singing. The manifestations continue for several weeks, during which time the shaman exercises the most violent activity with scarcely a pause. After the performance he must not show any signs of fatigue, because he is supposed to be sustained by the "spirits," and,

Klavdiy Vasilievich Lebedev,
The Conquest of the New Regions in Russia, 1904.
Watercolour on paper, 42 x 27 cm.
Art Museum of Vologda, Russia.

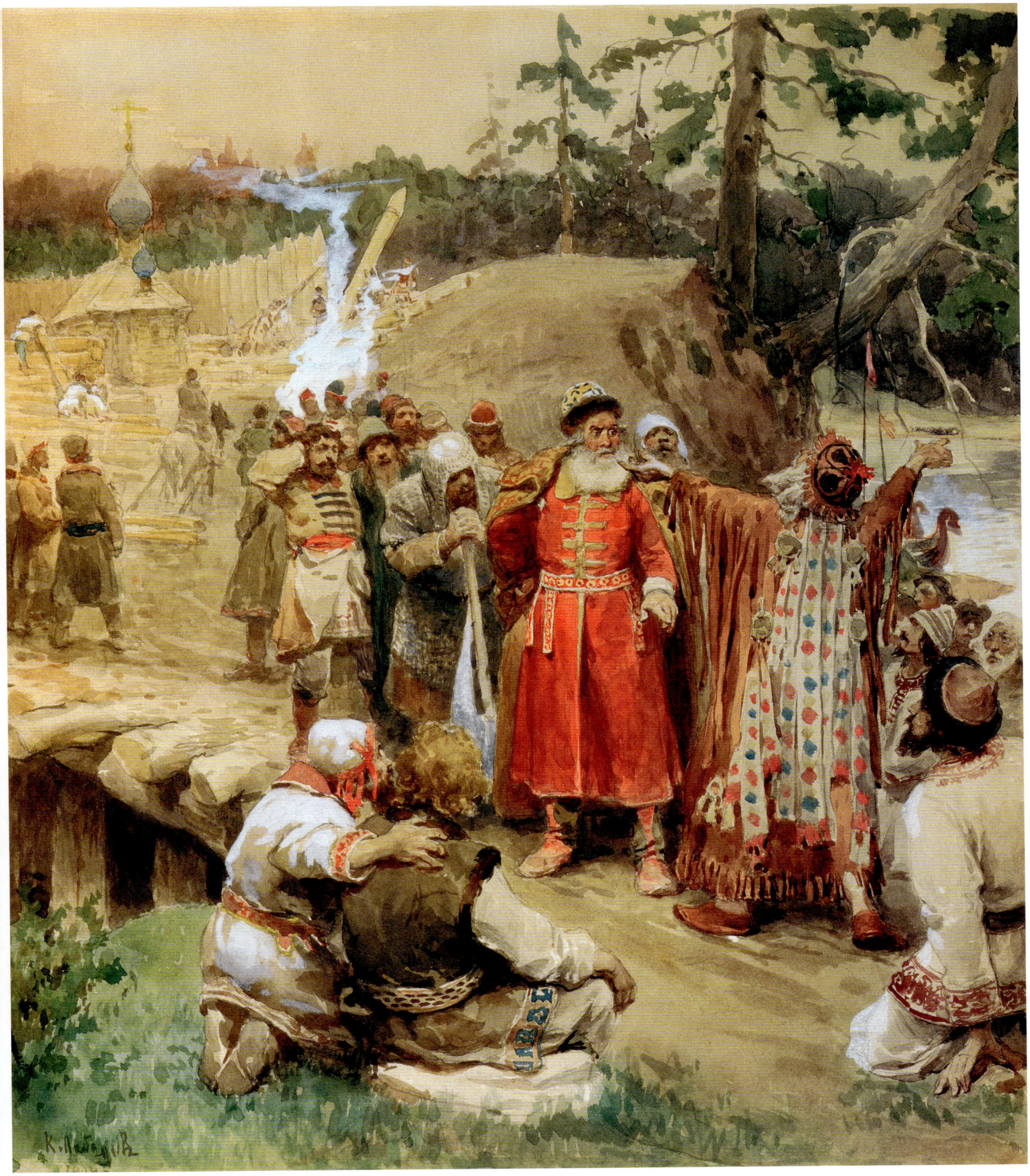

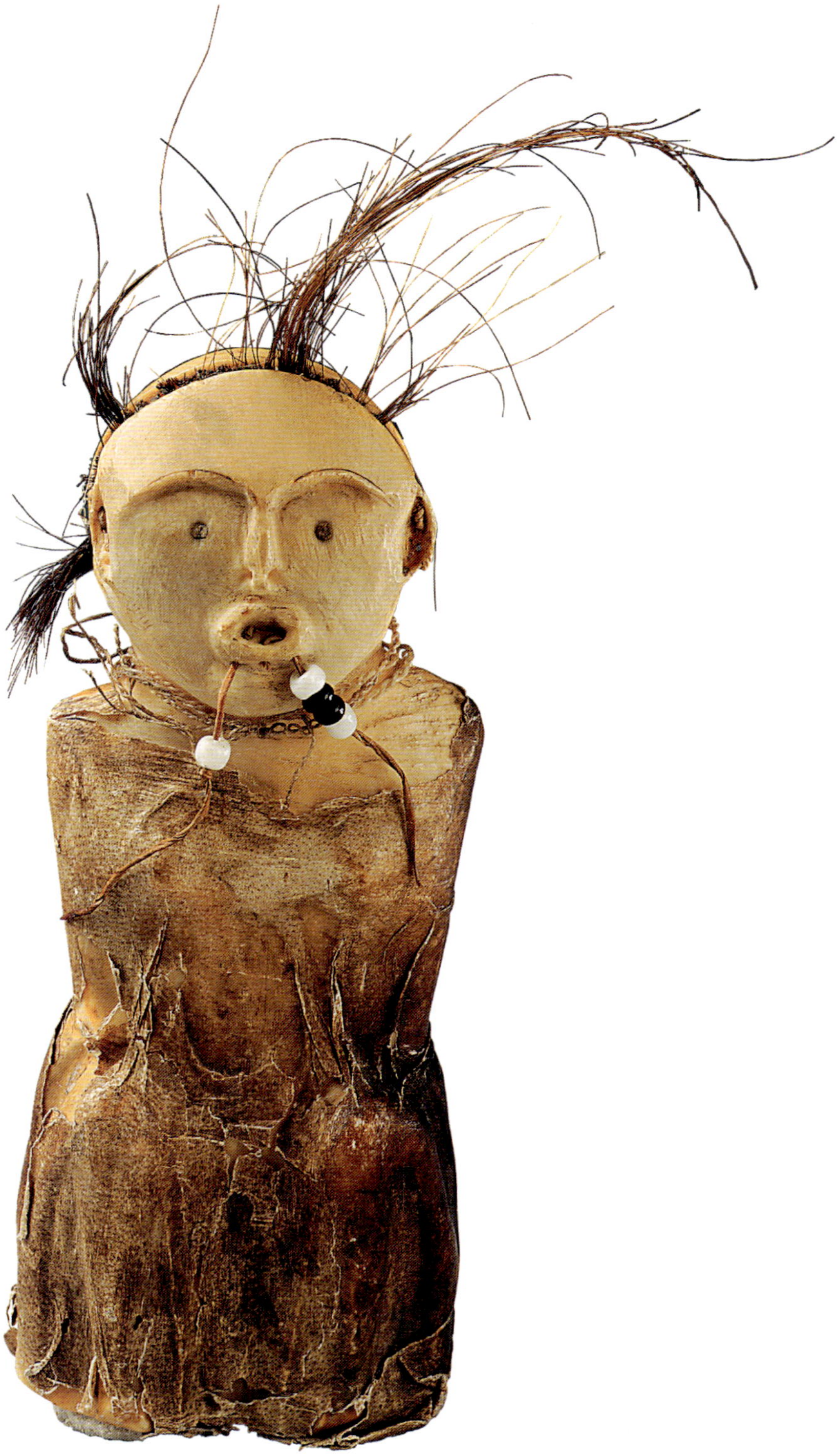

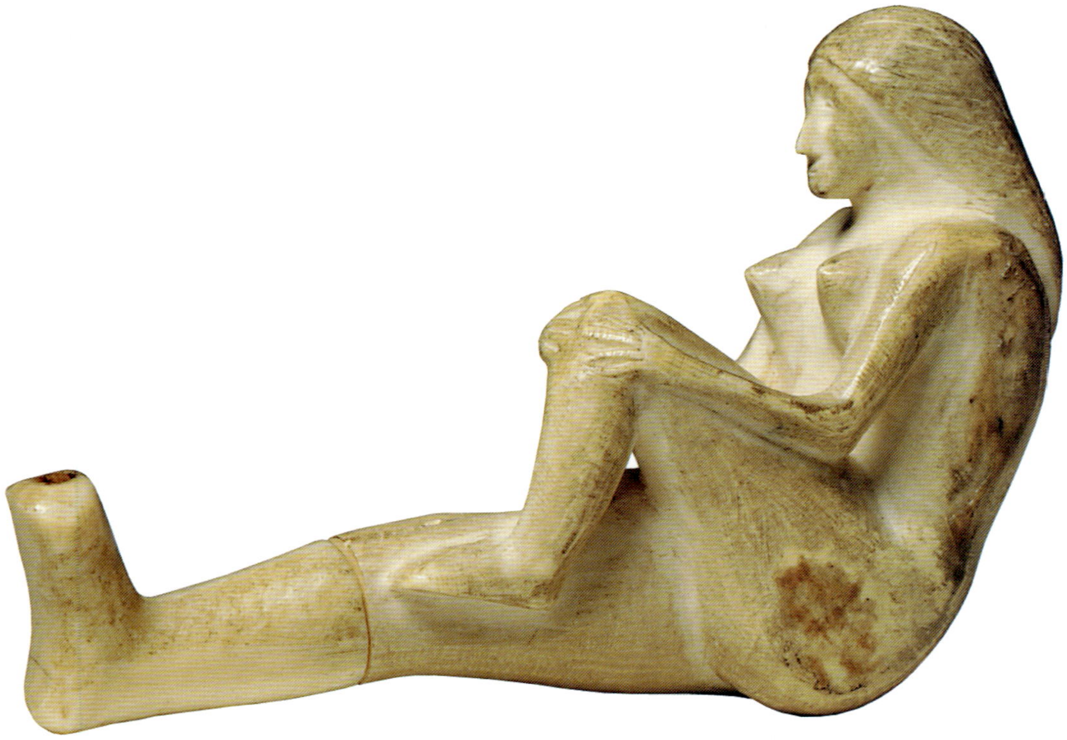

moreover, the greater part of the exercise is asserted to be the work of the spirits themselves, either after entering the shaman's body or while outside his body. The amount of endurance required for all this, and the ability to pass quickly from the highest excitement to a state of normal quietude, can, of course, be acquired only by long practice. Indeed, most shamans say that they had to spend a year, or even two years, before sufficient strength of hand and freedom of voice were given to them by the spirits. Some asserted that, during all this preparatory time, they kept closely to the inner room, taking up the drum several times a day, and beating it as long as their strength would allow.

Have the novices any teachers? One would suppose that they must have, if only to learn the difficult magical tricks, but it is hard to get any detailed information on this point, because the natives ascribe all the cleverness of the shaman to the 'spirits.' Sometimes the old men teach the young shamans. The man who gives a part of his power to another man loses correspondingly, and can hardly recover the loss afterwards. To transfer his power, the older shaman must blow on the eyes or into the mouth of the recipient, or he may stab himself with a knife, with the blade of which, still reeking with his 'source of life' (*telkeyun*), he will immediately pierce the body of the recipient.

Aleut,
Amulet, late 19th-early 20th century.
Bone, beads, hair, marine mammals intestines, sinew thread, 12 cm.
Russian Museum of Ethnography, St. Petersburg. Aleutian Islands.

Koryak,
Pipe in the form of woman's figure, 1906.
Walrus tusk ivory, 6.5 cm x 4.5 cm.
Russian Museum of Ethnography, St. Petersburg.

We find the practice of transfering power among Eskimo women, who were taught by their husbands, and whose children were taught by their parents. In one family, the shamanistic power has been retained through a succession of generations, evidently having been transferred from father to son.

"There are many liars in our calling," the shaman Scratching-Woman said. "One will lift up the skins of the sleeping-room with his right toe and then assure you that it was done by 'spirits;' another will talk into the bosom of his shirt or through his sleeve, making the voice issue from a quite unusual place."

The Gilyak.

Shamans do not play so important a role among the Gilyak as among some neighbouring tribes, yet still their power among this folk is almost unlimited. A Gilyak shaman said that before he had entered on his vocation he had been very ill for two months, during which time he was unconscious, lying quite motionless. Sometimes, he said, he almost regained consciousness, but sank again into a swoon before recovering his senses. "I should have died," he explained, "if I had not become a shaman." During these months of trial he became "as dry," he said, "as a dry stick." In the night he heard himself singing shaman's songs. Once there appeared to him a bird-spirit, and, standing at some distance from it, a man, who spoke to him in these words: "Make yourself a drum and all that pertains to a shaman. Beat the drum and sing songs. If you are an ordinary man, nothing will come of it; but if you are to be a shaman, you will be no ordinary one." When he came to, he found that he was being held by head and feet close to the fire by his friends, who told him that they had thought him already dead, carried off by the evil spirits (*kekhn*). Forthwith he demanded a drum, and began to beat it and sing. He felt half dead, half intoxicated. Then for the first time he saw his spirit-protectors, *kekhn* and *kenchkh*. The former told him, "If you see any one ill, cure him. Do not trust *kenchkh*. He has a man's face, but his body is a bird's. Trust us only."

Another story involves a boy of twelve. In spite of his youth he had two souls, being the son of a great shaman, Chanikh, who had as many as four souls (one from the mountains, another from the sea, a third from the sky, and a fourth from the underworld). Once on being suddenly awakened from sleep, Koïnit began to throw himself about, and to shout aloud in different pitches or intonations of the voice, as shamans are accustomed to do. When this was over, the boy's face looked worn and tired, like that of an old man. He said afterwards that, during the sleep which had preceded his outbreak, two *kekhns* had appeared to him. He knew them for his father's *kekhns*; and they said to him: "We used to play with your father - let us play with you also."

Passing from the Palaeo-Siberians to the Neo-Siberians, we notice that the shaman's protectors among the latter are highly developed beings.

Three kinds of 'spirits' are associated with a Yakut shaman, namely, *änägyat*, *yekyua*, and *kaliany*. *Änägyat* is the indispensable attribute of every shaman and it is also the name of the iron breast-circle, the sign of the shaman's dignity. Even the weakest shamans possess *änägyat* and *yekyua* - the latter is considered the 'mother animal,' and is said to be 'sent from above, animal picture, bewitching spirit, devilish devourer' (*Yekyua oïun abassyuah, simah abassyuah, üssüttan ongorudh*). The *yekyua* is carefully hidden from the people. Only wizards can see *yekyua*; to ordinary people they are invisible.

Once a year, when the snow melts and the earth is black, the *yekyua* arise from their hiding-places and begin to wander. They hold orgies of fights and

Yakut,
Shaman's outfit, late 19th-early 20th century.
Dressed reindeer skin, metal, 82 cm.
Russian Museum of Ethnography, St. Petersburg. Yakutia.

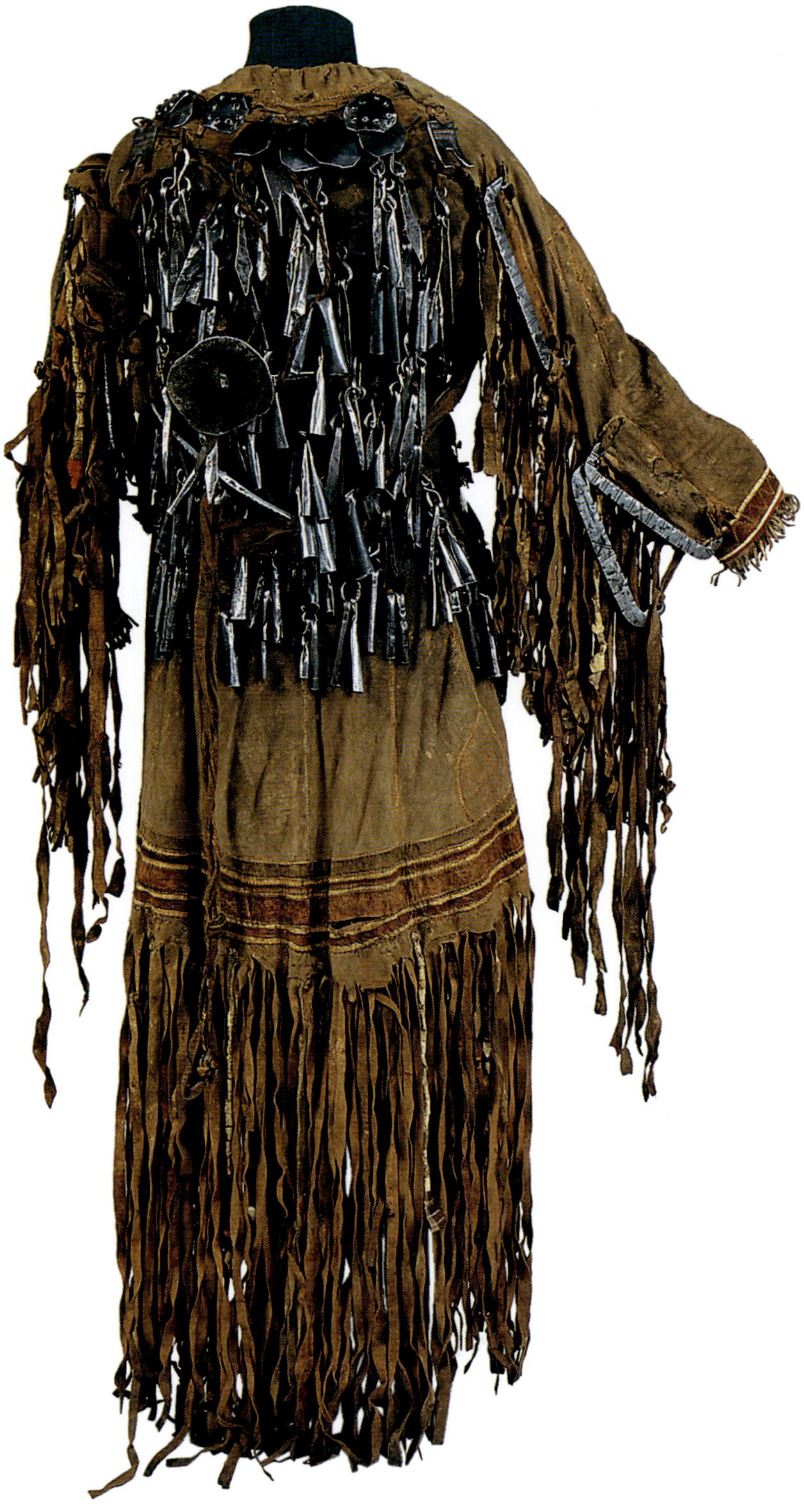

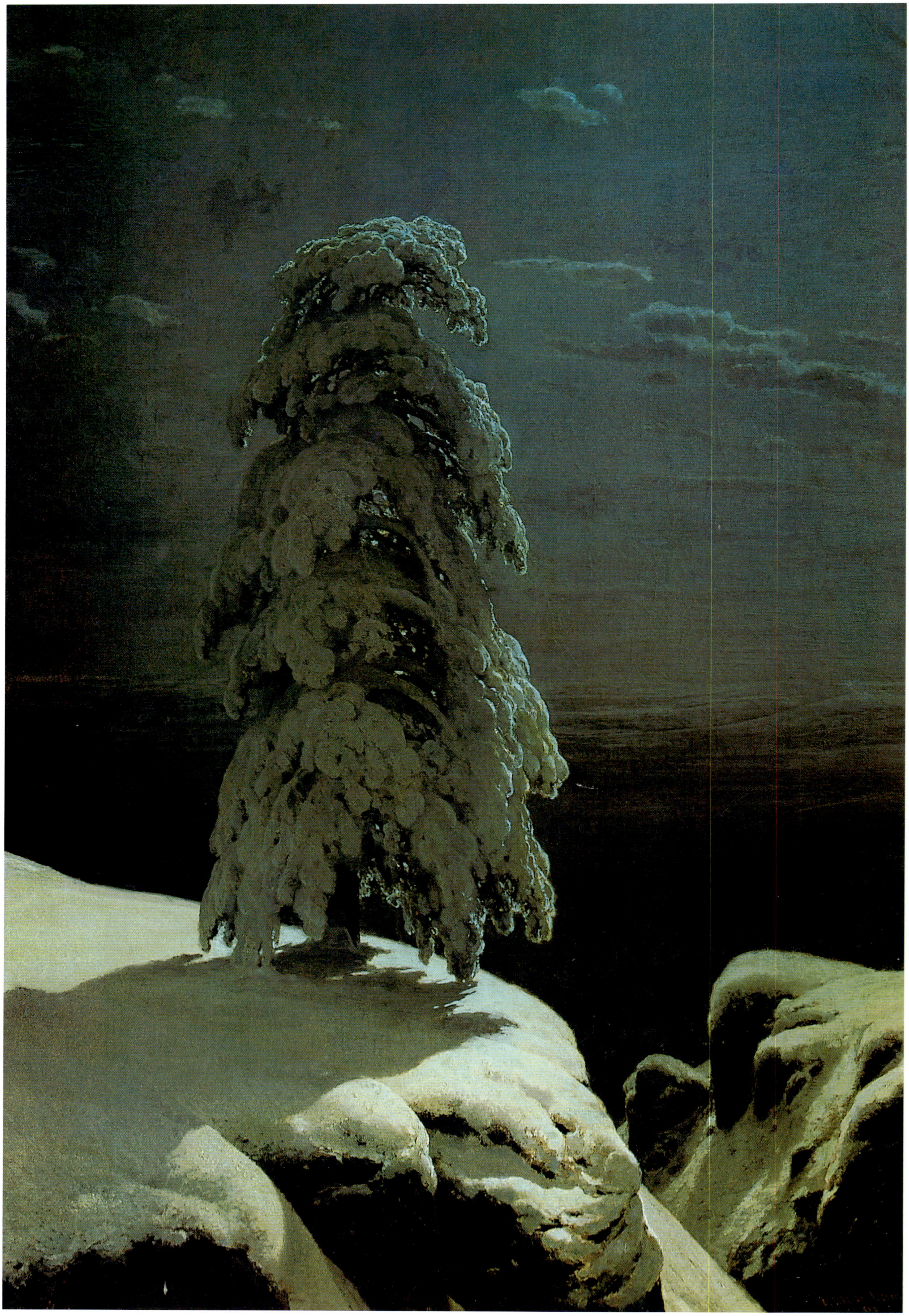

noises, and the shamans with whom they are associated feel very ill. Especially harmful are the *yekyua* of female shamans.

The weakest and most cowardly are the *yekyua* of dogs; the most powerful are those of enormous bulls, stallions, elks, and black boars. Those shamans who have as their animal incarnation a wolf, bear, or dog, are the must unfortunate; these animals are insatiable; they are never satisfied, however much the shaman may provide for them. The dog especially gives no peace to his two-footed fellow; he "gnaws with his teeth the shaman's heart, tears into pieces his body." Then the shaman feels sick and suffers pain. The crow is also a bad *yekyua*; the eagle and hairy bull are called 'devilish fighters and warriors' (*abassy keiktah*). This title is the most flattering one for a shaman. When a new shaman appears, the other shamans recognize him at once by the presence of a new *yekyua*, whom they have not seen before. If one of these animals kills another of its species, then the corresponding shaman will die. The shaman incarnates his *kut* only during the time that he is actually shamanizing.

Whereas the 'black' animal-protector of the *yekyua* seems to be of a totemic and personal nature, to a certain extent 'of one blood and flesh' with his protégé, on the other hand *ämägyat* strikes us as being a more impersonal power.

It is in most cases 'the spirit of a deceased shaman,' or, in some rare cases, one of the secondary heavenly beings. But it seems that the term 'spirit' is used here quite vaguely: The human body cannot contain the power of great gods, and so the spirit-protector remains always near the beloved man (outside of him) and willingly comes at his call; in difficult moments it helps him, defends him, and gives him advice. "The shaman sees and hears only through his *ämägyat*," says the shaman Tiuspiut.

Ämägyat comes to a shaman through an accident, or as a heavenly destiny. 'When I was travelling in the north,' says Tiuspiut, 'I came upon a heap of wood (*saïba*) in the mountains, and as I just wanted to cook some dinner, I set this on fire. Now under this heap was buried a well-known Evenki shaman (Tiuspiut was a Yakut), and so his *ämägyat* leapt into me.' If the great shamans at death take their *ämägyat* to heaven, they are transformed into heavenly beings; but if the *ämägyat* is not removed to heaven, then it will appear on the earth sooner or later.

Besides the two so-called spirits mentioned above, there comes to the Yakut shaman, during shamanistic performances, still another kind of spirit, a rather mischievous one, which forces the shaman to talk and to imitate various, often indecent, gestures. These spirits are called *kaliany*, and their representatives may be a Russian devil or a devil's daughter with a devilish groom, who, being blind, is in the habit of groping about in the dark.

Only a person whose *sür* has obtained a suitable education can become a shaman.

The sür of a 'white' shaman is educated under the care of one of the *aïy*, and the *sür* of a 'black' shaman studies with an *abassy*. How the *sür* of a white shaman is educated among the Yakut is not known to us. The sür of a black shaman lives with his tutor on the ninth floor (underground - in their ideal division of the universe). If the *sür* is educated on the ninth floor, then a most powerful shaman will arise from it; if on the eighth floor, then the shaman will be of medium power; if on the third floor, then the shaman will be only a sorcerer. The education consists in the *sür's* learning the habits, character, and behaviour of *abassylar* and shamans.

As to the education of a shaman himself, and his initiation, the Yakut shaman is taught by an older shaman, who consecrates him by placing on him the

Ivan Shishkin,
In the Wilds of the North, after Mikhail Lermontov's verse The Pine,
1891.
Oil on canvas, 161 x 118 cm.
Museum of Russian Art, Kiev.

ämägyat. This sign is taken away by the shaman from a person who does not wish to be a shaman any longer. There is in the Yakut language a word *usüi,* which means to teach the art of shamanizing and to consecrate a shaman.

The consecration of a shaman among the Yakut proceeds as follows: the old shaman leads his pupil up a high mountain or into a clearing in the forest. Here he dresses him in a shaman's garment, gives him a rattle, and places on one side of him nine chaste youths, and on the other nine chaste maidens. Then the shaman puts on his own garment, and directs the youth to repeat after him certain words. He demands of the novice that he shall give up all that is most dear to him in the world, and consecrate his life to the service of the spirits who shall come at his call. He tells his pupil where certain 'black' spirits dwell, what diseases they cause, and how they may be propitiated. Finally the young shaman must kill a sacrificial animal, and sprinkle himself with its blood. The flesh is eaten by those who have been present at the ceremony.

A child chosen to be a shaman is recognized among the Buryat by the following signs: he is often absorbed in meditation, likes to be alone, has mysterious dreams, and sometimes has fits during which he is unconscious. According to the Buryat beliefs, the soul of a child is then in process of being trained, among the 'West Tengeris' if he is to be a 'white' shaman, among the 'East Tengeris' if he is to become a 'black' one. Living in the dwelling of the gods, his soul, under the tutelage of deceased shamans, learns the various secrets of the shaman's vocation; the soul must remember the names of the gods, the places where they live, the means by which they may be propitiated, and the names of the spirits which are subordinate to the high gods. After a period of trial the soul of the child returns to the body, which for a time resumes its normal life. But on his reaching adolescence, peculiar symptoms show themselves in the person who has undergone these experiences. He becomes moody, is easily excited into a state of ecstasy, leads an irregular life, wandering from *ulus* to *ulus* to watch the shamanistic ceremonies. He gives himself up with great earnestness to exercises in the shamanistic arts, for which purpose he segregates himself, going to some high mountain or into the forest, where, before a great fire, he calls on the spirits, and afterwards falls into a swoon. In the meanwhile, to prevent him from doing himself an injury, his friends keep watch over him unobtrusively.

While the novice is preparing himself for his new life, his relations call in a good shaman, who makes a sacrifice to propitiate the spirits and induce them to help the young shaman-to-be. If the future shaman belongs to a poor family, the whole community helps to procure the sacrificial animals and other things which are indispensable for the ceremonies.

The preparatory period lasts for several years, its length depending largely on the capacity of the young man. He cannot, however, become a shaman until he reaches the age of twenty. Finally he undergoes a purification ceremony. One such ceremony does not confer all the rights and powers of a shaman; there are, in fact, nine. But very few shamans go through all these purifications; most only undergo two or three; some, none at all, for they dread the responsibilities which devolve upon consecrated shamans. To a fully consecrated shaman the gods are very severe, and punish his faults or mistakes with death.

The first consecration ceremony is preceded by a purification of water. For this an experienced old shaman, called the 'father-shaman,' is chosen, together with nine young men to be his assistants. These are spoken of as his 'sons.' The water for the ablution must be drawn from a spring - sometimes from three springs. They go in the morning of the day of consecration to fetch the water, taking with

Eveni,
Doll-woman, 1910.
Reindeer fur, woolen and cotton fabric, beads, dressed reindeer skin, 16 cm.
Russian Museum of Ethnography, St. Petersburg. Primorskaya Oblast, Anadyr Krai.

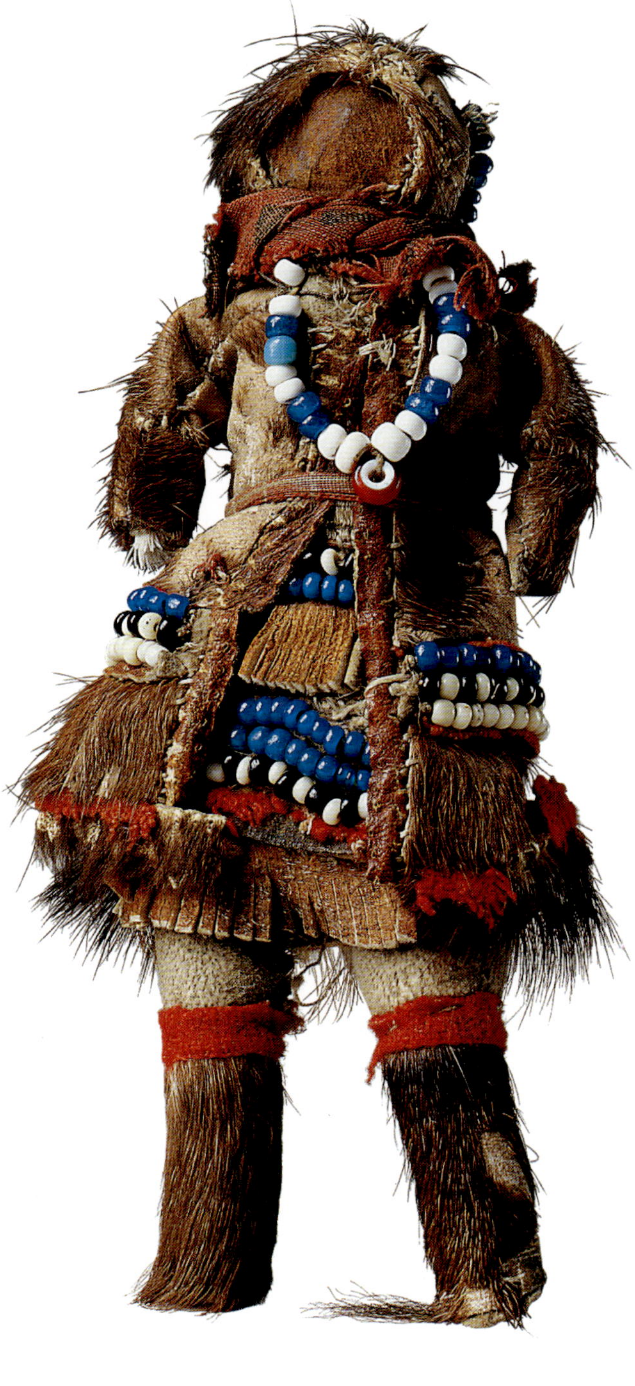

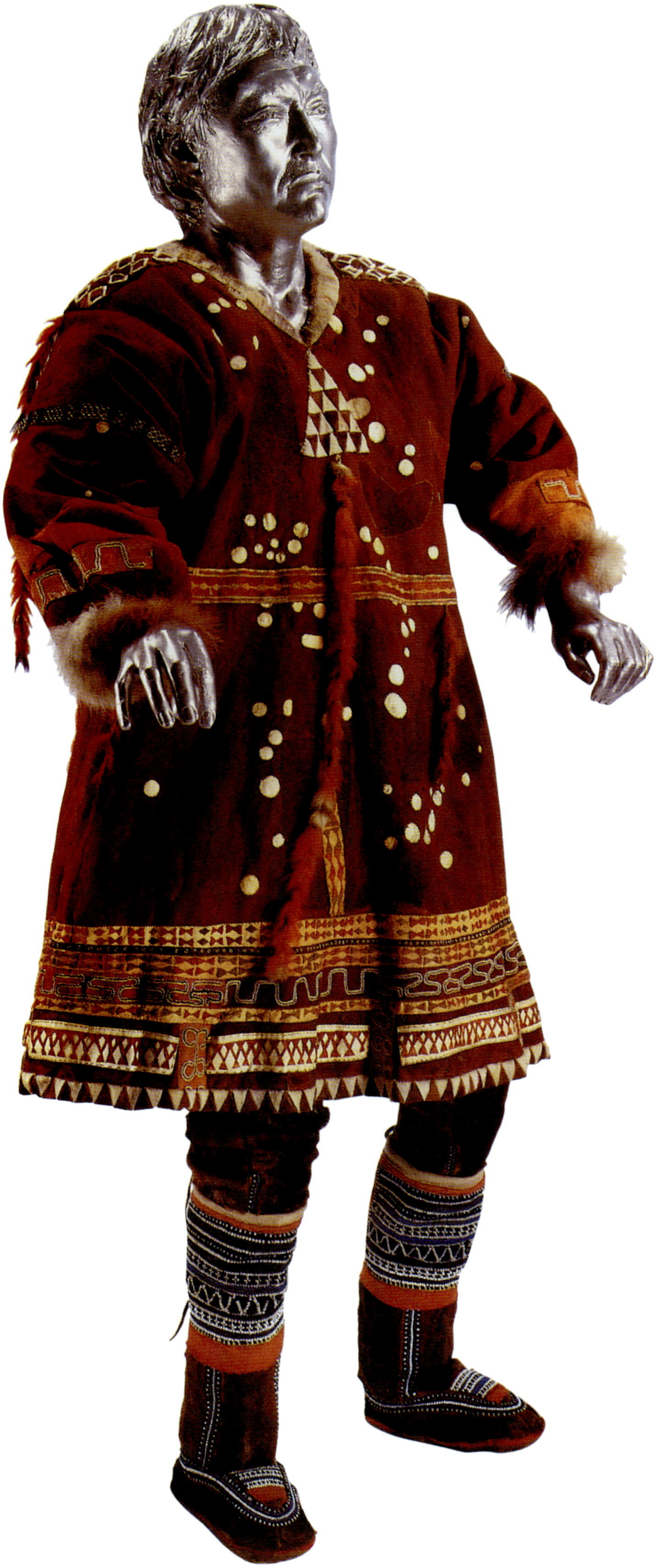

them *tarasun*, with which they make a libation to the master and mistress-spirits of the spring. As they return, they pluck up from the earth birch-seedlings, of which they make a broom, and take it to the house of the novice. Next the water is heated over a fire, and into it are thrown certain herbs and pieces of bark. Then from the ears of a male goat prepared beforehand, they cut pieces of hair, and some shavings from its horns and hoofs, and throw these also into the pot. The goat is then killed in such a manner that its blood drips into the pot. Then only is the water ready for the consecration ceremony. The flesh of the goat is given to the women present, who cook and eat it.

Now the father-shaman foretells the future from a sheep's shoulder-blade. He summons the shamanist ancestors of the novice, and offers libations of wine and *tarasun*. Then he dips the birch-broom into the water and beats the candidate on his naked back, as do also the nine 'sons' of the 'father-shaman,' saying at the same time: "When thou art called to a poor man, ask little in return for your trouble, and take what is given. Take care of the poor always, help them, and pray to the gods to defend them against the power of evil spirits. If thou art called by a rich man, go to him riding on a bullock, and do not ask much for your trouble. If thou art called at the same time by a poor and by a rich man, go first to the poor." The candidate repeats these precepts after the shaman, and promises to observe them.

Then follows a libation of *tarasun* to the guardian spirits; this closes the ceremony. The purification of a shaman by water is performed at least once a year, but sometimes once a month, at the new moon; or else at any other time when he considers himself to have been defiled, e. g. by touching some unclean object. If the defilement is especially extreme, then purification is performed with blood. The shaman also purifies himself after a death has occurred in the *ulus*.

This ceremony is followed after some time by the first consecration, called *kherege-khulkhe*, the expenses of which are shared by the community. Again a 'father-shaman' and nine 'sons' are chosen, and they, accompanied by the novice, ride on horseback from *yurt* to *yurt*, collecting offerings. Before each *yurt* they stop and announce their coming with a shout. They are hospitably entertained, and offerings of different kinds - votive handkerchiefs, which are tied to a birch staff carried by the novice, and sometimes money - are brought to them. They buy wooden cups, little bells tied to horse-staves, and wine, among other things. The day before the ceremony a certain number of stout birches are cut from the groves by the 'sons' under the direction of the 'father-shaman;' from the straightest of these they make horse-staves. The grove from which these are taken is one in which the dead of the *ulas* are buried, and for the propitiation of the spirits there they make offerings of mutton and tarasan. At the same time they prepare the shaman's accessories, and meanwhile other shamans of similar standing with the 'father-shaman ' summon the spirits. In the morning of the day of the consecration the birch-trees cut the day before are planted. The stoutest birch, which has its roots still attached to it, they plant in the south-west corner of the *yurt*, where the ground is left bare for the fire; the top of the tree projects through the smoke-hole above. This birch represents symbolically the porter-god who allows the shaman ingress into heaven. It points the way by which the shaman can reach the sky, and remains permanently in the *yurt* as a sign that the dwelling is that of a shaman.

Among the *Samoyed* and *Ostyak* of the Turukhan country the future shaman spends his youth in exercises which stimulate his nerves and excite his

Koryak,
Ceremonial shaman's coat, 1900-1901.
Dyed seal pup fur, dyed reindeer skin, hair embroidery, cotton thread, cloth, dog fur trim, leather, 96 cm.
American Museum of Natural History, New York. Kushka.

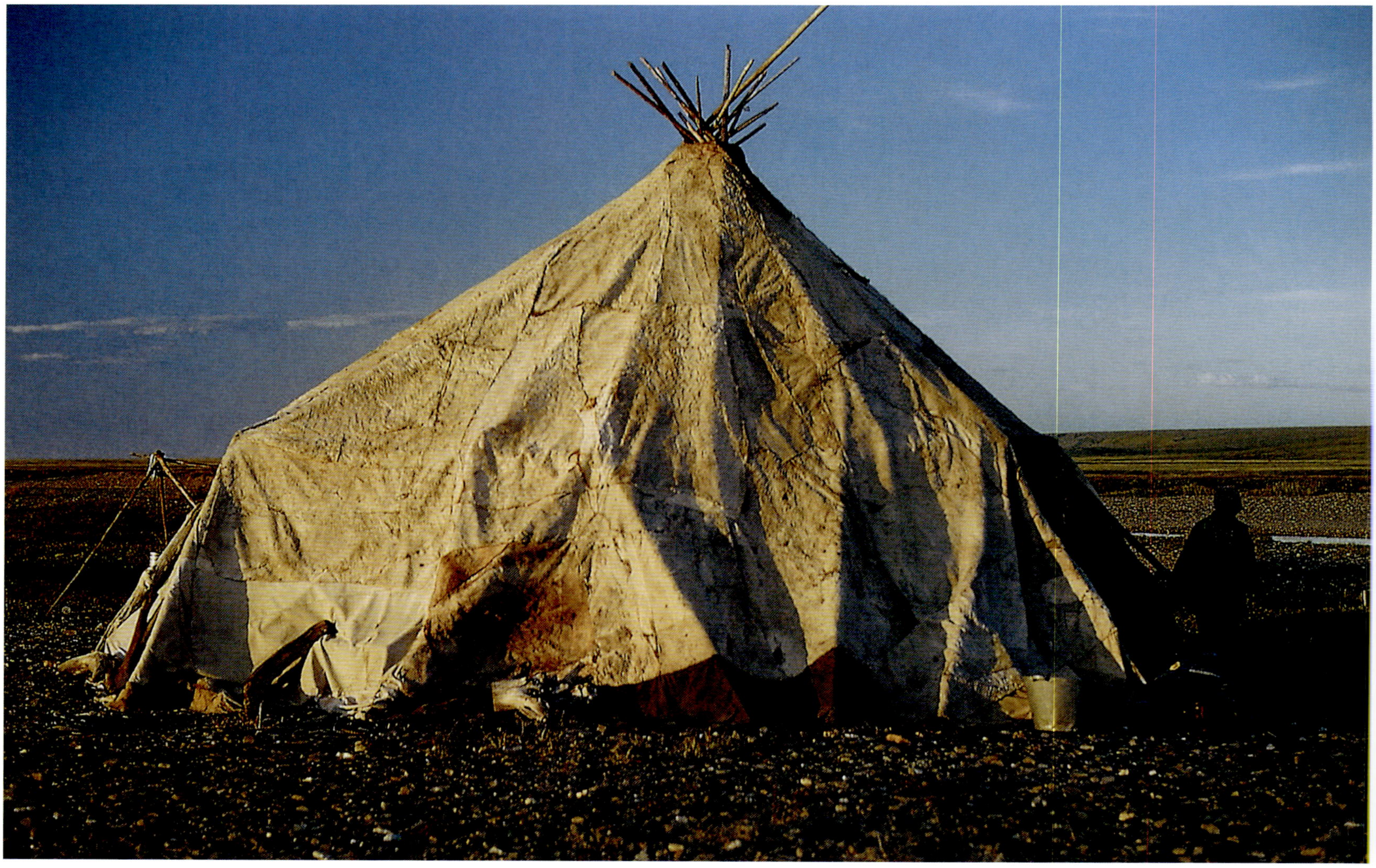

Chukchi yurangas on the tundra,
1998.
Reindeer skin, wooden poles.

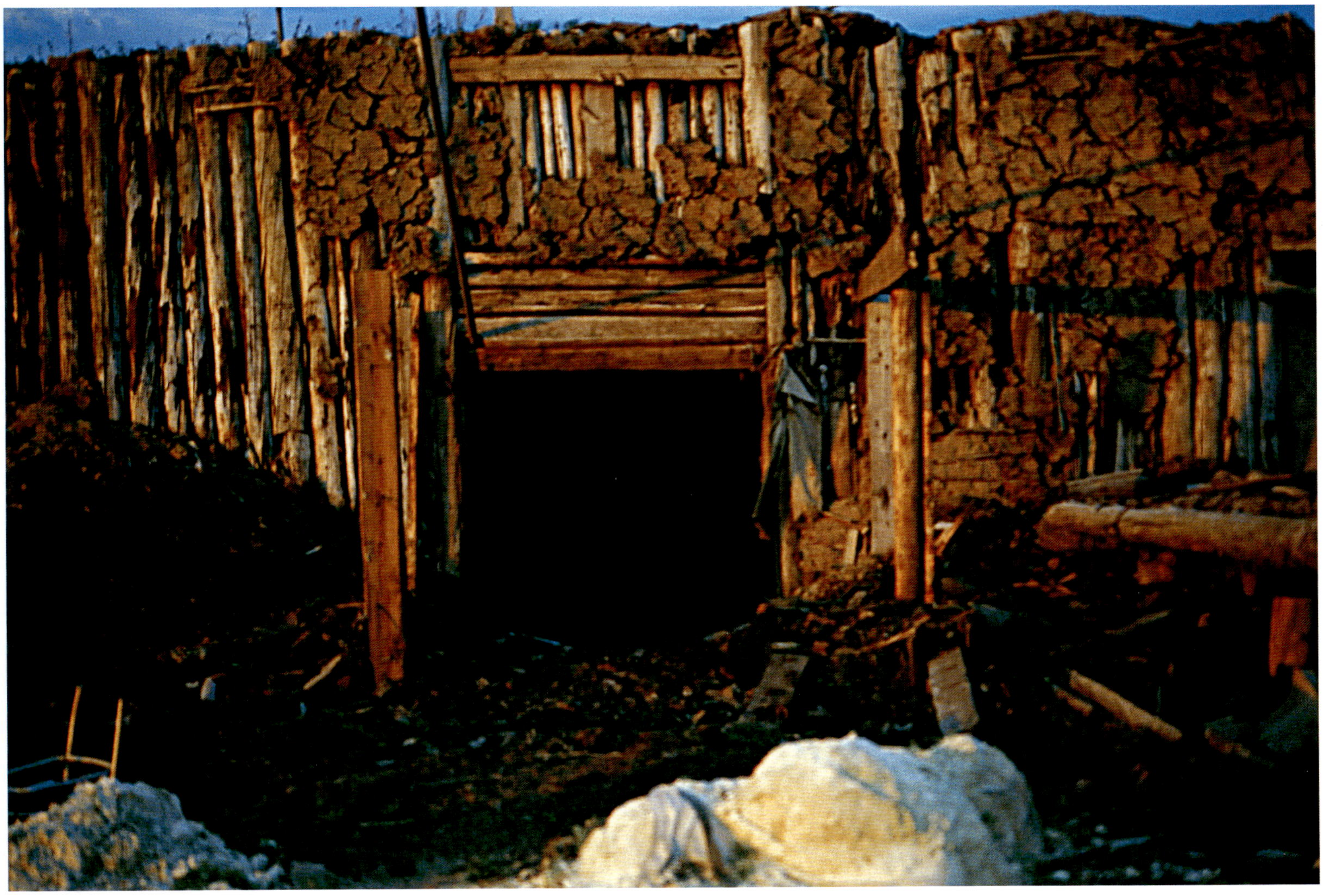

Yakut summer encampment at haymaking time.

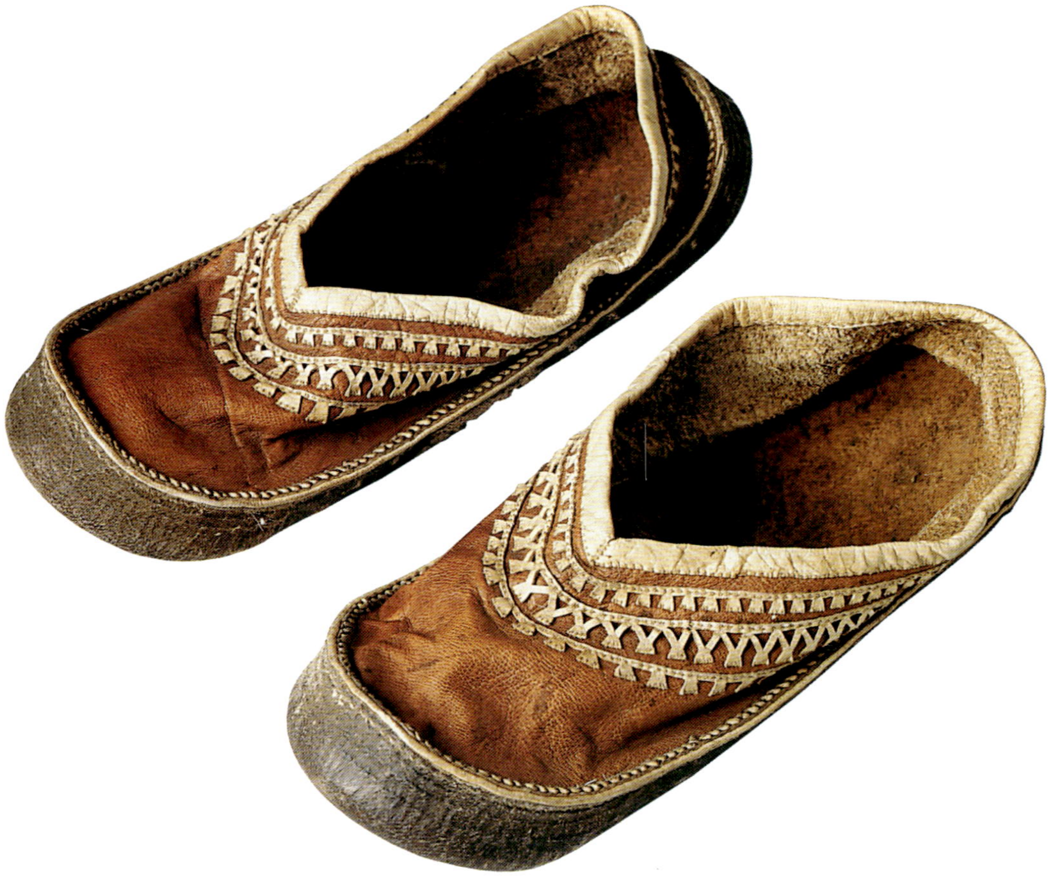

imagination. At the consecration of a novice, he must stand with his face towards the west, while the officiating shaman asks the Dark Spirit to help the candidate and to give him a spirit to serve him. At the end of the ceremony the shaman sings a hymn in praise of the Dark Spirit, and the novice repeats it after him. The beginner is tested by the spirits, who require of him certain sacrifices, as of his wife or son, and he has to promise them various other sacrifices.

One of the Samoyed shamans told of how he was entrusted to the care of an old shaman for training when he was fifteen, as he (the candidate) came of an old shamanist family. The means of education was as follows: Two *tadibey* (shamans) blindfolded him with a handkerchief, and then beat him, one on the back of the head and the other on the shoulders, till his eyes were dazzled as with too much light, and he saw demons dancing on his arms and feet. It must be remembered, of course, that he had been taught beforehand about the Samoyed world of spirits. In former times, Lapland was a school of Shamanism, and all neighbouring tribes sent youths thither to be trained as shamans. At present only among Russian Lapps are *noyda* (shamans) to be found, and they are but degenerate copies of their predecessors.

Unknown,
Shoes.
Russian Museum of Ethnography, St. Petersburg.

Evenki,
Costume for a shaman, 1915.
Fabric, deer skin, bird claws and feathers, 115 cm.
Russian Museum of Ethnography, St. Petersburg. Eastern Siberia, Vitim and Olekma river basin.

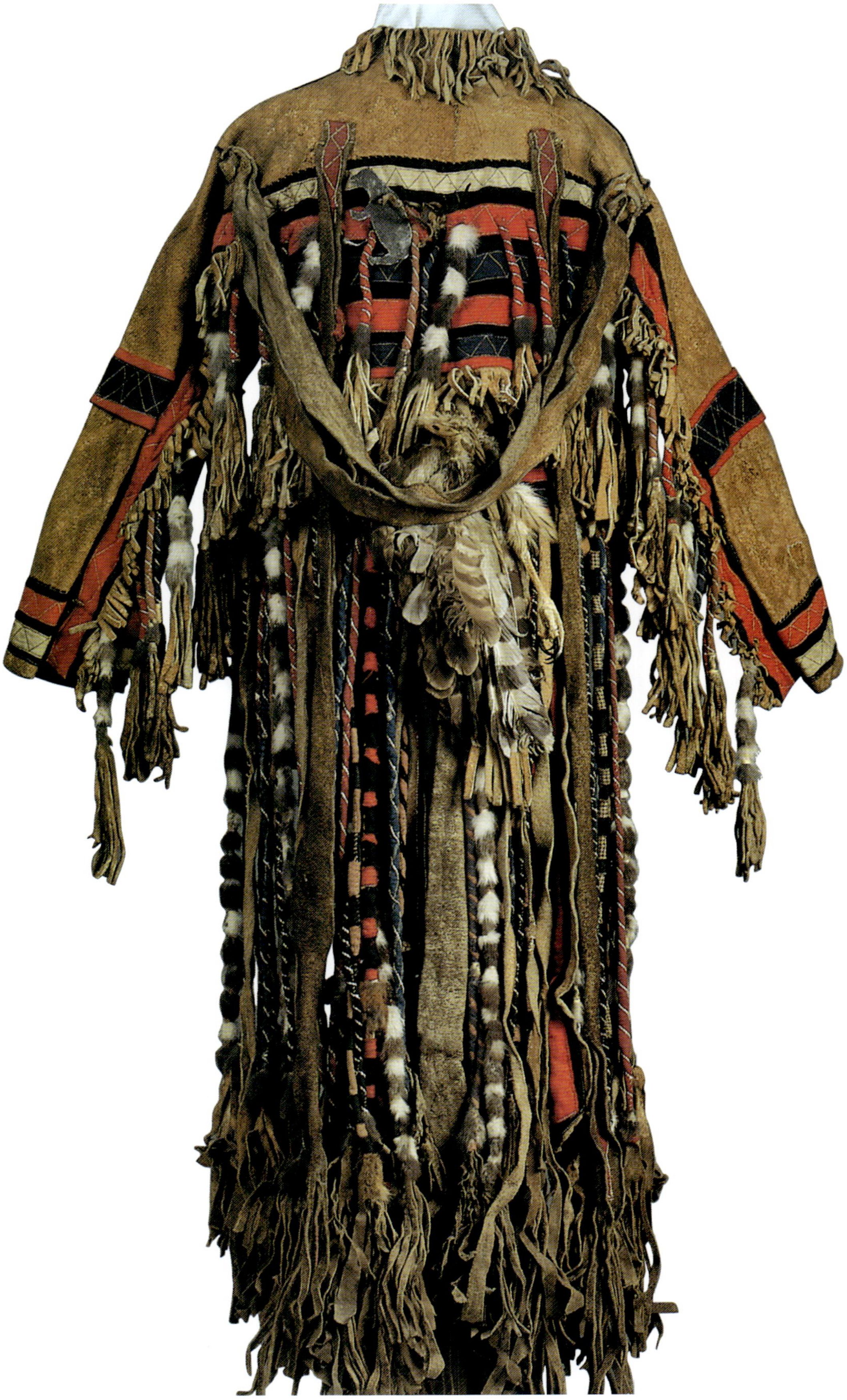

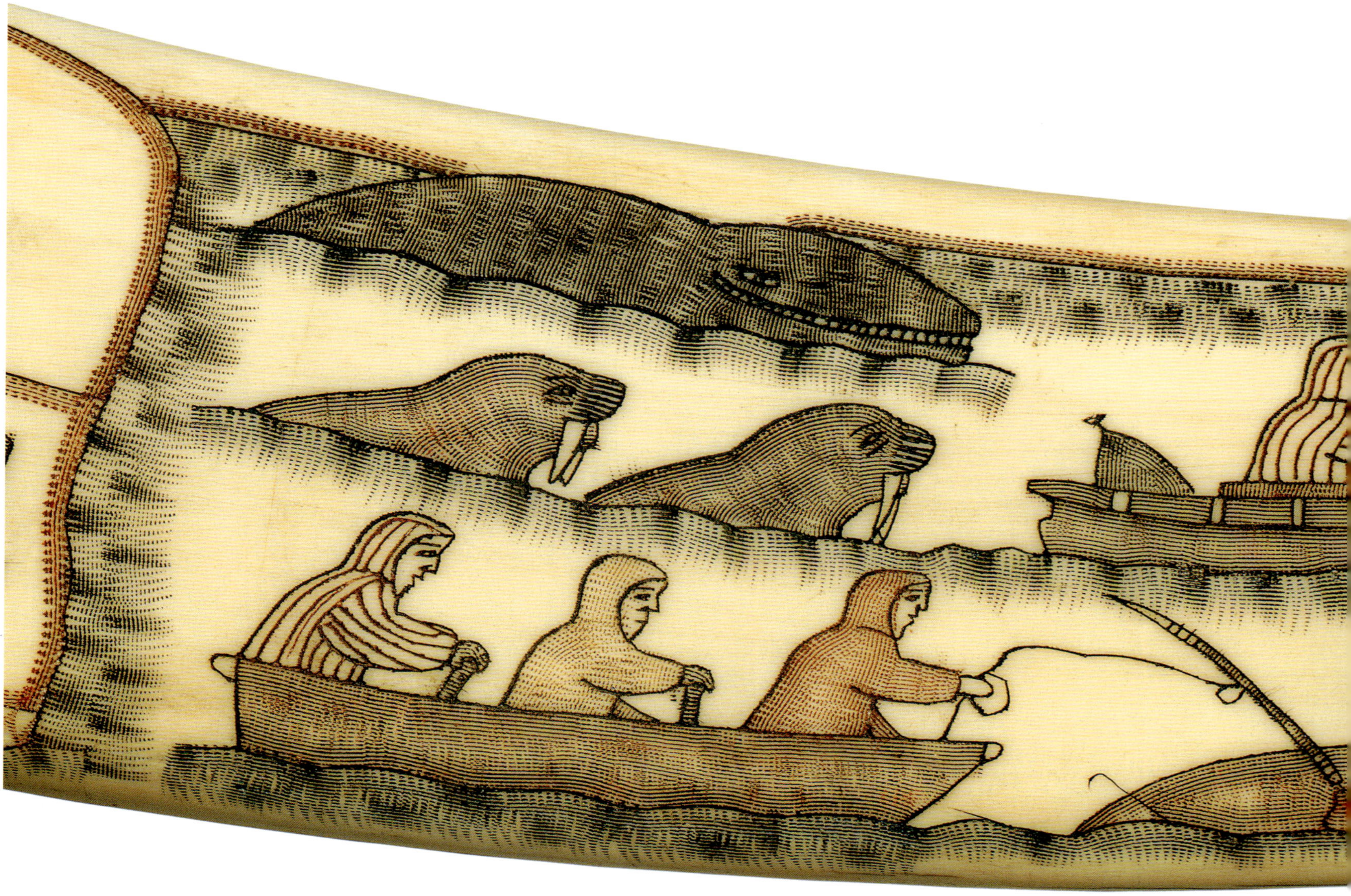

Chukchi,
Tusk with coloured engraving
(2nd side), fragment, 1930s.
Walrus tusk ivory, 51 x 7 cm.
Russian Museum of Ethnography,
St. Petersburg. Chukchi Peninsular.

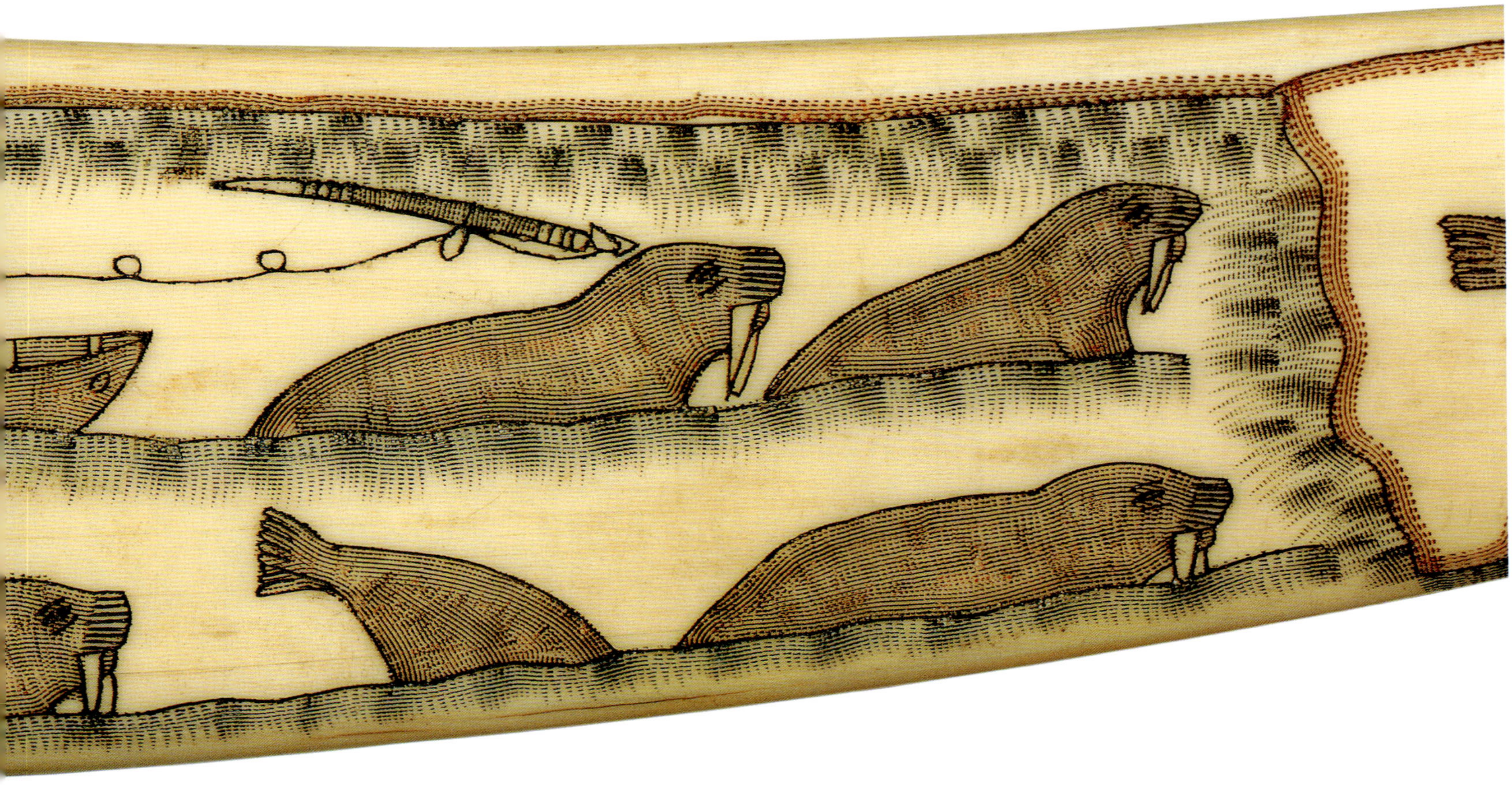

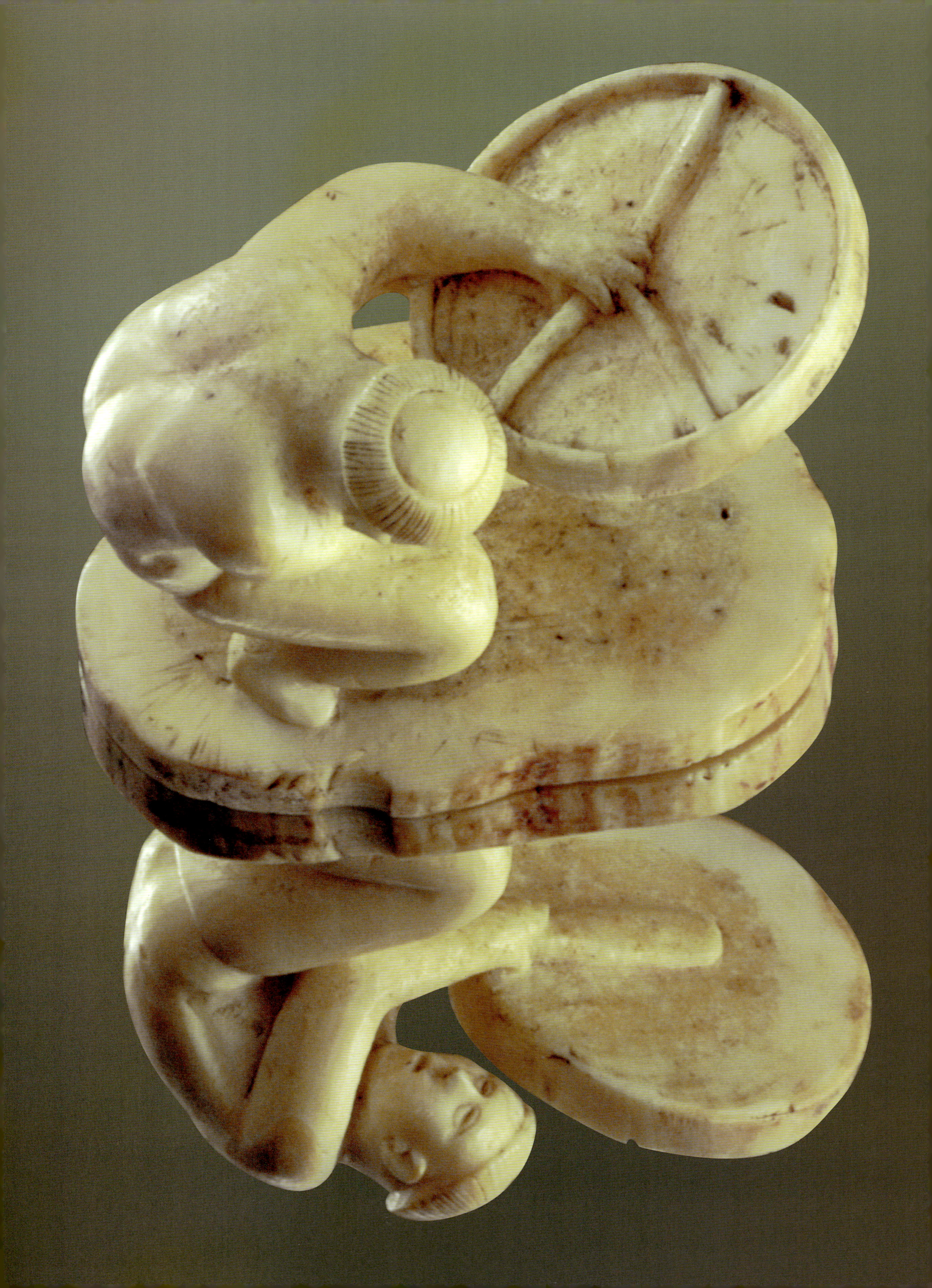

B. TYPES OF SHAMANS

"The shaman Galmuurgin was said by the Chukchi to be '(with) only his (own) body' (em-wikilin), because no other beings helped him with their inspiration. When giving a séance, he began by beating a drum and singing, then, drawing a few long, almost hysterical breaths, would immediately proceed to foretell the future."

In this chapter, which deals with the different types of shamans, the duties of a shaman will be enumerated. In nearly all the more advanced tribes we shall see that certain shamans specialize in one sort of duty or another, while among the more primitive peoples each performs many different kinds of duties - a state of things made possible by the less complex nature of those duties. The high conception of a shaman's duties among certain tribes may be seen from the ideal picture of a Buryat shaman. He is a priest, a medicine-man, and prophet. As a priest, he knows the will of the gods, and so declares to man what sacrifices and ceremonies shall be held; he is an expert in ceremonials and prayers. Besides the communal ceremonies at which he officiates, he conducts also various private cerenionials. As medicine-man, the shaman performs certain ceremonies to expel the evil spirit from the patient. As a prophet, he foretells the future either by means of the shoulder-blade of a sheep or by the flight of arrows.

This ideal type of shaman was probably rare even in the nineteenth century, for accounts say that a shaman was not present at all communal sacrifices. It is the same with some family sacrifices: the *ongons* are fed by the master of the house; and certain other sacrifices, as, for instance, those offered at child-birth, are made without the assistance of the shaman.

The fact that a communal or family ceremony is sometimes presided over by the head of the commune or family, or that a private individual occasionally performs divination, does not alter the fact that the original type of Buryat shaman had the performance of all these rites in his hands.

The Koryak.

Among the Koryak, as among the Palaeo-Siberians and most Neo-Siberian tribes, we may distinguish family shamans and professional shamans.

Family Shamanism is connected with the domestic hearth, whose welfare is under its care. The family shaman has charge of the celebration of family festivals, rites, and sacrificial ceremonies, and also of the use of the family charms and amulets, and of their incantations.

Professional shamans are those who are not definitely attached to a certain group of people. The more powerful they are, the wider is the circle in which they can practise their art.

There is no doubt that professional Shamanism has developed from the ceremonials of family Shamanism. It seems, however, necessary to add another category of communal shamans, forming a transitional class between family and professional shamans. These shamans have to deal with a group of families taking part in important ceremonials. The admission of this third category must not be taken to mean that we agree unconditionally with the idea that the professional

Siberian School,
Shaman beating drum.
Ivory, 6.4 cm.
American Museum of Natural History, New York.

Yakut,
Wedding bag, 1909.
Reindeer fur, beads, seed beads, dressed reindeer skin, 79 x 55-62 cm.
Russian Museum of Ethnography, St. Petersburg. Yakut Oblast, Boturuski Ulus.

Evenki,
Box for crockery, 1962.
Wood, dressed reindeer skin, reindeer, sable and bear furs, woolen cloth, tarpaulin, 17 x 33 cm.
Russian Museum of Ethnography, St. Petersburg. Dalnevostochni (Far-Eastern) Krai, Sakhalin Oblast, Eastern Sakhalin district, Val village.

shaman is a development from the family, or the communal, shaman, though many practices, and the opinions of serious investigators, lend some weight to this notion.

It was among the Koryak that professional shamans were first affected by Christianity.

The Chukchi.

Among the Chukchi, the above division into family and professional shamans needs to be supplemented, since we find that there exist three categories of professional shamans: Ecstatic shamans, Shaman-prophets, and Incantation shamans. Of course, the duties of the shamans of all these categories merge into each other; still, a certain specialization is to be observed.

A. The ecstatic shaman communicates with 'spirits' and is called *kalatkourgin*.

This includes all kinds of intercourse with spirits which become apparent to the listeners; that is, the voices of spirits talking through the medium of the shaman, ventriloquistic performances, and other tricks - generally speaking, the whole spectacular part of Shamanism, which forms the main content of the shamanistic *séances*. As observed above, all this is often considered merely as a kind of jugglery. For performances of this sort, young people are said to be better adapted than older ones. With increasing years some of the shamans discontinue most of these tricks.

B. The shaman-prophet is known as the one who is 'looking into,' *hetolatirgin*.

This branch of Chukchi Shamanism is held in the highest veneration, because the shaman possessing it has the faculty of seeing the danger lying in wait for the people, or the good in store for them, and accordingly he is able to advise them bow to avoid the first and to secure the second. Most of the instructions given are of a ritualistic kind, and refer to certain details of ceremonials, which must be arranged after a certain manner in order to secure the desired result.

There are shamans who, though they have *kelet* at their disposal, cannot give any advice; while others, on the other hand, cannot communicate with spirits, but give magical advice as a kind of internal subjective inspiration, after self-communion for a few moments. These, notwithstanding the simplicity of their proceedings, usually enjoy the highest consideration of their neighhours.

C. Incantation shamans (*ewganva-tirgin*, 'producing of incantations') carry on the more complicated practices of Shamanism.

Incantations, together with spells, form the greater part of Chukchi magic. The incantations may be of a benevolent or malevolent character. Hence there are two types of shamans in this class:

1. 'Well-minded' (*ten-cimnulin*), who play their art in order to help sufferers.
2. 'Mischievous' (*kurg-enenilit*, or *kunich-enenilit*, literally 'mocking shamans'), who are bent on doing harm to people.

Good shamans have a red shamanistic coat and bad shamans a black one. The same colours are used by the Yukaghir shamans.

The majority of shamans, however, combine in themselves the gifts of all these categories and in the name of spirits perform various tricks, foretell the future, and pronounce incantations.

The Yakut.

The division of shamans into black and white is the most essential division among all Siberian tribes, though many travellers speak of shamans in a general way as if there were only one kind. It would seem, however, foolish to overlook the distinction between the religious conceptions of the Palaeo-Siberians and

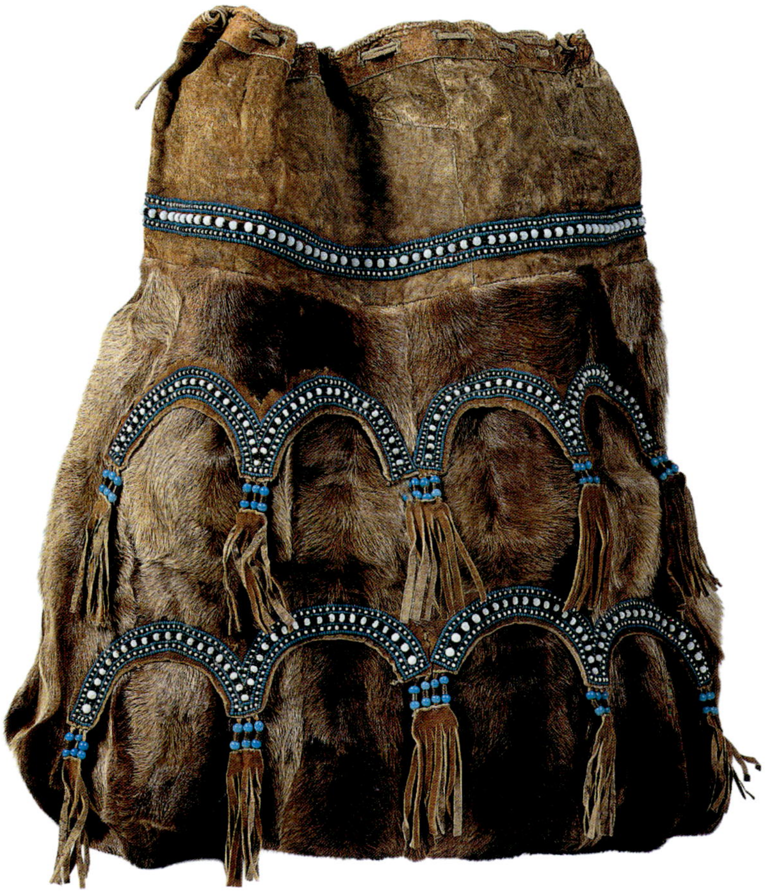

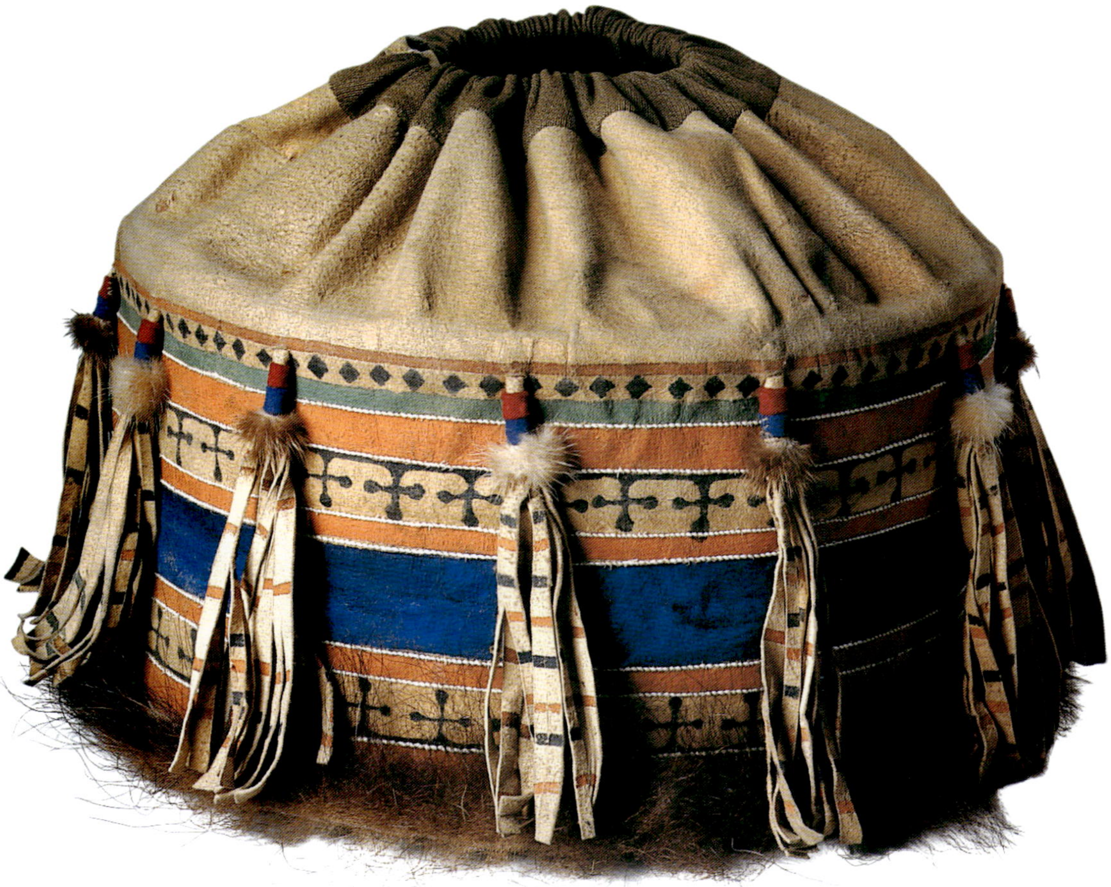

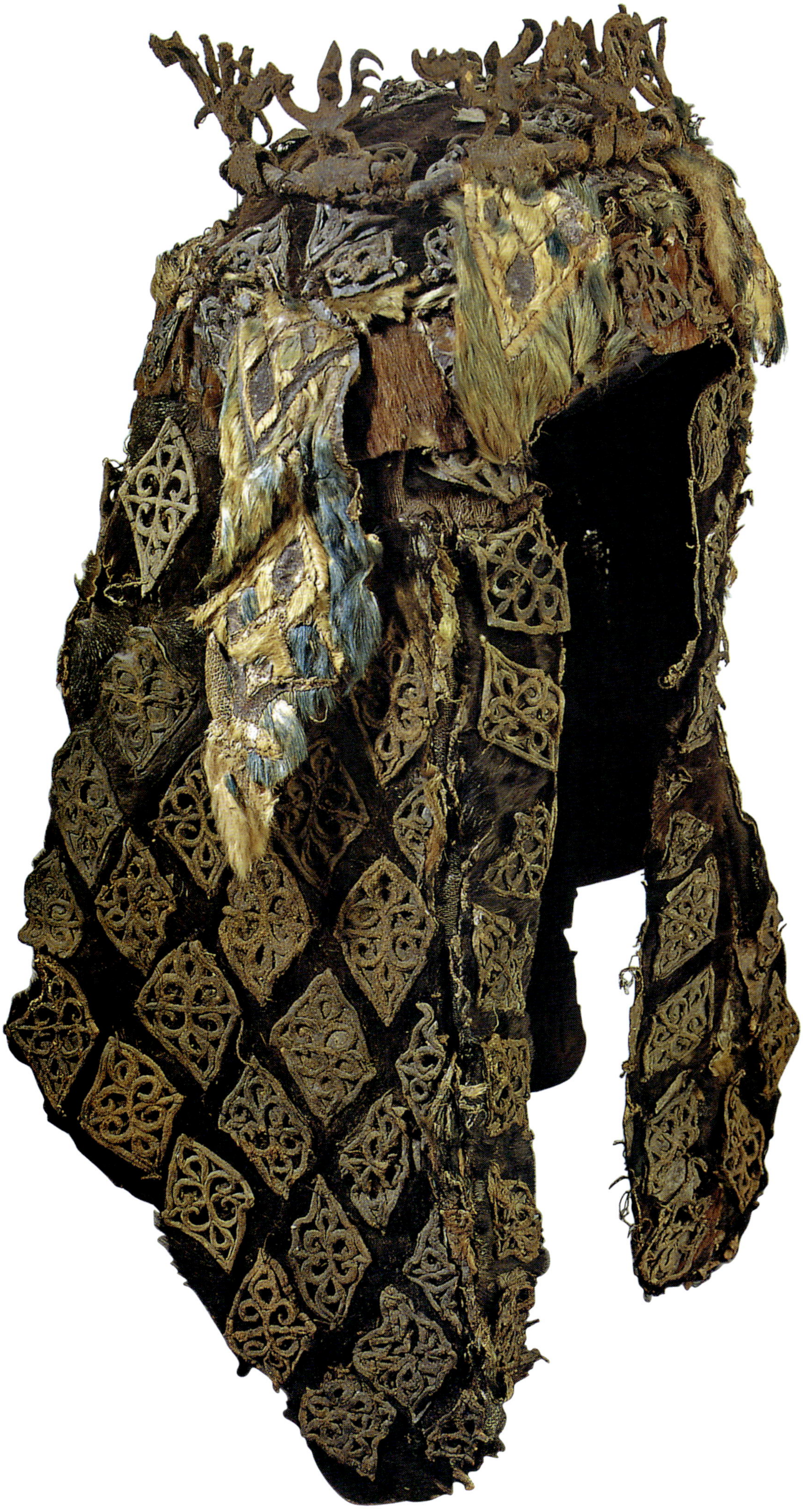

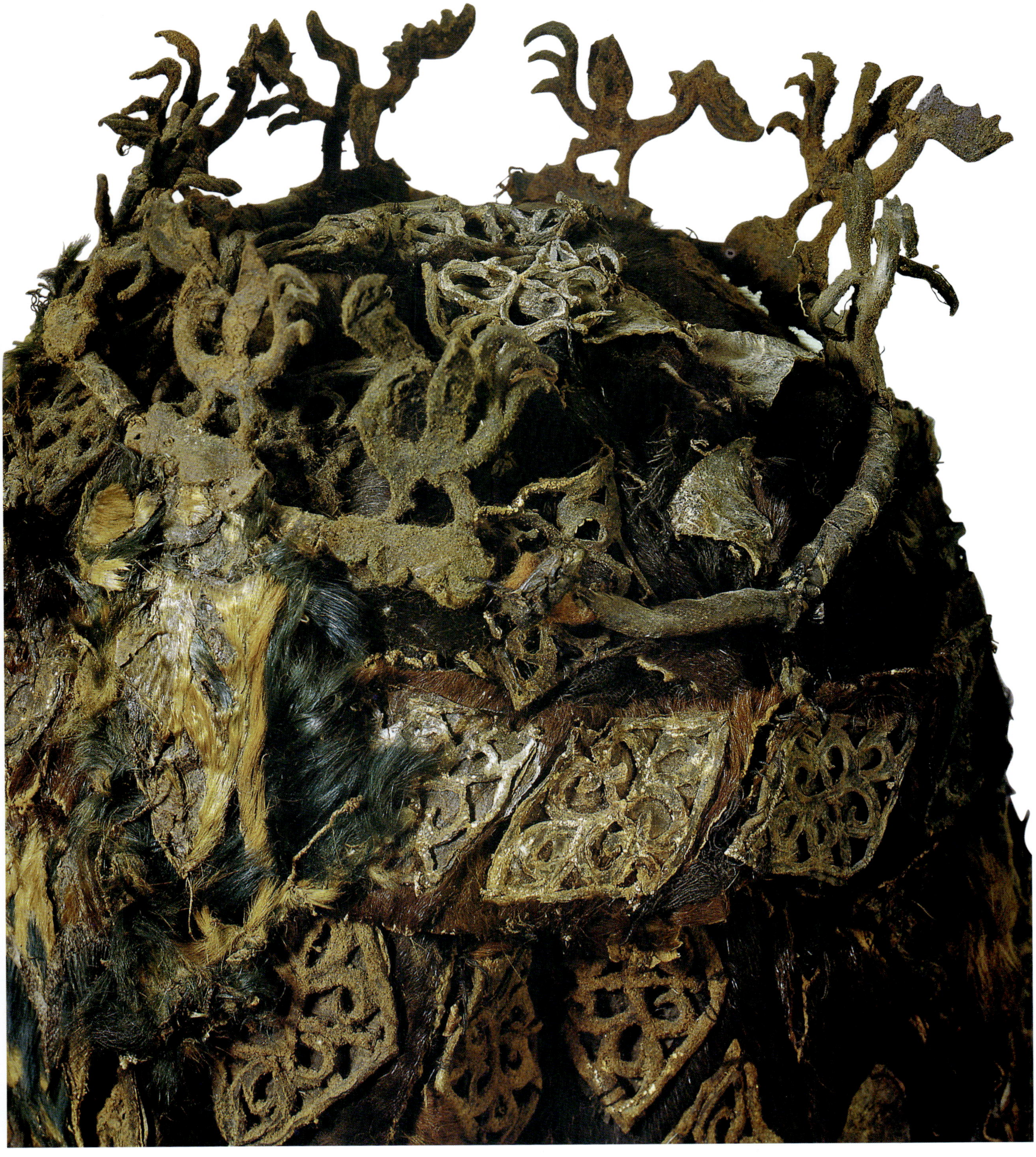

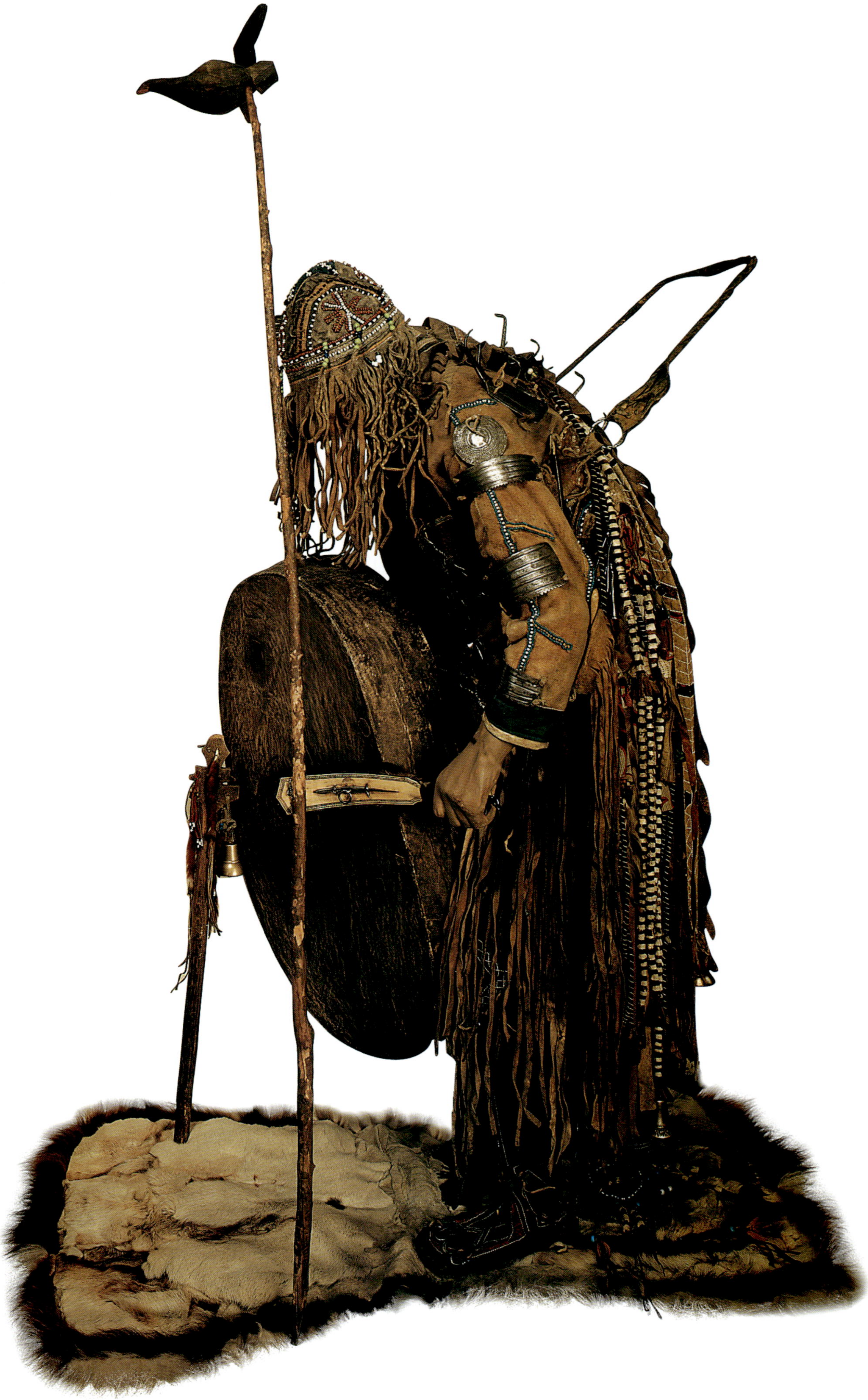

those of the Neo-Siberians. They live under different environmental conditions; and, besides, the Neo-Siberians have undoubtedly been to some extent influenced by contact with the higher Asiatic religions.

It is among the Neo-Siberians that magico-religious dualism appears more distinctly. Again, within the class of Neo-Siberians themselves differences are found. Among the Yakut the black shamans predominate, the white hardly existing; while among the Votyak the white are almost the only shamans now to be found, as the cult of the bright god has almost entirely displaced that of the black.

The Yakut white shamans are called *aïy-oïuna*. They take part in the spring festivals, marriage ceremonies, fertilization rites, and the curing of diseases, in cases where *kut* has not yet been taken away from the patient.

We read in a certain tale that at one wedding there were present nine *aïy-oïuna* (white men-shamans) and eight *aïy-udangana* (white women-shamans). White shamans also ask, in cases of the sterility of women, the *maghan sylgglakh* to descend to earth and make the women fertile. At the autumn fishing, in former times, they lighted torches made of wood cut from a tree struck by lightning, purged the waters of all uncleanness, and asked the *ichchi* (spirit-owner) of the lake for a benefit. This was certainly done by white shamans, if only for the reason that the ceremony was held in the daytime. Only the spring festivals were called *aïy-ysyakh*; the autumn festivals were known is *abassy-ysyakh*. Hence the ceremony of fertilization of the lake must have been performed by black shamans, *abassy-oïuna*, in spite of the fact that this ceremony was held in the daytime.

As to the characters of the two kinds of shamans, the 'black shaman' among the Yakut is only professionally 'black,' and his attitude has no particularly evil character, and that he helps men no less than the white shaman does. He is not necessarily bad, though he deals with evil powers, and he occupies among the Yakut a higher position than among other Neo-Siberians.

Black shamans offer sacrifices to *abassylar* and shamanize to maintain their prestige. They foretell the future, call up spirits, wander into spirit-land, and give accounts of their journeys thither. At the present day there are among the Yakut special storytellers and also special sorcerers (*aptah-kisi*).

According to the degree of esteem in which they are held by the people, shamans are classified as follows: The Great Shaman - *ulahan-oïun*, The Middling Shaman - *orto-oïun*, The Little Shaman - *kenniki-oïun*.

A 'great shaman' has the *ämägyat* from *Ulu-Toïen* himself. A shaman of middling power also possesses *ämägyat*, but not of so high a quality or to so great an extent as the former. A 'little shaman' does not possess *ämägyat*. He is not, in fact, really a shaman, but a person in some way abnormal, neurotic, or original, who can cure trifling illnesses, interpret dreams, and frighten away small devils only.

With regard to the classification of shamans into 'white' and 'black,' some suggest that these two classes of shamans originated and developed independently. One might imagine that the class of white shamans came into existence first, and that it derived from the class of heads of families and clans. The custom of the choice of one shaman leader for common ceremonies or sacrifices may have helped in this evolution of the white shaman from the heads of families. The wisest and most respected member of the community would probably have the best chance of being chosen, as he could please not only the people but also the spirits.

Buryat,
Woman's head covering,
5th century B.C.
Leather, feathers, gold, 50 x 30 cm.
State Hermitage Museum,
St. Petersburg.

Buryat,
Woman's head covering, detail,
5th century B.C.
Leather, feathers, gold, 50 x 30 cm.
State Hermitage Museum,
St. Petersburg.

Evenki,
Shaman. Part of the exposition 'Nations of Siberia', late 19th-early 20th century.
Russian Museum of Ethnography,
St. Petersburg. Eastern Siberia.

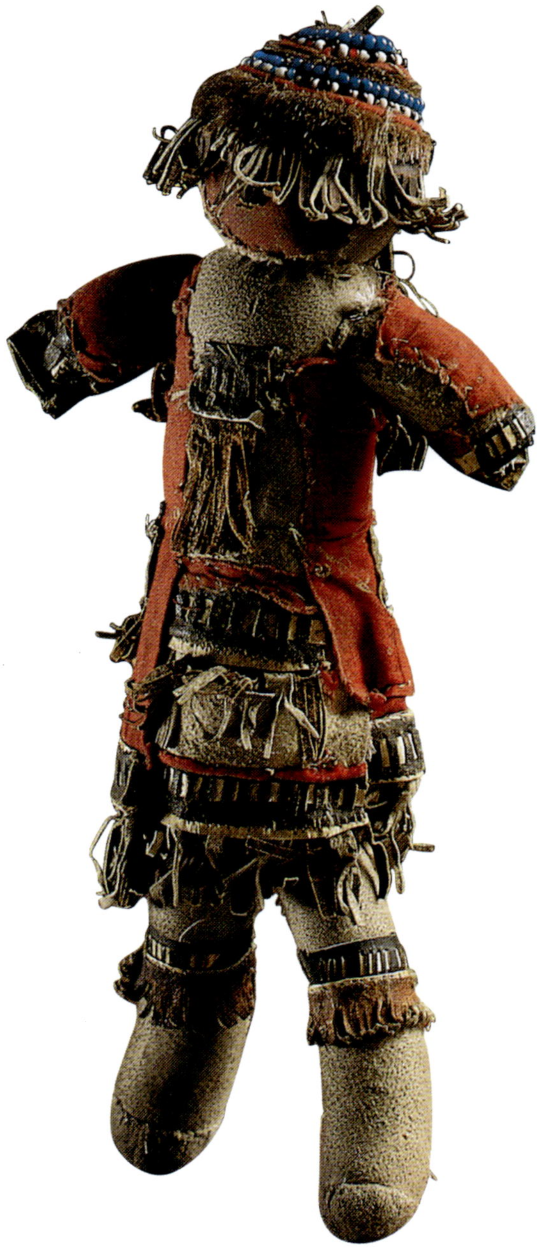

Eveni,
Shaman doll, 1904-1907.
Reindeer fur, glass beads, fabric, metal, 35 cm.
Russian Museum of Ethnography, St. Petersburg. Chukotka, Anadyr.

Eskimo,
Carpet, 1926.
Sealskin, reindeer underneck hair, fur, Diameter: 95 cm.
Russian Museum of Ethnography, St. Petersburg. Chukchi Peninsular.

Evenki,
Cover for a saddle-bag, 1905.
Reindeer fur, woolen cloth, velveteen, beads, 61 x 38 cm.
Russian Museum of Ethnography, St. Petersburg. Primorskaya Oblast, Okhotsk Okrug, Inya territory.

The same persons might then have been chosen repeatedly, and presently a class of white shamans might arise for the communal cults and sacrifices. In the meantime the head of the family could still keep his priestly power in his own home, until the professional shaman took his place. The white shaman may be a woman, in cases where the woman stands as family head.

Now as to the black shamans, we assert that they were originally women, and the following linguistic and sociological particulars are made to act as evidence in support of this hypothesis.

What is the essential meaning of the word shaman? In Sanskrit *sram*=to be tired, to become weary; *sramana*=work, religious mendicant. In the Pali language the word *samana* has the same meaning. These two latter words have been adopted by the Buddhists as names for their priests. But the word *shaman* originated in northern Asia: *saman* is a Manchu word, meaning 'one who is excited, moved, raised;' *samman* (pronounced *shaman*) and *hamman* in Evenki, have the same meaning. *Samdambi* is Manchu: 'I shamanize,' i.e. 'I call the spirits dancing before the charm.'

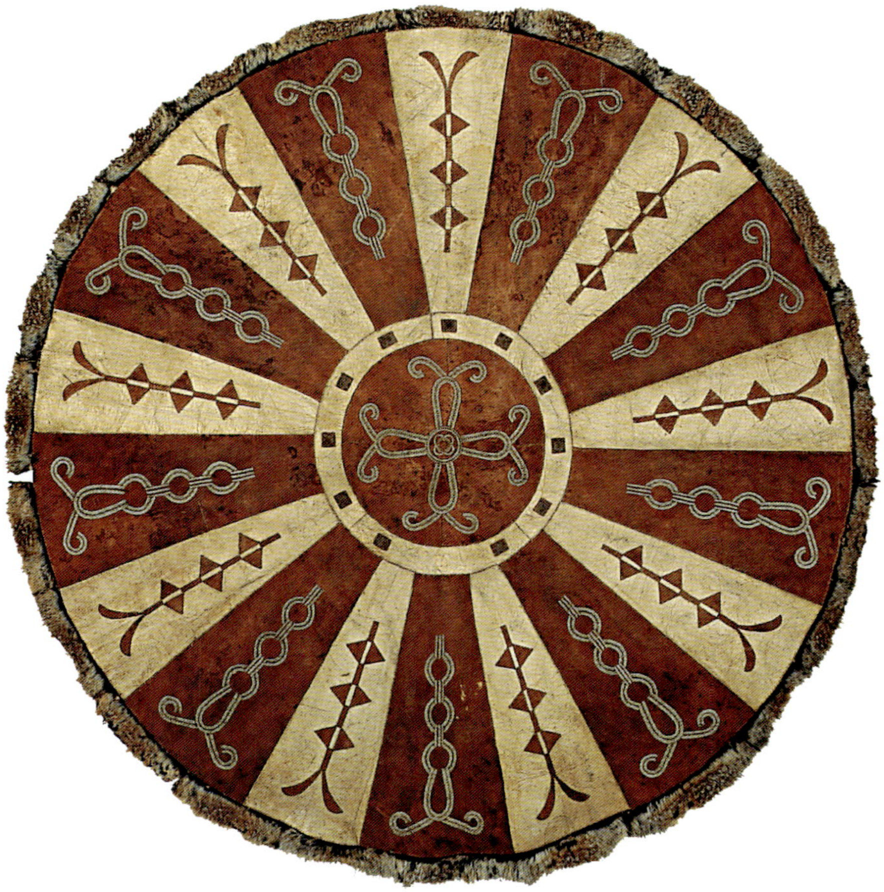

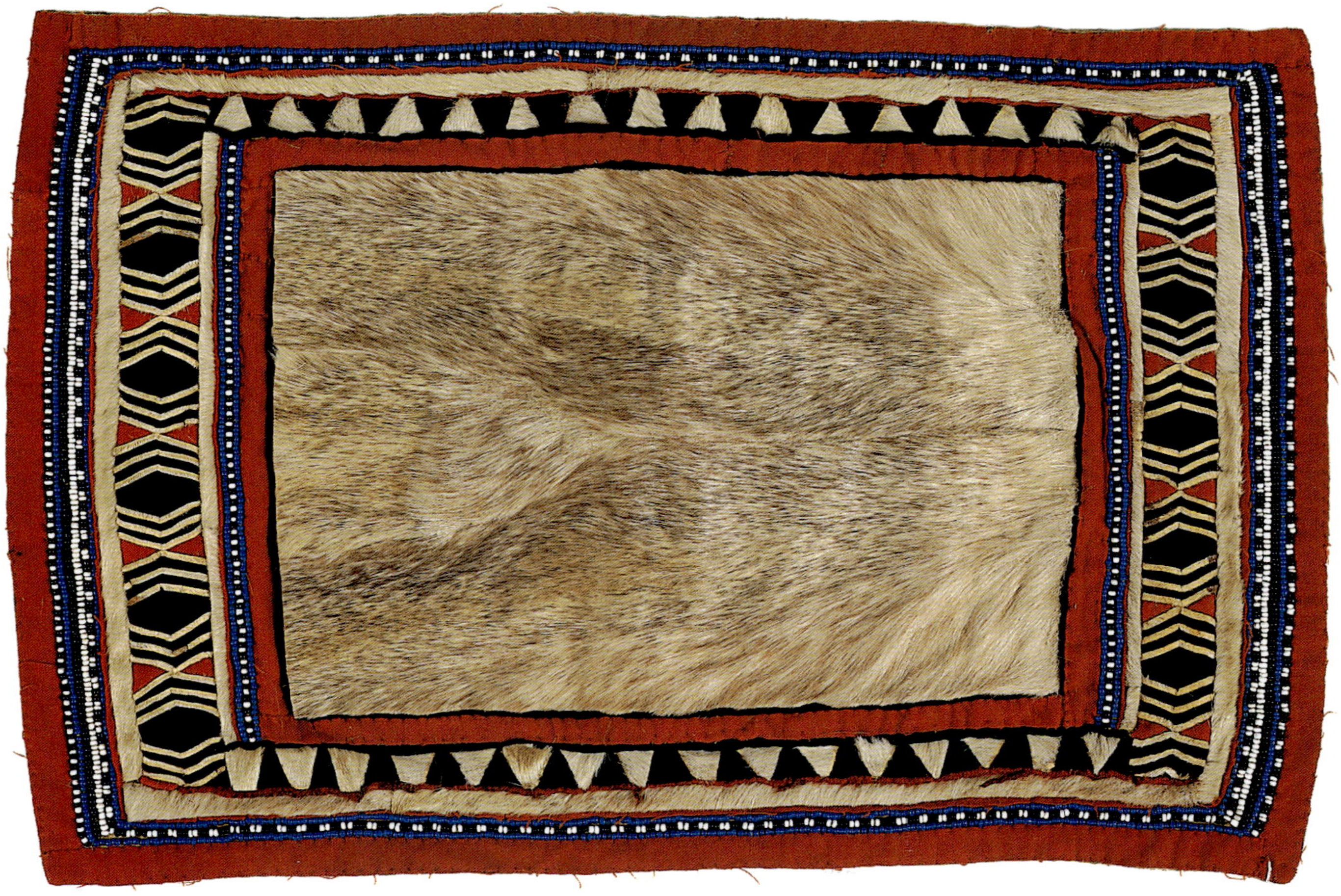

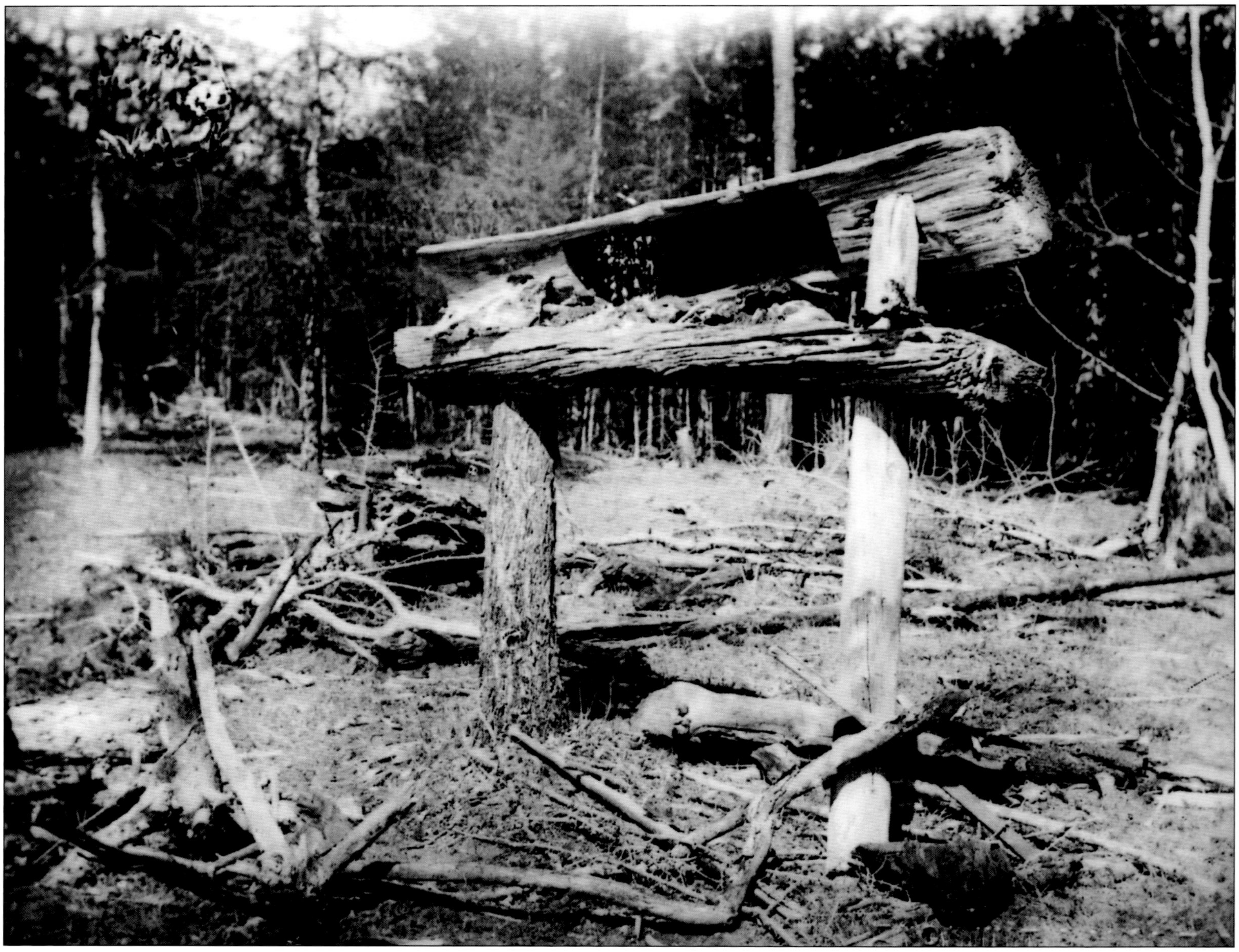

Yakut,
'Aerial' coffin, early 20th century.

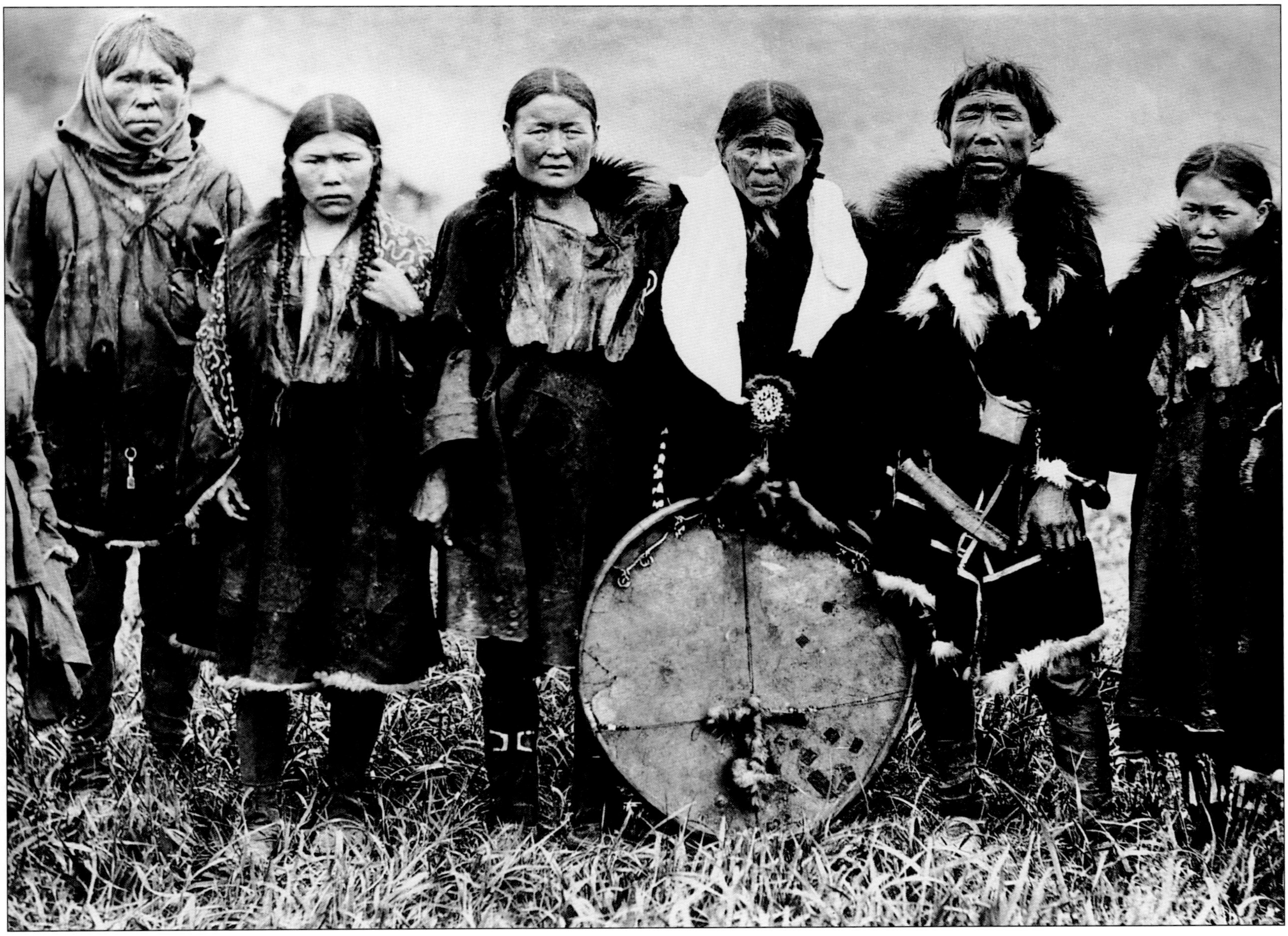

Koryak,
Female shaman with drum surrounded by villagers.

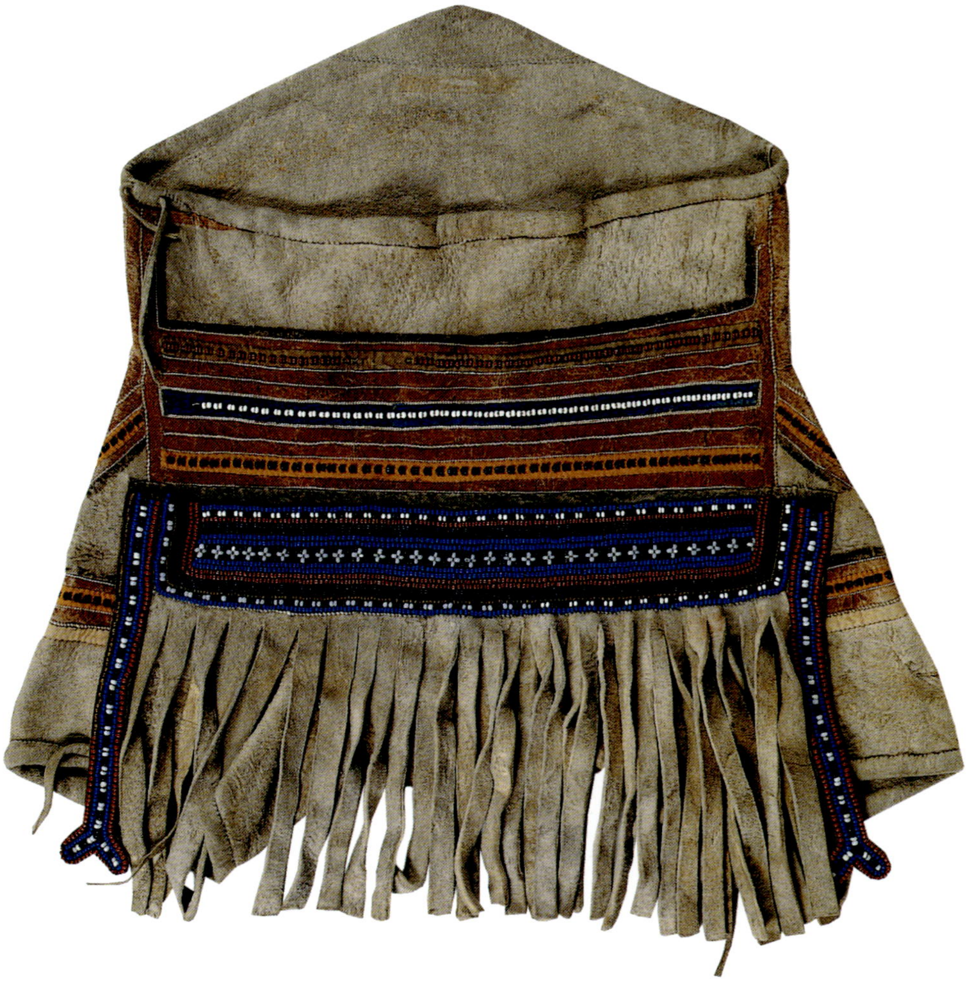

Evenki,
Man's back panel, 1908.
Dressed reindeer skin, beads, cotton fabric, reindeer hair, 38 cm.
Russian Museum of Ethnography, St. Petersburg. Yenisey Gubernia (province), Yenisey Uyezd (district), the Podkamennaya Tunguska river basin.

From the above we see that the essential characteristic of a shaman is a liability to nervous ecstasy and trances. Women are more prone to emotional excitement than men: among the Yakut most of the women suffer from *menerik* (a nervous disease, one type of the so-called 'Arctic hysteria ').

But the only conclusion - if any - that we could draw from this would be that women are by nature more disposed to shamanizing than men. And why should this make her the original black shaman? Only one piece of evidence is adduced to connect women with 'black' shamanizing, and that is taken from Itelmen life. Among the most primitive Itelmen, where there were only women (or *koek-chuch*) shamans, these practised only black Shamanism, summoning evil spirits.

There is also religio-social evidence, drawn exclusively from the Yakut, in support of this hypothesis of the evolution of the 'black' man-shaman from the 'black' woman-shaman: on the Yakut shaman's apron there are sewn two iron circles, representing breasts. The man-shaman dresses his hair like a woman, on the two sides of the head, and braids it; during a performance he lets the hair fall down. Both women and shamans are forbidden to lie on the right side of a horse-skin in the *yurt*. The man-shaman wears the shaman's costume only on very important occasions; in ordinary circumstances he wears a girl's dress made of the skin of a foal. During the first three days after a confinement, when Ayisit, the deity of fecundity, is supposed to be near the woman who is lying-in, access to the house where she is confined is forbidden to men, but not to shamans.

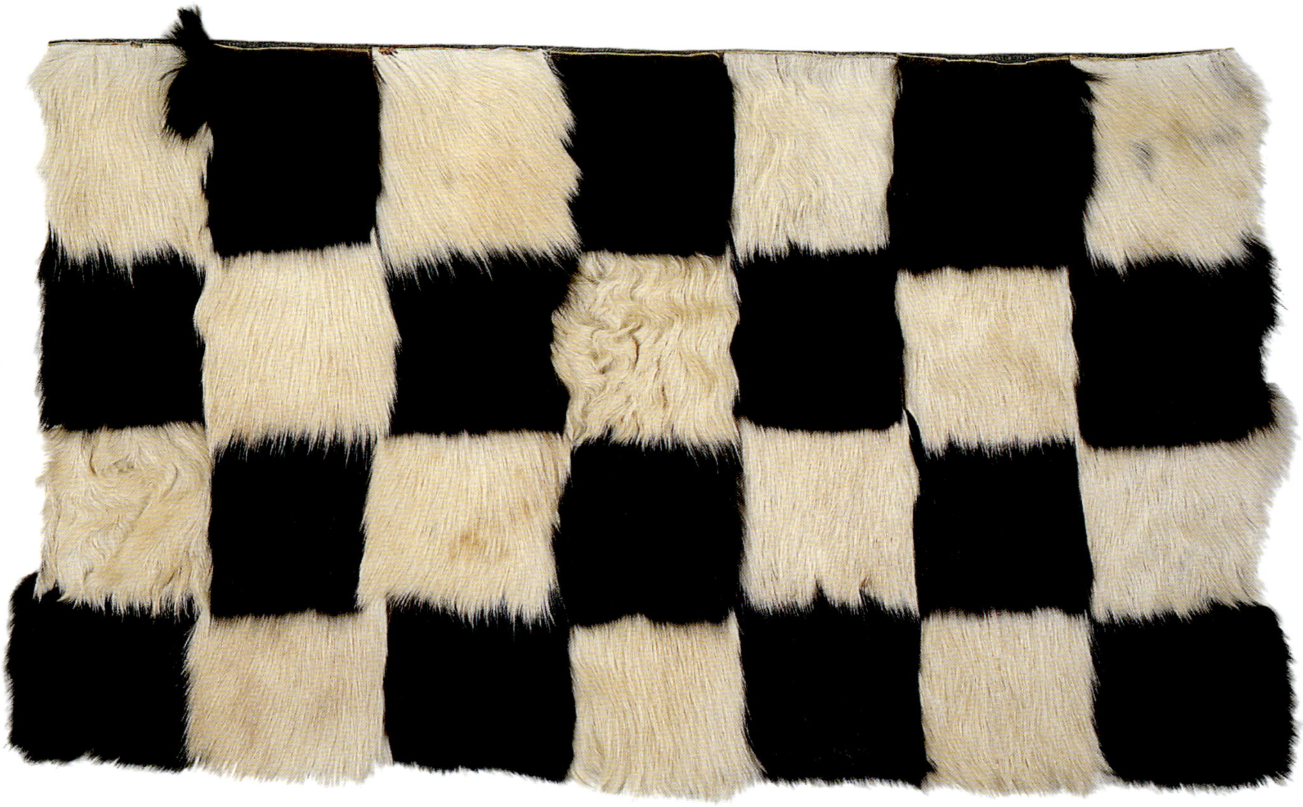

How the female black shaman was displaced by the male black shaman is explained as follows, again using exclusively Yakut evidence:

The smith who made the ornaments for the female shaman's garment acquired some shamanistic power. He was in contact with iron, which was of magical importance, and power came to him through this contact. (The smiths were, like the shamans, 'black' and 'white,' but among the Yakut one hears more of 'black' smiths than of 'white.') Thus the similarity between the vocation of a shaman and that of a smith becomes close, especially when the calling of smith descends through many generations in the same family. Smiths come to be considered as the elder brothers of shamans, and then the differences between them finally disappear, the smith becoming a shaman. The woman, then, since she could not be a smith, had eventually to give up her place to the man.

This hypothesis of women being the first black shamans is, however, not borne out by the evidence. Even if we allow that the above quotations, especially that containing the linguistic evidence, tend to show that women were shamans before men, it does not follow that they were the first black shamans.

The Altaians.

Among the Altaians, besides the shaman, called *kam*, there are also *rynchi*, who, during attacks accompanied by pain, can foretell the future; *telgochi*, or 'guessers;' *yarinchi*, or those who can divine by means of the blade-bone;

Yakut,
Rug, 1978.
Horse fur, cotton fabric, 105 x 58 cm.
Russian Museum of Ethnography,
St. Petersburg. Yakut ASSR, Yakutsk.

koll-kurechi, who divine from the hand; *yadachi,* who control the weather by means of a stone, *yada-tash,* which is found in narrow mountain defiles, where winds blow continually. To obtain these stones a *yadachi* must swear away all his possessions. Hence he is poor, lonely, and usually a widower.

The Buryat.

Among the Buryat, shamans are divided into hereditary shamans and shamans of the first generation. Another division is into real and false shamans. Again there are white (*sagan-bö*) and black (*haranïn-bö*).

The white and black shamans, the Buryat say, fight with each other, hurling axes at one another from distances of hundreds of miles. The white shaman serves the West *tengeri* and West *khats,* and has charge of the ceremonies held at birth and marriage. He wears a white coat and rides a white horse. A famous white shaman was Barlak of the Balagansk district, to whose grave his descendants still go to worship.

The black shaman serves the *tengeri* and *khats* of the East. These shamans are said to have power to bring illness and death upon men. They are not liked, but much feared, by the people, who sometimes kill black shamans, to such a point does this dislike develop. The grave of a black shaman is usually shaded by aspens, and the body is fastened to the earth by a stake taken from this tree. There are also a few shamans who serve both good and bad spirits at the same time.

The Samoyed.

The Samoyed shamans are not divided into distinct classes, black and white, as among the Buryat, but serve both for good and bad ends, as occasion arises. The Lapps likewise make no strict distinction between good shamans and bad. Some of the Lapp *noyda* (shamans) are known as 'Big,' and others as 'Little,' *noyda.*

The Votyak.

The whole Votyak hierarchy arose from the white shamans. The chief of the shamans is the *tuno.*The *tuno* is the chief upholder of the old religion.

As the soul of a *tuno* is 'educated' by the Creator, he is without doubt a white shaman. Besides the *tuno,* there are priests, chosen either by himself or by the people under his advice. In most cases the profession and knowledge of a *tuno* descend from father to son, although any person who has the opportunity of acquiring the knowledge necessary to a *tuno* can become one. In former times black shamans also were to be found among the Votyak, but they have given way to the white, just as among the Yakut the white shaman has been largely displaced by the black.

Among the Votyak there is a classification of shamans into permanent and temporary. The latter are chosen to perform some particular sacrifice. Besides these there are secondary priests appointed by the *tuno* and called *töre* and parchis.

The Votyak black shaman of former times has been converted into an ordinary sorcerer. He is called *pellaskis,* and he can aid the sick, and find lost cattle through his incantations; but all this without any connexion with the deities. Another kind of sorcerer is called *vedin.* He is feared and hated by all.

When the *tuno* has finished his education under *Kylchin-Inmar* (the Creator), the latter takes his pupil to a place where the candidates for the position of sorcerer reside. He examines them, and to those who answer satisfactorily he gives permission to enchant and destroy men.

Woman cleaning the bones of a reindeer sacrificed during the traditional festival of the Koryak reindeer-herders.

Lake Baikal.

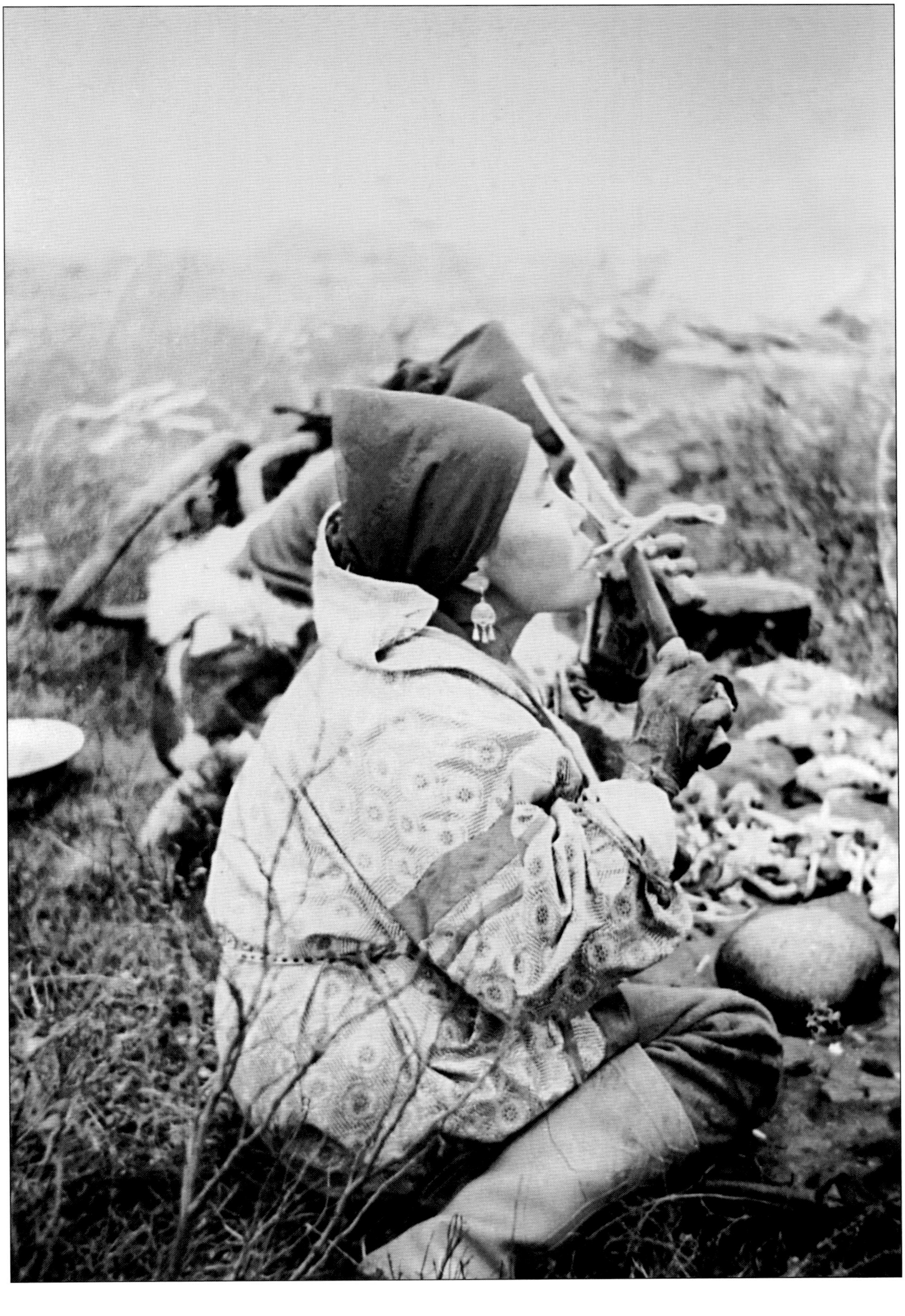

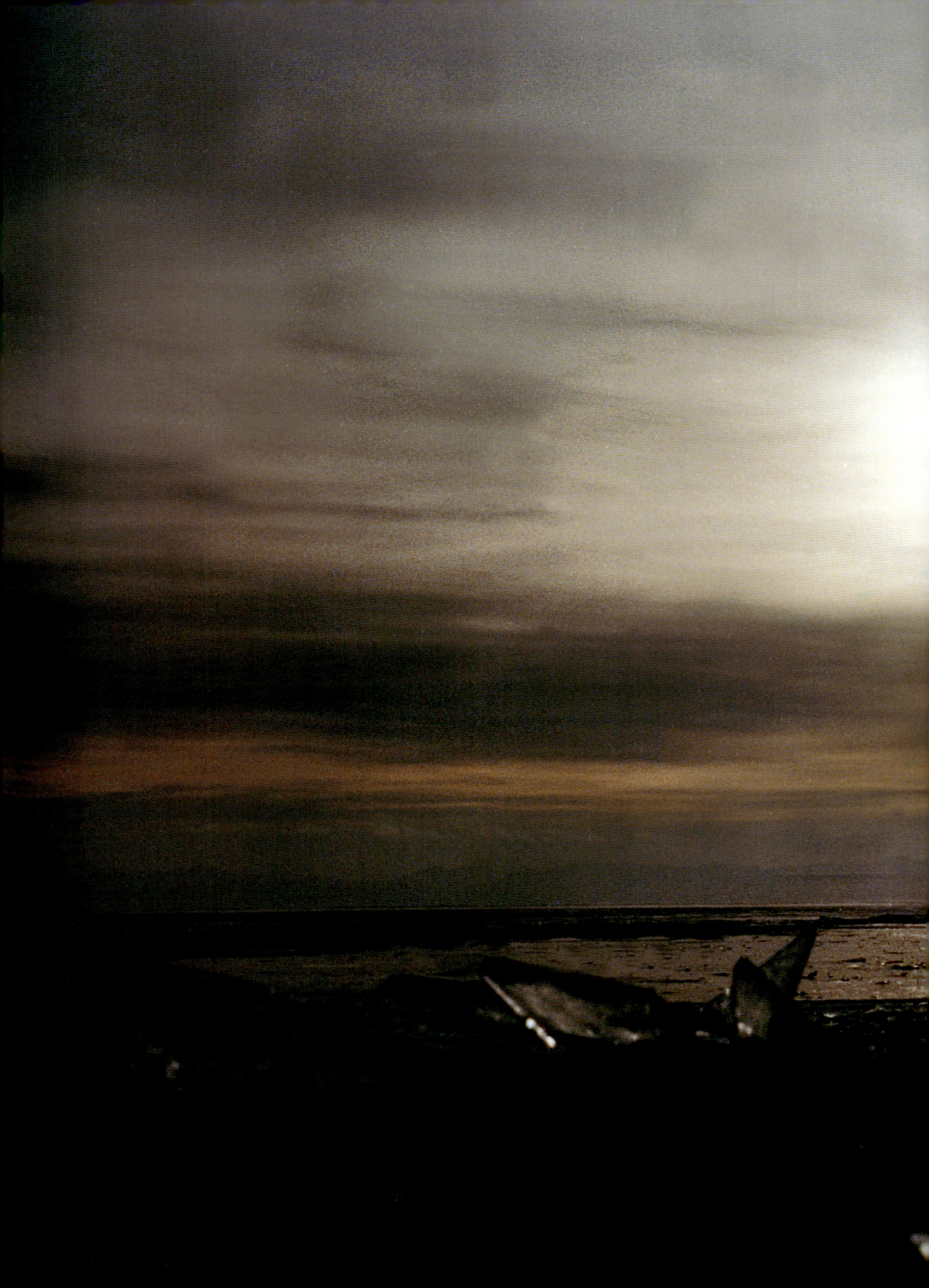

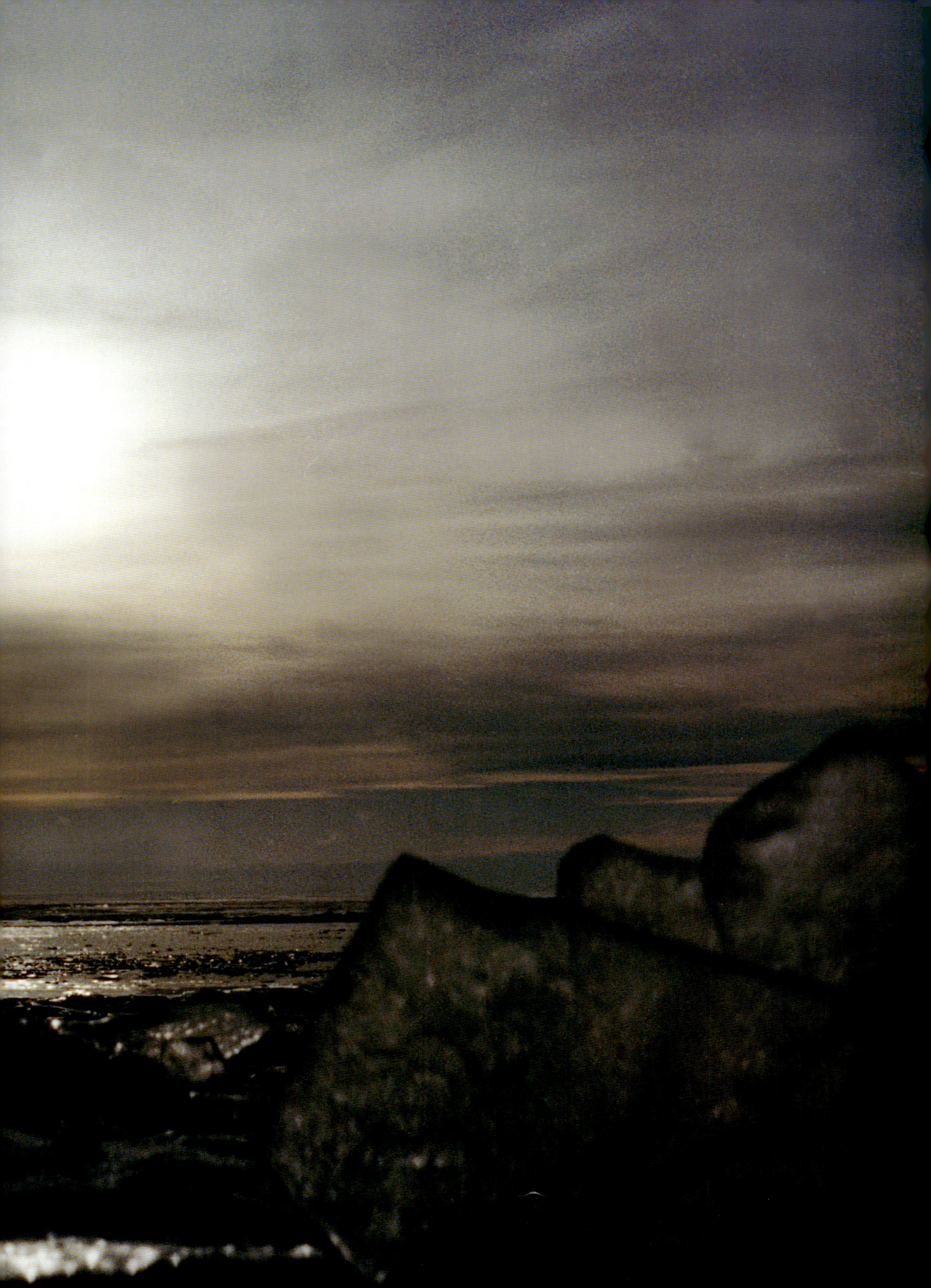

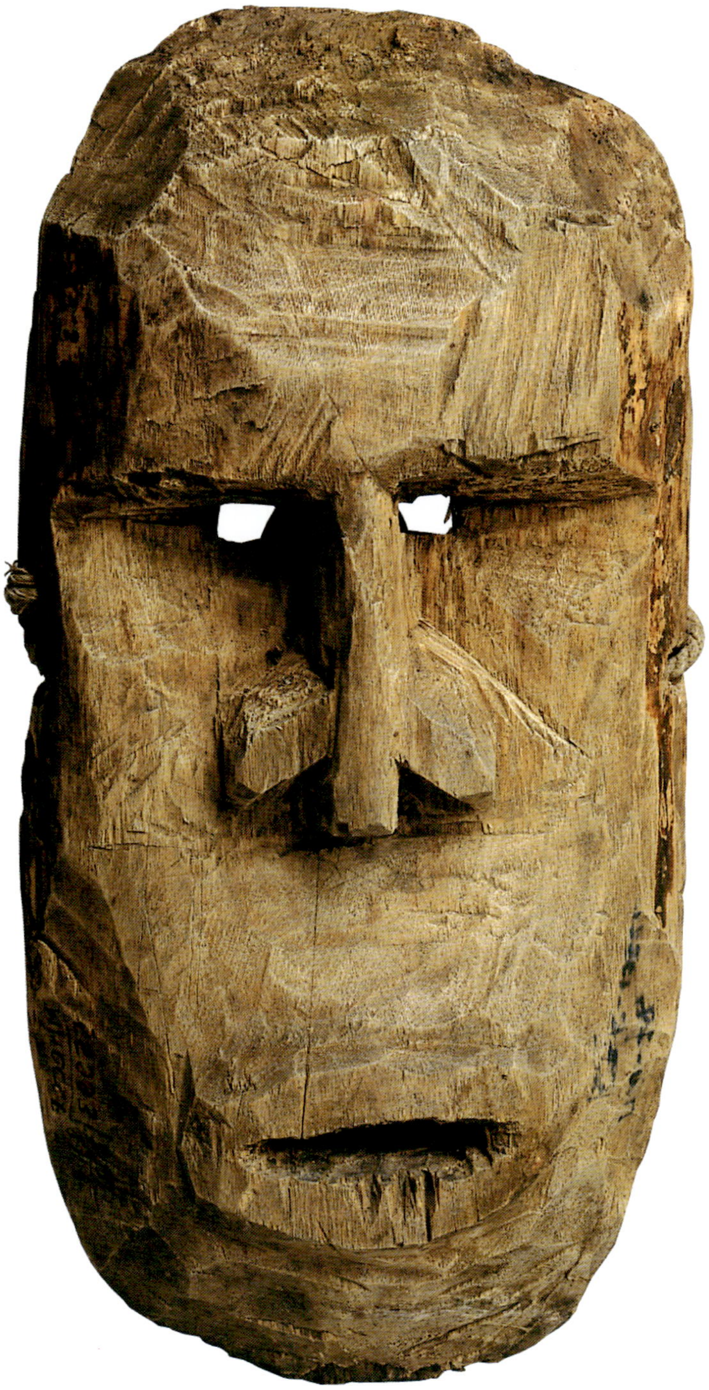

C. THE ACCESSORIES OF THE SHAMAN

"The drum has the power of transporting the shaman to the superworld and of evoking spirits by its sounds."

In everyday life the shaman is not distinguishable from other people except by an occasionally haughty manner, but when he is engaged in communicating with spirits he has to make use of a special dress and special instruments. Of these the most important and the one in most general use is the shaman's drum. It may be said that all over Siberia, where there is a shaman there is also a drum.

It is important to pay great attention to the shaman's accessories. Though they have probably only attracted notice because of their picturesque characteristics, yet their descriptions are very valuable in view of the modern attempt to reach the primitive mind through its symbolical forms of expression.

The following items are indispensable to the shaman's dress all over Siberia: the coat, the mask, the cap, and the copper or iron plate on the breast. The Samoyed *tadibey* substitute for the mask a handkerchief tied over the eyes, so that they can penetrate into the spirit-world by their inner sight. This use of a handkerchief is also mentioned for the shamans of northern Altai, who wear one round the forehead to keep the hair out of their eyes.

These four accessories - the coat, the mask, the cap, and the iron plate - are used by the Neo-Siberians only, since among Palaeo-Siberians the dress is much less complicated.

Each tribe has, moreover, some particular object which plays the chief part in the shamanistic ceremony.

In the Evenki shaman's costume, over the usual shamanistic garment an apron, adorned with iron, is also worn; his stockings, likewise remarkable, are made of skin ornamented with iron. Among the Gilyak and the Olchi it is the shaman's girdle which is of the greatest significance; among the Buryat, the horse-staves. Iron and copper objects seem also to be especially associated with the Neo-Siberians.

The whole costume with its appurtenances used during shamanistic performances throughout Siberia has a threefold significance: The shaman wishes to make a profound impression on the eyes of the people by the eccentricity of his costume. The ringing of the bells and the noise of the drum impress their sense of hearing. Finally, a symbolic meaning is attached to these accessories and adornments, a meaning known only to believers, especially to the shamans, and closely connected with the religious conceptions of Shamanism.

But this interpretation does not bring out the whole importance of the relation of these objects to the spiritual world. They are of great importance, for the spirits will not bear the voice of the shaman unless the right dress and implements are used, and the drum beaten; they are sacred because of their contact with a supernatural and often dangerous power.

Being sacred, these accessories must not be used by any one but a shaman, otherwise they are impotent to produce any result. It is only a good shaman, a real one, who can possess the full shaman's dress.

Among the Palaeo-Siberians it is usually the shaman himself who makes all accessories, and that only when the spirits give their permission. Among the

Koryak,
Ritual mask, 1930s.
Wood, sinew, 30.7 x 16 cm.
Russian Museum of Ethnography,
St. Petersburg. Kamchatka.

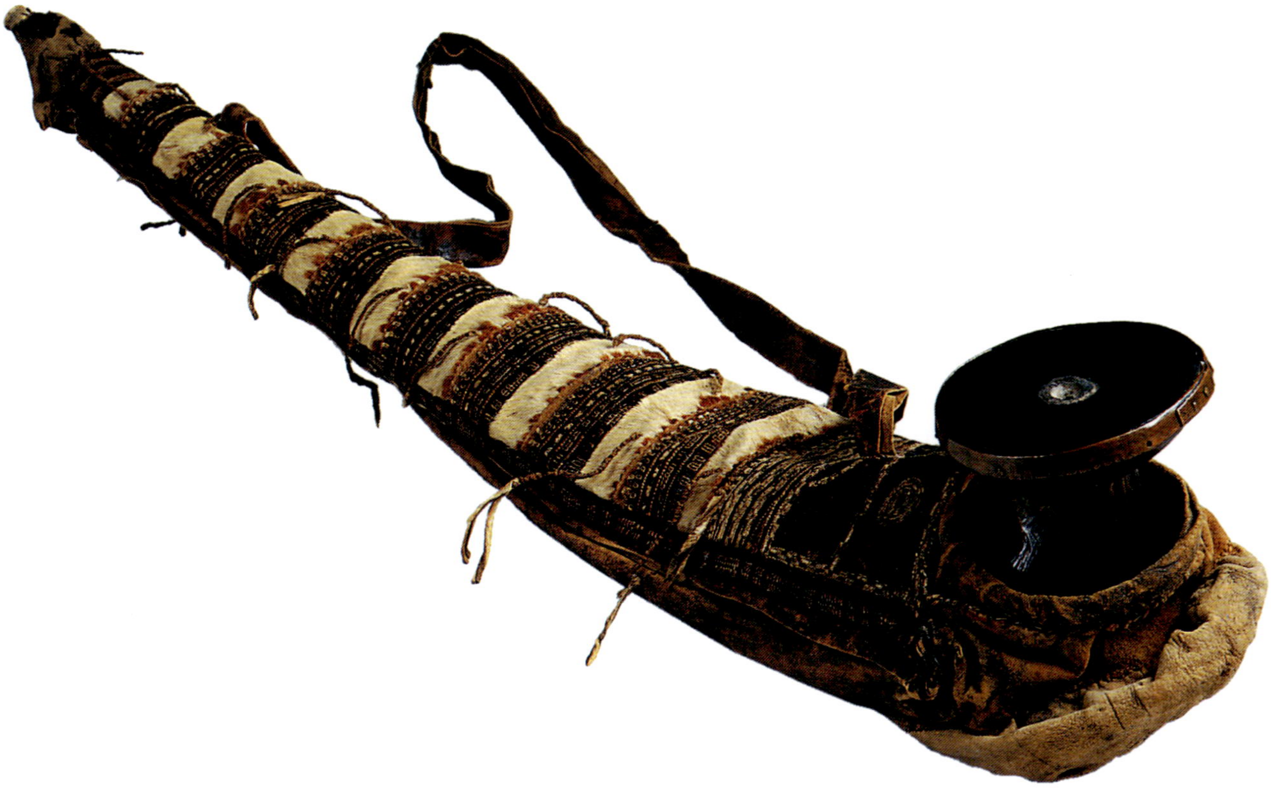

Chukchi,
Pipe for smoking tobacco during public gatherings, late 19th-early 20th century.
Wood, antler, dressed reindeer skin, sealskin, reindeer underneck hair, metal, 87.5 cm.
Russian Museum of Ethnography, St. Petersburg. Primorskaya Oblast, Anadyr Krai.

Koryak,
Pipe, 1906.
Walrus tusk ivory, 14.2 cm.
Russian Museum of Ethnography, St. Petersburg. Primorskaya Oblast, Anadyr Krai.

Koryak,
Pipe, fragment, 1906.
Walrus tusk ivory, 14.2 cm.
Russian Museum of Ethnography, St. Petersburg. Primorskaya Oblast, Anadyr Krai.

natives of Altai it is not all shamans who have the right to wear *manyak* (the coat) and the owl-skin cap.

Among the Yakut even the blacksmith who undertakes the ornamentation of the costume, must have inherited the right. If the blacksmith who makes a shamanistic ornament has not a sufficient number of ancestors, if he is not surrounded on all sides by the noise of hammering and the glow of fire, then birds with crooked claws and beaks will tear his heart in pieces. For this reason the blacksmith's vocation comes next in importance to the shaman's. In modern times it is practically impossible among the Yakut for the shaman's coat to be made, since there is now no class of hereditary blacksmiths. There is an instance of a shaman who had no cap because the old one was burnt and the spirits would not grant him a new one. Many Buryat shamans do not possess drums, since the spirits withold permission to make them, and two long sticks which are struck crosswise against each other are therefore substituted at the performance.

With the degeneration of Shamanism, the number of people who know bow to prepare the sacred instrument, the drum, with due regard to magical custom is decreasing. This, however, is not the true explanation of the disappearance of the drum among the Buryat, for the importance of the other chief Buryat accessory, the horse-staves, which demand equal care in the making, must also be taken into account. Without them the shaman cannot perform any of the principal rites.

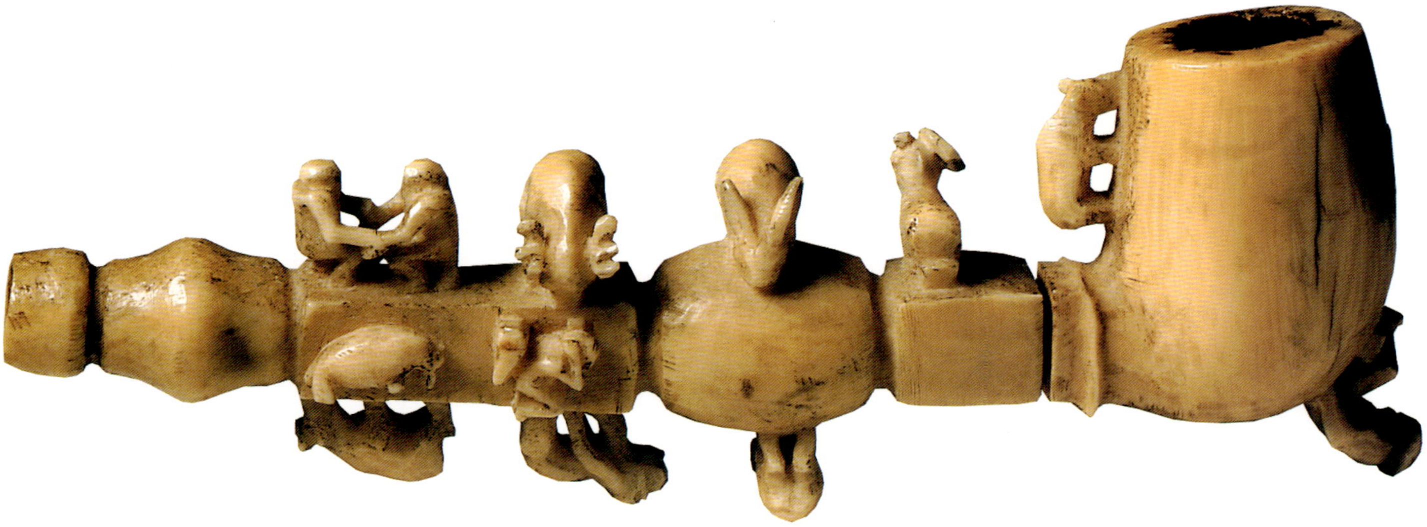

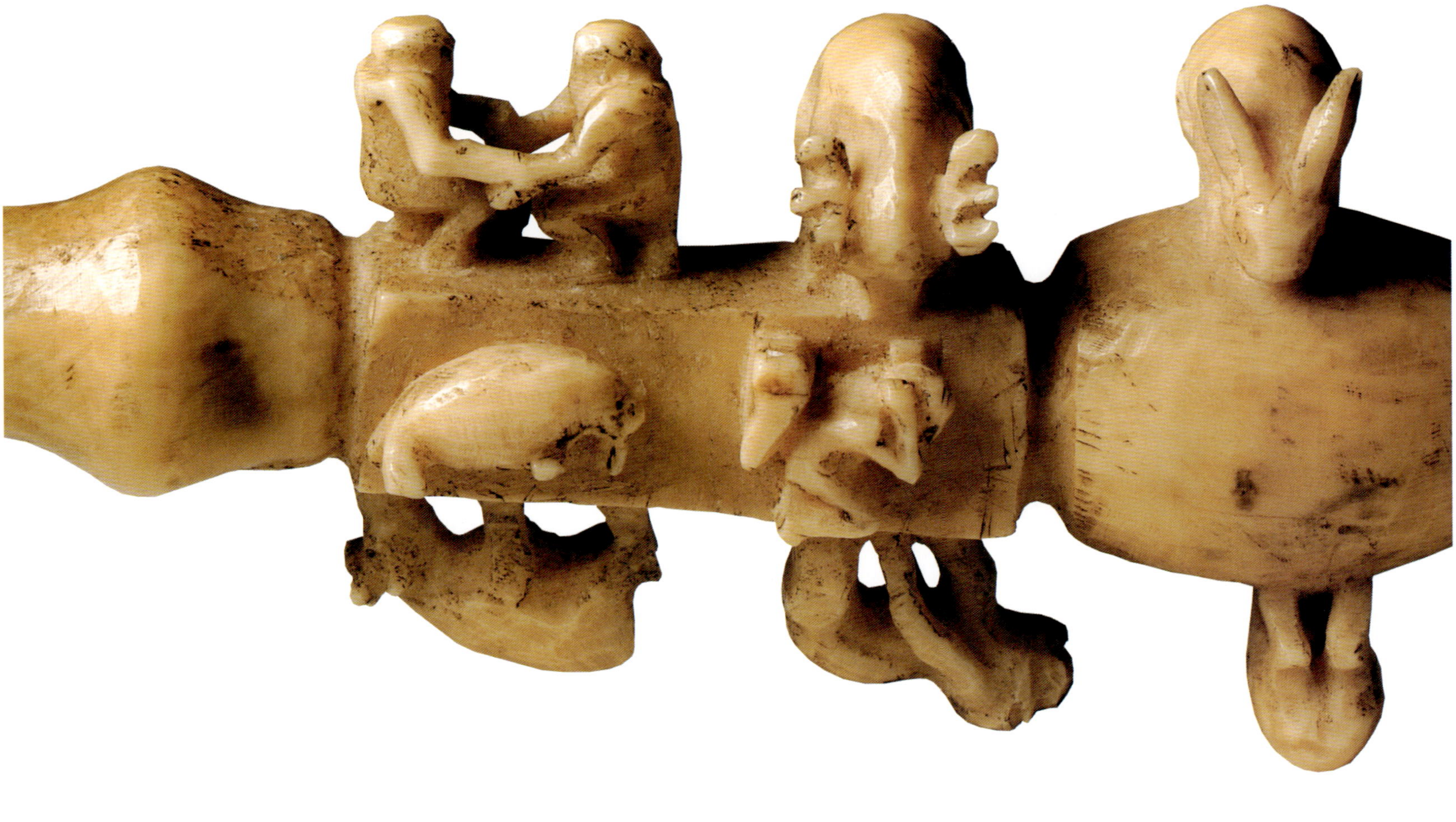

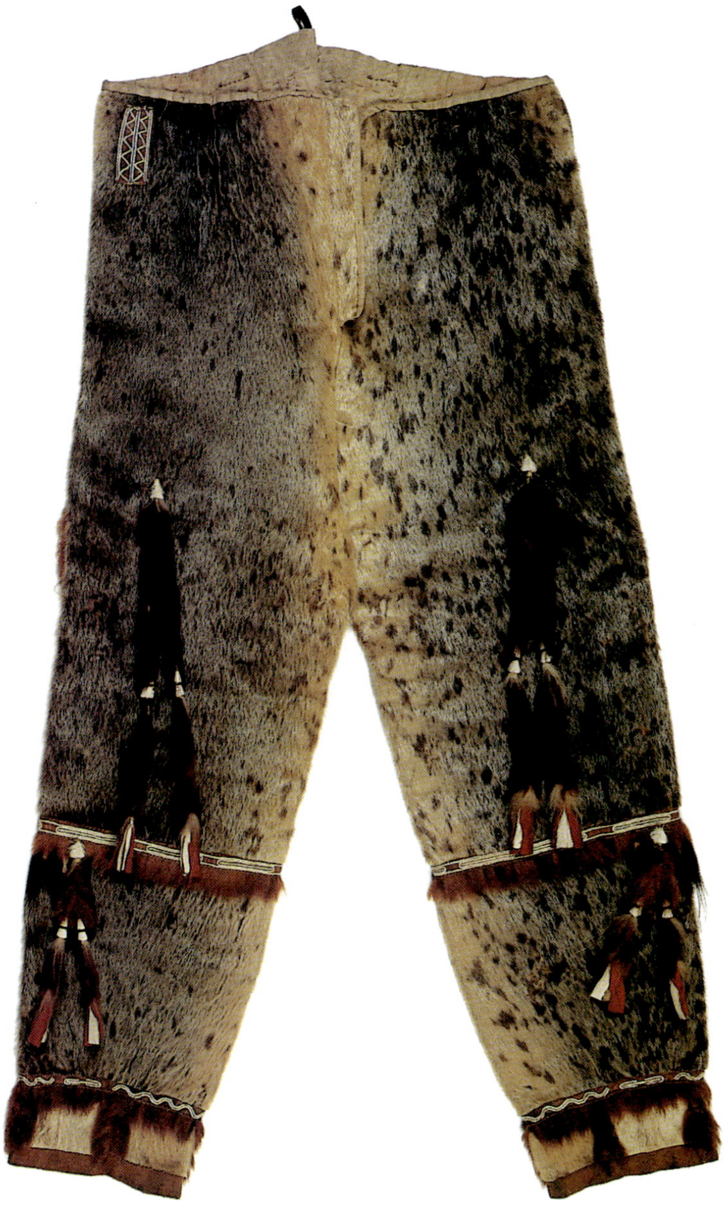

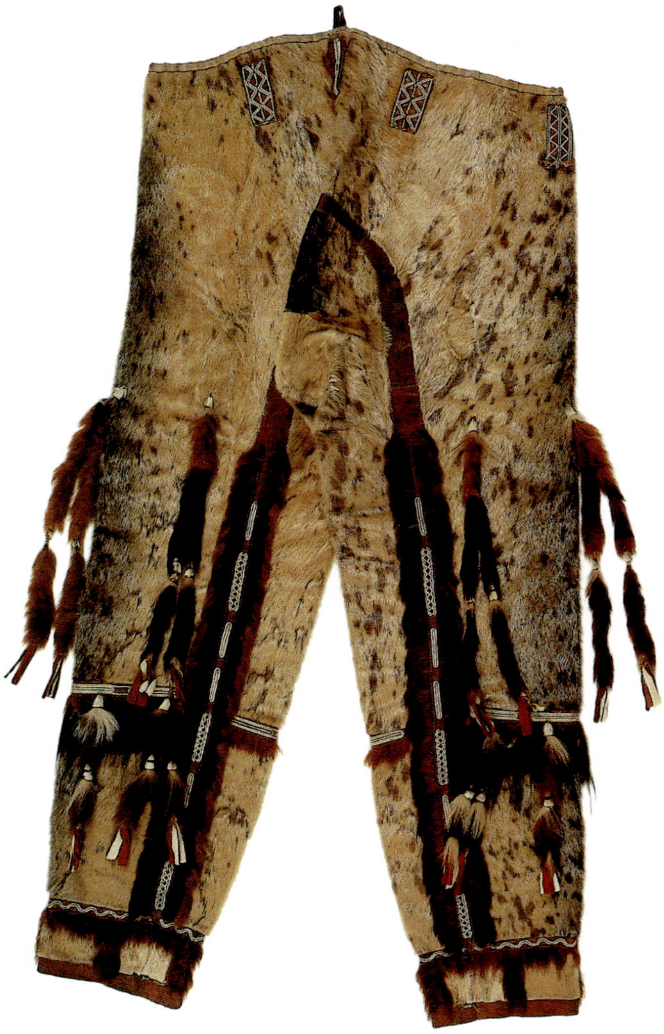

They are usually made of birch-wood, no one but a shaman who has passed his fifth consecration being allowed to use iron horse-staves. The Lapps take great care of their drum and keep it covered up with furs. No woman may touch it.

The Chukchi.

Among Palaeo-Siberians there are no strict regulations as to the shape and quality of the shaman's dress. Originality of costume is what is most sought after, and the Chukchi shamans sometimes adopt some old coat brought from the American shore. The Chukchi have nothing similar to the well-known type of coat covered with fringes and images, which is in general use among the Yakut and Evenki, and which probably was borrowed from the latter by the Yukaghir and perhaps also by the Itelmen.

The absence of a peculiar shaman's dress among the Chukchi may be accounted for by the fact that the shamans perform their ceremonies in the darkness of the inner room of the house, in an atmosphere so hot and stifling that they are obliged to take off their coats and to shamanize with the upper part of the body quite naked.

The only shamanistic garments elsewhere are a coat and a cap. Among several neighbouring tribes also, female shamans have no outward distinguishing mark, nor do they use the special shamanistic garb which is assigned only to the male shamans.

The custom among certain tribes of the adoption by the male shaman of the clothes and manner of a woman appears still more strange. The shamanistic coat is characterized by a fringe round the sleeves a little above the opening, or round the neck a little below the collar. This coat may be adopted by the shaman or by the patient. Besides the fringe there are slits ornamented with cured leather. These slits and fringes are usually said to represent the curves and zigzags of the Milky Way.

But if we remember the many other ways in which the Chukchi shaman imitates the Evenki shaman, we may conclude that both slits and fringes in the shamanistic coat are but another instance of the same imitation. Some garments feature an image of *tetkeyun*, that is, 'vital force,' which resides in the heart and assumes its form. It is made like a leather ball and filled with reindeer-hair. The other figure, likewise of leather, represents a *rekken*, or 'assisting' spirit of the shaman.

The shamanistic cap is also supplied with fringes, with a tassel on the top and a long double tassel on the left side. The tassels are of the type adopted for magic purposes, that is, they are formed of alternating pieces of white and black fur. Another cap with the opening on top, and likewise fringed and tasselled, was used by the shaman as a remedy against headache.

In addition to these garments, the Chukchi shaman uses in his performances many small instruments, such as the knife, the handle of which is embellished with magical objects, and a small flat piece of ivory, which is said to be usually employed when cutting open a body. The ivory of the shaman 'Scratching-Woman' had three leather images fastened to it. One was said to represent a *kele* from the 'direction' of the darkness, with the arms longer than the legs. The middle image with only one arm and one leg, and with the two eyes one above the other, represented the *kele lumetun*. The third image represented a crawling 'spell' sent by an enemy of the shaman, who interecpted it on the way and thoroughly subdued it so that it began to do his bidding. These different amulets, the form of pendants and tassels, are made of skin and beads by the shaman himself, and are fastened to various parts of the body or dress. Such are also the

Koryak,
Man's holiday trousers, front view,
1909-1911.
Seal hide and undercoat, alder-tree bark, fabric, reindeer underneck hair, sealskin, 101 x 48 cm.
Russian Museum of Ethnography, St. Petersburg. Kamchatka.

Koryak,
Man's holiday trousers, back view,
1909-1911.
Seal hide and undercoat, alder-tree bark, fabric, reindeer underneck hair, sealskin, 101 x 48 cm.
Russian Museum of Ethnography, St. Petersburg. Kamchatka.

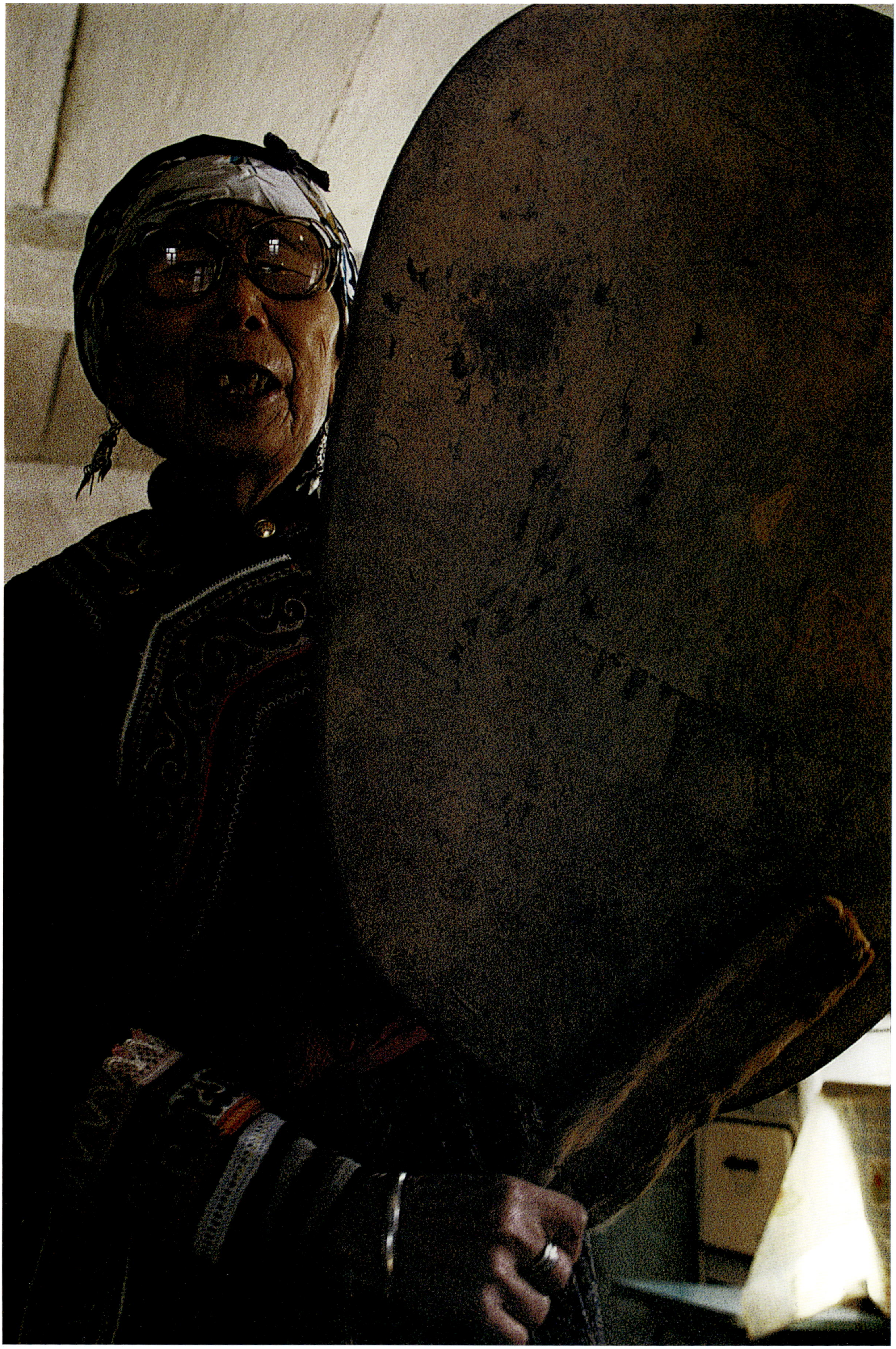

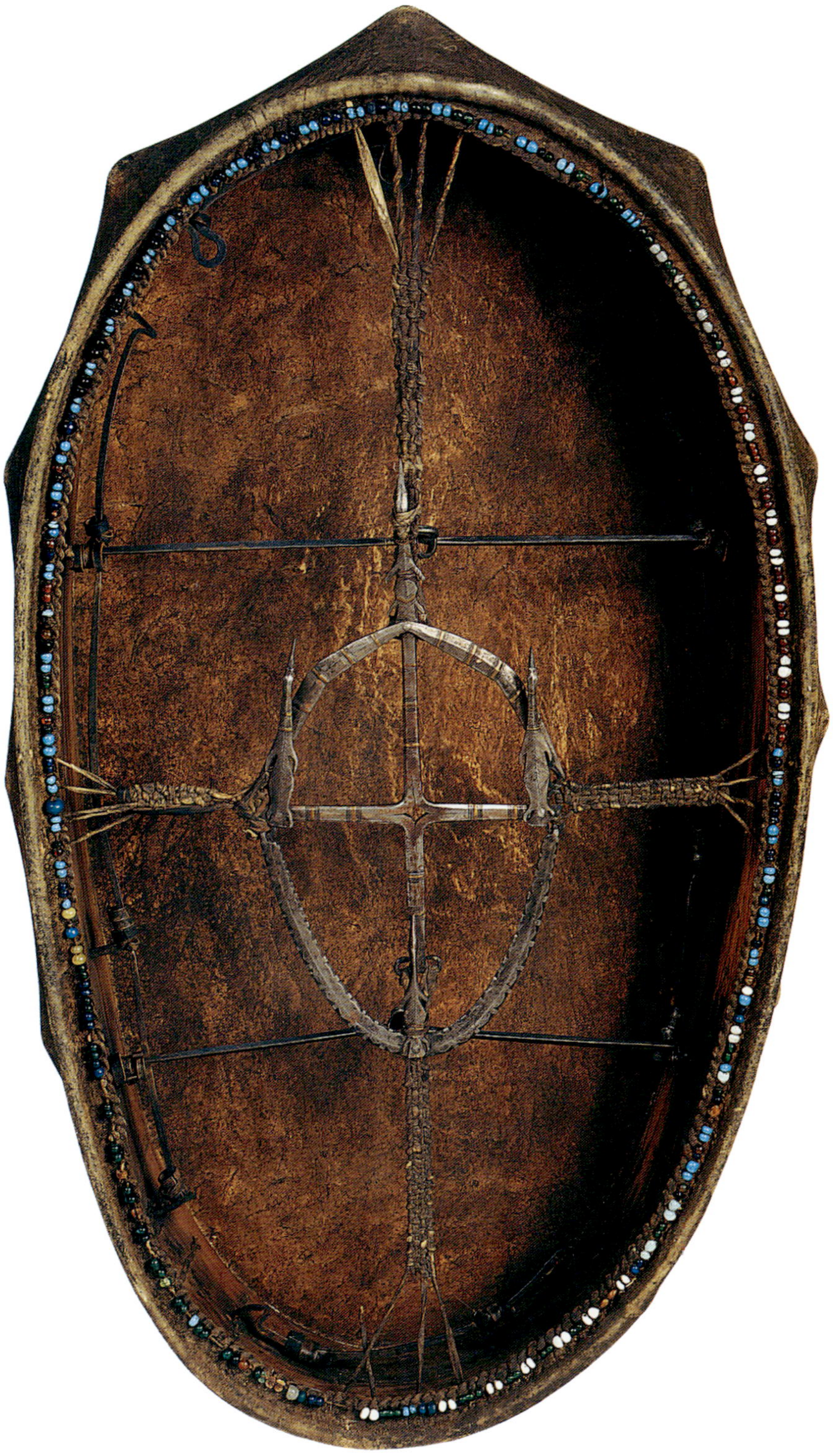

round patches of skin, often with a tassel in the centre, which are considered highly effective amulets among the Chukchi, the Koryak, and the Asiatic Eskimo. They are sewn to the coat, on the breast or on the shoulders, or against the affected part of the body. An image of the 'guardian' is placed in the middle, and is often replaced by an ornamental figure of a woman, of a dancing man, or of a warrior. These objects, as well as those already mentioned, serve both a magical and an ornamental purpose.

The most important object in shamanistic performances all over Siberia is the drum. Thus the Chukchi use the drum which is common to both Asiatic and American Eskimo. The drum used by the reindeer-herding and coastal Chukchi is different from that adopted in north-western Asia by the Yakut, Evenki, Koryak, Itelmen, and Yukaghir, which is rather of a southern type.

The southern drum is large and somewhat oval in shape, and is held by four loose bands, which are fastened to the hoop of the drum on the inner side. The other ends of these bands meet in the middle, where they are tied to a small wheel or a cross, which is without any other support. When these are grasped by the hand the drum hangs loosely, and may be shaken and its position changed at will. The drum-stick is made of wood and covered with skin or with cured leather.

The Chukchi drum has a wooden handle which is lashed with sinews to the wooden hoop. The diameter of the hoop, which is nearly circular in shape, measures from 40 to 50 centimetres. The head is made of very thin skin, usually the dried skin of a walrus's stomach. In order to stretch the skin it is moistened with water or wine, and the edge is then tied with sinew cord. The ends of this cord are fastened to the handle. The drum is very light, weighing from half a pound to a pound and a half. The drumstick varies according to its purpose. It is either a narrow, light strip of whalebone from 30 to 40 centimetres long, or a piece of wood from 60 to 70 centimetres long, which is sometimes adorned with fur tassels. The former is used during the magical performances held in the inner room at night, the latter during ceremonials performed in the outer tent during the day.

When the family is moving from place to place, the cover of the drum is removed, folded, and fastened to the hoop to be replaced when needed. In the winter house the drum remains in front of the sleeping-place, and in the summer tent it hangs near the sacred fire-board.

The Koryak.

The shaman accessories of the Koryak, another Palaeo-Siberian tribe, are described as follows: The Koryak shamans have no drums of their own; they use the drums belonging to the family in whose house the shamanistic performance takes place. It seems that they wear no special dress; many shamans wear ordinary clothing.

One embroidered jacket is very much like the ordinary man's dancing-jacket used during the whale ceremony, but more elaborate. The Koryak drum, *yyai*, is oval in shape and covered with reindeer-hide on one side only, its diameter being 73 centimetres. The drum-stick is made of thick whalebone, wider at the end with which the drum is struck, and this end is covered with the skin of a wolf's tail. Inside the drum at four points in the rim a double cord of nettle fibre is fastened and joined below to form the handle. These cords run towards one side of the drum. On the top of the inside rim is attached an iron rattle. This custom of attaching the rattle has been borrowed from the Evenki and not all Koryak drums possess it.

Nanai,
Woman shaman Linza Beldi, 1992.

Evenki,
Shaman tambourine, early 20th century.
Leather, wood, metal, beads,
95 x 50 cm.
Russian Museum of Ethnography,
St. Petersburg. Siberian Krai.
Krasnoyarsk Okrug, Turukhan
District, the Nizhni (Lower)
Tunguska river basin.

Yukaghir,
Hat of a "transformed" shaman, detail,
1900-1901.
Reindeer skin, hair embroidery, dyed
seal pup fur tassels, sinew, 91 cm.
American Museum of Natural
History, New York. Markovo.

Yukaghir,
Shaman's hat, 1907.
Reindeer skin, dyed seal pup fur,
beads, fabric, dog fur, brass, hair
embroidery, 61 cm.
American Museum of Natural
History, New York.

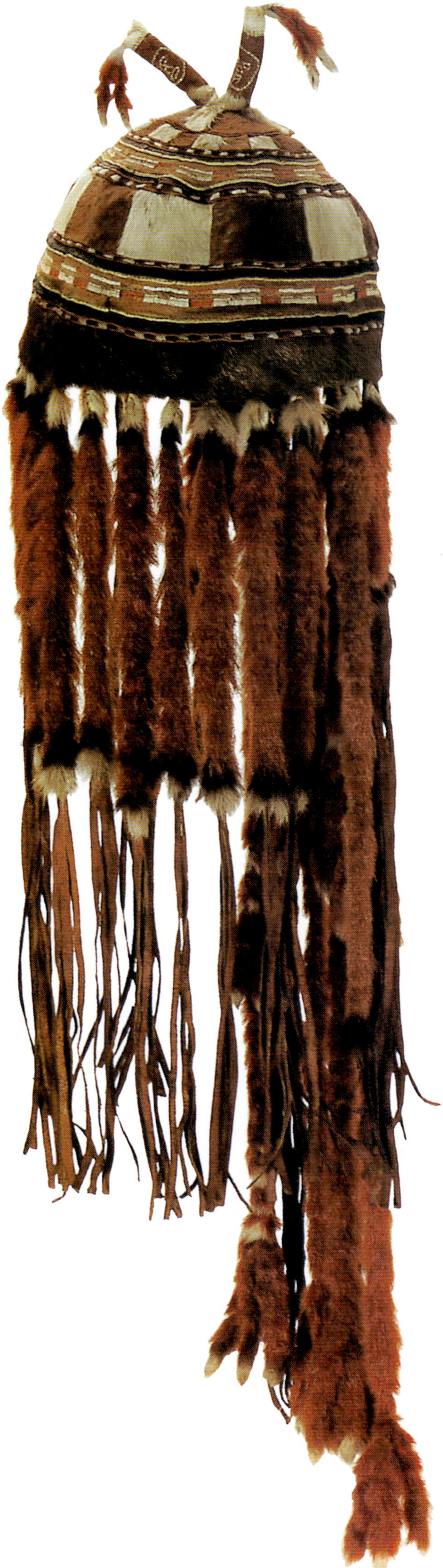

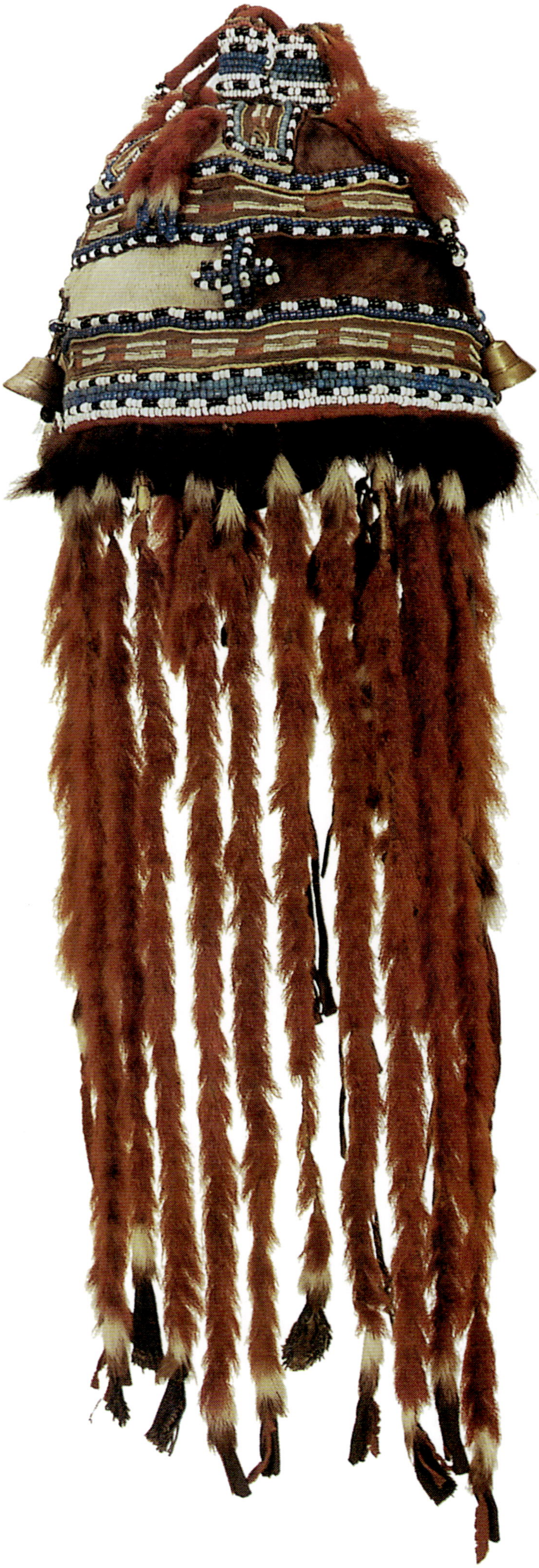

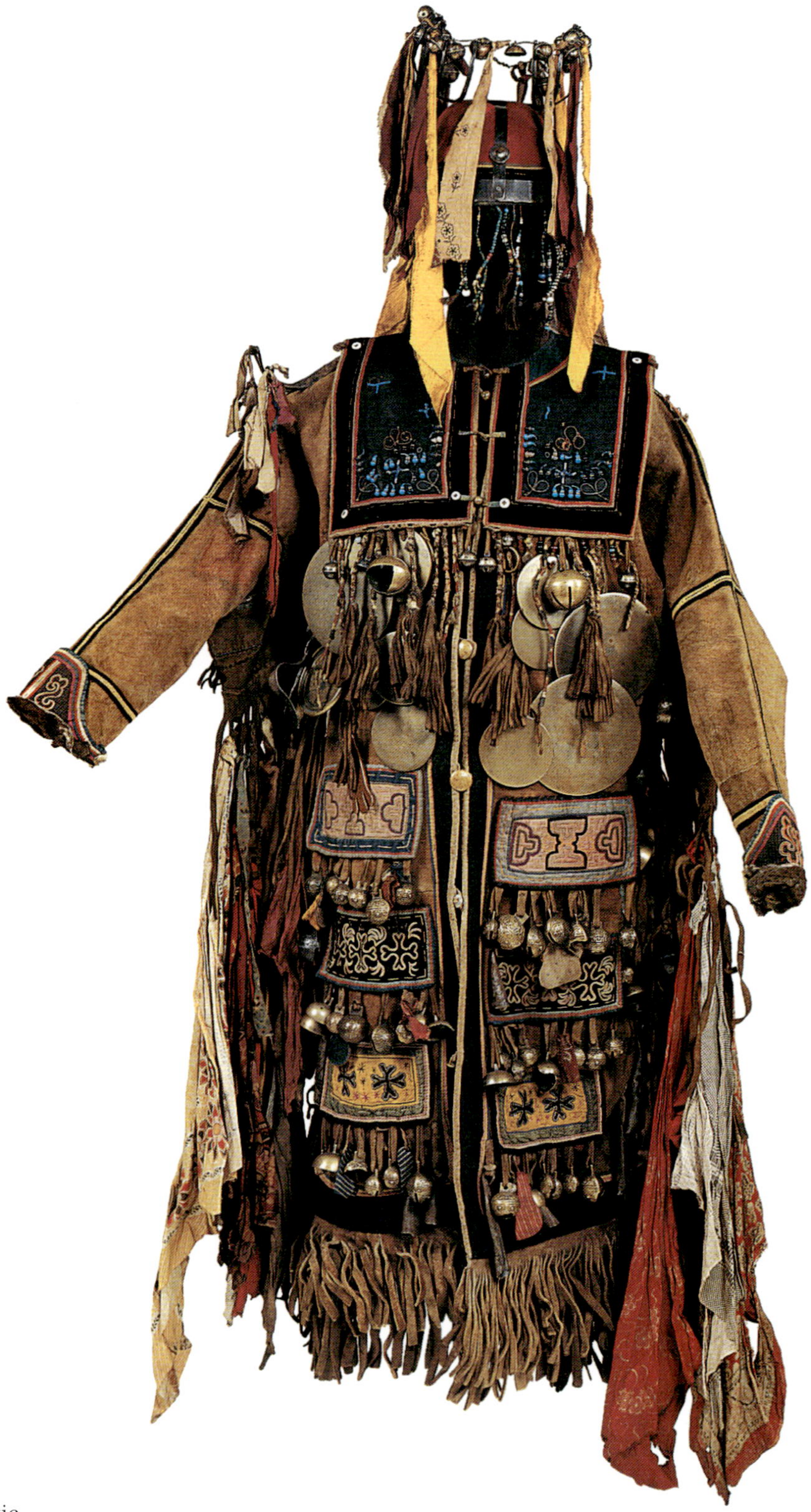

Manjagir,
Shaman outfit, front view, late 19th-early 20th century.
Elk leather, fur, velveteen, plastic buttons, metal, seal skin, fabric, beads, seed beads, felt, Caftan: 104 cm;
Collar; 57 x 36 cm;
Head gear: 20 x 21 cm.
Russian Museum of Ethnography, St. Petersburg. Dalnevostochni (Far-Eastern) Krai, the Zeya river basin.

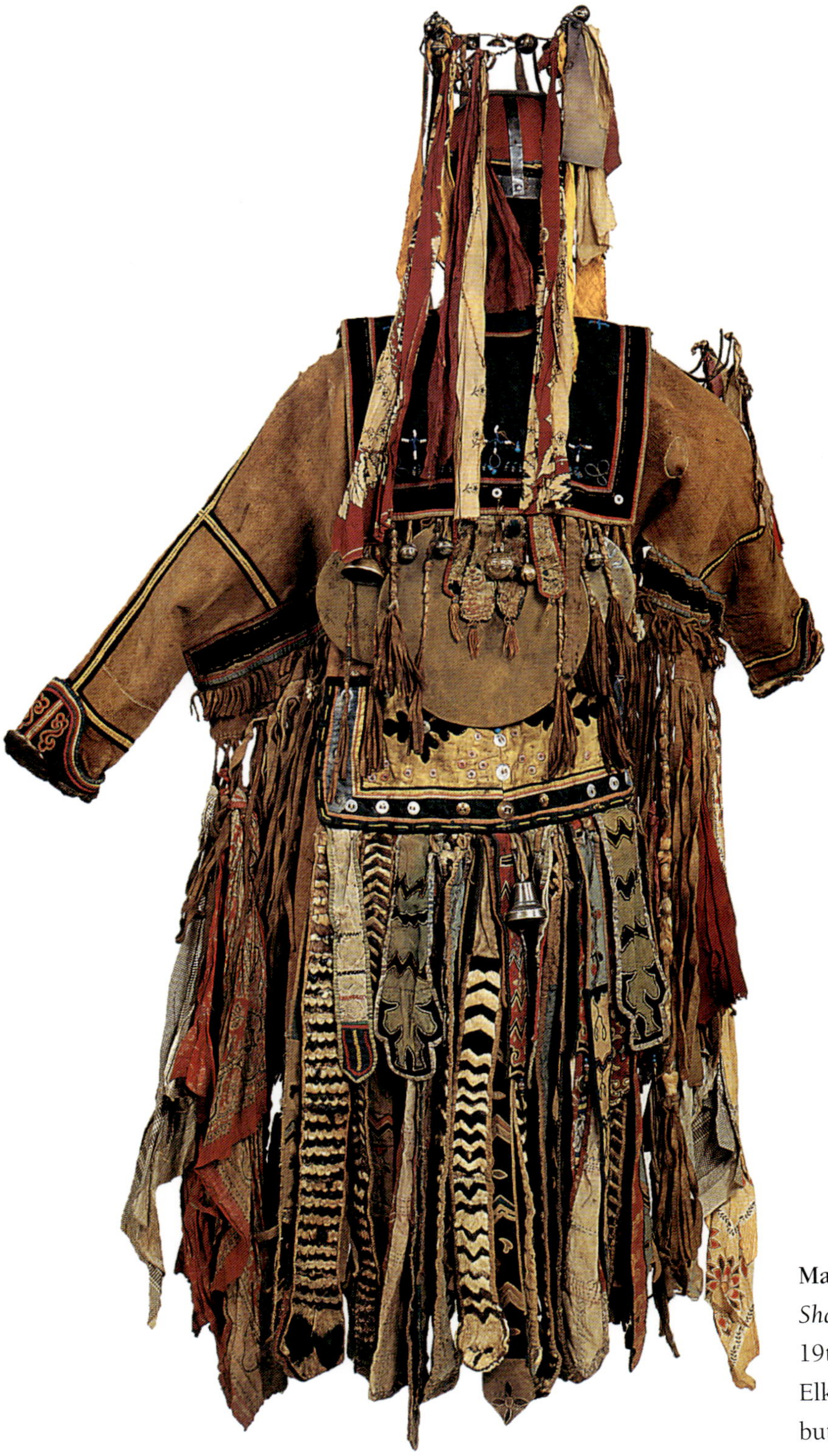

Manjagir,
Shaman outfit, back view, late 19th-early 20th century.
Elk leather, fur, velveteen, plastic buttons, metal, seal skin, fabric, beads, seed beads, felt,
Caftan: 104 cm;
Collar; 57 x 36 cm;
Head gear: 20 x 21 cm.
Russian Museum of Ethnography, St. Petersburg. Dalnevostochni (Far-Eastern) Krai, the Zeya river basin.

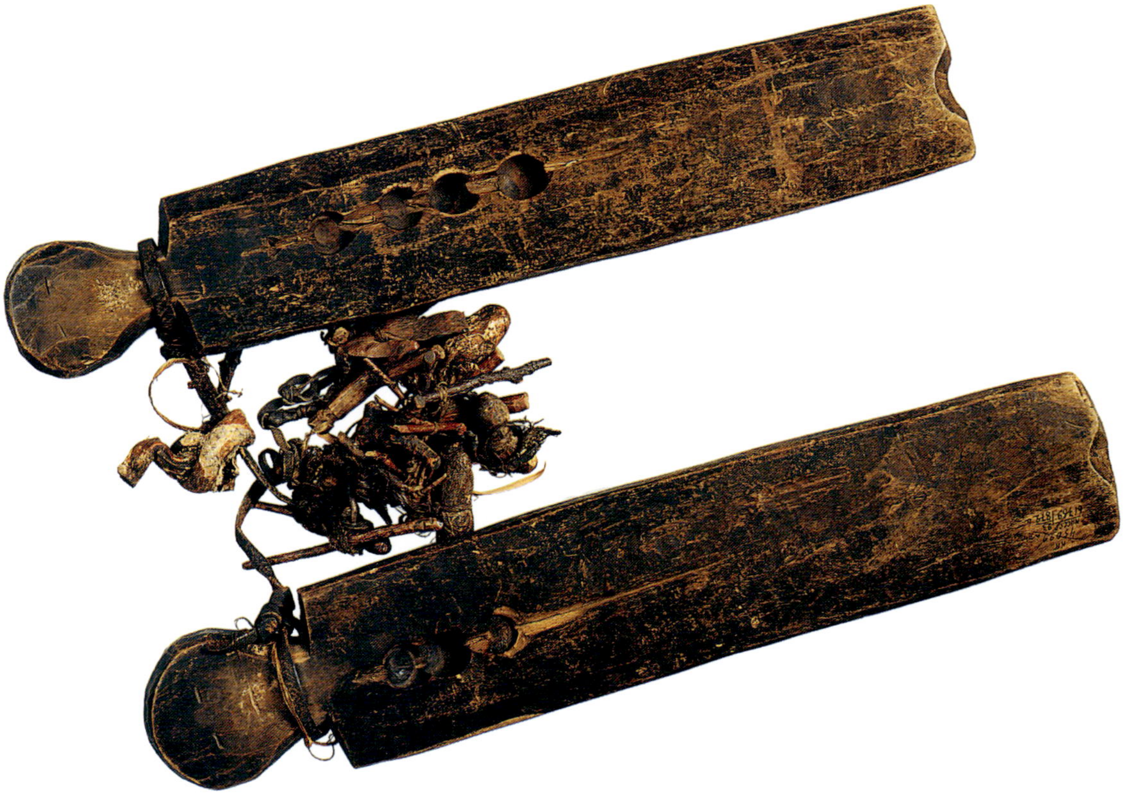

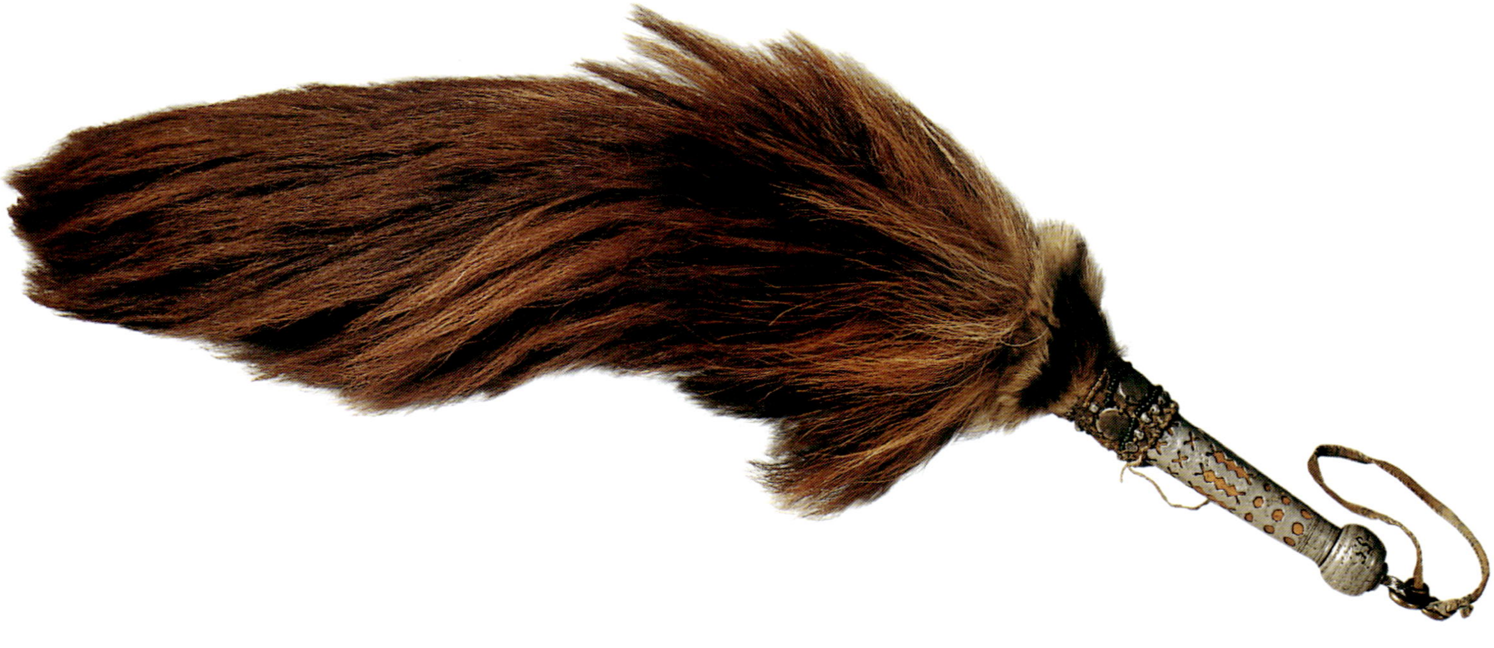

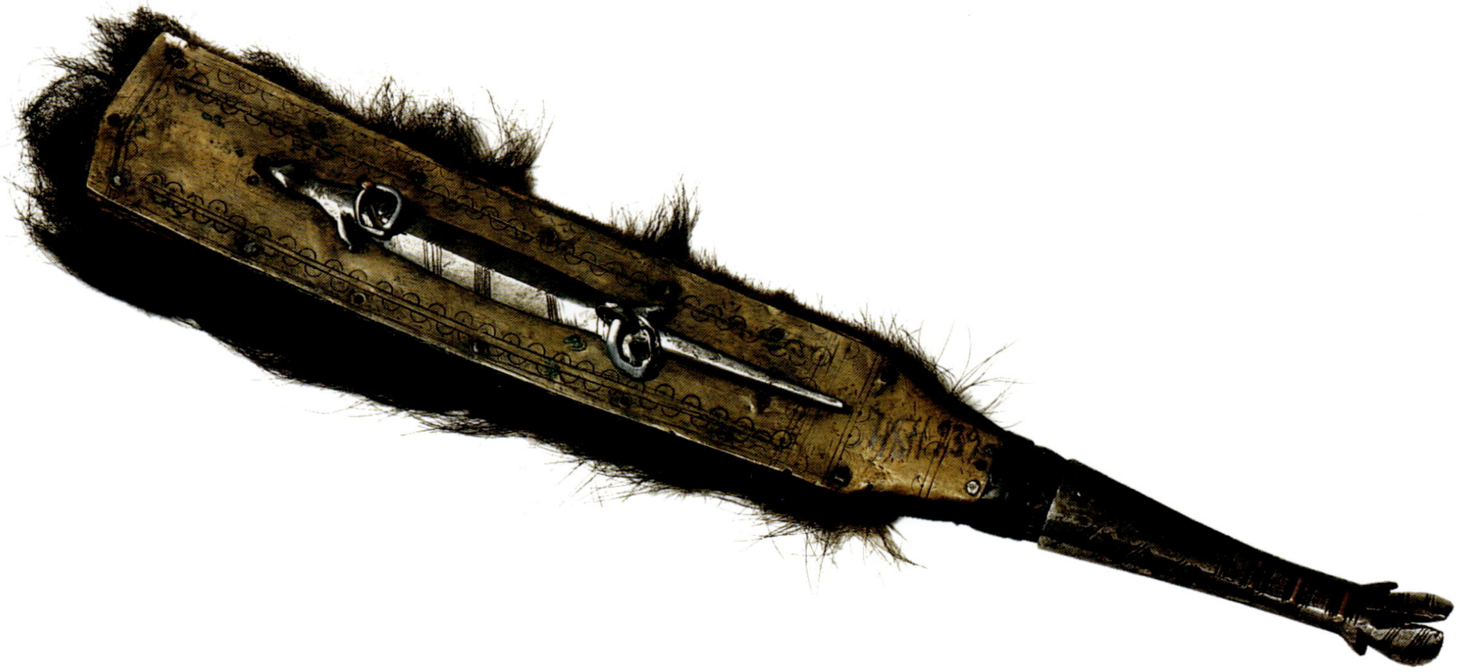

Chukchi,
Appliances for making fire by friction with a bunch of family charms, 1896.
Wood, leather, reindeer sinews, 58 x 11 cm.
Russian Museum of Ethnography, St. Petersburg. Chukchi Peninsular.

Yakut,
Flapper for fanning mosquitoes away, 1908.
Wolverine fur, wood, beads, metal, beads, leather, Length: 50 cm; length of handle: 13 cm.
Russian Museum of Ethnography, St. Petersburg. Yakut Oblast, Vilyuy Okrug.

Evenki,
Mallet for shaman's tambourine, early 20th century.
Wood, bear fur, metal, 39.5 x 4-5 cm.
Russian Museum of Ethnography, St. Petersburg. Siberian Krai, Krasnoyarsk Okrug, Turukhan District, the Nizhni (Lower) Tunguska river basin.

The Itelmen (Itelmen).

Among the Itelmen there is apparently no shamanistic garment or drum. Everybody, especially women, can shamanize, and hence this occupation is not professional enough to demand a special dress.

The Yukaghir.

The Yukaghir drum is a rough oval. It is covered with hide on one side only. Inside the drum there is an iron cross near the centre, which serves as a handle. The ends of the cross are fastened with straps to the rim, to which four iron rattles are attached. There is a great similarity between the Yukaghir and the Yakut drum, not only in the iron rattles, iron cross, and general shape, but also in the small protuberances on the outer surface of the rim, which according to the Yakut represent the horns of the shaman's spirits. The stick is covered with the skin of a reindeer's leg. In Yukaghir traditions the drum without metallic additions is still traceable, the iron pieces having been borrowed from the Yakut.

The Yukaghir word for drum is *yalgil*, which means 'lake,' that is, the lake into which the shaman dives in order to descend into the shadow-world.

The Gilyak.

The most important accessories of the Gilyak shaman are the drum, *kas*, and the shaman's girdle, *yangpa*. First of all the drum is heated by the fire, to make the hide taut, so that the sound might be more sonorous. The drum is made of the skin of a goat or reindeer, and while it is being prepared, the shaman makes himself ready. He takes off his outer garment, puts on the so-called *koska*, a short apron, and ties round his head a band of grass, the end of which hangs over his

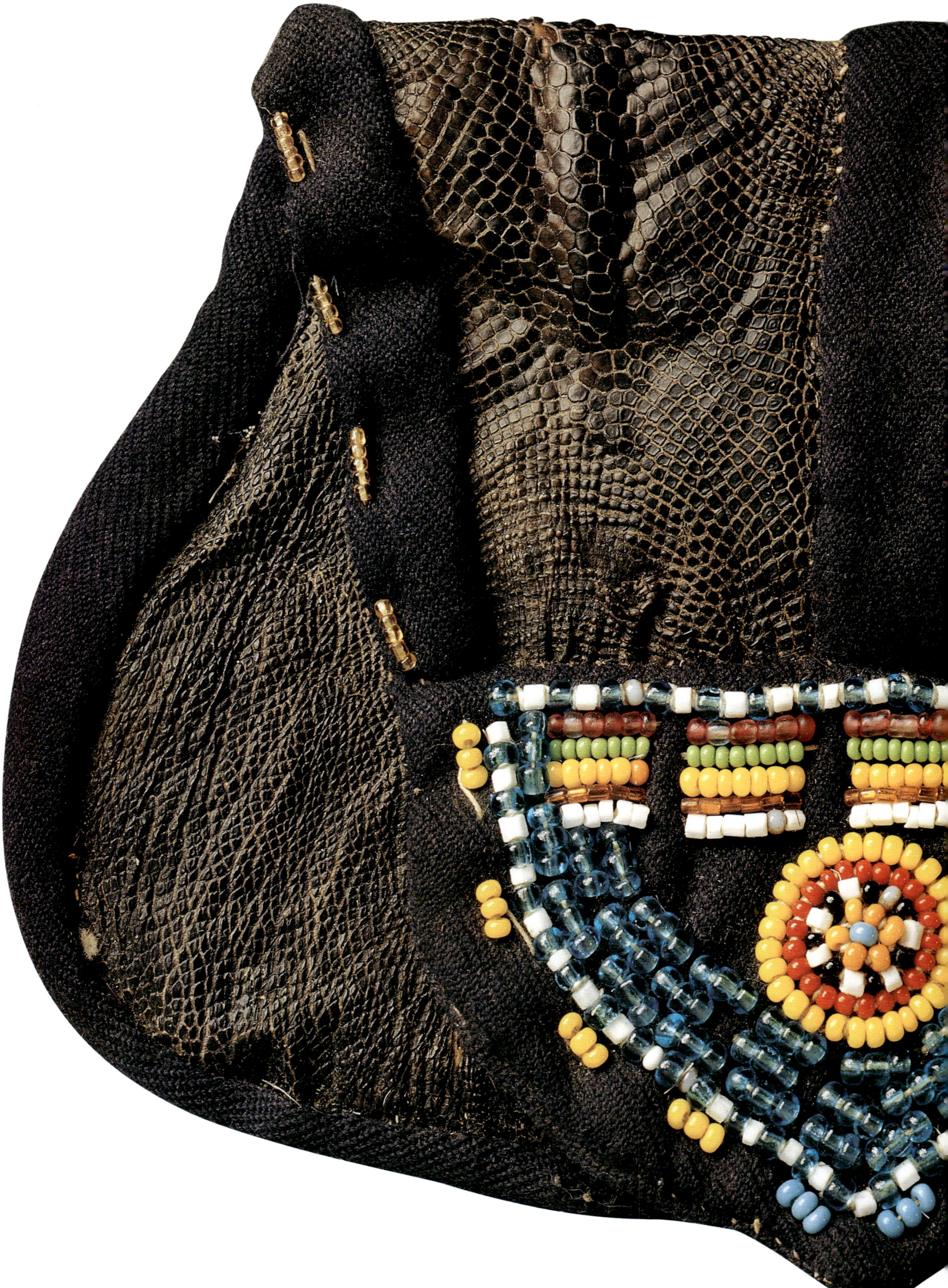

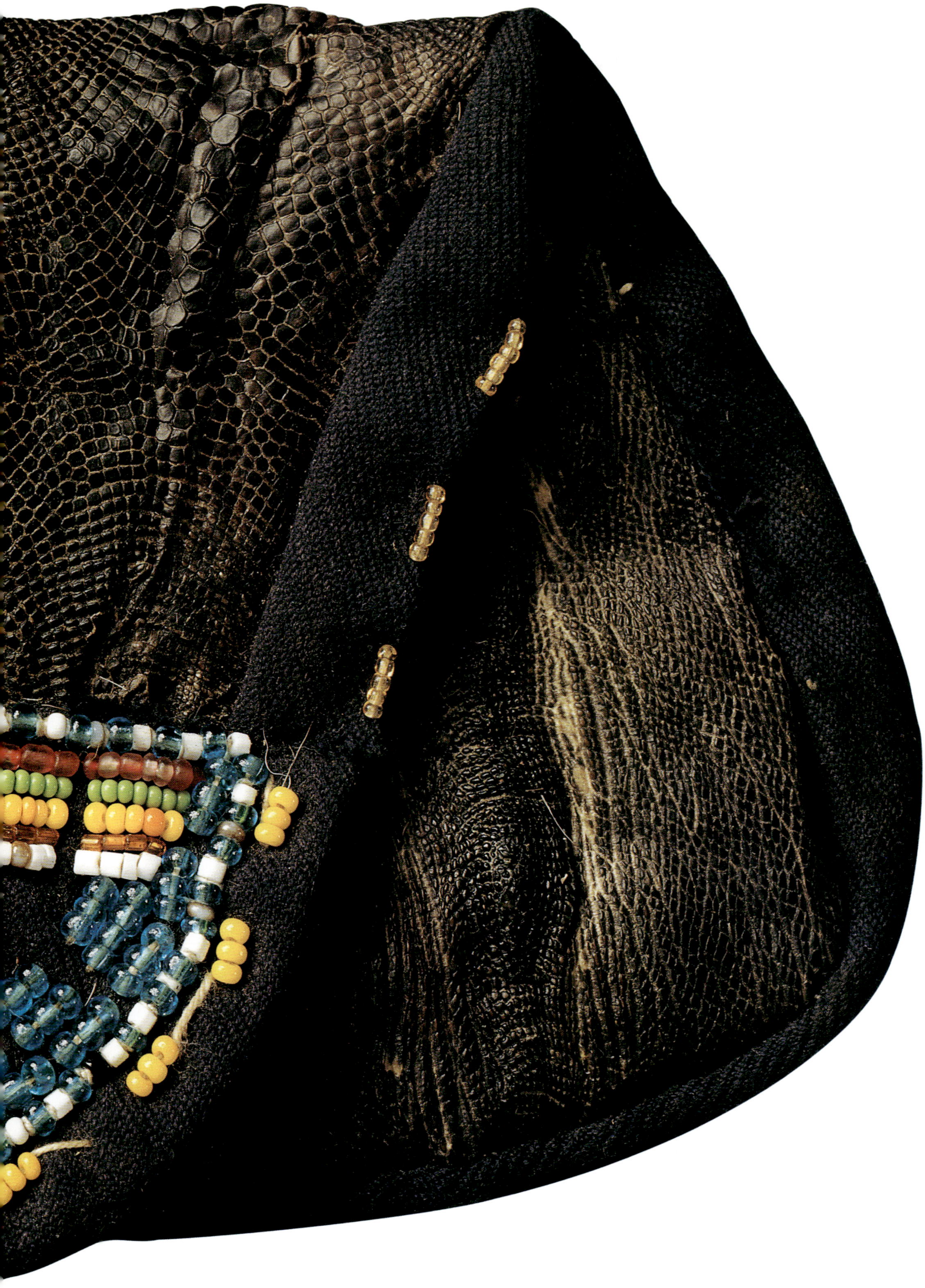

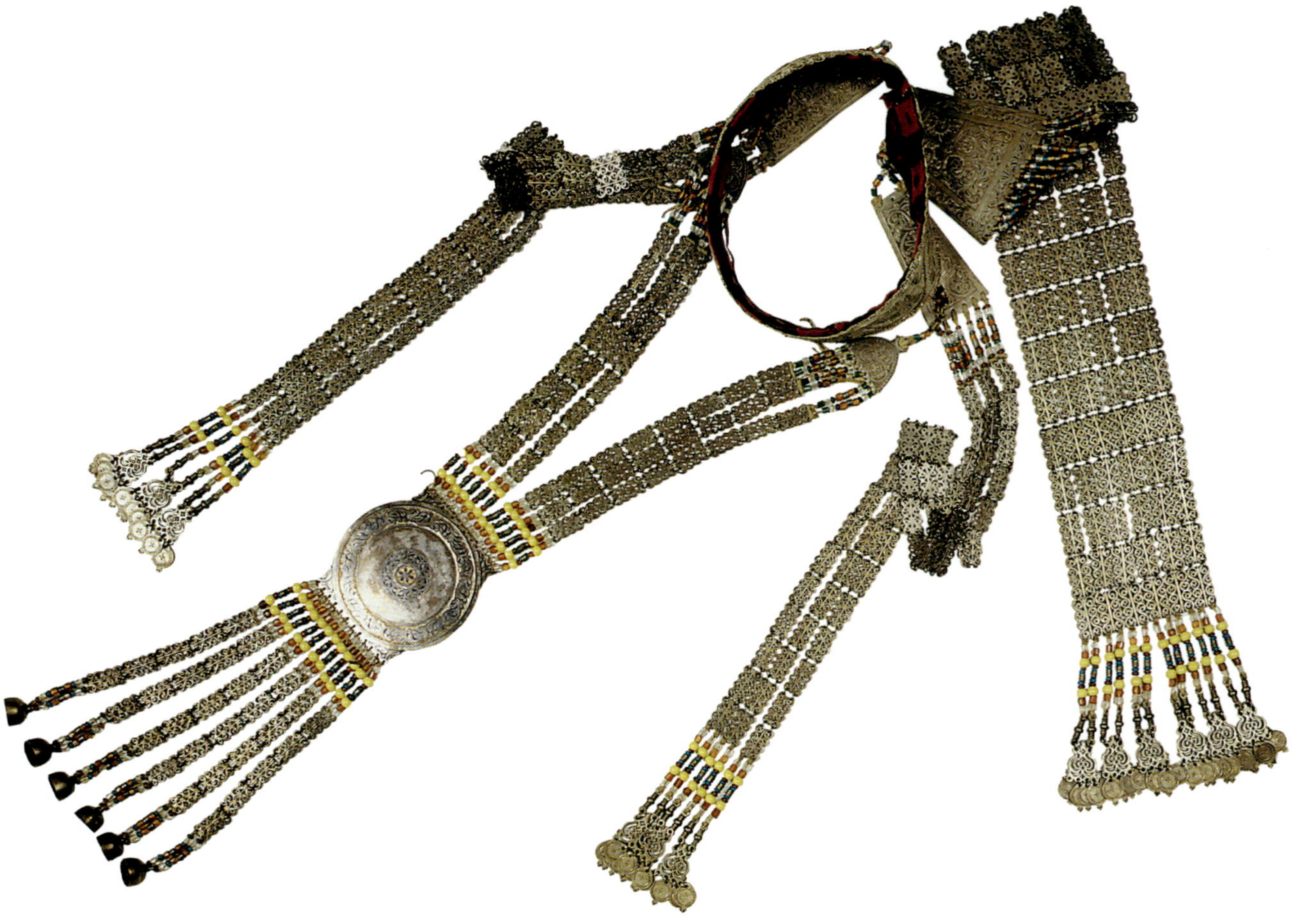

Yukaghir,
Small bag for woman's fancy-work tools, 1982.
Swan leg skin, beads, woolen cloth, 21 x 13 cm.
Russian Museum of Ethnography, St. Petersburg. Yakut ASSR, Verkhnekolyma District, Nelemni village.

Yakut,
Head adornment, 1903.
Silver, fabric, beads, 97 cm.
Russian Museum of Ethnography, St. Petersburg. Yakut Oblast.

Evenki,
Shaman's clothing.
Metal, skin, and feathers.
Russian Museum of Ethnography, St. Petersburg.

shoulders like a tress of hair. Then he takes the shaman's leather girdle, with many iron plates, copper hoops, and other metal pendants, which produce a loud clanking noise during the shamanistic dances. This girdle is called in Olcha dialect *yangpa*. Its chief pendant is a large copper disk with a small handle ornamented in relief, showing Manchu influence; this circle, called *tole*, makes the most important sound. There are also many iron links called *tasso*, and many irregular pieces of iron called *kyire*, which make a very loud noise; a few rolled iron plates called *kongoro*, and, finally, some small copper bells without tongues, called *kongokto*. When the girdle is put on all these objects hang together at the back. This shamanistic girdle is of considerable weight.

Although the Gilyak belong to the Palaeo-Siberians, the metal accessories seem to be of Evenki origin, as are some other features of their culture. We learn from a description of the costume of an Evenki shaman that he wears over the ordinary dress an apron ornamented with iron. This suggests that this apron-form of the shaman's coat was borrowed either by the Gilyak from the Evenki, or vice versa.

Among the Neo-Siberians, their entire philosophy of life is represented symbolically in the drum, and great significance is also attached to various parts of their dress.

The Yakut.

Among the Yakut even those who, like the blacksmith, help in the adornment of the shaman's garment occupy a half-magical position, being

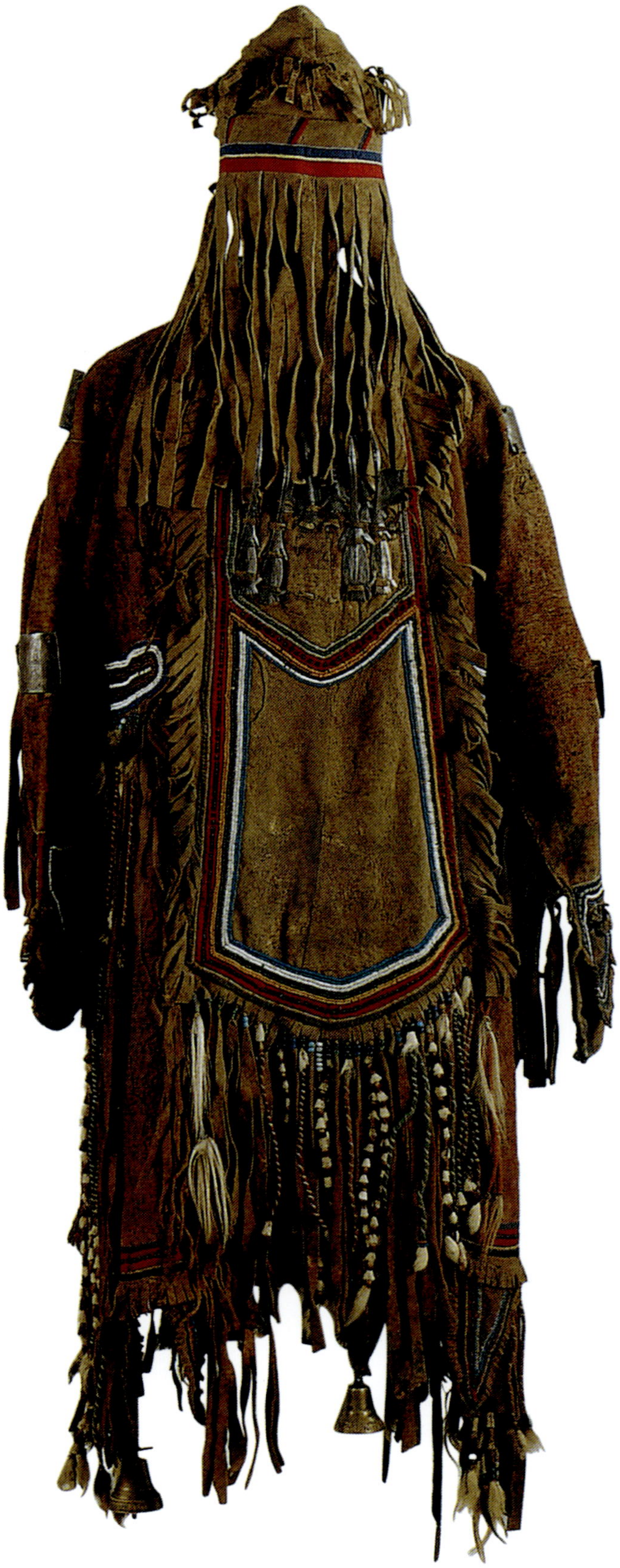

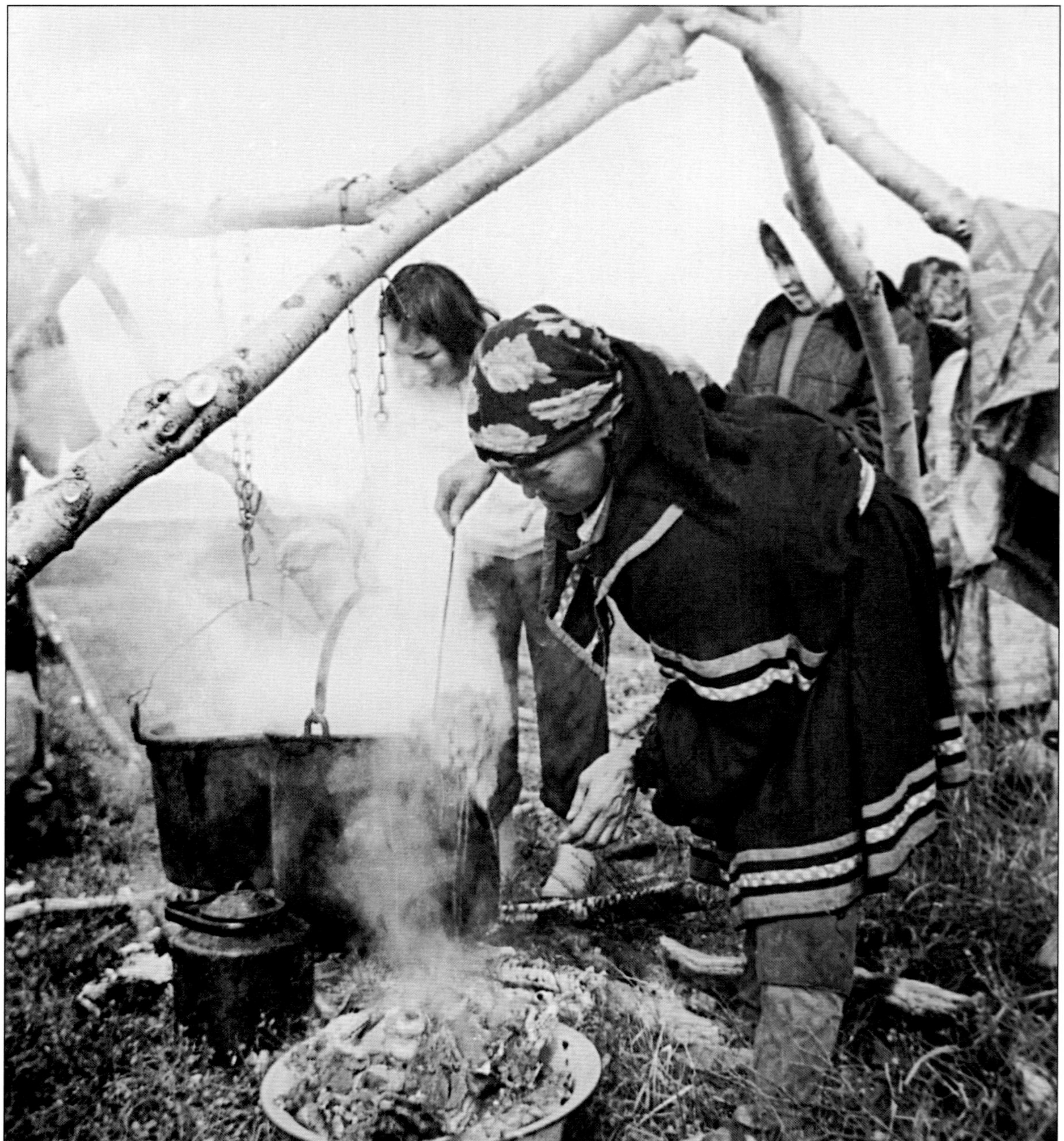

credited with 'peculiar fingers.' The hereditary blacksmiths have tools with 'souls,' *ichchylakh,* which can give out sounds of their own accord. The blacksmiths are those who approach most nearly to the shaman in their office, and are, in a way, related to them. "The blacksmith and the shaman are of one nest," says a proverb of the Kolyma district. "The smith is the elder brother of the shaman." Blacksmiths can sometimes cure, give advice, and foretell the future, but their knowledge is simply a matter of cleverness and does not possess magical value. The profession of blacksmith is mostly hereditary, especially in the north; in the ninth generation the blacksmith first acquires certain supernatural qualities, and the longer his line of descent, the greater his qualities. The spirits are generally afraid of the iron hoops and of the noise made by the smith's bellows. In the district of Kolyma the shaman will not shamanize until the blacksmith had removed his case of metal instruments, and even then attributes his bad luck to them: "The spirits are afraid of the blacksmith and that is why they do not appear at my call."

The shaman's dress consists chiefly of a coat. It is of cowhide, so short in front that it does not reach the knees, but touching the ground at the back. The edges and the surface of this coat are ornamented at the back with different objects, each having its own name, place, and meaning. The shaman's coat, which is not an indispensable part of the ritual costume arnong Palaeo-Siberians, is most elaborate among the Neo-Siberians.

Linguistically also there is a curious point connected with the terms for coat and drum. While the drum has a common name (with dialectic differences) among most Neo-Siberians, *tünür, tüngür,* the term for the shaman's coat varies: *kumu, ereni, manyak.* This seems to show that the ceremonial coat is a comparatively newer invention than the ceremonial drum.

What follows is an account of the meaning of the coat ornamentation. A good shaman's dress requires about 35 to 40 pounds of iron. According to general belief, the iron and the jingling pendants of the shaman's coat have the power to resist rust, and possess a soul-*ichchite.*

1. *Küngeta* (the sun), a round, smooth, shining disk, the size of a small saucer, hanging between the shoulders, on a short strap of leather which passes through the hole in the middle of the disk.
2. *Oibon-Künga* (hole-in-the-ice sun), a disk of the same shape and size as the first, but with a larger hole in the middle. It hangs above or below the first plate on a long leather strap.
3. *Kondei kyhan,* rolls of tin about the size of a thumb, but longer, banging at the back on the metal rings or loops.
4. *Chilliryt kyhan,* flat plates as long as fingers, hanging in great numbers at the back, above the waist.
5. *Hobo,* copper bells without tongues, suspended below the collar, like a crow's egg in size and shape and having on the tipper part a drawing of a fish's head. They are tied to the leather straps or to the metal loops.
6. *Biirgüne,* two round flat disks, similar to those which adorn the woman's cap, *tuskata,* but without any design on them; they are tied like an epaulet on the shaman's shoulders.
7. *Oiogos timiria,* two plates about the breadth of four fingers and a little shorter, fastened on both sides of the body.
8. *Tabytaua,* two long plates two fingers broad, which are fastened to both sleeves.

Koryak woman preparing to cook the meat of a reindeer that has been sacrificed.

9. *Ämägyat, abagyta ämätiat* (in many places called *emchet*), a copper plate as long as the first finger and half as wide as the palm of the hand. It is covered either with a drawing of a man, with feet, hands, head, nose, mouth, eyes, and ears, or with an engraving in relief on a copper medallion, having a man's figure in the middle.

Only a blacksmith who has nine generations behind him can without danger to himself from the spirits, make an *ämägyat,* a copper plate such as has been described, which the shaman, when he begins to shamanize, hangs on his breast. What exactly *ämägyat* means, whether it is a personal or an impersonal power, it is difficult to determine. We shall go on to review the various references to this subject, since the word *ämägyat* is used in the double sense of an invisible power and of a visible symbol. In this chapter we shall confine ourselves to the latter. The absence of *ämägyat* differentiates the less important shamans, called *kenniki oyuun,* from those who possess it and who are known as *orto oyaun.* The power of those in partial possession of *ämägyat* varies according to 'the strength of their *ämägyat.*' The great shamans are said to be those whose spirit-protector was sent them by Ulu-Toyen himself (*ämägyatitiah ulytoër ulutoënton ongorulah*).

The shaman implores the assistance of his *ämägyat* and of other protecting spirits, and it is only when the *ämägyat* descends upon the shaman that he begins his frenzied dances. Whenever a family numbers a shaman among its members, it continues to do so, for after his death the *ämägyat* seeks to re-embody itself in someone belonging to the same clan (*aya-usa*).

The human body cannot endure the continuous presence of a power equal to that of the great gods; hence this spirit-protector (if *ämägyat* can be so called) resides not within, but close beside the shaman, and comes to his assistance at critical moments, or whenever he needs him. The shaman can see and hear only with the help of his *ämägyat.* Possession of the *ämägyat* does not in any way depend upon the shaman; it comes either by an accident or by a decree from above. Tiuspiut obtained his *ämägyat* (of Evenki origin) quite accidentally.

The great shamans at death take their *ämägyat* with them, and thus change into heavenly beings, most of whom are ex-shamans; if the *ämägyat* does not depart in this way, then sooner or later it will show itself on the earth. The most important ornament of the Yakut shaman's coat is *ämägyat,* which represents a man. On some coats there is an *ämägyat* on the left side made of molten copper. On orther coats *ämägyat* were on both sides of the breast and made of tin.

Speaking of the preparatory stage of the shaman, it is noteworthy that the Yakut shaman is taught by an older shaman, who initiates him by suspending round his neck the *ämägyat.*

In the Mongolian language, *ämägäldzi* signifies the figure of the protective genius of the house, family, and goods, and is made of tin. This word is derived from ämägän, grandmother.

10. *Balyk-timir* (the fish), a plate a metre long, two fingers wide, made in the form of a fish with head, fins, tail, and scales. It hangs on a long leather strap. In some places, like the district of Kolyma, it drags on the ground to entice the secondary spirits, which run after it and try to catch it.

11. *Choran,* small hollow copper balls, fastened to the ends of long leather straps reaching to the heels and hanging like a fringe from the lower edge of the coat. This fringe is called *bytyrys* (the weed).

The coat fastens on the breast with leather straps, and under the chin with a buckle in the form of a colt's tongue (*kulun tyl kurduk*). On the front of the

Aleut,
Woman's cloak, 1912.
Grass-wrack, woolen yarn,
74 x 46 cm and 181 cm.
Russian Museum of Ethnography,
St. Petersburg. Aleutian Islands,
Umnak Island.

Evenki,
A shaman's footwear.
Salmon-skin.

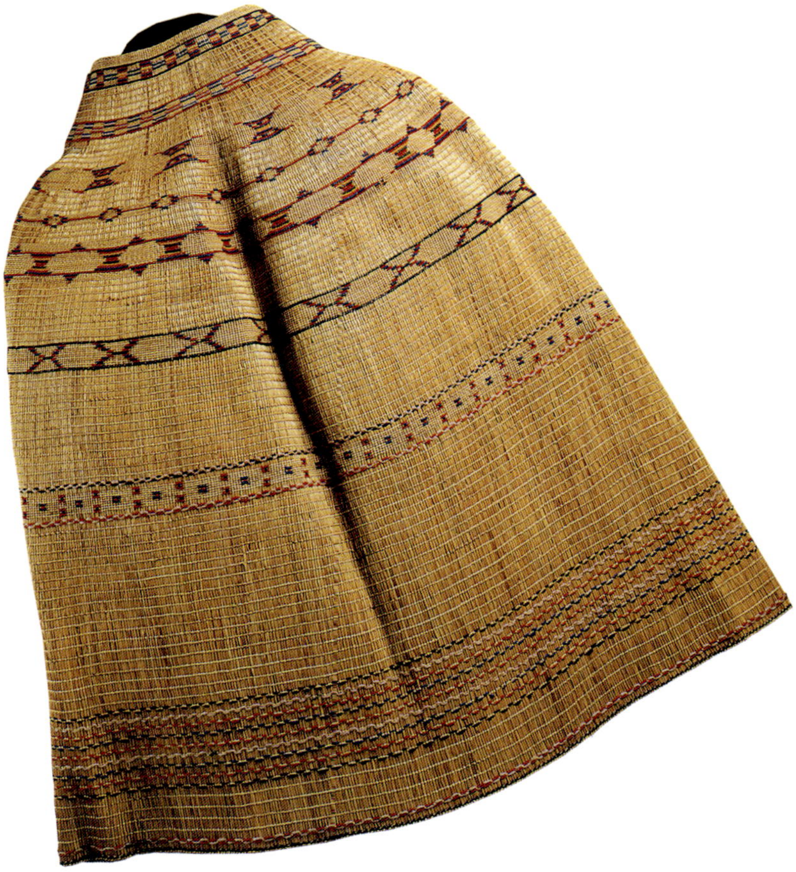

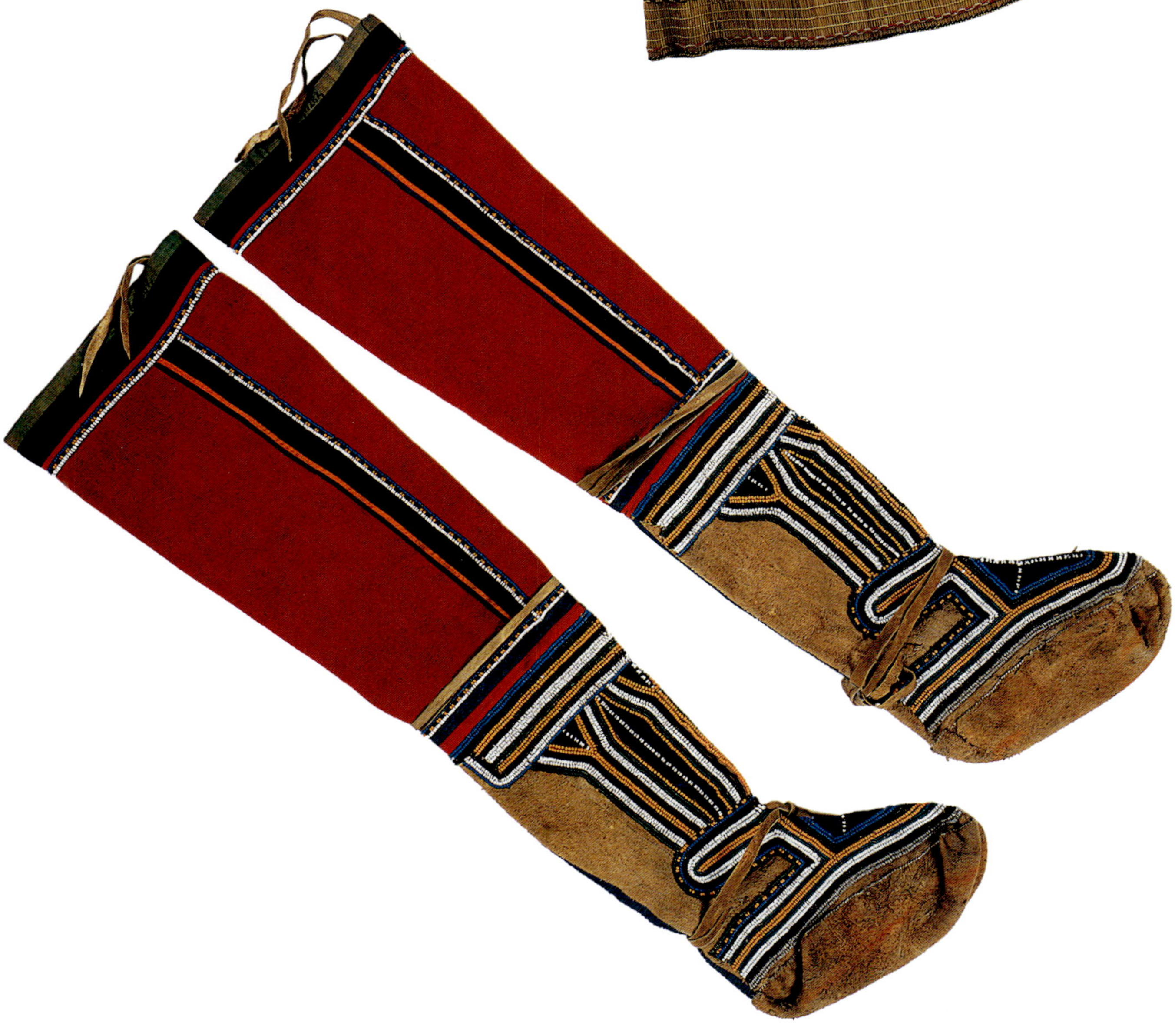

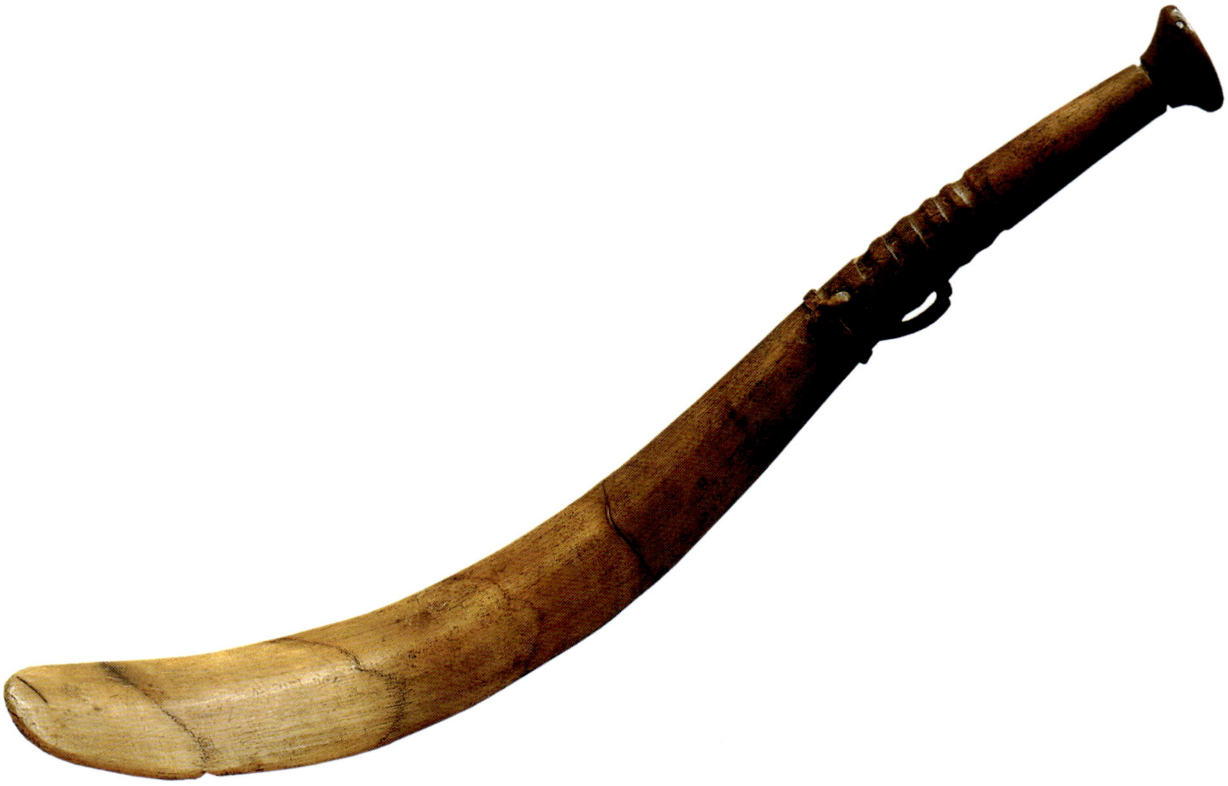

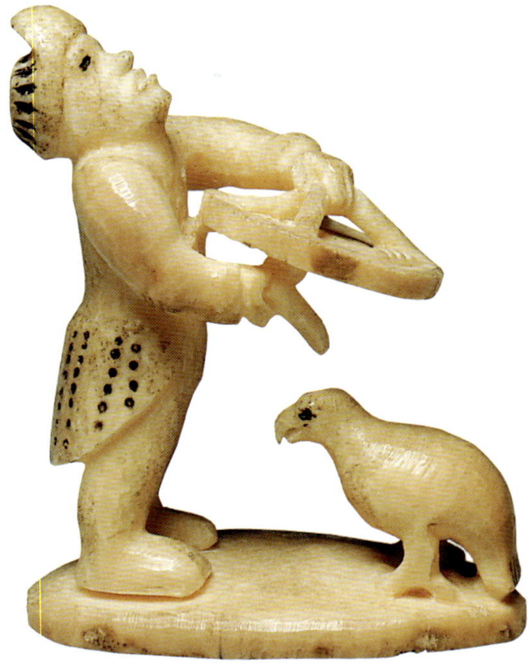

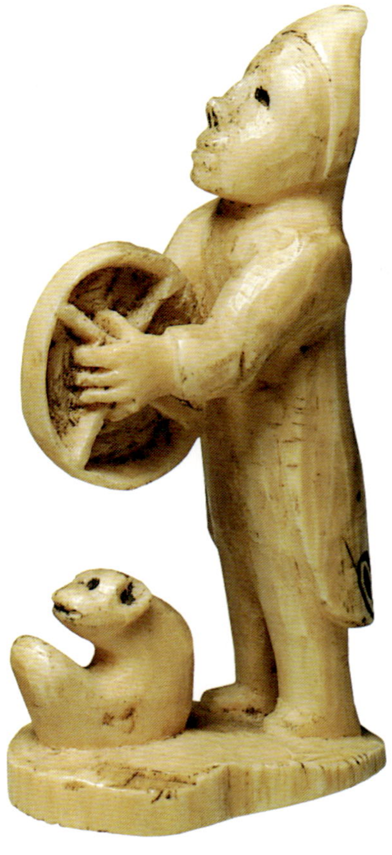

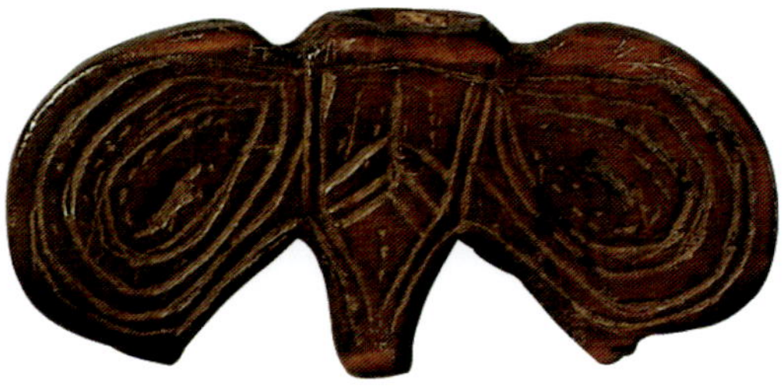

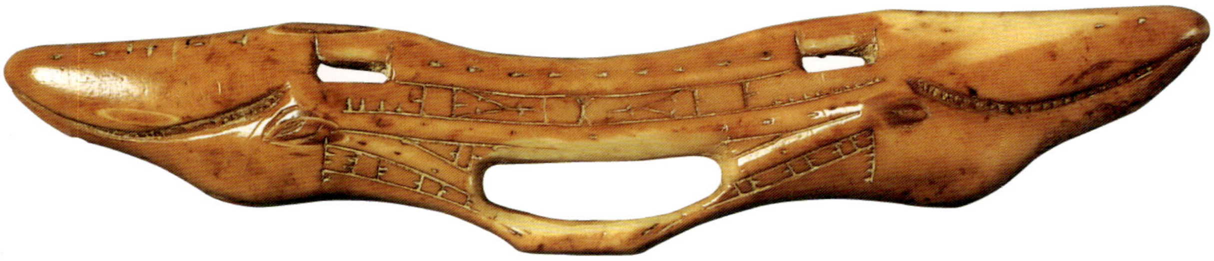

coat are sewn figures of animals, birds, fishes; various disks; images of the sun, moon, and stars; and also some iron representations of the human skeleton and bowels.

In the north, in case of the absence of this costume, the shaman wears the woman's *sangyniah*, a coat of calf's skin, with the hair outside, on the feet of which are occasionally hung some of the most important iron accessories, like the two 'suns' (or sun and moon), the fish and the *bürgüne*; sometimes two round circles, which represent the breasts, are hung in the front.

Among the Yakut, white and black shamans have different coats. The coat of the white shaman has no animal pictures on it, because his spirit-protectors belong to the *aiy* (good spirits), which are not symbolized by animal pictures. The coat of the black shaman should not have representations of the sun, for these are peculiar to white shamans.

Tribal and clan differences exist in the shaman's coat, and it would be difficult to say whether a sharp line can be drawn between black and white shamanistic garments.

On a shaman's coat of the Uriankhai tribe, among other properties, there was a small doll with a minute drum in its left hand. On the same string to which the doll was tied there was another small figure of an animal resembling the sacrificial animal of the real shaman. The significance of this is, of course, obvious. The shaman's ancestor resides in a symbolic form in the shaman's coat. Thus the small doll of the Uriankhai shaman's coat takes the place of the *ämägyat* of the Yakut, if we are to take *ämägyat* as the symbol of the shaman's ancestor.

Koryak,
Snow-flapper for 'shaking down sins' from the deceased person, 1956.
Argali horn, 43.5 x 5.5 cm.
Russian Museum of Ethnography, St. Petersburg. Kamchatka Oblast, Tigilskiy District, Sedanka village.

Koryak,
Small plastic artworks 'Shaman with the eagle as a spirit-protector' and 'Shaman with the animal as a spirit-protector', 1903.
Walrus tusk ivory, Heights: 1) 6.8 cm 2) 7.8 cm; Dimensions of supports: 1) 4.4 x 3 cm 2) 3.8 x 2.5 cm.
Russian Museum of Ethnography, St. Petersburg. 1) Primorskaya Oblast, Gizhiginski Okrug; 2) Kamchatka Oblast.

Eskimo,
'Winged object' and handle, 3rd-4th century AD.
Walrus tusk ivory, 1) 6.2 cm 2) 13.7 cm.
Russian Museum of Ethnography, St. Petersburg. Chukchi Peninsular.

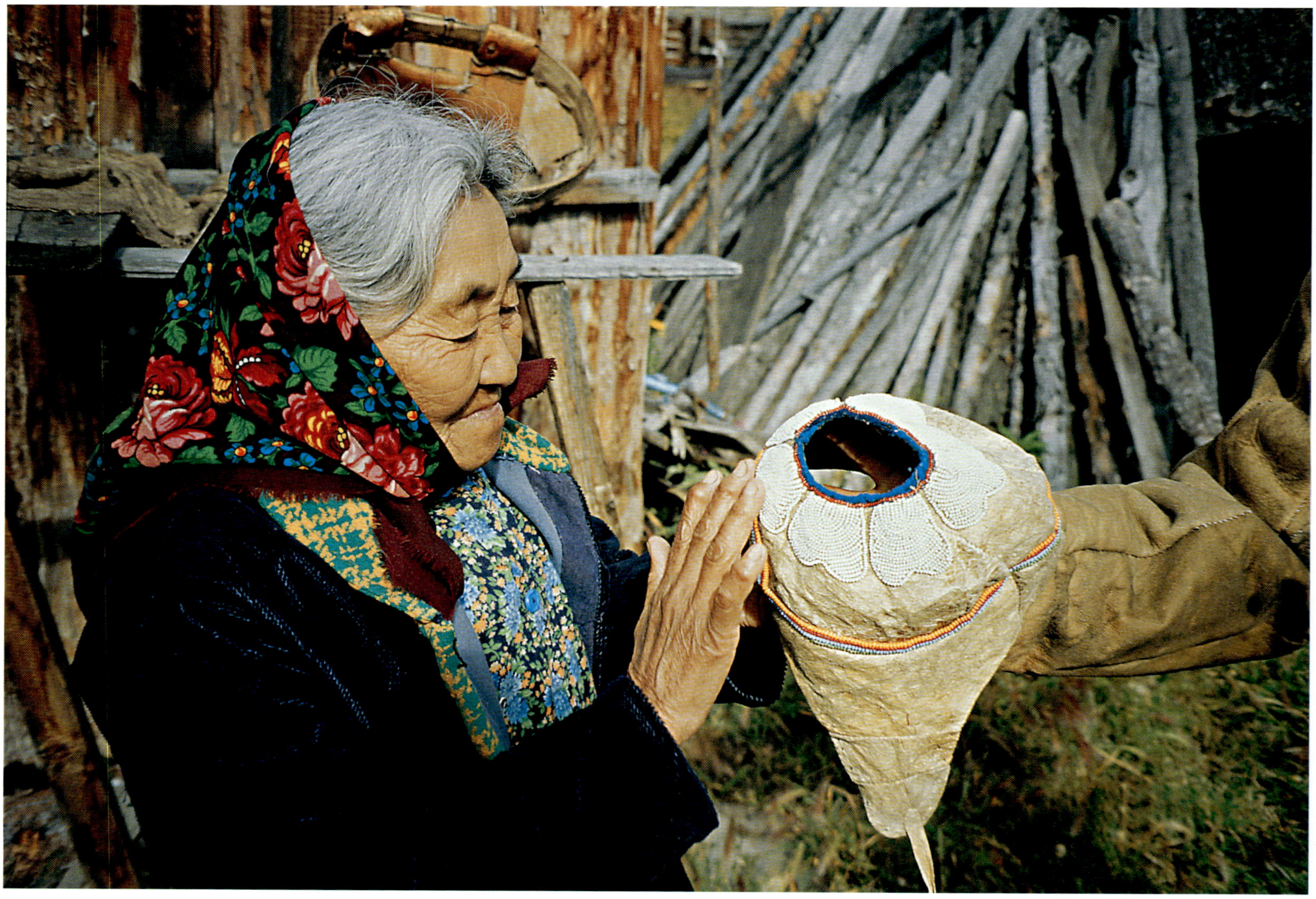

Yukaghir story-teller – despite being a woman, renowned for her hunting prowess and her artistic skills.

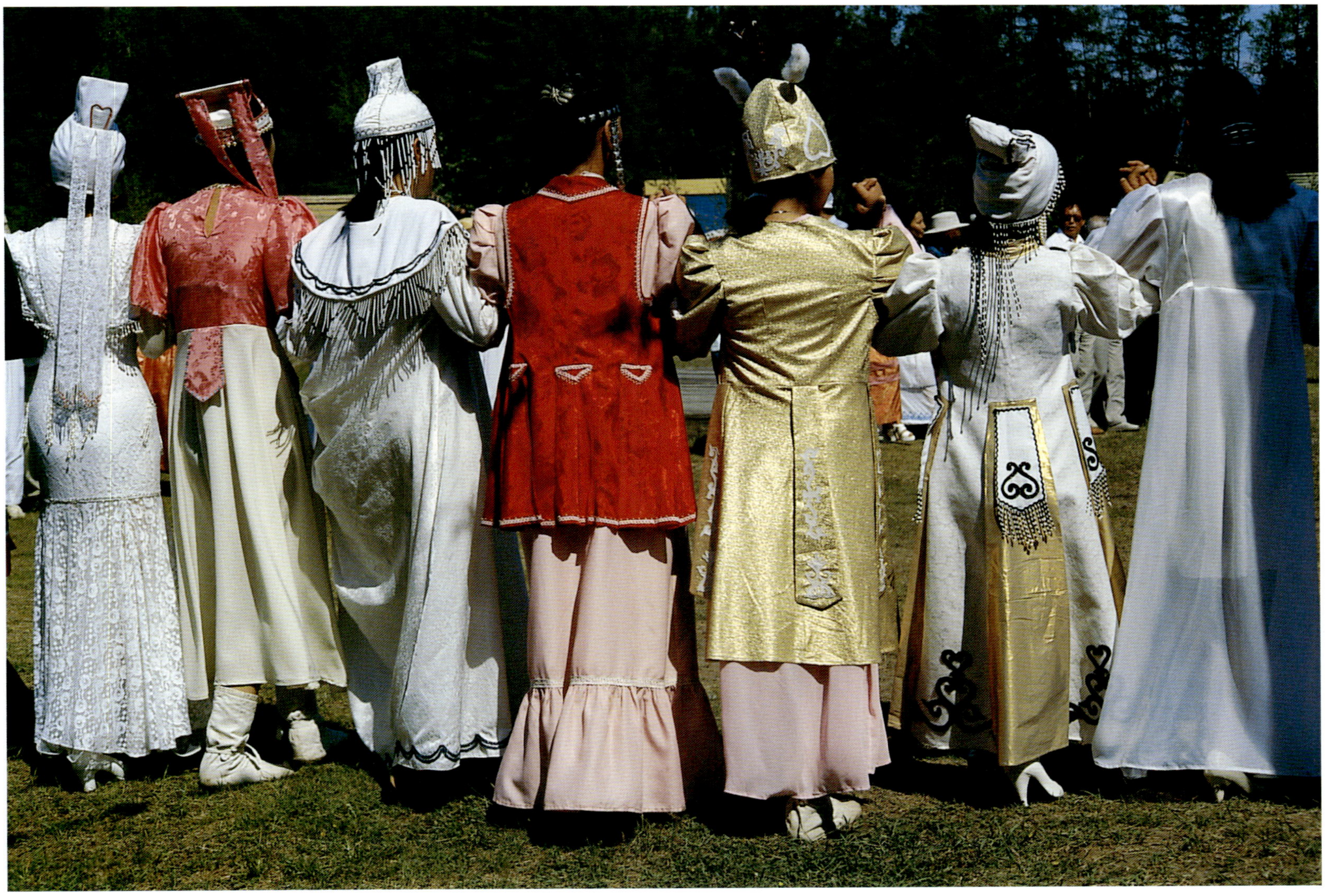

The dance ohuokhai, the Yakut festival of Isahar.

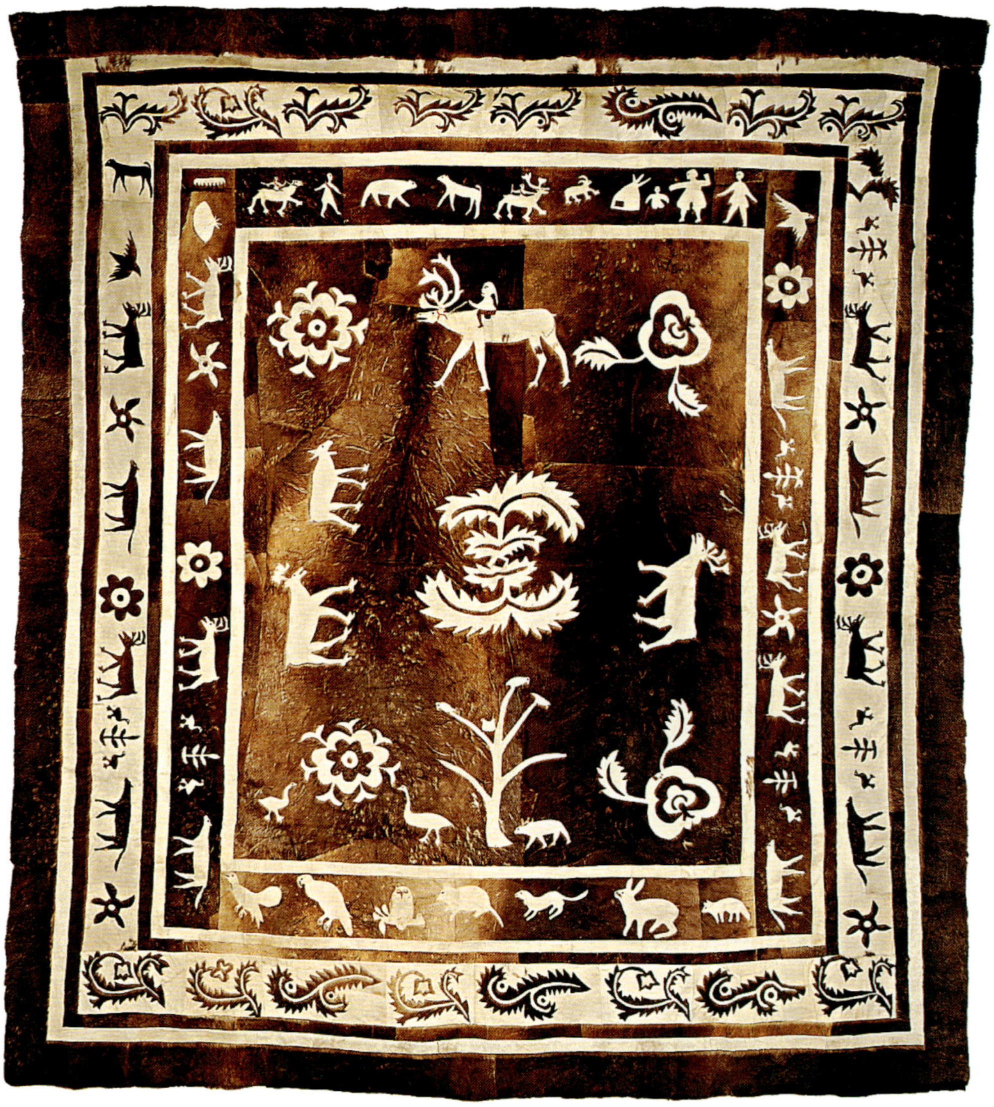

The skeleton which often figures on the shaman's coat must probably also be ascribed to the shaman's ancestor, for quite near it are usually sewed hawks' wings, and none but a shaman can fly or be represented by wings.

One might suppose from what has been said above that we have here to deal with three ways of representing the shaman ancestor: by the doll, the ämägyat, and the skeleton. It would be interesting to know, however, whether or not the ämägyat is to be found side by side with either of the other symbols. If so, it is possible that ämägyat is not a symbol of the ancestor spirit, but has a meaning of its own. On the Yakut coat the skeleton exists independent of ämägyat. On the Altaian coats, the doll is found side by side with the ämägyat.

The coat possesses an impersonal power of itself. It is said to bear the names of *ongor* (Mongol) and *tanara* (Yakut) in addition to the classified names for the coat. The coat as a whole is a *tanara* of the shaman, and each symbolic picture on the coat is also his *tanara*, i.e. protector.

By assuming this coat the shaman receives supernatural power, which allows him to go to the upper and under-worlds to meet spirits and deal with them. It is called 'shaman's horse' among the Yakut.

Another interpretation of the coat is that the picture of a perforated sun and a half-moon represents the dusk which reigns in the kingdom of the spirits. The strange animals, fishes, and birds which hang on the coat indicate the monsters that are said to inhabit the spirit-land.

Markovians,
Wall carpet, 1910.
Reindeer fur, 236 x 219 cm.
Russian Museum of Ethnography, St. Petersburg. Kamchatka Oblast, Chukchi Okrug, Markovo village.

Koryak,
Wooden shaman doll used in reindeer ritual, 1992.

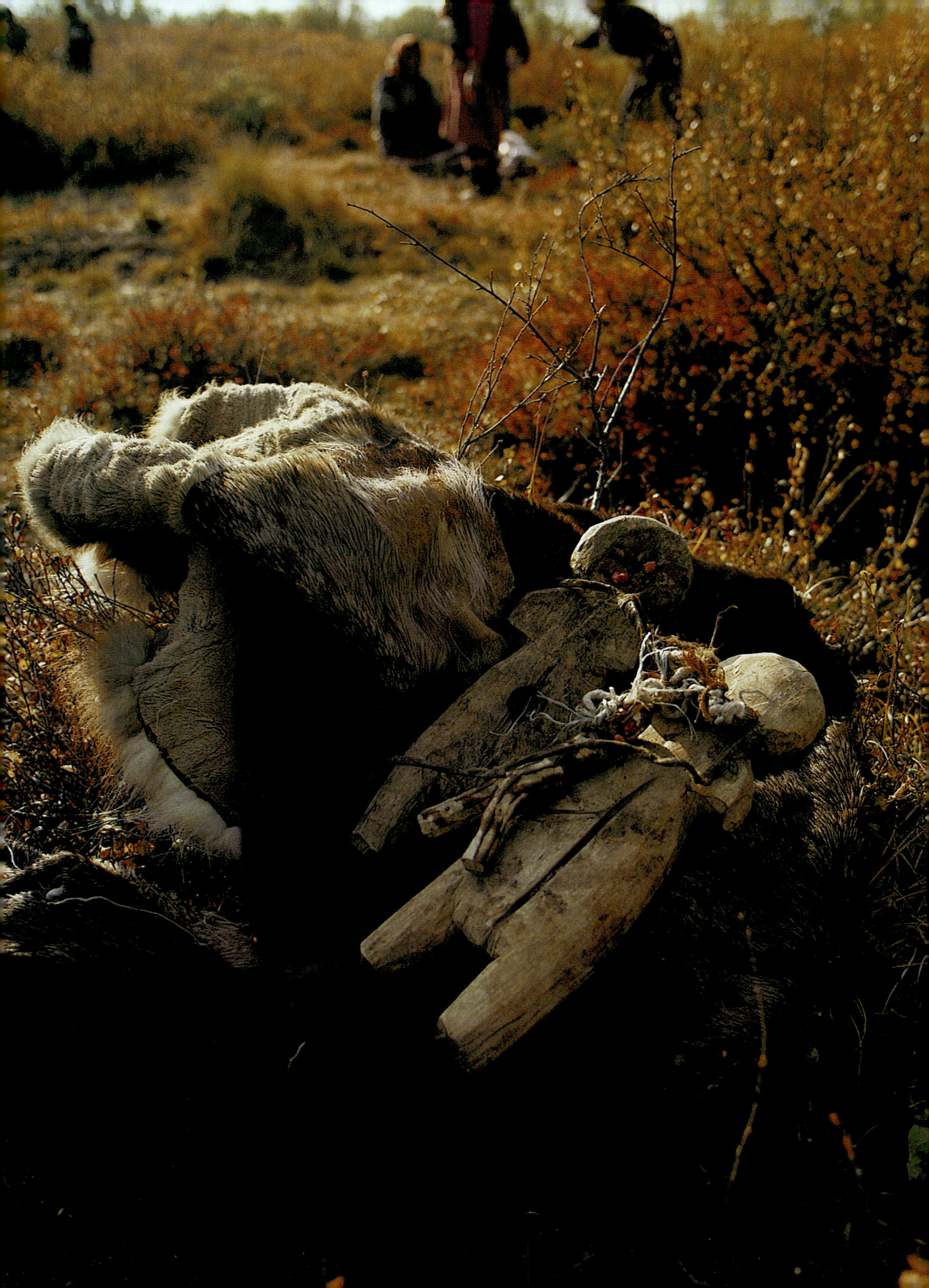

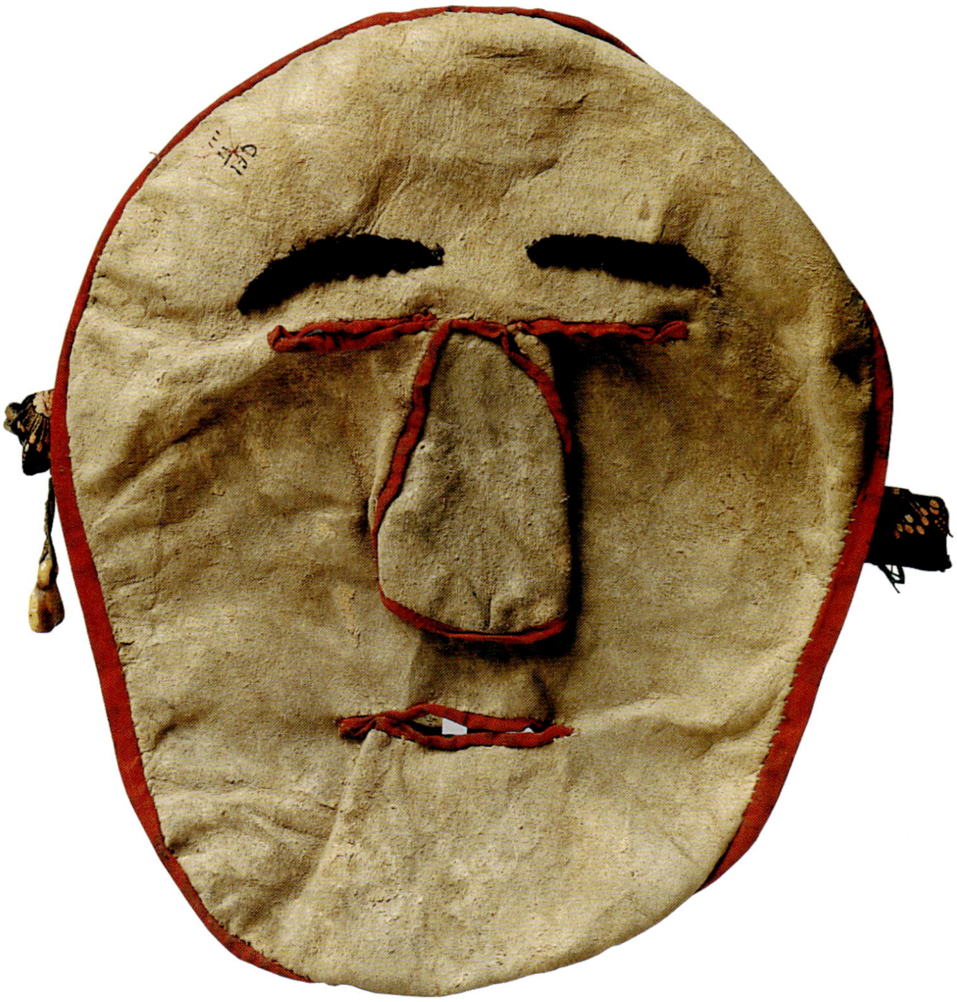

The iron chain hanging on the back signifies, according to some, the strength of the shaman's power, and according to others, the rudder which he uses in his journeys through the spirit country. The iron disks are there to defend the shaman from the blows of the hostile spirits.

The shaman wears his magical coat next his skin, and receives it from the hand of a *kuluruksuta* (page or assistant), whose duty it is to shout during the performance: *seb! kirdik! choo! o o!* (well! true! choo! o o!), and who helps the shaman in other ways, such as preparing the drum.

The drum is always egg-shaped, and is covered with the bide of a young bull. Its longest diameter is 53 cm., the width of the rim 11 cm., and the length of the stick 32 cm. The wider part of the stick is covered with cowhide. Sometimes there are twelve raised representations of horns on the drum, while in other cultures, they are always found in odd numbers, 7, 9, or 11. The cross inside is attached to the rim by means of straps. Little bells, jingling trinkets, and other rattles of iron and bone are attached inside round the rim, especially in the places where the straps are fastened.

Among the Yakut, there are two names for the drum, *tünür* and *donkür*. The Yakut of Viluy, in addition to the tünür (drum), have also a stringed instrument, *dünür*.

Besides the drum, the shaman uses two other musical instruments, one of which is a stringed instrument like the Russian balalaika (a kind of banjo), the other an instrument like that known as a Jew's harp, a small frame with a long wooden or metal tongue, which is moved by the finger; the narrow end of the instrument is held between the teeth, so that the mouth acts as a sounding-board.

Among the Buryat from Irkutsk, this instrument is called *khur*, and is used only by the shamans. This is also true of the Uriankhai. The Soïot call it *komus*, but the Altaians (using the term in the narrowest sense), who also have the word *komus*, use it to designate the stringed instrument resembling the Russian balalaika, which only shamans play. The Kirgis call the shaman's drum *kobuz*. The Altaians use the two-stringed *kabys* or *komus* as an accompaniment to the recital of heroic tales.

There are sometimes minor shamanistic performances without the drum and without the special garments. The shaman sits in his everyday dress on a small chair in the middle of the room and holds in his hands a branch ornamented with bunches of white horsehair, of which there may be three, five, or seven, but never an even number. The fire is not put out for these performances, and some of the horsehair is thrown on to it. The shaman does not dance, but sings and whirls about.

Natives of Altai.

The shaman's coat is made of goat or reindeer hide. All the outer side is covered with pendants of varying length in serpent form, and has pieces of many-coloured stuff stitched on to it. The pendants, which terminate in serpents' heads, hang freely. Bundles of reindeer leather straps are also attached here and there. The term *manyak*, is applied by the natives of Altai to the small pendants as well as to the coat as a whole.

There can further be found on the coat various symbolic figures and jingling pendants, such as iron triangles or a small bow and arrow to frighten hostile spirits. On the back and sometimes on the front of the coat there are sewed two copper disks. One *kam* (shaman) had four empty tobacco-bags hanging on his coat with imaginary tobacco inside, which he offers to the spirits whilst he is wandering in their country.

Koryak,
Ritual mask, 1911.
Dressed reindeer skin, fabric, walrus tusk ivory, 27 x 22 cm.
Russian Museum of Ethnography, St. Petersburg. Kamchatka.

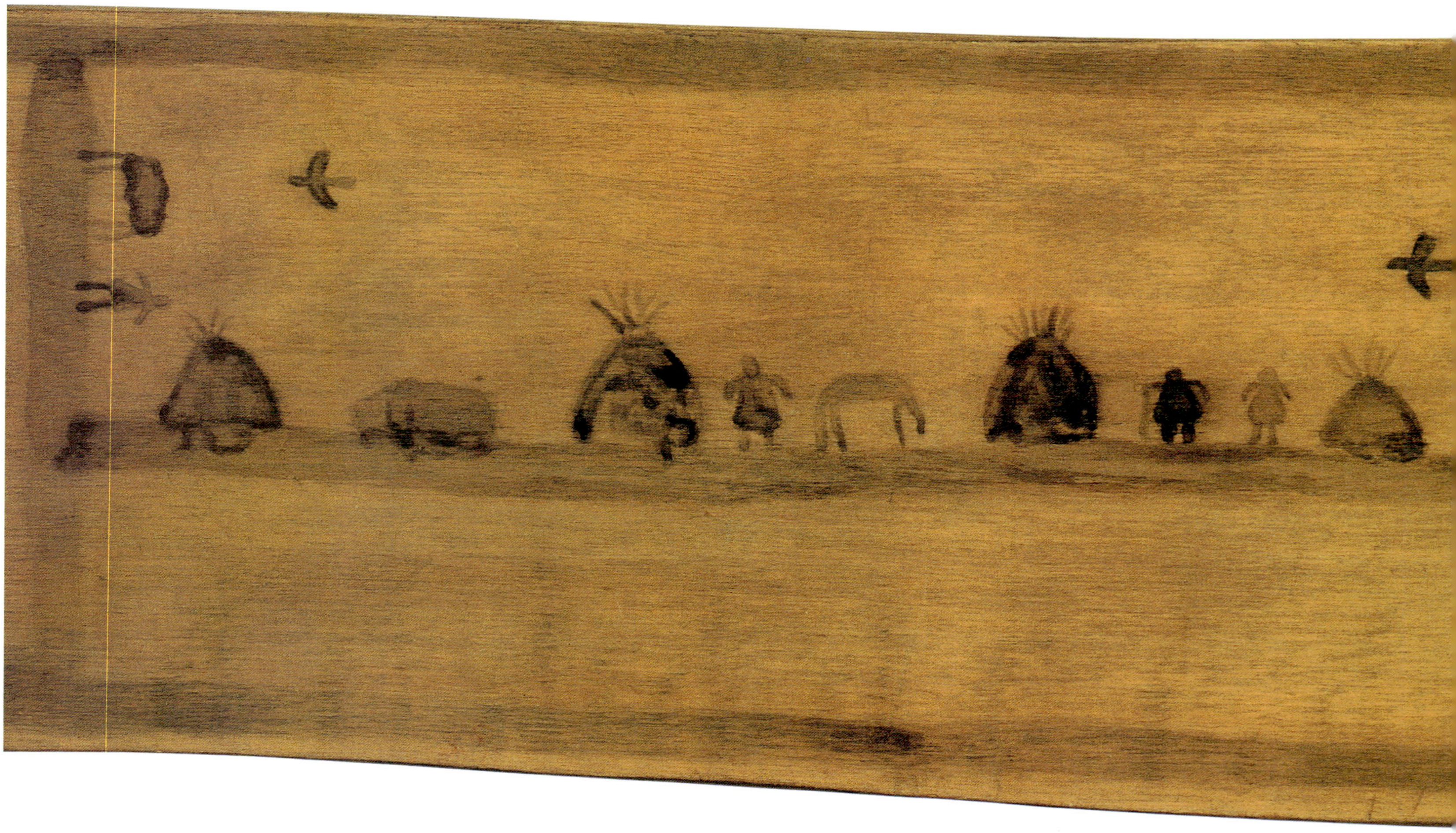

Chukchi,
'Boards of conjuration' for performing of rites at holidays, fragment,
1904-1907.
Wood, paint, 62.2 x 10 cm.
Russian Museum of Ethnography,
St. Petersburg. Chukchi Peninsular.

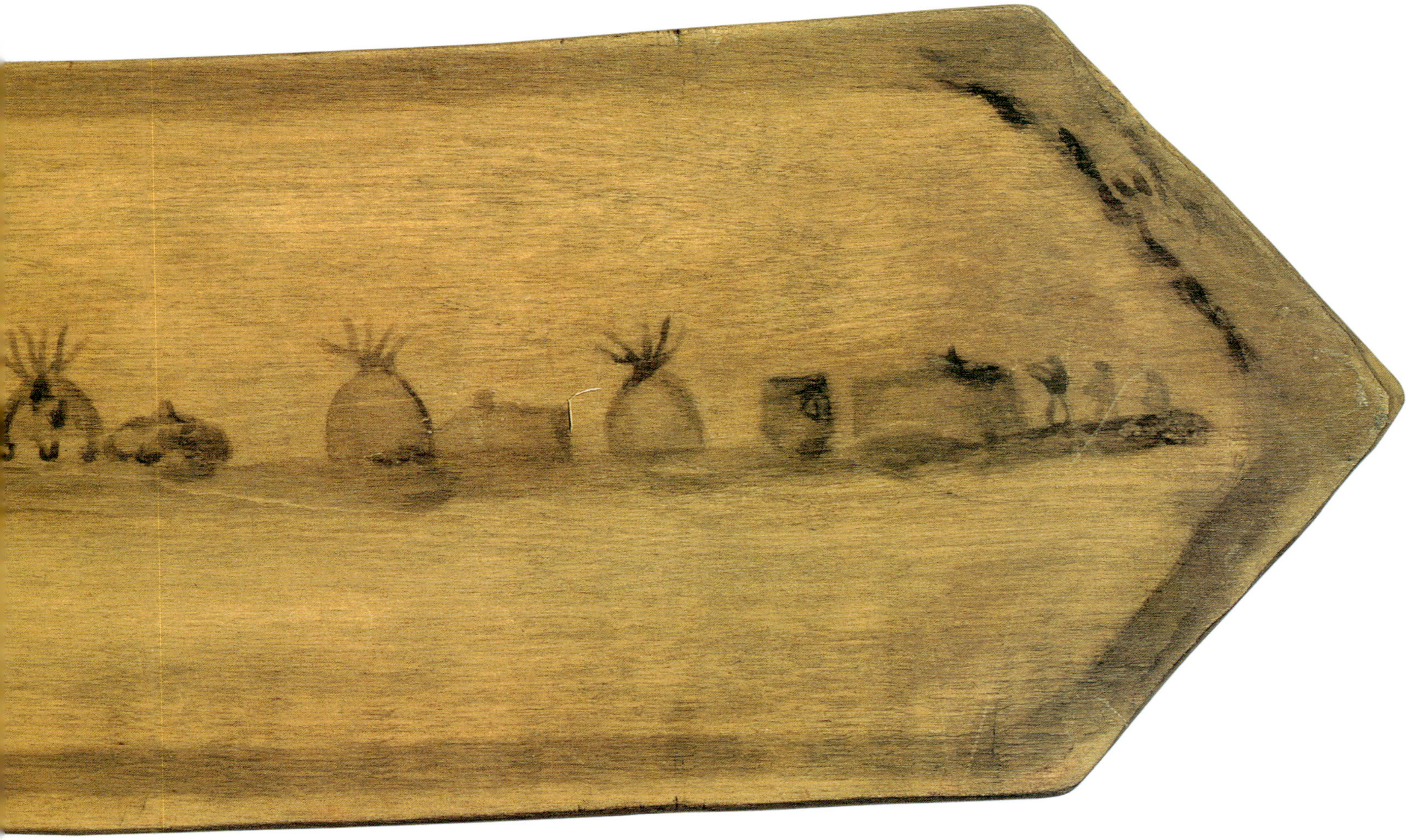

The collar is trimmed with owl's feathers. One *kam* had seven little dolls on his collar, which were heavenly maidens.

A few bells are sewed on here and there; the more prosperous shamans have as many as nine. The ringing of the bells is the voice of the seven maidens whose symbols are sewed to the collar calling to the spirits to descend to them.

The cap of the Altaian shaman is formed of a square piece of the hide of a reindeer calf. On one side there are two buttons and on the other two loops. On the top, bunches of feathers are sewed, and from the lower edge bangs a fringe made of string and shell-fish. This is placed on the head with the two sides buttoned to the back, thus forming a cylindrical cap on the shaman's head. If the hide is hard, the top of the cap with its feathers sticks up like a coronet.

Among some shamans of the Teleut, the cap is made of brown owl skin; the feathers remain as ornaments, and sometimes also the bird's head.

It is not all shamans who can wear the *manyak* and the owlskin cap. The spirits generally announce to the chosen man when he may wear them.

Among the Tartars of Chern the shaman wears a mask (*kocho*), with squirrels' tails for eyebrows and moustaches. Among the same people one might observe the use of two crutches; one of them is a crook, the other is supposed to be a horse, similar to the horse-staves of the Buryat.

All the drums which we see among the natives of Altai and north-western Mongolia are round in shape. The Tartars of Chern have oval drums resembling the egg-shaped drum of the east Siberians.

The Altai drum has a hoop as large as the palm of one's hand, covered on one side with hide. Inside the drum there is a vertical wooden stick and a horizontal iron *chord* with rattles attached. The drum is held by the wooden stick, and not at the intersection of the stick and the iron crossbar.

The wooden vertical stick is called *bar* by the natives of Altai. Among other north-western tribes it has various names. The *bar* has a man's head and feet at the two ends. The upper part is often carved, the eyes, the nose, the mouth, and the chin being cut with great exactness. The horizontal iron stay is called by the Altaians *krish*, and from it hang various iron rattles called *kungru*. The number of *kungru* varies according to the ability of the shaman. It is a guide to the quantity of *chayu* possessed by the shaman, since the more *chayu* the shaman possesses, the more *kungru* are found in his drum.

Under the chin of the figure on the wooden bar are fastened long strips of gaudy material called *yauasua*.

On the hide of the drum, sometimes on both sides, sometimes on the inner side only, circles and crosses and other lines are drawn with red dye.

Some Altai drums have drawings of animals on them, like those on the drums of the North-American Indians.

The drums of the Chern and Kumandinsk Tartars differ from those of the Altaians; instead of *bar*, *krish*, and jingling plates there are here representations of the two worlds, above and underground, separated by a horizontal line, which divides the drum into two parts, an upper and a lower.

On the outer side of the drum of the Chern Tartars, pictures of animals and plants are found. On the upper and larger part an arch is drawn, with indications of sky, inside of which are two trees with a bird on each. To the left of the tree are two circles - the sun and the moon - light and darkness. Below the horizontal line are pictures of frogs, lizards, and snakes. These drawings have a particular importance, since the symbols described show more than any others the shamanistic view of the natural and the supernatural.

The Lena under ice and snow.

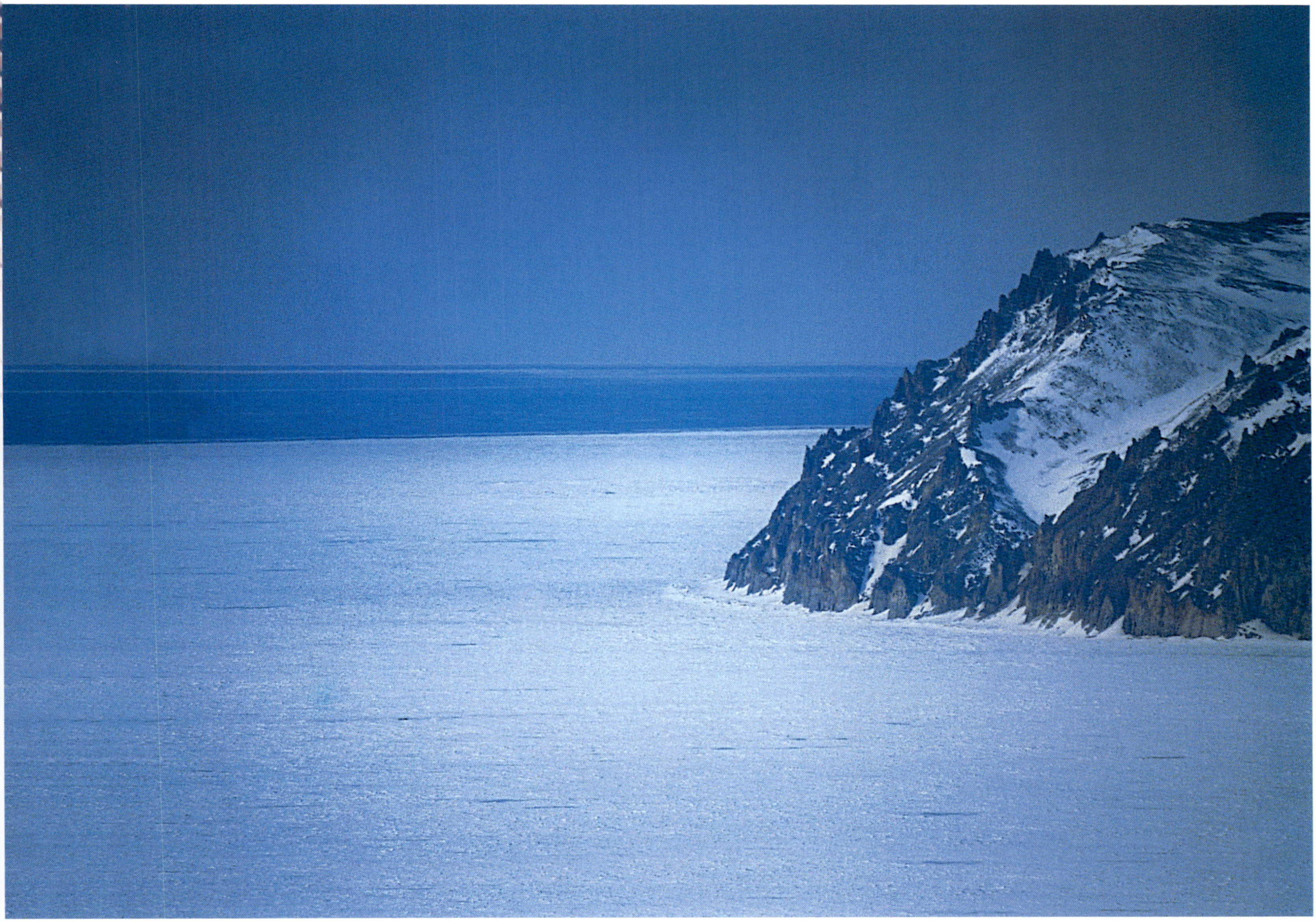

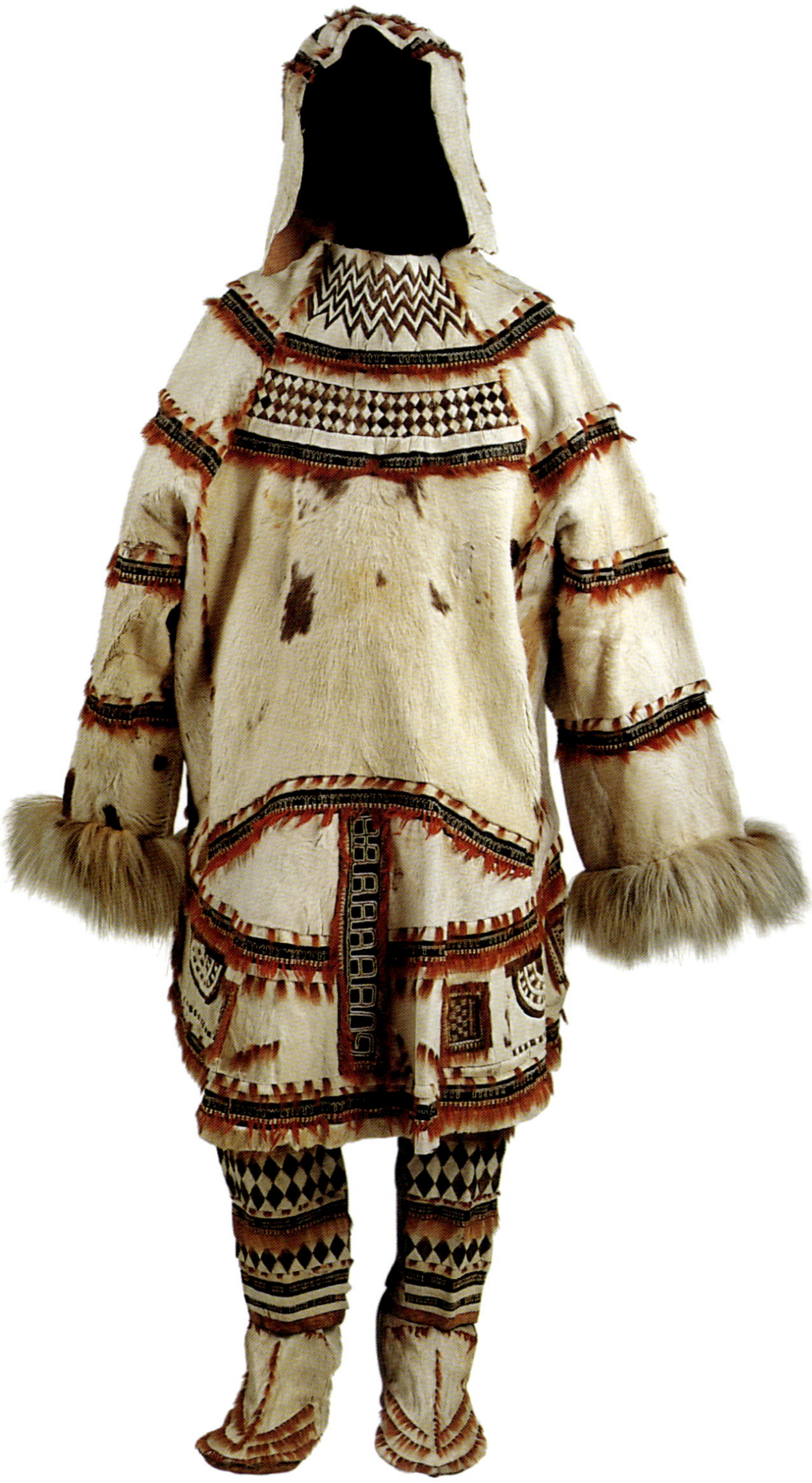

Koryak,
Man's burial outfit, front view,
1904-1911.
Reindeer hide and leg fells, dog fur, seal skin and undercoat, alder-tree bark, reindeer underneck hair, Parka: 98 x 94 cm; Trousers: 86 cm; Shoe soles: 23 cm; Height of boot: 17cm.
Russian Museum of Ethnography, St. Petersburg. Dalnevostochni (Far-Eastern) Krai, Kamchatka Okrug.

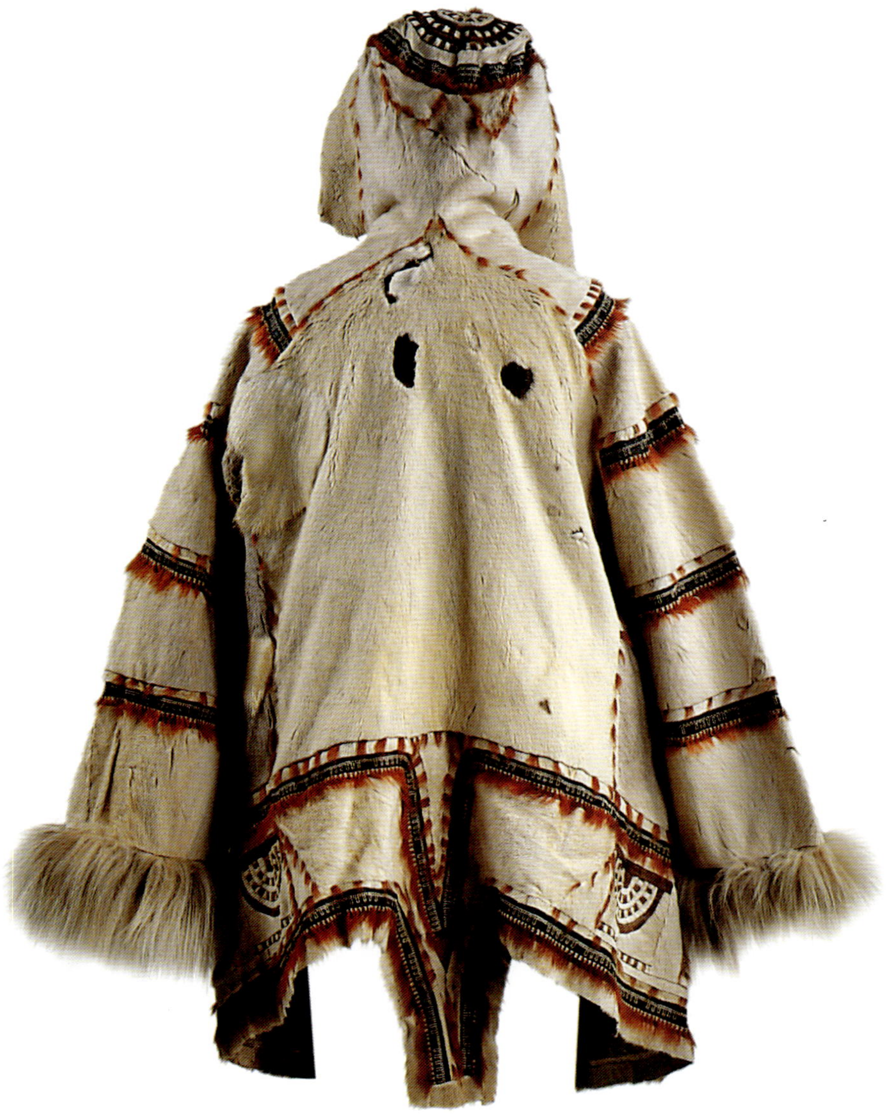

Koryak,
Man's burial outfit, back view,
1904-1911.
Reindeer hide, dog fur, seal undercoat and skin, alder-tree bark, reindeer underneck hair, 98 x 94 cm.
Russian Museum of Ethnography, St. Petersburg. Dalnevostochni (Far-Eastern) Krai, Kamchatka Okrug.

Evenki,
Shaman tambourine, fragment, early 20th century.
Leather, wood, metal, beads, 95 x 50 cm.
Russian Museum of Ethnography, St. Petersburg. Siberian Krai. Krasnoyarsk Okrug, Turukhan District, the Nizhni (Lower) Tunguska river basin.

The Buryat.

An example of the Buryat shaman's costume belonged to a female shaman, who was accompanied by her husband and two other Buryat, each of them holding a magical drum. She herself held in her hand two sticks, ornamented at the top end with a carving of a horse's head surrounded by small bells. From the back of the shoulders reaching to the ground hung about thirty snakes, made of white and black skin, in such a way that the snakes seem to be composed of white and black rings. One of the snakes was divided into three at the end, and was accounted indispensable to each Buryat female shaman. The cap was covered with an iron casque having horns with three branches, projecting on both sides like those of a deer.

Also worth describing is a costume of another old and revered female shaman near Selenginsk. Her costume was hanging in her *yurt,* but, according to her account, was not complete. Among other things, there was a box, full of strips of

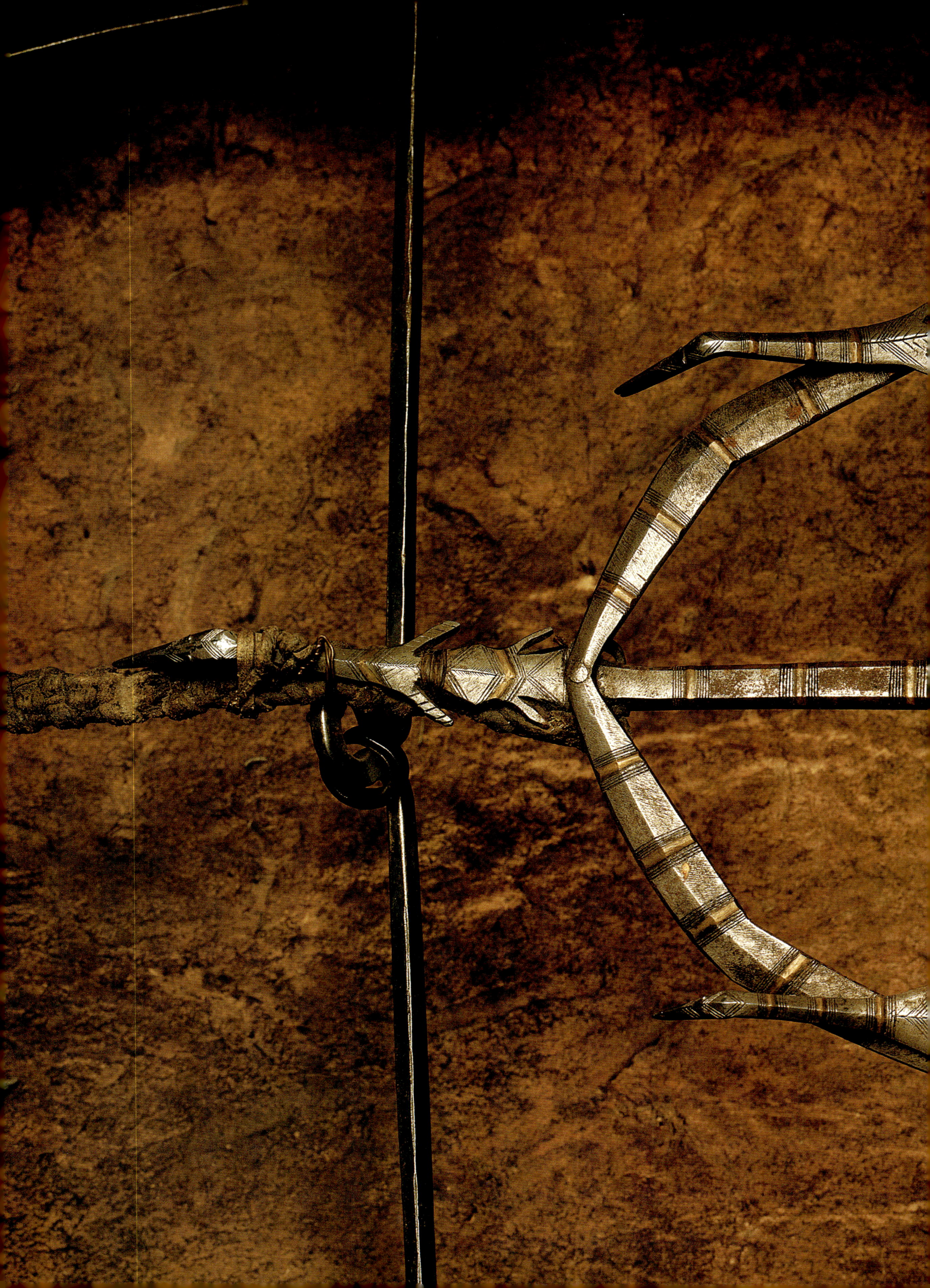

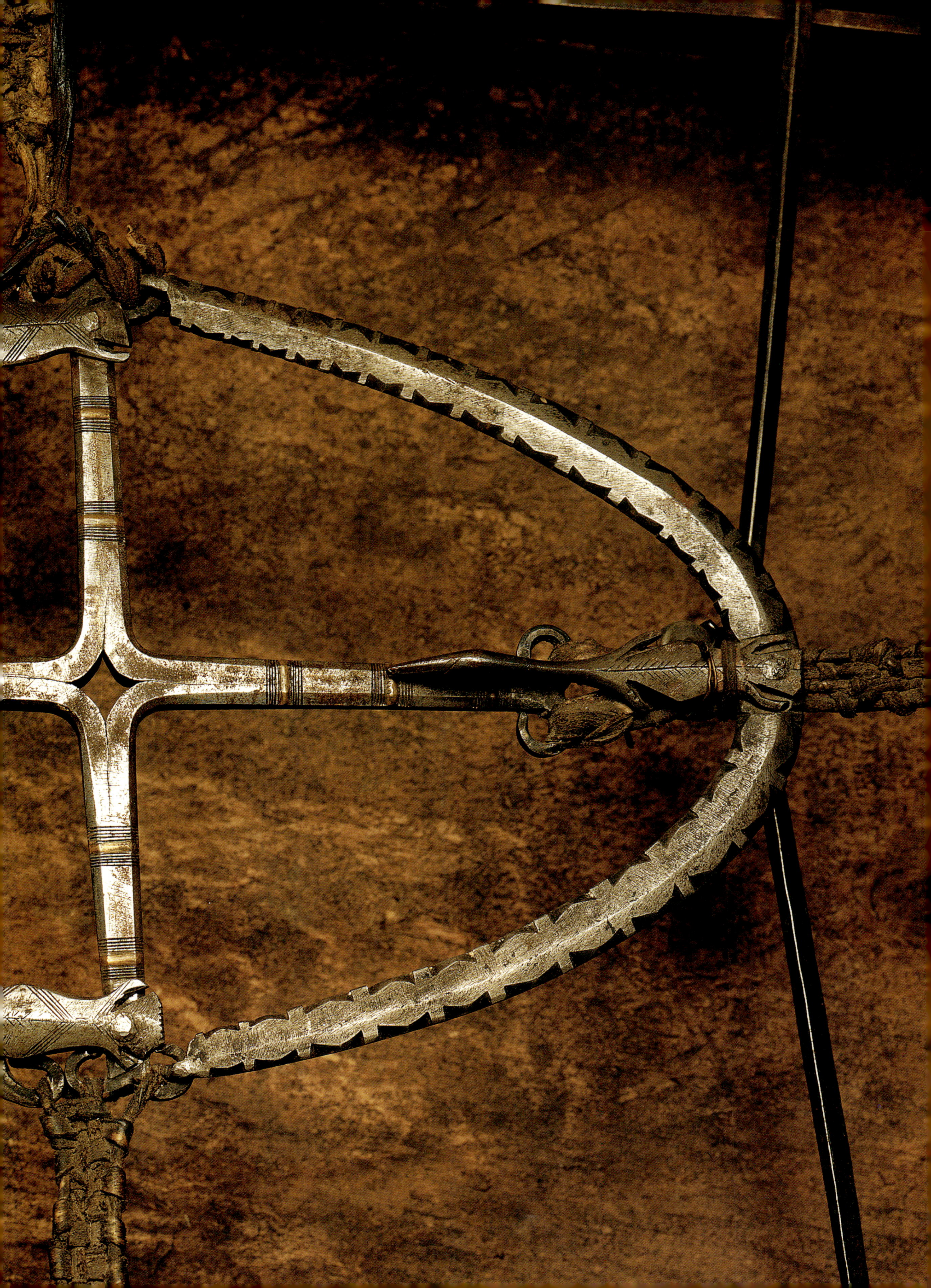

cloth, small stones, thunderbolts, which she used for magical purposes.There was also a felt bag full of various felt idols.

The coat (*orgoy*), the cap, and the horse-staves *morini-khörbö* are the chief appartenances of a shaman in these communities.

The *orgoy* is of white material for the white shaman, and of blue for the black shaman. Its shape does not differ from that of the ordinary coat.

The old-fashioned *orgoy* was shorter than that of the present day. The front of the coat is covered with metal figures of horses, fishes, birds. The back is covered with twisted iron representing snakes, with rattles hanging from them (*shamshorgo*), together with a whole row of little bells and tambourine bells.

On the chest above the thin plates used to hang little shining copper disks, and on the sleeves were also hung thin iron plates, in imitation of the bones of the shoulder and forearm.

The cap, which is peaked, is made of lynx skin, with a bunch of ribbons on the top. After the fifth consecration the shaman can wear the iron cap; it is composed of a crown-like iron hoop with two half-hoops crossing each other, above which is an iron plate with two born-like projections.

In the place where the intersecting hoops are tied to the hoop round the head, there are three groups of *khoubokho*, or *kholbogo*, conical weights of iron. From the back of the hoop hangs an iron chain composed of four links and ending in small objects resembling a spoon and an awl.

This cap is sort of the metal diadem, consisting of an iron ring with two convex arches, also of iron, crossing one another at right angles, and with a long jointed chain which hangs down from the nape of the neck to the heels.

The horse-staves (*morini-khorbo*) are to be met with among all the Buryat of Baikal, but among the Buryat of Balagan they are not used. Each Baikal shaman possesses two. They are made of wood or of iron; but the iron staff is only given to the shaman after the fifth consecration, when he also receives the iron cap. The wooden horse-staves are cut for the novice the day before his first consecration, from a birch-tree growing in the forest where the shamans are buried. The wood for the horse-staves must be cut in such a way that the tree shall not perish, otherwise it would be a bad omen for the shaman.

This implement is 80 cm long; the upper part is bent and has a horse-head carved on it; the middle part of the stick forms the knee-joints of the horse, and the lower end is fashioned into a hoof.

Little bells, one of which is larger than the rest, are tied to the horse-staves. Likewise small conical weights of iron, *khoubokho*, or *kholbogo*, blue, white, yellow and red-coloured ribbons, and strips of ermine and squirrel fur. To make it look more realistic miniature stirrups are also attached.

The iron horse-staves are not very different from the wooden ones. They represent the horses on which the shaman rides to the upper and lower worlds.

It is in the drum that the horse, on which the shaman makes his flight, is symbolized. This drum is covered with horse-hide fastened to the back with leather straps. However, the drum, *khese*, is very little known among the Buryat, who substitute the horse-staves for it, and the little bell is sometimes also called *khese*; nevertheless, among the Mongol Shamanists and the Mongolized Uriankhai, the drum is in use.

The Buryat Buddhists use in their divine services either drums covered on both sides with hide, like those found among the North-American Indians, or those with hide on one side only. These drums are round, and have leather handles attached to the outer edge of the rim.

Yakut,
Ancient tomb of a shaman,
early 20th century.
Yakutia.

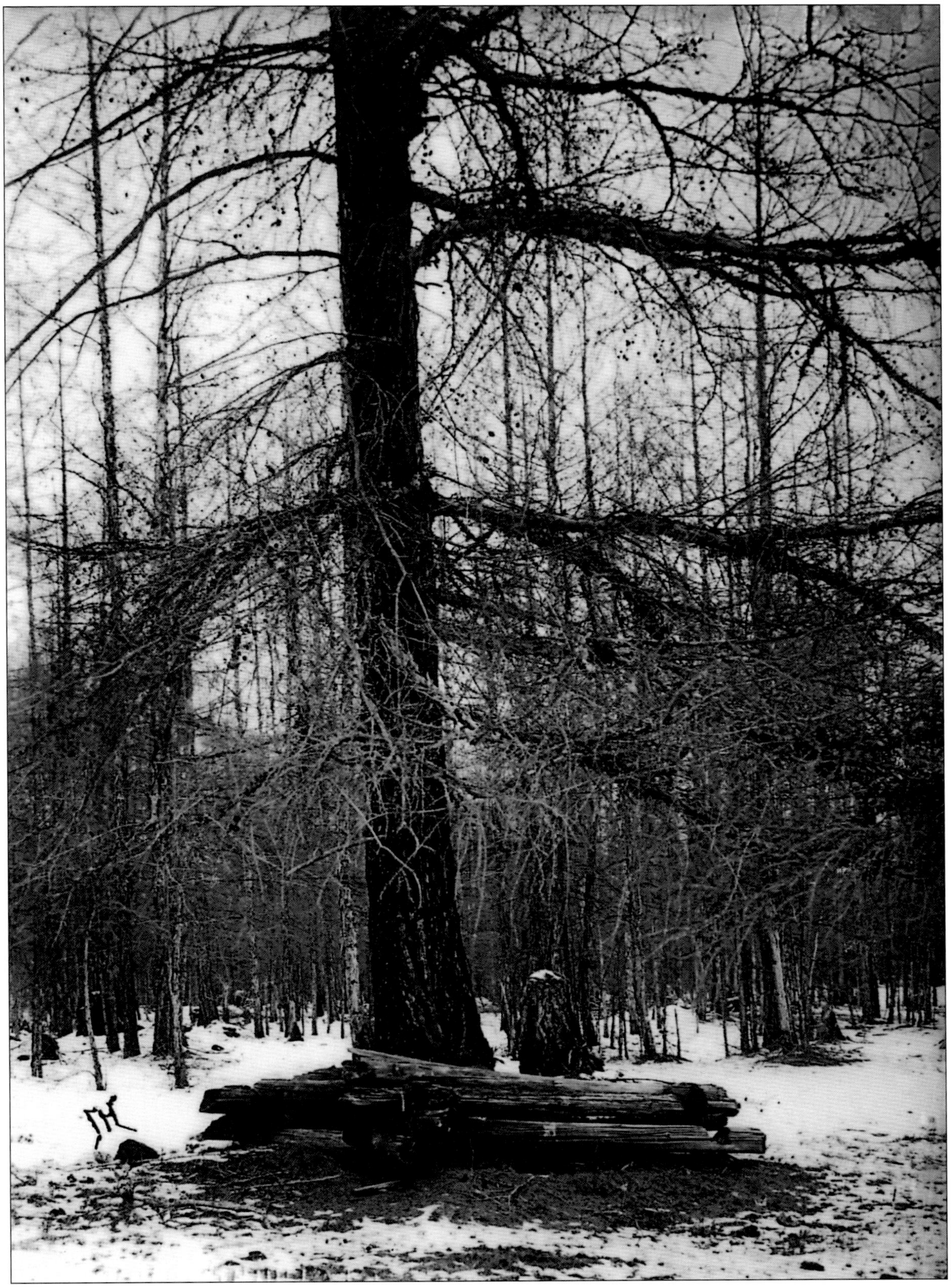

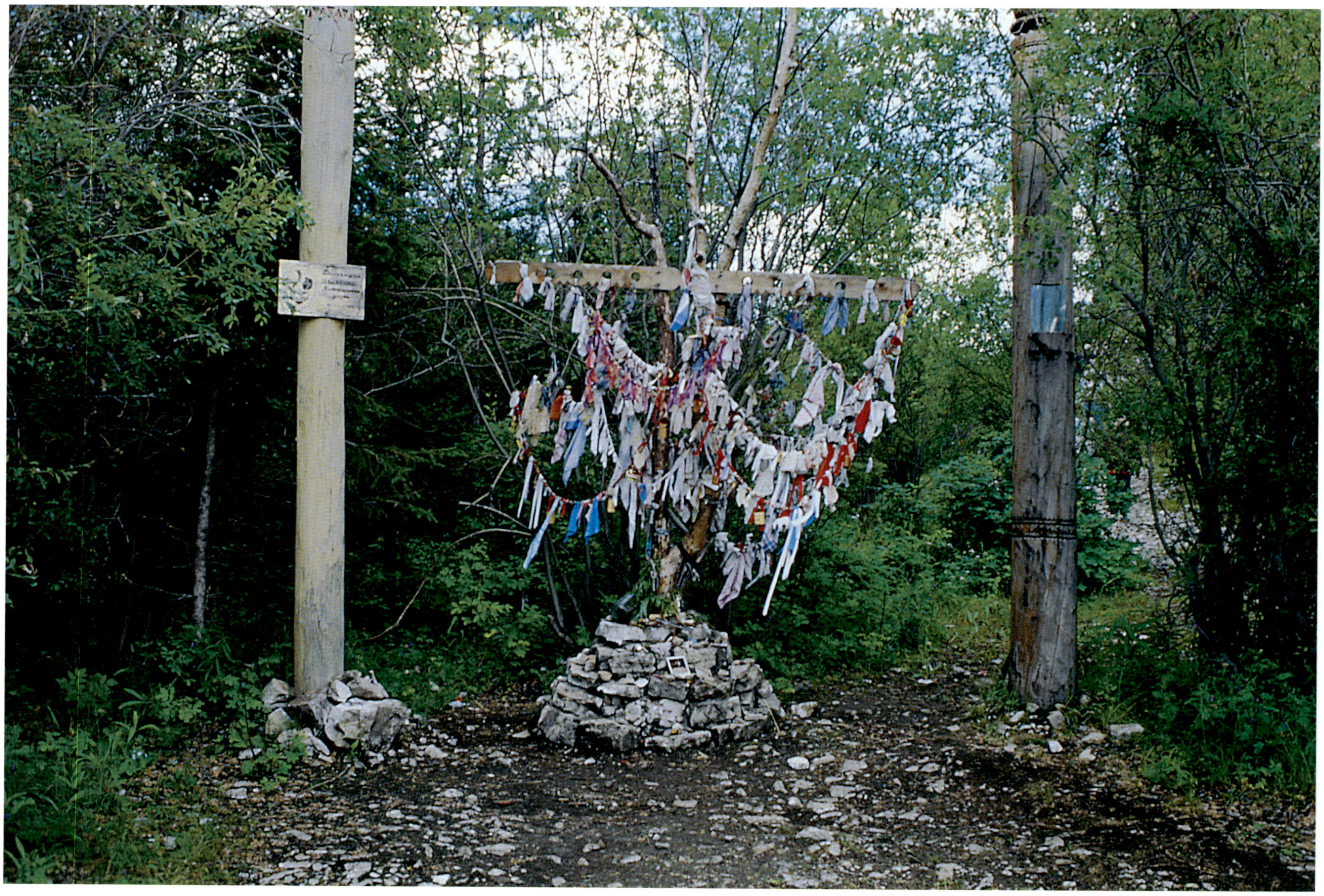

The sacred tree of a shaman.

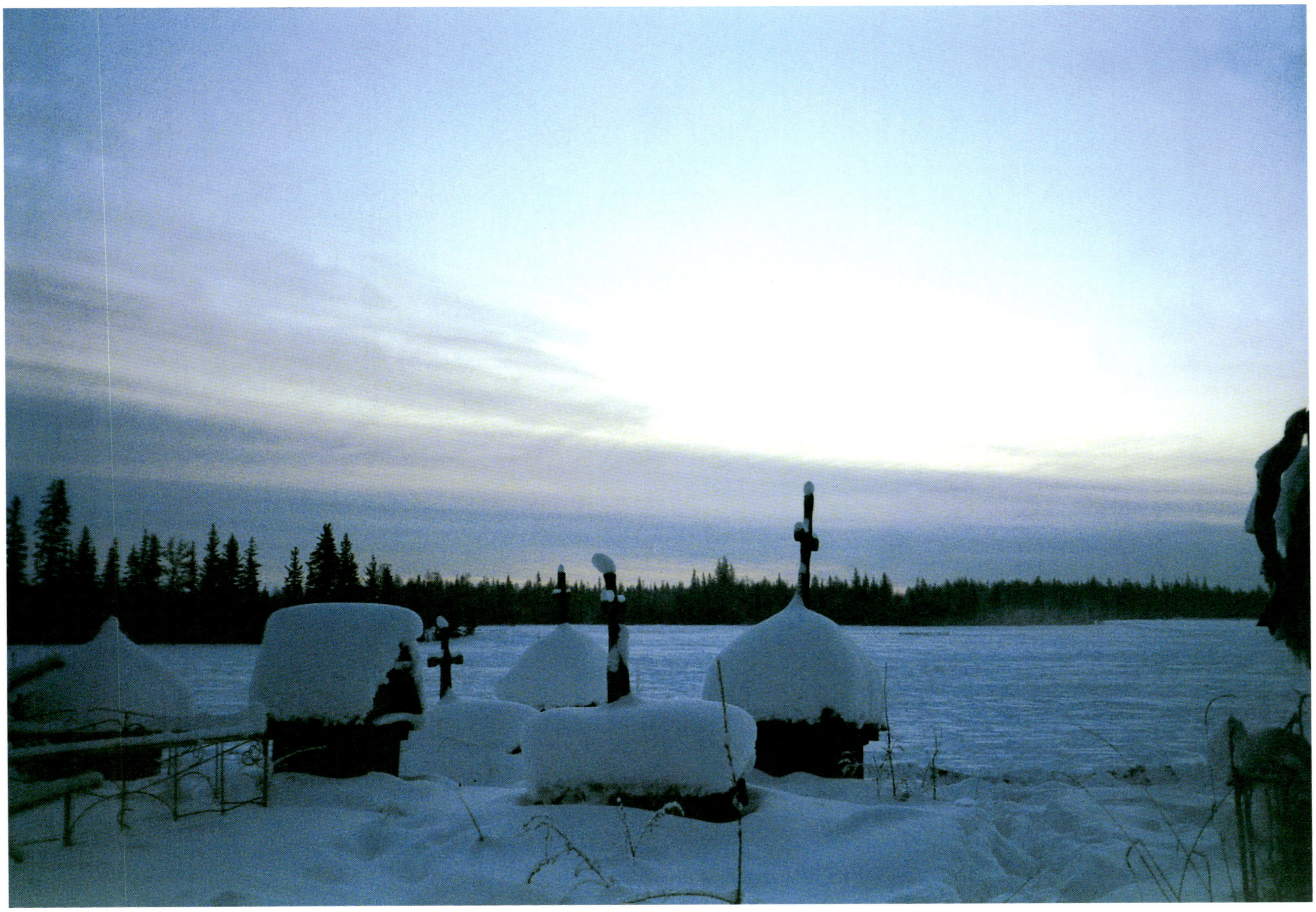

Tombs in the taiga.
Yakutia.

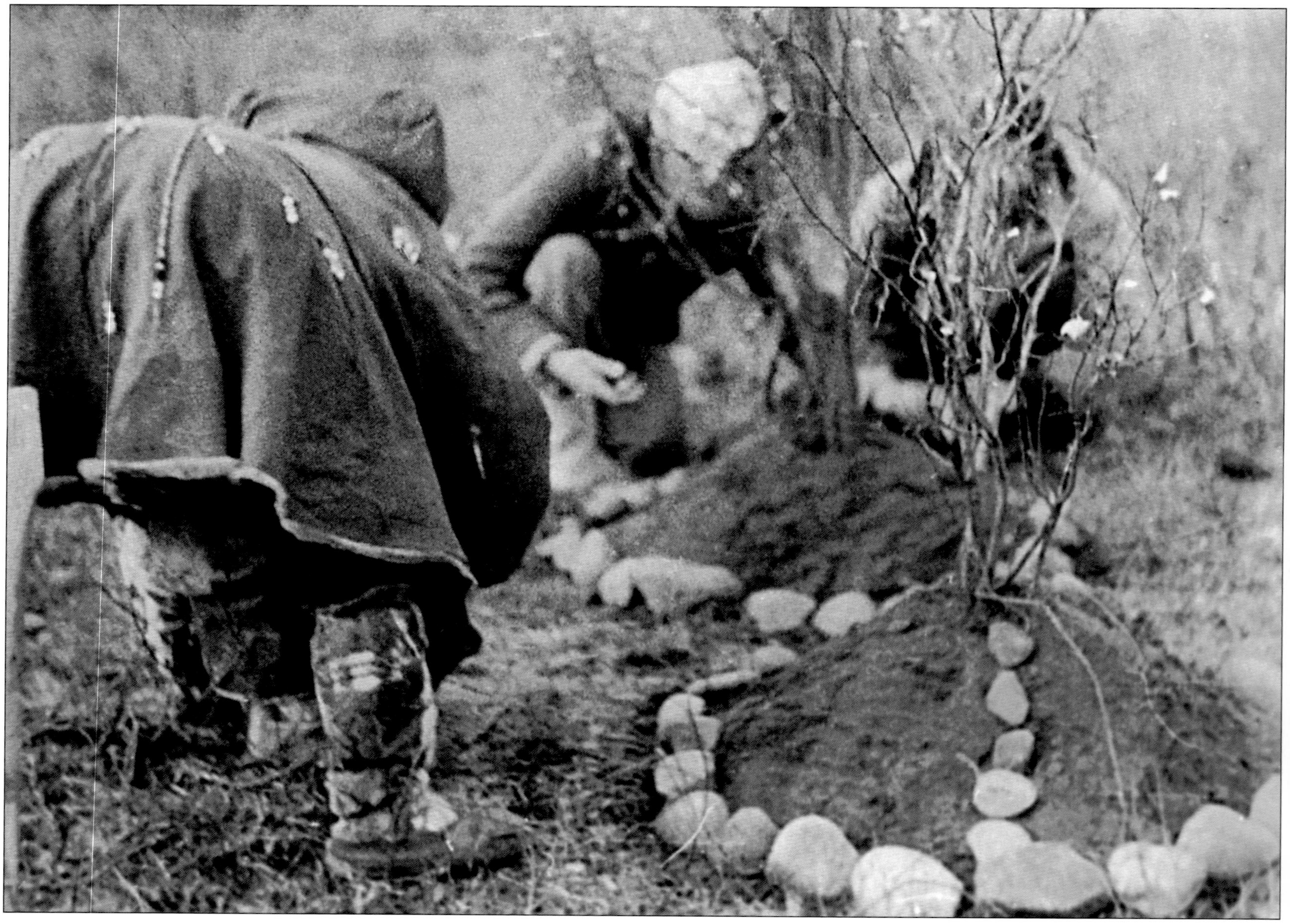

The next accessory of the shaman is the *khur*, a 'tuning-fork,' with a wire tongue between the two side-pins, an implement largely in use among shamanists. It may be met with from the sources of the Amur to the Ural, and from the Arctic Ocean down to Tashkent. Here and there it is merely a musical instrument.

The Olkhon Buryat have one other property, called *shire*. It is a box three and a half feet long and one foot deep, standing on four legs, each two feet high. On the box are hung ribbons, bells, strips of skin, and on one of the long sides different figures are carved or painted in red. Usually on the right side is represented the sun, and on the left, the moon. The sun is depicted as a wheel, and in the middle of the moon there is a human figure holding a tree in one hand. In the middle of the long side there are three images of secondary gods, one woman and two men, in whose honour wine is sprinkled several times a year. There are also war implements—bow and quiver and sword, and under each human figure there is a horse. The *shire* is used to hold horse-staves, drums, and other ritual implements. The shaman acquires the right of carrying the *shire* after the fifth consecration. It is asserted, that with every new consecration up to the ninth, the height and other dimensions of the *shire* increase.

There are two other articles worth mentioning: *abagaldey*, a monstrous mask of skin, wood, and metal, painted, and ornamented with a great beard; and *toli*, a metal looking-glass with representations of twelve animals on it, which is hung round the neck and worn on the breast; sometimes it is sewed on the shaman's coat.

Occasionally the Buryat shaman has also a whip with bells, but generally all these implements have tended to disappear in modern times.

Two other ethical and linguistic groups, which, although they live only partly in Siberia, yet belong to the Neo-Siberians, are the Samoyed and the Finnic tribes, and a survey of their shaman accessories is of special interest in connexion with those of the Mongolic, Turkic, and Evenki shamans.

The most important belonging of a *tadibey* (Samoyed shaman) is his *penzer* (drum), which he prepares according to a special set of rules. He must kill a male reindeer-calf with his own hands, and prepare the skin in such a way that no veins are left on it. In these preparations *inka* (i. e. a woman), being considered unclean, cannot assist.

The drums, which are ornamented with metal disks and plates, and covered with transparent reindeer hide, are round in shape and of various sizes. The largest drum was nearly two feet in diameter and two and a half inches in height.

The drums of the Samoyed and of the Ob-Ostyak are like the Altai drums, round, broadrimmed, covered on one side only, and with a diameter of from 30 cm to 50 cm.

The shaman's costume consists of a chamois-leather coat called *samburzia*, ornamented with red cloth. Eyes and face are covered with a piece of cloth, since the *tadibey* is supposed to penetrate into the spirit-world with his inner sight. Instead of a cap there are two bands round his head to keep the cloth over the face in position. An iron disk hangs on his breast.

In certain places the *tadibey* uses a cap with a visor, and over the leather coat jingling trinkets and little bells and strips of cloth of various shades are hung. In this ornamentation the number seven plays an important role.

Koryak woman in the process of making welcome the spirit-masters of the semi-domesticated reindeer at the traditional autumn festival of Koryak reindeer-herders.

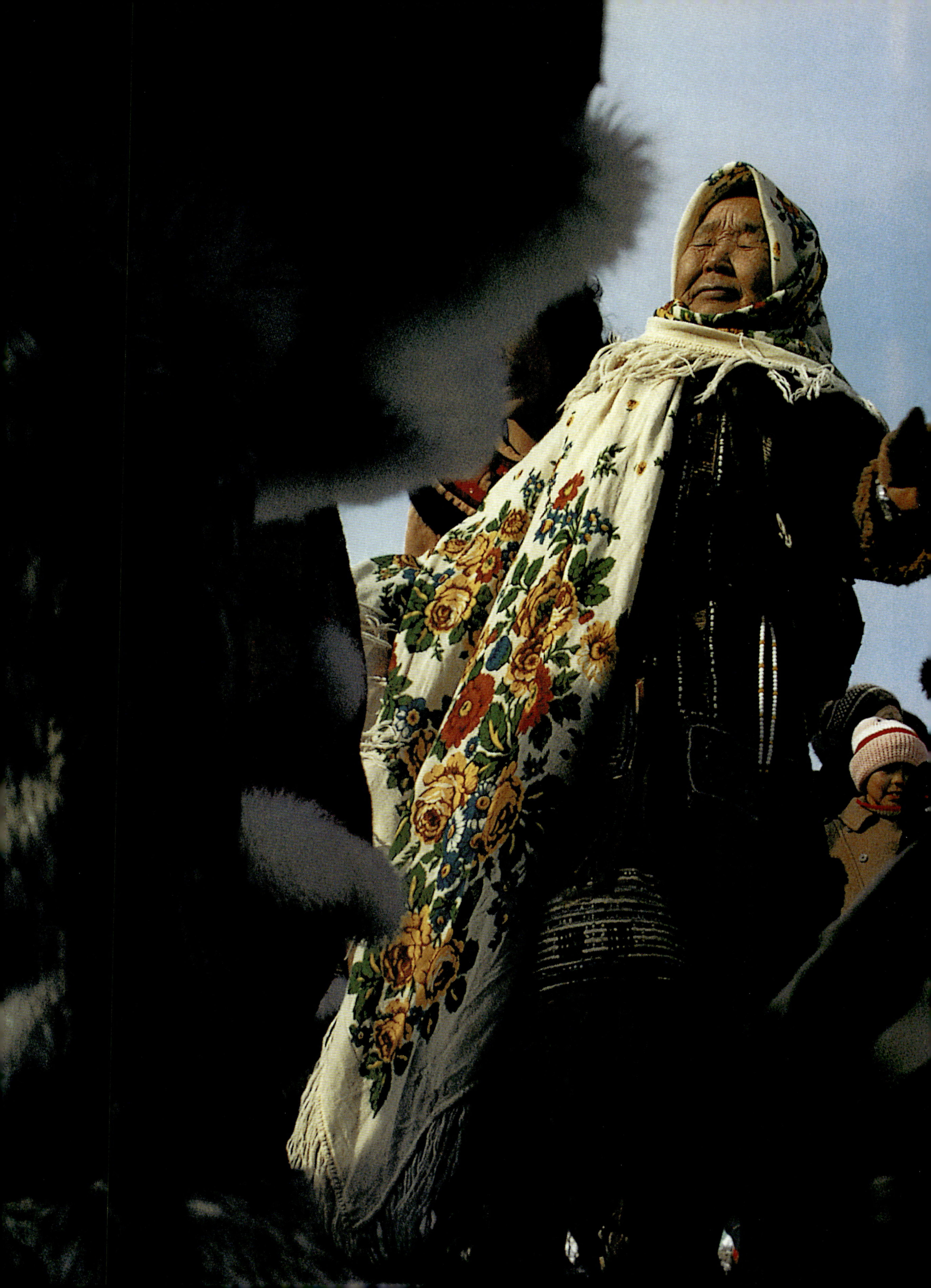

D. THE SHAMAN IN ACTION

"After his introductory interview with the spirits, the shaman sometimes 'sinks;' he falls to the ground unconscious, while his soul is wandering in the other worlds, talking with the 'spirits' and asking them for advice."

Since the performances of shamans as professionals called in to treat diseases, to answer inquiries, for soothsaying and other similar purposes, are very much the same among the different tribes of Palaeo-Siberians, we shall confine ourselves to giving a few typical examples of these performances. The same procedure will be followed with regard to the Neo-Siberians.

The Koryak.

Professional Shamanism among the Koryak is at a most primitive stage of development, yet at the same time, thanks to the influence of European culture, it is also decadent.

Among the Koryak, two shamans performed the following rituals:

Both of the shamans were young men, and neither enjoyed special respect on the part of his relatives. Both were poor men who worked as labourers for the rich members of their tribe. One of them was a Maritime Koryak from Alutor. He used to come to the village of Kamenskoye in company with a Koryak trader. He was a bashful youth, his features, though somewhat wild, were flexible and pleasant, and his eyes were bright. The people put out the oil-lamps in the underground house in which he stopped with his master. Only a few coals were glowing on the hearth, and it was almost dark in the house. On the large platform which is put up in the front part of the house as the seat and sleeping-place for visitors, one could discern the shaman in an ordinary shaggy shirt of reindeer skin, squatting on the reindeer skins that covered the platform. His face was covered with a large oval drum.

Suddenly he commenced to beat the drum softly and to sing in a plaintive voice; then the beating of the drum grow stronger and stronger; and his song - in which could be heard sounds imitating the howling of the wolf, the groaning of the cargoose, and the voices of other animals, his guardian spirits - appeared to come, sometimes from the corner nearest to the listener, then from the opposite end, then again from the middle of the house, and then it seemed to proceed from the ceiling. He was a ventriloquist. Shamans versed in this art are believed to possess particular power. His drum also seemed to sound, now overhead, now on the ground, now behind, now in front of the rapt audience. The shaman was moving around, noiselessly stepping upon the platform with his fur shoes, then retiring to some distance, then coming nearer, lightly jumping, and then squatting down on his heels.

All of a sudden the sound of the drum and the singing ceased. When the women had relighted their lamps, he was lying, completely exhausted, on a white reindeer skin on which he had been sitting before the shamanistic performance. The concluding words of the shaman, which he pronounced in a recitative, were uttered as though spoken by the spirit whom he had summoned, and who declared that the "disease" had left the village, and would not return.

Itelmen,
Ritual celebration at a religious festival, 1992.

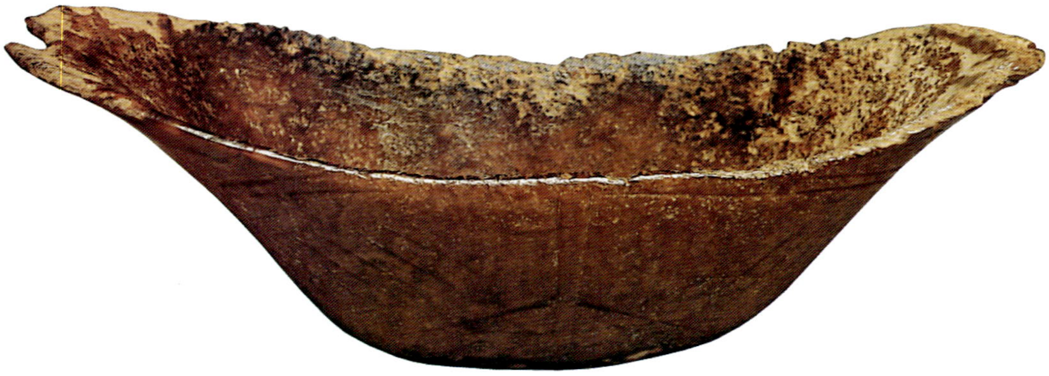

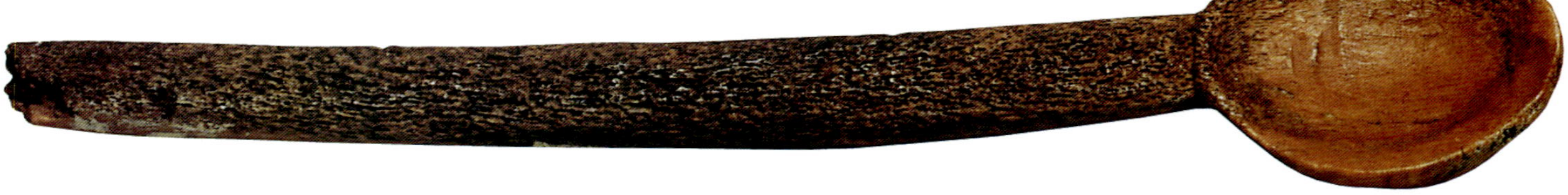

Eskimo,
Ritual spoon and cup in the form of a boat, 3rd-4th century AD.
Walrus tusk ivory, Spoon: 12.7 cm; Cup: 10.3 x 2.2 cm.
Russian Museum of Ethnography, St. Petersburg. Chukchi Peninsular, Enmillen village.

Chukchi,
Quiver for arrows, fragment, 1904-1907.
Dressed reindeer skin, sealskin, reindeer underneck hair, wood, 88 x 21.5 cm.
Russian Museum of Ethnography, St. Petersburg. Primorskaya Oblast, Anadyr Krai.

The other shamanistic ceremony was performed by a shaman for the purpose of divining whether travellers would reach home safely.

Someone gave him a travelling knife, which was sharp and looked like a dagger. The light in the tent was put out; but the dim light of the Arctic spring night (it was April), which penetrated the canvas of the tent, was sufficient to allow me to follow the movements of the shaman. He took the knife, beat the drum, and sang, telling the spirits that he was ready to carry out their wishes. After a little while he put away the drum, and, emitting a rattling sound from his throat, he thrust the knife into his breast up to the hilt. However, after having cut his jacket, he turned the knife downwards. He drew out the knife with the same rattling in his throat, and resumed beating the drum.

Then he said to the traveller that he would have a good journey, and showed through the hole in his coat the blood on his body. The common Koryaks are sure that the shaman actually cuts himself, and that the wound heals up immediately.

The Chukchi.

Among the Chukchi, a typical shamanistic performance is carried on in the inner room of the house, when it is closed for the night. This room, especially among the reindeer Chukchi, is very small. Sometimes the performance here described is preceded by another, held in the outer room, in daylight, and usually connected with a communal ceremonial.

When the drum is tightened and moistened, and the light is put out, the shaman, who is often quite naked down to the waist, begins to operate. The shaman beats the drum and sings tunes; at first slowly, then more rapidly. His

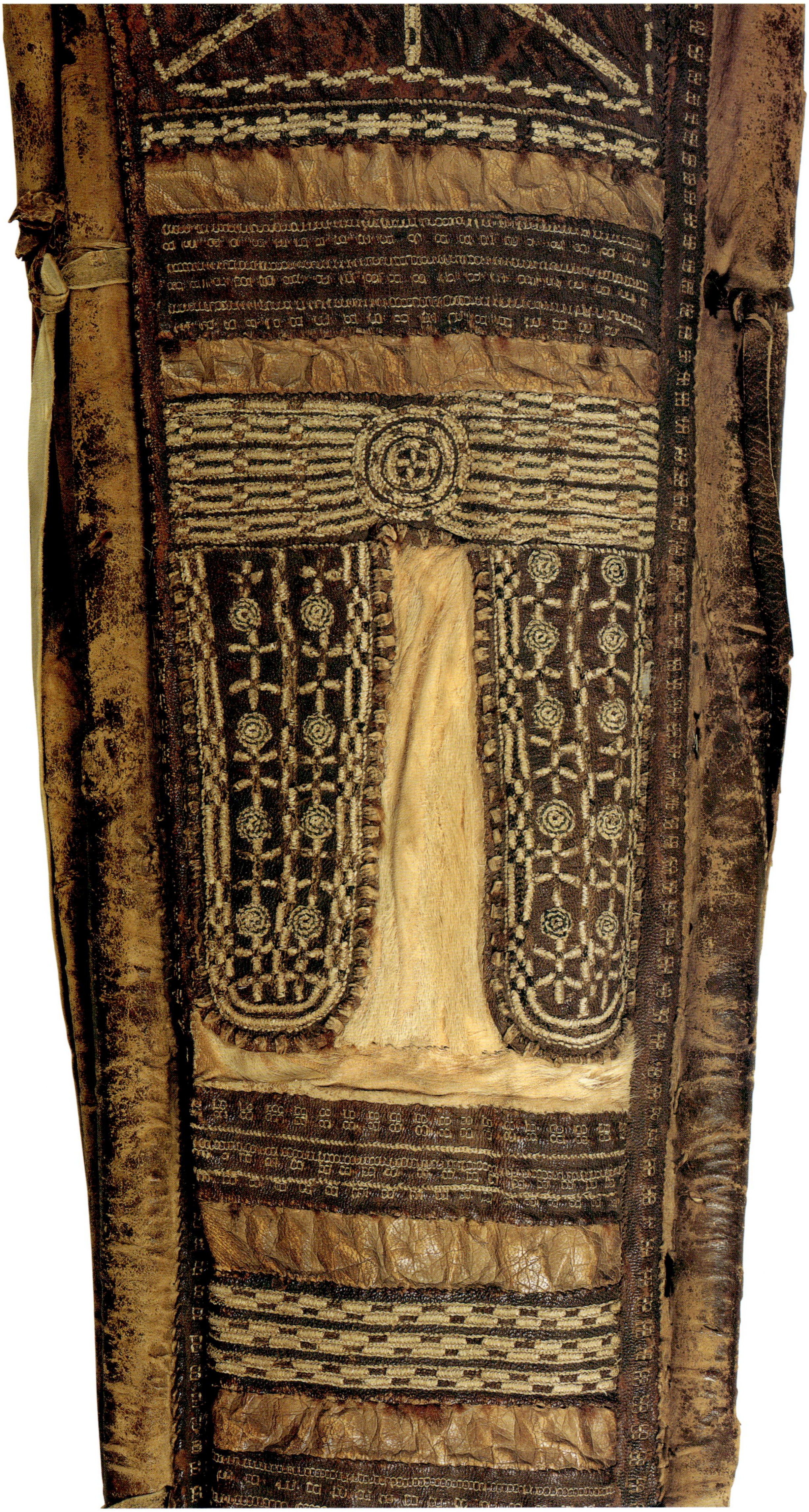

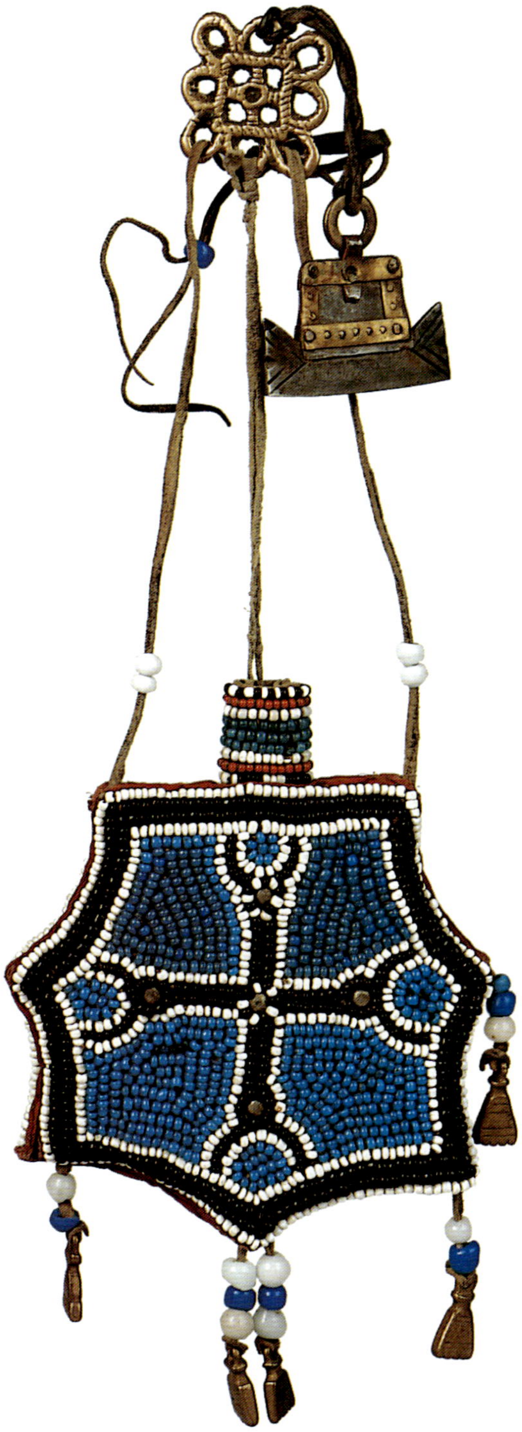

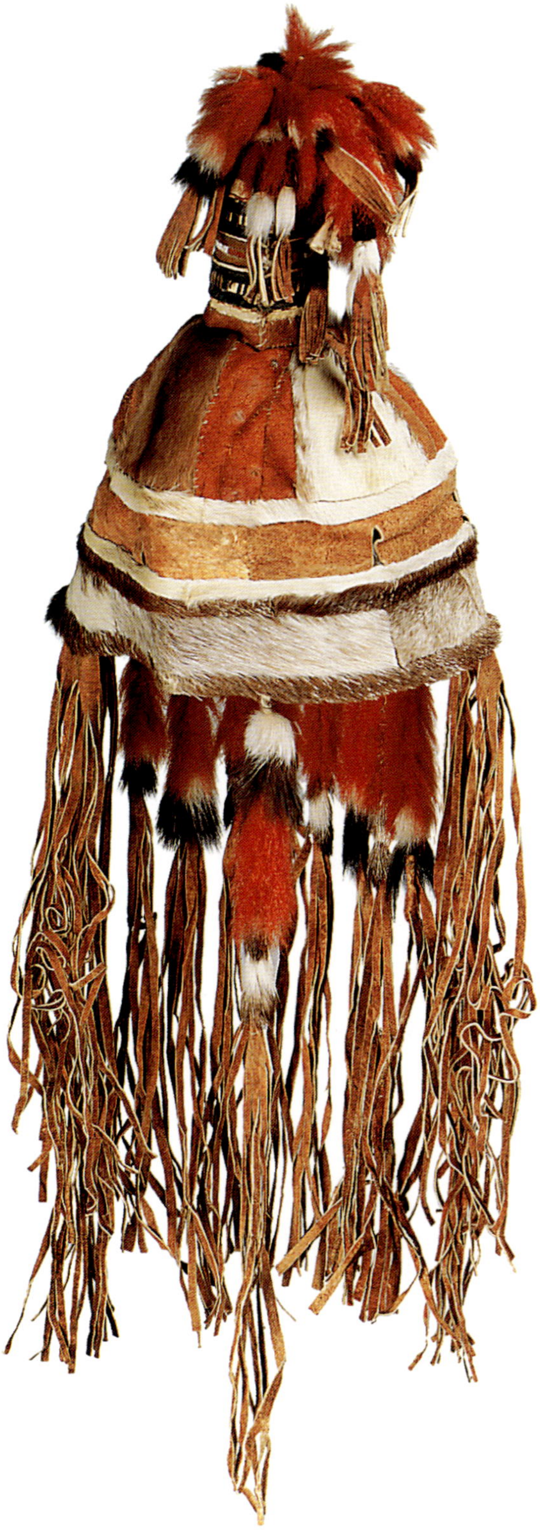

songs have no words, and there is no order in their succession. Though the audience take no actual part in the ceremony, they are in fact of some assistance, as forming a very primitive 'chorus.' Their frequent exclamations encourage the shaman's actions.

Without an *ocitkolin* ('to give answering calls': the audience) a Chukchi shaman considers himself unable to perform his office fittingly; novices, therefore, while trying to learn the shamanistic practices, usually induce a brother or a sister to respond, thus encouraging the zeal of the performer.

In modern times Chukchi shamans imitate the Evenki shamans in smoking a pipe filled with strong narcotic tobacco.

Among the Asiatic Eskimo, the wife and other members of the family form a kind of chorus, which from time to time catches up the tune and sings with the shaman. Among the Russianized Yukaghir of the lower Kolyma, the wife is also the assistant of her shaman husband, and during the performance she gives him encouraging answers, and he addresses her as his 'supporting staff.'

When the *kelet* come to the shaman, he acts in a different way, according to whether he has or has not a ventriloquistic gift. If the shaman is only 'single-bodied,' the *kelet* will sing and beat the drum through his body, the sound only of the shaman's voice being changed. When he is a ventriloquist, the *kelet* appear as separate voices.

Shamans could, with credit to themselves, carry on a contest with the best practitioners of similar arts in other countries. The voices are successful imitations of different sounds: human, superhuman, animal, even of tempests and winds, or of an echo, and come from all sides of the room; from without, from above, and from underground. The whole of Nature may sometimes be represented in the small inner room of the Chukchi.

Then the spirit either begins to talk or departs with a sound like the buzzing of a fly. While it stays, it beats the drum violently, speaking in its own language, if it happens to be any animal except the wolf, fox, and raven, which can speak in the language of men; but there is a peculiar timbre in their voices.

Usually it is not only one spirit which appears, and this part of the performance might be called a dialogue. Sometimes the shaman does not himself understand the language he is using, and an interpreter is necessary. There are cases when spirit-language, comprising a mixture of Koryak, Yakut, and Yukaghir, has to be translated into Russian for the Russianized shamans and natives, especially those of the Kolyma district.

A Evenki shaman nicknamed Mashka, had 'spirits,' being of Koryak origin, who spoke through him in that language. An observer relates:

> *"I asked him several times to dictate to me what his spirits were saying, and he would invaribly reply that he did not remember, that he forgot everything after the seance was over, and that, besides, he did not understand the language of his spirits. At first I thought that he was deceiving me; but I had several opportunities of convincing myself that he really did not understand any Koryak. Evidently he had learned by heart Koryak incantations which he could pronounce only in a state of excitement."*

There is no regular shamanist language among the Chukchi, merely a few special expressions. Among the north-western branch of the Koryak, the spirits are said to use a special mode of pronunciation, similar to that used by the south-eastern Koryak and the Chukchi. A few words are also said to be peculiar to them.

Eveni,
Case for fire-making flint and steel, 1920s.
Leather, beads and seed beads, woolen cloth, metal, 12 cm.
Russian Museum of Ethnography, St. Petersburg. Dalnevostochni (Far-Eastern) Krai, Sea of Okhotsk coast.

Eveni,
Head-dress of a seriously ill patient, 1910.
Dressed reindeer skin, reindeer fur, seal hair, 31 x 61 cm; length of pendants: 35 cm.
Russian Museum of Ethnography, St. Petersburg. Primorskaya Oblast, Anadyr Krai.

Eveni,
Woman's chest panel, 1907.
Dressed reindeer skin, beads, metal, woolen cloth, reindeer hair, 112 x 64 cm.
Russian Museum of Ethnography, St. Petersburg. Yakut Oblast, Kolyma Okrug.

Eveni,
Fragment of woman's chest panel, 1907.
Dressed reindeer skin, beads, metal, woolen cloth, reindeer hair, 112 x 64 cm.
Russian Museum of Ethnography, St. Petersburg. Yakut Oblast, Kolyma Okrug.

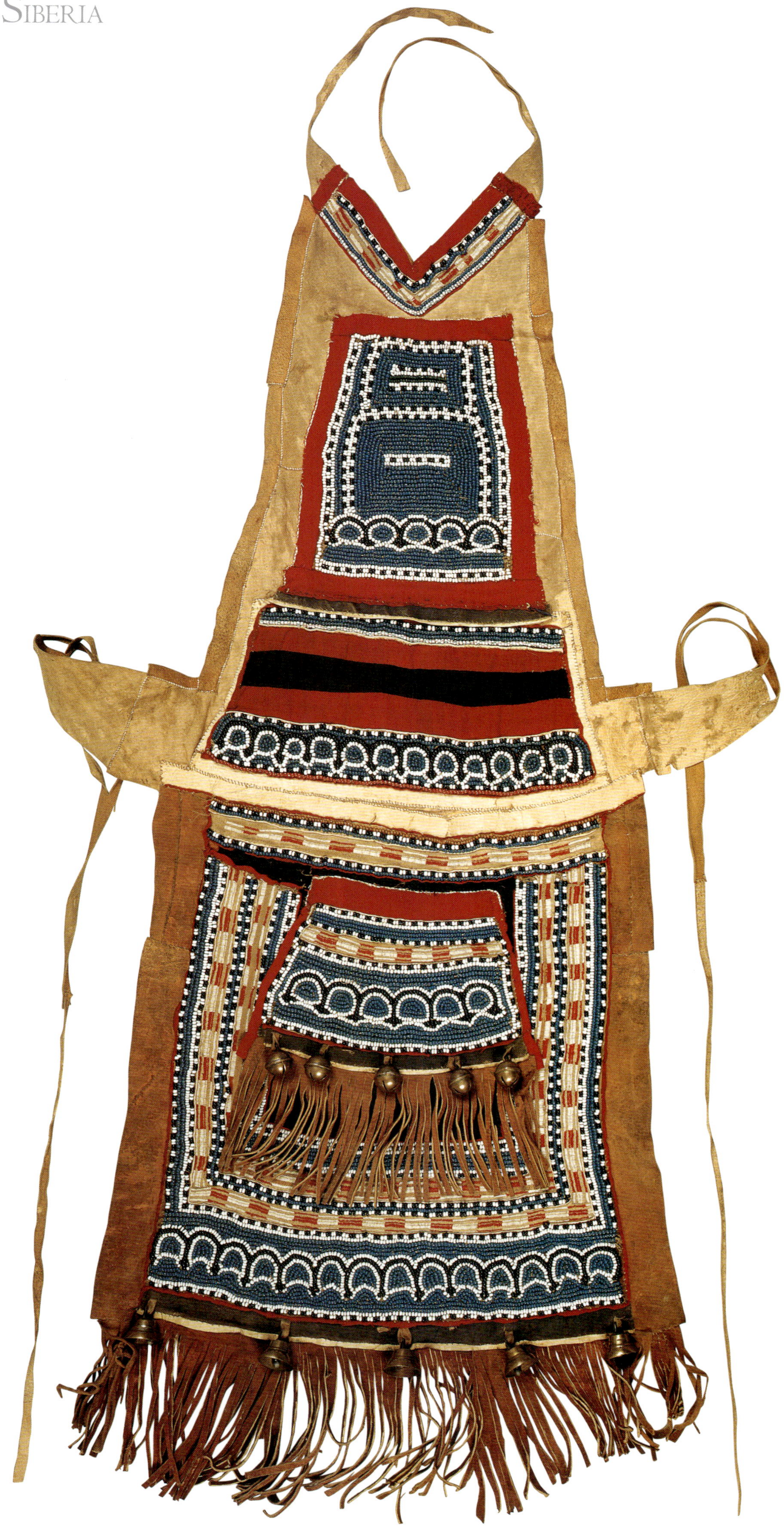

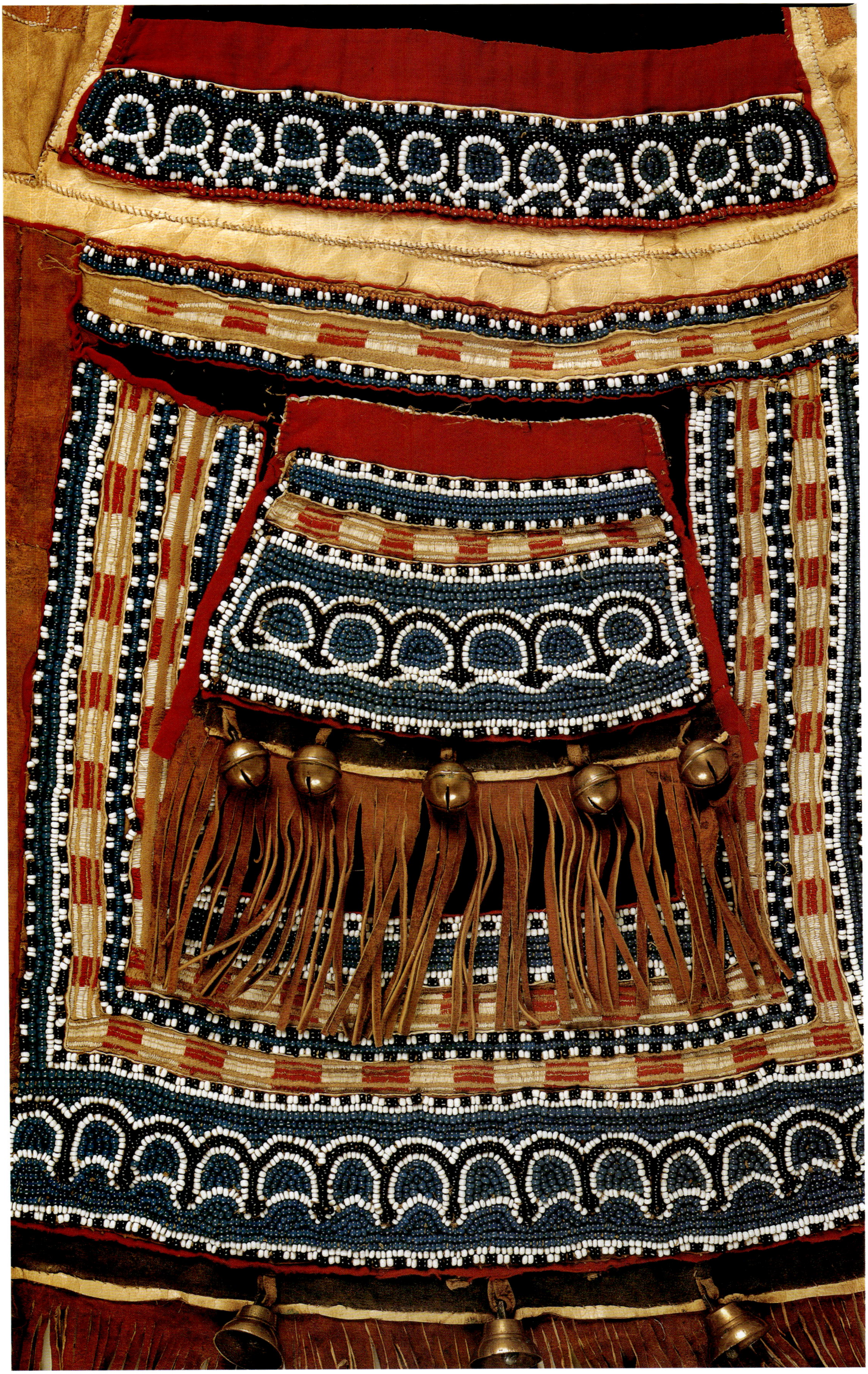

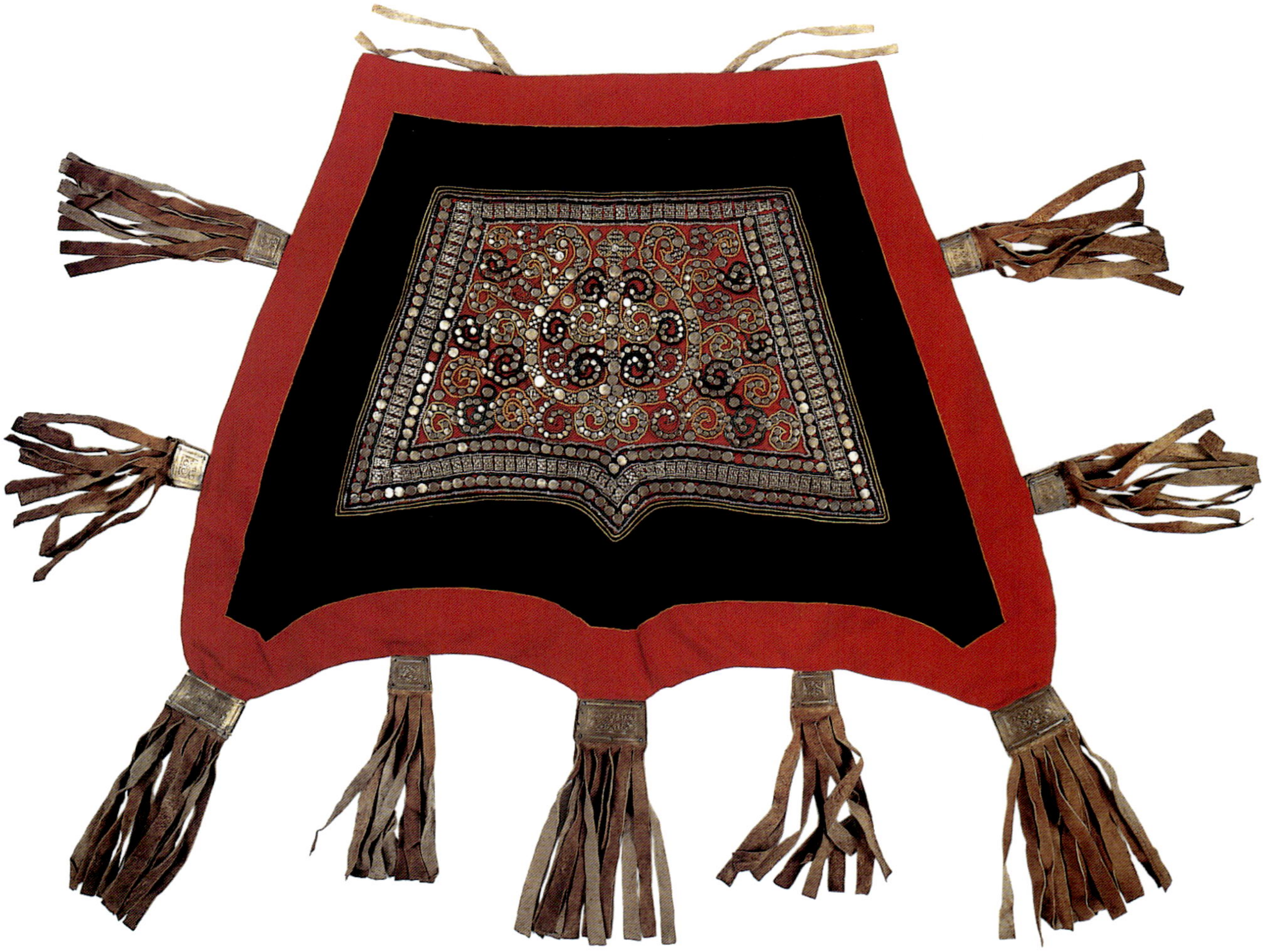

Yakut,
Shabrack, 1959.
Woolen cloth, metal, beads, dressed reindeer skin, 74 x 101 cm.
Russian Museum of Ethnography, St. Petersburg. Yakut ASSR, Yakutsk (city).

Koryak,
Small plastic artwork 'Dressing of reindeer head', 1911.
Walrus tusk ivory, 6 x 6.5 cm.
Russian Museum of Ethnography, St. Petersburg. Kamchatka Oblast.

Koryak,
Small plastic artworks 'Wrestlers', 'Game of Chess', 'Outweighing of stick', early 20th century.
Walrus tusk ivory, 1) 4.8 x 8 cm; 2) 4.7 x 5.5 cm; 3) 6.4 x 2 cm;
Dimension of support: 1) 4 x 3.2 cm.
Russian Museum of Ethnography, St. Petersburg. Kamchatka Oblast, Chukchi Peninsular.

Among the Asiatic Eskimo the spirits are said to have a special language. Many words of it are analogous to the spirit language known to various Eskimo tribes of America, both in Alaska and on the Atlantic side.

Sometimes the spirits are very mischievous. In the movable tents of the reindeer people an invisible hand will sometimes turn everything upside down, and throw different objects about, such as snow and pieces of ice.

The audience is strictly forbidden to make any attempts whatever to touch the spirits. These latter highly resent any intrusion of this kind, and retaliate either on the shaman, whom they may kill on the spot, or on the trespassing listener, who runs the risk of having his head broken, or even a knife thrust through his ribs in the dark.

After the preliminary intercourse with the spirits, the shaman, still in the dark, gives advice and utters prophecies. For example, at one ceremony, the shaman Galmuurgin prophesied to his host that many wild reindeer would be at his gate the following autumn.

"One buck," he said, "will stop on the right side of the entrance, and pluck at the grass, attracted by a certain doe of dark-grey hair. This attraction must be

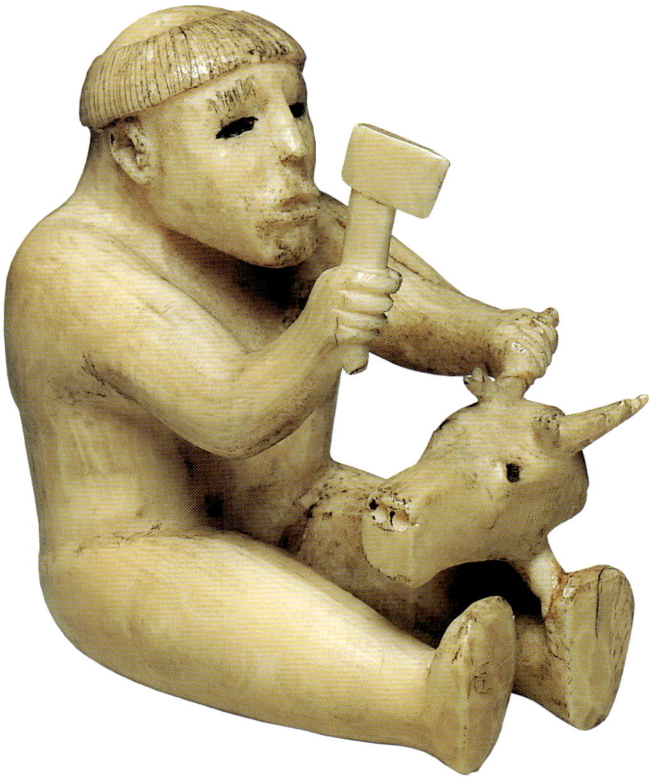

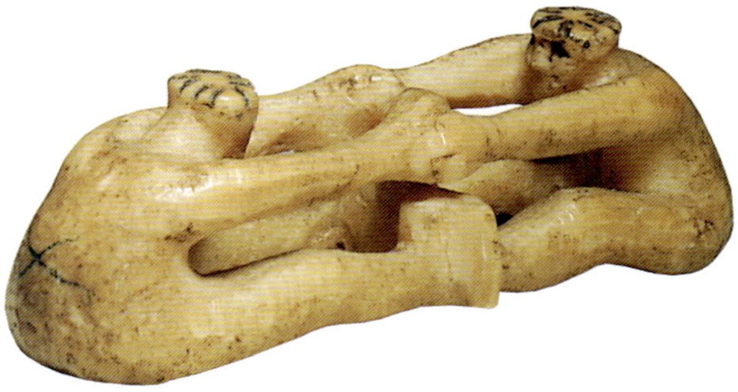

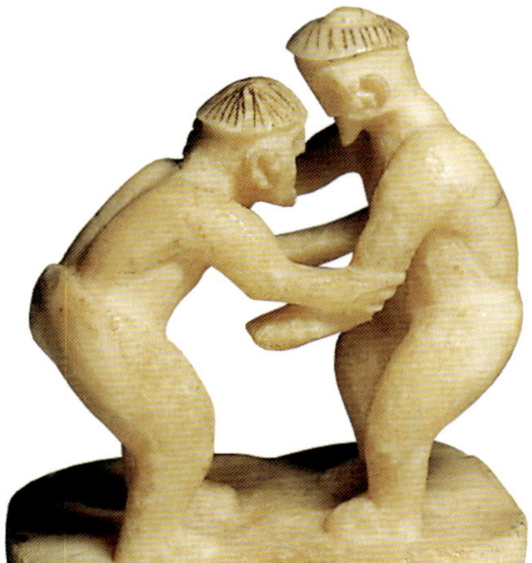

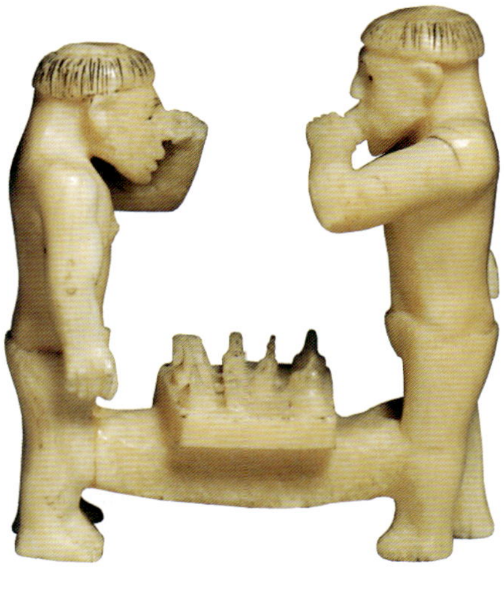

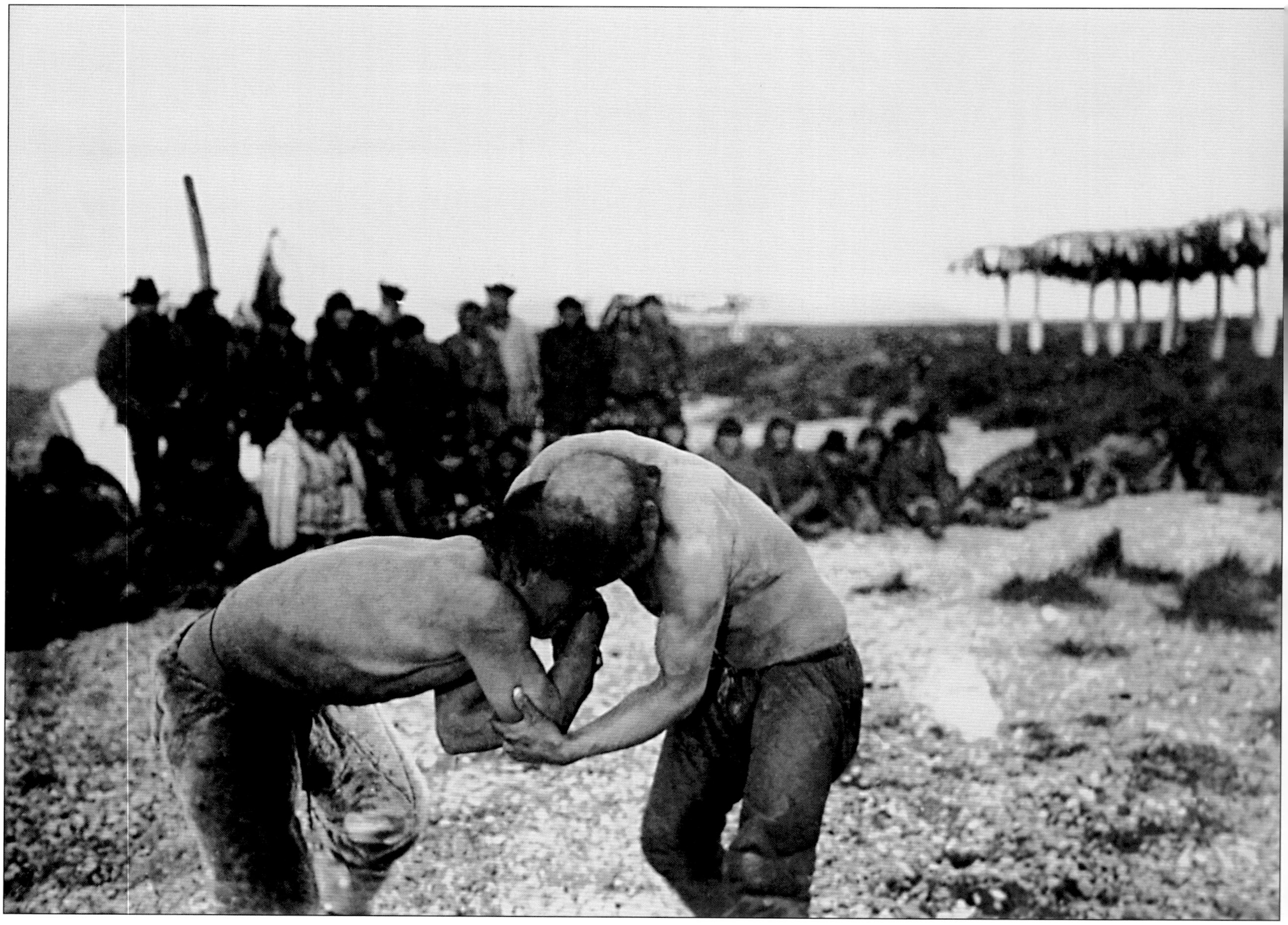

strengthened with a special incantation. The reindeer-buck, while standing there, must be killed with the bow, and the arrow to be used must have a flat rhomboid point. This will secure the successful killing of all the other wild reindeer."

When shamanistic performances are connected with ceremonials, they are carried on in the outer room. Ventriloquism is not practised on these occasions, and the *kele* is bent on mischief, and among other things seeks to destroy the life which is under his temporary power.

Upune, the wife of a dead Chukchi shaman, possessed wonderful shamanistic power; she herself declared that she had only a small part of her husband's ability. In a shamanistic performance she took a large round pebble of the size of a man's fist, set it upon the drum, and, blowing upon it from all sides, began to mumble and snort in the same *kele*-like manner. She called attention by signs - being in the possession of the *kele*, she had lost the faculty of human speech - and then began to wring the pebble with both hands. Then a continuous row of very small pebbles began to fall from her hands. This lasted for fully five minutes, till quite a heap of small pebbles had collected below, on the skin. The larger pebble, however, remained smooth and intact.

The female shaman repeated this feat with the same success, and all the upper part of the body being naked, it was easy to observe her movements. The practice of stabbing oneself through the abdomen with a knife is universal in shamanistic performances; Itelmen and Eskimo, Chukchi and Yukaghir, even the Neo-Siberian shamans of northern Asia, are familiar with this trick.

It would be difficult to describe all the tricks performed by the shamans: some of the commonest are the swallowing of burning coals and setting oneself free from a cord by which one is bound.

The Yakut.

For comparison with the Palaeo-Siberian methods of shamanizing, we shall take a Yakut shaman in action. Outwardly, shamanistic ceremonies are very uniform. The ceremony now described is the part of the shamanistic ceremony which remains always and everywhere unchanged, and, sanctioned by custom, forms, so to speak, the basis of the rite.

When the shaman who has been called to a sick person enters the *yurt*, he at once takes the place destined for him on the *billiryk agon*. He lies on his white mare's skin and waits for the night, the time when it is possible to shamanize. Meanwhile he is entertained with food and drink.

When the sun sets and the dusk of evening approaches, all preparations for the ceremony in the *yurt* are hurriedly completed: the ground is swept, the wood is cut, and food is provided in larger quantity and of better quality than usual. One by one the neighbours arrive and seat themselves along the wall, the men on the right, and the women on the left; the conversation is peculiarly serious and reserved, the movements gentle.

In the northern part of the Yakut district the host chooses the best latchets and forms them into a loop, which is placed round the shaman's shoulders and held by one of those present during the dance, in order to prevent the spirits from carrying him off. At length every one has supper, and the household takes some rest. The shaman, sitting on the edge of the *billiryk*, slowly untwists his tresses, muttering and giving orders. He sometimes has a nervous and artificial hiccough which makes his whole body shake; his gaze does not wander, his eyes being fixed on one point, usually on the fire.

The fire is allowed to die out. More and more deeply the dusk descends on the room; voices are hushed, and the company talks in whispers; notice is given that

Wrestling-match for Chukchis during a festival.

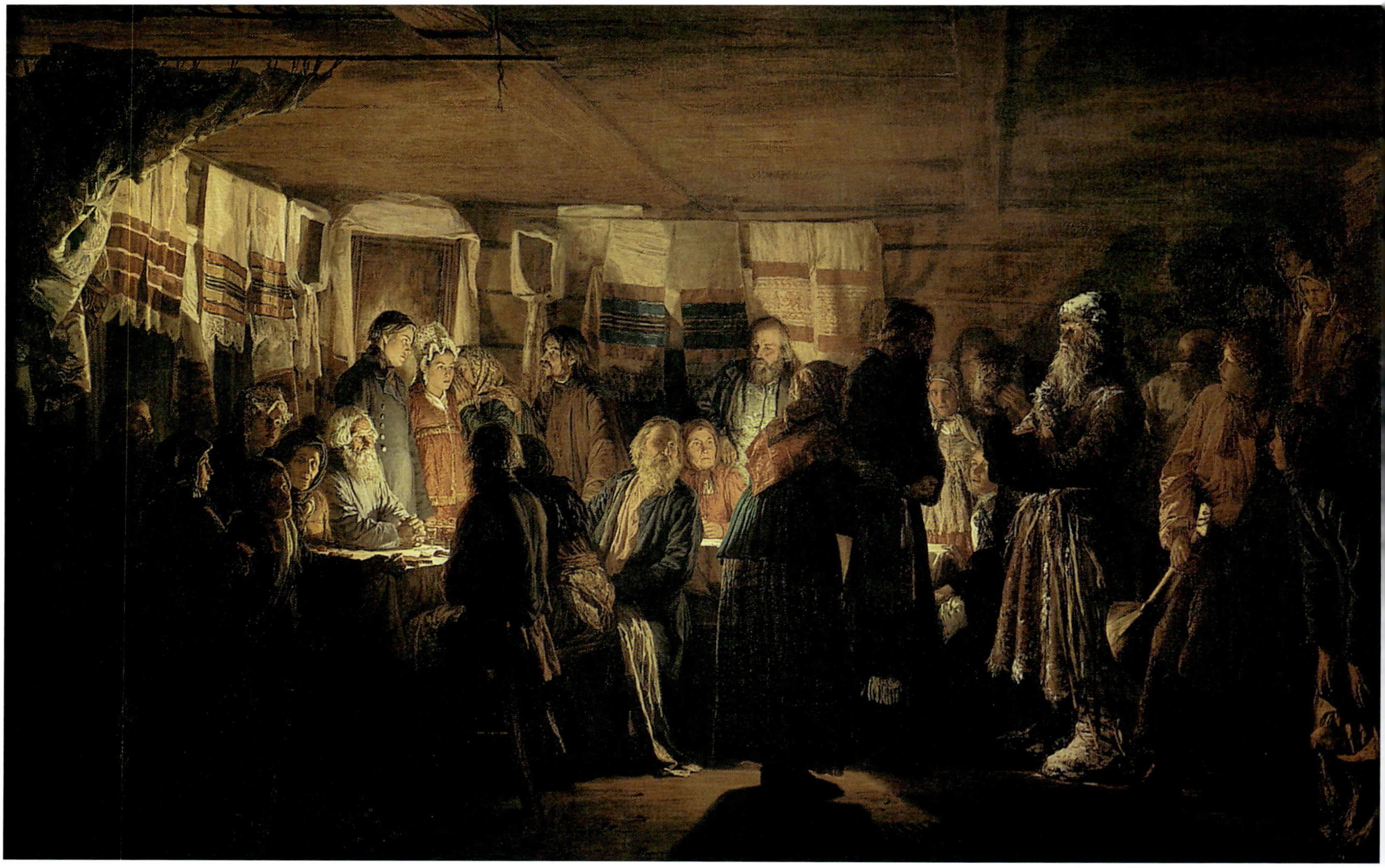

Vasily Maximov,
Sorcerer Coming to Peasants' Wedding,
1875. Oil on canvas, 116 x 188 cm.
Tretyakov Gallery, Moscow.

Chukchi,
Tusk with coloured engraving (2nd side), fragment, 1930s.
Walrus tusk ivory, 57 x 6 cm.
Russian Museum of Ethnography,
St. Petersburg. Chukchi Peninsular.

Aleut,
Bucket grip, early 20th century.
Walrus tusk ivory, 27 cm.
Russian Museum of Ethnography,
St. Petersburg. Aleutian Islands.

Chukchi,
Walrus tusk showing Kelet myth,
1951. Walrus tusk ivory, 65 cm.
Museum of Anthropology and
Ethnography, Moscow. Uelen.

anybody wishing to go out must do so at once, because soon the door will be closed, after which nobody can either go out or come in.

The shaman slowly takes off his shirt and puts on his wizard's coat, or, failing that, he takes the woman's coat called *sangyniah*. Then he is given a pipe, which he smokes for a long time, swallowing the smoke; his hiccough becomes louder, he shivers more violently. When he has finished smoking, his face is pale, his head falls on his breast, his eyes are half-closed.

At this point the white mare's skin is placed in the middle of the room. The shaman asks for cold water, and when he has drunk it he slowly holds out his hand for the drum prepared for him; he then walks to the middle of the room, and, kneeling for a time on his right knee, bows solemnly to all the four corners of the world, at the same time sprinkling the ground about him with the water from his mouth.

Now everything is silent. A handful of white horsehair is thrown on the fire, putting it quite out; in the faint gleam of the red coals the black motionless figure of the shaman is still to be seen for a while, with drooping bead, big drum on breast, and face turned towards the south, as is also the head of the mare's skin upon which he is sitting.

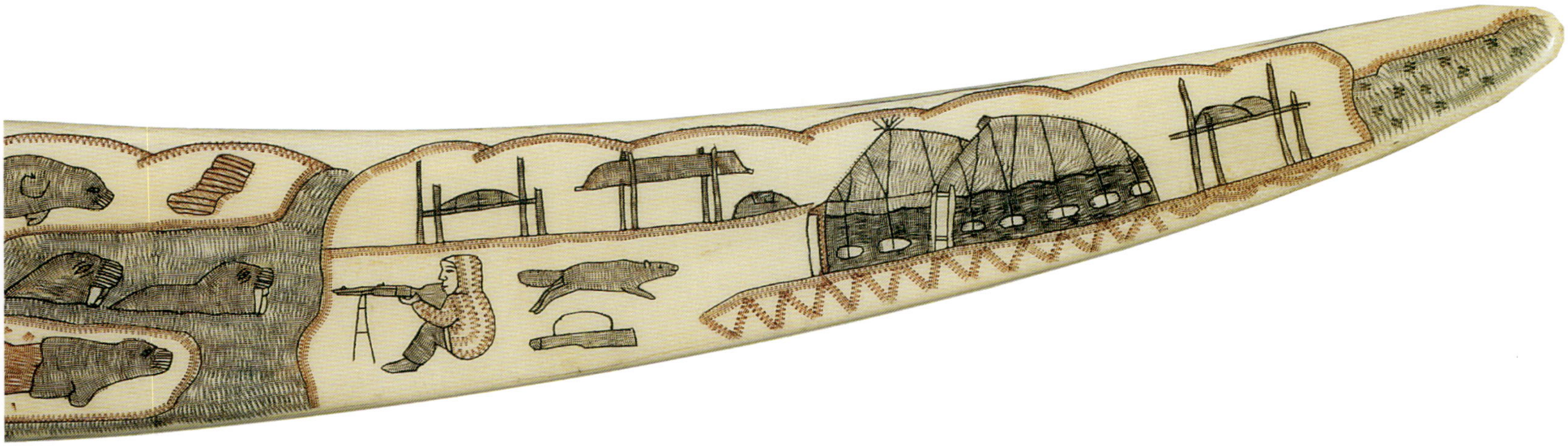

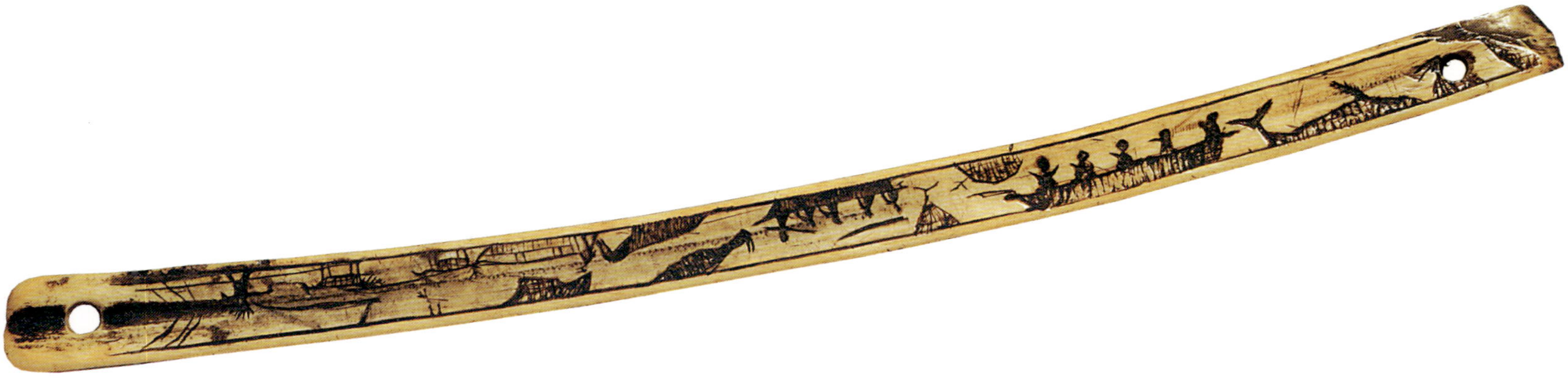

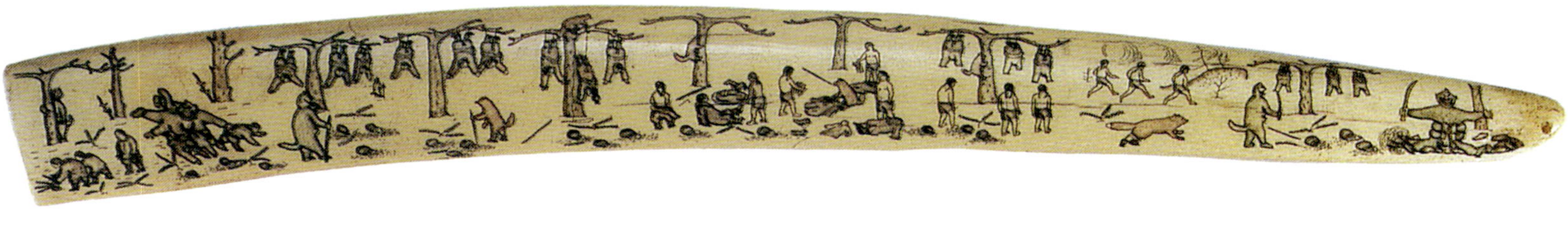

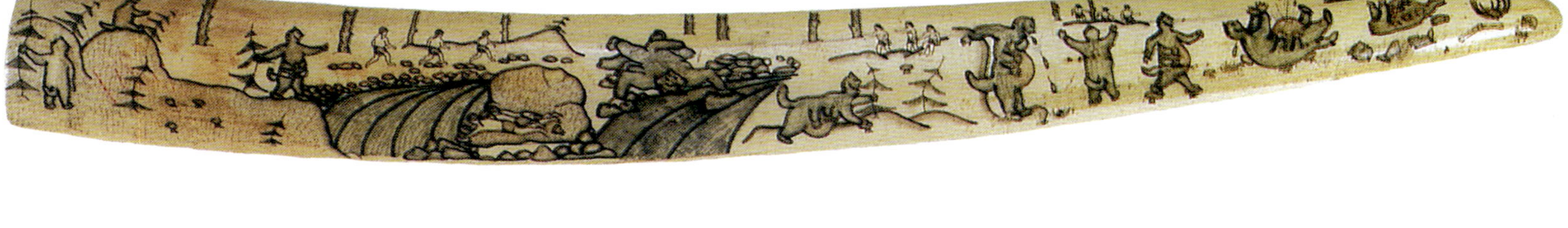

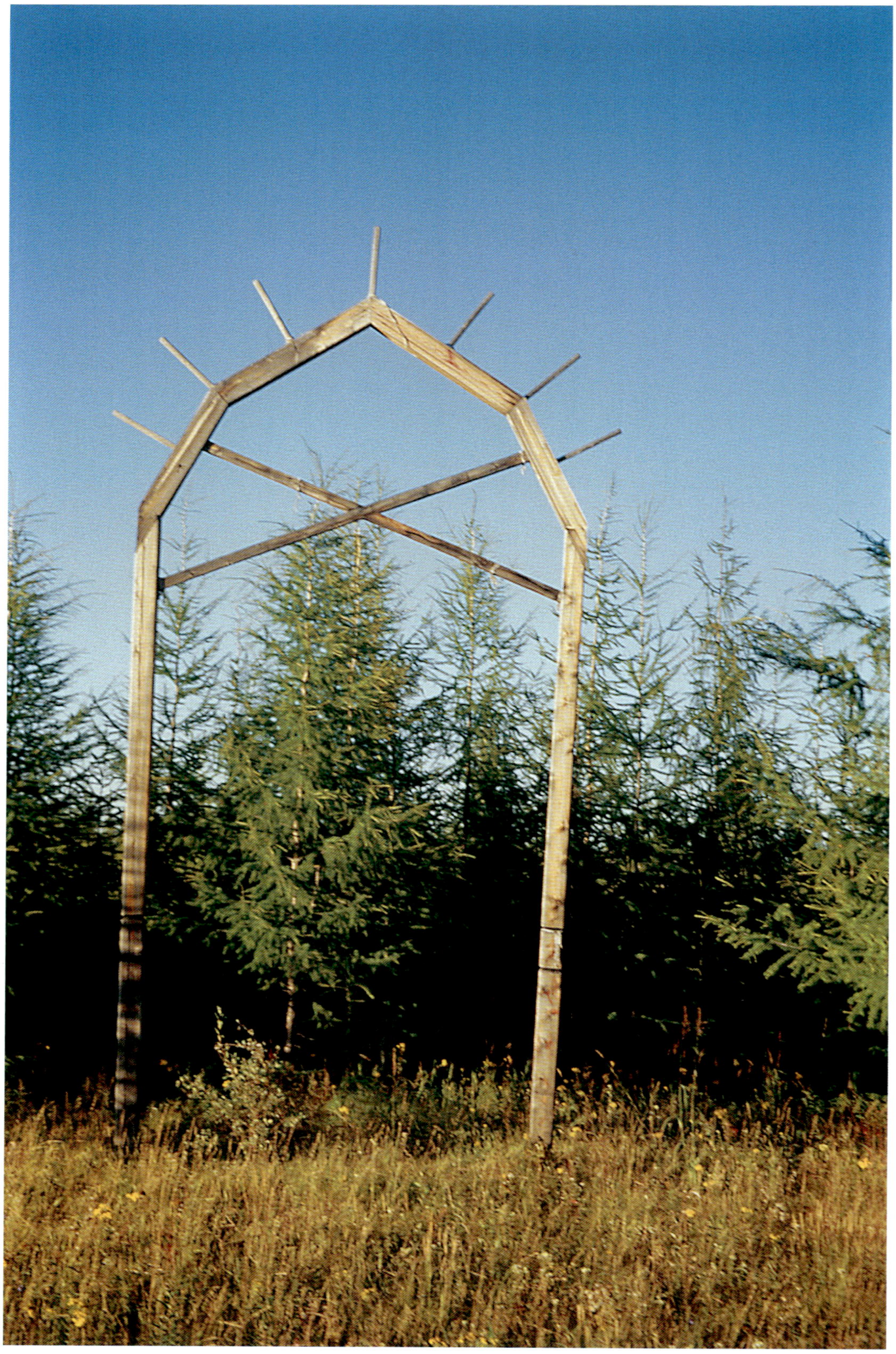

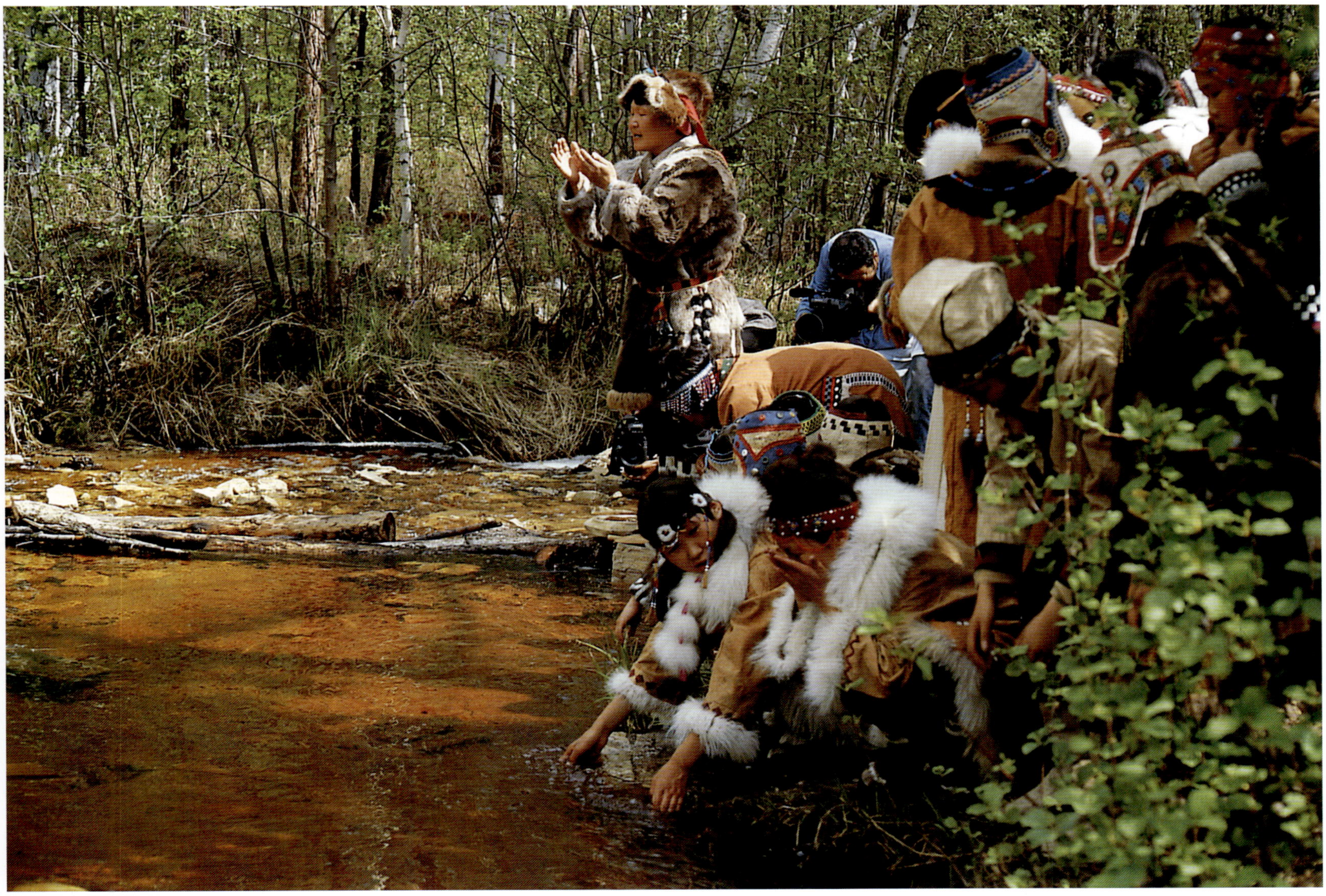

Complete darkness follows the dusk; the audience scarcely breathes, and only the unintelligible mutterings and hiccoughs of the shaman can be heard; gradually even this sinks into a profound silence. Eventually a single great yawn like the clang of iron breaks the stillness, followed by the loud piercing cry of a falcon, or the plaintive weeping of a seamew - then silence again.

Only the gentle sound of the voice of the drum, like the humming of a gnat, announces that the shaman has begun to play.

This music is at first soft, delicate, tender, then rough and irrepressible like the roar of an oncoming storm. It grows louder and louder and, like peals of thunder, wild shouts rend the air; the crow calls, the grebe laughs, the seamews complain, snipes whistle, eagles and hawks scream.

Bow related to the solar cult among the Yukaghirs of the taiga (Nelemnoe).

Eveni,
Rite of the spirits of water, performed during the summer festival of The Minor Peoples of the North.
Yakutsk.

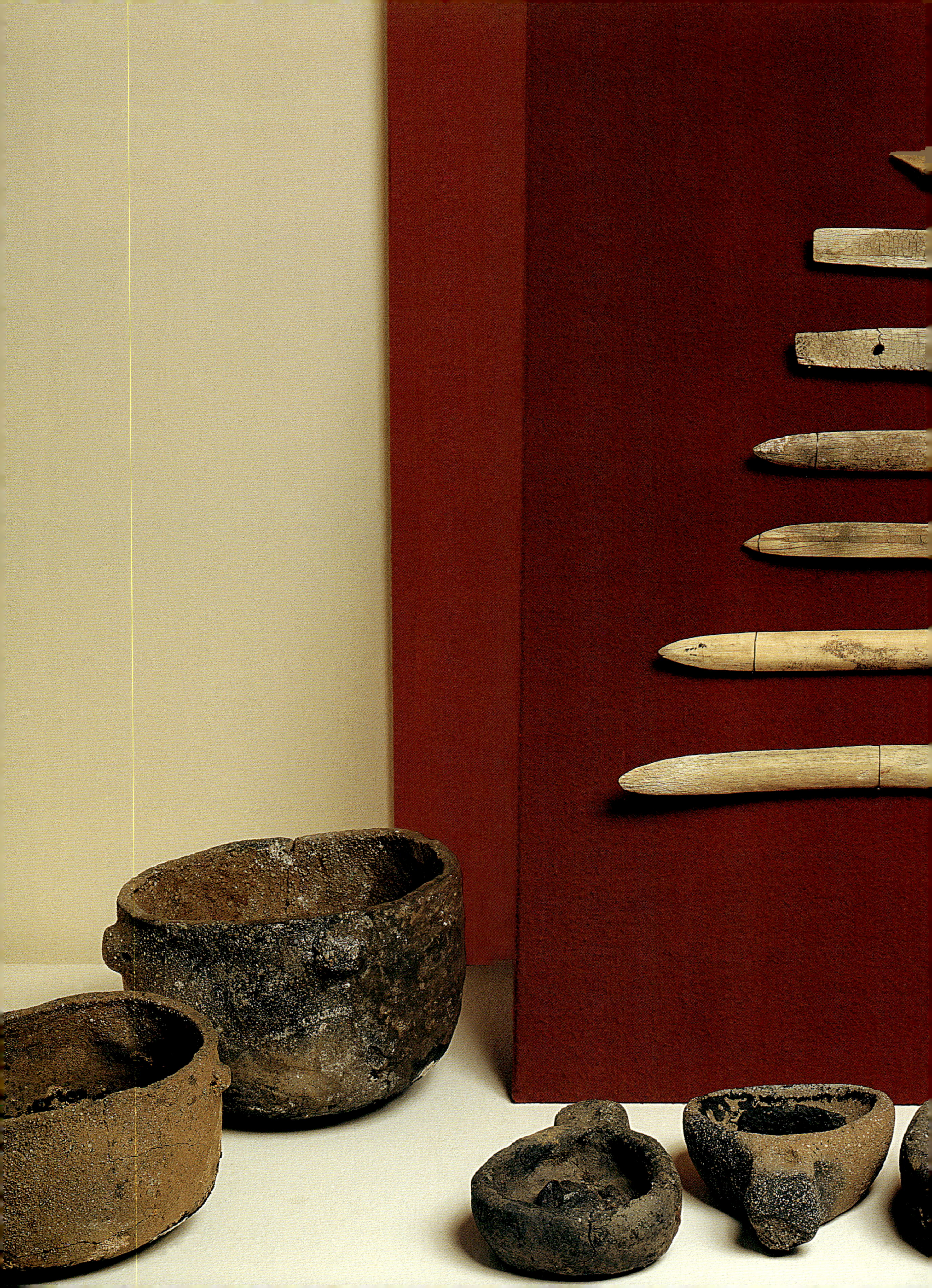

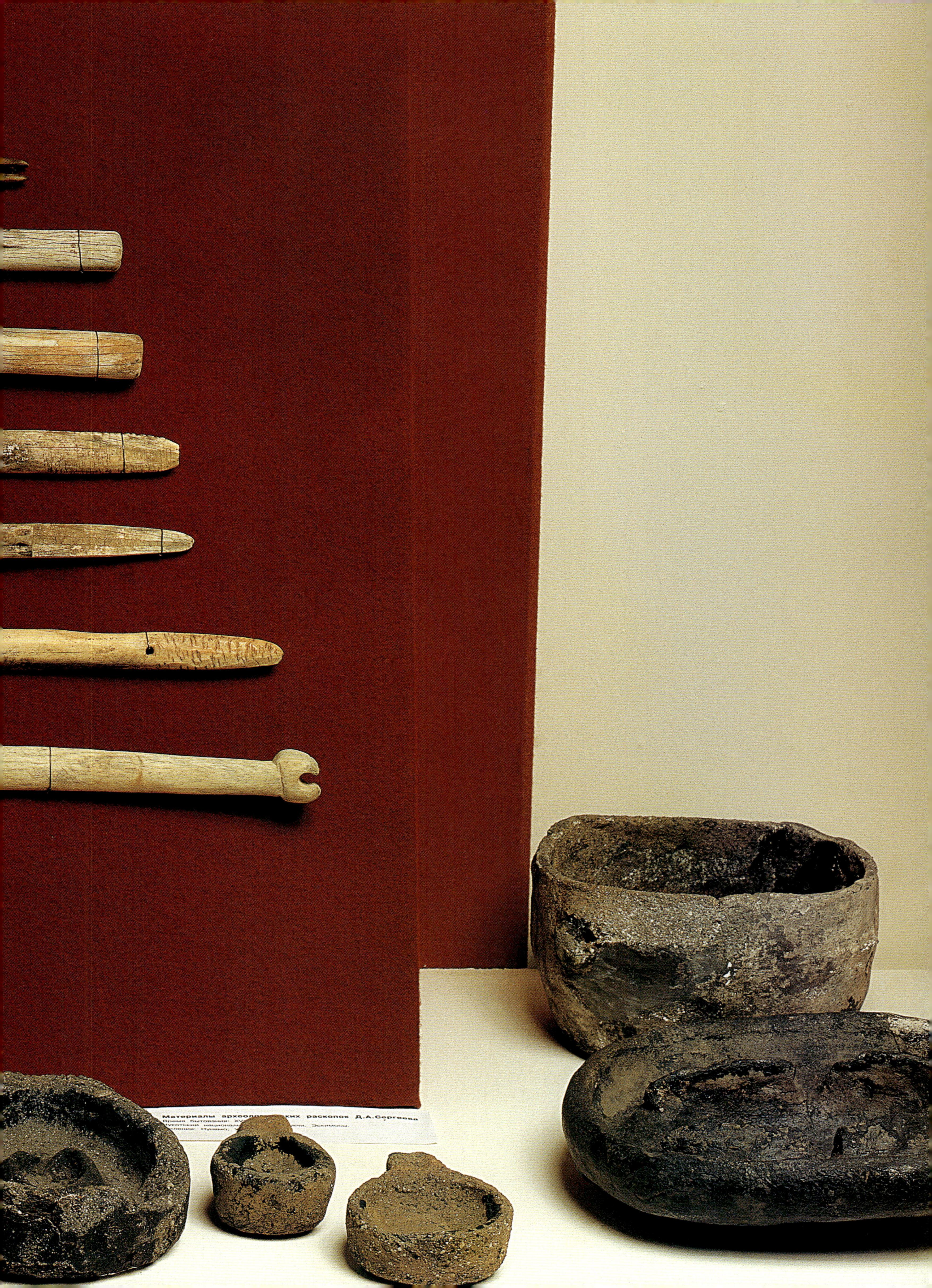
Материалы раскопок Д.А.Сергеева
Время бытования:
Эскимосы.

The music swells and rises to the highest pitch, the beating of the drum becomes more and more vigorous, until the two sounds combine in one long-drawn crescendo. The numberless small bells ring and clang; it is not a storm - it is a whole cascade of sounds, enough to overwhelm all the listeners. All at once it breaks off - there are one or two strong beats on the drum, which, hitherto held aloft, now falls to the shaman's knees. Suddenly the sound of the drum and the small bells ceases. Then silence for a long moment, while the gentle gnat-like murmur of the drum begins again.

This may be repeated several times, according to the degree of the shaman's inspiration; at last, when the music takes on a certain new rhythm and melody, sombrely the voice of the shaman chants the following obscure fragments:

1. 'Mighty bull of the earth . . . Horse of the steppes!'
2. 'I, the mighty bull . . . bellow!'
3. 'I, the horse of the steppes . . . neigh!'
4. 'I, the man set above all other beings!'
5. 'I, the man most gifted of all!'
6. 'I, the man created by the master all-powerful!
7. 'Horse of the steppes, appear! teach me!'
8. 'Enchanted bull of the earth, appear! speak to me!'
9. 'Powerful master, command me!'
10. 'All of you, who will go with me, give heed with your ears! Those whom I command not, follow me not!'
11. 'Approach not nearer than is permitted! Look intently! Give heed ! Have a care!'
12. 'Look heedfully! Do this, all of you, all together . . . all, however many you may be!'
13. 'Thou of the left side, O lady with thy staff, if anything be done amiss, if I take not the right way, I entreat you - correct me! Command! . . .'
14. 'My errors and my path show to me! O mother of mine! Wing thy free flight! Pave my wide roadway!'
15. 'Souls of the sun, mothers of the sun, living in the south, in the nine wooded hills, ye who shall be jealous . . . I adjure you all . . . let them stay . . . let your three shadows stand high!'
16. 'In the East, on your mountain, lord, grandsire of mine, great of power and thick of neck-be thou with me!'
17. 'And thou, grey-bearded wizard (fire), I ask thee: with all my dreams, with all comply! To all my desires consent . . . Heed all! Fulfil all! . . . All heed . . . All fulfil!'

At this point the sounds of the drum are heard once more, once more wild shouts and meaningless words - then all is silent.

Adjurations similar to the above are used in all the Yakut districts and all ceremonies begin with them. There is, however, another formula still longer and more complicated. The ritual which follows this formula consists of an improvisation appropriate to each person and occasion.

In the ensuing prayers the shaman addresses his *ämägyat* and other protective spirits; he talks with the *kaliany*, asks them questions, and gives answers in their names. Sometimes the shaman must pray and beat the drum a long time before the spirits come; often their appearance is so sudden and so impetuous that the

Chukchi, Eskimos,
Archaeological section of the exhibition 'My friends – sea hunters', dedicated to the memory of the Director of the Museum D.A. Sergeev,
Russian Museum of Ethnography, St. Petersburg. Chukchi National Okrug, Chukchi District, Magadan Oblast.

Kamchatka,
Dancing at a harvest festival, 1992.

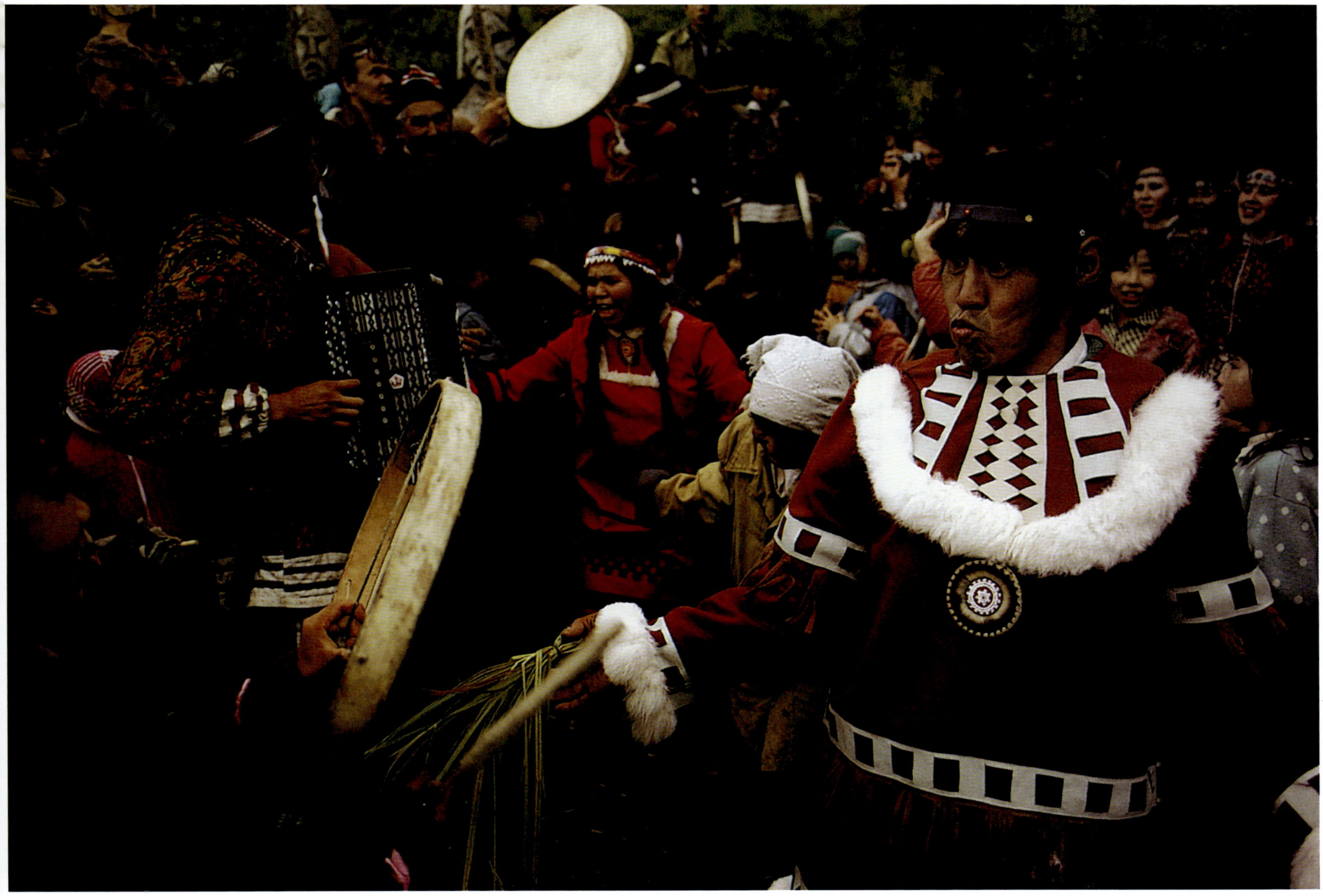

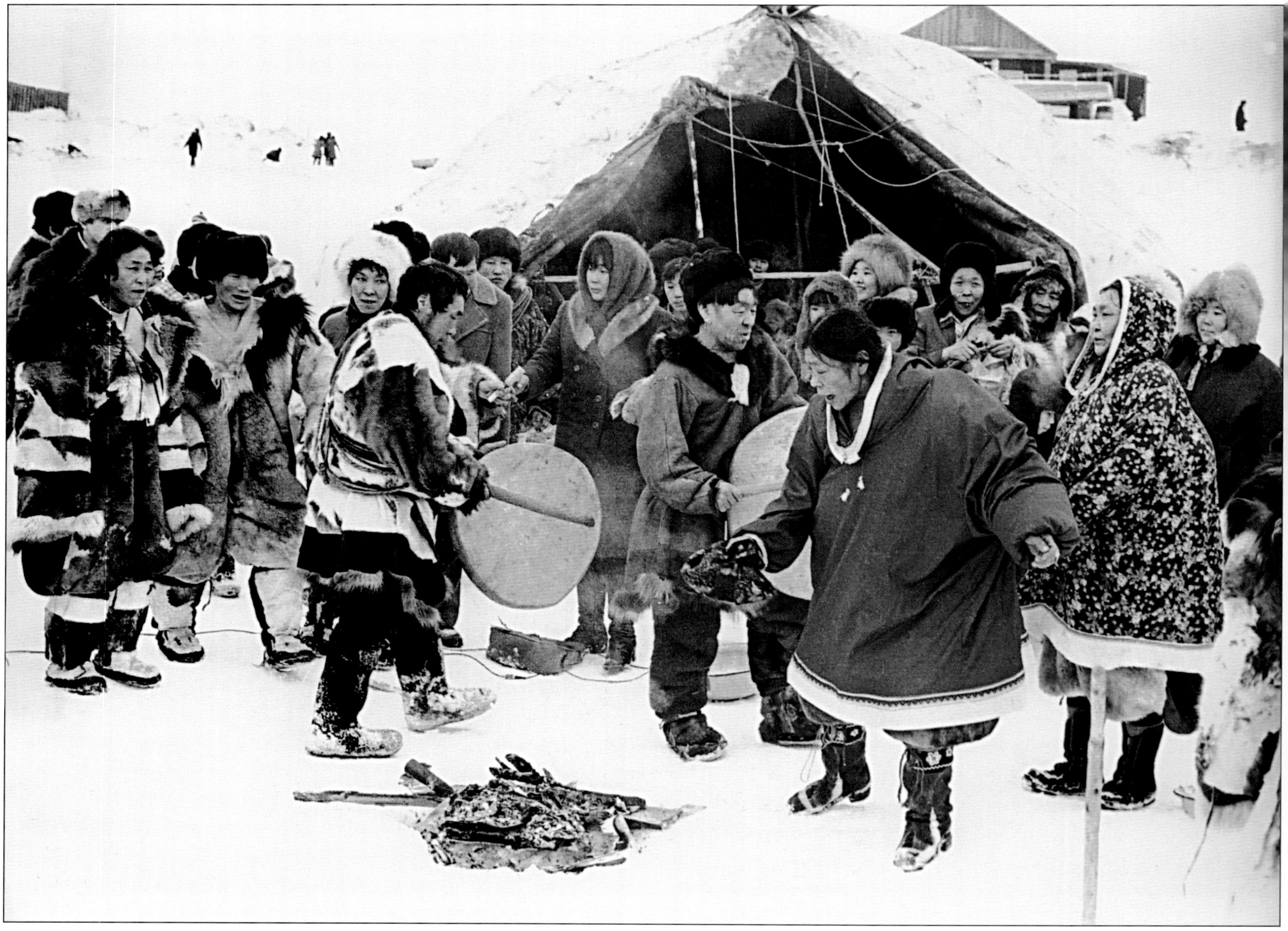

shaman is overcome and falls down. It is a good sign if he falls on his face, and a bad sign if he falls on his back.

When the *ämägyat* comes down to a shaman, he arises and begins to leap and dance, at first on the skin, and then, his movements becoming more rapid, he glides into the middle of the room. Wood is quickly piled on the fire, and the light spreads through the *yurt,* which is now full of noise and movement. The shaman dances, sings, and beats the drum uninterruptedly, jumps about furiously, turning his face to the south, then to the west, then to the east. Those who hold him by the leather thongs sometimes have great difficulty in controlling his movements. In the south Yakut district, however, the shaman dances unfettered. Indeed, he often gives up his drum so as to be able to dance more unrestrainedly.

The head of the shaman is bowed, his eyes are half-closed, his hair is tumbled and in wild disorder lies on his sweating face, his mouth is twisted strangely, saliva streams down his chin, often he foams at the mouth.

He moves round the room, advancing and retreating, beating the drum, which resounds no less wildly than the roaring of the shaman himself; he shakes his jingling coat, and seems to become more and more maniacal, intoxicated with the noise and movement.

His fury ebbs and rises like a wave; sometimes it leaves him for a while, and then, holding his drum high above his head, solemnly and calmly he chants a prayer and summons the 'spirit.'

At last he knows all he desires; he is acquainted with the cause of the misfortune or disease with which be has been striving; he is sure of the help of the beings whose aid he needs. Circling about in his dance, singing and playing, he approaches the patient.

With new objurgations be drives away the cause of the illness by frightening it, or by sucking it out with his mouth from the afflicted place: then, returning to the middle of the room, he drives it away by spitting and blowing. Then he learns what sacrifice is to be made to the 'powerful spirits,' for this harsh treatment of the spirit's servant, who was sent to the patient.

Then the shaman, shading his eyes from the light with his hands, looks attentively into each corner of the room; and if he notices anything suspicious, he again beats the drum, dances, wakes terrifying gestures, and entreats the 'spirits.'

At length all is made clean, the suspicious 'cloud' is no more to be seen, which signifies that the cause of the trouble has been driven out; the sacrifice is accepted, the prayers have been heard - the ceremony is over.

The shaman still retains for some time after this the gift of prophecy; he foretells various happenings, answers the questions of the curious, or relates what he saw on his journey away from the earth.

Finally he is carried with his mare's skin back to his place of honour on the *billiryk.*

The sacrifice offered to the 'spirits' varies according to the importance of the occasion. Sometimes the disease is transferred to the cattle, and the stricken cattle are then sacrificed, and ascend to the sky. It is this journey to the sky, together with the spirits and the sacrificed animal, which the dance symbolizes. In the old days (according to the native accounts) there were, in fact, shamans who really did ascend into the sky while the spectators saw how on the clouds there floated the sacrificed animal, after it sped the drum of the shaman, and this was followed by the shaman himself in his wizard's coat.

There were also wicked and powerful shamans who, instead of a real animal, carried up into the sky a mare formed of cloud, but the evidence for the

Request for future abundance during a ritual for Chukchi reindeer-herders.

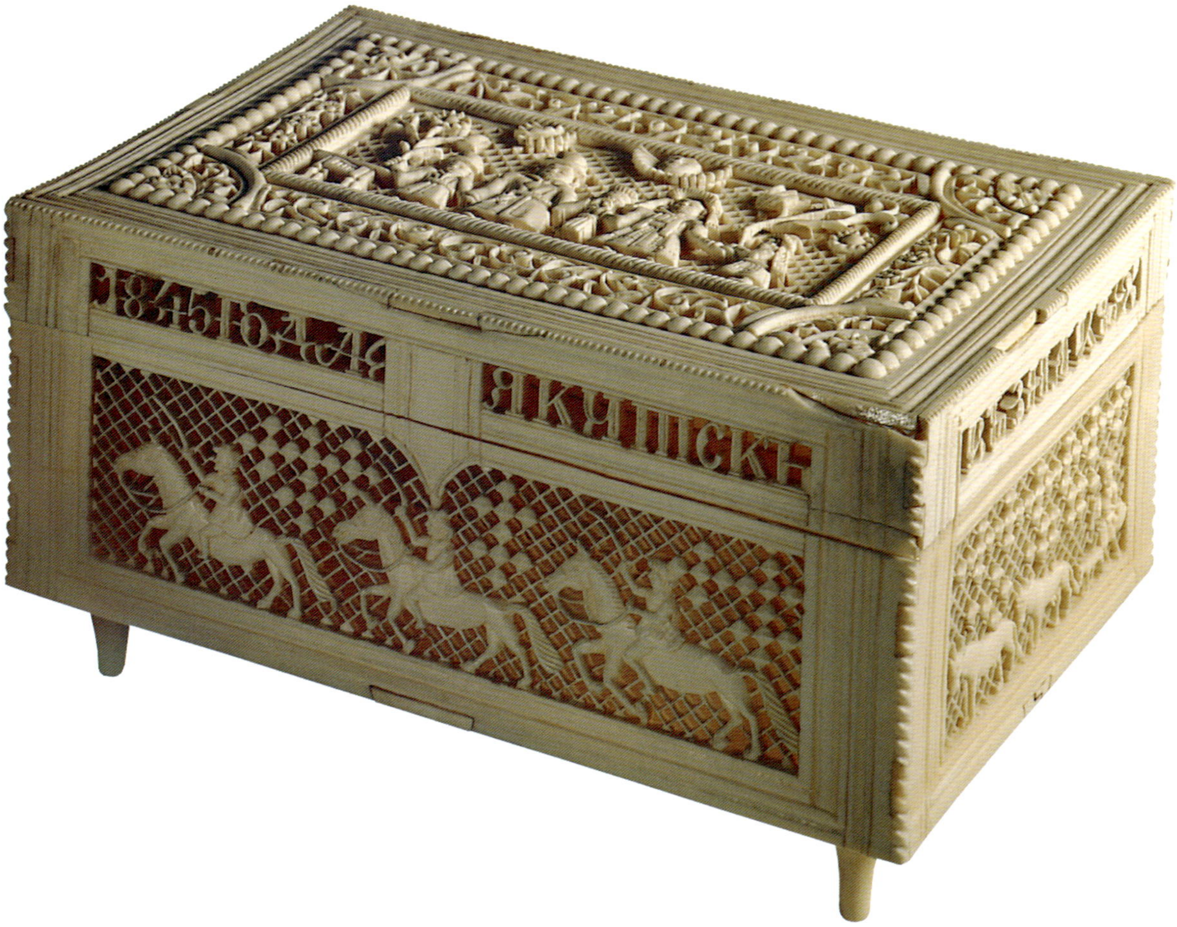

Yakut,
Casket, 1845.
Mammoth bone, 16 x 10.5 x 6.5 cm.
Russian Museum of Ethnography,
St. Petersburg. Yakutia, Yakutsk (city).

Koryak,
Man's cremation costume, 1900-1901.
Reindeer skin, dyed seal pup fur,
sealskin, yarn, hair embroidery, silk
thread, bead, dog fur, Coat: 132 cm;
Leggings: 63 cm.
American Museum of Natural
History, New York. Mikino, Talovka.

existence of these shamans is indefinite. During this difficult and dangerous journey every shaman has his places of rest, called *ouokh* (*olokh*); when he takes a seat during the dance, this signifies that he has come to an *ouokh*; when he rises, he is ascending further up into the sky; if he falls down, he is descending under the earth.

Every shaman, however far he may have proceeded on his journey, knows where he is, on which *ouoloh*, and also the route taken by every other shaman who is shamanizing at that moment. Sometimes the leading of the ' spirit' and the sacrificed cattle into the sky forms a separate ceremony performed a few months after the first, in which they had promised this sacrifice. The sacrifices are either bloody, when the shaman tears to pieces the body of the animal with rage and fury, or bloodless; for instance, when some grease or meat, or other material, such as hair, is offered up.

The Samoyed

On arriving at the *yurt* the shaman takes his seat on a bench, or on a chest which must contain no implement capable of inflicting a wound. Near him, but

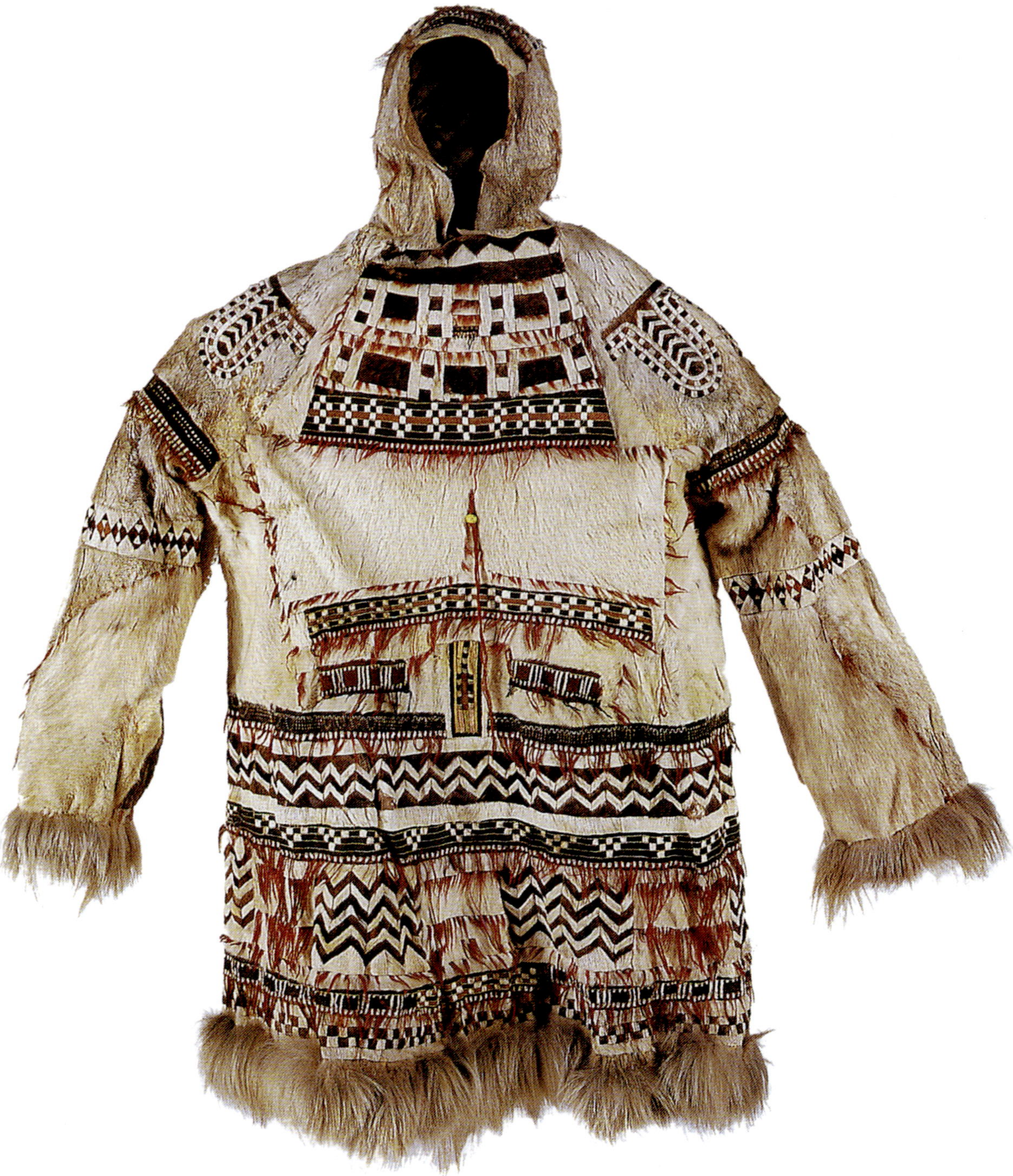

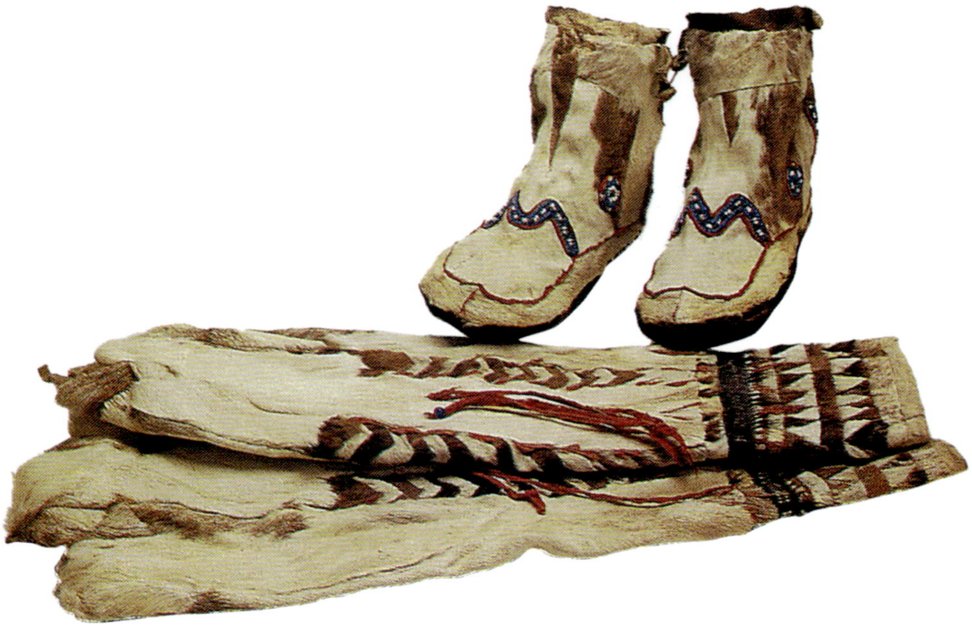

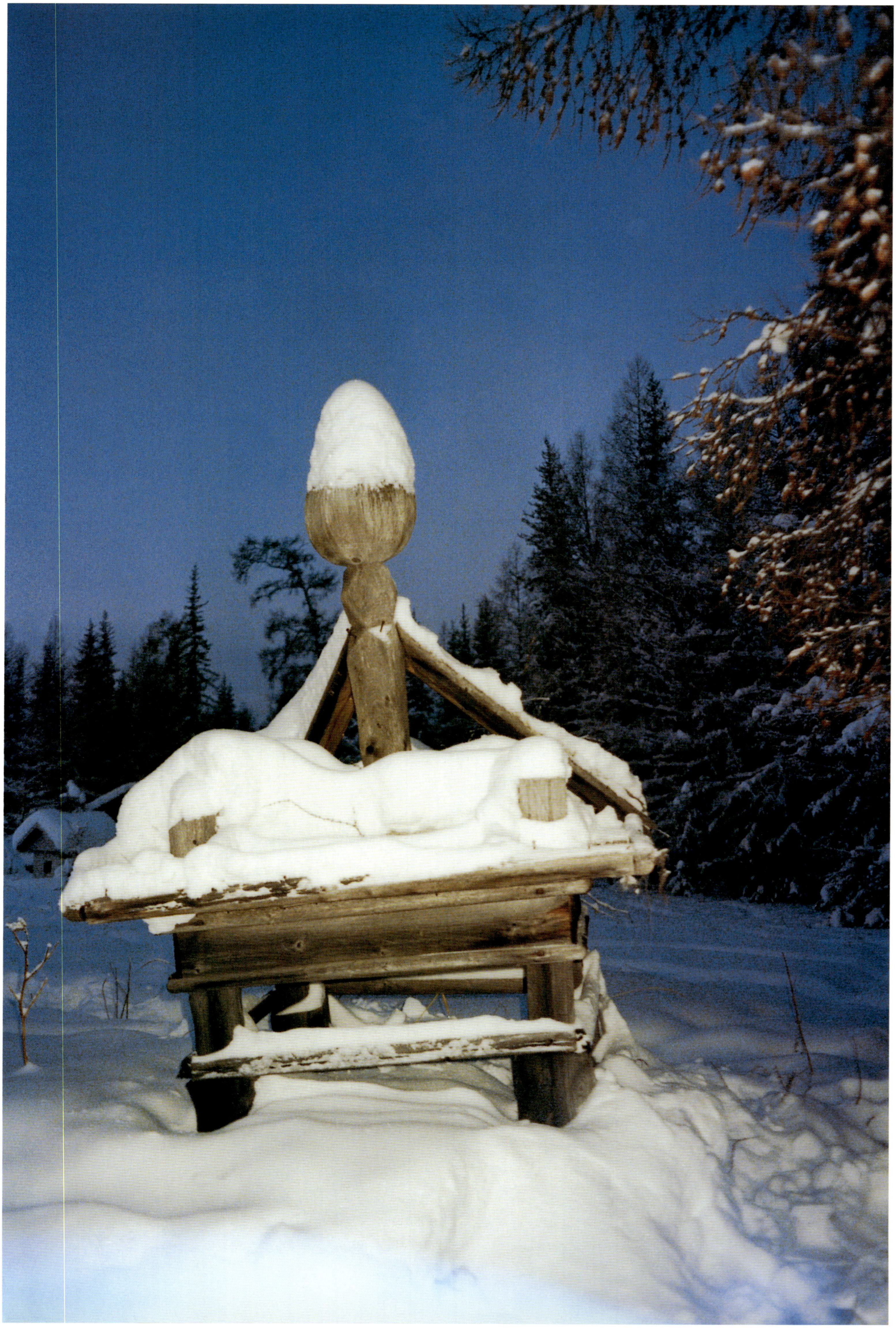

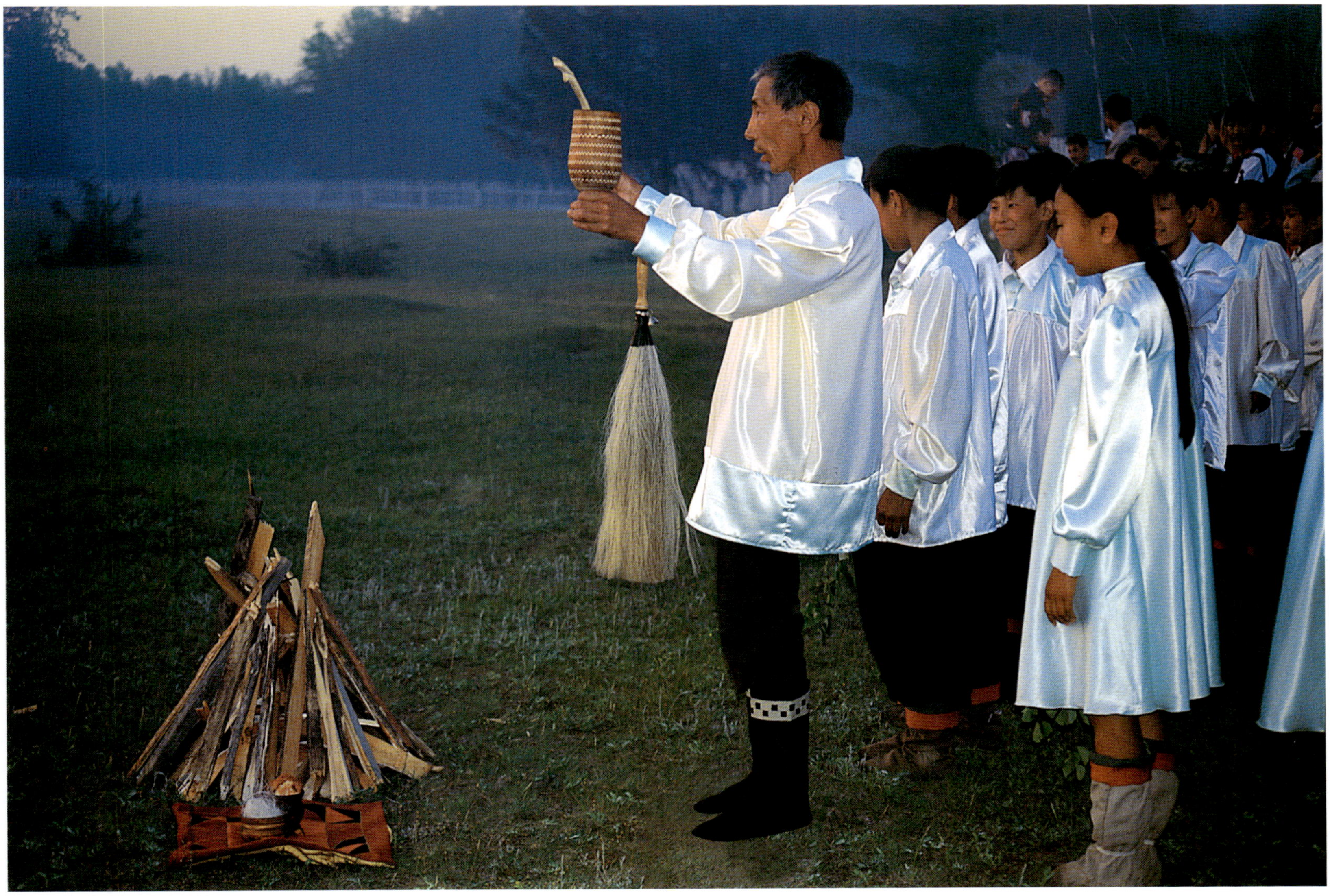

not in front, the occupants of the *yurt* group themselves. The shaman faces the door, and pretends to be unconscious of all sights and sounds. In his right hand he holds a short staff which is inscribed on one side with mystic symbols; and in his left, two arrows with the points held upwards. To each point is affixed a small bell. His dress has nothing distinctive of a shaman; he usually wears the coat either of the inquirer or of the sick person. The performance begins with a song summoning the spirits. Then the shaman strikes the arrows with his staff, so that the bells chime in a regular rhythm, while all the spectators sit in awed silence. When the spirits appear, the shaman rises and commences to dance. The dance is followed by a series of complicated and difficult body-movements. While all this is going on the rhythmical chiming of the bells never ceases. His song consists of a sort of dialogue with the spirits, and is sung with changes of intonation denoting different degrees of excitement or enthusiasm. When his enthusiasm rises to a high pitch, those present join in the singing. After the shaman has learnt all he wishes from the spirits, the latter communicate the will

Unknown,
Tomb in the taiga.
Yakutia.

Ceremony at sunrise at the beginning of the traditional Yakut festival of Isahar.
Russian Museum of Ethnography, St. Petersburg.

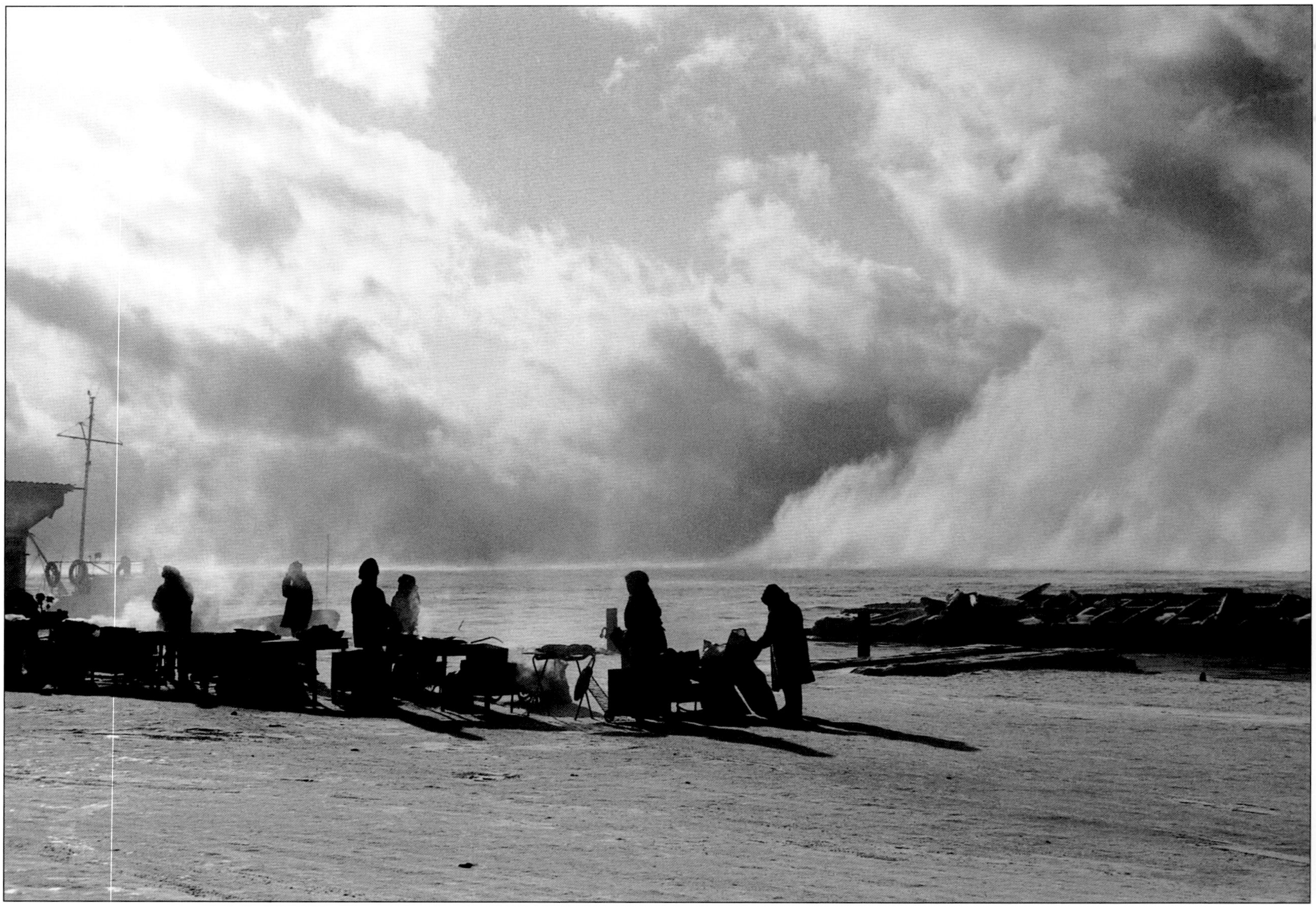

Lake Baikal: the traders of Omul.

Evenki,
Tomb of an ancestor, early 20th century.

Unknown,
Chest panels: 1) woman's 2) man's, 1925, 1914.
Dressed reindeer skin, beads, horsehair, metal, seed beads, cotton fabric, 1) 57 x 16-27 cm; 2) 72 cm.
Russian Museum of Ethnography, St. Petersburg. 1) Turukhan Krai, the Sym-river; 2) The Nizhni (Lower) Tunguska river basin.

of the god to the people. If he is to foretell the future, he employs his staff. He throws it on the ground, and if it falls with the side inscribed with mystical signs turned upward, this is a good omen; if the blank side shows, ill-fortune may be looked for.

To prove his trustworthiness to those present, the shaman uses the following means. He sits on a reindeer skin, and his hands and feet are bound, The room is completely darkened. Then, as if in answer to his call to the spirits, various noises are heard both within and without the *yurt*: the beating of a drum, the grunting of a bear, the hissing of a serpent, the squeak of a squirrel, and mysterious scratchings on the reindeer-skin where he sits. Then the shaman's bonds are untied, he is set free, and every one is convinced that what they heard was the work of the spirits.

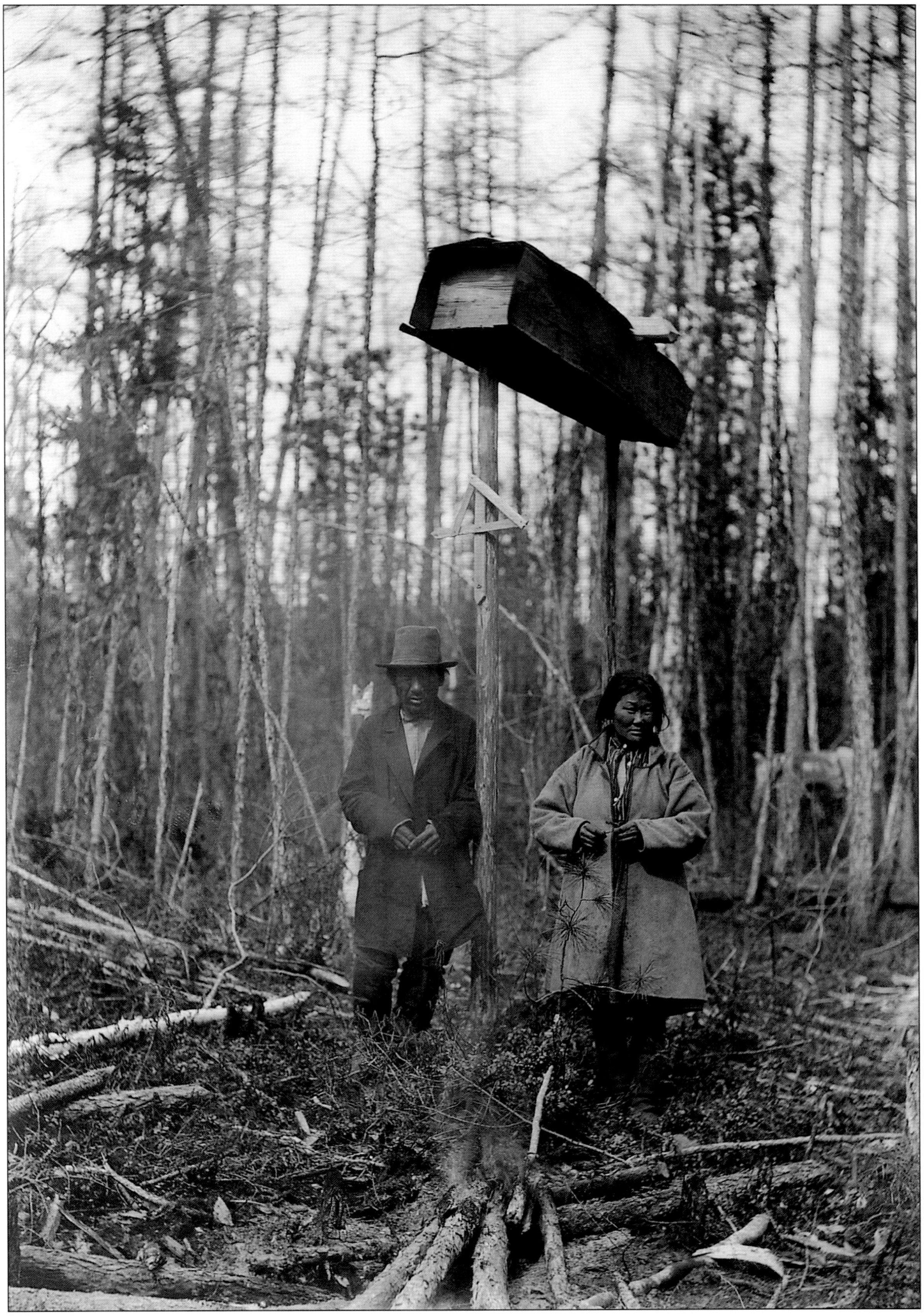

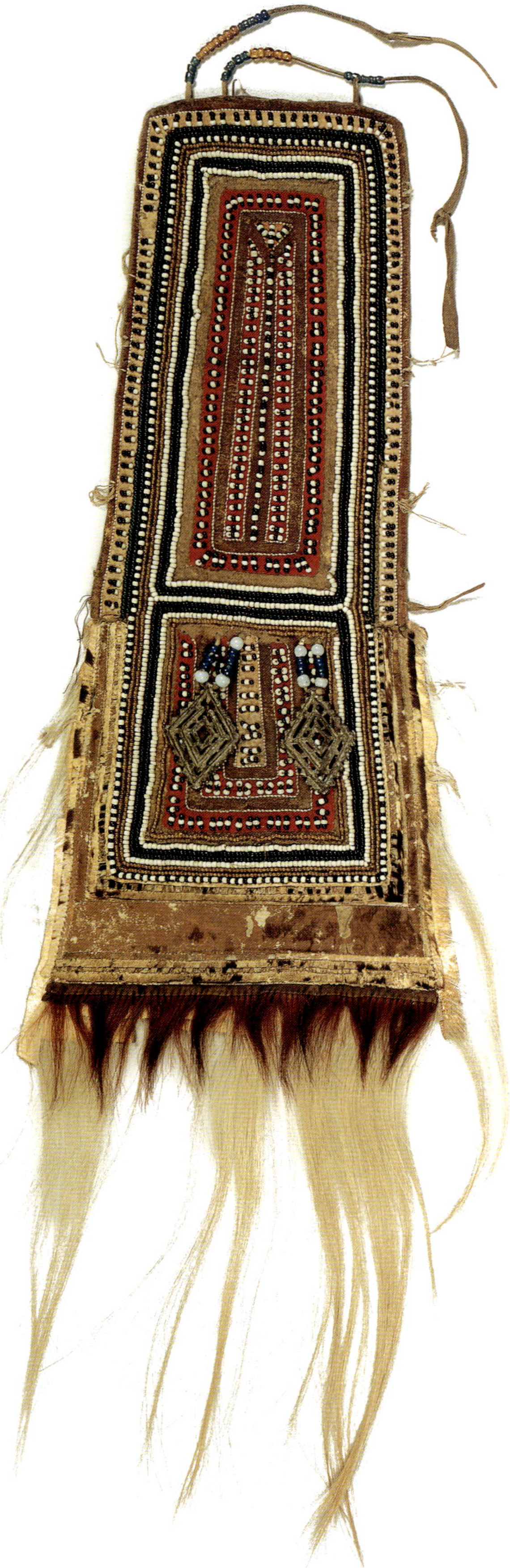

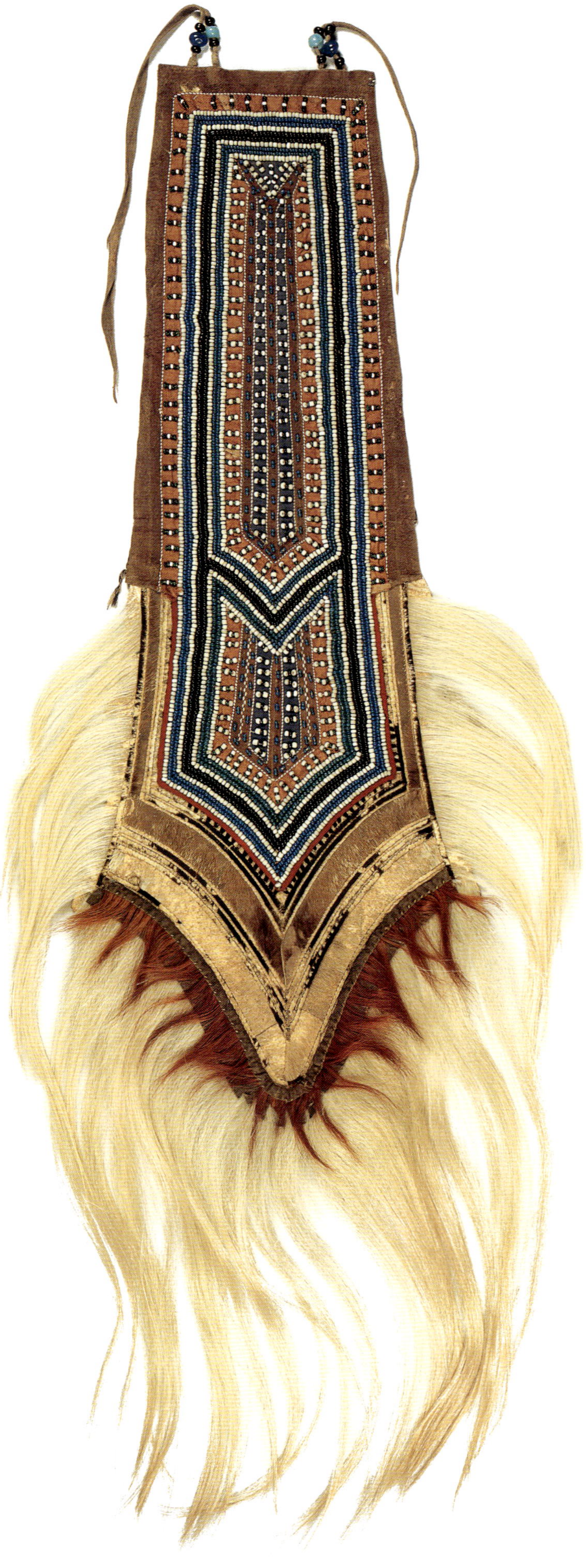

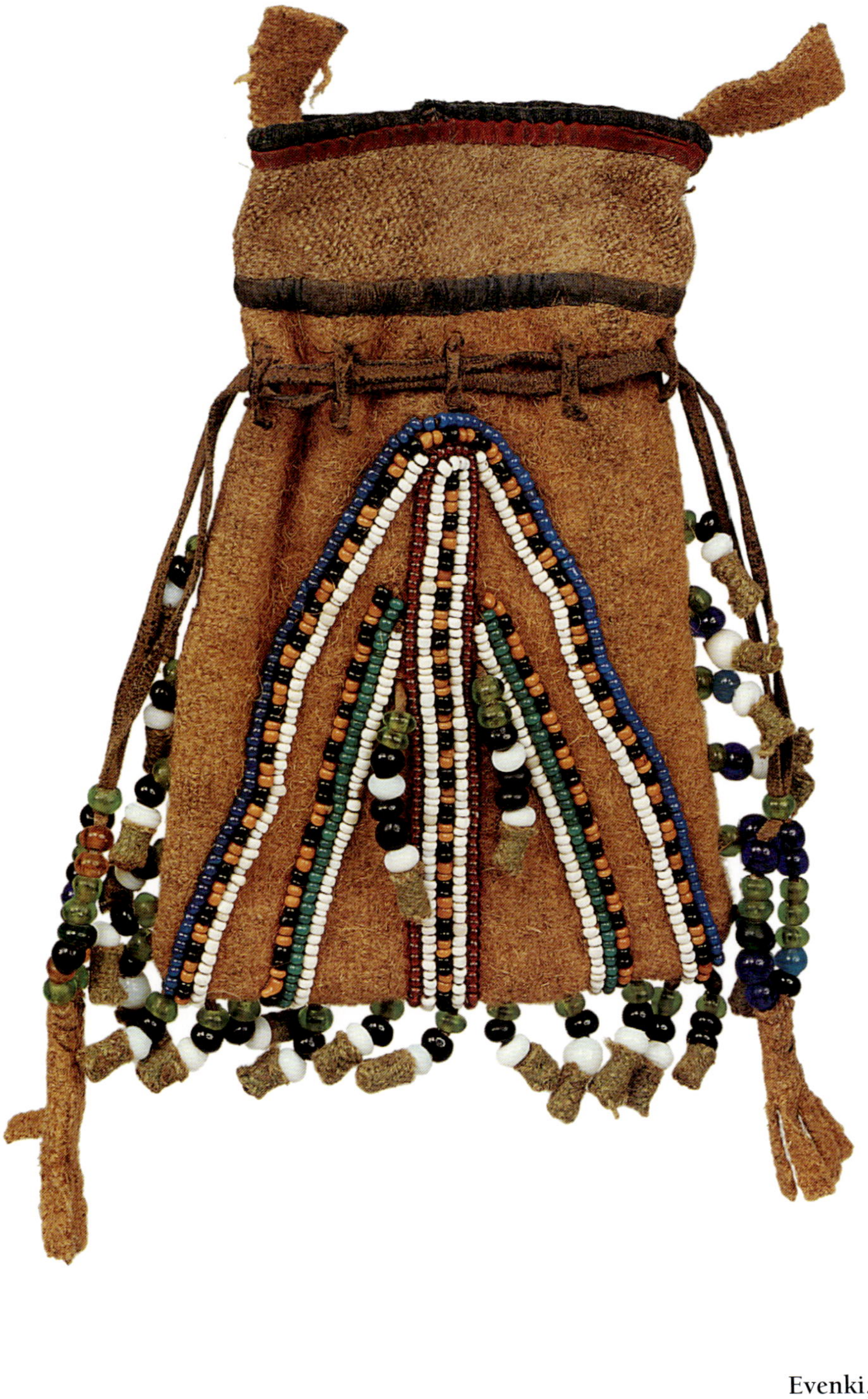

Evenki,
Tobacco pouch, 1913.
Woolen cloth, beads, seed beads, leather,
Russian Museum of Ethnography,
St. Petersburg. Yenisey Gubernia
(province), Turukhan Krai, the
Nizhni (Lower) Tunguska river basin.

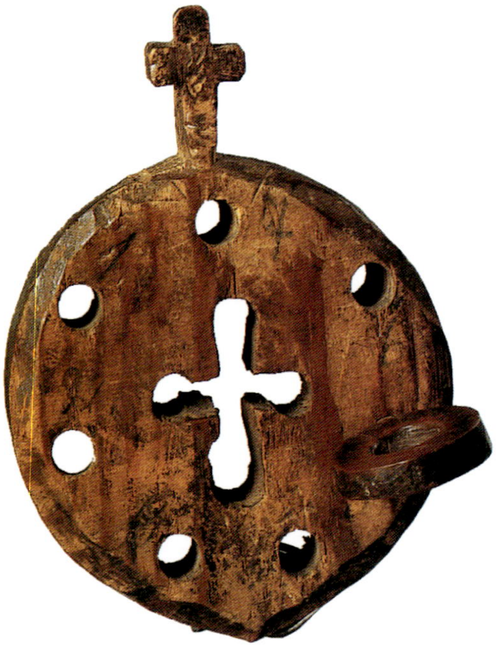

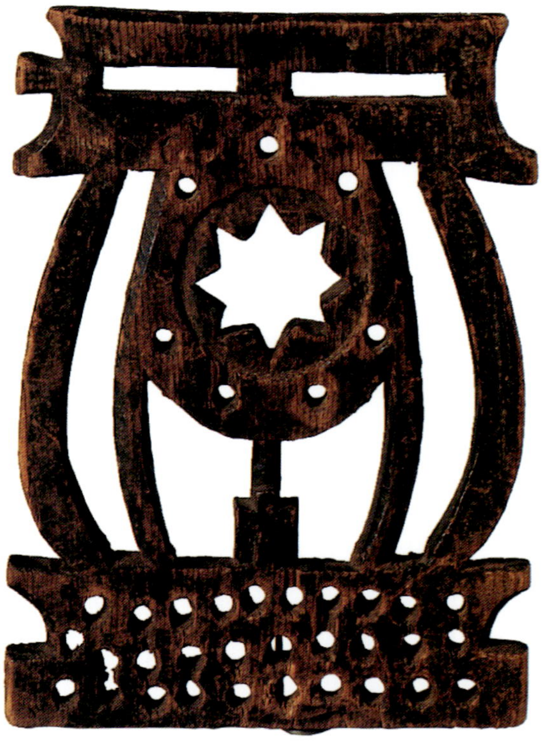

Yakut,
Calendars: 1) weekly 2) monthly and weekly, 1906.
Wood, 1) diameter: 15.2 cm;
2) 15.2 x 11.5 cm.
Russian Museum of Ethnography, St. Petersburg. 1) Yakut Oblast, Yakut Okrug, Boturuski ulus, Terasinski settlement; 2) Yakut Oblast, Yakut Okrug.

Aleut,
Rug, fragment, 1909-1910.
Grass-wrack, woolen yarn, leather, 155 x 39 cm.
Russian Museum of Ethnography, St. Petersburg. Aleutian Islands.

The Altaians

The *kams* (shamans) of the Turkic tribes of the Altai have preserved with great strictness the ancient shamanistic ceremonial forms. This was evident in a shaman named Enchu, who lived by the River Talda. Four stages, each marked by a different posture of the shaman, characterized his performance: in the first, he was sitting and facing the fire; in the second, standing, with his back to the fire; in the third, a sort of interlude, during which the shaman rested from his labour, supporting himself with his elbow on the drum, which he balanced on its rim, while he related what he had learned in his intercourse with the spirits; and in the fourth, a final shamanizing, with his back to the fire, and facing the place where the drum usually hangs. Enchu declared afterwards that he had no recollection of what happened while he was shamanizing with his back turned to the fire. While he was in that position he had been whirling about madly in circles on one spot, and without any considerable movement of his feet; crouching down on his haunches, and rising again to a standing posture, without interrupting the rotating movement. As he alternately bent and straightened his body from the hips, backwards and forwards and from side to side, with lively movements or jerks, the *manyak* (metal pendants) fastened to his coat danced and dangled furiously in ill directions, describing shining

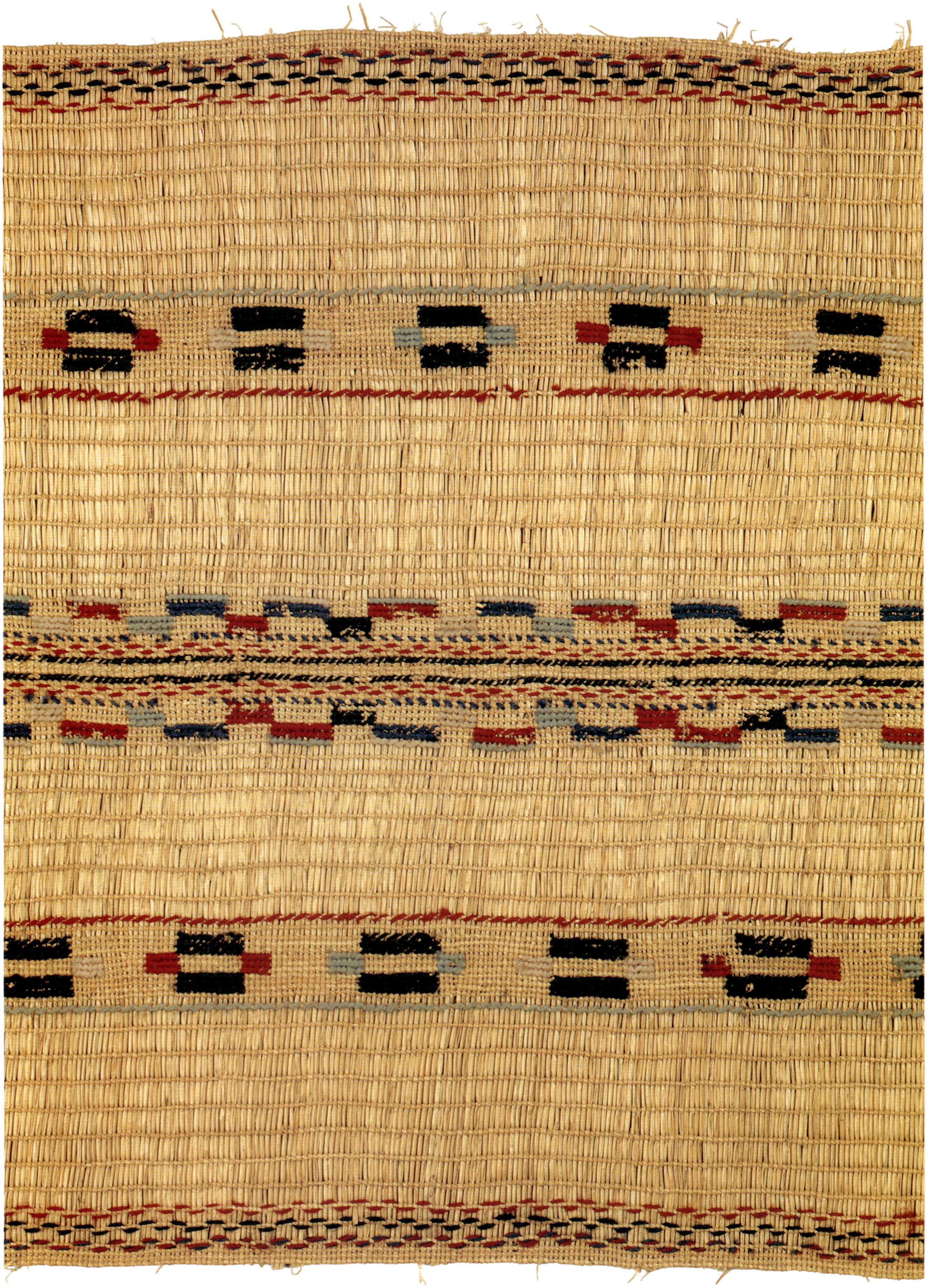

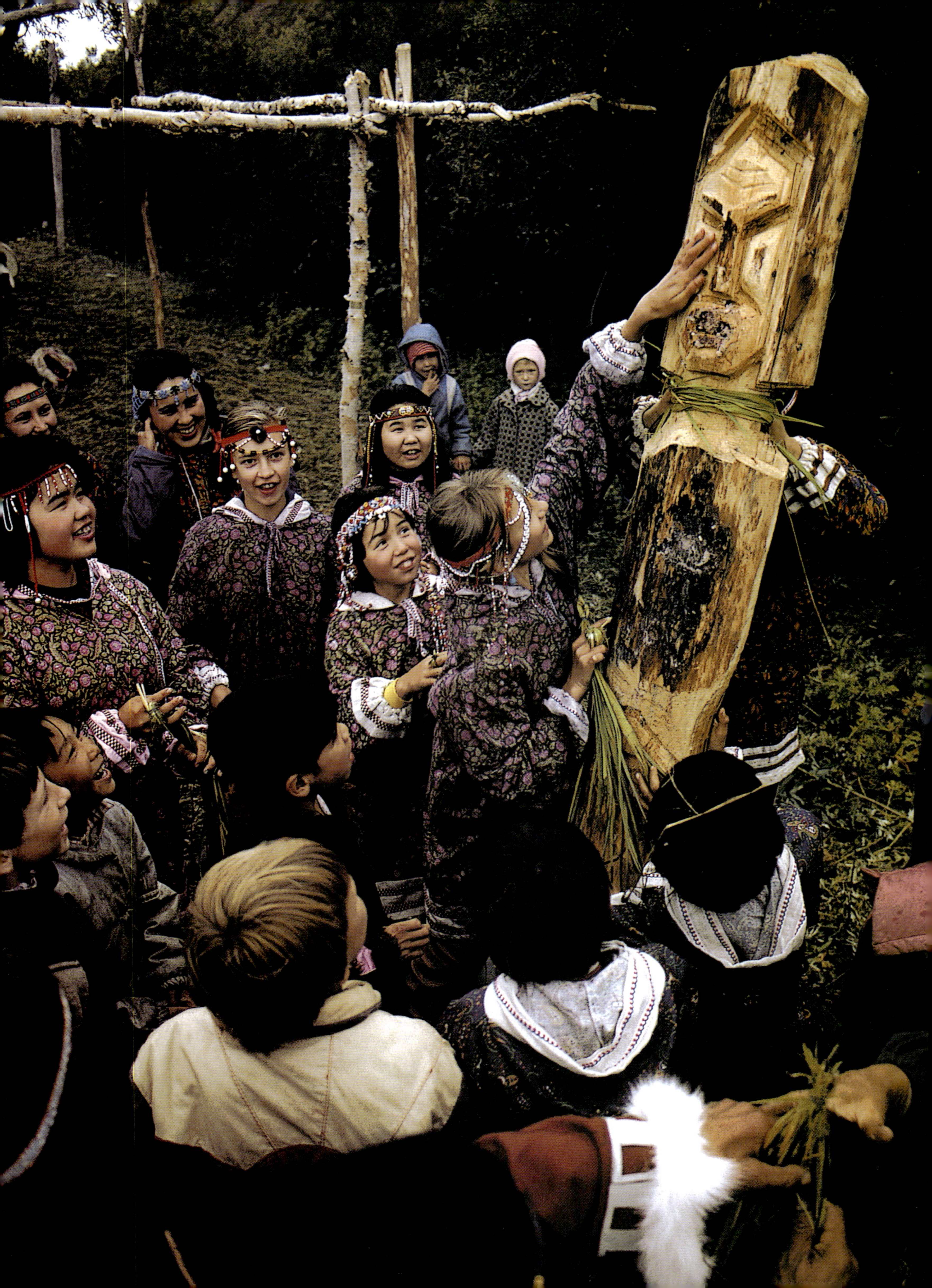

circles in the air. At the same time the shaman kept beating his drum, holding it in various positions so that it gave out different sounds. From time to time Enchu held the drum high above his head in a horizontal position and beat upon it from below. When the shaman held the drum in that way, he was collecting spirits in it. At times he would talk and laugh with some one apparently near by, but invisible to others, showing in this manner that he was in the company of spirits. At one time Enchu fell to singing more, quietly and evenly, simultaneously imitating on his drum the hoof-beats of a horse. This was to indicate that the shaman, with his accompanying spirits, was departing to the underworld of Erlik, the god of darkness.

In this spiritual journey, the *kam* directs his way towards the south. He has to cross the Altai Mountains and the red sands of the Chinese deserts. Then he crosses a yellow steppe, such as no magpie can traverse. "Singing, we shall cross it," says the *kam* in his song. After the yellow steppe there is a 'pale' one, such as no crow can pass over, and the *kam* in his imaginary passage once more sings a song full of hopeful courage. Then comes the iron mountain of Tamir Shayha, which 'leans against the sky.' Now the *kam* exhorts his train to be all of one mind, that they may pass this barrier by the united force of their will. He describes the difficulty of surmounting the passes and, in doing so, breathes heavily. On the top he finds the bones of many *kams* who have fallen here and died through failure of power. Again he sings songs of hope, declares he will leap over the mountain, and suits the action to the word. At last he comes towards the opening which leads to the underworld. Here he finds a sea, bridged only by a hair. To show the difficulty of crossing this bridge, the *kam* totters, almost falls, and with difficulty recovers himself. In the depths of the sea he beholds the bodies of many sinful *kams* who have perished there, for only those who are blameless can cross this bridge. On the other side he meets sinners who are receiving punishment suited to their faults; for example, an eavesdropper is pinned by his ear to a stake. On reaching the dwelling-place of Erlik, he is confronted by dogs, who will not let him pass, but at last, being appeased by gifts, they grow milder. Before the beginning of the shamanistic ceremony gifts have been prepared for this emergency. Having successfully passed these warders, the *kam*, as if approaching the Yarta of Erlik and coming into his presence, bows, brings his drum up to his forehead, and says, "*Mergu! mergu!*" Then he declares whence and why he comes. Suddenly he shouts; this is meant to indicate that Erlik is angry that a mortal should dare to enter his yurt. The frightened *kam* leaps backward towards the door, but gathers fresh courage and again approaches Erlik's throne. After this performance has been gone through three times, Erlik speaks: "Winged creatures cannot fly hither, beings with bones cannot come: how have you, ill-smelling blackbeetle, made your way to my abode?"

Then the kam stoops and with his drum makes certain movements if dipping up wine. He presents the wine to Erlik; and makes a shuddering movement like that of one who drinks strong wine, to indicate, that Erlik has drunk. When he perceives that Erlik's humour is somewhat milder under the influence of his draught he makes him offerings of gifts. The great spirit (Erlik) is moved by the offerings of the *kam*, and promises increase of cattle, declares which mare will foal, and even specifies what marking the young one will have. The *kam* returns in high spirits, not on his horse as he went, but on a goose - a change of steeds which he indicates by moving about the *yurt* on tiptoe, to represent flying.

Itelmen,
Dancing at a Kamchatka religious festival, 1992.

THE SONG OF THE SHAMAN

(By V.A Dolgounov)

Hoyaw-koo! Hoyaw-koo!
My spirit, my Master,
My companion, my likeness,
Spirit-soul,
Take possession of your mistress,
Of your beautiful grandmother -
Stir with all your strength,
Shaking her until she starts frothing,
Beating her until she bubbles over.

Hoyaw-koo! Hoyaw-koo!
A dread misfortune will surge forward.
A feared misfortune is about to break.
A great misfortune has come to shore.

Hoyaw-koo! Hoyaw-koo!
You who act as shaman in this great tidal roar,
My beloved little father,
My protective shell,
My loyal helper -
If you can manage it of yourself,
What do you say?
What is the price I will have to pay?

Hoyaw-koo! Hoyaw-koo!
My little mouse of a shaman,
My dearest sister,
My protective shell,
My loyal helper -
If you can manage it of yourself,
What do you say?
What is the price that I will have to pay?
Hoyaw-koo! Hoyaw-koo!
You who lived so gloriously in times now gone,
My poor little grandmother,
To confront what afflicts us now,
If you can manage it of yourself,
What do you say?
What is the price I will have to pay?

Hoyaw-koo! Hoyaw-koo!
My mistress,
You, my beautiful grandmother -
Skimming the surface of the water,
Riding on one of the white horses,
Flying above the liquid ice,
Sporting a badge at his harness-breast,
With a watch on his wrist,
With a mirror in his pocket,
Holding the law in his clenched hand,
Reading his destiny from his palm,
A blade hooked into his sword-belt,
It is your Prince of Amyhaakh.

If from his wife,
Spirit-soul,
From the white and opaline Me-khe-jay
I manage to get through to myself,
Even if I die,
I will not be looking for death.
Hoyaw-koo! Hoyaw-koo!
My very own little bird -
Darting its eyes all around,
Shining with all its fiery light,
It can be seen on the plain
With its steaming breath,
With its loud neighing,
With its gleaming caparison:
Even if I owned such a horse,
What would happen then?

Hoyaw-koo! Hoyaw-koo!
It can be seen in the byre,
With its shaggy coat,
With its well-curved back,
With its horns thrusting forward,
With its flattened hooves:
Even if I owned such a cow,
What would happen then?

Hoyaw-koo! Hoyaw-koo!
It can be seen in the taiga,
Treading with a step that snaps,
With its soft fur,
Feeding on mosses,
With hooves from which combs are made,
With antlers on the top of its head:
Even if I owned such a reindeer,
What would happen then?

Hoyaw-koo! Hoyaw-koo!
Even if I had clothing that was
Threadbare through being worn,
Even if I had money
That goes and that comes,
Even if I had coins
Stamped with the Eagle,
What would happen then?

Hoyaw-koo! Hoyaw-koo!
See how I am now,
With my face all pale,
With my brittle bones,
With a feeble tread -
Isn't that how I am?
With fat cheeks,
With a bulbous Russian nose -
See the man that I am!

Hoyaw-koo! Hoyaw-koo!

THE PEOPLES OF SIBERIA

ALEUTS

Number: nearly 2,000 in the USA; 700 in Russia
Location: Aleutian Islands (south-west of Alaska, USA, towards Kamchatka); Commander (Komandorski) Islands (Russia: Bering Sea)
Livelihood: residential; hunting sea mammals, fishing
Religion: Shamanism
Language: (Eskimo-)Aleut group

BURYATS

Number: 421,000 in Russia; 70,000 in Mongolia; small communities in the north-east of China
Location: around Lake Baikal; Republic of Buryatia; Autonomous Buryat District of Ust' Orda in Irkutsk Oblast; Autonomous Buryat District of Aga in Chita Oblast
Livelihood: Mongolian-style nomadic rearing (of cattle, horses, sheep, goats, camels) to the east of Lake Baikal; semi-residential rearing to the west
Religion: Buddhism in the east; Shamanism in the west
Language: Mongolian family

CHUKCHIS (THE CHUKCHI PEOPLE)

Number: 15,000
Location: Autonomous District of the Chukchis; the northern part of the Autonomous District of the Koryaks; the north-east of Yakutia
Livelihood: Ankalynes of the coastal area, residential: hunting of marine mammals; Chaochus of the tundra, nomadic: reindeer-herding
Religion: Shamanism
Language: Chukchi-Koryak-Kamchatka group

DOLGANS (THE DOLGAN PEOPLE)

Number: 6,945
Location: northern Yakutia, the Taimyr Peninsula
Livelihood: semi-residential; reindeer-herding, hunting, fishing
Religion: Orthodox Christianity; elements of Shamanism
Language: Turkic family

EVENI (THE EVENI PEOPLE; THE LAMUT)

Number: 17,000
Location: north-eastern Yakutia; Khabarovsk Region; Chukotka; Kamchatka
Livelihood: nomadic in the tundra; reindeer-herding and -hunting semi-residential in coastal areas; fishing, hunting marine mammals
Religion: Shamanism
Language: Tungusic family

EVENKI (THE EVENKI PEOPLE)

Number: 30,164
Location: Autonomous District of the Evenki (Krasnoyarsk Oblast); Khabarovsk Region; the Republics of Yakutia and Buryatia, in Irkutsk, Chita and Amur Oblasts
Livelihood: nomadic; reindeer-herding and -hunting
Religion: Shamanism
Language: Tungusic family

KETS (THE KET PEOPLE; 'YENISEY-OSTYAKS')

Number: 1,113
Location: strip centring on the Yenisey River south of Turukhansk, Baikit Oblast (Krasnoyarsk Region)
Livelihood: residential; hunting and fishing
Religion: Shamanism
Language: apparently unrelated

KHANTY (THE KHANTY PEOPLE; OSTYAKS)

Number: 22,521
Location: Autonomous District of the Khanty-Mansi;
Autonomous District of the Yamal-Nenets, Tomsk Oblast
Livelihood: nomadic reindeer-herding in the tundra – hunting and fishing in the taiga;
rearing of various animals (goats, sheep, pigs, etc.) in southerly areas and on the Ob River
Religion: Shamanism; bear cults
Language: Finno-Ugric family

KORYAKS

Number: 9,000
Location: Autonomous District of the Koryaks;
Autonomous District of the Chukchis, Magadan Oblast
Livelihood: nomadic reindeer-herding in the tundra;
residential fishing and hunting of marine mammals in coastal areas
Religion: Shamanism
Language: Chukchi-Koryak-Kamchatka group

MANSIS (THE MANSI PEOPLE;
THE VOGUL PEOPLE)

Number: 8,474
Location: Autonomous District of the Khanty-Mansi
Livelihood: hunting and fishing; reindeer-herding now almost died out
Religion: Shamanism
Language: Finno-Ugric family

THE NANAI PEOPLE (THE GOLD PEOPLE)

Number: 12,000 in Russia; around 1,000 in China
Location: the extreme east of Russia,
in the lower course of the Amur River (the Regions of Khabarovsk and of the Primor'ye);
the island of Sakhalin
Livelihood: residential; hunting and fishing
Religion: Shamanism
Language: Tungusic family

THE NEGIDAL PEOPLE

Number: 622
Location: the lower course of the Amur River (Khabarovsk Region)
Livelihood: residential; hunting and fishing
Religion: Shamanism; bear cults
Language: Tungusic family

THE NENETS

Number: 34,000
Location: Autonomous Districts of the Nenets (Archangel Oblast), of the Yamal-Nenets,
and of the Dolgan-Nenets
Livelihood: nomadic; reindeer-herding in the taiga and the tundra
Religion: Shamanism
Language: Samoyedic family

NIVKHI (THE NIVKHI PEOPLE; GILYAKS)

Number: 4,673
Location: the lower course of the Amur River; the island of Sakhalin
Livelihood: residential; fishing, hunting, hunting of marine mammals;
crop-farming, rearing of dogs
Religion: Shamanism; bear cults
Language: apparently unrelated

OLCHI (THE OLCHI PEOPLE)

Number: 3,200
Location: the extreme east of Russia,
in the lower course of the Amur River (Khabarovsk Region)
Livelihood: residential; hunting and fishing
Religion: Shamanism; bear cults
Language: Tungusic family

THE OROCHON PEOPLE

Number: 915
Location: Khabarovsk Region, Amur Oblast
Livelihood: residential; hunting and fishing
Religion: Shamanism
Language: Tungusic family

OROKI (THE OROKI PEOPLE)

Number: 190
Location: the island of Sakhalin
Livelihood: semi-residential;
fishing and the hunting of marine mammals in coastal areas; hunting in the taiga
Religion: Shamanism
Language: Tungusic family

THE TUVA PEOPLE (TUVINIANS; THE URYANKHAI; THE SOYOT)

Number: 235,000
Location: Republic of Tuva (south of Siberia on the border with Mongolia,
between the Ob and Yenisey Rivers); Mongolia; China
Livelihood: nomadic; horse-, cattle- and camel-breeding
Religion: Tibetan Buddhism (Lamaism); Shamanism
Language: Turkic family

UDEKHE (THE UDEKHE PEOPLE)

Number: 2,011
Location: the Regions of Khabarovsk and of the Primor'ye
Livelihood: residential; hunting and fishing
Religion: Shamanism; tiger cults
Language: Tungusic family

UIT (THE YUIT)

Number: (Inuit:) 35,000 in the USA; 26,000 in Canada; 45,000 in Greenland;
(Yuit:) 1,700 in Russia
Location: as above – but in Russia: the eastern side of Chukotka; Wrangell Island
Livelihood: residential; hunting marine mammals,
shooting and trapping birds, fishing, crop-farming
Religion: Shamanism
Language: Eskimo(-Aleut) group

YAKUTS

Number: 382,000
Location: Republic of Sakha (Yakutia)
Livelihood: residential; rearing of horses and domestic livestock
Religion: Shamanism
Language: Turkic family

YUKAGHIRS

Number: 1,142
Location: northern Yakutia, Kolyma and Magadan Oblasts
Livelihood: nomadic and residential; hunting, reindeer-herding, breeding hunting-dogs
Religion: Shamanism
Language: Yukaghir-Chuvantsi group

BIBLIOGRAPHY

Armstrong, T.. *Northern peoples of ths U.S.S.R.*. Cambridge: Scott Polar Institute, 1989.

Balzer, Marjorie Mandelstam. "Flights of the Sacred: Symbolism and Theory in Siberian Shamanism." *American Anthropologist.* Article 98(2):305318. 1996.

Balzer, Marjorie Mandelstam, ed.. *Shamanic Worlds: Rituals and Lore of Siberia and Central Asia.* Armonk, New York: North Castle, 1997.

Clutton-Brock, Juliet. *Domestic Animals from Early Times.* Austin: University of Texas Press, 1981. British Museum of Natural History, London.

Crowell, Aron and William W. Fitzhugh. *Crossroads of Continents: Cultures of Siberia and Alaska.* New York: Smithsonian, 1988.

Czaplicka, Maria Antonina. *Aboriginal Siberia: A Study in Social Anthropology.* Oxford: Clarendon, 1914.

Dahl, J.. "Indigenous Peoples of the Soviet North." *International Workgroup for Indigenous Affairs.* Document no. 67. 1963.

Doeker-Mach, Gunther, Ed.. *The Forgotten Peoples of Siberia.* New York: Scalo, 1993.

Jochelson, W.. *Peoples of Asiatic Russia.* New York: American Museum of Natural History, 1928.

Kempe, Frederick. *Siberian Odyssey: A Voyage into the Russian Soul.* New York: G. P. Putnam's Sons, 1992.

Kennan, George. *Tent Life in Siberia and Adventures among the Korak and Other tribes in Kamchatka and Northern Asia.* New York: Putnam, 1910.

Lagardere, Genevieve and Catherine Varlot. *Derniers chasseurs de rennes de Sibérie.* Musée Departmental de Prehistorie de Solutré, 1992.

Stadling, Jonas. *Through Siberia.* Westminster: Constable, 1901.

LIST OF ILLUSTRATIONS

Q/R

S